Troubleshooting Your PC Bible, 5th Edition

Troubleshooting Your PC Bible, 5th Edition

Jim Aspinwall and Mike Todd

IDG Books Worldwide, Inc.
An International Data Group Company

Foster City, CA ✦ Chicago, IL ✦ Indianapolis, IN ✦ New York, NY

Troubleshooting Your PC Bible, 5th Edition

Published by
IDG Books Worldwide, Inc.
An International Data Group Company
919 E. Hillsdale Blvd., Suite 400
Foster City, CA 94404
www.idgbooks.com (IDG Books Worldwide Web site)

ISBN: 0-7645-3510-2

Printed in the United States of America

10 9 8 7 6 5 4 3 2

1B/SZ/QY/QQ/FC

Distributed in the United States by IDG Books Worldwide, Inc.

Distributed by CDG Books Canada Inc. for Canada; by Transworld Publishers Limited in the United Kingdom; by IDG Norge Books for Norway; by IDG Sweden Books for Sweden; by IDG Books Australia Publishing Corporation Pty. Ltd. for Australia and New Zealand; by TransQuest Publishers Pte Ltd. for Singapore, Malaysia, Thailand, Indonesia, and Hong Kong; by Gotop Information Inc. for Taiwan; by ICG Muse, Inc. for Japan; by Intersoft for South Africa; by Eyrolles for France; by International Thomson Publishing for Germany, Austria, and Switzerland; by Distribuidora Cuspide for Argentina; by LR International for Brazil; by Galileo Libros for Chile; by Ediciones ZETA S.C.R. Ltda. for Peru; by WS Computer Publishing Corporation, Inc., for the Philippines; by Contemporanea de Ediciones for Venezuela; by Express Computer Distributors for the Caribbean and West Indies; by Micronesia Media Distributor, Inc. for Micronesia; by Chips Computadoras S.A. de C.V. for Mexico; by Editorial Norma de Panama S.A. for Panama; by American Bookshops for Finland.

For general information on IDG Books Worldwide's books in the U.S., please call our Consumer Customer Service department at 800-762-2974. For reseller information, including discounts and premium sales, please call our Reseller Customer Service department at 800-434-3422.

For information on where to purchase IDG Books Worldwide's books outside the U.S., please contact our International Sales department at 317-596-5530 or fax 317-572-4002.

For consumer information on foreign language translations, please contact our Customer Service department at 800-434-3422, fax 317-572-4002, or e-mail rights@idgbooks.com.

For information on licensing foreign or domestic rights, please phone +1-650-653-7098.

For sales inquiries and special prices for bulk quantities, please contact our Order Services department at 800-434-3422 or write to the address above.

For information on using IDG Books Worldwide's books in the classroom or for ordering examination copies, please contact our Educational Sales department at 800-434-2086 or fax 317-572-4005.

For press review copies, author interviews, or other publicity information, please contact our Public Relations department at 650-653-7000 or fax 650-653-7500.

For authorization to photocopy items for corporate, personal, or educational use, please contact Copyright Clearance Center, 222 Rosewood Drive, Danvers, MA 01923, or fax 978-750-4470.

Library of Congress Cataloging-in-Publication Data

Aspinwall, Jim.
   Troubleshooting your PC bible / Jim Aspinwall and Mike Todd. -- 5th ed.
     p.   cm.
   New ed. of Troubleshooting your PC /
Jim Aspinwall and Mike Todd. 4th ed. c1999.
   Includes index.
   ISBN 0-7645-3510-2 (alk. paper)
   1. Microcomputers--Maintenance and repair.
2. Microcomputers--Upgrading. I. Todd, Mike.
II. Aspinwall, Jim. Troubleshooting your PC.
III. Title.
TK7887 .A87   2000
004.165--dc21   00-057499

is a registered trademark or trademark under exclusive license to IDG Books Worldwide, Inc. from International Data Group, Inc. in the United States and/or other countries.

ABOUT IDG BOOKS WORLDWIDE

Welcome to the world of IDG Books Worldwide.

IDG Books Worldwide, Inc., is a subsidiary of International Data Group, the world's largest publisher of computer-related information and the leading global provider of information services on information technology. IDG was founded more than 30 years ago by Patrick J. McGovern and now employs more than 9,000 people worldwide. IDG publishes more than 290 computer publications in over 75 countries. More than 90 million people read one or more IDG publications each month.

Launched in 1990, IDG Books Worldwide is today the #1 publisher of best-selling computer books in the United States. We are proud to have received eight awards from the Computer Press Association in recognition of editorial excellence and three from Computer Currents' First Annual Readers' Choice Awards. Our best-selling ...*For Dummies*® series has more than 50 million copies in print with translations in 31 languages. IDG Books Worldwide, through a joint venture with IDG's Hi-Tech Beijing, became the first U.S. publisher to publish a computer book in the People's Republic of China. In record time, IDG Books Worldwide has become the first choice for millions of readers around the world who want to learn how to better manage their businesses.

Our mission is simple: Every one of our books is designed to bring extra value and skill-building instructions to the reader. Our books are written by experts who understand and care about our readers. The knowledge base of our editorial staff comes from years of experience in publishing, education, and journalism — experience we use to produce books to carry us into the new millennium. In short, we care about books, so we attract the best people. We devote special attention to details such as audience, interior design, use of icons, and illustrations. And because we use an efficient process of authoring, editing, and desktop publishing our books electronically, we can spend more time ensuring superior content and less time on the technicalities of making books.

You can count on our commitment to deliver high-quality books at competitive prices on topics you want to read about. At IDG Books Worldwide, we continue in the IDG tradition of delivering quality for more than 30 years. You'll find no better book on a subject than one from IDG Books Worldwide.

John Kilcullen
Chairman and CEO
IDG Books Worldwide, Inc.

IDG is the world's leading IT media, research and exposition company. Founded in 1964, IDG had 1997 revenues of $2.05 billion and has more than 9,000 employees worldwide. IDG offers the widest range of media options that reach IT buyers in 75 countries representing 95% of worldwide IT spending. IDG's diverse product and services portfolio spans six key areas including print publishing, online publishing, expositions and conferences, market research, education and training, and global marketing services. More than 90 million people read one or more of IDG's 290 magazines and newspapers, including IDG's leading global brands — Computerworld, PC World, Network World, Macworld and the Channel World family of publications. IDG Books Worldwide is one of the fastest-growing computer book publishers in the world, with more than 700 titles in 36 languages. The "...For Dummies®" series alone has more than 50 million copies in print. IDG offers online users the largest network of technology-specific Web sites around the world through IDG.net (http://www.idg.net), which comprises more than 225 targeted Web sites in 55 countries worldwide. International Data Corporation (IDC) is the world's largest provider of information technology data, analysis and consulting, with research centers in over 41 countries and more than 400 research analysts worldwide. IDG World Expo is a leading producer of more than 168 globally branded conferences and expositions in 35 countries including E3 (Electronic Entertainment Expo), Macworld Expo, ComNet, Windows World Expo, ICE (Internet Commerce Expo), Agenda, DEMO, and Spotlight. IDG's training subsidiary, ExecuTrain, is the world's largest computer training company, with more than 230 locations worldwide and 785 training courses. IDG Marketing Services helps industry-leading IT companies build international brand recognition by developing global integrated marketing programs via IDG's print, online and exposition products worldwide. Further information about the company can be found at www.idg.com.   1/26/00

Credits

Acquisitions Editor
Ed Adams

Project Editors
Sharon Eames
Martin Minner

Technical Editor
Jeff Wiedenfeld

Copy Editors
Lane Barnholtz
Julie Campbell Moss
Nancy Rapoport
Michael D. Welch

Proof Editor
Patsy Owens

Project Coordinators
Danette Nurse
Louigene A. Santos

Proofreading and Indexing
York Production Services

Cover Image
Lawrence Huck

Graphics and Production Specialists
Bob Bihlmayer
Darren Cutlip
Jude Levinson
Michael Lewis
Victor Pérez-Varela
Ramses Ramirez

Quality Control Technician
Dina F Quan

Media Development Specialist
Brock Bigard

Permissions Editors
Carmen Krikorian
Jessica Montgomery

Assoc. Media Development Specialist
Megan Decraene

Media Development Coordinator
Marisa Pearman

Media Development Manager
Laura Carpenter

Illustrators
Rashell Smith
Gabriele McCann

About the Authors

Jim Aspinwall writes to support his PC habit, and he conveys his experiences to others as author of *IRQ, DMA, & I/O* and as *Computer Currents* magazine's "Windows Advisor" columnist. He brings to this fifth edition of *Troubleshooting Your PC Bible* several years of experience with PC utility software, PC diagnostic software, telecommuter-networking technical support, and online support. He has worked for DiagSoft, Vertisoft, TuneUp.com, Quarterdeck, and various high-tech firms. A consummate tinkerer, Jim still finds a few moments away from the keyboard to spend at his workbench in a dusty mountaintop radio shack or on a cold steel tower to build and maintain amateur-radio repeater systems.

Mike Todd founded the Internet Society Los Angeles Chapter, the Capital PC User Group in Washington, DC, the IBM Special Interest Group on CompuServe (also on The Source and on Unison), and has promoted the development of computer user groups around the world. Along with Professor Sumpei Cumon, Mike spoke in 1985 at the inauguration of the NEC PC Value Added Network, which was one of the first public networks established in Japan. . Before retiring from the U.S.Navy, Mike fostered the development of the Navy's Microcomputer User Group and trained the people who manage public education in how to use their PCs at each of the regional offices of the U.S. Department of Education. Most recently, Mike, along with a few new friends, has founded the Internet Society Los Angeles Chapter (ISOC-LA). At one of the first ISOC-LA sponsored events, which provided a free clinic for anyone having problems with their computer, Mike even helped a few MAC users upgrade their computers so that they could connect to the Internet. Mike's interests include developing communities and commerce over the Web, information systems technology, health care administration, applications in business and government, programming, computer consulting, hiking, body surfing, bicycle riding, and travel.

Contacting the Authors

Jim Aspinwall: Internet: wb9gvf@raisin.com or through www.raisin.com

Mike Todd: Internet: Mike.Todd@miketodd.com, www.miketodd.com, or mtodd@ISOC-LA.org.

The *Troubleshooting Your PC Bible* Web site can be found at www.typc.com.

To my wife, friend, and favorite PC user, Kathy.
To my family and friends. To PC users everywhere.

—Jim Aspinwall

To Kristi, my wife and best friend. To my sons,
and to countless PC users, members of the online
communities, and Internet users around the World.

—Mike Todd

Preface

If you are a PC technician, *Troubleshooting Your PC Bible, 5th Edition* will help you better educate your customers, which should make your job easier. It will help you get their computers back into operation much quicker, and then they will be more satisfied with your work.

If you are an experienced PC user, this book will remind you of those things that have helped you get you to where you are now, and it will provide a solid reference for some of the issues you may not have dealt with in the past.

This book really is not to be read from cover to cover in one or two sittings, like a novel, although we encourage you to try it that way, too. We have organized the information so that you can use this book as a reference guide. If something is not working right, reach for this book, find the section that deals with that problem, find the information you need, and follow the steps to solve the problem.

You and your computer might encounter some misleading and baffling problems at some time in your relationship. Hopefully, those will be few and far between. For the most part, a little familiarity, the willingness to try, and a handy reference like this one should be all you need to explore the inner workings of your system and to find and fix what ails it.

Feel free to use *Troubleshooting Your PC Bible, 5th Edition* as either a reference for looking up what you need to know or as a tutorial to help you become much more familiar with your PC and to help you handle any common problem—and some of the uncommon ones, as well!

How this Book is Organized

Problem Index. The place to quickly find Solutions to Problems you have identified by their Symptoms and the components you Suspect.

Part I: Getting Started

You'll find the "Getting Started" chapters in Part I. While these chapters are mostly oriented to folks who are new to PCs, many seasoned PC veterans have found great value in this perspective. A refresher seldom hurts.

✦ **Chapter 1: Troubleshooting.** We cover the general concepts of troubleshooting and demystify the process of finding and solving problems in your system.

✦ **Chapter 2: Tools of the Trade.** We describe the hardware and software tools you need to work on your PC, including emergency diskettes, prerecovery preparations, recovery tools for Windows, program removal tools, and hand tools.

✦ **Chapter 3: Protecting Yourself and Your PC.** We cover erased file protection; virus protection; communications problems; data recovery; and ways to protect yourself, your files, and programs.

✦ **Chapter 4: Your Personal Computer.** Chapter 4 provides an overview of your PC system; definitions of the major components, subsystems, and other items found inside your PC; and definitions and examples of PC peripherals

✦ **Chapter 5: Physical Versus Logical Devices.** What's physical, what's logical? Chapter 5 answers this, and it discusses translating logical devices into physical addresses, associating IRQ assignments with logical names, and how Windows handles device names and addresses.

Part II: The Soft Side of your PC

Part II delves into the soft side of you PC by taking you through the legacy of DOS and early versions of Windows, the current manifestations of Windows 2000 and Windows Millennium, and then it takes off into Networks and the Internet.

✦ **Chapter 6: Operating Systems, File Systems, and User Interfaces.** This chapter covers control programs and procedures, and ways that both can take full advantage of the power of PCs. This small introduction helps you prepare to install, configure, and use the devices that integrate into our PC systems.

✦ **Chapter 7: DOS Parts.** Chapter 7 starts with a brief history of DOS, introduces configuring your operating system, surveys DOS Shells, and ends with multi-tasking user interfaces.

✦ **Chapter 8: Windows for Home and Desktop.** Chapter 8 departs a bit from this book's presentation style. As a premise, we start with an old PC, one that began life as a 386, DOS system, and we upgrade it all the way to Windows NT/2000, installing Windows 3.1, Windows for Workgroups, Windows 95, and Windows 98 along the way.

✦ **Chapter 9: Windows for the Enterprise.** Windows NT Workstation, Windows 2000 Professional, Windows NT Server, Windows 2000 Server, and Windows 2000 Advanced Server are presented primarily from the standpoint of installing and configuring. Of course, we do address problems but, aside from some new and exciting installation challenges, these Windows versions are much more stable than any earlier version of Windows.

✦ **Chapter 10: Networking.** Networking has become a function of just about every PC. This chapter starts with the reasons to share files, printers, and other resources. Windows networking is emphasized because it is installed or installable on the majority of PCs in use and being sold today. While this chapter is not meant to provide comprehensive network management and optimization information, it does address the types of problems that can prevent access to networks, and it offers solutions.

✦ **Chapter 11: The Internet.** Chapter 11 builds on the networking introduction in Chapter 10 and takes some of the mystery and complexity out of setting up your system to connect with the Net. It does not attempt to make you an instant expert on the Internet, but it does address common setup and trouble-shooting issues. Chapter 11 also address Internet security and encourage you to use a personal firewall.

Part III: The Hard Side of your PC

Part III starts with applying the power to your PC and continues on with hardware installation and configuration, and it spends time on system boards and memory.

✦ **Chapter 12: Bootup Problems.** This chapter begins by discussing what happens when you turn on the power to your PC, and it continues on into problems related to the AC and DC power used by your system. It deals with battery problems; portable and handheld computers; and general system problems, such a video, CMOS, memory, motherboard, and hard disk system problems related to starting your computer.

✦ **Chapter 13: Configuration Problems.** Chapter 13 addresses configuring your PC through its startup files. Because DOS is where PCs started, this is where we begin. We provide a basic look at configuring and starting your system, using the multiboot options to give you the ability to use multiple operating systems, and we take a look at configuration conflicts. The focus is on the CONFIG.SYS and AUTOEXEC.BAT files, but many concepts still apply to problems found in Windows, OS/2, and even Unix and mainframe systems. Windows configuration problems are covered more directly in Chapters 8 and 9.

✦ **Chapter 14: System Boards.** Regardless of which operating system you decide to use, the system board in your PC is the platform on which it runs. This chapter introduces you to all of the components and features that compose the system board, as well as explaining how they work together. We also cover the connections to the system board, including the system bus; and I/O connections, including Universal Serial Bus, the FireWire, keyboard, and mouse. We present ways to make Plug and Play work for you and your computer, or at least ways to keep it from preventing you from using your hardware. The BIOS setup gets the full treatment, and we even cover how to work with Flash ROM and how to use special recovery procedure, if you run into problems. We wrap up this chapter with the problems you may encounter and how to fix them, of course.

✦ **Chapter 15: System Memory.** This chapter describes ROM, RAM, and other types of memory (CMOS, VRAM, cache, and even virtual). It discusses memory parity and how to test your system's memory leads to memory configuration, as well as exploring common problems and solutions. We also help you upgrade your memory for optimum performance.

Part IV: Disk Drives

Part IV is dedicated to disk drives and explores their variety, as well as their commonality. Because computers are not very useful without reliable data storage, we help you make sure your investment in disk drives is protected and optimized.

✦ **Chapter 16: Disk Drive Basics.** This chapter comprehensively describes disk drive types, BIOS and DOS limitations and features, disk partitioning, and formatting. We delve into the technology that makes your hard disk, CD-ROM, and diskette drives work.

✦ **Chapter 17: Disk Drive Utilities and Diagnostics.** Chapter 17 presents disk drive utilities and describes how they keep drive systems running at top performance.

✦ **Chapter 18: Hard Drives.** Chapter 18 covers installing, adding, or changing hard drives; partitioning and formatting hard drives; and, of course, hard drive problems.

✦ **Chapter 19: Diskette, CD-ROM, and other Drives.** Chapter 19 is about working with diskettes, CD-ROM drives, and alternative drives. This chapter covers taking care of drives and disks, and it covers comprehensive presentations of the problems and solutions for fixing drive systems.

Part V: Other Parts of Your PC

Part V deals with the components of PCs that provide the means to actually use them. Screens, keyboards, speakers, microphones, printers, scanners, modems, and wireless devices are covered. How to install, configure, and integrate these components into a functional unit is the goal.

✦ **Chapter 20: Sights and Sounds.** Chapter 20 starts with a little history of PC video to help with orientation, standards, and terminology. We cover new video capabilities, installing sound and video, common video and video-display problems, sound card installation, and common audio problems.

✦ **Chapter 21: Basic Input and Output.** Chapter 21 addresses the devices most often connected to your computer for getting information and data into and out of your computer system. We start with printers, which, outside of video, is the most common way of viewing your computer's information. We also discuss mice, trackballs, and pen pads, even though they provide few problems. Small Computer System Interface (SCSI) provides some configuration challenges, so we cover these problems, as well. Scanners can also be a challenge, but careful setup and configuration can produce rewarding results. The USB provides some new problems, but the solutions make sense.

✦ **Chapter 22: Serial Input and Output.** This chapter deals with installing, configuring, and using computer serial ports. Because the use of modems is the most common use of COM ports, the majority of this chapter deals with modems and the types of problems you may encounter when using them. We also deal with the problems associated with phone lines and connecting modems. We round out the chapter with alternate ways of engaging serial communications.

Part VI: Maintaining Your PC

Part VI wraps up the concept of avoiding troubleshooting with a proactive approach to building barriers to problems and maintaining the ability to respond more quickly to the inevitable challenges that you may face at one time or another.

✦ **Chapter 23: Do it Yourself — With Confidence!** This final chapter surveys types of diagnostic and utility software, and it explores how this software provides information about your system, analyzes your system, diagnoses problems, and in some cases, fixes those problems. We also cover software used to diagnose and fix Year-2000 problems and show where to find this software. We cover do-it-yourself advice that helps you prevent problems and keep your system running smoothly. Much information and a form to document your system are provided to help you get the right kind of support, even if you provide it yourself. We end with recommendations for upgrading your computer for optimum performance.

Appendixes

All through *Troubleshooting Your PC Bible* we offer advice to help you install, configure, and optimize your PC and its components. We lead you into problem solving by way of identifying Symptoms that lead you to the Suspects contributing to the problem, and then we provide the Solutions that get your PC back into operation.

Use the Problem Index at the beginning of the book to help you locate discussion of specific problems in the chapters. In these discussions you'll find not only the solutions to problems, but also the background information that will help you avoid further problems.

Use the Glossary to expand your vocabulary and learning quotient.

Use the Appendix section to find specific details regarding memory, IRQs, keyboard codes, the ultimate ASCII-EBCDIC-Binary-Octal-decimal-HEX-PC character-code chart, Video colors and modes, hard drive types, beep codes, error messages, cabling diagrams, your very own Technical Support Form, and our favorite and most helpful Internet sites.

Appendix J contains the guide to the files on the CD-ROM.

Suggestions for Using This Book

If you read Chapters 1 and 23 before trouble arises, you will probably feel much more comfortable when you have to open your PC's box for the first time. After reading these chapters, removing the cover of the system, checking the wires and their connections, running the utility software, finding the right parts at a computer store, and finding help without wasting much time or money will be mysteries you already know how to solve.

If you want to build your own PC or learn how to become a full-time service technician, there are very good texts and courses on the subject. We are proud that this book is one of them — but our aim right now is to get you and your computer up and running.

In addition to Chapter 1, you may want to read Chapters 2 through 5 to become familiar with the components of your PC and the methods and simple tools used to fix and maintain it. You should also read Chapter 23 to begin a planned program of preventive maintenance for your system. Check the Appendixes for items of interest to you. Browse the front matter and the remaining chapters just to see what is in the book.

Your familiarity with this book will come in handy when you find yourself in the midst of a long night or weekend and something goes wrong. The better you have taken care of your system, maintained its documentation, and kept up with logging system status (hardware and software configuration and settings), the easier it will be to take care of a problem.

If you are pretty sure that the problem is related to startup, configuration, memory, or one of the other main areas to which an entire chapter is devoted, turn to the Problem Index organized by chapters. Find the Problem Statement that appears to be related to your current situation. Turn to that section in this book and get ready to solve the problem.

You may need the documentation for your hardware and software for information unique to your particular system. If you have maintained your own documentation of hardware and software installed in your system, make sure you have that available, too.

The rest of what you will need to do will depend on the circumstances and how well your problem matches those we have documented in this book.

Symptoms, Suspects, and Solutions are a special feature of this book. If you want to skip over all the explanatory text of each chapter and get right to solving specific problems, look for these sections:

Symptoms

▶ The things your system tells you through onscreen messages or other methods.

Suspects

▶ The parts of your system that may be the cause or may be related to the problem to which the symptoms point.

Solutions

▶ What you can do to fix the problems you have found.

 Remember this piece of information. It could help you save time or energy later on.

 Warning, caution, and take care! Some of the solutions we suggest should be attempted only after you have taken the proper precautions that we provide. Also, taking actions to solve a problem in one area of your system may cause problems in another. This icon serves as a yellow light to slow you down in those areas.

 Note this fact.

 We call this our "Look elsewhere" icon. It appears whenever we refer you to other areas of the book for more information.

 There are many cool demos of useful products in this book's CD-ROM. This icon in the text will tell you when a product we've discussed is on the CD-ROM. You can also check out the "What's on the CD-ROM" appendix in the back of this book.

For your benefit, some key words, most of them defined in the text and/or in the Glossary, appear in *italics*. Executable program names and internal DOS commands appear in UPPER CASE. DOS and CMD command lines appear in a `monospace font`, as well as onscreen messages, as they would appear on your screen.

By informal convention, where DOS disk, directory, subdirectory, and filename specifications are indicated, as in

    `d:\path\filename`

or

    `d:\sub-directory\filename`

the `d:` is meant to be replaced by the designation for your specific disk drive, such as `A:`, `B:`, `C:`, and so on. The `\path\` or `\sub-directory\` is meant to be replaced by your particular subdirectory path or structure where the filename of interest is located, for instance \UTILITIES\NORTON\. And filename is meant to be replaced by the executable or working file of interest, such as NDD.EXE, or simply NDD for an executable file; or MY_TEXT.DOC for a document file. You will see this type of expression throughout many software manuals and books about PCs.

Most numeric address expressions are in hexadecimal, as noted by a lower case "h" following the number, such as ###h, or 0x###, the same number (because the "0x" preceding the number means it is a hexadecimal number too), also by convention. In cases where the "h" or "0x" may have been left off, as in "378" when referring to a port designation, we mean "378h" (or "0x378"), unless we have specifically noted that the number is in decimal or another numbering system. Bitmapped indications, such as 0101 are in binary (base 2) and not meant to represent "101h" or "101" (one hundred one, decimal, base 10).

Just to keep the numbers straight, as explained in the text and Glossary. Following, though, are some definitions:

>   A byte is 8 bits, a word is 16 bits or 2 bytes.
>
>   A kilobyte, abbreviated as KB or K, equals 1,024 bytes.
>
>   A megabyte, abbreviated as MB or M, is 1,024 KB; or 1,024 × (times)
>   1,024 bytes = 1,048,576 bytes, or 8,388,608 bits.

The numbers start getting really large. Have you seen a petabyte number lately? It is composed of 50 digits.

It's now time to get on with the job of fixing your computer and increasing your understanding of PCs. Use this book to document your system, diagnose its problems, and get to work troubleshooting and fixing those problems.

Acknowledgments

Jim about Mike

A mutual friend and prior coauthor of ours was my inspiration and first "PC guru" who got me involved first online and then into PCs full-steam ahead. I first met Mike through that online experience, while I was researching the best way to proceed with getting into PCs (I was using an Apple IIc at the time). Mike was then the "sysop" of the IBMSIG forum on the now defunct "The Source" online service. What I found was truly an online *community* of users from throughout the world. The nature of this community, its open sharing of PC technical and simplified use information, recommendations of hardware and software, and its wealth of fix it and upgrade tips truly impressed and inspired me to go further.

The experience of learning about and then diving into PCs, with so few really good books on the subject, and really only the online help available from folks like Mike, led to the idea of us together crafting a better PC users' guidebook. We made an online "date" and then traveled to California to meet Mike in person and discuss this hair-brained scheme further. The meeting in person was followed by months of online chatting. After several rejections of the original text, Brenda, then an editor at M&T Books, got us into creating *The PC Users Survival Guide*.

We had found through the experience of creating this book that we had very similar "voices" and complimentary approaches to explaining the intricacies of PCs to almost anyone who would ask or listen. Several online communities, several thousand downloadable files put into online libraries, a few innovations that we ended up developing together, and four editions later, we've managed to maintain our sense of community and to continue fostering PC help for educational, commercial, charitable, and general purposes. Through Mike and my other online neighbors, I probably learned more about and felt comfortable with learning to "program" a little, as well. Something about "carrying the torch," of making PC use easier and more fun, just seems to drive Mike nonstop. Thanks!

Mike about Jim

We have been working together for so long, I forgot that we had not started on our publishing ventures until after I had retired from the Navy and moved to California. Our first face-to-face meeting was around a picnic table in my backyard in Long Beach to discuss writing a book we would name *The Uncomplicated PC*. Even though we never got that one past the initial publisher reviews, it did open the door to write our first book together that Jim mentioned in the preceding acknowledgment. Little did we know that we had formed a partnership that would last more than a decade. It will probably last a good deal longer, too!

The many letters and e-mail messages we have received from PC users around the world have provided the encouragement we needed to keep striving for the best way to help all PC users, not just those that have the newest computer on the block. We hope to continue to be the definitive source for just about everything a PC users needs in order to keep their computer running and problem free. We also hope to continue to provide computer technicians and professionals the information they need to best support their clients and customers. Let us know if there are things you would like to see in future versions of this book that would be even more helpful.

One of these days, I may even get my radio license, if for no other reason than to show Jim that he really has had some influence on me. (By the way, if you are a HAM operator, Jim's Internet ID is his call sign . . .)

Thanks to you too, Jim!

Special thanks to the folks at IDG Books

No book gets into print without the tremendous efforts of the copy editors. We give our special thanks to Lane Barnholtz, Julie Campbell Moss, Nancy Rapoport, and Michael Welch. Also lending a hand was proof editor Patsy Owens. KC Hogue also provided proofreading in-house for those files we didn't get to proofreading in time. AND — the person at the helm — the person who forced everything to come together — our editor, who deserves the biggest THANKS! — Sharon Eames.

Contents at a Glance

Contents

• •

Part I: Getting Started · 1

Part II: The Soft Side of Your PC   83

Part III: The Hard Side of Your PC — 253

Part IV: Disk Drives   417

Problem Index

The Problem Index is a shortcut for finding the Solution to a current problem you've encountered with your PC. It contains the symptoms from the "Symptoms, Suspects, Solutions" (SSS) sections from the chapters. They are presented in the order in which they occur in the book.

This Problem Index is not a traditional index. Alphabetical order means nothing here. If you want to do an alphabetic search for terms that might relate to your PC's current problem, use the traditional index near the end of *Troubleshooting Your PC Bible, 5th Edition* to do your search. The Problem Index has the Chapter number, title, and brief list of the contents followed by the symptoms from the SSS sections. Only the chapters with SSS sections are included in the Problem Index.

If your problem is with a particular part of your PC, such as the screen or printer, go to the section of the Problem Index that has the chapter number and title that relates to, in this case, your screen or printer. Again, in this case, that would be Chapter 20: "Sights and Sounds" for the screen or Chapter 21: "Basic Input and Output" that contains information about printer problems.

If you have no idea what your problem may be, skimming through the Problem Index will take a lot less time than skimming through the whole book (except that the Problem Index does not have any pictures). In the Problem Index you may find a phrase or sentence that seems to hit very close to the kind of problem you've encountered. Then, when you find your problem, you can flip to the chapter in which it's located for the suspects and solutions and background information.

> **Tip** The symptoms are in the same order here in which they appear in the chapters.

Chapter 8: Windows for Home and Desktop

Problem #1: Common Windows 3.x Problems
+ Windows will not run — It indicates that a device cannot be run in Standard mode.
+ Windows will not run — It indicates that a device must be run in Standard mode.
+ Windows will not run — It indicates that a device cannot be run in 386 Enhanced mode.
+ Windows will not run — It indicates that a device must be run in 386 Enhanced mode.

Problem #2: More Windows 3.x Problems
+ Windows will not run at all.

Problem #3: Windows 3.x Standard Mode Problems
✦ Windows will not run in standard mode.

Problem #4: Windows 3.x Real Mode Problems
✦ Windows will not run in Real mode.

Problem #5: Windows 3.x Enhanced Mode Problems
✦ Windows will not run in 386 Enhanced mode.

Problem #6: Windows 3.x Setup Problems
✦ Insufficient memory error running SETUP from DOS.

Problem #7: Windows 3.x Memory Problems
✦ Insufficient memory errors.

Problem #8 Windows 3.x Memory and Mode Problems
✦ Cannot run applications in the background.

Problem #9 Windows 3.x Program Conflicts
✦ Unrecoverable Applications Error message (Windows 3.0).
✦ General Protection Fault error message (Windows 3.1).

Problem #10 More Windows 3.x Program Conflicts
✦ Windows gives you a dialog box indicating that your application has corrupted the system or the Windows environment and that you should stop running your system.

Problem #11: Common Windows for Workgroups Problems
✦ Insufficient memory to run application.
✦ General Protection Fault errors in one or more applications.
✦ Darkened, incomplete program icon display in open program group(s).

Problem #12: Windows 95 and 98 Device Problems
✦ Windows 95/98 does not recognize some devices during installation.

Problem #13: Windows 95 and 98 Bootup Problems
✦ Pressing F4 does not enable bootup into prior DOS version after installing Windows 95/98.

Problem #21: Network Cabling and Configuration Problems
✦ No LINK light on network card.
✦ Workstation can ping itself but not the rest of the networked devices.
✦ Workstation cannot see other systems on the network.
✦ Workstation cannot log on to server.
✦ "No domain server available" message appears at logon.
✦ Network functions erratically.

Problem #22: More Network Configuration Problems
✦ Workstation can ping itself but not the rest of the networked devices.
✦ Workstation cannot see other systems on the network.
✦ Workstation cannot log on to server.
✦ "No domain server available" message appears at logon.
✦ "No DHCP server" message appears after startup.
✦ Network driver or Windows indicates an IP address conflict with another interface.

Problem #23: Network Setup and Workgroup Configuration Problems
✦ Network Neighborhood does not show all servers/workstations.

Problem #24: Logon and Workgroup Configuration Problems
✦ Network resources are visible when browsing the network, but you are unable to access and use them.
✦ Messages indicate that your user name or password is incorrect or that you do not have rights to the server, domain, or resources.

Chapter 11: The Internet

Problem #25: Modem Connection Problems
✦ Dial-Up Networking reports that the modem is in use or not available.
✦ Dial-Up Networking reports no dial tone.
✦ Rapid-busy error signal when dialing.

Problem #26: Network Configuration, Connection, and Congestion Problems
✦ Unable to negotiate a proper set of protocols with the server.
✦ Unable to authenticate with server.
✦ A connection is established but drops suddenly.

Problem #27: Network Configuration and Availability Problems
✦ Browser, e-mail, or other Internet applications indicate an inability to find the host name/address in DNS lookup.
✦ Unable to connect to server/site, or you get "host not responding" messages.
✦ Data requests go out and host connections appear to be made, but no data returns or you get "invalid host/destination" messages.

Problem #28: Web Page Access Problems
✦ A VPN connection dialog box appears when you try to access a Web page or use another Internet connection.

Problem #29: Dial-up Connection Problems
✦ Dial-up connection does not happen automatically as it used to.
✦ Dial-up connection happens automatically but is not desired.

Problem #30: Web Page Display Problems
✦ Tearing, distorted, incomplete graphics display on Web pages. A reload or refresh of the page may not clear up the display.

Problem #31: More Web Page Display Problems
✦ Unusual or blotchy color on Web pages that are clear and crisp on other systems.

Problem #32: JavaScript Error Messages
✦ You see JavaScript errors after a Web page appears to load correctly.

Problem #33: More Web Page Display Problems
✦ Data in HTML forms disappears after the screen-saver/blanker activates, and then display is restored.

Problem #34: Browser Helper and Plug-in Application Problems
✦ Errors occur when trying to view graphics files from Web pages.
✦ You get a browser message indicating that no viewer or helper application is associated with the file type you are trying to view.
✦ The wrong application opens when trying to view graphics files from File Manager/Explorer or selecting links to them from Web pages or e-mail.

Chapter 12: Power and Startup Problems

Problem #35: AC Power Problems
✦ Error messages 01x or 02x
✦ Intermittent system operation/failure
✦ Printer, CRT, or accessory problems

Problem #36: DC Power Supply Problems
✦ Power-on indication but no operation; flickering LEDs
✦ Fan starts and stops
✦ Error messages 01x or 02x
✦ Nonspecific or intermittent system failures or lockups
✦ After successful startup or seemingly successful startup attempt, computer turns off automatically

Problem #37: CMOS Setup Problems
+ Loss of date/time, memory, disk, or system information
+ Error messages 01x, 02x, 102, 103, 161, 162, 163, 164, 199, or 17xx
+ Long beep at startup, followed by the preceding messages
+ CMOS RAM error
+ Memory size error
+ Disk drive configuration error

Problem #38: Video Display Errors
+ One long and two short beeps
+ Error messages in 4xx, 5xx, 24xx, or 74xx ranges

Problem #39: Display Problems
+ Screen flickers or shrinks
+ Display is wiggly, pulsing, blurred, too large, or too small

Problem #40: Common Memory Errors
+ Memory size error (AT and higher systems)
+ Not enough memory (PC, XT)
+ Two short beeps and/or error message 2xx (PC, XT, AT)
+ Parity check 1 or 2, or ????? message
+ System hangs up

Problem #41: Floppy Disk Errors
+ Error messages in the 6xx or 73xx range

Problem #42: Hard Disk Errors
+ Error messages in the 17xx or 104xx ranges

Problem #43: DOS Disk Errors
+ Non-system disk or disk error

Problem #44: General Disk Errors
+ General failure reading drive x
+ Invalid drive specification
+ Drive not ready

Chapter 13: Configuration Problems

Problem #45: Problems in CONFIG.SYS

✦ Bad or missing commands or drivers in CONFIG.SYS indicated by one or more of the following messages:

✦ System Message: "Unrecognized command in CONFIG.SYS."

✦ System Message: "Bad or missing d:\subdir\driver.sys" ("drive:\path\driver filename" of a driver supposedly installed in your system).

✦ System message: "Label not found."

✦ System boots okay, but some things may not be just right, such as an inability to open enough files, the system runs slow, or a device (printer, network connection, plotter, expanded or extended memory, or other system extension) does not function.

Problem #46: Problems with Driver and Programs in CONFIG.SYS

✦ System locks up in CONFIG.SYS.

✦ System stops before executing the AUTOEXEC.BAT file.

✦ Some CONFIG.SYS command results (messages) may be onscreen, but your system does not respond.

✦ Ctrl+Break, Break, Ctrl+C, Esc, Ctrl+Alt+Delete, and other keys normally used to get out of problem situations do not have the expected effect. Your system is locked up.

✦ You may see a message containing "System Halted."

Problem #47: Problems Executing AUTOEXEC.BAT

✦ Bad, missing, or wrong COMMAND.COM indicated by one of the following:
  • "Invalid COMMAND.COM, system not loaded"
  • "Bad or missing command interpreter"
  • "Cannot load COMMAND.COM, system halted"
  • "Incorrect DOS version"

✦ System message: "Label not found".

✦ Your version of DOS may display a different message than the preceding message, but it will have a similar meaning.

Problem #48: Problems with the AUTOEXEC.BAT File

✦ Missing or wrong AUTOEXEC.BAT file (wrong in the sense that it is not doing what you expect and assuming you may have more than one).

✦ Your system asks for the date and time before displaying the DOS prompt.

✦ Your system boots, but the system setup you expect to use does not appear.

Problem #49: Problems with Commands and Programs in AUTOEXEC.BAT

✦ Bad commands, or missing files or programs in AUTOEXEC.BAT.
✦ Onscreen message: "Bad command or filename."
✦ Onscreen message containing the following:
  • "file not found"
  • "missing"
  • "not installed"
✦ Your system boots, but the system setup you expect does not appear.
✦ Your system might become locked up, but only after it gets past loading the devices and parameters in CONFIG.SYS and you see some of the results of your AUTOEXEC.BAT file.

Problem #50: Memory Problems in Configuration

✦ Onscreen message containing "insufficient memory"

Problem #51: Bad, Corrupt, or Missing Device Drivers

✦ Some device or accessory is not running or available after booting up your system.
✦ Message onscreen containing one or more of the following:
  • "device not found"
  • "device not installed"
  • "unable to access"
  • "unavailable"

Problem #52: Bad Batch File or Script

✦ "Infinite loop" problem. (The computer keeps doing the same thing over and over again):
  • Repeating messages onscreen
  • Executing the same program repeatedly
  • Initializing one or more devices repeatedly
✦ The computer may continue indefinitely or, eventually, crash or lock up.

Problem #53: Problems with Bad Commands or Programs in Batch or Script Files

✦ Your batch file never ran.
✦ You have a batch file that contains the commands needed to do a particular job, but the job does not get done.
✦ A program is executed by your batch file, but the batch file should be doing more.

Chapter 14: System Boards

Problem #54: Bootup and Lock-up Problems

◆ System does nothing at startup.
◆ System suddenly hangs up.
◆ Windows will not run.
◆ System reboots when you try to run or exit from Windows.

Problem #55: System and Application Speed Problems

◆ Games and programs run too fast.
◆ Time-out errors from applications.
◆ Divide-by-zero errors.

Problem #56: System Board-related Memory Problems

◆ Memory size error (AT).
◆ Not enough memory (PC and XT).
◆ Two short beeps, error message 2xx, or both (PC, XT, and AT).
◆ "Parity Check 1 or 2," or "Parity Check ?????" message.
◆ System hangs up.

Problem #57: Math Chip Problems

◆ Error message "Coprocessor not found."
◆ Application failure.
◆ Hardware lock up.
◆ Diagnostics fail or do not show math coprocessor interrupt.

Problem #58: Clock Problems

◆ Date and time are wrong, fast, or slow.
◆ CMOS/clock battery does not last more than a few days or weeks (expected life is one to five years).
◆ Error messages 01x, 02x, 102, 103, 161, 162, 163, 164, 199, or 17xx occur.
◆ Long beep at startup, followed by previous messages.
◆ CMOS RAM error.
◆ Memory size error.
◆ Disk drive configuration error (drive not found, no boot device available, or similar messages).

Problem #59: System Board Related Keyboard Problems

◆ Keyboard is locked or inactive.
◆ System prompts for a password.
◆ Keyboard error message at startup.
◆ Keyboard errors during testing.

Problem #65: Memory Configuration Problems
✦ Error messages about insufficient or no memory of a specific type
✦ Error messages containing the letters DPMI, VCPI, DOSX, or another name that refers to a DOS extender

Chapter 18: Hard Drives

Problem #66: Disk Hardware Failures
✦ Drive will not start spinning or it groans.

Problem #67: Disk Drive Motor or Electronics Problems
✦ Drive spins up and down erratically.

Problem #68: Disk Drive Crash or Soon to Happen
✦ Drive makes high-pitched noise.

Problem #69: Power-On Self-Test Disk Drive Messages
✦ Any of the following numeric error messages appear, usually during the POST:
- 1701   Controller/cabling/drive/drive select jumper/CMOS
- 1702   Controller
- 1703   Controller/cabling/drive/jumpers
- 1704   Controller or drive
- 1780   First physical drive (0:) failure
- 1781   Second physical drive (1:) failure
- 1782   Controller
- 1790   First physical drive (0:) error
- 1791   Second physical drive (1:) error
- 10480   First physical drive (0:) failure (PS/2-ESDI)
- 10481   Second physical drive (1:) failure (PS/2-ESDI)
- 10482   PS/2 ESDI controller failure
- 10483   PS/2 ESDI controller failure
- 10490   First physical drive (0:) error (PS/2-ESDI)
- 10491   Second physical drive (1:) error (PS/2-ESDI)

Problem #70: Disk Drive Performance Issues
✦ Slow performance

Problem #71: Disk Drive Partitioning, Formatting, or Cluttered Problems
✦ Drive fills up too fast.

Problem #72: Disk Cache, Buffering, and Intermittent Problems
✦ Files are partially or improperly written.
✦ Files are not saved on the disk.

Such a message indicates that the FAT is defective on the disk in question. The solutions are the same as those for the "File Allocation Table Bad, Drive *x*" message.

Problem #116: COM Port Conflicts

✦ The modem dials out, but nothing else happens.

✦ The serial printer does not print or prints only pieces of what is expected.

✦ Your mouse gets lost or causes your cursor to move around the screen as your system locks up.

✦ Your voice synthesizer speaks with a garbled or unintelligible voice.

✦ Someone calls your computer's modem and gets connected to the modem, but your computer (communication program) does not respond or know that a connection exists.

Problem #117: Modem Initialization Problems

✦ Your communication program and modem are not working together.

✦ The communication program never knows when the modem is connected to the other end. (Modem CD control or communication program connect message setting. Check modem &C command.)

✦ You cannot make the modem hang up the phone or, if the phone is hung up, the program thinks it is still connected. (Modem CD control and DTR control or communication program hang-up string. Check modem &C and &D commands.)

✦ The speaker is too loud or too quiet. (Modem Speaker control and volume settings. Check modem L and M commands.)

✦ The communication program cannot communicate with your modem. You see numbers printed on your screen when the modem connects, resets, or hangs up, but the communication program does not realize the change in status. (Modem use of numeric or verbal command responses coupled with your communication program settings for the expected responses from your modem. Check modem V and W commands).

✦ The communication program cannot connect with your modem. You see commands such as CONNECT, RING, and NO CARRIER printed on your screen but the communication program does not realize the change in status. (Modem use of numeric or verbal command responses and the corresponding settings in your communication program. Check modem V command setting.)

✦ You expect your modem to make an error correcting connection (for example, MNP or V.42bis), but this does not happen. (Modem error correction protocol settings. Check modem &Q or \L or \O or other commands dealing with error correction.)

✦ Your modem does not dial, even when you know the communication parameters (COM port assignment, bps rate, parity, data bits, stop bit, and so forth) are all set correctly. (Dial command string in your communication program, usually ATD or ATDT coupled with a dialing command suffix that is usually a carriage return represented by a symbol such as ! or ^ or |.)

✦ Your modem does not answer the phone when you think it is supposed to. (Modem answer command and number of rings settings. Check the modem S0 (zero) register setting and/or an A command to answer the phone.)

✦ Your modem answers the phone when you think it should not. (Modem answer command and number of rings settings. Check the modem S0 (zero) register setting and/or an A command setting.)

✦ Your modem is supposed use pulse dialing, but it is not. (Modem dial mode command. Check for T or P command in your modem initialization string.)

✦ Your modem takes a long time to dial a number. The dialing tones are long and there seems to be a long delay between dialing tones. (Modem dial tone register setting. Check your modem S11 register setting.)

✦ Your modem dials so quickly that the phone cannot respond. (Modem dial tone register setting. Check your modem S11 register setting.)

✦ Your modem dials a number but hangs up the phone before a connection is made. (Modem and communication programs wait for connect time settings. Check your modem's S7 register setting.)

✦ Your modem is supposed to adjust to the communication speed of the computer you called or the computer that has called your system but it does not happen. (Check both the flow control and protocol mode selections in both your modem — usually &K and &Q or &B, &H, and &N commands — and your communication program.)

✦ You are trying to use your modem with hardware flow control but it is not working. (Modem and communication program hardware flow control commands and settings. Check your communication program settings and your modem initialization commands, usually &K and &Q or &B, &H, and &N commands.)

Problem #118: Flow Control Problems

✦ Your PC does not make a connection to or does not continue to communicate with the serial device on the other end.

✦ Data is lost during a serial connection due to one side or the other continuing to transmit data when the opposite side is not ready.

Problem #119: Erratic Communications Problems

✦ Line noise or unwanted or poor signals getting into your modem.

Problem #120: Erratic connection problems

✦ Crosstalk or interference. If you hear other conversations or tones on the line while you are using the telephone, you are hearing crosstalk. This is the effect of one line's information being induced into another.

Problem #121: Modem Connections Too Slow

✦ Impatience, frustration, headaches from stressed deadline pushing, and envy for the faster modem and serial printer in the other person's office.

Problem #122: High-Speed Transfer Problems

✦ When operating your serial port at 9600 bps or faster or when using your serial ports under a multi-tasking operating system, files lose characters or file transfers are slowed down due to multiple retries.

✦ Your communication connection occasionally locks up or the connection gets dropped or fails when using high speeds or working under a multi-tasking environment.

Problem #123: Bad Cables, Poor Connections

✦ "It used to work and I have added no new hardware or software, and all the serial port and parameter settings are correct, but nothing happens."

✦ Same situation mentioned earlier, but the data transferred or received from the device or system on the other end is missing data or contains "garbage characters" mixed with what should be transmitted or received. (Again, this includes serial printers, modems, your mouse or track ball, and other serial devices.)

Problem #124: Null Modem Problems

✦ Data transmitted from one end of the serial cable is not received at the other end.

✦ Hardware flow control signals are ignored.

✦ Neither side knows the other is connected.

Problem #125: Universal Serial Bus Problems

✦ Your PC has a USB port but the device you plug in does not work.

Now that you've reached the end of the Problem Index, especially if you have not found the specific problem you've encountered, please go to the chapter or chapters about the part of your PC that is not working properly. That chapter, and others that have not been included in this index, contain background and descriptive information that will help you diagnose and fix the problem.

Please let us know if encounter a new kind of problem. We're all in this, together!

Getting Started

Even if you are new to PCs or feel you need much help getting started, you're in the right place. Earlier editions of this book have been used as a recommended reference for certification training programs, such as the A+ Certification, and have also been used as a text in courses to teach non-technical students how to become PC support technicians.

If you are impressed by a person who can solve a PC problem by just tapping a few keys; if you are surprised by a person who can tear a system down to the plastic standoffs that hold the system board in place, and rebuild it in 20 minutes; or if you wish you could do it — you are in luck!

Anyone with even modest mechanical skills, the ability to insert and remove diskettes, and the ability to type on a keyboard, can do 90 percent of the repairs a PC might need. Understanding the basics is the first step.

Part I starts you on the path to troubleshooting your own PC. So what are you waiting for? Get started with Chapter 1.

Troubleshooting

If you are one of those people who marvel at folks who can just tap a few keys and make everything better, or you envy those who can tear down a system to the plastic standoffs and rebuild it in 20 minutes, this book can help you achieve those same skills. You will see that anyone with even modest mechanical skills and the ability to insert and remove diskettes and type on a keyboard can do 90 percent of the diagnosis of PC problems and make most of the repairs a PC might need. If you can read and follow instructions and diagrams, you are on your way to becoming a PC expert. Understanding the basics is the first step.

Troubleshooting Defined

Troubleshooting is the process of evaluating, in an orderly fashion, the purpose, function, normal operational behavior, and apparent symptoms of a piece of equipment, program, or system, with the objective of identifying malfunctions and arriving at a solution that places your system back in proper, usable condition. Fixing the problem is a separate process that logically follows troubleshooting. A final aspect of repairing a problem is verifying that you indeed fixed it, which is a step easily overlooked after the frustration of having the problem and the headaches of fixing it. Problem solving is the integration of both troubleshooting and repairing, and, we might also add, taking steps to prevent problems. If you do not take the last step in repair — verification or validation — you will miss a crucial problem prevention step.

If you are already familiar with your PC system, where internal and external cabling and accessories plug in, and what they do, you may wish to skip ahead to Chapter 2 in order to learn about the tools you'll need to begin working on your PC.

The goal of this book is to help you solve problems by leading you through the basics of troubleshooting and diagnosing.

You will have to work with your system and some tools to determine what the problem is and how to fix it. However, our mission is to help you keep the system running from the day you buy it until the day you send it to the big PC retirement home in the sky.

Few of you who use PCs lack the ability to troubleshoot. You may not be able to design, construct, or program a PC, but if you have used a PC for more than a few days or weeks, remember that compared to someone who has not yet tried to work with a PC, you are already an expert.

You can do it!

It is important to realize that you can do most of the things you may ever need to do with a PC and do them in just a few minutes of actual work. The hard part may be waiting on the telephone for technical support, standing in line to buy the part for the repair, or finding something else to do while your system runs formatting or diagnostic tests.

 If you feel ready, skip ahead to the "Basic Troubleshooting" section of this chapter.

Temper this with your own and others' awareness that you cannot and should not be expected to know and do everything with a PC. Some folks can fix the dickens out of any motherboard problem but cannot read the first line of a batch (.BAT) file, while some of the most brilliant programmers should be kept away from tools and electrical components for their own safety and that of others. We all fit somewhere in the extremes of this highly technical world. Reaching beyond our means can be as unproductive as not reaching out to them at all.

Apart from diagnosing and resolving some of the more obscure problems, you should be able to fix (replace or repair) most of the components or files in your PC system. The components are simply mechanical devices that must fit together by design and form to create electrical and mechanical attachments. Similarly, there is a design, form, and function to the organization of memory, disks, and files; though they may not be mechanical or visible, they can be visualized, which is often the first step in solving a particular problem.

Electrical and file-related (or "soft") issues seem to be the most confusing or forbidding to many users. Hazardous electrical items should be well contained within the power cords, outlets, and power supply boxes. You should be wary of them and heed specific warnings. The delicate items that handle the high-speed bits and bytes require an advanced level of awareness as well.

We do not delve deeply into electrical theory in this book, but we do warn you of potentially harmful procedures and issues that you must handle with care handle with care in order to ensure proper operation and to prevent damage to sensitive components. Many components are as vulnerable to your actions as you may feel they are to the electrical environment in which your PC lives. PC system components (not the power supply and monitor) operate at far lower voltage than anything that can harm you. That is the good news. The precaution is that everything we use today—including your computer, printer, and various other components—relies on the potentially lethal electrical properties connected with every wall switch in the rooms around us.

As for those things you cannot see or feel, and must deal with using the components of the computer, this book will avoid a lot of mumbo-jumbo about tricky analog signals and multiplexing data and addresses, or shifting bytes of numbers around to compress or read files.

Be prepared

As long as your personal computer works as you expect it to, you probably take it for granted, as you would any other reliable tool, and give little thought to those building blocks and how they work together. But when something goes wrong, it helps to understand and know how to work with your system's separate elements.

That is where we come in. Whether your hard drive crashes, your power supply blows a fuse, or your printer suddenly begins to spit out nonsense characters, this book will guide you through the various problem-solving steps you need to take in order to get your trusty computer up and running again.

Basic Troubleshooting

When you decide that something needs to be fixed, you have already completed much of the troubleshooting process by identifying that something is wrong. At this point, you are well on your way to solving the problem. For want of a little more information and maybe a new part, you could be back up and running in a matter of minutes. Most repairs take no more than a couple of hours, if you have access to the right resources.

 Caution   Lack of information is a dangerous thing. Make sure you take the time to figure out what the problem is before you attempt to fix it.

Recognizing that something is wrong is the first step. What happened, when it happened, and the effects it has on the rest of your PC system are the key pieces of information you need.

This section covers some basic items to consider as you try to determine the source, cause, and remedy for PC problems. The chapters that follow describe more specific methods for determining the cause of a problem.

The problem-solving process

Solving a problem requires first recognizing that there is one — which may be somewhat obvious — logically determining where the problem could be, and then narrowing things down from there. More experienced folks may appear to go right from problem to solution and make the process look all too easy. But between the problem and solution is a set of learned and practiced analysis — you just do not see the wheels spinning in their heads. That is what experts are for.

If it ain't broke, don't fix it!

This phrase establishes a philosophy and sets the tone for things to come. The worst thing you can do is jump right from having a problem into taking some action, which may or may not be appropriate for the problem at hand.

Sometimes simply shutting things down and restarting the system is *the* solution to one or more otherwise unexplainable problems. Actually, the problems are explainable, given the right tools, time, and circumstances to analyze the situation, but more often than not, we do not have that luxury, nor can anyone else provide an easy explanation. More on that when we get into program lockups, Windows crashes, and so on.

Rules to live by

Somewhere between the unexplainable, the obvious, the oversimplified, and the wrong solutions is a set of rules, experiences, assessments, analysis, and actions that lead to the right solution. We are going to take you down that path as we explain the processes and go through problem examples throughout this book.

1. Understand the task at hand. Know what your goal is to be. Are you trying to print a file, upload it to a BBS, or just create it with a text editor?

2. Understand how to accomplish those tasks. What methods must you use to reach the goal, and what components or bits, paper, disks, programs, modems, sound, or motion are involved?

3. Determine whether there really is a problem.

   a. Did it ever do what you think it is not doing now?

   b. When did it last do what it should?

    c. How does it do it differently?

    d. Does it work for some things and not for others?

4. Identify the problem. What are the circumstances around the problem? Which of those circumstances are involved in the problem and which have nothing to do with it?

5. Consider the activities, use, and conditions around the system. Have you made any recent changes?

6. Correct items that are found defective.

7. Correct items that could cause a problem in the future.

The keys to solving these problems include the following:

1. Knowing and understanding your system

    a. What type of processor does it use?

    b. How much and what type of memory?

    c. How many and what kind of disks?

    d. What options and adapters does it have (serial ports, modems, and so on)?

    e. Is the system configured correctly — both in terms of hardware and software or configuration files?

2. Understanding enough about DOS or Windows to boot up a system and run a program

3. Understanding how the software you use is supposed to function

4. Knowing what components are in your system and where they are located

5. Knowing how to remove and insert the components, as well as knowing how to operate any switches or change their jumpers

6. Being able to recognize textual, visual, and audible clues that indicate potential problem spots

7. Being familiar with your system's documentation and keeping handy the technical support number(s) for the components in your system and its software

8. Taking each aspect of the system and your work step by step and eliminating what does not fit the problem

9. Having patience and a will to do it

10. Having the proper hand tools to open and change parts in your system

What you do not need to be or have are listed here:

1. An electrical engineer, electrician, astrophysicist, brain surgeon, programmer, radio/TV technician, or psychic (though we wonder if the latter would be the most valuable to the process)

2. A box of fancy tools, meters, plugs, cables, scopes, and so on (the simple tools should suffice)

Cross-Reference

See Chapter 2 to learn what tools you'll need for the work at hand.

3. Panic and stress

In short, the basic strategy is to divide and conquer. Any good, successful, and respected service person will tell you that the worst thing you can do is jump into the middle of a problem and start diddling with anything and everything you can get your hands on.

When your computer does not do what you asked it to do, this book will serve as your reference guide and support. Following the approach in these chapters, attack the problem with a calm, step-by-step approach. Check out one symptom at a time, in a logical sequence, until you have identified — and cured — the disease.

Don't rush!

The first technique is to avoid assumptions, working from the middle or inside steps to outer or inner steps, jumping to conclusions, or just "fixing" something that may not affect the problem.

Second, the simple rules we learned for crossing the street apply just as well to troubleshooting and problem solving — *stop, look, and listen*. Do not step out before you are sure the road is clear or that you have checked the basic items first.

Where to start

Always, *always* begin with good, solid information. This is a step you can take when the system is working fine — from learning what normal things happen as the system starts up to making a report or log of the system's configuration information. Creating your own audible, visual, and configuration reference point gives you a goal to work toward.

Cross-Reference

It will be to your advantage to read Chapter 5, which introduces the relationships between names, such as COM, and the technical things, such as addresses and IRQs.

✦ Note visual clues:

- Error messages on display

- Fan speed

- Display or LED flickering or not operating

- Inspect cables for broken or cracked insulation, cuts or abrasions, misaligned or dirty connectors or pins

- Inspect add-in cards and connections for proper seating and the alignment of connectors and brackets

- Look for loose or missing screws, or items that may have fallen into circuits, causing shorts or failure of a device that is missing the screw(s)

✦ Note audible clues:

- Sound of the fan

- Noises from disk drives, with or without diskettes inserted

- Error code beeps from the speaker

- Snapping or popping sounds from inside the display or power supply

✦ Check the outlet the system is plugged into to be sure it works. Use a lamp or another device as a basic power indicator.

✦ Swap the system power cord for another.

✦ Be sure the system has "room to breathe" and that it is not dirty inside. Most dirt would be visible at the inlet vents, at the edges of the chips inside the system, and around the fan inlet at the power supply.

✦ A slow-turning fan may be hard to recognize unless you are familiar with how the air moved or the fan sounded before the current problem. A worn-out or weak fan may have caused this problem. A weak power supply, or poor AC power to the system could also be the cause.

✦ If the fan does not turn (no air coming out or rushing-air sound) but the system runs, the fan itself may be bad. Repairing this usually entails replacement of the entire power supply, unless you are technically inclined and can find a replacement fan and install it in the supply.

✦ Failure of the fan can result in shutdown of the power supply or the system due to excessive heat. Excessive dirt or blockage of the air vents around the system may also cause excess heat or fan failure.

✦ Erratic disk drive operations or various failures, such as system resets during use or lockups might indicate a weak power supply.

✦ Weak AC power to the system will typically show up in a pulsating or flickering display or erratic "tearing" of the displayed image (much as you would see on a television set with misadjusted horizontal or vertical hold).

✦ Clues indicating a weak or insufficient power supply include occasional slow starting, noticeable "groaning" when the system starts up, or a slow response from a disk drive.

✦ If you have noticed that a disk drive is slow or that it has given you data errors or frequent error messages ("Drive Not Ready" or "General Failure"), your problem is most likely in that single disk drive.

✦ If just one part of your system is affected, you may have a loose connection. If your system has been moved or worked on often, the pins at the individual connections may be poorly connected.

You can check this last point by "wiggling" the connector, or unplugging it and inspecting the pins. You might find that the round female pins on disk drive power connectors have become enlarged and need to be compressed to their original size in order to make good contact. On the motherboard power connectors, the pin connections may have flattened away from making good contact. A small screwdriver or knife blade might be useful in reshaping the pins.

Data cables are more difficult to troubleshoot because there are so many connections, often hidden from view. Replacement of suspect cables is often the best method to diagnose (fix) the problem.

Isolate possible causes by the process of elimination. It is possible that one or more items may be interfering with other data or that something is overloading the power supply, causing loss of power to other items. This process involves disconnecting cables or removing different parts until the system begins to function.

Begin with the least critical items and work your way into the system details. If you suspect problems with the power supply, begin to unload the drain from it by removing or disconnecting the following items, in order of their necessity to run the system:

1. Serial and/or parallel port cards

2. Clock/calendar card

3. Additional memory card(s)

4. Hard disk adapter card (run your system from a diskette to the test it. You should expect an error on the the screen regarding the missing hard disk.)

5. Power from the hard disk drive

6. The diskette drive adapter card (try the system without disks, expect an error on the CRT)

7. Power from the diskette drive(s)

During this process, if removing one or more serial or parallel adapters enables the system to begin working properly, reinstall one adapter at a time until the problem reappears. The last card you install before the problem reappears is likely defective.

This process works as well for isolating some errors with programs "hanging up" with data or interrupt conflicts because of a hardware problem. The card or device that you disconnect may cause the symptom to disappear, indicating some type of conflict with that item and the rest of your system.

Summary

In this chapter, you learned the fundamentals of troubleshooting your PC. Here are important things to remember:

✦ Troubleshooting need not be a mystery.

✦ The best place to start is before your system develops a problem.

✦ Making and keeping good records of what is in your system will be a *big* help.

✦ Don't fix something unless it is really a problem.

✦ Be sensible — use your senses. What do you see? What do you hear? What do you smell? What do you feel? Relate these to your experience before the problem.

✦ Use help if it is available.

✦ Don't get frustrated, lose your patience, or get mad. Success is more fun!

✦   ✦   ✦

Tools of the Trade

Before you take the cover off of your system, you should make sure you have a few simple tools to help you along. Even better, you may be able to "look" inside the system without removing screws and panels. Without X-ray vision, the next best thing is diagnostic and utility software. Listed in the "Your Software Toolkit" section are some of the more popular and effective software tools that may not only be capable of determining the source of a problem, but often repair problems inside your system as well. More detailed coverage of these tools can be found in chapters covering specific problems and in Chapter 23.

Your Software Toolkit

If you forget one of the most important messages this book has to offer — *backup* — this section may be the one that comes to your rescue. From the time you turn on your system, a few guideposts help to keep your data on the proper route, and if your data strays, there are some simple pointers to getting it back on track quickly.

For the big blowout on the freeway, a spare, a jack, and a little time are all it may take to get rolling again. However, there is always the 17-car pileup threat, and if you are lucky all you need is the big yellow truck to pull you out, if you remembered to keep its number (disk) handy.

Tip

Here we come to one of the most important messages in this book — have a few diskettes stashed safely away that enable you to at least boot your system and run a diagnostic or file recovery program. Without these, you may as well be in the middle of the desert without water.

Startup diskettes. These are typically bootable diskettes that would include at least the CHKDSK, FORMAT, FDISK, and SYS (for older systems) programs. We recommend also including the DOS EDIT program to use for creating and editing various configuration files. If you are running Windows 98, Microsoft Windows Millennium Edition (Me), or Windows 2000, these operating systems provide robust facilities for creating startup diskettes for your system.

System utilities. If your system comes with a special set of programs for configuring or testing your system, you should maintain a working copy of these files with your DOS or bootable diskettes. If you use a program such as EZ-Drive, OnTrack, or some other special disk partitioning software, or software that enables you to use a disk drive larger than the one supported by your system BIOS, by all means keep this software handy! The same goes for any software used to compress your disk drive (the old Stacker, or any version of DriveSpace).

Basic utilities and diagnostics. A wide choice exists with the utility and system enhancement packages available from Norton/Symantec, Gibson Research, Network Associates (formerly McAfee Associates, and encompassing Helix Software's Nuts&Bolts utilities). Since many of these packages cannot be run from the original diskettes, the software should be installed onto a hard disk and selected files copied to diskettes, or install the software on diskettes. You may also benefit from certain public domain or shareware programs.

Advanced diagnostics. Beyond the popular or more common utilities, such as Norton Utilities, you may find an occasion to use a more detailed diagnostic program to rigorously test individual parts of your system. Packages, such as PC-Doctor from Watergate Software, offer a range of system diagnostics, from user-friendly to technician-level, that can pinpoint specific chips or boards that may be defective. For use in Windows, PC-Doctor for Windows from Watergate offers considerable help in verification and system testing.

 A trial version of PC-Doctor is available on the CD-ROM that accompanies this book.

Diagnostics are used in the quality control verification of each one of your system components, from the time a new disk drive or chip is invented, through development, the factory assembly line, and by the vendors who sell PC systems. These once "for technicians only" programs are becoming friendlier and more helpful, and are a part of many technical support efforts.

As you will see throughout the various sections of this book, diagnostic software plays an invaluable role in finding and fixing many types of PC problems. If you are looking for software to help you with your system, you will want a package that can trace problems all the way back to the origins of the parts you are testing. Do not neglect the many fine programs available for download from bulletin-board systems and online services. Support of these shareware and public domain programs and their authors lead to some powerful and successful software products.

Emergency diskettes

The following sections cover utilities for your disk drives. Disk drives are relatively easy to work with because, unlike memory and chips, the data is usually still on the disk drive — perhaps scrambled a bit after a system crash, but utility software can usually retrieve the data. We do not have that luxury with the dynamics of memory, chips and such, but some progress has been made in preventing crashes, as you will see toward the end of this section.

A handful of diskettes may be all it takes to save your files. Considering the investment is all of a couple dollars (for the disks), plus whatever you decide to invest for utility software (Norton, Nuts&Bolts, and so on), and the time it takes to create this "toolkit," it is good insurance.

Note   Even if your A: drive is a 1.2 or 1.44MB drive, it is a good idea to use low-density (360K or 720K) diskettes just in case the CMOS RAM setup (hardware configuration area on 286, 386, 486, and Pentium systems) is lost and somehow the parameters default to the lower density. You will be unable to read and, therefore, unable to boot from the high-density diskettes if the drive parameters default to low density. Although early versions of DOS provide two powerful disk utilities, CHKDSK and RECOVER, and later versions of DOS include scaled-down versions of Symantec/Norton programs (notably, SCANDISK), there are faster, safer, and less troublesome utilities that are recommended, such as the full version of Norton Utilities.

We do recommend that you obtain at least one utility and one diagnostic package to complement each other. Alas, these off-the-shelf, aftermarket utilities are not free or even economical, considering you already get some utilities with DOS; however, they will make life *much* easier for isolating and solving common and uncommon file and disk problems. Which ones you prefer is up to you and your budget, and your technical expertise and requirements. Seek recommendations and product information and consider the reputation of the company providing the package.

Emergency diskette recommendations for older systems

We strongly recommend that you have at least a bootable/system DOS diskette handy. It should contain at least the following files and be verified as bootable (try booting with the diskette after formatting and copying the files.).

✦ IO.SYS (MS-DOS) or IBMBIO.COM (PC-DOS)

✦ MSDOS.SYS (MS-DOS) or IBMDOS.COM (PC-DOS)

✦ COMMAND.COM

✦ CHKDSK.COM or SCANDISK.EXE

✦ FORMAT.COM

✦ FDISK.COM

✦ SYS.COM

This diskette is most easily made with the FORMAT *drive letter*:/S command. Use the COPY command to place SCANDISK, FORMAT, FDISK, and SYS on the diskette. With these files, you should be able to reformat and make your hard disk bootable, check for lost files, and begin any necessary recover operations.

For gaining access to your CD-ROM drive in order to reinstall, say, Windows Me, you will need a copy of the DOS driver for your CD-ROM drive and the MSCDEX.EXE program copied onto the diskette, and include references to them in your CONFIG.SYS and AUTOEXEC.BAT files, respectively.

You should also store a set of diskettes for the utility suite of your choice with the previously listed files. You will not be able to use some master/original disks for these utilities because many of the files are compressed before installation. Copy the executable files from your hard disk installation. If you use Norton Utilities, copy the program file NDD.EXE to your boot diskette, or use its Create Rescue Diskette utility.

If you use special hard disk partitioning software, OnTrack's Disk Manager, or Storage Dimension's SpeedStor (commonly used in drives larger than 32MB and in DOS 3.3 or earlier, or for drives larger than 512MB on later DOS systems), you preferably will have the original copy, or at least a working copy, of these. The special driver file for this software, which goes into your CONFIG.SYS file, should be on your bootable DOS diskette and loaded with the CONFIG.SYS file from that diskette in order to make any future recovery easier.

Also keep handy the following:

✦ A diskette containing any special driver or utility files for your hard disk controller card. These may fit onto the DOS diskette.

✦ A diskette containing the CMOS RAM setup program for your BIOS. A generic one usually comes with many diagnostic programs, but BIOS is highly customized for each system. For EISA-type and IBM-PS/2 systems, you will need the respective configuration and reference diskettes that come with these systems.

✦ A diskette with the backup program of your choice. One of these, preferably bootable, should also be kept with your backup diskettes or tapes.

We recommend that you invoke "disk imaging" program (IMAGE from Norton) on a regular basis, either with your AUTOEXEC.BAT file or before shutting the system down.

These utilities store a snapshot of the critical areas of your drive (Boot sector, File Allocation Tables, and directory structures), making recovery much faster, more reliable, and the resulting files usable. Also use the partition-saving option with these utilities to make disk partition restoration easier.

Note If you use Disk Manager or SpeedStor, the images of the hard disks will be significantly different than normal DOS images, especially where the partition tables are concerned. Data recovery may be quite difficult in some cases, especially if you have not used one of the snapshot utilities or have booted without loading the special driver file.

If you have an *old* PC, XT, or AT system, you may need the DOS DEBUG program or the utilities for your disk controller in case you have to resort to a low-level format of the hard disk. You will lose all of your existing data in the process, but you will get the system up and ready for a restoration of the backup, if possible.

Write-protect the diskettes and tuck them away in their own "guru" box. If you keep them safely locked away with your backups, you will have everything you need, unless you have a massive, unrecoverable hardware failure.

Armed with these tools, you stand a much greater chance of surviving a hard drive disaster. Without them you may have to write off the drive or files and find some outside help to get your system functioning again.

One sure sign that this method is important is that Windows 95/98 and NT ask users to create emergency diskettes upon installation, and they recommend that you update the diskettes frequently and especially after you make changes in your system.

Note The preceding procedures, with the exception of the recommendation to have additional utility programs available on diskette, are pretty much replaced by the Emergency Repair Disk procedures for Windows 95/98/Me/2000 and NT.

Getting to a DOS prompt at bootup

Sometimes you have to revert to a boot diskette—keep one handy! Most of the time Windows (DOS) displays "Loading Windows 9x . . ." when a system first boots up. If you see this, press F8, and you should get a Windows boot menu (not the DOS boot menu you make in CONFIG.SYS and AUTOEXEC.BAT.)

The menu will show you a few startup options, such as "Normal", "Safe Mode", and "Command-prompt only". Most of the time selecting "Command-prompt only" is the option you want.

Making startup and bootable DOS diskettes

Okay, hiding DOS behind a fancy graphical interface is fun, until you really need to get at things before Windows gets in the way or crashes.

Creating a startup diskette

If you're setting up Windows for the first time, go ahead and make your startup disk when you set up. If you've already set up Windows, you can still create a startup disk using the Add/Remove Programs feature of the Control Panel.

Tip   You can access the "Add/Remove Programs" feature by double-clicking the "My Computer" icon, located on your desktop, and then opening the "Control Panel".

Creating a bootable DOS diskette

Once you've got your startup disk, follow the next few steps with another blank diskette in order to create your bootable DOS diskette:

1. Place the blank diskette in your A: drive and format it in DOS with the /S command switch. Or, in Windows using Explorer, right-click on your diskette (A:) drive, select Format, and do a complete format, including placing the system files on the diskette (See Figure 2-1).

Figure 2-1: Formatting a diskette in Windows Explorer

2. Copy the following files from the Windows\Command folder on your hard drive to the diskette (A: drive):

   C:\WINDOWS\COMMAND\ATTRIB.EXE

   C:\WINDOWS\COMMAND\EDIT.COM

   C:\WINDOWS\COMMAND\FDISK.EXE

   C:\WINDOWS\COMMAND\FORMAT.COM

   C:\WINDOWS\COMMAND\MSCDEX.COM

   C:\WINDOWS\COMMAND\SYS.COM

3. If you're so inclined and know which file is the right DOS/Config.sys driver for your CD-ROM drive, copy it to the diskette too. If you do not copy it, you will have to reinstall your CD-ROM while in a DOS environment in order to get that particular file identified. You will not be able to use your CD-ROM without it again if it is required.

This will provide you with the basic files for booting your system to DOS and, as you will see in the next section, you can get your CD-ROM to work, too — which is essential for installing Windows.

Startup diskette with CD-ROM drivers

At some time in your work with Windows, you will probably want to reinstall the program. However, you may be unable to figure out how to get your CD-ROM recognized in DOS so that you can install Windows from the CD.

If you use the following directions, you may be able to avoid having to load your CD-ROM drivers unless you reformat or change your hard drive. After you have created a startup diskette using the steps in the "Creating a bootable DOS diskette" section, follow these steps in order to get your CD-ROM drive working:

1. Run the EDIT program, loading it from your hard drive or from the diskette. You will start working with a blank file that we will call CONFIG.SYS. Save it to the A: drive.

2. Type in the following line in the EDIT program box:

DEVICE=MYCDROM.SYS /D:MSCD001

Replace the characters MYCDROM.SYS with the actual, full name of the proper CD-ROM driver file for your CD-ROM drive. Remember, the characters that appear after the /D: — the characters can be almost anything, but Microsoft typically uses MSCD001 — will be used in the next step. If you perform this procedure *before* you have modified your working system, you can get the names of the CDROM.SYS and the specific version of MSCD001 for inclusion in your A:\CONFIG.SYS file.

Diskette versus Floppy

The term diskette, especially when accompanied by size and density measurements, is a much better term to use than "floppy." The floppy term came from the early days of computing when flexible media was used instead of the hard platters or drums available today for data storage. The floppy material is the flexible disk inside of the sleeve or package on which the recording is stored. Because so many sizes and densities of recording media exist, more definitive terms than floppy better identify specific recording media. So the term Floppy applies to the package as well as the material inside the case.

3. Press Alt+F and then X in order to close the file. You will be prompted to save the file. Name it A:\CONFIG.SYS. Next, click OK and then exit the EDIT program.

4. Run the EDIT program again, loading it from your hard drive or from the diskette. You will start working with a blank file that we will call AUTOEXEC. BAT and saving it to the A: drive.

5. Type the following line in the EDIT program box:

MSCDEX /D:MSCD001

Both command lines have a /D:MSCD001 designation. The device driver gives this virtual name to the CD-ROM drive, and then the MSCDEX program accesses this CD-ROM by its name. This designation *must* be the same in both lines!

6. Press Alt+F and then X in order to close the file. You will be prompted to save the file. Name it A:\AUTOEXEC.BAT and click OK to save the new file and exit the EDIT program.

Using DOS-level device drivers with Windows may leave your entire disk system running in real/compatibility-mode, possibly with decreased disk performance. Why? Because some CD-ROM drives or their drivers do not provide enough support or compatibility with Windows and will not run without a DOS driver, and the older drivers are not Windows-friendly, keeping Windows from managing the IDE (Integrated Drive Electronics) interface devices, including the hard disk drive, in full 32-bit mode.

Hint: get a late-model ATAPI-compliant IDE CD-ROM drive. It will not require DOS-level drivers and will install automatically as long as your system's BIOS is also up to date.

The result should be a CONFIG.SYS file on your A: drive that contains

```
DEVICE=MYCDROM.SYS /D:MSCD001
```

and an AUTOEXEC.BAT file on your A: drive that contains

```
MSCDEX /D:MSCD001
```

Restarting your system with this diskette in the drive should give you access to your CD-ROM drive as Drive D: or on a drive letter following the last DOS-partition drive letter of your hard drive. For example, if the last DOS-partition drive letter of your hard drive was F:, then your new access to your hard drive will be through Drive G:.

Helpful utilities

Many of the utility packages for DOS systems include recovery or disk imaging tools that record information about your disk drive, partitions, boot information, directories, and files, storing them for later use by programs that diagnose and reconstruct corrupt disks and files.

Use of these utilities greatly eases recovery from accidental erasures, formats, drive errors, glitches, and gremlins that tend to work against our systems. These utilities are not all-powerful or sure things, but they do help in 99 percent of the cases normally encountered.

Caution

Having multiple recovery tools invoked before and used after a known error situation is still no guarantee of success in recovery. Current backups are your only real hope of data recovery, and often the restoration process is faster than the utility recovery process.

The usual weak sector, mistaken erasure, accidental format, or other common mistakes and incidents are recoverable. It is doubtful that most users would ever subject their systems to the level of new or beta testing that we do, or to intentional trashing of a system in order to test recovery practices. And users who do have no excuse for not backing up just before testing.

The emergency diskettes mentioned earlier in this chapter are key to using available recovery techniques. Some of these utilities even create diskette-based emergency files because these files are vulnerable on the hard drive. Of course, if you do not even include the recovery tools in your AUTOEXEC.BAT file before you shut your system off, you stand little chance of recovering from even simple disasters.

One of the most common utilities for recovery aid is Norton Rescue Diskette service, which creates recovery files on a diskette and your hard drive. This is similar to the creation of the bootable disks covered earlier, but it is coupled with the other recovery features of Norton Utilities and makes creation of the disks an easier task.

For routine drive checking and protection, there are utilities you should run daily, weekly, or monthly in order to verify drive and data integrity. Some of these include the following:

✦ Norton Disk Doctor

✦ Gibson's SpinRite—extremely thorough testing and repair of disk drive surfaces

The data recovery process

The actual recovery from a disk incident is a fairly straightforward process. That is probably why the programs that provide these services have been so successful and are worth purchasing!

Again, the process is much easier and faster if the recovery utility has access to the appropriate pre-recovery files for use as references to put things back in their places. Not much more can be said than to call the utility from DOS and follow the prompts in order to select the drive of interest and the operation to perform. This is not an oversimplification—much work has gone into making the process easy.

If you are running Windows 95/98/Me, you should run the recovery utility from within that environment. However, if your Windows environment has also been destroyed, your only alternative may be that last backup you performed. Another less-promising alternative may be to install a new hard drive in your system, install your Windows on that new drive, and then try to recover the damaged drive from your new Windows environment. Reinstalling Windows on the damaged hard drive may destroy any chance of recovering the damaged data.

There are a few precautionary measures to take prior to any utility operations on disk drives, from formatting to defragmenting, compressing, recovering, or unerasing files. These measures are meant to *disable* any resident or running software or utilities, including those in the following two lists.

For DOS and Windows 3.*x* systems:

✦ DOS's FASTOPEN

✦ Cache or delayed-write options of any disk cache software

✦ Automatically timed disk-head parking

✦ Disk and virus protection software that alerts you to or prevents disk-write operations that you know or expect these utilities to perform (and they will do many of them!)

✦ Any activity, scheduler, or appointment reminder program that is likely to try to access the system without being aware of the primary activity you are doing

For Windows 95/98/Me systems

✦ Windows' FastFind and FindFast utilities

✦ Norton's Speed Utility

✦ Software "uninstaller" programs

✦ Crash prevention software (CrashGuard, Crash Preventer, and so on)

✦ Disk and virus protection software that alerts you to or prevents disk-write operations that you know or expect these utilities to perform (and they will do many of them!)

✦ Any activity, scheduler, or appointment reminder program that is likely to try to access the system without being aware of the primary activity you are doing

✦ Resident communications software, FAX receiving software, and so on

✦ Disable sharing of local disk drives and printers with others on your network

These measures are not of any concern if you have booted from your emergency diskette and have loaded nothing from the hard drive. Having the information handy from the low-level format, partitioning, and DOS (or NTFS or HPFS file system) format can be useful if the recovery process is only partial, or you need to manually intervene with a disk sector editor, or you are prompted for information that can help the programs along.

Basically, let the utility software run its course and do as much as it can automatically. Occasionally, if there is severe damage, you might see a display that asks you if it should save some undefined file or directory, displayed with an assumed name of %#)*^!2{."]/ or similar gibberish. This is *not* a file or directory name according to the rules of DOS and no attempt should be made to save this particular information as a file or directory.

If such an error message is the only recovery information you obtain, and you appear to be getting little else out of the process, try another recovery utility, if you have one. If not, determine whether you absolutely need to recover the information, which may mean finding a specialist in data recovery, or if you should simply reformat the drive and work from a previous backup set.

Prerecovery preparations for DOS and Windows 3.x

For DOS/Windows 3.x systems, it is normally recommended that you include some prerecovery tools in your AUTOEXEC.BAT file so that the condition of your system at BOOT is saved. These prerecovery tools make an image of the system as you left it before shutdown, and they will not create another image until you reboot again (if you do so during the course of your work) or until the next day's bootup. Just running it as part of your startup routine is great for saving what happened the day before, but not for saving what happens while or after you use your system. To give you a better snapshot of your system immediately after you use it for the day, let the prerecovery utility run after you complete your work in Windows.

Using prerecovery tools gives the recovery tools a working reference. Using the recovery tools without their prerecovery counterparts may or may not be better than marginal tools, such as the SCANDISK program included with DOS. The DOS programs make no attempt to re-establish the name, directory, or complete File Allocation Table assignments of an erased or partially destroyed file. At least the after-market utilities search for more logical and useful information and can interact with you to piece together entire files, if need be.

Here is an example of an AUTOEXEC.BAT file using Norton Utilities version 3.x IMAGE utility, run before Windows:

```
rem THIS IS AUTOEXEC.BAT
ECHO OFF
CLS
```

```
PATH=C:\;C:\DOS;C:\WINDOWS;C:\NORTON
SET TEMP=C:\TEMP
C:
CLS
C:\NORTON\IMAGE C: D: E: F: G: H:
WIN
```

To make an image part of both your startup and shutdown routines, you can use it both before and after Windows (or the other programs you use) loads in your AUTOEXEC.BAT file as follows:

```
rem THIS IS AUTOEXEC.BAT
ECHO OFF
CLS
PATH=C:\;C:\DOS;C:\WINDOWS;C:\NORTON
SET TEMP=C:\TEMP
C:
CLS
Rem You will need your rescue diskette to do this...
C:\NORTON\IMAGE C: D: E: F: G: H:
ECHO Saved a current image - remove the rescue diskette.
PAUSE
ECHO Thanks! - Time to start Windows
WIN
Rem substitute your local DOS menu or other
Rem programs for the WIN command above as desired
C:\NORTON\IMAGE C: D: E: F: G: H:
ECHO Saved today's image - remove the rescue diskette.
PAUSE
ECHO Thanks! - Done for the day!
```

We have embellished the file slightly with a few comments so that what is happening is more clear. Using this technique, you get a fresh disk image before you run Windows, so you will have it available if Windows or something else crashes your system while you work. When you are done, you get another image that includes all the changes done in Windows.

Use this prerecovery step after you make major directory or file changes and if you ever compress, defragment, or reorganize each drive. All utility packages recommend that you back up your drives before their installation, and then regularly thereafter. This should tell you something about the potential for data loss, even when installing the tools that are supposed to prevent it!

Note that the equivalent functionality for Windows 95/98 runs at startup and runs as a part of those environments in order to accommodate the new, long filename and FAT-32 file systems, and they have no DOS-level programs that do much good here.

Recovery tools for Windows 3.*x*

Microsoft Windows 3.*x* presents more complex problems to most users because of the way new programs are installed and the way they affect the many configuration files on a system. Windows 3.*x* uses INI and GRP files to control the system and user-interface behavior. For all versions of Windows, a plain-text editor program (NOTEPAD.EXE) is quite adequate for viewing and changing the INI files.

Windows 95/98/Me and NT/2000 depend on and use a new configuration file set — the system Registry. To manage these configuration items, you need software tools. Norton provides some of these, but if you want to dig around for yourself, you need to use the Windows REGEDIT.EXE or Norton's Registry Editor program to view, search, and edit the special Registry files. Keep your Windows and application program CD-ROMs or diskettes handy — just in case something really goes wrong somewhere along the line (unfortunately, with Windows 95 it usually does at some point).

A relatively new breed of system crash prevention or recovery tools has come along that monitors your system activity, alerts you to low drive space and low memory, reminds you when you need to create fresh disk images, looks over your configuration and Registry, checks for viruses, and so on. Some tools even intercept Windows and application crashes and attempt to regain control of the system so that you can save any data that may be at risk. Products from Norton (Norton System Doctor and CrashGuard), CyberMedia (FirstAid), and Quarterdeck (RealHelp, formerly Vertisoft's Fix-It, but dramatically beefed up) all do some level of active system diagnosis and crash protection.

Windows 98 and Me Registry protection

Windows 98 introduced a utility that should have been in Windows 95 all along — ScanReg. Both DOS and Windows have versions of this utility. Windows 98 and Me automatically create backups of your current Registry database and keep up to five prior copies on your hard drive in the C:\Windows\Sysbckup folder. They appear as RB001.CAB files. (CAB is a compressed file format used by Microsoft for many setup and backup file purposes.)

If at Windows startup you see error messages about the Registry, Windows is telling you to restart your system in DOS mode and then to run the SCANREG program from a DOS prompt. SCANREG enables you to make a fresh copy of your Registry or select a prior Registry backup file to restore. Typically, you want to restore the Registry from a version saved one or two days earlier – or whenever the system was last running okay.

Note   DOS mode is an option that appears on the startup menu if you press F8 after seeing "Starting Windows"

Note   You won't be able to restore your Registry to a recent version if you don't back up regularly. If there's one message we can get through with this book, it's to be sure you have a good backup plan!

Restoring from a previous Registry backup may cause you to lose some software and Windows settings, but this is far less severe than reformatting your hard drive and reinstalling Windows and your applications. And consider the data you may have lost!

Windows configuration evaluation

Norton's WinDoctor and Cybermedia's FirstAid offer services called conflict or con-figuration assessment, which survey your system. During the survey, these utilities collect data from the files and Registry about installed programs and drivers, and then the utilities compare the data to see if anything is missing, if paths to the files are correct, and so on. Results are displayed, and in some cases problems with incorrect paths or Registry entries can be corrected if all of the pieces exist. If you are missing drivers or files, you will have to reinstall the program of interest or per-haps all of the operating system in order to set things right.

Caution   Windows NT Version 4.0 does not provide the means to completely reinstall the operating system while retaining the data and configurations in your system. If you end up needing to reinstall Windows NT 4.0, a complete backup of your system will be the only way to fully recover from an NT 4.0 crash. Fortunately, this is a rare occurrence, and Windows 2000 is supposed to correct this problem.

Windows crash prevention

The most annoying and critical things about Windows 95 and 98, as well as with Windows 3.x, are unpredictable crashes. You know the routine—you are working away in some important document and suddenly you get a Windows dialog box indicating that a program has experienced or caused an Invalid Page Fault. At that point, perhaps all you can do is click OK or Close and try the program again. Worse, you get the "blue screen of death" from an exception error and there is almost noth-ing you can do to recover, so you have to hit Reset or turn the system off in order to get back to work. We all hate it when that happens.

You can experience several types of crashes with Windows—and dare we say that most of them are caused by inadequate memory management or outright bugs in one program or another that stomp all over the memory used by another program. These usually show up as invalid page faults indicated in a Windows dialog box and are simply programs that bumped into each other in memory. One has to give way and be closed to the rest of the environment in order to carry on undisturbed.

The exception errors you see as blue-screen exception errors are more violent symptoms of one program invading another's memory space. In these situations, the memory data that should have been program data may be incorrectly interpreted because the CPU expected an instruction and received garbage instead. The CPU then indicates that it cannot go any further. Invalid page fault errors are usually high-level environment crashes that are not fatal to the entire system, whereas a CPU crash is a lower-level crash, but it can lead to more problems.

Windows 95 and 98 are smart enough to see some of these errors and thus are able to give you these warning messages. Crash intervention programs, such as the Crash Defender that accompanies Quarterdeck's RealHelp and Crash Guard offered by Norton, sit on your system and monitor the activities in memory and of Windows, and they try to alert you to conditions before the conditions cause a program to crash. They also try to warn you before an invalid instruction goes to the CPU. We must say that although these warnings are good ideas, as often as not, left to their own devices, many program and Windows crashes sort out these problems. Furthermore, Windows waits until one program or the other gives up and you get the default Windows dialog box, or it waits until the program unfreezes itself. The details display in Windows from the crashed programs' dialog box is almost useless. Although it is supposed to offer useful debugging information, considering all the variables in systems and their configuration, do not count on this information to help you out in any technical support calls.

Because this is probably one of the most significant and annoying aspects of PCs and Windows, we will cover Windows configurations, memory management, and system crashes more as we go along.

Program removal tools

Little is worse than not being able to get rid of a program you no longer want on your system. Tools such as Symantec's CleanSweep, one of many "uninstaller" programs, provide much system management service. These utilities can monitor new software installations, keep records of configuration files before and after installations, and enable users to undo software installations and to restore system files to their previous conditions, in case you change your mind or encounter a problem with new software that might mess up Windows.

Uninstallers came about late during the Windows 3.x era as tools to help extract the many fragments and changes that various programs leave in systems during their installation and use. Although Windows 95 and 98 contain some program removal service with the Add/Remove Programs applet in the Control Panel, and many programs come with their own uninstall feature, these offerings are far from thorough in tracking and removing every program's presence. CleanSweep uses much reference information and some powerful methods for tracking not only which files are installed during an installation, but also many Registry and file changes after installation. Its removal process is perhaps the safest and most complete of any such tools on the market.

In all cases, these tools load and must be running most of the time, especially during the installation of new software (the software they will be able to remove best). They prompt you as they detect a SETUP or INSTALL program operation so that they can begin their tracking of the process, and they prompt you after the process is complete so that they can ensure that everything is logged properly. Perhaps these prompts and some of the time delays these programs cause are a bit annoying, but unless you learn more about the Windows Registry and many of the nooks and crannies of your system, these are good tools that can save you time and frustration later on.

Hand Tools

Solving problems with PCs involves not only using the tools and power of the computer itself, through error codes and utility software, but often the use of a few common hand tools as well. These tools are available at almost any hardware store. The only exception may be that some manufacturers use Torx-style screws, identified by a 6-cornered, indented screw head. A Torx tool may be provided with the system by the manufacturer, if you must have one to work on that PC. Otherwise, the appropriate tool will have to be sought and purchased.

Before you purchase any tools, you should review the following lists, consider how much work you expect to do in and around your PC system, look at the connectors and fasteners on your system, and buy tools that will fit the job, your hands, and your abilities.

Your basic PC toolkit should include each of the following:

✦ #0, #1, and #2 Phillips or crosshead screwdrivers

✦ $\frac{3}{32}$-, $\frac{1}{8}$-, and $\frac{3}{16}$-inch wide flat-blade screwdrivers

✦ $\frac{3}{16}$- and $\frac{1}{4}$-inch hex nut drivers

✦ Small, long-nosed pliers

✦ #15 and #20 Torx-blade drivers (as needed)

✦ Specific metric-sized tools that might be needed

Additionally, the following items are helpful when it comes to basic computer and electronic repairs:

✦ 4- to 6-inch long tweezers (for gripping and removing small parts)

✦ An IC removal tool (a U-shaped handle with fingers that hook under chips)

✦ CPU removal tools (these look like wide, flat crowbars or short combs)

✦ A 1-inch-wide brush (for dusting off parts)

✦ A can of pressurized air with a nozzle (for blowing dust off parts and dirt out of small places, such as keyboards)

Most of these tools can be found in prepackaged PC toolkits sold in computer stores or through mail order for between $12 and $30.

Caution Do not use magnetized screwdrivers or other magnetized tools. It is possible that these tools will damage diskettes and other magnetic recording media. Even being careful cannot guarantee that a magnetized tool will never be in the wrong place at the wrong time!

In order to work with the differences between 25-pin and 9-pin serial connectors, you may wish to carry a variety of cable adapters that come in molded block form or as cable sets, including these:

✦ 9-pin D male to 25-pin D female

✦ 9-pin D female to 25-pin D male

✦ 9-pin D male to 9-pin D male (otherwise known as a gender changer)

✦ 9-pin D female to 9-pin D female (also a gender changer)

✦ 25-pin D male to 25-pin D male (also a gender changer)

✦ 25-pin D female to 25-pin D female (another gender changer)

✦ 25-pin D male to 36-pin Centronics female (printer adapter)

✦ 9- and 25-pin null modems

Cross-Reference See Chapter 22 for examples of some of these connectors.

You can make many of these cable adapters yourself or buy them prepared at most computer or electronics supply stores. The null modem can be useful for determining if internal wiring is incorrect. Incorrect wiring can lead to many errors or failed communications between systems.

Cross-Reference Appendix G includes a schematic of a correct, multipurpose null modem.

If you expect to make or repair common PC cables, you will also need these items:

✦ A 25- to 60-watt (700 degrees F) electronic-grade soldering iron with a ¹⁄₁₆–⅛-inch tip. A stand to hold the iron, preferably one with a sponge for cleaning the soldering tip, is handy.

✦ A small amount of electrical solder (This solder is commonly labeled as "60/40," representing the tin-to-lead content ratio. If you can find solder labeled "63/37," this is much better to work with, enabling better connections, especially for those new to soldering.)

✦ A small-pin crimping tool, used for connector pins, often referred to as *AMP pins*, for attaching pins to cable wires

✦ A small-pin removal tool

✦ A pair of wire strippers and a pair of small electronic-wire cutters

If you are so inclined or technically qualified, you may also wish to have an inexpensive digital voltmeter (DVM) to use for testing AC and DC voltages and locating shorted wires in cables. Common units have a resolution of 3½ digits with an accuracy of 0.1 to 3 percent. The meter should be capable of indicating the readings of three significant digits. For the 5-volt DC supply leads, you should be able to see a reading of 5.*xx*, not just 5 or 5.0. For the 12-volt leads, you should be able to see 12.*x*, not just 12. For the 120 volt AC power readings, you should be able to read 12*x*, and perhaps be able to see 12*x.x*.

The common voltage measurement ranges are 0 to 2, 0 to 20, and 0 to 200 volts. Units that have ranges of 0 to 4, 0 to 40, and 0 to 400, or ranges from 0 to 1, 0 to 10, 0 to 100, and 0 to 1000 are not common or generally suited to the accuracy of readings that we would like to perform. A digital voltmeter is preferred for better accuracy and easier reading versus an analog or dial-reading multimeter. Suitable units may be purchased for as little as $20.

To make your system installation neater in appearance and organization, you should arrange and carefully wrap and secure cables with plastic wire ties or tie-wraps. It is always handy to have a package of 25 to 100 of these in your tool kit.

If you are comfortable enough with troubleshooting and repairing to the extent of opening chassis, power supplies, and monitors, you will also want to have a variety of fuses available. Common fuse values worth having are 1, 2, 3, 4, 5, and 6 amp values rated for 250 volts in both the common U.S. size (3AG or ¼ × 1 inch) and the metric size of 5 × 20 millimeters.

Summary

The main focus of this chapter is to provide a comprehensive description of the software and hardware tools you may need if you want to work effectively on your system. This chapter also includes valuable suggestions concerning how to prepare your system and yourself to handle the most common problems that can prevent effective use of your PC. If you read this chapter and follow its recommendations while your system is running correctly, you may be able to avoid a system crash. More importantly, if a crash occurs, you should be able to recover with less chance of total loss of your important data and capabilities.

✦   ✦   ✦

Protecting Yourself

✦ ✦ ✦ ✦

In This Chapter

Erased file protection

Virus protection

Communications protection

Data recovery services

Backup software and services

✦ ✦ ✦ ✦

In addition to reviewing the software, the hand tools, and a number of recommended procedures we covered in the previous chapter, in this chapter we also cover how to avoid or at least mitigate the damage associated with several common problems and how to repair the problems, if they arise.

Erased File Protection

The ability to undo a file deletion is a common utility these days. An early version of Norton Utilities included a utility called Erase Protect. Such a feature was deemed valuable enough that Microsoft includes it in all new versions of Windows — known as the Recycle Bin. This feature sets aside a "trash can" area or a special protected directory on your hard drive and runs a resident or internal program to intercept any file deletion operations you perform, saving the "deleted" files in this special trash-can area for a period of time you can specify. (Figure 3-1 shows the slide rule that controls the size of your Recycle Bin.) This is considerably better than taking a chance on your system's capability to unerase a deleted file later on.

Saving data by assigning it to the trash can enables you to recover a file intact, if you act within the trash can's dumping period. The alternative is to use the undelete or unerase features of a utility package such as Norton Utilities. In this case, you have to hope that the operating system did not overwrite the space used by the erased file and that you can remember or reestablish the first character of the filename.

Note   Why do you need to know the first character? Because the first character is all that really changes when a file is erased.

Figure 3-1: Set the size of your Recycle Bin through the Recycle Bin Properties dialog box.

Recovering an erased file is what made Peter Norton of Norton Utilities famous, but it cannot be accomplished successfully if the erased file's space is reused, as DOS will do when it needs space to save the next file. The best time to recover an accidentally erased file is *immediately* after you have erased it!

The Recycle Bin is not a utility you would use often, but it does not intrude on your use of your computer, as do other types of utilities, and it is a great "just-in-case" feature to have around.

Virus Protection

Computer viruses are a serious problem, warranting discussion wherever they are likely to be found. Because most viruses come and go, and "live" on disks or online services and other networks, they can be truly obnoxious, if not detrimental to your computer.

Viruses can attack *any* executable file on any disk in your system; this includes embedded macros in Microsoft Word and Excel document templates. They can scramble or erase bootup information, directory information, drive partitions, or any piece of information you have in memory, including wiping out the CMOS RAM data where your system information is stored (286 and higher systems). Some viruses simply reformat your hard disk, or part of it, while other activity continues. As a result, nothing looks wrong until later.

The latest rash of viruses are e-mail messages with a file attachment that auto-executes if you open the message. These e-mail messages, in addition to performing various forms of damage, read your e-mail address list, duplicate themselves and then mail these duplicate viruses to people on your address list as a message from you. The viruses takes advantage of people in your e-mail address book who may be unaware of the danger posed by receiving a message from you. Because so many of us use e-mail these days, a virus propagated this way quickly infects systems around the world. Major corporations around the world have had their e-mail systems inundated by such messages, effectively removing their e-mail capabilities until the virus is removed. This is in addition to the damage that the programs themselves may perform.

The most common type of attached file for these e-mail viruses is one with a .vbs extension. Microsoft's Visual Basic Script provides the capability to auto-execute a program upon opening the file. Because an e-mail message can be programmed to automatically open attachments after the e-mail has been opened, this is a vulnerable part of your system.

E-mail systems are being updated to detect these types of viruses in an attempt to reduce their impact. Some virus utilities are also being updated to help protect personal computers, but best protection is to refuse to open an e-mail message, even if it is from a close associate or family member, if it has an attached file. You can always check with the sender in order to make sure that the person sent you a valid message with the attached file in question.

Protection against and recovery from viruses is concentrated on disk drives and files by utility software of several kinds. The most popular seems to be the VirusScan series of programs from Network Associates (formerly McAfee Associates), as well as Symantec's Norton AntiVirus. These programs and their virus-definition files are updated on a regular basis.

Numerous known viruses and at least several hundred strains or variations from the known viruses can affect PC systems. Enough exist to allow one virus for every two programs kept in any extensive public-domain and/or shareware library available to the public. The virus creators have been almost as busy as legitimate software authors. If we estimate that another 1,000 commercial PC programs are available, not counting those written for less public consumption, that estimate comes to one virus for possibly every four programs you may be using. From that perspective the threat is quite serious.

Fortunately, the majority of Web site, BBS (bulletin board system), and online system librarians check all uploaded or mailed-in programs before making them available to the general public. We do not know for sure if the commercial vendors routinely check their systems or not. A few have not in the past and have found out the hard way that a virus can get into any system and out the door in new shrink-wrapped products.

Many online-service file systems check uploaded files automatically. From our experience as system operators (sysops), we know intimately the time and effort it takes to make sure bad code is not shared with others. While these operations are not usually visible and operate as system utilities in the background, rest assured that most reputable sites perform these checks automatically, just like most workplace computer systems.

Fortunately for the general-user population, the process is not time-consuming or difficult. You have many options for protecting your system, from a quick few-minute scan of each drive to installing antivirus software that checks each file as it is accessed and that checks each unusual request to write to special disk areas.

Note   Taking precautionary antivirus measures on your system is second in importance only to backing up your files in order to keep you out of trouble. The process should be done every time you receive new software from a commercial dealer, from a friend, or from a BBS system. Having a resident antivirus utility running when you format a new batch of diskettes is also a good idea.

The mechanisms used and the types of harm done by viruses vary widely and are too involved for coverage in a single chapter, much less a part of a chapter. Perhaps inaccurately labeled as viruses, there are some nonharmful but quite annoying attacks from "bad code" that fall into the categories of pranks, Trojan horses, or other definitions. These are no more legitimate software efforts than are intentionally destructive programs. They can be found and eliminated a number of ways.

Your best protection against viruses is to employ the following safe-computing practices:

✦ Use virus detection programs, such as VirusScan or Norton AntiVirus.

✦ Obtain regular updates of these programs from the antivirus program vendor's Web site.

✦ Use these programs on a regular basis, *especially* when you exchange disks or files with others (online or via networks), obtain new software, and so on.

✦ Do not open or read a message with an attached file (not from anyone) unless you are expecting that person to send you a file.

✦ Back up your system regularly (which, unfortunately, may carry a virus with it, but it buys you some time on timed-execution viruses).

✦ Refresh your DOS SYSTEM and program files after a backup or restore.

This last point requires that the disk *not* have a Volume Label, meaning the disk cannot be named. Also required is the use of the SYS.COM program with DOS, run from a diskette used to boot your computer. You can eliminate the Volume Label with the DOS LABEL program and replace it later. (For versions of DOS later than 5.0, you will have to use the FORMAT command to create a bootable system diskette from your hard drive because you cannot use the original DOS diskettes for anything but a full DOS installation — which is one way to refresh the DOS files.)

Cross-Reference   Refer back to Chapter 2 for a refresher on the bootable DOS diskette.

In all versions of Windows, Disk Label is one of the parameters you will see when you display the Properties for that particular drive. Whether you use the My Computer icon on your desktop or the Windows Explorer to display your drives, after you right-click on the drive and select Properties, a Label field appears that either displays the current name of that drive or, if empty, will allow you to give it a name.

Many companies restrict the use of shareware and public domain (PD) programs (generalized as *downloaded files,* in many cases) and tightly control the inventory of software that exists on in-house systems. Of course, keeping your systems completely isolated is one way to reduce the chances of exposure. This would have to include prohibiting portable systems or disk exchanges between home systems (for those who work outside of the office) and prohibiting exchanges between customer-site systems. These are serious and restricting methods, and not necessarily good alternatives to providing a PD/shareware library on CD-ROM for all employees and providing antivirus software to all users with every system.

Outside exposure is not the only threat. Bad code can originate from any number of sources, and the most damage could be inflicted from a source located *inside* an organization that relies too heavily on avoiding outside threats. Safe, informed, positive attitudes toward the work at hand and developing good employee abilities are responsible approaches to any situation.

Communications Protection

In addition to virus protection, many vendors offer additional products or enhanced versions of their products that monitor your system and connections for suspicious network traffic and possible security violations. The following list includes some of these products:

✦ ZoneAlarm (free) from ZoneLabs (`www.zonelabs.com`)

✦ BlackICE Defender from Network ICE (`www.networkice.com`)

✦ ConSeal Private Desktop from Signal9 (`www.signal9.com`)

✦ Secure Desktop from Sybergen (`www.sybergen.com`)

✦ Guard Dog from Network Associates/McAfee (`www.mcafee.com`)

✦ eSafe Protect from Elia Shim (`www.esafe.com`)

Outsiders can affect your computer in many ways besides attaching viruses to files you download from them, so a quick overview of these methods is in order.

With so many things happening on the Internet these days, you are wise to be wary when connected to the Internet, or any other computer system. You should be aware of the kinds of connections that can be made with your computer and the things that can happen with various application types, connections, sites, and downloads. To help sort things out a bit, the lists that follow will give you a heads-up of what to be careful of and what you need not worry about on the Internet as far as damaging or nuisance file types.

Be careful of those connections

Although not specific or limited to the Internet, this section covers the overall class of application types that help individual users privately connect their computers to other systems through a modem, a network connection, or an Internet connection. If you are concerned about security and your personal computer, you should get to know anything and everything that dials or connects your computer to another computer system. We don't want to start rumors or get everyone worried, but does anyone *really* know what the software that CompuServe, AOL, Prodigy, ICQ, Microsoft, or anyone else provides to us is doing with the information on our systems?

Some potentially harmless examples are listed here:

✦ **Registration wizards.** These send your information to hardware and software vendors after you install a new application. When you are connected to the site that accepts the form you filled in, what other information could be sent?

✦ **Online banking software.** These have to be audited by the U.S. Treasury Department and a few other folks to ensure as much security and accuracy as possible—but do we know exactly what information they are being accurate about?

✦ **Automatic software-updating agents.** These are those nifty little utilities that check the version of our current software and enable us to download updates. Certainly, in order to tell if we need an update, these have to know something about the software on our system. Are they peeking at the Windows Registry, the Web-browser cookies, or history files, too?

✦ **Software from an Internet service provider.** Users may also tend to over-trust the software given to them by online or Internet service providers.

✦ **Remote-control connections.** Symantec's pcAnywhere remote-control application is one of a few communications applications that enables others to connect to your system, operate it through keyboard and mouse actions, and see your screen as if they were right there. These connections are handy for remote technical support, but if abused, they can be dangerous. Usually you would set up these connections only for known users with passwords and whom you want to allow access to your system. Because you pass out the passwords, you have some control over your guests.

✦ **Remote system-management services.** Many companies have a keen interest in maintaining the hundreds and thousands of PCs that they use in day-to-day business. Like remote-control connections, these remote system-management services allow administrative access to files on the system, so these connections must be taken quite seriously by users and support people alike.

Of a potentially more dangerous nature are the following:

✦ **Trojan horses.** BackOrifice (BO) is perhaps the most well-known Trojan horse program to hit the wires. Others exist, but BO is the king. It is placed onto your system by running other programs that contain the BO installer files. BO is essentially a well-hidden and powerful remote-control program that can also capture and store keystrokes and data from your system and, therefore, enable someone else to take control of the system—to execute programs, transfer or delete data, or disable your system. If your PC is networked with other systems, BO can use recorded keystrokes to gain access to other systems on your network, using your logon and password information.

✦ **Malicious ActiveX and Java applets.** Some of these may or may not fall into the virus category, but many are detected by and removed or blocked with some of the virus and online protection products available. These are executable pieces of program code that can be sent to your PC by Web site operators. They can do much damage by installing other viruses or by intercepting passwords and data traveling to other sites.

✦ **Cookies.** Anything in moderation can be okay, even a handful of Mrs. Field's oatmeal raisin cookies (a favorite here) or a benign marker (Web cookie) placed onto your computer to enable faster or better access to commonly used resources on a Web site. Because you do not normally log directly into a Web site, but instead simply ask the Web server to display a specific Web page, there is no other interactive way for a Web site to be personalized for you without putting this little marker file on your hard drive and asking for it later. Yes, it is essentially possible to place personally identifiable information into the data a cookie stores. But it is highly improbable for it to be done if you do not allow a malicious ActiveX program to be downloaded and run on your PC or if you do not catch a virus or Trojan horse program from a downloaded and executed program. If in doubt about a Web site or cookies, turn them off in your browser or, at the very least, turn off the Web site you suspect.

✦ **Unsecure transaction sessions.** Never, ever give out financial information through a Web connection that is not secured by a recognized authentication and encryption method. Hesitate when giving any personal information over an unsecured connection. Basically, know what data is going, where it goes, and why. Secure transactions are indicated in your Web browser by a little padlock icon closing or being highlighted. However secure the browser-to-server connection may be, you still may not be able to trust the security at the back end of the system. If hackers cannot get into the Web site, can they get into the company's private network?

✦ **Port scanners.** Before hackers actually try to get into your system, they have to assess the opportunities and chances of success. This is typically done by running a program that scans your Internet connection, looking for available Internet communications protocols, such as TCP (Transmission Control Protocol) or UDP (User Datagram Protocol), ports that they can try to gain access through. A port scan by itself is harmless, but it can be a precursor to a real attack. The real attack may not actually come for days, weeks, or months, and it may not come from the source of the port scan. The Internet is tricky and provides tremendous resources to create anonymity for its users. A port scan from an Internet connection on the East Coast may or may not be related to an actual hack attack from a connection on the West Coast.

Any caution about Internet-based or Internet-enabled software is well warranted. Find out what interaction the software has with your system and theirs. There are many good, secure software sources and Internet communications out there. If the application's and the vendor's Web sites pass a security audit, you should be in good shape.

There have been few reports of a legitimate service provider or application abusing a questionable amount of information from your PC activities. One such incident was caused by a flaw in RealNetworks' software, which has since been fixed. You may want to check out Steve Gibson's (of Gibson Research Corporation, writer for InfoWorld and other publications, and inventor of the light pen) Opt Out program at www.grc.com for more up-to-date information in this area.

Things on the Internet that may annoy but don't affect your system

The following Internet features may be viewed as annoyances, but do not present any danger to your system:

✦ **Unwanted e-mail messages, a.k.a. spam.** These may annoy you and waste your time. They are in essence a form of denial of service (because you cannot or do not do anything else when you are wasting time on unwanted sales pitches), but they are not detrimental to your hardware, software, or disk files.

✦ **File attachments in e-mail messages.** Attachments themselves are not a hazard—unless you actually open or execute ones that are truly executable programs (EXE, COM, VBS) or that contain bits that can manipulate files (Microsoft Word and Excel documents with embedded macros). However, most virus protection programs can automatically scan all files written to your disk drives. Virus protection is your best protection against these hazards. Microsoft has posted several notices and updates about vulnerabilities in their e-mail programs – check them out.

Caution

Do not open an e-mail message, even from someone you know, if it has an attached file and you were not expecting that person to send you a file. Your best bet is to save the attachment to your hard drive and run your virus-scanning program on the file prior to opening it. As a matter of fact, just go and get the latest security fix files from Microsoft (it seems there will always be a new fix update) to make sure you have the latest protection.

✦ **JavaScript activities within Web pages.** These are not executable programs per se, and they do not have the capability to read or write files on your system. They can simply open annoying windows and create cute button activities, both of which exist for appearance's sake only. JavaScript is a good and bad—you almost need to have it enabled in order to use many Web sites these days, but you'll want it turned off for sites that create annoying pop-up windows. Malicious JavaScripts can cause so many separate windows to open that your browser may crash or your operating system will run itself out of memory trying to make all of the windows and fill them up.

Things on the Internet that can affect your system

A variety of application types found on Web sites are routinely downloaded to computer systems in order to enhance the user's experience with a particular site. By far the majority of them are good, decent, trustworthy applications—but a bad element can exist in any environment. Your precaution here—be sure you trust the site that you receive applications from and use a resident virus-protection program.

✦ **Java and ActiveX applications.** These are full-blown executable programs that have access to your local hard drive. Most do not do anything harmful, and many do offer nice features for various Web sites. Still, they should be protected by a virus-scanning program.

✦ **Plug-ins and helper applications.** Examples are RealAudio and various video viewing programs that launch when you select certain files on Web pages. These are full-blown executable programs that have access to your local hard drive. Most are not harmful, and many offer nice features for various Web sites. However, these programs should also be protected by a virus-scanning program.

✦ **Denial-of-service attacks.** This is a classification of activity in which someone else attempts to make a connection to or alter the connection of your networked computer system. This is not quite "hacking into" your system, but it is imposed by someone taking advantage of weaknesses in your operating system or network connections. Windows 95 and Windows NT can be particularly vulnerable if you do not apply various fixes to prevent the attacks from being effective. These attacks come in many forms and usually affect servers and systems with permanent or predictable connections to the Internet. Dial-up Internet connections are occasionally affected.

These attacks are caused by executing one of any of a dozen or so programs (such as WinNuke) or by simply sending many plain-old Internet ping (Packet Internet Groper) packets with invalid values to your PC's Internet Protocol (IP) address. The quantity of data sent to the computer under attack simply swamps the network connection or confuses its networking software. Microsoft's site and other Web sites provide details, preventive measures, and patches that can ward off these attacks.

✦ **Be aware of what goes on around you.** Finally, to protect yourself against fraud over the Internet, the one really effective precaution is to be aware of what is going on around you. According to a seasoned police officer speaking at a recent meeting of the Internet Society, Los Angeles Chapter, your best possible protection against fraud on the Internet is to avoid offers of products or income-producing activities that seem too good to be true. Fraud on the Internet is not that different from the fraud that has plagued people throughout history. However, the main problem with fraud over the Internet is that because so many people can be contacted in such a short time, even the smallest fraud can provide a criminal with a large reward.

More connections to come

As people become more and more connected to the outside world through their PCs, they will see more and more connection types and services becoming available. For every advantage, though, there are potential disadvantages. Yes, it would be convenient to monitor your home security system, start dinner, or program your VCR while you are at work or on the road, but that means some part of your home or computer must be open to an outside connection. It is up to each of us to weigh the options and the risks, and to know as much about these connections, their power, and vulnerabilities as possible. The only real secure solution is to stay disconnected — but then look at all the fun and value we would be missing!

As more and more people enjoy *always-on* DSL (Digital Subscriber Line) and cable-modem connections to the Internet, they are also more vulnerable because most of these connections provide assigned IP addresses, making it easier for malicious people to return to your system anytime they want. Of course, those who decide to hack others from their always-on connections are easily identifiable by their host name and IP address through their Internet service provider (ISP).

 Cross-Reference   While some protection methods have been discussed in this section, more are discussed in Chapter 11.

Data Recovery Services

Three or four of the data recovery firms that advertise in the popular PC magazines can do a fantastic job of reading data from burned, crushed, or otherwise very damaged drive surfaces, even if the case is broken, melted, or otherwise damaged in a way that leaves the drive mechanism unusable.

If your drive is not physically damaged, there may be good news — it is possible that you may not need to resort to the expensive recovery services. Through the Data Advisor utility, provided free from OnTrack Data International, you can see if your drive is damaged and then connect via modem to OnTrack Data International's data recovery service for an initial assessment and recovery estimate.

The cost of these services reflects the complexity and time involved in the process of extracting the media, testing it, and determining where the data might be and what type of data it is. Even after using one of these services, you may have to spend hours evaluating millions of bytes of information in order to regain anything useful. Still, if you need the data, the few hundreds to few thousands of dollars spent to retrieve the data from a destroyed drive onto tape or CD can be *much* more economical than re-entering the data from paper records (if any), and it can be much less embarrassing than calling your clients and telling them you lost their data.

Backup Software and Services

For all of the utilities, tools, toys, widgets, and techniques available to help PC users, none is perhaps so basic, yet inelegant and boring, as simply backing up all of your data to a tape, Zip, Jaz, or CD-ROM. Redundancy has its value to the personal-system user, just as it does to the big network and server systems online, in small offices, or in corporations. Quite simply, nothing beats a good backup — one that is performed and refreshed as frequently as possible.

Backups can be performed in a number of ways. You can copy files to a local diskette, duplicate hard drive, or other media, or use tape backup software, such as Seagate's Backup Exec. You also can send your data across a local area network to a central backup system, or send your data off to one of a few Internet-based backup services, such as driveway (shown in Figure 3-2), located at www.driveway.com.

After having fires, floods, or other incidents literally char or soak everything imaginable in their PC systems, many people became convinced of the value of keeping offsite backups. It is much easier to have your backup stored off-site than to deal with the time and expense of the recovery services.

As we said, backing up your data is kind of boring. It takes 20 to 40 minutes to copy the image of even a small system's 540MB disk drive to a local tape cartridge in order to do a full backup. If you select just your critical data files, the time is less. A network backup takes a little more time, but your network administrator can schedule that after working hours so that you are not disturbed. An Internet backup can take awhile longer, but it is recommended that you copy off only data and critical system files, which you can recover from nearly any system that has the right software (free!) and Internet access — quite a convenience for travelers.

Figure 3-2: The home page of driveway, an online backup service

The best preventive medicine for your potential PC problems is to get the important stuff safely away from your system so that you can get to it later, and Internet backup services and secure offsite storage vaults are two of the best alternatives going today.

Summary

Now you know what troubleshooting is all about, you know about the problem-solving game plan, and you may have started to think about your own disaster-recovery plan.

In the next couple of chapters, we will take you into what a PC is supposed to do when you turn it on, and if it does not, how you can make it work again. Following the divide-and-conquer strategy, keeping in mind what you know about your system already, and what you have learned so far, specific problems should be easy to track down and repair.

✦   ✦   ✦

Your Personal Computer

This chapter provides an overview of the different parts
and some important problem-solving aspects of your
personal computer system.

Getting to Know Your Personal Computer

Since the previous edition of this book, more things about the
PC have changed in a shorter period of time than ever before.
The PC system, its components, and the software you use still
contain simple building blocks that together form a tremendously powerful, global tool. Whether you use this tool to
print a letter on paper or control a satellite in orbit, the PC
and its software are still just a tool.

If you are already familiar with your PC system — where
internal and external cabling and accessories plug in — and
what they do, just make sure you are familiar with basic
troubleshooting, the tools of the trade, and protecting
yourself, covered in Chapters 1, 2, and 3. Then you're ready
to move on to Chapter 5, which discusses physical and logical devices.

The basic components of your PC have been and still are:

✦ A main system board, containing various components
  such as the CPU, memory, and I/O (input/output)
  connections

✦ A screen

✦ A keyboard interface

✦ Clocks to keep the time and to synchronize the activities
  of the CPU, memory, and I/O devices

Through the years many PC system functions have shifted from being performed by add-on devices to being built in to the main system board because almost every system today needs them. Here are some examples:

✦ Serial and parallel I/O ports (still legacy devices)

✦ A standard pointing device connection (mouse port)

✦ Diskette and hard disk drive adapters

Note   The hard drive I/O bus adapter portion moved onto the system board and the hard drive controller portion moved onto the disk drive. The diskette functions remain quite the same as their 1980-vintage counterparts.

Over time, various other functions have been moved or added to the basic system board because they, too, have become commonplace and much cheaper to provide on the main board than with separate add-in cards, such as the following:

✦ Basic high-fidelity sound recording and playback features

✦ Higher-speed serial I/O interfaces, such as the Universal Serial Bus and IEEE-1394

✦ Disk drive interface improvements, such as ATA-66, for more than 20 times the data transfer performance of the original AT systems

In addition, the basic system BIOS has taken on a new set of features and functions, among which are:

✦ The ability to self-configure (Plug-and-Play)

✦ Environmental monitoring (temperature and disk drive status)

✦ Power consumption management

As long as your personal computer works as you expect it to, you probably take most of it for granted, just as you might any other reliable tool, and give very little thought to those features, functions, and building blocks, and how they work together. But when something goes wrong, it helps to understand and know how to work with your system's basic elements.

That's where this book comes in. Whether your hard drive crashes, your power supply blows a fuse, or your printer suddenly begins to spit out nonsense characters, this book is meant to guide you through the various problem-solving steps you need to take to get your computer running again.

What the *Box* Is

The *box* may be referred to as anything from the PC chassis to what IBM calls the *System Unit*. It has six sides, at least one of which is removable to enable you to get to the insides. More than 120 million PC systems reportedly exist in the world today. Of this enormous number of systems, it is likely that many of them are outdated systems that are no longer in use. This chapter describes nonstandard boxes such as laptops and other forms of PCs as well, but concentrates on the larger desktop systems with large enough pieces that you can get to without microsurgery.

As technology, marketing, and user needs develop and change, so do PC configurations. Every few weeks, companies develop or announce major changes and new products. Not even the weekly PC journals can keep up with this activity. Hardware and software firms work around the clock to provide and support new features.

Shown in Figure 4-1, the following are key exterior elements of your box:

✦ On the front of the box are slots for your diskette drives, access for a tape drive if you have one, perhaps an indicator light or two, and maybe a keyboard lock, reset button, and turbo (CPU speed) button. Some systems even have a digital display indicating processor clock speed or some mode of operation. If your system is a tower or upright unit, its power switch also may be on the front panel. The front of the unit is where you will find many systems' air-inlet vents, as well.

✦ The back of a PC contains the cable connections. Most units' exhaust air vents also are on the back.

Note With so many configurations in use today, your system may not exactly match everything we discuss here. Figure 4-1 shows the front and rear views of a typical PC system. The basic elements will be present, but what they look like can vary greatly. If you cannot find an exact match for some of the elements illustrated in this book, check your system's documentation, or call the manufacturer or dealer to verify items, part numbers, terms, and functions.

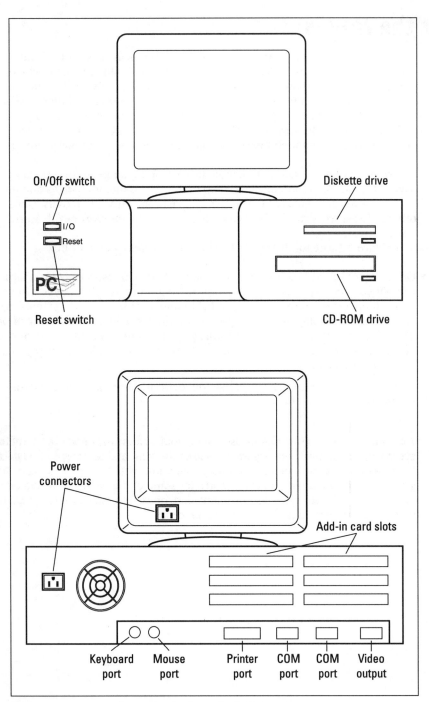

Figure 4-1: Front and rear views of a typical PC system

Case Care

Your PC's case performs several functions, each of which deserves some consideration.

First, the case is the structural housing for all of the system components. The fit and proper position of various components depends on the integrity of the case dimensions and shape. The original and many subsequent desktop-style PC cases could easily handle the weight of the smaller, simpler 10- to 14-inch monitors of years gone by. A typical monitor today weighs much more than the PC system unit, and the case is simply not designed to handle this load. Heavy items placed on top of the system unit can depress the top, causing contact with the disk drives and add-in cards, pinching cables inside the unit, or damaging plug-in cards.

Second, the case is part of the component cooling system. It is designed to route airflow to the fan inside the machine for cooling components. Avoid running the computer without the cover. Never block your air-inlet vents. Allow 4 to 6 inches of free space behind your system unit to accommodate its air vent and cabling, and don't allow cabling to bundle near the air-exhaust vent.

The rear panel may contain power outlets and connectors for keyboard, serial, parallel, or mouse ports. Most systems provide up to eight slots for add-in cards. If you don't have an add-in card in one of the slots, the slot should be covered over with a blank slot filler bracket. Proper cooling airflow depends on keeping these slots blocked off so that air exhausts properly through the power supply vent.

Finally, the case and many of its pieces form an electromagnetic shield. This shield is necessary to keep various electronic signals generated by the components from radiating beyond the case to nearby radios or other devices. Similarly, the case can keep interfering signals out of the PC components.

Defining the Box

A computer system is made up of several basic subsystems and components. Most of these pieces are readily identifiable as bigger items (from the case to the monitor to the keyboard), smaller components (a disk drive or I/O card), or parts of larger item (the CPU or RAM chips on a system board).

The computer's chassis or system unit holds most of the computer's working parts, but users don't have much direct contact with it or the pieces inside. At most we may change diskettes or CD-ROMs, turn on the power, or hit the reset switch on occasion. If we do open the box, we will find myriad cables, connectors, screws, chips, and various shiny pieces of all sizes. Among these:

✦ A **central processing unit** (CPU) that works with the data that you, your programs, and your files provide and generates results based on a set of rules.

In this context, this unit comprises a powerful microprocessor chip, either an Intel Corporation–designed 8088, 8086, 80286, 80386, 80486, Pentium-class processor, or a compatible chip from Cyrix, AMD, or IDT. Yours may be an IBM or Texas Instruments version of a Cyrix CPU.

✦ **Storage** for instructions and data for the processor. This is commonly in two forms: electronic memory that is active only when the computer is in use (the RAM and ROMs of the system), and the storage media you use for programs and data that supply the electronic memory during use (such as diskettes and hard disks, CD-ROMs, and tape systems).

✦ **Input and output (I/O)** connections to the external mechanisms for you to provide data input and retrieve results. I/O usually connects the inside of the computer to a keyboard, a video display, a printer, and possibly a network or phone-line connection for a modem.

✦ Computers need a set of logical **rules** to govern how input and output are handled, and how to perform the job to be done. The rules come from the software and the logic designed into the electronic chips used in the system.

✦ An **energy source** to power the components.

An IBM-compatible PC system both expands and integrates these major subsystems or functions into a variety of features and options to provide a very flexible, customizable computer system. At the risk of some redundancy, but to provide a different perspective or analogy, the basic subsystems in a PC break down into the following modules or components:

✦ **Processing.** This includes the CPU and interface circuits to the other subsystems, modules, and components. The ROM BIOS (*Read-Only Memory* containing the *Basic Input/Output System* software) may be considered an integral part of the processing system because it provides the rules that give the processing system its functional hardware foundation. ROM is a program storage area, but it is typically permanent and necessary for the x86 processing system to behave like an IBM PC. Similarly, the CMOS RAM used to store system option and parameter information is an integral part of the processing system. All the other systems and functions within your computer must interface with the processing system in some way—either directly, on the system board, or through connectors to external or add-on devices.

Note

Intel 8086-based CPU (x86) chips can be used for other things besides PCs. For instance, versions of the x86 chip are used in automobile ignition and security systems, security and building air conditioning control systems, and communications control equipment—such as the very popular 3Com (formerly USRobotics) TotalControl system that accepts your dial-up modem calls to your ISP to connect you to the Internet.

✦ **RAM.** Volatile or temporary memory is used to store the data and instructions that make up the operating system (the programmatic interface between a system's hardware and the applications people use), your application programs, and data generated while you are using your PC.

This memory is called RAM, for *Random Access Memory*. RAM normally exists on the motherboard, along with the CPU. Additional RAM may be added to your system by installing either add-in cards and discrete chips (on much older PCs), SIMM or DIMM plug-in boards, or modules.

To learn how to add RAM to your PC, go to Chapter 15.

✦ **Data storage.** We could also call this rotating magnetic storage because it differs from memory chip or electronic storage of information. This is longer-term storage or memory for saving and using application programs and data. Disk storage is comprised of two or more types of disk drives — removable media drives such as diskettes, Zip, or LS-120 cartridges, and hard or fixed disk drives, or other special devices such as CD-ROM and tape drives. Unlike RAM storage, which is cleared when you turn off the machine, data stored on these media is considered nonvolatile or semipermanent.

All typical storage devices and media will lose their data storage capability over time.

✦ **Keyboard and other human interface devices.** These are part of the Input/Output subsystem, but are treated differently in both hardware and software. A mouse, trackball, document scanner, bar code reader, and voice recognition interfaces are examples of other input devices. Most of these latter units cross over into the serial I/O portion of your system as well.

✦ **Video display.** This is part of the Input/Output subsystem. With the variety of components and applications of video display items available, this becomes a significant factor in any PC system.

✦ **Serial I/O devices.** As it encompasses a variety of options and applications, this portion of the I/O subsystem is also significant and handled differently than other I/O devices in your PC system. This category now includes such devices as the Universal Serial Bus (USB) and the IEEE 1394 external serial bus, or FireWire.

✦ **Parallel I/O devices.** The parallel I/O portion of your PC system is generally used for output only, such as to a printer. Many vendors have developed new products to make some use of the input circuitry available as part of many parallel port interfaces, called a bidirectional interface. You may find PC-to-PC file transfer applications, disk drive interfaces, or special control interfaces available that use the input as well as the output functions of parallel I/O. A prime example of this is the ever-popular LapLink with its special cable that enables you to hook two PCs together via either parallel or serial connectors. In addition, the Small Computer System Interface (SCSI) connections for disk drives and other devices are also parallel in nature. Some companies such as Adaptec and Belkin provide adapters to turn a parallel port into a SCSI port.

✦ **Other I/O devices.** A PC system provides a great deal of flexibility in what may be designed and programmed to operate within the parameters of the I/O features and connections. On the typical PC today, you will find speaker and microphone connections as I/O devices for sound cards.

You may also find an adapter that sends your PC's video display signal out to a TV set or other video device, or one that takes TV or other video signals to display or record them onto your PC. You may also encounter special interfaces for networks, laboratory or factory equipment control, test equipment, data collection, or security systems. These latter specialty items typically connect to the bus or directly interface to the processing system.

✦ **Power supply.** This is the energy source required by all portions of your PC system. Desktop or tower systems contain a power supply that converts power from common AC wall outlets to specific DC voltages required by the computer's components. Laptop and notebook computers get their energy from batteries. The battery power is controlled within the PC system so the internal components receive the proper voltages.

✦ **Software.** Along with the CPU and BIOS, software is part of the "rules" portion of your system. The lowest-level rules are determined by the internal design of the microprocessor chip. The microprocessor design and its internal micro code dictate the first level of software interface to the world outside of the CPU chip. The world outside of the chip communicates with the chip in what is known as *machine code*. Every program ever run on your PC system ultimately speaks in machine code no matter whether it was written in Assembler, BASIC, C, Pascal, Java, or another higher-level programming language, and whether or not it runs in a DOS, Unix, or Windows operating system.

Every computer program must ultimately be constructed in a specific manner to work with a specific type of computer chip. Usually, this construction or compilation is handled by the tools used to process raw program language information into an executable program. Relatively few people deal at the machine-code level of a PC system or its processor, but the most efficient programs are those that are written in a language similar to that which the CPU understands directly. The basis for most of the DOS and Windows operating systems and applications, written mostly in C or C++ languages, would be much more efficient if written in assembly language.

Apart from what happens inside the CPU chip, but close to the hardware functions, the BIOS program that runs when you first turn on your system is the next step in the hierarchy of the rules. The BIOS may be created using assembly language or C programming tools, but ultimately the chip contains machine code that the processor understands. The BIOS is the first interface between the processor and the system user, assessing what equipment is installed in the system and then allowing activities such as reading bootup data from adiskette.

At the user level we are mostly concerned that the BIOS runs properly with hardware, and that the operating system loads and runs properly so we can use application programs. The rules/software that we may use are those established at the operating system level or in the applications. This level of the rules for the computer you're using is commonly accessed from a diskette or hard drive, but more and more software may be distributed and run only as needed over a network rather than being stored on a local hard disk.

We have just completed our first divide-and-conquer session by looking at how the five subsystems of a basic computer system are divided into smaller or more specific components for handling specific parts of the computer's functions. From here, we'll move on to identifying and describing the actual modules and components that make up a typical PC system.

Looking Inside the Box

Your PC system chassis contains some or all of the essential subsystem components of your system. Unless it is a laptop or portable system, the only common items outside of the system unit are a keyboard, mouse, and a display device. You could also have an external modem or storage unit, page scanner, printer, or some other peripheral. Figure 4-2 illustrates the view inside a typical PC system.

The PC's various subsystems may be integrated in different ways. The CPU is generally considered to be inclusive with the motherboard, unless you have an interchangeable CPU card. The motherboard also contains support circuits for the CPU, memory, and I/O. Some memory is contained on most motherboards, but may extend also to an add-in card. Part of the video subsystem, as well as parallel and/or serial input and output may be installed on the motherboard. We will discuss these items in a functional context.

Interior components usually consist of the following:

✦ The power supply

✦ The motherboard or system board

✦ The video display adapter, either as a card or as part of the motherboard

✦ The disk drive controller, either as a separate card or as part of the motherboard (this controller provides an interface between the computer and either the diskette drives, the hard drive, or both; separate cards may exist for the diskette and hard drives)

✦ The I/O ports — serial and parallel port adapter cards, which may be add-in cards or, again, an integral part of the motherboard

✦ The pointing device interfaces — most IBM-PS/2 and many late model compatibles include the mouse interface as part of the motherboard, but they might use one of the serial ports

✦ The PC speaker or a beeper

✦ Interface cables between the system board, I/O cards, disk adapters, and the drives

✦ DC power cables from the power supply to the motherboard and disk or tape drives and other internal components

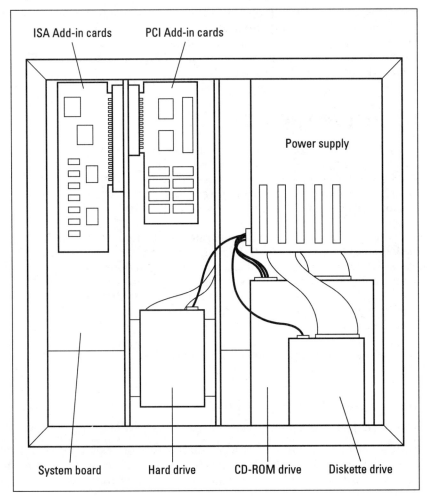

Figure 4-2: A view inside a typical PC system

Optional devices may include these items:

✦ Fax/modem, network, or other interface cards

✦ Disk drives — diskette drives and/or hard drives, CD-ROM, DVD, and high-density removable media (such as Zip and LS-120 drives)

✦ A tape drive

✦ Add-in memory expansion cards (a possible add-in for PC, XT, 286, and 386 systems)

✦ An add-in clock/calendar card (a typical add-in for PC and XT systems)

✦ A battery package for a clock/calendar and/or the CMOS RAM

All you need for your computer to function at a basic level are the following:

✦ A power supply

✦ The motherboard with some memory on it

✦ A video-display adapter and monitor

✦ A diskette drive interface and at least one diskette drive

✦ A keyboard

These are the items you will have to leave in your system if the troubleshooting process calls for removing everything you possibly can in order to run tests with the simplest system possible. A couple of tests may also require removing either the disk controller or the video adapter, or both, in which case you will have only the PC speaker to rely on for some test result information (in the form of beeping sounds).

The power supply

Your PC needs specific DC voltages that it gets from its internal power supply unit. If you have a laptop, its power supply is some form of battery pack that feeds voltage to regulator circuits for the various parts of the system.

The power supply may include a main system power switch, marked with a 1 for ON and a 0 for OFF, or the power switch is wired to the front panel.

At least four cable sets originate at the power supply. Two of these connect to the motherboard, and the others are available for disk- or tape-drive connections. If you have only two cables for disk and tape drives, but have more than two drives, the extra drives may be accommodated with a splitter or Y cable on one of the connectors.

The power supply converts the AC wall outlet power to specific regulated DC voltages required by the motherboard, any add-in cards, and the disk drives. If any one of these voltages is out of tolerance (too high, too low, or missing), the system will probably not operate.

 You will find more about power supplies and voltages in Chapter 12.

The system board

The system board or motherboard, as shown in Figure 4-3, is the actual computer in your system. It contains the microprocessor and support chips, usually some memory; and at least a few plugs, slots, and sockets for more memory, add-in cards, the keyboard, or other items. Most, older motherboards also contain switches or jumper posts for selecting video display mode, port addresses, amount of memory, number of disk drives, and other features.

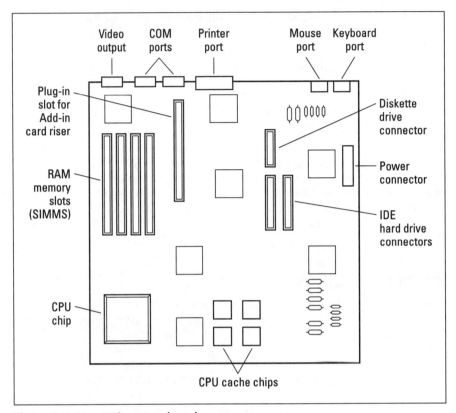

Figure 4-3: Your PC's system board

Your motherboard may also contain an empty chip socket or two, intended to accommodate a math coprocessor chip (older models), additional memory, or special program chips.

There is nothing unique or exclusive about the components for IBM PC and compatible computers. The basic computing design closely follows designs that Intel defined for the 8086 processor chip in the 1970s. Basically, IBM refined a new design for add-on devices, used an 8088 processor, and originated the BIOS code that makes a PC an IBM-compatible personal computer. Microsoft was sought out along the way to provide the operating system that provided the "glue" between the hardware system and user programs.

All PCs, up to and including the 80486- and Pentium-based personal computers of today, perform the same basic functions as the 8088-based IBM Personal Computer. Later models added the capabilities of multitasking and *much* faster operation, and are complemented by several new peripheral and interface designs that give the concept of *turbo* a new meaning.

The system board is held in place by spacers, insulators, and standoffs that provide mechanical support and electrical isolation where needed. Sometimes you have to remove all the wires and fasteners from the board in order to gain access to the sockets for memory or the math chip.

Early motherboards were built from individual chips and components plugged into sockets or soldered into the board. Today, most of the separate, discrete components have been combined into a few densely packed single chips soldered to the board with connections so small that technicians must use magnifiers to work on them.

You usually cannot repair the motherboard at the component or chip level. Most failures occur in the board itself, or in a manufacturer's unique integrated circuits, for which you will not find too many commonly available or safely replaceable parts. In either case, repair of motherboard or CPU-related problems is more economical by complete board replacement.

Disk drives

Your disk drive, especially your hard disk drive, is usually the most personally critical part of your PC system. Nearly anything else can fail and not cause as much headache and heartache as the unit that holds your software and data, and what may be days, weeks, months, or even years of your work.

Tip   It's always a good idea to back up your data regularly, even if your computer is brand new.

Disk drives are delicate. The speed and tolerances with which they work are very precise. Many of the mechanisms that make up the essential parts of the drive system are easily damaged by shock, vibration, or static electricity. Disk drives should be left flat on their bottom side, or vertically on the left or right side, and in some cases, not on the front or back side. Older drives could not be run when upside-down, but this is acceptable for many newer drives.

It is fairly simple to install or remove a disk drive. The key connections of a disk drive are shown in Figure 4-4. An IDE hard drive has one 40-pin cable, and a SCSI drive typically has one 50-pin flat data cable connecting it to the disk adapter or motherboard and another to connect it to the power supply. Floppy disk drives use one 34-pin flat ribbon data cable and one power cable. The connections to a CD-ROM may also include a small cable to the sound card.

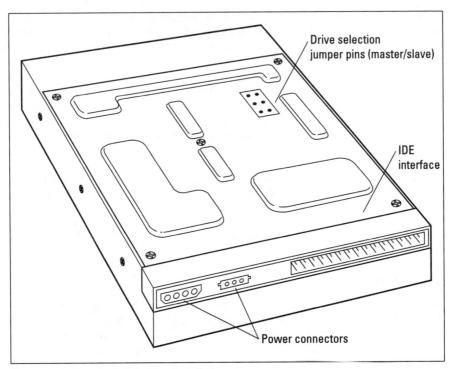

Figure 4-4: A typical disk drive installation

Fragile – Handle with Care While in Operation

Never move or jar your disk drive while it is operating. Severe shock can cause the following problems:

✦ The delicate balance of airflow between the surface of the disk and the read/write head is upset or the heads will be forced to hit the disk surface. When the head makes contact with the disk surface, it causes physical damage to the material and makes that part of the disk unusable.

✦ The bearings that keep the disk platter aligned while it is spinning can be damaged. A damaged bearing can make the disk drive very noisy to operate and the disk rotation will become unstable.

✦ The electrical connections that carry power and data can break, causing loss of one or more drive functions.

How a disk drive is mounted varies between systems. It used to be safe to say that mounting a disk drive was much easier in 286 and later computers. It was easier because they had slide-in rail-mounting systems and front retaining clips and screws versus the side panel screws used for PC and XT systems. Now mounting a drive may require all sorts of tricks in solid geometry to get it in place. Some of the side-mounting screws may be blocked by the system board or other internal parts. It is easy to drop these screws inside your system, where they are likely to rattle around and cause some trouble, so be careful.

 Caution   Be very careful with any screws or metal objects in and around your computer. If you leave something inside, you are likely to find it later, probably after something has gone wrong as a result.

Add-in cards

Within the limits of what will fit in the box, add-in cards of nearly every shape, color, function, speed, connector orientation, and manufacturer imaginable exist in the PC market. All of these cards, however, must fit the system unit height and length restrictions imposed by most of IBM's first designs, and must comply with at least one of three or four motherboard connector styles.

The standard and new IBM-compatible motherboard connector arrangements are as listed here:

- ✦ 8-bit interface for PC, XT, and AT systems (ISA)
- ✦ 16-bit interface for AT systems (ISA)
- ✦ 8-bit interface for PS/2 systems (MCA)
- ✦ 16-bit interface for PS/2 (MCA)
- ✦ 16-bit interface for EISA systems
- ✦ 32-bit interface cards for VESA Local bus
- ✦ 32-bit and 64-bit interface cards for PCI systems
- ✦ Advanced Graphics Port (AGP) interface
- ✦ PCMCIA/PC Card interface

Some early style add-in video cards will work with the 8-bit PC/XT interface even if they also connect to the 16-bit AT interface. Cards for PS/2 Model 30 and similar systems are unique to that product series. Cards for the PS/2 Micro Channel systems are unique to that product series (some exceptions exist with manufacturers who have designed cards that may be interchanged within the PS/2 series). Cards that match the PC, XT, and AT systems comply with the Industry Standard Architecture (ISA). Cards for the PS/2 series are part of the Micro Channel Architecture (MCA) or Micro Channel standard.

Advances in technology through the existence of the PC since 1981 have brought four new interface styles to consider. First, in 1984–85, Compaq and others introduced the Enhanced Industry Standard Interface (EISA), which is compatible with some of the ISA connections and added extended contacts for deeper EISA motherboard add-in sockets. EISA connectors support both 8- and 16-bit cards as well as EISA-specific cards.

In 1990–91 an enhanced interface for external devices for portable computers, PCMCIA, began to emerge. PCMCIA (short for Personal Computer Memory Card International Association, a technical standards group) provides an interface to portable memory packs, miniature disk drives, modems, network interfaces, and interconnection with radio and cellular telephone systems. A PCMCIA interface resembles a thick credit-card-sized slot with a miniature connector inside.

In 1992, in an effort to speed up video subsystem performance, the VESA Local Bus (VL) interconnection method became popular. Local Bus provides a more direct route between the CPU circuits and I/O devices, and can be used within the motherboard to connect integrated video and disk interfaces.

Note   VESA, the Video Electronics Standards Association, is still involved with PC video modes and programming interfaces, but the Local bus I/O convention has given way to the more versatile and universal PCI standard.

The Peripheral Component Interconnect (PCI) bus is an enhancement in performance between the CPU and I/O devices used mainly for video, disk drive, and network I/O interfaces. PCI is also intended to provide for the exchanging of I/O devices between different types of computers — existing ones such as new versions of the Apple Macintosh and Power PC, and newer developments by other manufacturers. This is a significant step as personal computers begin to share more and more features and performance benefits, and it is more economical for manufacturers to make the most of development and manufacturing costs. The PCI bus in PCs also provides for *IRQ Steering* that enables multiple PCI devices to share a single hardware IRQ assignment.

As Figure 4-5 illustrates, the distinction between 8-bit ISA cards and 16-bit EISA cards is the 16-bit cards' cut-out and extra connector area. EISA cards are similar in this regard, but the connector areas extend out farther from the main body of the card. PCMCIA devices are not internal cards, but small external devices. Local Bus and PCI-style cards resemble 16-bit ISA cards.

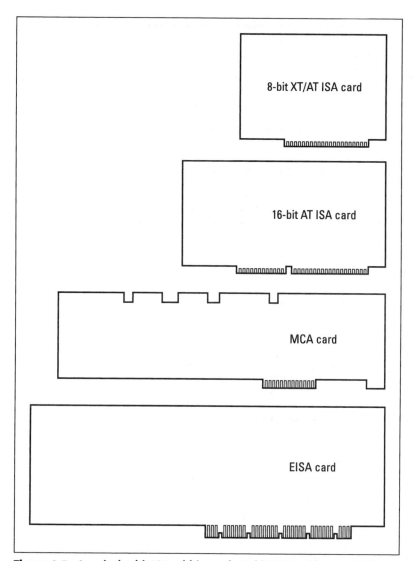

Figure 4-5: A typical 8-bit ISA add-in card, 16-bit EISA add-in card, Micro Channel card, and EISA card

Figures 4-6 through 4-9 illustrate other critical add-in cards: a VESA Local Bus add-in card, a PCI add-in card, an AGP add-in card, and a PCMCIA device, respectively.

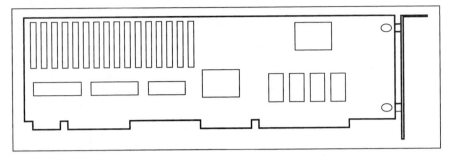

Figure 4-6: A typical VESA Local Bus add-in card

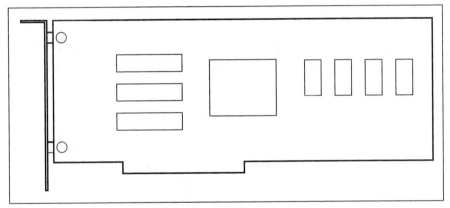

Figure 4-7: A typical PCI add-in card

AGP Bus Video Adapter

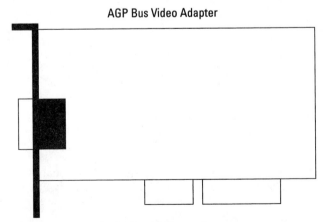

Figure 4-8: A typical AGP add-in card

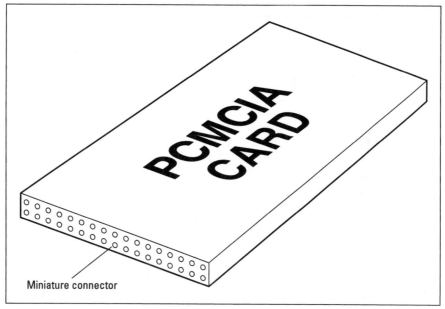

Figure 4-9: A typical PCMCIA device

Many manufacturers provide extended interfacing for 32-bit memory or I/O cards, using a third connector beyond the 16-bit connector portion or extending the 16-bit portion so that the card cannot be plugged into 16-bit ISA sockets. These cards are proprietary designs and may be used only with matching motherboards made by specific manufacturers. They either cannot or should not be plugged into 8- or 16-bit slots.

The following sections point out the appearances and features of some typical or generic add-in cards — from disk controllers, serial ports, parallel ports, video adapters, and modems to clock/calendar/port and memory expansion cards.

Video adapter

Your video adapter card usually can be identified by the presence of at least a single female connector on the rear bracket, most likely with two or three rows of holes. DIP switches may be accessible through the rear bracket of some of these cards. Monochrome, Hercules, CGA, and EGA adapters all have 9-pin female sockets to accept the cable from the video display monitor. A VGA-only adapter, either analog, digital, or multisync, will have a three-row, 15-pin female connector on its rear bracket, as shown in Figure 4-10.

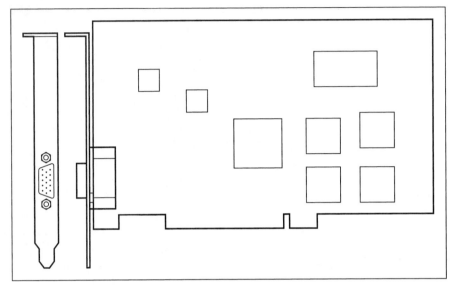

Figure 4-10: A typical VGA video adapter

If you have a CGA or combination CGA/EGA video adapter, you may also have a circular jack called an RCA or phono jack that provides a composite video signal for use with a television adapter or some early types of monitors.

If your video adapter is a combination CGA/EGA and VGA card with selectable options, you may have both a 9-pin female connector and a 15-pin female connector. The 15-pin connector is distinguishable by its three rows of pins that are smaller than those for the standard 9-, 15-, and 25-pin monitor, game, and serial connections.

Most monochrome video adapter cards also contain a parallel printer adapter (a 25-pin female socket on the rear bracket). Some brands of video cards also have a connection for a mouse or pointing device. This connector is a 6- to 9-pin circular female socket.

Some common manufacturers of video adapters are ATI, Matrox, Number Nine, Diamond, Orchid, and Hercules. Common chip identifications to look for are S3, Cirrus, Tseng, and Western Digital.

Disk drive adapters

Disk drive adapters come in various sizes and with various features. This item used to be referred to as a *controller* instead of an *adapter* because this I/O device used to contain a lot more circuitry and "intelligence" as part of the entire disk subsystem. Now the controller portion resides mainly on the disk drive, and the interface portion is just a method of connecting or adapting the CPU I/O bus to the disk drive.

Disk adapters are now usually built into the system board to take advantage of new chipset features and PCI bus speeds for higher performance.

Your system may have a combination diskette/hard disk controller, or separate cards for each type of disk drive. The original IBM PC system came with a diskette-only controller that included a 37-pin female socket on the rear panel, to which you could attach external diskette drives. This connector was also useful for some external tape drives.

All current system boards provide either or both of the disk adapters for hard drives and diskette drives, to facilitate higher-speed data transfer and to save space and cost. It is possible to have multiple hard drive adapters or connections for two or more IDE hard drives, CD-ROM drives, or SCSI devices, or a mix of both SCSI and IDE devices.

Diskette drives interconnect with their controllers by a 34-pin flat ribbon cable and either edge (open slot) or header (straight pin) connectors. Hard drives use a 34-pin flat cable and a 20-pin flat cable (for ST-506/MFM and ESDI drives), a 40-pin flat cable (for IDE drives), or a 50-pin flat cable (for SCSI type 1 and 2 devices). Newer SCSI-2 and SCSI-3 devices use a very high-density D-shaped connector and special flat cables.

Most SCSI host adapters provide an external connection of either a 25-pin D-type connector, a 50-pin "printer-style" connector, or a high-density D-shaped connector for use by external devices.

Serial (COM) ports

If you have a mouse, external modem, serial network connection, or scanner, or use a serial cable interface to your printer, your system will have at least one serial port. This port may be included on the motherboard, or may reside on a dedicated or shared add-in card. Many older systems had dual-purpose cards that included one or two serial ports and a parallel port.

Several varieties of IBM PC-compatible serial port cards exist. Many of these can provide two serial ports, as either COM1 and COM2, or COM3 and COM4, depending on how you configure your system (*COM* stands for communications). A variety of vendors now provide enhanced, or "smart," serial port cards that can provide more than the first four ports, and may speed serial communications. Mostly we will be dealing with the "plain-Jane," straightforward types of COM ports.

The keys to identifying a serial card are in the connectors used and, if you can identify it, the main serial port chip, called a UAR/T (for Universal Asynchronous Receiver/Transmitter). The connector will be either a 9- or 25-pin male plug on the rear bracket of the computer's case, or add-in card, or a 10-pin pad (two rows of five pins) on the motherboard, that connects to an adapter cable leading to a 9- or 25- pin socket.

One of the confusing aspects of any option on a PC system is the set of switches or jumpers used to select its address, hardware interrupt (IRQ), or operating condition of that option.

A serial port can have one of four possible port addresses, simplified to COM1, COM2, COM3, or COM4, and usually only one of two possible hardware interrupt settings: IRQ3 or IRQ4. Sometimes the COM port address switching is used to control the IRQ switching as well. Based on the original PC standards, COM ports, no matter how they are addressed, always start with COM1 — even if the port has an address normally expected to be COM2, COM3, or COM4. Refer to Chapter 5 for more detail on this situation.

Beyond the documentation itself, another helpful guide is a system-information program such as Microsoft's MSD.EXE or Watergate Software's PC-Doctor, which shows you what options exist in your system. Using a trial-and-error method of changing the switches and using a system information program to identify what ports you have set in the system is a time-consuming but sure way to decipher your options. Most of the cards themselves are generic imports, so you will not be able to rely on finding common or brand names. The View by Connection/Properties option in the Windows Device Manager display, found in the Control Panel in the Device Manager or System icon, depending on your version of Windows, will list all of the IRQs and to what they are attached.

Chips to look for to help identify serial ports have, for example, numbers similar to 8250, 82C50, 16450, 16C450, 16550AFN, 16C550AFN, 16C650, or a multipurpose chip by SMC marked 37C665.

Parallel (LPT) ports

Parallel ports are considerably easier to deal with than serial ports. The parallel ports are normally associated with printers, and how they are addressed and configured reflects this. PC systems can support up to three parallel ports, commonly labeled for printers as LPT1, LPT2, and LPT3 (*LPT* stands for line printer).

A provision for a hardware interrupt (IRQ) assignment to these ports, though available, is rarely, if ever, used, unless you are using IBM's OS/2 or another operating system or a sophisticated printer system that requires the LPT port to have an IRQ connection.

On these I/O ports you are usually given only one set of parallel port selections, most commonly LPT1 or LPT2. If you have only one printer port in your system, even though it may be configured as LPT2, it will function as LPT1 because the BIOS will try to make sure that any printer is available as the default and only printer. Refer to Chapter 5 for more information on this situation.

Parallel ports are typically one-way or output-only devices. They were intended to send 8-bit data to printers and obtain up to five different and separate bits of status information from printers. Since the original PC, XT, and AT systems, developers have created two new types of parallel ports. One, often called a Type 2 parallel port, provides not only 8-bit output data, but also can accept 8 bits of input data in parallel. Another port enhancement, often called the Type 3 parallel port, provides two-way 8-bit transfer and other programmable functions. You may see indications of these different types in your system's CMOS setup and port assignments.

Enhanced parallel ports have been developed that may be used for data transfer interconnections between systems or external devices, but these are not being used as widely as hoped. We will see higher-speed serial interfaces in common use very soon (as we already see in USB and FireWire, for instance).

With some creative programming it is possible to use the five status bits for two-way data transfer. Two less common uses for the parallel ports are file transfers between PC systems using a special cable and software (such as Traveling Software's LapLink), some external tape and disk drives, a portable sound adapter, or control of external hardware for special applications. Some of these uses are more effective with either of the two enhancements made to parallel ports in the past few years.

Parallel ports have only one easily identifiable characteristic: The connector is a 25-pin female socket. If this socket is mounted on the back of your PC chassis and has a cable that connects it to the motherboard or parallel adapter card, that cable will be a 26-pin flat ribbon cable with a 26-pin (two rows of 13 pins each) header connector at the other end. This connector may be confused with some older SCSI adapter connectors — check the labeling of the card. If the card label contains the name Adaptec, Always, Bustech, Buslogic, Trantor, Seagate, UltraStor, Western Digital, or possibly others, the chances are this is a SCSI adapter and not a card containing a parallel printer port.

Parallel port cards are akin to serial cards in that no common manufacturers or brand names are associated with them.

Keyboard and mouse ports

The typical keyboard connection on older machines uses a 5-pin circular or DIN connector built onto the system board. To save space, when IBM introduced its PS/2-series systems it provided a new-style mini-DIN circular connection. Many people now recognize this as being identical to the new-style mouse connections. Both types of connections work the same way, and are interchangeable with various adapter plugs and cords so that almost any PC-compatible keyboard may be used on the PC.

Until IBM introduced its PS/2-series systems, if you had a mouse, it connected to either a serial (COM) port or to a special adapter card (from Logitech or Microsoft). The introduction of the PS/2 provided that new port connection on the back of the PC, the mini-DIN connection, which is identical to and often confused with the mini-DIN keyboard connector.

The keyboard and mouse connections actually use the same device on the system board—what we know from the "old" days as the 8250 keyboard controller chip. This chip provides two serial interfaces that are specifically programmed inside the controller chip to work with PC keyboards (they cannot be used as additional COM ports). You will find that there may be only one mini-DIN connection provided on some laptops, but this single connection can be used for either a mouse or a keyboard, for your convenience. You can also buy a Y splitter that lets you attach both a mouse and a keyboard to the mini-DIN connection.

Network interface cards

Network interfaces are more varied than serial or video adapters because at least five different connector types are used for various networks. Figure 4-11 shows some of the possibilities. Today it is likely that you will find network cards with only a 10- or 100-BaseT RJ-45 connector on them.

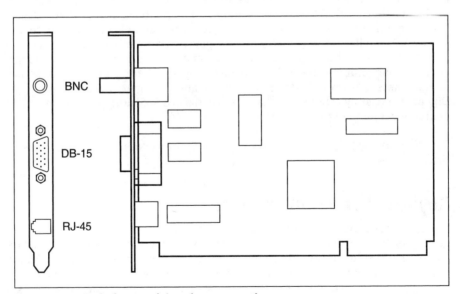

Figure 4-11: Typical network interface connections

Jumpers to look for may indicate "10BaseT" and "BNC" to specify the type of cabling used, or any of several address options (280, 2A0, 300, 320, 340, or 360), a few IRQ selections (2, 3, 5, 7, 9, 10, 11, or 12) and possibly DMA channel settings (1, 3, 5, or 7). Recent versions of add-in cards typically use a software configuration method rather than hardware jumpers.

Some of the more common manufacturers associated with network adapter cards are 3Com, D-Link, LinkSys, and Intel. Almost certainly if the card has a chip with the numbers 8390 on it, it is a form of network adapter.

A network card is becoming a very important part of many PC systems because it is the pipeline for data flowing between a PC and other computers on a local network and the Internet.

It may be easy to confuse the RJ-11 or 15-pin connectors with other adapters, such as game ports (for joysticks or paddles). Modems are easier to identify (see the section that follows). The only easy way to tell the difference between a network adapter and a game adapter is a brand name or a sticker that indicates a network node address, and that the 15-pin network connection is coupled with distinctive bracket clips where the game adapter will have common hex-shaped extended screw sockets.

Modem cards

Modems are most easily identified by their one or two RJ-11 telephone-style modular jacks on the rear bracket, and almost certainly by a 1–2-inch square, flat speaker attached to the card. The telephone-style jacks may be labeled PHONE, LINE or WALL to indicate which connection is supposed to go to which device.

Another indication may be the labeling of switches or jumpers that refer to COM1, COM2, COM3, or COM4; IRQ3 or IRQ4; and related abbreviations such as DTR, DSR, RTS, CTS, RD, or CD that refer to the modem-status signals. Some modems may also contain a UAR/T chip, mentioned previously, but in most modems, the UAR/T function is built into other chips.

Look for brand names such as Creative Labs or Diamond, or chips labeled Creative, ESS1688, or Sierra, which can be obvious indicators that a particular card is likely a sound card.

Sound cards

Multimedia or sound cards are most easily identified by two, three, or four ⅛-inch miniature round jacks on the back, labeled OUT, LINE, MIC, SPKR, or something similar.

Some multimedia cards also have 34-, 40-, or 50-pin connector rows for connecting CD-ROM drives, and small plastic shrouded pins for CD-ROM drive audio connections.

You may also see a lot of jumper pins and blocks with labeling for 220 or 240 as addresses, several IRQ or interrupt selection jumpers, and three or four DMA channel jumpers.

Look for brand names such as Creative Labs, Diamond, or chips labeled Creative, ESS1688, or Sierra, which can be obvious indicators that a particular card is likely a sound card.

Memory cards

Add-in memory cards are rare if nonexistent in today's PCs, but PC, XT, AT, and some 386 systems often have additional memory provided through add-in cards. They are pretty easy to identify. They will have distinct rows and columns of chips and sockets, usually grouped in rows of 9 or 18 sockets. Boards with rows of nine sockets should have a single 8-bit bus connector at the bottom of the card. Boards with rows of 18 sockets should have an 8-bit connector and the additional 16-bit connection at the bottom, unless the 18 sockets are organized in two rows of nine sockets each.

The majority of integrated circuits will be RAM chips with common numbering similar to 4164, 4464, 41256, and 44256. The 64 and 256 refer to the number of thousands of bits the chip can store. These numbers are sometimes followed by a hyphen (-) and a number such as 4, 7, 8, 10, 15, 20, 70, 80, 100, 150, or 200, which indicates the speed rating of the chip (usually in nanosecond units).

If your memory is a Single Inline Memory Module (SIMM) or Single Inline Package (SIP) style, you should see three or nine small chips mounted on a small circuit board or encased in a plastic molding. These will likely have numbers reflecting 256K, 1-, 4-, 16-, 32-, 64-, or 128-megabyte capacity, and they plug into small plastic brackets or a single row of small pin sockets. SIMMs, resembling small add-in cards, come in 8-, 9-, 32-, or 36-bit wide capacities, with 30 or 72 connection pins along their edge. Dual-Inline Memory Modules (DIMM), resembling small add-in cards, have 168 connector pins, and may be installed on a card or on the motherboard.

Older memory boards usually have at least one set of switches or jumpers to configure the amount of memory present on the card and the address where that memory starts. Aside from generic or clone memory cards, your old memory board may be from a specific manufacturer such as AST, Everex, Intel, Compaq, Northgate, or Dell. Add-in memory cards are nonexistent for newer systems that use 30- or 72-pin SIMM or 168-pin DIMM modules because the memory components need to be interfaced closely to the CPU in high-speed systems; using an add-in card is less reliable for this critical system element. Memory is covered in much greater detail in Chapter 15.

Clock/calendar units

A real-time clock and calendar was not included with the early PC and XT systems until IBM provided it in the PC/AT system. If you did not want to bother with setting the date and time each time you turned your PC on, you had to add this function as a standalone module or as part of a multifunction card.

If your system is not an AT or higher-class PC, or one of a few new XT versions with a dedicated clock and calendar function, you could have any one of three or four different styles of add-in clocks. One type of clock unit plugs in between a diskette drive and cable and contains a lithium battery holder and clock chip. Other units plug into one of the ROM sockets on the motherboard, and some are on a small card that plugs into the standard add-in card slots.

The most distinguishing feature to look for is a lithium or mercury battery. These battery types are usually in the form of a large button-cell (about the size of a quarter), or a small NiCad battery pack that resembles a bumpy cylinder, half an inch in diameter and about half an inch to two inches long.

Later model systems contain integrated clock and battery modules, usually from Dallas Semiconductor. These devices are black-cased, block-like plug-in modules. They may be replaceable, and should be available at many computer and parts resellers. Most systems today have the clock functions built-into other onboard components, such as the Intel 440BX and similar chipsets that link the CPU, memory, and I/O functions together.

Multifunction cards

Also a rarity in today's systems, except to combine multiple COM and LPT ports, are multifunction adapter cards that provided everything from additional memory to clock and calendar, diskette, and disk drive interfacing, serial and parallel ports, and game interfaces.

These cards are usually three-quarter to full-length cards containing any or all of the distinguishing features mentioned previously for the items supported by the card. You can expect to find a selection of jumpers, switches, and connectors for each function the card provides.

AST Research and Intel made a popular series of cards that can add extra DOS, LIMS-EMS, or expanded memory to your system and provides an extra serial, parallel, and clock function. You could find similar products from Everex and many of the generic clone or import vendors.

Multifunction cards contained serial, parallel, and game port adapter functions, as well as diskette and IDE hard disk interfaces. Today these functions are built onto the main system board.

PCMCIA/PC card slots

Found mostly on laptop systems, the PCMCIA slots are the connection points for add-in disk drives, memory cards, serial, parallel, or SCSI devices, modems, and network adapters. When these devices are connected they often appear to the system as additional logical devices. To better support mobile computing and keep your office and mobile computers synchronized, add-on boards for PCs exist that will use the PCMCIA cards.

Infrared port

Appearing as a mysterious small, dark-red panel on the edge of many laptop systems and handheld computers, an infrared port is most often configured as an additional serial (COM) port on these systems. It enables cordless communications between other portable and personal digital assistant units, and some peripheral devices such as printers.

Universal Serial Bus port

The PC can now expand beyond the limits of its usual four COM ports (eight for Windows 95/98 and 255 for Windows NT) and three LPT ports, and provide interconnection for myriad other peripheral devices. The port electronics are usually built onto the system board, but connect to the outside world by a new-style four-wire connection. Figure 4-12 shows the various ports on a typical ATX system.

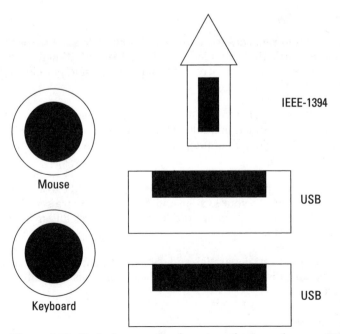

Figure 4-12: Typical connection layout on the rear of a new ATX system

A Universal Serial Bus (USB) port can connect up to 255 external devices to your PC, communicate several times faster than a conventional serial port, and even provide a modest amount of power to those devices. Until recently only a handful of peripheral devices were available with USB, but more are on the way. Today a lot of gaming/recreation and multimedia devices take advantage of USB as well as an even faster serial connection — IEEE-1394, or FireWire.

IEEE-1394 port

The port for IEEE-1394, FireWire, i.Link, or whatever you call it, is finally starting to appear on PC systems. IEEE-1394, or 1394, is a super-fast serial communications link designed for moving large amounts of imaging data, such as that from video cameras, to editing systems. It is also very useful for add-on storage accessories such as disk drives, and is finding its way to scanners and printers. IEEE-1394 ports have been seen on some new PC systems from Compaq and Sony, and are available with PCI-bus add-in cards. We're still waiting for Dell, Hewlett-Packard, Gateway and others to get IEEE-1394 onboard as a standard component, rather than an add-on.

Cross-Reference For more information about general I/O systems, USB and IEEE-1394, go to Chapters 20 and 21.

FireWire . . . i.Link . . . Whatever!

The reason for the "whatever" naming confusion is that Apple Computer had been one of the original driving forces behind making use of this technology, and because "IEEE-1394" is quite a mouthful and a little too technical for consumers, Apple gave it a name: FireWire. The name caught on informally but to be associated with products requires permission from Apple — and the PC industry is not too keen on licensing from rival vendors, even if it is free.

Sony Corporation felt that the name IEEE-1394 didn't work for its marketing efforts, and saw the advantages of the interface for its imaging products. Consequently, Sony called the interface *i.Link* — for *image link* or *eye link*.

Confusing the landscape a little further is the fact that Sony uses the i.Link name for three different but related aspects of its implementation of IEEE-1394. One aspect is quite simple — i.Link is just a nicer name for IEEE-1394. Another is a secure data transfer protocol that Sony implements to protect material with restricted distribution from being copied. This does not affect the 1394 electronic interface or interoperability with other devices and systems, but it could confuse the market a little. Finally, Sony does confuse the physical implementation of "1394" by using smaller non-1394-standard connectors on many of its cameras. The function is the same, electronically and in the data transfer process, but it is not a "1394" connector.

Things Outside the Box

Most of the things inside your PC system ultimately connect to things on the out-side of the PC—those items that you can touch and interact with, and those from which you simply get data or to which you send data. These are known as the *peripheral* devices, and usually fewer of these exist than do different devices inside your system.

Video displays

The video display monitor resembles a small TV set, and it probably sits on top of the box. It should have at least a power switch, a power indicator, and brightness and contrast controls near the front of the unit.

Many units place the horizontal and vertical controls near or under the front edge, or behind a small door under the display area. Less thoughtful manufacturers bury the controls at the back of the unit, possibly requiring a special screwdriver to get to them through small holes. The really sadistic manufactures place the controls inside the unit, which makes them very difficult to adjust.

It is best to leave the insides of your display monitor to skilled technicians, because several places inside the display housing carry extremely high voltages. The voltage that attracts electrons on the inside of the screen's face can be any-where from 12,000 to 30,000 volts or higher. This voltage is supplied at a very low current, but it can be dangerous. It is this portion of the high voltage inside your display that can cause arcing, snapping, and popping, and that electrical smell that signals the buildup of dust or humidity inside the case.

Two types of power plugs are common on display monitors. One requires a stan-dard three-wire American-style AC outlet, and the other uses an international equip-ment plug that can connect to an outlet at the back of your power supply. For $3 to $7 you can buy a short adapter cable that converts the standard three-wire AC plug to the protected three-wire international-style plug that fits into the back of most PC power supplies.

Some monitors could be configured to serve as CGA, EGA, or VGA monitors. Dep-ending on the application and the video adapter card to which your monitor is con-nected, you may find an adapter plug attached to the end of the video cable. This plug is used to convert the wiring of a CGA or EGA connection to that of a VGA con-nection. If your system does not require this adapter, you should keep it in a safe place in case you need to test the monitor on another system, or if you sell the monitor to someone else who needs a different type of connection.

Keyboards

Probably the closest thing to you when you are using your computer is the keyboard. It is the component most likely to get dirty, and it may drink more coffee than you do some days. You may also find that this is where most of your staples and paper clips go when you are not looking.

About the only thing you need to know about your keyboard is whether or not it has a switch that configures it to be used with PC XT systems or AT and higher systems. If it does not have a switch, it is either a PC or XT keyboard that can also be used on AT systems, or it is an AT-specific keyboard that cannot be used on PC or XT systems. Selector switches are usually located on the bottom face of the keyboard, and should be clearly marked. Your keyboard may also have a switch that selects the function of the Control and CapsLock keys.

Your keyboard contains a small microprocessor and some other circuits that receive power from and communicate with your main computer. Enhanced keyboards have some programming capabilities built in that enable you to select key combinations for character-repeat speed (the *typematic* rate) and the time delay before a key begins repeating. You may also be able to program the keyboard to swap the Control and CapsLock key functions, lock the period and comma keys regardless of the shift status, or program a function key to send specific key sequences to the computer.

Your keyboard may require some care and cleaning from time to time. Check the documentation for your keyboard before attempting any cleaning or disassembly.

Caution

If you have an early version of a true IBM keyboard, do not take it apart! If you open only the housing you will not get very far into the switches and buttons and may be tempted to remove the metal cover from the back of the electronics. If you do this, do it over a large baking pan, or towel. You will be very surprised at the number of springs and small pieces that pop out, and it will take you 15 to 20 minutes to find them all and put them back into place. It will take you another 10 to 15 minutes to put the metal cover back on — if you are very dexterous or have a cooperative third hand available. (Yes, we have learned the hard way. You only do it once!)

Mice and other pointing devices

Few computers are without that odd-looking widget, connected to the end of yet another wire plugged into your system unit, that enables you to move an arrow symbol around on your screen to point and click at objects representing programs or documents you want to use.

Although they are generically called *pointing devices*, most users have a *mouse* — a small device about the size of a bar of soap, with two or three buttons at one end. Some users prefer a stationary device called a *trackball*. Still others prefer to use a *tablet* and *pen positioner*.

As with your keyboard, the pointing device you choose requires some periodic care and cleaning to keep it functioning smoothly. Nothing is worse than a bumpy or scratchy-feeling mouse or trackball to mess up the alignment of graphics or text in your work.

You may find wireless pointing devices that are meant to point at the PC system for the signal to get inside, much like a TV or VCR remote control, and these may have mouse-like bottoms or trackballs for cursor location as well. These use a special infrared light coupling, like the remote control for a television, and thus have an infrared eye or special adapter for their connection to the PC. These are easily spotted by the existence of a flat, shiny, red plastic "eye" that seems to do nothing. They are found most often on a wireless mouse, wireless printer, or personal data assistant (PDA).

Summary

By this point you have discovered what an IBM-PC-compatible system contains, and have seen what some of the pieces look like. From here we take you into the realm of what you really have a PC for — to run applications within an operating system — and discuss these operating systems so you know what to expect from them and how to deal with them when they go wrong. But first, let's tackle the confusion over physical and logical devices in Chapter 5.

✦   ✦   ✦

Physical Versus Logical Devices

As you can see, your computer contains a lot of physical items with a lot of different names, and different functions. It may seem a bit odd at first to use the parallel port, typically thought of as the printer port, for connecting to a network or an external disk drive, just as a serial port can be used for a modem, a mouse, or connecting your computer to another computer. But those are functional issues. It can be more confusing to understand the complexity of device names, numbers, addresses, IRQs, and how these things relate to one another.

Many technical support and system setup issues revolve around naming conventions and the addressing of devices in the PC. Before we go much deeper into the PC and common problems, it seems appropriate to discuss this issue, which goes beyond whether a device exists or if it functions properly, because first it must be set up correctly.

While it might be easy to think that Plug-and-Play and Windows do away with having to know about these technical details, think again. The Plug-and-Play BIOS must *know* what devices to tell Windows about. Windows, driver software, and most application programs still refer to these everyday connections and devices by their original designations. If you own and use a PC for any length of time, you will need to be familiar with these items at some time.

Perhaps the most common and confusing issue is how COM or LPT ports are named and assigned. This often brings up the question of why a system configuration you have performed does not turn out the way you thought it should. This issue is most often encountered when adding a new device, building and setting up a new system, or using an existing device with a new piece of software.

What's *Physical*?

Physical devices are the actual hardware that make up a serial communications port, a parallel (printer) port, disk drive interface, video adapter, keyboard port, or mouse port. These devices convert the CPU's data and address signals into data usable by other devices. The CPU knows these devices by their addresses, and interacts with their interrupt request (IRQ) and Direct Memory Access (DMA) signals.

Your computer must have some way to distinguish each of these items from one another. To do this, each item, from memory to disk drives, has a unique address so the CPU knows which device to send to or get data from. Most have an interrupt signal to let the CPU know they need attention; only a few have DMA signals.

Although most of these assignments were predefined by IBM in 1980, it is possible for different devices to use addresses normally intended for some other purpose. Appendix B contains a detailed listing of the IBM-standard addressing assignments that manufacturers and users should follow for the PC and most of its software applications to work properly.

What's *Logical*?

The CPU refers to devices using addresses such as 3F8h. Such addresses are not exactly friendly or easy for humans to remember, so devices are given names such as COM1 that are much easier to remember. They are easier to remember because their names closely or more *logically* resemble the function of the device or I/O port.

Drive C:, *LPT*, *COM*, and similar designations are merely human-oriented names for the devices. They are not designations for the electrical or physical properties that a computer uses to get signals to and from them.

We don't see too many device addresses unless we install a new device and the documentation lists addresses with the device name or number — COM3 and 3E8h, for example. We just want to add the function of a new COM port; the address should not matter to us, but it does. Similarly, software, at least Windows software, should not need to be too concerned about addresses; it simply needs to know which port to talk to. But remember that a CPU does not understand COM3 or MODEM; it needs to know addresses. So a conversion or translation layer exists between the hardware and the software — the BIOS.

Translating Logical Devices into Physical Addresses

To match up device names and address numbers, the system BIOS and DOS, or for Windows, device drivers, work together to provide you with named functional devices to work with, regardless of address numbers. The BIOS provides us an automatic translation or conversion layer to isolate us from hardware details. It is good that BIOS can un-complicate things. It can be confusing that BIOS provides this translation automatically without telling us about it or how it works, because the translations may not appear to make sense.

The hardware address-to-device name translation follows a few simple rules. It is important to understand that IBM established the rules in 1980. The rules are not perfect, but they must be maintained and adhered to for proper and consistent PC configuration. If the rules were changed, then PC systems would become incompatible and further confuse the issue.

The hardware addresses and device names are not tightly bound together. They do not need a direct one-to-one correlation, as the many device name and address tables imply. Device names are assigned dynamically when the system boots up, and in order, by the first suitable device found.

The rules assign the COM1 logical name to address 3F8h, but if a physical device does not exist at that address, it will give the name to any serial port device it finds in this order: 3F8h, 2F8h, 3E8h, and then 2E8h. If the first physical device the BIOS finds is at address 3E8h, that device will get the name COM1. Logical device naming is dynamic, so if another device with address 2F8h is added later on, it will be given the name COM1, and the device at address 3E8h will be given the name COM2.

This dynamic naming applies to almost every device in the system, and also means that you cannot reserve or preset fixed names for devices. Thus you cannot have a device named COM2 unless you have a COM1 first; subsequently you cannot have a third (COM3) or fourth (COM4) port unless you have the first and second ones. In the case of floppy disk drives, you cannot have a B: drive unless you have an A: drive.

Associating IRQ Assignments with Logical Names

Despite the name versus physical or electrical separations, any software, device or function that requires an IRQ (hardware interrupt line) assignment usually expects this assignment to be associated with the BIOS name or logical device rather than the physical address. The expected and desired BIOS translations for LPT and COM ports are as follows:

Logical Device	Physical Address
COM1	3F8
COM2	2F8
COM3	3E8
COM4	2E8
LPT1	3BC
LPT2	378
LPT3	278

What if you want a COM2 to "save" COM1 for a later assignment? You address your serial port for 2F8, install it, set your software to use COM2, and you're ready to go, right? Wrong! Try setting the software for COM1 instead—it works! What gives? BIOS will not let you have a second device without the first. BIOS does not "know" that 2F8 "should be" COM2, and will not let it be. Here's the result:

Logical Device	Physical Address
COM1	2F8
COM2	None
COM3	None
COM4	None

Add a "COM" addressed device at 3E8 and you end up with a COM2. You cannot have a third device without having a second.

Logical Device	Physical Address
COM1	2F8
COM2	3E8
COM3	None
COM4	None

Add a "COM4" device at 2E8 instead of the "COM3" device and you have a COM2. You cannot have a fourth device without having a third. You do not have a third device and cannot because you do not have a second device, so what you thought was to be COM4 ends up being your second device at COM2, as follows:

Logical Device	Physical Address
COM1	2F8
COM2	2E8
COM3	None
COM4	None

Add a COM1 device of 3F8 and you have COM1 where it should be, COM2 where it should be, and the COM4 device ends up as COM3. You have two devices, but you cannot have the fourth without having a third one, and the BIOS knows that 3F8 should be COM1 and 2F8 should be COM2, so it cleans up those assignments to what we expect them to be:

Logical Device	Physical Address
COM1	3F8
COM2	2F8
COM3	2E8
COM4	None

This logic works the same way for LPT port assignments and diskette drives. The BIOS is often friendly enough to tell us if we mixed up a drive assignment, but it was never programmed to tell us about unexpected LPT or COM assignments.

This situation can get more complicated because operations involving serial ports also need to use an interrupt request (IRQ) hardware signal, which BIOS expects to be associated with the logical device, not the physical hardware.

Some DOS-based software programs, mostly communications software, ignore BIOS and work directly with the hardware so that they run faster. In this case you may not notice the BIOS mix-up, unless you have changed the IRQ assignment to match the BIOS logical device rather than the physical device to which the IRQ might normally be set. If things get too mixed up, software does not work correctly. Or, if two programs try to use the same port and neither program works, you have a mess.

Windows' Handling of Device Names and Addresses

Up to this point this discussion probably started making sense until you saw in the Windows "Device Manager" a COM5 port assignment for a newly installed modem when the system originally had only COM1 and COM2. We've not discussed a COM5, much less associated it with an address or an IRQ, but here it is. How can you have a fifth something without having the third or fourth? Does Microsoft know something that we don't?

Obviously, we didn't just gain two extra ports so we could have a fifth one, because we do not see a COM3 or COM4, just COM1, COM2, and now COM5. And no, Microsoft does not know something that we do not — they made it up. It has been Microsoft's goal to do away with the old BIOS method of configuring and using devices for quite some time. Not that they did not like IBM's way of doing things, but they recognize, as many others do, that the original methods of configuring and associating physical hardware with user-friendly functional names is clumsy and inadequate for all the devices that have been added to the PC.

The system BIOS will not simply go away because Microsoft wants it to, however, so it subverts or replaces much of the BIOS with its own device driver software — and much more so in Windows NT and 2000 than in Windows 9x/Me. Under Windows NT and 2000, this is called the Hardware Abstraction Layer, or HAL. It is essentially a programmatic way for the operating system to take control of the hardware, and prevent direct access to hardware by device drivers and software. One intent of this is security. Another is improving stability and management of the PC environment.

Using HAL and device drivers means that Windows can take advantage of new devices that use previously unused or ignored addresses, and translate them into new or additional names. IBM also provided for more COM ports with additional addresses when it introduced its PS/2-series products; sometimes these are used, more often not.

Overall, it is best if you are aware of and follow the BIOS rules, and build and configure your system logically according to the tables shown previously unless you have some specific need to create or use software that ignores the BIOS. Bending or ignoring the rules for the BIOS and these devices is helpful or necessary in some cases, but limits exist to the amount of bending you can or want to do or that you want software programs to do for you.

Some of this discussion will continue in other chapters as it pertains to the specific operation or problem at hand. By mentioning it here, in the context of what's in your system and how the pieces work together, hopefully some problems will be solved more quickly.

Summary

Now that you have a clearer picture of your computer, by taking this short look at the physical items that may be referred to using logical names, we will take you into the realm of why you got a PC — to run applications within an operating system. In Part II we'll give some history (because some of the older operating systems are still being used) of DOS and Windows, address problems with installation, configuration, and, of course, troubleshooting.

✦   ✦   ✦

The Soft Side of Your PC

P A R T

♦ ♦ ♦ ♦

In This Part

Chapter 6
Operating Systems,
File Systems, and
User Interfaces

Chapter 7
DOS Parts

Chapter 8
Windows for Home
and Desktop

Chapter 9
Windows for the
Enterprise

Chapter 10
Networking

Chapter 11
The Internet

♦ ♦ ♦ ♦

You didn't get your PC for its good looks. Well, that may have changed with the designer PCs on the market lately. However, you probably got that PC so you could do some work, manage some data, play some games, and communicate with the world. This requires an operating system, software, your own data, and some work on your part. Your own data and your work are the most important part of this mix. You *do* need a functioning hardware platform and functioning software to get to that most important part.

To understand where PCs are now, it is best to have a good picture of where they started and what paths they took along the way. Part II begins with a brief history of DOS and Windows before running headlong into the current milieu of operating systems, software, and configurations out there today.

If you need to skip ahead to a particular version of Windows or need to get on with troubleshooting your network or Internet connection, feel free to go directly to the chapter and section that best fits your need. Just remember, if you run into too much new terminology, you can always back up and get a better orientation.

Operating Systems, File Systems, and User Interfaces

Whether you work with your PC through a screen full of icons or from the DOS prompt, you are using some form of user interface. User interfaces may be "bare bones," such as the infamous C:\> prompt, or they may be so powerful that almost all you need to know about your PC is how to turn it on and how to select what you want.

User interfaces are intended to help you make better use of your PC or isolate you from the underlying technical details of the operating system, but they also come with unique sets of technical problems. Before Microsoft Windows and OS/2, the most common PC user interfaces were text-mode shells, or text-mode multitasking interfaces, such as Path-Minder, QDOS, Norton Commander, Tree86, XTree Gold, or DESQview (do *you* remember any of these old names?). Even a graphical interface such as Microsoft Windows 95 is a shell or dressing on top of at least part of the old DOS. Microsoft Windows NT and 2000 are graphical user interfaces embedded into the operating system and are true, preemptive, multitasking systems.

This chapter presents a brief look at the legacy of DOS and early Windows to set a perspective. Chapter 7 presents this history in a little more detail. Chapter 8 delves deeper into the current Windows operating systems for personal use, installing and configuring them, and highlights some common problems you may encounter. Chapter 9 is more oriented to the business side of Windows.

Defining Operating Systems

An *operating system* is a control program that provides user access to the capabilities of the hardware devices and utility functions of a computer system through application programs. Operating systems usually provide a few applications of their own to help users manage the system and perform basic functions with the computer system. Every computer must have an operating system or monitor program that manages the access to and use of the hardware it supports.

In embedded, or single-function, computers, such as those used in electronic thermostats, alarm panels, and microwave ovens, the operating system and the application program are very tightly coupled, and the operating system *is* the user interface.

The operating system in a mainframe computer does not have much of a user interface except very sparse console or terminal interfaces to monitor system status. Instead, users interact with a mainframe through application programs, some of which may be administrative or system operator programs that provide access for installing software or configuring system resources.

Minicomputers, and subsequently personal computers, are the first computer systems that provide access to and interact with the operating system from applications or services available directly through the system's primary console port. For most minicomputers this is still a character-based terminal interface. The PC broke this tradition by integrating terminal or console functions into the low-level code close to the CPU, and providing keyboard and video functions within the computer system instead of through an external box such as a separate data terminal. In essence, the computer system also performs the data terminal functions. Unix workstations are a mix of these two methods, providing both basic terminal port connections (a serial port for character-based operation) and internal data terminal (keyboard and video) support. No separate character-based terminal function or connection port exists within a PC; you have to provide a video adapter, monitor, and a keyboard to the PC system in order to work with it.

Managing Storage Media

In addition to the basic communications with the computer itself, an operating system is used to manage storage media (disk drives), establish and manage the data storage file system (directories, filenames, and so on), and other basic functionality such as providing for serial and parallel data ports. This is what DOS, a disk operating system, does for us — provides us with access to the system's hardware resources.

Why Is It Called "DOS"?

Why "DOS" and not just "OS"? First, specifically, it is either MS-DOS or PC-DOS to give the operating system some brand identification (Microsoft or IBM). Second, the "D" indicates the operating system is disk-based, rather than embedded or ROM-chip-based, although there have been implementations of DOS in ROM chips made to look like virtual disk drives.

DOS gives us some tools to establish and maintain disk drives and their file systems (with the FDISK, FORMAT, SYS, CHKDSK, SCANDISK, MKDIR, DIR, RMDIR, COPY, DEL, and XCOPY programs), manage memory (with HIMEM.SYS and EMM386.EXE), perform basic text editing functions, and use a BASIC programming language interpreter to run programs. However, DOS's main purpose in life is to enable us to invoke application programs we buy from other sources to perform work we want to do with an IBM-compatible personal computer.

DOS is an almost-derivative mixture of various aspects of Unix and CP/M. You can see it in some of the commands and the file system. It is a simple, text-based system but may be considered cryptic by all but the most avid user.

The operating system is just one key element of a computer system. In a car, lug nuts, spark plugs, distributors, and brakes are crucial elements — you need to be aware that they exist and to recognize their significance and maintenance requirements. But for the most part, these components are *not* the reason you bought the car. In the same manner, you did not purchase the operating system so you could use the computer it supports. Yes, occasionally you have a flat tire, need to get the oil changed, or should wash your car, and similarly, you or someone will also have to do specific tasks to keep your PC running properly. If it was simple, it would not be a PC, and it would not deliver as much flexibility or value.

Defining User Interfaces

A *user interface* is the portion of the operating system that enables the user to interact with the computer and where most programs are launched. The user interface provided by operating systems such as DOS and Unix, including the underlying DOS portions of Windows 95/98/Me and the command prompt under Windows NT/2000, are sparse, line-by-line text interfaces. These command-line presentations to the user feature no graphics, no pointing devices, little or no color, and so on. Yet the text-based command-line and screen feedback is a user-interface. See Figure 6-1 for the blank stare of the Windows 2000 Cmd prompt, the familiar C:\> prompt, at which you may enter commands and get results.

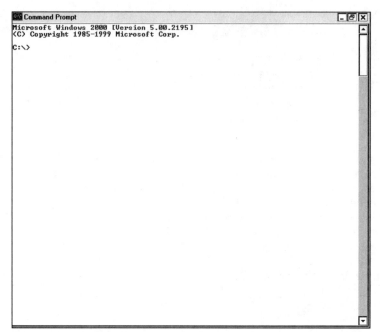

Figure 6-1: The Windows 2000 Cmd window—a command-line
(C:\> prompt) interface

From the text-based command line, we can build various text-based menu schemes
or run another user interface program—a DOS shell, a graphical user interface (GUI)
such as Windows, or different implementations of the X-Windows interface, such as
OpenWin for Sun and other Unix workstations. These may give a more pleasing and
colorful visual experience and provide pointing devices rather than cumbersome
and cryptic commands. Figure 6-2 shows a typical GUI screen containing a company
logo and icons that you may double-click to run various programs or applications.
However, any Unix aficionado will tell you that learning a command-line interface and
the line editor are the only way to run a computer system. Sometimes that's true.

The user interface for the PC started with DOS. DOS by itself or with a fancy interface such as Windows 3.x is rarely seen in use today. However, to keep the proper
perspective, Chapter 7 takes a quick look at the oldest DOS versions, with a short
discussion of the main elements added to each new version. After that, Chapters 8
and 9 discuss the most popular Windows operating systems being used at home
and in small businesses today.

Figure 6-2: A Windows 2000 screen — a typical GUI interface

Summary

This quick introduction to PC interfaces has covered the most important reasons to use PCs. Operating systems provide us with an interface that gives us access to our data (files and their programs) and many ways to accomplish goals by creating, collecting, storing, and manipulating information.

Now we can get into some of the history, so we understand how we got here, and then get into making sure you are setting up your PC so it will get the work done you expect. Chapter 7 covers DOS and multitasking user interfaces, the precursors to the robust operating systems we use today.

✦   ✦   ✦

DOS Parts

Every modern computer, even small computer-driven
devices, such as Palm Pilots, or appliances, such as digi-
tally controlled washing machines, requires an operating system. One of the most important features of a computer is its
ability to work with data and files. The PC's first encounter
with an operating system was DOS — the Disk Operating
System. This chapter focuses on DOS, but we'll move on to
the newer operating environments commonly used on PCs
as we move through this part of the book.

A Brief History of DOS

An operating system provides rules and access to hardware
and to predefined basic computing services upon which applications may be built. The first PC applications were either written in assembly language or Beginner's All-purpose Symbolic
Instruction Code (BASIC) language. Since the first days of PCs,
there has been a specific operating system designed to accompany the hardware. The details of the various versions of the
increasingly powerful and flexible disk operating system
(DOS) for PCs are provided in this section. DOS, as MS-DOS
(Microsoft), PC-DOS (IBM), or DR-DOS (Digital Research/
Novell), is not the only operating system that can run on
IBM-compatible PCs, but it was the most popular and is still
"under the covers" in Windows 9*x*.

Note   There are at least three popular variants of the Unix operating system available for PCs, as well as operating systems
and environments that require DOS to start up on the PC
before providing a user interface or running applications.

DOS 1.0

The DOS 1.*x* series is most notable for what it does not support. For example, 160K diskettes (320K with DOS 1.05 or 1.1)
provide about all the diskette storage space you can access.

Filenames may contain the slash (/), less than (<), greater than (>), and pipe (|) characters because a directory structure does not exist for your files, nor is there redirection of program output to and from files or piping of program output to another program. You cannot use extended or expanded memory, even if you have a 286 or 386 processor, because there is no way to install device drivers. In other words, DOS 1.*x* has no CONFIG.SYS file. Even the method of storing files on double-sided diskettes was changed for DOS 2.*x*.

Virtually no one still uses a 1.*x* version of DOS, unless they work on a computer that they bought in 1981 or 1982. However, it is possible to grab an old diskette that was formatted with DOS 1.*x* and boot your computer. If you do, your computer will not seem like the same one you were using before you rebooted. Maybe the program on the diskette runs, but you will not find your hard disk, nor will you have access to all of your memory.

DOS 2.0

Most DOS programs that run on IBM PCs and compatibles require DOS 2.1 as a minimum. Version 2.1 is essentially the same as 2.0 but with bugs fixed. The features include the CONFIG.SYS configuration file, tree-structured directories, hard disk support, 360K diskette (9 sectors) support, redirection (< and > commands), and piping (the | command). Many of the new commands (ASSIGN, BACKUP, FDISK, MKDIR, RMDIR, CHDIR, PATH, RECOVER, RESTORE, TREE, and VOL) were provided to handle the new disk-drive capabilities. Others (BREAK, CLS, CTTY, GRAPHICS, PRINT, PROMPT, SET VER, and VERIFY) were added to improve DOS usability. The DOS batch language was extended, too (ECHO, IF, FOR, SHIFT, GOTO). To handle new capabilities, some commands (CHKDSK, COMP, DEBUG, DIR, DISKCOPY, DISKCOMP, EDLIN, ERASE, and FORMAT) had to be changed. Finally, support for two additional printer ports (LPT2: and LPT3:) and an additional serial communications port (COM2:) was added. This information is not intended to document DOS differences, but to show that there were extensive changes to DOS in the upgrade to 2.1.

DOS 3.0

The several releases of DOS in the 3.*x* series provided DOS support for 3½-inch diskettes, 1.2MB 5¼-inch diskettes, networks, and the capability for a DOS program to open more than 20 files. Some commands were changed to accommodate these new capabilities and new commands were added.

Most of the changes to DOS since the release of DOS 3.3 have provided specific new features. Few DOS programs require a version of DOS newer than DOS 3.3.

Accessing a Larger Hard Disk with DOS 2.0

At the time DOS 2.0 was released, a hard disk with 32MB of space was considered a large drive for a PC. Drivers were developed by some hard-disk manufacturers and developers to enable access to larger volumes, but DOS 2.1, by itself, cannot access a hard-disk volume larger than 32MB. This is probably the most common problem with DOS 2.1. The solution is to use a hard-disk driver or upgrade to a later version or a new operating system.

DOS 4.0

The major changes provided in DOS 4.0 were access to hard disks up to 2.2GB in a single volume, and the MS-DOS Shell. The MS-DOS Shell is a graphic user interface that appears to be a cross between the Windows File Manager and Microsoft Works.

The producers of hard disks provided access to large hard disk volumes for many PC users with device drivers and software. If your hard disk is supported by your system's ROM BIOS, you may save some DOS memory by using DOS 4.01 or 5.0 rather than the device driver provided with your hard disk.

Cross-Reference

See Chapter 15 for more information on ROM BIOS.

Software developers have satisfied our need for easier access to the capabilities of the PC through the many DOS manager utilities, menu systems, and operating environments such as Windows. Though it does not appear to have caught on, the MS-DOS shell (in its DOS 4.0 implementation) shows that Microsoft and IBM had recognized this need.

Other than the MS-DOS shell and the DOS 4.0 programs themselves, almost no DOS programs require a version of DOS later than 3.3.

DOS 5.0

DOS 5.0 has significant improvements over its predecessors. DOS 5.0 can use the high memory area (HMA), which is the 64K of memory immediately above DOS' first megabyte, to load and run a part of itself. DOS 5.0 can also load and use device drivers and terminate-and-stay-resident (TSR) programs in the upper memory area, which is the top 384K of DOS' first megabyte of memory. Unfortunately, DOS only uses about 45K of this memory, which still leaves about 30 percent of it unusable.

Other improvements included the following:

✦ Significant improvements to the MS-DOS shell

✦ Added file protection with an Unformat and Undelete capability

✦ Online help for all DOS commands

✦ A full-screen editor, which is also the QBASIC editor, DOS' BASIC language feature

✦ The capability to use large hard disk partitions (up to 2.2GB) without having to use the SHARE program

✦ The capability to install more than two hard disk drives

✦ A DOSKEY function to access and use your command-line history, including the ability to build and use macros

✦ A SETVER command so that programs that require a specific version of DOS may be run without problems

✦ Improvements to the DIR command

✦ The capability to search for files through multiple levels of directories (DIR/S)

✦ The capability to use 2.88MB disk drives

Figure 7-1 presents a DOS help screen, showing how DOS has matured through changes such as these.

```
Command Prompt                                                    _ ☐ ✕
DOSKEY    Edits command lines, recalls Windows 2000 commands, and creates macros.
ECHO      Displays messages, or turns command echoing on or off.
ENDLOCAL  Ends localization of environment changes in a batch file.
ERASE     Deletes one or more files.
EXIT      Quits the CMD.EXE program (command interpreter).
FC        Compares two files or sets of files, and displays the differences
          between them.
FIND      Searches for a text string in a file or files.
FINDSTR   Searches for strings in files.
FOR       Runs a specified command for each file in a set of files.
FORMAT    Formats a disk for use with Windows 2000.
FTYPE     Displays or modifies file types used in file extension associations.
GOTO      Directs the Windows 2000 command interpreter to a labeled line in a
          batch program.
GRAFTABL  Enables Windows 2000 to display an extended character set in graphics
          mode.
HELP      Provides Help information for Windows 2000 commands.
IF        Performs conditional processing in batch programs.
LABEL     Creates, changes, or deletes the volume label of a disk.
MD        Creates a directory.
MKDIR     Creates a directory.
MODE      Configures a system device.
MORE      Displays output one screen at a time.
MOVE      Moves one or more files from one directory to another directory.
-- More --
```

Figure 7-1: Windows 2000's Command Prompt window, showing a section of the HELP command

Tip

DOS 5.0 provides considerable documentation for customizing your system and handling problems. A feature of DOS 5.0, one that has been quite helpful in dealing with problems, is its ability to uninstall itself. If you follow the excellent documentation and installation instructions to preserve your old version of DOS, you can restore your system to its previous state by using the uninstall feature.

DOS 6.0 and higher

The versions 6.*x* of DOS — MS-DOS by Microsoft and PC-DOS by IBM — offer many improvements over DOS 5.0, some of which are listed here:

✦ A multiple-configuration option that provides a preboot menu. It enables you to select different configurations without a third-party utility program that maintains multiple copies of CONFIG.SYS and AUTOEXEC.BAT files. This provides a menu for various configurations at bootup, with an automatic default configuration selection that runs after a preset period of time with no response.

✦ Two much-needed preboot command keys, F5 and F8, enable you to completely bypass loading CONFIG.SYS and AUTOEXEC.BAT (F5) and provide the ability to step through each line of these files to control their execution (F8).

✦ Enhanced memory management with the EMM386.EXE and MEMMAKER (MS-DOS) programs provide more upper memory for device drivers and TSR programs. PC-DOS 7.0 provides RAMBOOST to automatically optimize conventional memory in order to give your programs more memory.

✦ Bundled disk-compression utilities enable expansion of available disk space. This is DoubleSpace with Microsoft DOS 6.0, debugged DoubleSpace in MS-DOS 6.20, no DoubleSpace in MS-DOS 6.21, and DriveSpace in MS-DOS 6.22 and higher. IBM provided a version of AddStor's SuperStor with PC-DOS 6.10 and 6.30, and Novell provided Stacker with Novell DOS 7.0.

✦ PC-DOS 7.0 also provides Restructured Extended Executor (REXX) support for writing DOS and OS/2 programs, docking support for "hot and warm" Plug-and-Play operation, Scheduler to support unattended operations, the new E editor, PenDOS, and many more new features.

✦ Microsoft and IBM have opted to provide most of the DOS documentation in file form to reduce the amount of seldom-read paper documents shipped with the products. Finally someone got the message in this high-tech age of electronic information systems, but it only helps if you can get the system booted with the drive and files intact.

✦ The first-boot core of Windows 95, 98, and Millennium is fundamentally a new version of DOS. In many aspects, DOS 6.22 was more robust because of the help it provided in creating batch files and using the command line for the internal and external services of DOS. When Windows 95 was introduced, much of the power of DOS was diminished in favor of the Windows GUI and file system. Because the removal of significant help and documentation for DOS was the first step toward its demise, the introduction of FAT-32 as a much-needed upgrade to the limited partitioning schemes of DOS is the most significant change in the DOS operating system family. FAT-32 raised the bar on file-system and disk-size limitations that troubled the DOS/Windows world for so long.

✦ DOS 7.0 brought support for the Long File Name system (a big feature with Windows 95), which maintains two filename directories — one for the old DOS 8.3 file-naming limitations and one for the longer-string, 256-character filenames.

DOS has a long and illustrious history, but it's not very interesting, even in a picture. Figure 7-1 shows a section of the "HELP | MORE" command — "help," followed by a vertical bar, and then "more," separated by spaces — which will display one screen of text and wait for you to press a key before displaying more text. This shows that even DOS has progressed to the point of providing some useful information at the command prompt.

Prettier Faces on DOS

A *shell* is a program that provides an interface to the command line, disk, and file services of DOS. This kind of interface saves you from having to remember specific commands and options, makes it easier to find programs and files, and it may help to keep you from overwriting or erasing files you want to keep.

Shells can be implemented and used in a number of ways. A program might be designed as a pop-up or memory-resident shell to help you only when you need or want it, or it may be the only thing you see onscreen when you are not using your applications for specific tasks.

Some users employ shells as the primary user interface for selecting and running programs, rather than using Windows. Others use only the powerful tools for disk and file management that some shells provide.

Not all shells are file managers, but most file managers provide shell functions, even if the file manager does not function as your user interface to DOS. The shell function — to get to DOS or to run other programs — should be an integral part of any application you run on your system.

Tip   It is a good idea to use a file manager or shell program to help manage the files and organization of a hard disk. Shells can save dozens of keystrokes and help avoid any number of problems you might encounter when running DOS at the command line.

Powerful and popular shell programs of the past have included the following:

✦ PathMinder from Westlake Data Corporation

✦ QDOS from Gazelle

✦ Norton Commander, by John Socha, from Symantec/Norton

✦ Tree86 from The Aldridge Company

✦ XTree from Executive Systems

Each of these shell programs enables to you to copy, move, and delete files and sub-directories, providing easy-to-use power for file management, as well as providing the capability for it to function as your interface for selecting other applications.

Some shells, such as XTree Gold, provide advanced file viewing for many file formats, including spreadsheet, database, word processing, and many graphics file formats. They also provide ASCII text and hexadecimal-level editing of files. A special feature of XTree Gold is the built-in capability to create, open, view, and extract files from the popular ARC and ZIP compressed-file formats.

The Norton Commander approaches menu and file tools with a TSR pop-up method that enables much display format and sorting flexibility, and it uses a small amount of DOS memory. Many people miss the ability to use the Norton Commander because it provided side-by-side displays of files in different directories and different drives – and it will not run properly with the newer file systems.

Tip

The real benefits of shell programs are in the file and disk management services they provide. Shells do not always serve as practical menu or user interfaces for DOS programs. This is because shell programs, like most DOS menu programs, continue to occupy a portion of DOS RAM when you select and run another application from the shell.

Cross-Reference

See Chapter 15 for a discussion of memory, its various forms, and addresses.

Depending on the technique used and the amount of RAM the shell program occupies for itself, this can cost you from 7K to 30K of DOS RAM that you might prefer to have available for your application and data. If your system is already squeezed for memory with only your application program and data, consider running some programs from batch files at the DOS prompt rather than through a shell program.

Multitasking User Interfaces for DOS

A *multitasking user interface* is a control program that allows the operation of more than one application at a time on the same computer using the same screen, keyboard, and other system resources to display and control multiple program operations. Prior to OS/2 and Windows NT, the alternatives presented here may have been considered *environments* rather than operating systems because they require DOS to boot the system and to provide access to hardware resources.

Most multitasking environments provide shell-like features, helping you with the more mundane and cryptic aspects of using computers. Multitasking environments have developed out of a family of control programs known as task switchers. A *task-switching* control program enables you to switch manually between programs, using memory or disk-drive space to store the application and data you are not using at the moment. Task switchers, such as Carousel from SoftLogic Solutions, are obsolete, having been replaced by newer programs designed for newer computer systems.

The shell-like features of multitasking programs also provide a home for underlying automatic program-swapping features, memory management, networking services, and a friendlier appearance or graphical user interface (GUI). If you are going to spend time using many different applications, something should ease the eyestrain and improve the recognition of program and data items. The GUI does that.

DESQview was one of the first multi-program operating environments available for the PC and the first to implement preemptive multitasking. Microsoft Windows is one of two early graphical environments for the PC, the other being the GEM environment supported by Digital Research (now Novell). A lesser-known graphical interface called GeoWorks appeared for a couple of years and was the graphical basis of some DOS-based applications, such as the interface for the early DOS versions of America Online.

Microsoft Windows became popular and practical as the population of 80386-based PCs grew. Attempts to use Windows in its 8088/86 and 286 versions were frustrating at best. Windows also gained popularity because some PC users related to it better, much as Apple Macintosh users prefer the Mac operating system and environment.

Note   All of these graphical interfaces have partial roots in early research by Xerox Corporation, the folks who introduced the concepts of running applications in a window-like interface (very much like the windows used on the Mac, in Windows, and for other user interfaces such a X-Windows in Unix). They also introduced the pointing devices, which provided the basis for the Apple Macintosh and Windows user interfaces.

Although Windows became practical, when running it on a PC with the 80386 CPU, it still required DOS, an operating system for 8-and 16-bit computers. DOS and Windows simply run faster and somewhat better on 386 and newer systems. The desire to take advantage of not just faster CPUs and better memory control, but also the 32-bit power of the 386 and higher processors, led to development of 32-bit operating systems. The first of these was OS/2. OS/2 originated at Microsoft and was adopted by IBM. A variety of factors caused Microsoft to abandon OS/2 efforts in favor of their own operating system, resulting in the creation of Windows NT.

Technical details aside, Windows 95/98/Me, and Windows NT/2000 are designed for 32-bit (386 and higher) processors. They will not run on 80286 or earlier systems. Windows 95 requires a 386DX or higher, Windows 98 requires a 486 with 16MB of memory, and Windows NT needs a 486DX/33 or higher with 16MB of memory.

Note It's probably safe to say that most Windows users work with a Pentium-class CPU running at least 200 MHz and that has 32MB of RAM, if not 64 or 128 (for NT/2000).

Having full control over the 32-bit systems, memory, and I/O resources enables these new operating systems to run older 8- and 16-bit applications much faster, and they provide the capability to run newer, more powerful 32-bit applications. Windows NT was also available in versions for non-Intel-based (and therefore non-DOS) systems, creating one option for mixed-system, shared-resource computing environments.

At this point, with Windows 95/98/Me and Windows NT/2000, the operating system and the user interface become integrated into one package. There is no separate DOS to install, configure, and reconfigure to accommodate multitasking and graphics. Typical DOS or command-line services are available, so users can gradually transition from the character-based, DOS-only world to the new environments.

Of the currently popular operating systems, only Windows 95 and 98 provide a way to reach the DOS environment without running the graphical environment. Windows Millennium does not offer the choice to easily access a command prompt before the GUI loads. Windows NT provides a command-prompt mode for testing the system for NT installation or through a dual-boot option — which is fine if your disks are not partitioned for an NT file system. However, users still need to access the system resources without the graphics and multitasking, as older systems are adapted to run with newer software. We expect that quite soon the need for a command prompt will diminish, and all configuration, diagnostic, and utility software will be designed to work with the new, non-legacy hardware and within the graphics shell. Until then, with perhaps only a year or two left, users will have some form of access to the familiar C:\> command prompt.

Tip It is helpful always to keep a plain DOS diskette handy for running and testing your system without any special user interfaces. The startup diskettes you can make with Windows 95/98/Me and NT/2000 will serve this purpose in most cases. You may still want to keep your MS-DOS 6.22, IBM DOS 7.0, or other DOS bootable diskettes on hand.

Proper hardware configuration cannot be overstressed. It is all too often taken for granted, and it is the most frequent cause for technical support calls, user frustration, and failed operating-system activities. Operating systems, no matter how advanced, simply cannot function well with or overcome defective hardware issues. Without a solid foundation, the rest of the structure will suffer.

Cross-Reference Use the hardware-oriented Chapters 12 through 22 to understand and to properly configure your hardware, and to ensure that they function properly through DOS or through the installation of other operating systems.

Once you are sure the basic hardware is functional, you can address configuration and application issues. Exactly how, or how well, hardware issues may be addressed from within the various operating-system environments varies with the talents of the software developers and the stability of hardware standards in the industry.

Summary

This chapter has covered about 20 years of the history of the PC's disk operating system (DOS) and hopefully provided some background that will help explain what is going on under the covers of that beautiful, easy-to-use graphical-user interface you're using to manage your PC. In the next chapter, we'll take a brief step through some of the older versions of Windows because many people still use them, and then we'll move on to today's Windows PCs.

✦   ✦   ✦

Windows for Home and Desktop

Whether you work with your PC through a screen full of icons or from the DOS prompt, you are using some form of user interface. User interfaces may be basic, such as the infamous C:\> prompt, or they may be so powerful that almost all you need to know about your PC is how to turn it on and how to select what you want.

User interfaces are intended to help you make better use of your PC or to isolate you from the underlying technical details of the operating system, but they also come with their own unique sets of technical problems. Before Microsoft Windows and OS/2, the most common PC user interfaces were text-mode shells, or text-mode multitasking interfaces, such as PathMinder, QDOS, Norton Commander, Tree86, Xtree Gold, or DESQview — names that most people have probably forgotten. Even a graphical interface, such as Microsoft Windows 95, is a shell or dressing on top of at least part of the old DOS. Microsoft Windows NT and 2000 are graphical user interfaces embedded into the operating system and are true, preemptive multitasking systems.

This chapter presents a brief look at the legacy of early Windows in order to get a perspective. Then it delves deeper into the current Windows operating systems for personal use, examines how to install and configure them, and highlights some of the common problems you may encounter with them.

Windows: Operating System or User Interface?

Our tongue-in-cheek answer to this question is "yes." However, we need to qualify our answer by discussing the perception, context, and definition of each of these labels we use to describe Windows.

To be a little more specific, and we think many will agree (while others will argue over the gray areas), some versions of Windows are operating systems and some are not.

There is disagreement over whether Windows is a user interface or an operating environment, since all versions of Windows do provide a user interface and a specific operating environment to access and use PC system resources.

Indeed, we believe that every version of Windows before Windows 95 is *not* an operating system, as we would clearly define DOS, CP/M, OS/2, LINUX, FreeBSD, and so on as operating systems. Windows 1.0, 2.0, and 3.*x* all clearly required the presence and functioning of DOS in order to work, and they only provided many user interface features and some new and unique hardware access and utilization features.

This leaves Windows 95, 98, NT, 2000 and Me as what we believe are true operating systems. Windows 95/98/Me constitutes an interesting hybrid of operating system and user interface. Initially, these boot up with the familiar DOS. Then they evaluate the operating-system configuration to determine which way to go next — to the basic command-line interface and an 8/16-bit operating system, to a version of DOS (one over which we could also load and run Windows 3.*x* as a user interface), or to switching modes into a 32-bit operating system with a graphical user interface and just enough 16-bit functionality to enable backward compatibility. We still need to run some of the older DOS and Windows applications. This all makes Windows 95/98/Me seem more like the old DOS and Windows "trick" of booting in DOS and then switching to the Windows environment, but in fact these operating systems share as much in common with Windows NT/2000 as they do with the old DOS.

There can be almost no question that Windows NT/2000 is an operating system, since there is no DOS or command-line operation, or no direct-access-to-hardware or low-level functionality at all, until the operating system has fully loaded and initialized. Even then there is no real DOS, but instead a limited DOS-like command-line interface available within a window of the graphical user interface. Many old DOS programs, written for and with the specific features of DOS, do not run under Windows NT/2000. Many of the old, native DOS functions do not exist within the command-line interface program. Indeed, they should not, lest they undermine the hardware control and security that the overseeing operating system must have.

Indeed, every user interface or operating environment is just a fancy shell or protective cover for the complex and more technical inner workings of an operating system. More and more, these protective shells are necessary, if not also desirable, in order to enable easier access to the resources that users need and to improve the usability of the tools needed to get work done.

Microsoft Windows 3.x

Microsoft described Windows 3.x as "software that transforms the way you use your personal computer." When properly installed and set up, Windows 3.x does make your PC easier to use. Windows 3.x enables you to run more than one program on your computer at a time, and to share data easily between Windows applications, presenting these features in a somewhat pleasing, easy-to-understand user interface.

Early Windows ran on any of the family of Intel 80×86-compatible microprocessors, but its more advanced modes are available only on 386 and newer systems. You need a minimum of 2MB of memory, along with a 6–8MB minimum of free space on your hard disk. You also needed a graphics-capable monitor and some sort of pointing device (a mouse or trackball) to get the most out of Windows.

Windows 3.x uses a sophisticated installation program that makes it relatively simple to set up. You need to know some basic information about your system, such as what type of pointing device and monitor you are using, what kind of printer you have, and to which printer port your printer is connected. After a few minutes of changing floppy disks and answering a dozen or so questions and prompts, Windows should be ready to load and run.

From this point, you might encounter a variety of common and easily solved problems, as well as several obscure and system-specific problems. Many of the millions of PCs in daily use are designed, built, configured, and changed by their owners to be drastically different from anything we would call common. Therefore, your best sources for specific, uncommon tidbits of information may be Web sites and USENET news groups. The myriad of after-market and third party books covering Windows cannot be matched by the vast collection of user experiences and expertise available on online forums and Web sites for various hardware and software vendors.

Common Windows 3.x problems

If you are running Windows 3.x on your system, you may run into any of the following problems.

Symptoms

▶ Windows will not run, and it indicates that a device cannot be run in Standard mode.

▶ Windows will not run, and it indicates that a device must be run in Standard mode.

▶ Windows will not run, and it indicates that a device cannot be run in 386 Enhanced mode.

▶ Windows will not run, and it indicates that a device must be run in 386 Enhanced mode.

Suspects

▶ Device driver is incompatible with your version of Windows.

▶ Device driver is incompatible with the mode you are trying to use.

Solutions

▶ If you are starting Windows in Standard mode (WIN /S or WIN /2), try simply WIN or WIN /3 on the DOS command line.

▶ If you are starting Windows in 386 Enhanced mode (WIN /3), try simply WIN /S or WIN /2 on the DOS command line.

Some device drivers intended for 32-bit operation, such as those designed for the Extended Industry Standard Architecture (EISA), Peripheral Component Interconnect (PCI), or local bus systems may be developed under either Windows or Windows for Workgroups Version 3.1 or 3.11 exclusively (using the 32-bit extensions) and not tested under other versions. You may have to resort to using older, newer, or less capable modes or device drivers, or to installing another version of Windows to achieve some level of system operation. Contact your system or device vendor to obtain different driver files or at least report the problems you are having so that you might be able to obtain replacement files or hardware. Some vendors no longer support driver development for these older versions of Windows, but they usually have the last working copies available for download.

Symptoms

▶ Windows will not run.

Suspects

▶ Not enough memory.

▶ Not enough expanded or extended memory (for some applications).

▶ Not using an expanded or extended memory manager.

▶ File or buffer settings in CONFIG.SYS are insufficient.

▶ Installed options are incorrect:

• Wrong PC type (see the side bar on standard and 386 Enhanced modes that follows).

• Wrong screen type.

• Wrong keyboard type.

- ▶ A device specified in the SYSTEM.INI file is not on the disk or in the directory specified.

- ▶ SYSTEM.INI file is missing or corrupted (applies to every other problem).

- ▶ HIMEM.SYS is not loaded.

Solutions

- ▶ Reduce the amount of memory used by terminate-and-stay-resident (TSR) programs, disk caches, RAM drives, and device drivers or increase the amount of DOS (remember, you need 640K) extended or expanded memory in your system, depending on the type of memory the program uses.

- ▶ Ensure that you have the FILES= parameter set to at least 30 or up to 255 (with enhancements) in your CONFIG.SYS file if you run many programs at the same time under Windows. Windows opens 15 to 24 files for itself and adds more open files as applications are used. It often does not release these file records, even after you finish with an application.

- ▶ Turn off shadow RAM if it was on; turn it on if it was off. Different shadow RAM methods affect Windows differently.

- ▶ Establish a worst-case/best-case installation setup for Windows and reinstall Windows completely. If you install Windows on a bare system with no memory managers, disk caching, and so on, and then decide later to add QEMM, 386-Max, or other features to enhance your system, you could cause Windows not to work, even though you were trying to improve it. Be sure Windows is installed on the type of system and under the type of DOS environment that you will continue to use. Shifting things around is the most likely cause for Windows to fail.

- ▶ Consult Microsoft, or the creator of your memory manager or other enhancement software, for up-to-date tips on using enhancement applications with Windows. Often you will have to modify memory parameters or the SYSTEM.INI file to make things work together.

- ▶ Include DEVICE=C:\DOS\HIMEM.SYS or another suitable memory manager in your CONFIG.SYS file.

Windows Standard and 386 Enhanced Modes

Windows no longer uses the "standard" and "386 enhanced" modes for starting the Windows environment. These modes were created during a time when PCs were transitioning from the "archaic" 286 and earlier CPUs to the 386, 486 and Pentium-class processors. These modes were supposed to do a better job of using your PCs capabilities, especially hardware based memory management. Unfortunately, the mode was not always selected correctly and sometimes didn't work because of running on PCs with very mixed environments (part old and part new) or on systems with programs meant to help fool software into thinking your system had more capabilities than really existed.

Symptoms

▶ Windows will not run in standard mode.

Suspects

▶ "Will not run" options outlined previously apply here as well.

▶ Standard mode does not support non-Windows applications.

▶ You are not running Windows 3.1.

Solutions

▶ You need an 80286 or higher system with at least 1MB of conventional memory and 256K of expanded memory to be able to run Windows 3.x in standard mode and run multiple programs at the same time.

▶ Use DOSX.EXE or KRNL386.EXE instead of WIN.COM to start Windows 3.11.

Symptoms

▶ Windows will not run in Real mode.

Suspects

▶ If Real mode does not work but Standard or Enhanced (386) does, the problem is most likely settings in the SYSTEM.INI file or improper settings in the environment where you are running Windows. Every system that can run Windows should be able to run in Real mode.

▶ You are not using Windows 3.0+.

Solutions

▶ Check the suspected settings and correct as necessary. The error messages or other clues should point to the settings that may need to be changed and are likely covered in other sections.

Symptoms

▶ Windows will not run in 386 Enhanced mode.

Suspects

▶ Again, the "will not run" options apply.

Solutions

▶ You need an i80386SX, i80386, i80486SX, i80486, or Pentium grade central processing unit (CPU) and 1MB of memory. If you have less than 2MB of memory, your system may run more slowly than in standard mode. You may need to exclude some memory locations in the area above 640K (such as the location of ROM adapters) using the EMMExclude option in the SYSTEM.INI file.

Symptoms

▶ Insufficient memory error running SETUP from DOS.

Suspects

▶ Too little DOS memory is available before running SETUP.

▶ Too many OEMxxxxx.INF files in the \WINDOWS\SYSTEM subdirectory.

Solutions

▶ SETUP requires over 256K of free RAM to run properly — more if you have several or large INF files that provide details about your system options. Do not run SETUP through shells or with less than 384K of free DOS RAM (use the DOS MEM or CHKDSK programs in DOS, not within Windows, to see how much conventional/ DOS RAM is available). You may have to remove TSR programs from memory or reboot your system without loading unnecessary TSR programs or device drivers in order to free enough DOS RAM to continue with SETUP.

▶ It is not uncommon to have several OEM*.INF files in your Windows SYSTEM subdirectory if you have changed or added video cards, sound cards, or other accessories that require Windows configuration options. If there are more than five of these or if the options are large (greater than 5–10K), that may prevent SETUP from continuing with any option changes. You can view these files with a text view or edit program in order to determine and later remove any of the files that no longer apply to devices you have in your system.

Symptoms

▶ Insufficient memory errors.

Suspects

▶ Permanent or temporary swap file is too small.

▶ Too little available extended/XMS memory.

▶ Too many groups and/or icons on the desktop.

▶ Too many applications loaded or running at the same time.

Solutions

▶ Close or remove unnecessary program groups on the desktop.

▶ Remove unnecessary icons from program groups.

▶ If you are running multiple applications and the option to swap to disk is disabled or the TEMP variable is not specified, insufficient memory error messages may appear, indicating that an application cannot be run. Close other applications and try again. Windows does not function well, if at all, with 2MB or less of total RAM in the system. It is recommended that you have 4–8MB of RAM in your system. With 640K of RAM used by DOS, the little over 3MB of RAM left should be used by HIMEM.SYS as extended-memory-specification (XMS) memory. Do not allocate device drivers, disk caches, or other programs to occupy more than 512–1,024K of extended/XMS memory or expanded memory (if you also load EMM386). If you cannot close other applications or need to have them open at the same time, you may have to install more memory.

Cross-Reference See Chapter 15 for discussions of memory and the consequences of insufficient memory.

If you have enough disk space available (4–16MB), consider enlarging the swap file allocation (look for the 386 Enhanced icon in the Control Panel) to 4–8MB, disregarding Windows' warnings that it will not efficiently use a swap file larger than it recommends — it will. Do not fill all the empty space on your disk drive with the swap file. If you cannot create a swap file larger than 2MB but have much more than that amount of free space on your drive, use a disk defragmenting program to sort the files on the disk drive in order to make a single larger area of free space available to Windows. Reconfiguring the swap file may now work.

Symptoms

▶ Cannot run applications in the background.

Suspects

▶ You try to perform multitasking with Windows without using the 386 Enhanced mode.

Solutions

▶ Multitasking is not possible unless you run Windows in 386 Enhanced mode. Running non-Windows applications in a window, rather than in a full screen, requires 386 Enhanced mode.

You must have 0.5–1MB of free memory before starting Windows in order to run more than one program without swapping applications to disk and slowing the system severely. If you do not have enough disk space, Windows advises that it cannot maintain another open application and tells you to close one or more windows to accommodate your new request.

Symptoms

▶ Unrecoverable Applications Error message (Windows 3.0).

▶ General Protection Fault error message (Windows 3.1).

Suspects

▶ You are running an application that deletes or changes files that Windows uses, preventing Windows from functioning properly.

▶ The application you were running encountered a memory or device conflict with Windows from which Windows could not recover.

Solutions

These are not the same error conditions between the two different versions of Windows, but they can be as fatal to the work you are doing.

▶ First, you must quit the application, and often you must also reboot your system to recover from the problem.

▶ When you are able to run Windows again, check the Properties option in the Windows File Manager to be sure you are running the correct program when you select an icon to run an application. You should also create or edit a Program Information File (PIF) for the suspect application so that you can better control the PC resources that your program can use under Windows.

▶ The infamous Unrecoverable Applications Error (UAE) usually is a problem with Windows rather than with the application programs. UAEs are all but fixed in Windows 3.1 and later. If you are still running Windows 3.0, you are overdue for an upgrade.

▶ The General Protection Fault (GPF) is typical of an older application program that accesses your hardware or memory in a way that Windows 3.1 does not allow, or of an application that became corrupted because some other program, disk, or network operation was running before you loaded Windows. Usually a GPF indicates in which program the problem occurred, which is not always the program that caused the problem. Unfortunately, the most common way to recover from a GPF is to reboot. This does not cure the problem, but it does allow you to start over. If the problem occurs frequently, keep track of the programs you've run and the sequence in which you ran them. Chances are it is one of the last few programs or one of the last few operations that is the culprit. Start by upgrading programs and eliminating use of suspected programs, and see if these steps provide more lasting results.

Symptoms

▶ Windows gives you a dialog box indicating that your application has corrupted the system or the Windows environment and that you should stop running your system.

Suspects

▶ The application you were using required or took control of an input/output (I/O) device or memory area that was assumed to be under the control of Windows. If Windows loses the control it is supposed to have, it has no choice but to recommend that you shut down immediately and start over; otherwise, you could corrupt disk space and lose files.

Solutions

▶ Do as Windows recommends. Choose OK or CLOSE, close all open applications, and then exit from Windows in the normal fashion. When the DOS prompt appears, turn off your system, wait 30 seconds, and then turn it on again. These problems are similar to those for UAE and GPF conditions as indicated earlier. Often a background operation or disk operation has changed your system environment such that Windows does not know how to function properly. These errors are usually not reproducible and are hard to find.

Caution   Do not attempt to use CHKDSK, Norton Utilities, or any other program before you turn off the system. If you do run other programs, you do so with an unknown amount of memory available, quite possibly with several files open and at risk of being lost. This error condition is rare, but it is fatal if you ignore it and continue to use the system.

Windows for Workgroups

This section on Windows for Workgroups (WfWG), an enhanced version of Windows 3.*x* for the then-new Microsoft networks, points out some fundamental, overlooked, and not-so-obvious differences between WfWG and the other versions of Windows 3.*x*. The most significant of these is apparent in a higher percentage of memory-related issues during the installation and use of various applications. Applications that were seemingly flawless under other versions (Windows 3.0, 3.1, and 3.11) choke, sputter, and die under WfWG. Windows for Workgroups generally shares many of the same problems of Windows 3.*x*, but there are some new concerns as well.

Windows for Workgroup's biggest problem is that it requires more Windows resources, such as User, Graphical Device Interface (GDI), and so on to run—even if it is installed without networking support. True, there are a few more embedded OLE, DDE, and other common Windows interapplication features that come along with a WfWG installation, but you don't really see this except in the README files or unless you have a reason to dig for them. In addition, you can update Windows 3.*x* with various drivers to near-WfWG level operation and still *not* have the memory problems inherent in WfWG.

WfWG's memory issues come up in two places. Under Program Manager's Help/ About menu selection, note that available resources run 10 to 20 percent less with WfWG than in a comparable system using Windows 3.*x*, *and* you will see more desktop anomalies and "Insufficient Memory," "General Protection Faults," or "illegal operations" messages running a variety of applications. These are not benefits you would expect in a newer version of Windows, and the risks are not worth taking to get the meager networking support that you probably already have or that you may get from buying an add-in network driver product.

Common Windows for Workgroups problems

First, refer to the "Common Windows 3.x problems" section. WfWG is barely more than Windows 3.11, with additional network support.

Symptoms

▶ Insufficient memory to run application.

▶ General Protection Fault errors in one or more applications.

▶ Darkened, incomplete program icon display in open program group(s).

Suspects

▶ Too few Windows "resources" are available to support application loading (this is totally unrelated to the amount of RAM or swap file space configured in the system).

▶ An application which had been run and subsequently closed did not release resources.

▶ Too many program groups or program items in all groups.

Solutions

▶ Close as many program groups, icons, and applications as possible.

▶ Shut down, restart Windows, and then restart only the application(s) you need.

▶ Shut down Windows, shut down and restart the entire PC system (cold boot or warm boot), restart Windows, and then restart only the application(s) you need.

Windows creates and manages many areas of memory. Two 64K memory blocks, known as the Graphical and the User resource areas, are used to store information and data used for and between different programs. Each time you open a program group or folder, or load a program, these finite resources are used. Opening more folders, icons, and programs in the environment consumes even more of these resources.

How many program groups or program icons constitute "too many" is not specifically known. You can estimate the use of the Graphical resources by adding up the number of icons, each of which consumes 766 bytes. The maximum number of icons you could display would be 83, minus any Graphical resources taken up by window properties, the mouse cursor, and so on.

The total resources or memory limit that Windows looks for when opening new programs represents both the Graphical and User resources, so one could have plenty of memory available and the other could have none, resulting in the same symptom — insufficient resources. You can view the available resources with any number of utilities designed to display them or by using the Windows SYSMON. EXE program.

When a program group or application closes, the resources it used are supposed to be emptied and, therefore, made available for other programs. This does not always happen, causing an increasing resource drain, until eventually Windows will not load any more programs. Once this happens, your only recourse is to close down all programs and Windows, and then restart Windows. Hopefully, you will not lose work.

Utility programs, such as MagnaRAM, which is included with Versions 8 and 9 of Quarterdeck's QEMM, can monitor and often compress the contents of resource memory and ensure automatic recovery of unused resources when a program is closed.

WfWG is a memory hog in all respects. Use Windows 3.10 or 3.11 if you do not need the networking features of WfWG. Any combination of Windows devices, hardware-specific device drivers, the number of program groups or icons, and the size of the WIN.INI and SYSTEM.INI files, among other factors, affect Windows resources and its system memory use. Of course, there may be little accounting for poorly developed, misbehaving Windows application programs, down-revision device drivers, or cheap hardware.

Note   Many MS Office 6 applications require the presence of the DOS SHARE program or the Windows VSHARE driver. Other programs will not run when VSHARE is loaded at DOS. It is a dilemma. VSHARE is included with WfWG, but it can be added to Windows 3.x for free, leaving more DOS memory available and letting you use all your applications. Obtain the file WW1000.EXE or WW1000.ZIP from Microsoft, CompuServe, or some other online resource. Run the WW1000 program or unzip the files into a temporary directory. Follow the directions in that directory's README file. This way, you may enjoy WfWG-SHARE–free windowing with regular old "stable" Windows 3.x.

Microsoft Windows 95 and 98

In late August 1995, Microsoft released Windows 95. Almost everything rumored about it, both good and bad, came true or did not, depending on your perspective. Similar things can be said about Windows 98, though Windows 98 provided a significant improvement in stability that made up for many of the misgivings and lingering problems with Windows 95.

What Windows 95 gave us

Windows 95 significantly upgraded from the Windows 3.x environment in the following ways:

✦ Built-in support for 32-bit applications.

✦ A more flexible, more powerful user interface.

✦ Long filename support — great if you share your files only between Windows 95/98 or NT systems (which is not such a stretch today).

✦ Integrated support for Microsoft, Novell, and UNIX networking, including Internet (TCP/IP) connectivity.

✦ Mostly automatic (but not foolproof) detection, installation, and configuration of hardware devices.

✦ No need for complex CONFIG.SYS, AUTOEXEC.BAT, configuration files, or external device drivers. The operating environment/system provides access to the system devices and services, in most cases using full 32-bit drivers.

✦ Greater hardware recognition and support — for both legacy and new Plug-and-Play devices.

✦ Better memory protection, yielding fewer Windows 3-like protection faults and crashes.

✦ Higher performance for applications, networking, video, and multimedia.

✦ Also supports configuration for different multiple users, providing customized desktop appearances and privileges by user logins.

✦ Enhanced usability/accessibility features for various handicaps and disabilities.

✦ Network manageability and system administrator control over what can and cannot be reconfigured by the user, enabling more stable and uniform desktop support, especially for large, multiple PC environments.

What Windows 95 did not give us

Windows 95 attempted both to support the new 32-bit software environment and not leave DOS and Windows 3.*x* behind (Windows 98 does a better job) with the following improvements:

✦ Complete and exclusive 32-bit application support (maintains considerable 16-bit elements and limitations).

✦ Complete freedom from DOS — still leaves a common DOS layer for DOS and Windows program compatibility.

✦ Foolproof hardware configuration support or compatibility.

✦ Software remedies for hardware problems.

✦ One hundred percent compatibility of Windows 3.*x* applications (owing mostly to the old 8.3 filename convention, programmer's shortcuts, and tricks).

✦ Windows NT and Windows 95 applications are *not* the same. Windows 95 does not have all the capabilities of NT, and Windows NT does not support some of the unique features of Windows 95.

Expectations were that Windows 95 or any new advancement in operating systems might cure all the prior problems encountered with earlier operating environments. Compatibility is the biggest issue most users encounter when they upgrade to Windows 95. Success with Windows 95 depends greatly on a properly configured, smoothly running hardware platform. You may have worked around problems with DOS and Windows, did not know you had them, or blamed the problems on Windows itself. Windows 95 points out that something is wrong with the system, perhaps not exactly what but something, and you had better fix it before you can expect your system to work right.

For all of the problems users have encountered with Windows 95 applications and systems, Windows 95 is a success. This success required the participation of several thousand beta-testers supplying countless hours of quality assurance testing. There were more experienced Windows 3.x users who worked for free to make Windows 95 a success than for any other similar effort to date. Windows 95 can be a success for almost any user, corporation, or developer, *if* it is understood that a PC is only a PC. The PC must be in perfect working order and use all compatible hardware. Before you start, remember that no software can fix hardware incompatibilities, and you must plan adequately for success as well as for contingencies. One of those contingencies, of course, is that Windows 95 just may not work on your PC, in which case you would need to back out to Windows 3.x or install a new system board.

Windows 95 simply works, given the right resources to run it. Forget the specs on the box. With a properly configured 486DX2-66 or faster CPU; 12–16MB of RAM; a 500MB, 10 millisecond hard drive; a 800×600 SuperVGA display; and a couple of hours, you are almost home free. You still have to make sure all of your software works right.

Hardware and Software Issues

There are many exceptions in hardware and software to be aware of and prepare for when you use Windows 95. They are too numerous to mention here. For that reason, check out Bruce Brown's Web site, http://www.bugnet.com (his book *Windows 95 Bug Collection* is now out of print, but you may still get a copy from some bookstores) and regular publications, such as *Computer Currents,* that provide a list of newly found items on a regular basis. Fortunately, many hardware manufacturers have provided updated drivers to get around compatibility problems with Windows 95 and most of them are available on the Web. If Windows 95 has done nothing else for us, it has made the Web a frequently referenced and prolific source of technical information and tools about PCs, hardware, device drivers, tips, tricks, and applications.

What Windows 95 lacks, or what Microsoft has had to issue several patches and updates for, Windows 98 includes and improves on. The following is by no means a complete list of Windows 98 features, but it highlights quite a few improvements. We skip what will become the obvious differences, such as differing opinions about the Web-browser-like user interface (which can be altered to look more like Windows 95) and other frills. The emphasis here is on technical items.

Windows 95 original-equipment-manufacturer releases

When the general public learned that sub-releases of Windows 95 were made available to PC manufacturers, thousands scrambled to grab copies from their Information Technology departments, from friends, and from off the software-pirating sites on the Internet. Why? Because in some cases there were updated drivers and a myth of greater stability for unspecified and essentially nonexistent features or because you could download core patches for free from Microsoft.

Of course there were updated drivers — for the COMPAQ, Hewlett-Packard, IBM, Gateway, Dell, Toshiba, or other PC system for which specific original-equipment-manufacturer (OEM) releases were built, and as mentioned, a few patches that were free for downloading. As many found out, the OEM releases were problematic for many generic and home-built PC systems. Drivers were missing or different, chip-set support seemed lacking, and so on. Indeed, many owners were lucky and had the updated hardware that coincidentally matched some of the hardware bits that the manufacturers were using. On the flip side, owners of many OEM systems were disappointed by reloading retail versions of Windows 95 only to find out that sound features failed to work, video displays could not perform as advertised, and myriad other problems that drove people to jam technical support lines and PC manufacturers' Web sites.

There is a lesson to be learned here — if you have a name-brand system, stick with the Windows 95 operating system (OS) that came with it and look to the manufacturer for brand-specific support. The OEMs do some odd things to their systems in the quest to add features that they hope will make you love them even more. For our money, if you can pick and choose your optimum parts, do so. Built-ins and OEM limitations do not necessarily provide the optimum Windows experience. If you have a generic, home-built, or non-OEM system, stick with the retail version of Windows and seek proper support from individual hardware vendors and Microsoft. That's life with Windows 95. Trying to be leading edge sometimes turned into bleeding edge.

What Windows 98 makes up for that Windows 95 lacks

From a distance, Windows 98 does not look much different than Windows 95 with all of the latest upgrades. However, the following included upgrades make Windows 98 quite different from Windows 95:

✦ Enhanced network security and stability. Windows 95 is vulnerable to many different denial-of-service attacks via networking and the Internet. Patches are available for Windows 95, whereas Windows 98 includes prevention for denial-of-service attacks.

✦ Faster file system accesses. Windows 98 improves disk and file system I/O, which significantly enhances the performance of the system.

✦ A significant change in how those precious "resources" and apparent "low-memory" errors are handled. In Windows 3.x and Windows 95, three internal Windows resource pools were limited to discrete 64K sections of memory to hold information about operating-system presentation and interapplication data (System resources), application data (User resources), and graphical-display information (GDI resources). Resources were allocated in defined chunks, and if your configuration and applications used them up — poof — you were unable to load more applications or data, and the apparent "out of memory" or specific "out of resources" errors appeared.

In Windows 98, Microsoft redesigned the System and User resource methods so that the 64K areas of memory acted as holding places and pointers to areas of the much larger Windows memory pool — theoretically up to 4GB of RAM to play with. The GDI resource pool seemingly did not need to change. Now you can have as many icons, desktop widgets, and application convolutions as you want. Well, almost. Because the Resource Meter and measurement of resources were not updated to reflect what was now essentially immeasurable, these tools could not know what resource pools applications were using. In fact, resource use was still measured the old Windows 95 way- ignorant of the new resource pools. Thus "out of resources" errors still occur when applications become confused about what's what. Users get mistakenly concerned when programs actually use the resources Microsoft provides. Worse yet, Microsoft has not documented this.

✦ Support for many more devices, including Universal Serial Bus (USB). Microsoft did not issue as many readily available updates for new hardware and updated device drivers. Instead, with Windows 95 you had to visit various Web sites, deal with downloadable Service Packs from Microsoft, or find a copy of OEM Service Release 1 or 2 in order to get official, new drivers.

✦ Online registration and a semiautomatic update service for core and additional Windows components and drivers. With Internet connectivity nearly assumed these days, Microsoft encourages you to register your operating-system purchase online, which allows you access to Microsoft's automatic software and driver updating service. (This type of service is available from many free and subscription-based services, which covers hundreds more vendors than the Microsoft-specific offerings.) Considering how many security, Year 2000, and other bug fixes Microsoft has had to issue recently, embedding such a service into their operating system had to save them millions in technical support.

✦ Included and improved power management/energy-saving features.

✦ FAT-32 file system to support partitions larger than 2GB and provide greater disk space efficiency for drives up to 8GB, which is otherwise only provided in limited OEM distributions of Windows 95 Rev B.

✦ Registry database integrity checks, backup, and recovery. The plague of Windows 95 gets a shot in the arm with Microsoft's SCANREG utility, which keeps up to five prior versions of the Registry backed up and restorable from DOS. It is now possible to renew Windows back to a working state without reformatting and reinstalling everything!

✦ A startup disk that contains nearly every CD-ROM driver imaginable! Finally, you can restart the system from a DOS disk and get access to critical utilities and the CD-ROM drive should you ever need to reformat or reinstall.

For many of the good things about Windows 98, there are some things you cannot expect Windows 98 to do any better or worse than Windows 95 did because the industry and many standards did not change significantly in the three years between their releases. Windows 98 does not improve on Plug and Play, for example. It cannot — Plug and Play is only supported, not defined or controlled, by Windows.

Windows 98 second edition tides us over

There are at least two things to embrace in Windows 98 second edition (SE). The first addresses one of the promises of Windows — that it should work with anything. The variances between retail and OEM versions of Windows 98 and SE are minimal. In most cases, both have most of the hardware drivers available at the time of release. Perhaps the most significant difference is that some Microsoft-specific features, such as the TweakUI Powertoy utility, is missing from most OEM systems, and a version is not readily available from Microsoft's Web site, as it was for Windows 95. Some of the highlights of Windows 98 SE are the following:

✦ **IEEE-1394 (also known as FireWire or iLink) support.** This provides high-speed external device expansion capability, enabling the connection of video cameras and storage devices for professional-level production work.

✦ **Internet Connection Sharing.** This feature was once found only in shareware and third-party utilities, such as WinGate and WinProxy, but Microsoft finally caught on.

✦ **Revised hardware/driver support.** As more USB, Accelerated Graphics Port (AGP) video, and other devices came to market, Microsoft took the opportunity to roll in a few patches and updates for a new OS. No doubt, legal issues over Internet Explorer, Java, and general core operating-system security concerns had to be covered, as well.

Is Windows 98 SE better, more stable, cooler, or faster than Windows 98? Not really. Don't forget those patches! No, it still didn't get power management (suspend, sleep, auto-shutoff, quick-boot) features right, but this is not entirely Microsoft's fault. The PC industry has been trying to foolproof power management with varying standards and practices for years — there should be no expectation that Microsoft could or would fix it.

Windows Millennium

There is probably much to be said about Windows Millennium Edition, also known as Me. As of this writing, Microsoft has not completed Me, but we can offer a preview. In addition to appearing to be a significantly polished version of Windows 98 SE or a scaled-down version of Windows 2000, here is what we think we know about Windows Me:

✦ Windows Me is the home/personal upgrade path from Windows 98 and 98 SE. (Windows 2000 Professional is definitely the professional/enterprise upgrade for businesses, not homes.)

✦ Me includes a new user interface, which is more like the textured, fade-in, fade-out style of Windows 2000. (We are still waiting for the 3D/shadow-effect mouse cursor, though.)

✦ Me has made a further and quite successful attempt at burying DOS once and for all — but not quite. There is no default multiboot option — press F8 when it boots up and you get "normal" and "safe" modes. Microsoft has eliminated the real mode or DOS component of the bootup process so that Me can boot faster by avoiding significant memory mode changes and holding back 16-bit compatibility at this level. In other words, Me is the closest you will get to NT/2000 for a personal desktop OS without the security and administration overhead associated with using Windows 2000 Professional.

✦ Without real mode at the start, it takes less than 30 seconds from power up to logon prompt. Amazing!

✦ According to the following snippets from publicity information, Windows Me is chockfull of multimedia, Internet-experience, and gaming pizzazz:

• **Windows Movie Maker.** Enables home users to easily get, sort, and share their home videos. Users can import their footage directly from their VCR, too.

• **Windows Media Player.** Windows Media Player (WMP) does not simply play video or audio files, but it acts as a "digital media jukebox" that lets the user store, organize, and play audio and video files with optimal ease.

• **Windows Image Acquisition.** This feature makes it easy to acquire, process, manage, and share pictures from digital cameras and scanners to a PC.

- **Direct Play Voice Chat.** This option makes online gaming a richer experience for home users. Voice Chat allows two or more gamers to talk back and forth in real time while they play games with each other over the Internet.

- **Internet Explorer 5.5.** The next version of Internet Explorer (IE) will include increased performance, reliability, and frame download speeds. IE 5.5 also includes a Print Preview feature. (Expect it to be called IE 6 by release time, just to keep up with the competition!)

- **System File Protection.** A new feature said to proactively prevent system problems with core system files before they occur.

- **Microsoft's first implementation of Universal Plug and Play**. Universal Plug and Play (UPnP) simplifies Home Device Sharing. The OS will automatically identify new UPnP devices and easily connect them to the home network.

- **UPnP offers Enhanced Internet Connection Sharing.** Internet Connection Sharing (ICS) makes it easier to connect multiple PCs together and USB support makes it easier for users to connect devices to their PCs.

So what do you get here? Basically, a personal operating system beefed up for multimedia and entertainment — what Microsoft thinks the home computing market wants. We believe that despite this glitzy hype, somewhere amidst the fancy graphics is a stable, high-performance desktop OS that most people can enjoy. Beta 2 was buggy. Beta 3 looks better. The current release candidates look pretty good.

Still, we asked Microsoft (through its public relations agency) to comment on a few questions about Me. Following are the questions and the public relations firm's responses, or lack of response:

- ✦ *Question*: Does Me allow or support any pre-Windows drivers or programs, such as those typically loaded with CONFIG.SYS and AUTOEXEC.BAT?

- ✦ *Answer*: What we are doing in Windows Me is removing the ability to run your PC in real mode. This means that real mode device drivers will not be able to run and you will not be able to run applications in your AUTOEXEC.BAT file as you could previously.

- ✦ *Question*: Does Me provide any internal security features that make the operating system and applications less vulnerable to some of the types of security attacks so prevalent on the Internet today?

- ✦ *Answer*: To date, neither Microsoft nor its public relations firm have responded to this question.

- ✦ *Question*: What is PC Health supposed to do for the user? Are other vendors contributing to this effort? If so, which ones and how?

✦ *Answer*: Windows Me will include improvements that contribute to an easier, more reliable computing experience. With the removal of real mode, Windows Me's startup process is simpler, faster and more reliable. The *System Restore* feature allows users to roll back their computer to a date or time when it was working properly and simply begin using the computer from that point to bypass system crashes. The *System File Protection* feature of Windows Me actively searches the system's files for potential problems and corrects them, if such problems occur. The *AutoUpdate* function automatically downloads important Microsoft updates to the PC from its Web site.

Windows Me aims to provide a great out-of-the-box experience through simplifying the computing experience and streamlining maintenance of the PC. Windows Me will include System File Protection, which proactively prevents potential problems within the system by identifying them before they occur. Windows Me also provides support for "Easy PCs," computers that support the Easy PC push to make PCs easy to set up, use, expand, and maintain.

✦ *Question*: Can the user completely remove Internet Explorer from the operating system? If they can, and do, what about the many ActiveX and unique OS-kernel-embedded IE features? Are they also removed?

✦ *Answer*: To date, neither Microsoft nor its PR firm have responded to this question.

Recommendations for Me

Because Me is so new, well, not even fully developed or released at this point, we would rather not speculate further on specific troubleshooting issues. However, our position on creating and maintaining a properly configured, up-to-date hardware platform — including realistically current hardware and drivers, adequate CPU, RAM, and hard-disk capacity and performance — is firm. We strongly recommend the following:

✦ If your hard drive currently has less than 400MB of free space, get a new, larger hard drive before even considering an upgrade to Me — the installation requires much free disk space.

✦ If you have less than 32MB of RAM you need more — at least 32, if not 64MB.

✦ If your present hardware running Windows 95 or 98 still requires a DOS-level device driver, for example, to use your CD-ROM drive, buy and install a new ATAPI-compliant CD-ROM drive and do away with DOS drivers.

✦ If you need special disk partitioning software or drivers to make up for your system BIOS' inability to recognize a large hard drive (greater than 2 or 8GB), get a BIOS upgrade or a new system board.

✦ If your video card was made prior to 1997, you should consider an upgrade to a faster PCI or AGP bus card — you will need this to enjoy much better overall graphics performance.

Troubleshooting Windows

Windows 95 and 98 (and, as a matter of fact, Windows Me) are quite similar in the way they are installed and used, and in the problems you may encounter. For that reason, we will first cover items they share and then address issues specific to each version.

General Windows 95 and 98 hardware issues

Following is a list of common hardware issues to be aware of with Windows 95 and 98 (most references in this section apply equally to both Windows 95 and 98). Many of these issues are covered in Chapter 9 and in the appropriate chapter for a particular device or subsystem.

✦ **Interrupt-request (IRQ) conflicts.** Windows 95/98 disables conflicting devices if it finds an interrupt-request (IRQ) conflict. In many cases, you will have to find ways to use alternate IRQs by manually setting the add-in card, turning off Plug-n-Play capabilities, or allocating IRQs to "Legacy" support.

✦ **Proper IRQ and direct-memory-access assignments (serial and parallel ports, disk adapters, sound cards).** Because of Plug-and-Play support, Windows 95/98 is considerably more flexible in IRQ and direct-memory-access (DMA) assignments for various devices, often against the better judgement of legacy or Industry Standard Architecture (ISA) rules.

✦ **Proper physical and logical port assignments (serial and parallel ports, disk adapters).** Windows 95/98 will assign COM port devices beyond COM 4 to various Plug-and-Play devices that are capable of being addressed differently than legacy/ISA devices. This may provide you with more IRQs, or it may provide you with the challenge of experimenting with what combinations of turning off Plug and Play or reallocating IRQs to legacy devices will enable you to use all of your new and old devices.

✦ **Address overlap.** Be careful that no two devices are trying to share the same or overlapping addresses. Windows 95/98 disables overlapped devices; it cannot detect them. This can be a common problem with network and sound cards that offer a variety of address settings. Avoid 330h, 340h, and 360h, as these addresses may overlap common Small Computer System Interface (SCSI) and parallel ports. Sound cards at 220h or 240h may conflict with SCSI devices at 220h or 230h.

✦ **Early or incompatible Plug-and-Play or softset devices.** If Windows 95/98 does not properly identify or configure a Plug-and-Play (PnP) device, try to disable the PnP feature of the device, configure it manually, and let Windows 95/98 rediscover the device by choosing the Install New Hardware icon in the Control Panel. This is likely to be a problem with some network cards, such as the 3Com EtherLink III, but generally any software-configured device is susceptible to being disabled or improperly enabled. PnP devices such as video and disk adapters typically have well-recognized configurations and are rarely affected.

This problem may be accentuated if the Plug-and-Play BIOS in your system is not version 1.0a or later, or it is set to force conflicting values between the actual hardware in the system versus what Windows 95 is trying to detect or set. You may have to disable PnP in your system BIOS settings, and/or force the IRQ settings to ISA-mode for your hardware device, as well as force the configuration of the device at its hardware level with its setup program.

Tip

If you can, manually configure all your hardware device settings according to the standards established for BIOS and DOS devices (LPT, COM, mouse, and disk devices), set the configuration of nonstandard devices around the standard ones, and do not let your system PnP BIOS or Windows 95/98 soft set *any* configurations—simply let it detect what is there. Ensure that the configuration is valid and that the devices work properly as a basic hardware platform under DOS and Windows 3.*x before* the detection by Windows 95/98. Systems that come preloaded with Windows 95 should not have hardware configuration problems. Therefore, they should accept new devices without conflicts, if the manufacturer has not used up all IRQs, as Compaq has done with some models of the Presario line.

✦ **DOS-level Personal Computer Memory Card International Association services drivers.** Avoid using these in CONFIG.SYS or AUTOEXEC.BAT when running Windows 95. Windows 95/98 works extremely well with Personal Computer Memory Card International Association (PCMCIA) devices by itself without DOS-level device drivers, and it may only get confused, or the devices may be disabled, if you try to load the DOS-level drivers when you boot and run Windows 95 or 98.

✦ **Duplicate devices.** This is not so much something to avoid but be aware that it will happen in many systems. If your system board provides devices or ports that you believe you disabled in favor of ones on add-in cards, Windows 95/98 may detect both the system board device(s) and the add-in ones. The add-in ones that are active will usually be the ones Windows 95 uses, and the disabled ones, though detected, will be disabled, or Windows will indicate an exclamation point on a yellow-dot background to show that it knows the device exists but cannot determine its status. This is normal, although it may not appear to be correct. Indeed, Windows 95/98 found the device, but it did not find anything active attached to it. This will occur if you install an enhanced IDE disk adapter to use instead of the nonenhanced adapter built into the system board; the active adapter will appear okay and the inactive one will have the exclamation mark on it in the System Display found in the Control Panel. This may also occur if you have an SCSI host adapter plugged in that acts as your standard disk interface in addition to an inactive system-board IDE interface. Unfortunately, experimenting with various combinations of manually setting IRQs and memory addresses, along with selecting IRQs to be allocated to legacy support in your complimentary metal-oxide semi-conductor (CMOS) setup, are often the only ways to get all of your devices working.

You can often find these duplicates by running Win 9*x* in Safe Mode and checking the System icon contents in the Control Panel.

In general, the configuration items discussed in Chapter 13, the device tables in Appendix B, and the documentation for your hardware should be your ultimate guides for proper hardware configurations.

General Windows 95 and 98 software issues

The following is a list of common software items to be aware of with Windows 95 and 98:

✦ **Memory managers.** Be sure you have a memory manager that has been tested with or preferably designed for Windows 95. Using non-Windows 95 memory managers will most certainly result in page faults, illegal functions, and similar crashes of one or more applications running under Windows 95. If the Windows 95/98 Explorer program (basically the desktop) itself indicates a crash, you will want to reboot Windows to ensure no further data loss occurs. If all else fails, stick with the version of HIMEM.SYS that comes with Windows 95, do not use EMM386 at all, and keep the bootup configuration as simple as possible.

✦ **Windows 3.x software.** This is where Bruce Brown's bug list is invaluable. Every type of application, from games to multimedia production tools, appointment calendars to spreadsheets, and communications programs to system information programs, is eligible for Bruce Brown's list. The common issue is usually that a program developed for Windows 3.x may use undocumented workarounds or features found in Windows that are not in Windows 95, or developers have created their own internal versions of Windows functions that do not interface properly with Windows 95. Bruce Brown's bug list has grown up and offers mulch more help now, for all versions of Windows and more, and is available at `http://www.bugnet.com`.

✦ **Upgraded/updated Windows 3.x software.** Interim-release software or patches that are meant to get old Windows 3.x software somewhat in step with Windows 95/98 can be a waste of time and money. Accept only Windows 95/98-specific software versus patched Windows 3.x software. Microsoft introduced its "Designed for Windows 95" certification program for a reason — it helps consumers avoid software developer's tricks and shortcuts. Although there is good, legitimate Windows 95 software out there that has not yet been certified, the certification does indicate that the program passed some rigorous compatibility tests.

✦ The "Designed for Windows 95" certification program does have one minor flaw: It claims to require that all certified software be proven to run under both Windows 95 and Windows NT. In fact, programs that are built with Windows 95–only software creation tools do not necessarily provide support for Windows NT–specific features and functions, and Windows NT lacks some of Windows 95's limitations and features. Thus, perfectly good, clean, reliable Windows 95 and 98 programs may never run under NT. Microsoft is known to accept and certify Windows 95 software based on this situation. Similarly, Windows NT–specific software may never receive the "Designed for Windows 95" certification because 95 lacks NT features.

✦ **DOS software.** Most DOS programs work great under Windows 95 and 98, and even better than they did under Windows 3.*x*. This is mainly because Windows 95 handles memory much better (and Windows 98 better still) than Windoes 3.*x*, and when a DOS window is opened, it is better isolated (but not completely) from the rest of the applications. However, definitely avoid using hardware-level system information programs (CheckIt, QAPlus, and so on) and direct low-level disk utilities (for example, those from Norton or SpinRite) in DOS windows under Windows 95 or 98. As good as these programs may be at a pure DOS level, or even under Windows 3.*x*, they may crash the system hardware or corrupt disk data that should be left to Windows 95/98–specific programs.

✦ **Hardware utility software.** Because Windows 95/98 works dynamically in hardware detection and configuration, using any utility software to peek or poke at hardware items can really undermine the work Windows 95/98 is trying to do at the same time. The setup programs for your softset add-in cards (network cards, modems, and so on) should only be run under DOS and before Windows 95/98 loads, or Windows 95/98 could be confused about the configuration.

✦ **Disk utility software.** Because Windows 95/98 tracks two file-record systems, the original DOS File Allocation Table (FAT) and the Virtual File Allocation Table (VFAT), in order to provide long filename support, you should do *nothing* to your disk drives with a DOS or Windows 3.*x* application under Windows 95 or 98. Because DOS and Windows 3.*x* programs are unaware of the VFAT system (for the long filenames), tampering directly with files, disk sectors, and so on will place the FAT and VFAT systems out of sync, and data will be lost.

✦ **Memory utility software.** Avoid using utilities, such as SoftRAM, MagnaRAM, and so on unless specifically designed for use with Windows 95. Windows was not designed to have other utilities try to compress or reclaim resource memory for it. These utilities can rob system performance and conflict with your memory manager, Windows 95/98's own memory management, or other applications on your system. Although a novel concept, the FirstAid utility application, especially the Windows 3.*x* version, has not proven to be as beneficial as one might think. This type of background application can really decrease system performance. To date, aftermarket, third-party memory managers, such as QEMM, are not suitable for use with Windows 98.

Common Windows 95 and 98 problems

Once you have Windows 95 or 98 installed on your system, you may run into one or more problems similar to those that this section discusses. Many of the problems listed under Windows 3.*x* also apply to Windows 95/98. In this section, references to Windows 95 apply equally to Windows 98, unless stated otherwise.

Symptoms

▶ Windows 95/98 does not recognize some devices during installation.

Suspects

▶ Device is not supported directly by Windows 95 or 98.

▶ Device may require a vendor-specific driver to be installed under Windows 95 or 98.

▶ Device requires DOS-level driver to be visible to Windows 95 or 98.

Solutions

▶ Devices that are not currently in production, that have nonstandard uses, or that are of limited distribution may not warrant current support for Windows 95/98. Upgrade or replace the device with a supported version, if possible.

▶ Use the Add Hardware feature under Control Panel, do not let Windows 95/98 search for the device, and select the Have Disk option to browse and locate a vendor-provided driver for the device. The driver should come on a disk with the device, or you may have to obtain the driver from the vendor's online support presence.

▶ Use the DOS-level driver required by the device in the CONFIG.SYS or AUTOEXEC.BAT file as appropriate for the device to be available to DOS or Windows. This will be what is referred to as a real-mode driver, if it is visible under Windows 95/98's Device Manager dialog box (found under System in the Control Panel).

Although most users of Windows 95/98 have popular, widely distributed hardware that is generally known to Windows 95/98, even some recent devices by lesser-known vendors or those used for nonstandard applications may never be supported. Some "off-the-wall," proprietary CD-ROM interfaces, document scanners, early SCSI adapters, and so on are probably among those that Microsoft chose not to support, or the vendor is no longer in business and, thus, is unavailable to provide device or driver information.

Symptoms

▶ Pressing F4 does not enable bootup into prior DOS version after installing Windows 95/98.

Suspects

▶ The process of saving old DOS and Windows files so you can un-install Windows 95/98/Me may be the reason you cannot boot into the older version because the files were not stored individually, but in a single compressed archive file.

▶ Windows 95/98 FORMAT or SYS command performed on hard drive does not apply proper MSDOS.SYS parameters for multiboot feature.

Solutions

▶ Be sure to have bootable disks for both the old DOS version and for Windows 95/98. First boot up with a bootable DOS disk containing the SYS.COM program and then run the SYS program applied to the hard drive. Next, using a Windows 95 bootable disk, reboot the system and apply the Windows 95/98 SYS program to the hard drive. Reboot the system to Windows 95/98 and then use the Explorer to gain access to the MSDOS.SYS file in the root directory of the bootable (C:) drive. Select properties for this file and remove the Read-Only, System, and Hidden attributes from this file. Edit the MSDOS.SYS file to place the line BootMulti=1 under the [options] section of the file. Save the file and exit. BootMulti=1 tells Windows 95/98 at bootup that it should allow the swapping of critical boot files when you press F4 at the appearance of the "Starting Windows" message.

Symptoms

▶ Windows 3.x programs, groups, and properties are not as they were before installing Windows 95/98.

Suspects

▶ Windows 95/98 upgrade was not installed in the \WINDOWS directory.

▶ By default, Windows 95/98 does not retain all Windows 3.x properties.

Solutions

▶ After upgrade, manually add program groups to the Start Menu or your desktop in order to suit your preferences. This will involve selecting Start ➪ Settings ➪ Taskbar and clicking the StartMenu Programs tab. Use the Add button to locate and to select the disk drive, program folder, and the program icon for the programs of your choice and then move them to their target location on the Start Menu tree display.

▶ Before and after upgrade/installation, use a Windows 3.x-to-Windows 95 migration utility program, such as the Upgrade Assistant utility included with Vertisoft's Remove-IT, now a part of Quarterdeck's CleanSweep products.

As you may have seen, the Windows 95/98 desktop is not the same as Windows 3.x. This causes confusion for many users, who think they have lost their previous configuration and program groups. Instead of using a single Program Manager desktop, Windows 95 cleans up the desktop and puts program groups into a Start Menu, visible by clicking the Start button on the taskbar and selecting Programs, which should contain most all of your application program groups. However, you will not see the old Windows 3.x Main group because the features of Main are accessed elsewhere on the desktop in the Control Panel under My Computer and in Explorer folders for your disk drives.

To retain your old Windows 3.x desktop and program groups under Windows 95/98 when upgrading to the new operating system, first use a migration utility, such as the Upgrade Advisor provided in Quarterdeck's CleanSweep. This utility is used first under Windows 3.x to record your program group setups. It is to be used again after performing the Windows 95 or 98 upgrade to put that setup into the Windows 95/98 configuration. A handy utility, indeed, and one that Microsoft should have put in Windows 95 and 98. This utility is a must if you have installed Windows 95 or 98 in a new directory separate from Windows 3.*x*. Under this circumstance, Windows 95 or 98 knows nothing of your Windows 3.*x* setup, forcing you to build the Programs list on the Start Menu by hand if you want to get to the old applications.

Symptoms

▶ Windows 95/98 always or frequently boots up to its boot menu and recommends Safe Mode operation.

▶ Windows 95 never gets past the clouds and rolling color bar screen at bootup.

▶ The Windows 95 bootup logo clears, but Windows 95 never loads, leaving you with a blank screen and a blinking cursor.

▶ Windows 95 begins to load the desktop but stalls without presenting a network logon dialog box, or it never completes loading the desktop.

Suspects

▶ A device driver loaded at bootup or an application run in the foreground or background under Windows 95 may have reconfigured or misconfigured a device in your system, and Windows 95 is confused about or cannot use the device. Check for devices under Device Manager (found in System under Control Panel), shown with an exclamation point, to determine the offending device. If you cannot get Windows running, try starting in Safe Mode in order to get to your System icon in Control Panel so that you can check for hardware configuration problems.

▶ Your system crashed, was shut off, or encountered a power glitch before Windows was ready to shut down your system safely, thus, corrupting a device driver or configuration file.

▶ Your system is configured for a network that is not active, or it is misconfigured for the network it is on.

▶ An application or disk/file system error corrupted one or more copies of the Registry data files that Windows 95/98 uses to maintain system configuration information. Windows 95/98 depends on many different files for its configuration — some affect the entire installation, some affect only the appearance and behavior of Windows 95/98 for individual users of the system. Windows 95 provides background monitoring of the system, so it may identify any newly active hardware or changes in network conditions. Windows 95 frequently opens and closes these files, or it maintains your configuration in memory until it can store it to a file. Unlike Windows 3.*x*, Windows 95 keeps last known-good configuration file backups that it can use later to run the system. Like Windows NT, Windows 95 provides a safe shutdown sequence that you should use before turning the system off. This feature is intended to let you know when Windows is completely done running and has closed all its files, delaying an impatient user from accidentally corrupting files. Preventing misbehaving programs and system crashes from corrupting the current configuration has yet to be accomplished, but the backup copies of configuration files are a step in the right direction.

If you are configured for Microsoft Networking (this is not the Microsoft Network, MSN, online service) and have an incomplete network setup or conflicting drivers (such as both Microsoft TCP/IP and FTP Software's TCP/IP drivers), Windows 95 may not resolve the proper network communications, or it may receive conflicting network signals and then cannot communicate with one or more servers it expects to communicate with at bootup. It is important that you specify proper network addresses; workgroup, domain, and host names; and other network properties to match with the network system to which you are connected.

Solutions

▶ Remove all nonessential DOS-level device drivers and TSR/background/utility programs that may affect the disk drives or system devices. They may be confusing or conflicting with internal Windows 95 drivers. This solution may require booting the system with a DOS disk, or it may require stopping the boot by pressing F8 and selecting the Command Prompt option to enable you to edit out drivers from the CONFIG.SYS and AUTOEXEC.BAT files at DOS before rebooting into Windows 95.

▶ Clean up the power and connections to your PC. Shut it down properly only by selecting Shutdown from the Start menu. Clean your electrical contacts (plug and receptacles). Check for corrosion around batteries and their leads. Check for worn or frayed cables. Ensure that all boards and connectors are attached and seated properly.

▶ Use only Windows 95–specific device drivers, and few or none in CONFIG.SYS and AUTOEXEC.BAT.

▶ Use only Windows 95–specific utility programs.

▶ Use a Windows 95–specific antivirus program to scan your system and clean up any viruses.

▶ Run SCANDISK or Norton Disk Doctor for Windows 95 on your disk drives in Thorough Test mode in order to verify your disk drive system.

▶ Restart Windows 95 in Safe Mode (no networking support) by pressing F8 at the "Starting Windows 95" boot message. Then go to Networking in the Control Panel to set up your network properly. This may require information from your network system administrator.

▶ Reinstall Windows 95 from the DOS command prompt.

Symptoms

▶ Periodic or frequent disk activity occurs when not specifically accessing new files or programs.

▶ System is sluggish in saving files, opening applications, or swapping disk memory.

Suspects

▶ Excessive disk-memory swap-file activity is occurring, especially if system memory is less than 12MB.

▶ Disk drive or adapter is a bottleneck to file I/O speed.

▶ Virtual cache is too large or too small.

Solutions

▶ Add system RAM (increase to 12- or 16MB) to reduce reliance on disk-swap file.

▶ Upgrade your drive or disk-drive adapter to a faster model or to one with a higher-speed data path (Enhanced IDE versus IDE or older MFM; SCSI-III versus SCSI-II or SCSI-I; 16-bit EISA versus 8-bit ISA, Local Bus, PCI, and so on).

▶ Add or change disk-performance parameters in SYSTEM.INI, CONFIG.SYS, and the File System Properties dialog box to enable more frequent cache flushing. Retrieve the File System Properties dialog box by selecting Control Panel ⇨ System and then clicking the Performance tab in the System Properties window.

No matter how fast your CPU, if your disk system is sluggish, or you do not have enough RAM memory, Windows 95 will appear slow in comparison to the system capabilities because it is either swapping much data in and out of memory to the disk system, or the disk system is simply too slow to be acceptable.

Adding RAM was once an expensive proposition. Therefore, users may have tried to make up for the lack of RAM, as Microsoft and other operating systems do, by using virtual memory or a dedicated disk file. Today RAM may be found at discounted prices for 4MB 32-bit SIMMs and for 8MB 32-bit SIMMs. Price is now little excuse for not upgrading your system RAM. You can have too little and suffer lack of performance due to reliance on the virtual-memory swap file, or you may try to stuff your system full of RAM and not see any appreciable performance increase under normal conditions.

Side by side, two average 100–133 MHz Pentium systems run Windows no differently with 32MB or 16MB of RAM. Performance starts to fall off at 12MB, and it drops significantly with only 8MB of RAM. Increasing RAM above 32MB becomes beneficial with server applications or intensive graphics applications, or when you are running many applications simultaneously. Windows 95 and OS/2 should be run with 16MB or more of RAM. Windows NT runs quite adequately with 24–32MB. Because of Windows 95, 98, and NT memory-management features, it is possible to add too much RAM, as with situations where you do not have applications that require more than 64MB of RAM. In these cases, Windows can spend an inordinate amount of time managing much RAM when it could be processing your applications and data. Similarly, a slow disk drive (less than 10 millisecond average access time) is no match for a fast CPU system.

Improve Performance by Increasing Disk Speed

Using a faster disk system is a big plus for performance. Drives with access times greater than 12 milliseconds (average seek time to any track) will leave Windows 95 sluggish and nearly intolerable. Enhanced IDE drives of 540MB and larger capacity, and speeds under 10 milliseconds and low-cost Enhanced IDE (EIDE) adapters, provide a reasonably cost-worthy performance benefit.

Microsoft provides default settings for the obvious and not-so-obvious parameters that affect disk- and file-system performance for most systems. You could gain much performance by making simple changes in the values in the File System Properties dialog box and by experimenting with the [vcache] driver settings. Many disk drives provide their own buffering, as do many disk adapters. Late-model SCSI adapters also perform DMA transfers. Because these work at a hardware level, using the virtual/software cache drivers in Windows 95 or 98 may actually defeat the advantages of hardware caching. For most 486DX2-66 and above systems with recent models of disk drives, either EIDE or SCSI, the following seems to be a good starting place for increasing performance and decreasing annoying Windows 95 and 98 disk delays:

1. Go to My Computer ⇨ Control Panel ⇨ System and click the Performance tab.

2. Select Virtual Memory. Manually set the minimum swap-file size equal to half the amount of RAM in your system and the maximum swap-file size to twice the amount of RAM in your system. Windows 95 does not like you to manually set this value, but accept these settings and go on.

3. Select File System. Decrease the file-system parameter from its current default of 32K or 64K to something more modest, such as 4K or 8K.

4. Click on the Troubleshooting tab and disable "write-behind disk caching." Click OK several times until this series of dialog boxes is completely closed. When prompted to restart your system, choose No.

5. Edit the SYSTEM.INI file and below the entries under the [386Enh] category, add a category called [vcache]. Under that category, add the following two lines:

```
MinFileCache=256
MaxFileCache=1024
```

6. Save and close this file.

7. Edit your C:\CONFIG.SYS file, edit or add the line BUFFERS=6,0, and then save and close the file.

8. Restart your system from the Start menu by selecting Shutdown and then selecting Restart. You'll witness increased performance in a snap.

We have tried this trick on both Windows 95 and Windows 98 systems that seemed to operate sluggishly. Although no trick such as this will fix every system, it does point you to the parameters that most frequently affect the amount of time and resources your system devotes to trying to cache disk operations. If your usage opens a large number of small files, having your system use a smaller amount of memory for read-ahead cache for a larger number of files will increase its speed. On the other hand, if you use a small number of very small files, increasing the size of the read-ahead cache and reducing the number of files it handles will give you better performance. The only answer is to experiment with these settings in your own environment.

Symptoms

▶ Loss of proper desktop or folder icons (plain, generic box icons).

▶ Inability to launch applications when double-clicking on icons (main or shortcuts).

Suspects

▶ An unstable or incompatible application or memory manager has caused a system corruption.

▶ An unstable or defective disk system has caused configuration file corruption.

▶ Invalid or broken links exist between programs and shortcuts or links.

▶ There is general corruption of Windows 95 desktop, setup, or registry, and so on.

Solutions

▶ Reboot system from Shutdown, power off, power back on, and restart.

▶ Run SCANDSKW or NDDW to check the disk drive(s) for errors.

▶ Before going through the drastic step of reinstalling Windows, check the program shortcut link to see if the referenced program is still on the disk. Reinstall it if necessary.

▶ Reinstall Windows 95/98 with the SETUP.EXE program on the installation disk or CD-ROM, from the taskbar select Start ⇨ Run, and then copy over all or only the damaged files. This will cause Windows 95 to reestablish the desktop, folders, and all shortcuts and links, but only if they are still available.

These problems can occur if a program, memory manager, or disk error has occurred that caused Windows 95/98 to lose track of the program links and shortcuts. Also, a file may have been accidentally deleted. Because Windows 95/98 is always checking the system, including the Registry file and system configuration, for changes, this is a dynamic activity that can happen at almost any time.

Symptoms

▶ A Windows 95 system connected to a network appears to hang or freeze for extended periods of time.

Suspects

▶ System is set up with Microsoft networking and cannot find Workgroups or Internet domains.

▶ Network has heavy data traffic, reducing performance between other workstation or domain servers.

▶ Network driver is in real mode or loaded at DOS level, or it is incompatible with Windows 95.

Solutions

▶ Use only Windows 95 drivers, no DOS-level drivers. If your network card is not currently recognized or supported by Windows 95, upgrade it to a card that is supported by Windows 95..

▶ Upgrade network cabling for cleaner signals. Typically use CAT5 high-speed cables for 10BaseT and 100BaseT, and double-shielded, high-quality coax for 10Base2.

▶ Replace or upgrade your network card to a 16-bit or newer model. The network card may be causing signal noise on the network, or a defective network card on another system may be causing system noise.

▶ Determine excessive network response time or bad routing — usually a system administrator task. The Packet Internet Groper (PING) command (run in a DOS window or from the RUN option on the taskbar menu), gives you some idea of response times from your system to specific host IP addresses. Here is an example of a PING command:

```
PING myhost.mydomain.com[Enter]
```

• Local network connections should respond in under 10 milliseconds, routed network connections in 30 milliseconds or less, ISDN connections in 30 to 150 milliseconds, dialup networking in 100 to 350 milliseconds.

▶ Be sure you specify the Windows Domain name as the Workgroup name and be sure that the NT server providing this domain support matches this designation.

▶ Have your network system administrator verify that all file servers are active and accessible from your workstation.

This symptom may require that your system administrator intervene to review system routing tables or overall network design issues that may decrease your performance while accessing one or more servers. When Windows 95 is networked by using a Windows NT Domain server and/or third-party NFS file system driver (such as those from FTP Software or Hummingbird Communications), it is constantly searching the network for changes in server and drive systems. If there is a network system delay or failure to locate an NT domain or NFS file system server, the system will retry periodically, stalling normal desktop operations for 30 seconds or longer.

Windows Configuration Files

The Windows operating systems rely on several key files that define how the operating systems load into memory and run, what resources and applications are installed on a particular PC system, and how those resources and applications will be used. Without these files, Windows would probably be nothing more than a stupid, useless memory hog. Many other works on the subject cover in detail the various configuration files, what they do, and how to interact with them. We mention them here for their value in being able to properly install, configure, and use the operating systems, and for how to detect and recover from problems with them.

Windows 95 and 98 MSDOS.SYS file

Windows 95 introduced combining the separate functions of the IO.SYS (BIOS extensions) and MSDOS.SYS (DOS loader) files into one larger IO.SYS file, and it changed the purpose of the MSDOS.SYS file to be a configuration file that affects Windows startup.

On a Windows 95 or 98 system, the C:\MSDOS.SYS file is a plain ASCII/text file that is normally stored with the read-only, system, and hidden file attributes. To edit or view this file it is handy to remove these attributes with the following command-line instructions:

```
ATTRIB -r -a -s -h MSDOS.* [Enter]
```

You may also change the attributes using the Explorer property functions, if you have configured Explorer to show all file types and hidden files. After you have changed the attributes, you may use the DOS EDIT or Windows Notepad programs to view and edit this file. Windows may change the attributes on this file after reinstallation or other system changes, so do not be surprised if the file becomes hidden again. Before you edit the file you should know and understand the purpose and effect of each parameter in the file, as listed in Table 8-1. Sample MSDOS.SYS files are shown following the table.

Table 8-1
MSDOS.SYS Contents and Parameters

Attribute	Default Value	Optional Value	Purpose
AutoScan=*	1	0 or 2	1 = Always automatically run scan disk at startup, if the system was previously shutdown improperly. 0 = Do not prompt and do not run ScanDisk. 2 = Run ScanDisk on restart without prompting, even if with proper shutdown.
BootDelay=	5		The parameter is the number of seconds to delay.
BootFailSafe	0	1	0 = System does not boot into Safe Mode automatically. 1 = Forces the system to boot into Safe Mode.
BootGUI=	1	0	1 = Start Windows during bootup. 0 = Remain at Command Prompt after bootup.
BootKeys=	1	0	1 = The bootup function keys (F4, F5, F8, S+F5, C+F5, S+F8) are functional at startup. 0 = The bootup function keys are disabled at startup.
BootMenu=	0	1	0 = Do not display a startup menu (unless F8 key is pressed). 1 = Always display the startup menu at bootup.
BootMenuDefault=	1		Specifies the default selection of the options available in the startup menu.
BootMenuDelay=	30		Number of seconds that the startup menu will be shown before the default selection is activated.
BootMulti=	0	1	1 = Allows the boot menu option of loading your previous operating system, if it is still installed and available on the disk and if files IO.W40, MSDOS.W40 and COMMAND.W40 are still in the C:\ directory.
BootSafe=	0	1	1 = Forces the system to boot into Safe Mode.

Attribute	Default Value	Optional Value	Purpose
BootWarn=	1	0	1 = Show a warning dialog if Windows is run in Safe Mode. 0 = Do not warn the user when run in Safe Mode.
BootWin=*	1	0	1 = Forces booting Windows 98. 0 = Forces booting, old/prior O/S comes up.
DblSpace=	1	0	1 = Load the DoubleSpace disk compression driver. 0 = Do not load the DoubleSpace disk compression driver.
DisableLog=*	1	0	1 = Forces bootup logging process to C:\BOOTLOG.TXT. 0 = Disables bootup logging.
DrvSpace=	1	0	1 = Load the DriveSpace disk compression driver. 0 = Do not load the DriveSpace disk compression driver.
DoubleBuffer=	0	1	0 = Default w/o SCSI devices. DoubleBuffering is not loaded, regardless of SCSI device presence. 1 = Default w/ SCSI devices, or if disk controller, assumes a limit of 16MB of RAM or provides its own DMA controller. DoubleBuffering is loaded.
HostWinBootDrv=	C		This is the designation of the original system drive. If you compress your disk drive this will change to the host drive letter designation. C indicates an uncompressed boot drive.
LoadTop=	1	0	1 = Load COMMAND.COM, DRVSPACE.BIN, and/or DBLSPACE.BIN at the top of conventional memory. 0 = Do not load DOS at the top of memory. May be necessary for NetWare or other software.
Logo=	1	0	1 = Display the Windows startup logo (C:\WINDOWS\LOGOW.SYS) while booting. 0 = Do not display the Windows startup logo while booting.

Continued

	Default	**Optional**	
Attribute	**Value**	**Value**	**Purpose**
Network=	1	0	1 = Default value if network components are installed 0 = Default value if network components are not installed or if you do not want Windows to load network drivers at startup.
UninstallDir=	C:\		Enter the location of the WINUNDO.DAT and WINUNDO.INI files, if you elected to save your old O/S files during setup.
WinBootDir=	C:\ WINDOWS		Enter the location of Windows boot files (HIMEM, DRVSPACE, and so on). Will be different from WinDir if you compress your disk drive.
WinDir=	C:\ WINDOWS		Enter the location of the Windows installation.
WinVer=*	4.10.1998		Indicate the Windows version as specified.

* New for Windows 98

Following is a sample, default MSDOS.SYS file (the default values listed in Table 8.1 are in effect, unless otherwise specified in this file):

```
[Paths]
WinDir=C:\WINDOWS
WinBootDir=C:\WINDOWS
HostWinBootDrv=C
UninstallDir=C:\

[Options]
BootGUI=1
AutoScan=1
WinVer=4.10.1998
;
;The following lines are required for compatibility with other programs.
;Do not remove them (MSDOS.SYS needs to be >1024 bytes).
;xxxxxxxxxxxxxxxxxxxxxxxxxxxxxxxxxxxxxxxxxxxxxxxxxxxxxxxxxxxxxxa
;xxxxxxxxxxxxxxxxxxxxxxxxxxxxxxxxxxxxxxxxxxxxxxxxxxxxxxxxxxxxxxb
;xxxxxxxxxxxxxxxxxxxxxxxxxxxxxxxxxxxxxxxxxxxxxxxxxxxxxxxxxxxxxxc
;xxxxxxxxxxxxxxxxxxxxxxxxxxxxxxxxxxxxxxxxxxxxxxxxxxxxxxxxxxxxxxd
;xxxxxxxxxxxxxxxxxxxxxxxxxxxxxxxxxxxxxxxxxxxxxxxxxxxxxxxxxxxxxxe
;xxxxxxxxxxxxxxxxxxxxxxxxxxxxxxxxxxxxxxxxxxxxxxxxxxxxxxxxxxxxxxf
;xxxxxxxxxxxxxxxxxxxxxxxxxxxxxxxxxxxxxxxxxxxxxxxxxxxxxxxxxxxxxxg
;xxxxxxxxxxxxxxxxxxxxxxxxxxxxxxxxxxxxxxxxxxxxxxxxxxxxxxxxxxxxxxh
```

```
;xxxxxxxxxxxxxxxxxxxxxxxxxxxxxxxxxxxxxxxxxxxxxxxxxxxxxxxxxxxxi
;xxxxxxxxxxxxxxxxxxxxxxxxxxxxxxxxxxxxxxxxxxxxxxxxxxxxxxxxxxxxj
;xxxxxxxxxxxxxxxxxxxxxxxxxxxxxxxxxxxxxxxxxxxxxxxxxxxxxxxxxxxxk
;xxxxxxxxxxxxxxxxxxxxxxxxxxxxxxxxxxxxxxxxxxxxxxxxxxxxxxxxxxxxl
;xxxxxxxxxxxxxxxxxxxxxxxxxxxxxxxxxxxxxxxxxxxxxxxxxxxxxxxxxxxxm
;xxxxxxxxxxxxxxxxxxxxxxxxxxxxxxxxxxxxxxxxxxxxxxxxxxxxxxxxxxxxn
;xxxxxxxxxxxxxxxxxxxxxxxxxxxxxxxxxxxxxxxxxxxxxxxxxxxxxxxxxxxxo
;xxxxxxxxxxxxxxxxxxxxxxxxxxxxxxxxxxxxxxxxxxxxxxxxxxxxxxxxxxxxp
;xxxxxxxxxxxxxxxxxxxxxxxxxxxxxxxxxxxxxxxxxxxxxxxxxxxxxxxxxxxxq
;xxxxxxxxxxxxxxxxxxxxxxxxxxxxxxxxxxxxxxxxxxxxxxxxxxxxxxxxxxxxr
;xxxxxxxxxxxxxxxxxxxxxxxxxxxxxxxxxxxxxxxxxxxxxxxxxxxxxxxxxxxxs
```

A sample, modified MSDOS.SYS file with many of the defaults changed is shown here:

```
[Paths]
WinDir=C:\WINDOWS
WinBootDir=C:\WINDOWS
HostWinBootDrv=C
UninstallDir=C:\

[Options]
; we do not have or need the option to boot to old DOS
BootMulti=0
; by default we will load the Windows GUI at startup
BootGUI=1
; we want the boot Function keys to work
BootKeys=1
; we want to see the boot menu at startup
BootMenu=1
; we will delay the boot menu auto-selection only 5 seconds
BootMenuDelay=5
; we do not want to see the LOGOW.SYS file displayed at startup
logo=0
; we do not need either DBLSPACE or DRVSPACE drivers
DblSpace=0
DrvSpace=0
; we have SCSI and otherwise want to make sure DoubleBuffering is on
DoubleBuffer=1
;
BootWarn=1
; we do not want to load DOS at the top of memory
LoadTop=0
;
;The following lines are required for compatibility with other programs.
;Do not remove them (MSDOS.SYS needs to be >1024 bytes).
;xxxxxxxxxxxxxxxxxxxxxxxxxxxxxxxxxxxxxxxxxxxxxxxxxxxxxxxxxxxxxxa
;xxxxxxxxxxxxxxxxxxxxxxxxxxxxxxxxxxxxxxxxxxxxxxxxxxxxxxxxxxxxxxb
;xxxxxxxxxxxxxxxxxxxxxxxxxxxxxxxxxxxxxxxxxxxxxxxxxxxxxxxxxxxxxxc
;xxxxxxxxxxxxxxxxxxxxxxxxxxxxxxxxxxxxxxxxxxxxxxxxxxxxxxxxxxxxxxd
;xxxxxxxxxxxxxxxxxxxxxxxxxxxxxxxxxxxxxxxxxxxxxxxxxxxxxxxxxxxxxxe
;xxxxxxxxxxxxxxxxxxxxxxxxxxxxxxxxxxxxxxxxxxxxxxxxxxxxxxxxxxxxxxf
;xxxxxxxxxxxxxxxxxxxxxxxxxxxxxxxxxxxxxxxxxxxxxxxxxxxxxxxxxxxxxxg
```

```
;xxxxxxxxxxxxxxxxxxxxxxxxxxxxxxxxxxxxxxxxxxxxxxxxxxxxxxxxxxxxxxh
;xxxxxxxxxxxxxxxxxxxxxxxxxxxxxxxxxxxxxxxxxxxxxxxxxxxxxxxxxxxxxxi
;xxxxxxxxxxxxxxxxxxxxxxxxxxxxxxxxxxxxxxxxxxxxxxxxxxxxxxxxxxxxxxj
;xxxxxxxxxxxxxxxxxxxxxxxxxxxxxxxxxxxxxxxxxxxxxxxxxxxxxxxxxxxxxxk
;xxxxxxxxxxxxxxxxxxxxxxxxxxxxxxxxxxxxxxxxxxxxxxxxxxxxxxxxxxxxxxl
;xxxxxxxxxxxxxxxxxxxxxxxxxxxxxxxxxxxxxxxxxxxxxxxxxxxxxxxxxxxxxxm
;xxxxxxxxxxxxxxxxxxxxxxxxxxxxxxxxxxxxxxxxxxxxxxxxxxxxxxxxxxxxxxn
;xxxxxxxxxxxxxxxxxxxxxxxxxxxxxxxxxxxxxxxxxxxxxxxxxxxxxxxxxxxxxxo
;xxxxxxxxxxxxxxxxxxxxxxxxxxxxxxxxxxxxxxxxxxxxxxxxxxxxxxxxxxxxxxp
;xxxxxxxxxxxxxxxxxxxxxxxxxxxxxxxxxxxxxxxxxxxxxxxxxxxxxxxxxxxxxxq
;xxxxxxxxxxxxxxxxxxxxxxxxxxxxxxxxxxxxxxxxxxxxxxxxxxxxxxxxxxxxxxr
;xxxxxxxxxxxxxxxxxxxxxxxxxxxxxxxxxxxxxxxxxxxxxxxxxxxxxxxxxxxxxxs
```

The Windows Registry

Windows 95 introduced the Registry as the central repository for Windows configuration information to the end-user/personal desktop system. NT had a Registry first. Windows 98 and NT use a Registry, though NT's is more robust and complex because of the various security features involved. The Windows 95/98 Registry consists of two files, SYSTEM.DAT and USER.DAT. SYSTEM.DAT contains information common to the entire system, hardware, installed software, and so on. USER.DAT contains information relative to each user that logs on to the system. Different users can and usually do have different USER.DAT configurations (desktops, available applications, drive mappings, network logons, and so on). These files are read together to form the configuration database for the active system while it is booted, logged onto, and used.

Note   The Registry is designed to take the place of the slow, inadequate, more easily corrupted, and less easily cross-checked set of INI files found in earlier versions of Windows. Some INI files and their parameters remain in use under Windows 95 and 98 in order to maintain compatibility with older 16-bit Windows applications or as suits a particular program's author, but for the most part, Windows 95/98 can run without them.

The Registry is a hierarchical, referential database structure with hundreds of "many-to-many" relationships between system attributes and data values. It is specific to Microsoft and does not use any industry standard formats. Therefore, you cannot view it with SQL, xBase, or other common tools. Entries are typically made into, read from, edited from, or removed with Registry-specific functions available only through programs and functions provided by the operating system for access to the Registry from within other Windows programs.

Compatibility and the Registry in general

There are a couple of important things that are often confusing but need to be better understood about the Registry, and Windows 95, 98, and NT in general. The first is that none of these operating systems or environments "control" the system hardware. They can only deal with the hardware resource information provided to them by the hardware itself, and subsequently system BIOS and Plug and Play features of system BIOS, or device drivers provided by hardware manufacturers. Without a firm, solid, working, and properly configured system foundation, neither the operating systems nor the Registry information have the capability to correct hardware configuration problems.

The second is that successful, cooperative hardware and software design is a tricky thing at best, and it is amazing that most things work as well as they do when they do. Many of the hardware and driver issues related to the operating system are the responsibility of their respective designers, not Microsoft. That several major PC vendors have announced reluctance to distribute Windows 98 because of BIOS or hardware design issues with the operating system implies that these companies have made design mistakes of their own, rather than indicating problems with the operating system itself. Certainly Microsoft has and does contribute to a certain percentage of "hardware related" problems through its internal development policies and processes and a certain lack of openness about development tools and bugs, so Microsoft is certainly not to be held blameless in all cases. Industry standards help the cooperative processes considerably, but these do not dictate nor do vendors always comply with standards or wait for emerging standards to be accepted before trying to release a product.

Rather than trying to cover the Registry in depth, as John Woram has done in his highly recommended book *The Windows 95 Registry* (IDG Books Worldwide), we mention this significant aspect of these operating systems to encourage you to find and use a Registry backup utility. We cannot stress enough the importance of regular system backups and virus protection. No matter how good a system you have, how well maintained it is, or how good anyone is at fixing it, if your data is at risk, nothing short of having a copy of your work and the tools to get back to work will be sufficient.

For routine maintenance of the Registry, there are several Registry cleaner and validation programs available that can remove or correct bad, missing, or excess data entries in the Registry. This can be important for improving system performance (the combined Registry data set on many systems can be as large as 2MB, thus taking considerable time to open and read the file for information) and correcting application errors. Microsoft offers RegClean from its Web site, Symantec has the Norton Win-Doctor in the Norton Utilities Version 3.0, and Windows 98 has a Registry integrity scanner included with the operating system (the ScanReg programs, mentioned previously).

Our goal here has been to identify, define, and stress the importance of the Registry as a key to the proper functionality of the new Windows operating systems. We encourage you to learn more about the Registry, but more importantly, do what you can to ensure its integrity and recoverability, should disaster threaten your PC.

Registry Utilities

The most common available Registry backup utilities are available through Web sites such as www.shareware.com, www.download.com, www.cdrom.com, and others. Simply search with the keyword "registry" and pick from numerous choices, or retrieve one of the following files directly from their respective Web sites:

✦ WinRescue 98 v.2.04: www.superwin.com/rescue98.htm

✦ WinRescue 95 v.7.03: www.superwin.com/rescue.htm

✦ SysBack: www.crypto-central.com/sysback.zip

✦ And, of course, the Windows 98 ScanReg.exe and ScanRegw.exe programs replace the CfgBack.exe program that was used to backup and restore Registry files under Windows 95.

You can use these utilities to make unique backup sets of the critical Registry files for later recovery. As with various uninstall utilities that track system changes and can return most or all of the system to a prior working state, the capability to return to a Registry set that worked before can be beneficial and time saving. Both types of utilities have their benefits. You might prefer to use an uninstall utility instead of or in addition to a Registry backup tool so that you can restore more files to their "original" or prechange condition. However, you might not be able to use the uninstall utility until you can get a working Registry back in place.

The Upgrade Path to an Optimal Windows System

Why would anyone upgrade an old PC or work with obsolete computer parts? Looking back over the past 19 to 20 years of many new PCs and of upgrading some of them, we can come up with several reasons:

✦ To accommodate new hardware and software. This has remained a valid reason for upgrading from day one.

✦ To provide more program memory:

   • Expand DOS memory with the old DOS extenders to provide more memory to for DOS and Windows on early PCs (pre-386).

   • Add extended memory to PCs with the 386 and later processors.

✦ To enable upgrading to a new operating system. Consider the additional memory required for upgrading from DOS to a multitasking environment (first it was DESQview and then Windows). Or consider the change of a central processing unit to a 486/33, or faster system. How about changing a motherboard to accommodate a Pentium CPU and Windows/NT, 98, 2000, or Me?

✦ To increase capabilities for accomplishing work:

- Increasing speed with a faster processor

- Supporting running larger programs

- Working with multiple programs simultaneously by increasing memory and its speed as well as larger capacity, faster hard drives, and removable media.

✦ To add capabilities such as networking, multimedia, and new interfaces.

✦ To provide a PC to a family member, your favorite charity, or a community organization.

✦ And some PC users simply want to remain on the cutting edge. (Watch out for those sharp edges!)

Everyone's idea of the ultimate PC is probably just a little different. There are so many possibilities — so many different reasons to put together that ultimate system. While this book focuses on Windows because it is the predominant operating environment for the majority of PC users, many of the same considerations go into building the ultimate UNIX/Linux PC. You can build it by starting with a system you already own, put it together yourself from "off the shelf," or just go buy it once you have determined what you really need or want.

The point is, don't start by looking at computer ads in order to find the newest, fastest, latest, or most interesting items to make your upgrade decisions. Instead, start with as much description as you can to define what you want to accomplish with your new computer system. From that definition, you can compare what you need with what you already have and start making informed decisions about what you really need.

Chances are you may not have to buy a new computer system. You may be able to upgrade one you already have. One consideration should be cost. With the prices of PCs dropping all the time, you may be able to buy a new one for about the same cost as the upgrade, especially if the upgrade requires many new parts. This is where all the recommendations we have been giving you, such as to keep records of what is installed in your PC and how these items are configured, will pay off.

It also helps to know which hardware and software you need to accomplish your goals. You probably will not find general agreement about how to proceed with any particular job, especially among computer professionals, who have different experiences and biases.

If you primarily use your PC to manipulate text — typing letters, printing labels, and using small databases, for example — and your use of the Internet over a modem consists mostly of e-mails, transferring files, and maintaining your stock portfolio, the age of your computer and its operating environment are not very important. However, the technical requirements for high power and high speed are usually not found in such a system. If you have an older computer, you probably will be unable to use the latest versions of PC software because now most software is written only for Windows 95/98/Me, NT/2000, and CE.

Although Windows 95 can run on a 386 PC, it is not impressive in that environment. Windows 95 on a 386 PC requires the fastest and largest amount of memory your system can accommodate, as well as the fastest hard drive it can accommodate. Even at that, the 386 falls far short of expectations. Unix (FreeBSD and its Linux cousin) can run quite well on a 386, but the newer hardware is much more stable, and it can do more and do it more quickly.

There are ample reasons that the minimum processor for Windows NT, OS/2, and Windows 98 is a 486/33. For one, the 486 DX chip has the numeric data processor built in. Additionally, memory management is much better, supported by the newer and faster chips. Because you cannot buy a 486 CPU or system board today, your chances of getting stuck with anything less than a 300 MHz or faster Pentium-class system are pretty slim.

At the other end of the spectrum, following are technical reasons for having speed and power in your computer system:

✦ Sounds and 3-D graphics found in the newest games and the most sophisticated medical imaging systems require extra power and speed.

✦ Many multimedia systems, including the ability to converse with your computer, issue voice commands, and have it take dictation in normal, continuous speech, need much speed and power.

✦ Artificial intelligence systems that may be used to control complex systems also require large amounts of speed and power.

Most people and businesses may not run into these requirements in the immediate future. However, hardware and software advancements are continuous, and they always present opportunities to upgrade toward those future capabilities. If you play computer games, on your own system or over the Internet, or you experiment with the latest hardware and software to find better ways to get your work done, those requirements are real today.

Today you can buy PCs with processors that run at anywhere from 300–1,000 MHz. The bus speeds on motherboards available today operate between 100–133 MHz. This means you can expect your fast computer memory to actually operate at its highest speed. Faster I/O means a generally faster system overall. Today's 3-D graphics and sound boards have capabilities to even take over some of the processing required to produce fantastic visual and audio effects. Hard disk arrays are becoming so fast, especially with a large hardware cache using super-fast memory, and so large that they are becoming less of a liability in a PC's capability to compete with larger computer systems in overall speed.

However, do not throw away a computer that has a 386 or 486 processor. These will work just fine with FreeBSD and Linux, even for the things you would be doing with that powerful Windows machine. Non-profit and charitable organizations are always looking for computers and the old PCs will do just fine. They do fine in the corporate world too but they will not run the latest Windows operating systems and applications.

Upgrading from Windows 95 to Windows 98

If you believed all the ads and hype about Windows 98 (now 98 SE), you may have tried to install it on your computer without prior preparation. Oh, you may do a backup of your most important items. You might even consider checking your file system to see if you have enough free space. We try to make sure there are at least 200MB of free disk space on the target Windows 98 disk, but it can take up almost 300MB for a full installation!

If you are considering an upgrade to another system, such as FreeBSD, Linux, Windows ME, or Windows 2000, you may want to review the following list for pointers and other items to consider in preparation for that upgrade. After all, it is the hardware platform that is the focus for all of these installations, and the focus of this book, as well.

Tip

For an upgrade to Windows 2000, you may want to start with a review of Brian Livingston's and Bruce Brown's *Windows 2000 Secrets*, published by IDG Books. Also, if you have an older PC (more than a year or so), it is NOT a good candidate for installing Windows 2000.

Following are a few more items you may want to consider before you start an upgrade:

✦ Widen your knowledge of Windows 98 (or other system you wish to install) by using sources beyond just the popular press. You might find a comprehensive list of recommended actions, such as those presented in this list.

✦ Check your system against the Windows 98 or other OS requirements.

✦ Back up all of your data.

✦ Create a Windows 95 (your present OS) startup disk, in case you have to revert to the original operating system. However, if you are not careful, you can make it nearly impossible to go back. One major example would be reformatting or converting your hard disk to the new file system (FAT-32 or NTFS) which would prevent you from going back.

✦ Uninstall antivirus programs.

✦ Remove older disk-compression software, such as Stacker. This means that you will be uncompressing that drive, and you will have less space for the new installation.

✦ Give your system as much free space as possible. Remove nonessential applications.

✦ Run SCANDISK. This is important because Windows 98 will halt an ongoing installation if it runs into disk drive problems, corrupted files, or directories, and so forth, and you may not be able to start over or recover easily from this problem.

✦ Make sure you have your driver disks and CD-ROMs ready. Windows 98 makes good use of drivers.

Our experience has told us to go even further. Installing Windows 98 over Windows 95 magnified every problem we ever had with Windows 95. Installing Windows 98 over a "clean system"—only DOS—gave Windows 98 a clear runway, and the installation process took full advantage of it. Even though Windows 98 can take up more than double the space of a typical Windows 95 installation, it really did take less time to install. However, the initial release of Windows 98 was a little more stable than Windows 95, but it ran slower. Windows 98/SE fixed most of the problems slowing down Windows 98, and it is now the best version of Windows for the nonprofessional environment. Windows Me may take over that position once it is released *and* has received post release upgrades, which Microsoft products always require.

Following are some additional Windows 98 installation suggestions:

✦ You may have to redetect your modem because Windows 98 does not always "catch" its presence.

✦ You may want to use the FAT32 method of storing your files. If you think you might have to go back to an older version of Windows or DOS, it may not be worth the hassle of not having direct access to your hard drive because older systems cannot read files stored using FAT32. What this means is that there is no way back to an older operating environment if you choose to increase your drive space using the FAT32 file system. Your only alternative will be to wipe the disk drive, reformat, and then do a clean installation of the older operating environment. Hopefully, you'll have a complete backup of that older operating system and your full data/program backup!

Windows 98 really does give you the feeling of being on the Web. Windows, being painted on the screen, leaves the impression you are loading a page from an Internet site. Not to spoil the fun, but this should raise a red flag by telling you to be more observant. For example, what if you pasted a sensitive document into what you thought was your word processor and when you went to hit the Save button, you discover too late that you hit the Send button instead, e-mailing that really sensitive information to a competitor. This is not too far-fetched—we know someone who did this!

On a 486 system, Windows 98's screen painting seems to cause the program to run much slower than Windows 95. But this is not the case. We did some timing comparisons. Windows 98 really is faster.

Windows 98 is even more stable than Windows 95. It is not quite as stable as Windows NT, but it does offer more isolation between the programs and objects in your system than any previous, non-NT version of Windows.

Once all of the preparation is completed, the Windows 98 installation is pretty straightforward. As with Windows 95, you have to pay attention to what you are and are not installing on your computer. Aside from the information you need to provide that identifies your computer and its environment as well as your personal information, Windows 98 takes care of the rest. Just take a look at the startup installation screen in Figure 8-1. It gives you the impression of the Web interface that continues through installation and that continues after the installation is complete.

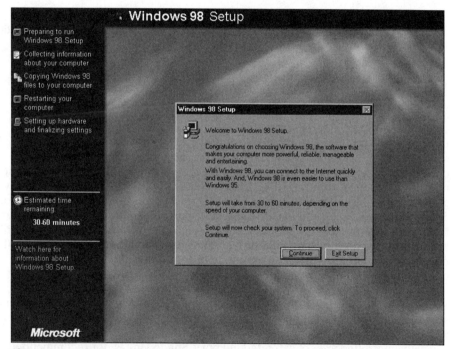

Figure 8-1: Windows 98 installation

Upgrading for Performance

Proper and efficient operation of Windows and most graphical user environments depends on four aspects of your system:

    ✦ Memory—for program loading and multitasking program swapping

    ✦ CPU type and speed—for program processing and memory control

✦ Hard disk space and speed—for program loading and swapping

✦ Video display adapter data path, video chipset, video memory, and speed

Typically, you may not have enough of any of these, individually or together, in order to be satisfied with your system, but there are ways to improve on what you have. The typical end-user, entry-level, off-the-shelf PC system intended for running Windows today has the following minimum specifications:

✦ Pentium-class CPU running at 450 MHz or higher

✦ 64–128MB of SDRAM

✦ A 10GB hard drive with 8–10 millisecond access time

✦ A Super Video Graphics Array (SVGA) video-adapter capable of at least 1,280 × 1,024-pixel resolution and 16- or 24-bit color depth, containing 8–16MB of video RAM

Memory

Memory is the food of graphical and multitasking environments, and these environments need much food during their operations. The more memory the better. For the rare (nongraphical) word processing and spreadsheet uses, 16–32MB of total system RAM is adequate. For graphics programs, larger spreadsheets and databases, and desktop publishing, 32–64MB of total system RAM is a must. The maximum that most users need at the present time is 64–128MB of RAM. However, graphics designers, system developers, and other power users will be much more efficient if they have a system with a fast processor and nearly unlimited memory. For server systems, 128–256MB is typical, though servers with more than 1GB of memory are becoming common. Although memory is not the only issue, it must be configured and used properly, requiring proper CMOS setup and a reliable memory manager.

Your system's CMOS setup may allow control over caching system ROM memory areas, caching CPU instructions (internal and/or external caches), and reserving RAM (for shadowing). Shadowing speeds up system operation by setting aside a specially controlled area of extended memory. Shadowing is not recommended, in deference to caching ROMs (a subtle but important difference to your system and Windows configurations) and enabling internal CPU and external instruction caching. A 64K external cache is quite adequate for a 486 CPU, and it certainly is better than none at all. For a Pentium system, 256K of external cache is a minimal performance requirement, and Pentium systems may have up to 1MB of cache. You simply have to keep that CPU fed!

HIMEM.SYS is a memory manager required and installed by Windows to provide 64K of high memory area in which DOS or some applications may load. This leaves more, lower memory for applications, and it provides management of your extended memory, converting it to what is then indicated as XMS memory.

HIMEM.SYS attempts to turn off the use of any shadow RAM for your system's ROM. Some systems may not operate correctly. If so, you will have to use the /SHADOW:off or other command-line options on the HIMEM.SYS line in your CONFIG.SYS file.

HIMEM.SYS does not load if the PATH in the DEVICE= line in CONFIG.SYS is incorrect or if the file is missing from your system.

CPU

While the CPU is not the most significant performance-determining factor in your system (a slow disk drive can take as much time to retrieve data from the platters into memory with a 100 MHz CPU as with a 500 MHz CPU), as more and more people explore the world of graphics and video with their home PCs, they'll definitely want a "hot" processor.

There are many ways to get that hot processor, and not all of them are healthy for your system. One way is to use a CPU that can be overclocked—such as some Intel Celeron CPUs and most AMD chips. But check the specs and what others have to say by visiting the www.sysopt.com or www.motherboards.org Web sites for details. All we can say is to choose your CPU and system board for all-around, maximum flexibility. There is no sense in getting a system board with a top-end CPU clock of 450 MHz if someday you could easily want an 800–1,000 MHz CPU chip. Similarly, there is little reason to scrimp $50 on a CPU chip in hopes of clocking it to the next level because sometimes it just does not work—or, if it does work, it literally may run so hot that it damages your system.

If you cannot get a new system board and CPU, at least check the specifications on your present system board to see what is the fastest CPU it will support and go that route.

Caution

Running your system at speeds it is not intended to support may cause heat-related failures of one or more system-board components or of the CPU.

Disk drives

A larger, faster disk drive is always desirable, especially for those who cannot bear to archive those old programs and files to floppy disks and for those who are tired of hearing the drive rattle and thrash for minutes at a time whenever a Windows program performs any operation. With drive prices falling well below fractions of a cent per megabyte and speeds running at or better than 9-millisecond access times (a lower number means faster access), you cannot avoid buying a new or additional drive.

New Monitor? Avoid Eyestrain

Upgrading your monitor will be considerably more expensive, maybe more so than the entire system itself, but your eyes may thank you in decreased eyestrain. Do not settle for a monitor with pixel or dot pitch greater than .28 millimeters. Above .28mm, that display begins to look unfocussed or fuzzy at resolutions of 800×600 and above. A .35, .38, .42, or .45mm dot pitch on a 15-, 17-, or 20-inch monitor will distract you to no end and increase your eyestrain. Such monitors are cheaper than higher quality models, but more expensive as far as your enjoyment and productivity. An unhealthy monitor is no bargain.

Video display and adapter

A couple of years ago, you were probably impressed with 256 colors and 800×600-display resolution in that new 16-bit Diamond video card with 1MB of RAM and an NEC Multisync 2 monitor. Now you have to see the difference that a new 128-bit, 32MB AGP video accelerator card makes. Plug in that 17- or 19-inch flat-screen monitor and take your system to the dazzling sharpness and speed of 1,280×1,024 with true colors. You will wish your television set was as sharp!

An older 8- or 16-bit video card with 256K or 512KB of video RAM, capable of only 16 colors at 640×480 or 800×600 resolution, is simply inadequate for the task of the operating system and multimedia tools available today. You need an upgrade. Even a 14-inch monitor seems like new with a new video card. Video card upgrades are relatively inexpensive, on the order of $40 to $150, depending on the make, model, and upgrade-capability of the card. Many cards with only 1MB of video RAM can be upgraded to 2MB or 4MB, which you might consider if you are going to use display resolutions higher than 800×600. The reason for the upgrade is not just display capabilities, but to take advantage of new circuits and driver technology that work better with and for Windows, and to get video data from the CPU to the screen on a faster data bus. Much work is being done for Windows 95/98/Me and NT/2000 to enhance the software and drivers for video and all multimedia performance to that of dedicated video games and real-time video presentations.

Summary

No matter which OS or user interface you choose or are required to use, it is important to understand that each one is being installed on your PC hardware platform. Each OS has its own list of supported devices. Each has different device drivers to accommodate supported devices. Each has its own installation procedures and capabilities. Each provides its own advantages and challenges. However, the hardware that combines to make your PC is the same for each of these OS alternatives, and that hardware must work together, regardless of which OS you install.

Multitasking, multimedia, and graphical programs, no matter which OS you use, require much higher computer speeds, better screens, more memory, and thus, more complexity than can be supported by the original DOS running on PCs. DOS by itself can be unforgiving of mistakes, and it requires you to be more knowledgeable of commands and limitations. However, it can be fast at many functions because it has no graphics- or multimedia-processing overhead. It is with user interfaces, if nowhere else, that a personal computer begins to take on and reflect the preferences and personality of its user.

This chapter has discussed user operating systems, from the original DOS to newest addition to the Windows family, Windows Me. It has mentioned Windows NT, 2000, and Unix-related operating systems, but chapters individually devoted to each of these systems delve into more detail. The focus of this chapter has been on small-business and personal use of the PC. Even from this perspective, the tremendous history of increased capabilities and performance is apparent.

Just remember, all of these environments, no matter which one you choose—DOS, Windows, or even Unix—require a solid hardware foundation. No computer is stronger than its weakest configuration. This cannot be stressed enough. You can set up and configure your computer to be the best fit to your requirements.

✦   ✦   ✦

Windows for the Enterprise

The primary focus of this chapter is the preparation for and completion of the installation of Windows NT and 2000, either from scratch or as an upgrade from a previous version of Windows.

Windows is, of course, the most prevalent operating system for many small- to medium-sized offices today. Which version you use can make a significant difference in your installation, planning, and applications.

For desktops there are the usual Windows 95, 98, 98SE, and Millennium (Me), though some organizations have chosen Windows NT Workstation and now 2000 Professional for stability, performance, and security.

For servers, most of us are probably still running some level of Windows NT 4.0 Server, pending a transition, forced due to application changes or otherwise, to Windows 2000 Server or Advanced Server. Windows NT or 2000 are perhaps the easiest way for homes and small offices to establish a server system for file and print sharing, or even to serve up Web pages and e-mail. Of course, Unix (FreeBSD) and Linux are making great headway in both business and home server usage, but that is a story for another place and time.

This chapter is not intended to cover enterprise desktops and servers in tremendous depth, especially because networking, either for simple print and file-sharing services or moderately complex Web sites, is a fairly involved field. Instead, this chapter provides a quick guide to issues you should be aware of and solutions that you should pursue by further using Microsoft and other resources.

Microsoft Windows NT Workstation and 2000 Professional

There are few reasons you would want to spend two or three times as much for one desktop operating system versus another, though the security and stability of your systems are reasons enough to consider desktop versions of Windows NT or 2000. The NT or new technology-based operating systems provide an enhanced level of 32-bit architecture and performance that enables them to have much better control over access to hardware and better control between applications and the system overall.

An operating system such as NT, or even Unix, that takes complete control over the hardware of the host system reduces incompatibilities between hardware, driver software, and the operating system—potentially making everything more stable. This also reduces the chances that an application, working within the operating system, could corrupt, crash, or disable hardware, which leads to an additional level of security.

Until Windows 2000 came out, Windows NT was available for several hardware platforms. In addition to what is known as *x86* or Intel-based systems, versions were available for Motorola Power PC, MIPS, and Digital Equipment's Alpha systems. Being an entirely 32-bit operating system enables a system to accommodate and maintain better control over more system memory and interapplication communications and improves performance—the operating system has more resources available to it faster, and it does not have to shift gears and bog down in order to handle 8- or 16-bit applications.

What you need

The basic system requirements for installing the workstation versions of NT or 2000 are roughly the same as for the consumer versions of Windows—a blazingly fast CPU with gigabytes of memory and unlimited available hard disk space (just kidding).

The following are the PC system requirements for Windows NT 4.0 Workstation:

✦ Personal computer with a Pentium or faster processor

✦ 16MB of memory; 32MB recommended

✦ Typical available hard disk space required: approximately 110MB

✦ CD-ROM drive or access to a CD-ROM over a computer network

✦ Video Graphics Array (VGA) or higher-resolution display adapter

✦ Microsoft Mouse or compatible pointing device

Here are the additional PC system requirements for Windows 2000 Professional:

✦ 133 MHz or higher Pentium-compatible CPU; also supports single and dual CPU systems

✦ 64MB of RAM recommended minimum; more memory generally improves responsiveness

✦ 2GB hard disk with a minimum of 650MB of free space

✦ A CD-ROM drive, a VGA display, and a mouse

If you can find Microsoft's system requirements for these operating systems, from which these lists were created, you will notice they seem incomplete or inconsistent. The reasons for this are changes in available systems — today almost no one uses just a Pentium CPU, and there are several non-Pentium (Intel) equivalents that work just as well in most cases (Cyrix, AMD). Also, CPU speeds tend to double or even triple within a year or so of the release of an operating system. When Windows NT 4.0 first came out, a Pentium PRO 180 was about the fastest CPU available. By the time most users had upgraded to NT 4, the slowest CPU available clocked in at more than 250 MHz.

Another example of apparent inconsistency is visible in Microsoft's list for Windows 2000 requirements. The list does not include a CD-ROM drive, a VGA, or a mouse — Microsoft assumes that anybody who wanted Windows 2000 would have these on their system.

If you install Windows NT or 2000 on a system with the minimum requirements, you quickly will be disappointed with the slow performance. The system will run, but if you are a Type A personality, you will quickly want to go back to DOS or perhaps you will seriously consider Linux as your next step. We offer a few enhancements to the original requirements lists by suggesting at least the following:

✦ A 266 MHz CPU — preferably a Pentium II or Pentium III — to obtain the larger L1 and L2 caches.

✦ 64MB, if not 128MB, of SDRAM for the desktop.

✦ Peripheral Component Interconnect (PCI) local bus VGA adapter with graphics acceleration. Accelerated Graphics Port (AGP) is not well supported on Windows NT, but it runs okay on Windows 2000.

✦ 2GB of free hard drive space. You will probably want to copy the installation files from the CD to the hard drive for faster configuration, and with seven levels of service packs and various hot fixes to apply, you will want to keep those handy, as well.

✦ Consider an ATA-33, an ATA-66, or a FastSCSI-2 hard drive with 9ms or faster access time — you will love the speed for all of the swap file operations that go on. Be careful of the system board you expect to run the ATA-33 or ATA-66 drives on — NT driver support is sparse for the UltraDMA modes under Windows NT, but this has improved with Windows 2000.

Allow a couple of hours for the installation. And allow time to find all of the configuration items (especially networking features) that are tucked away in various places, such as in drivers provided by Microsoft, in updates from manufacturers, in updates on Microsoft's Web site, and especially in drivers for older devices because neither Windows NT nor Windows 2000 are particularly fond of older hardware and drivers. Also, be aware that Windows NT and 2000 are arranged differently than Windows 95/98/SE and Millennium.

What, no DOS?

Windows NT is a high-end, power-user, not-for-everybody type of operating system. Something that you will notice about Windows NT and 2000, that you will also surely have discovered about Millennium is that no DOS or real mode is available at the startup of the operating system. This means that there is no CONFIG.SYS file; thus, there are no device drivers. This also means that there is no AUTOEXEC.BAT, so there are no tricky resident programs. Windows NT 4.0 and earlier versions have limited Plug-and-Play support, and they are rather particular about the number of different hardware devices supported. In addition to removing real-mode support, Windows NT attempts to do away with the basic input/output system (BIOS). It prefers to handle all hardware operations and access within the operating system.

This also means that any device drivers or special software needed to accommodate DOS-based or other special-mode games and graphics programs cannot be run on the system before it boots to Windows—the result is that you will lose the ability to run many old and some new graphical programs. To retain the ability to use these programs, you may have to consider configuring the system to dual boot between Windows NT/2000 and DOS or Windows 95/98/SE (but likely not Millennium).

Windows NT 4.0 looks much like Windows 95 and 98, and Windows 2000 and Millennium share some desktop graphics enhancements (though we prefer those in Windows 2000). NT enables applications to run faster and to share some resources between systems in its network environment.

NT file systems

Microsoft really mixes things up among the original DOS FAT-12 and FAT-16 file systems; the FAT-32 file system, introduced in Windows 95 OSR2; and Windows NT's NT file system (NTFS). FAT-32 is supported only on Windows 95 OSR2 and later and Windows 2000. NTFS is supported only on Windows NT and 2000. If you plan to configure your system for dual booting, you have to account for which file system(s) you will partition your disk drive with, if you want both operating systems to access the same files on the hard disk.

NTFS is much more secure and efficient than the FAT file systems. There is no way to access NTFS files booting the system with a DOS or non-NT disk because this requires Windows NT, and NT does not boot from disk. Similarly, you cannot access a FAT-32 file system with NT or versions of Windows prior to Windows 95 OSR2.

Built to network

The networking features of Windows 95/98/SE/Me and NT/2000, as workgroup tools or as part of an existing network configuration, are now more intuitive and easier to handle by intermediate to advanced users with some network experience.

Networking is a good thing in most cases, where people have to work together on shared projects, and sharing is the reason many people take their first steps into networking. Beginning with Windows for Workgroups, and greatly enhanced with Windows 95, small networks became relatively easy to setup. Unfortunately, sharing files and printers among only Windows 9x or NT workstations puts a tremendous burden on the processing and disk resources of the workstations sharing the resources. Also, any crash of a user's PC that is sharing resources causes all other users loss of that resource. At some point, setting up a server becomes necessary.

Caution   Typically, you will use only the Transmission Control Protocol/Internet Protocol (TCP/IP) network protocol with Windows, but be aware that Windows NetBIOS access to shared files and devices is available through TCP/IP, creating a security risk to your network if it is connected to the Internet.

To block this security hole, you can have your network firewall prevent IP Port 139 traffic between the Internet and your local area network (LAN). Or you can add the NetBIOS Enhanced User Interface (NetBEUI) protocol to the network configuration, bind NetBIOS to it, and unbind NetBIOS from TCP/IP. You can also set filtering on TCP/IP so that it only allows the IP ports and TCP protocols necessary for this system to communicate with other systems on your LAN or the Internet. A more extensive discussion about this is provided in Chapter 11 and on Gibson Research Corporation's Web site (www.grc.com).

When a system is to be networked, a few choices about workgroups and domains must be considered. The "Microsoft Windows NT and 2000 Servers" section discusses these choices.

Upgrading Your Desktop to Windows NT or 2000

If you get nothing else out of this chapter, here is a trick that will save you hundreds of hours trying to get any PC system working correctly. If you have the Windows NT/2000 CD-ROM, go to the \SUPPORT\HQTOOL directory and follow the directions in the README file. You will end up with a 3½-inch bootable disk that was designed to tell you if Windows NT/2000 can be installed on your computer. What you really get is just about the ultimate tool to diagnose the startup condition of your PC.

Here is an example. We were just about to install Windows NT 4.0 on a computer in order to upgrade from Windows 98 to Windows NT 2000. (This upgrade is discussed in more detail in the for the "Troubleshooting Windows NT and 2000" section.) We fed the PC the Windows NT Hardware Detection Tool (NTHQ) diskette, rebooted, and flipped through the multiple screens of information about every piece of hardware in the system. The report NTHQ generated contained tons of technical details, such as interrupt requests (IRQs) used, device capabilities, and overlapping resource assignments. Buried in this information we found a notice that the motherboard had virus protection implemented for the boot sector of the hard drive. That is normally good. However, when Windows NT installs, it modifies the boot sector of the hard drive. Therefore, Windows NT will not install on this PC until that feature is disabled. That bit of information probably saved us many hours of trying to figure out why this wonderful system that had already accepted everything from DOS to Windows 98 would not accept Windows NT.

Here is a copy of the section of the NTHQ.TXT file created by the NTHQ disk:

```
Hardware Detection Tool For Windows NT 4.0

Master Boot Sector Virus Protection Check
Hard Disk Boot Sector Protection: On.
Cannot write to MBR. You can not install Windows with it on.
```

One thing the report did not tell us was that Windows NT would not accept the video-screen driver that we were able to use with Windows 95 and 98 to get the maximum resolution out of the old Shamrock video monitor. On this old Super Video Graphics Array (SVGA) monitor, Windows NT would not support resolutions above 640×480. Higher resolutions would require replacing both the video adapter and monitor.

You do not need Windows NT in order to use the NTHQ disk created by this HQTOOL procedure. The bootable disk works on any computer with a 486 or higher processor, at least 12MB of memory, and a 3½-inch disk drive! No respectable PC repair toolkit should be without one of these wonderful disks!

If you need more information about this mysterious and wonderful world of IRQs and avoiding system conflicts, you may want to buy Jim Aspinwall's book, *IRQ, DMA, & I/O* (IDG Books Worldwide, Inc.). The HQTOOL gives you all the information about the hardware installed in your system. Jim's book covers the whole field, not just what is in your computer.

Once compatible hardware and software have been established, and all IRQ or memory location conflicts have been resolved, Windows NT can be installed so that there is little that can go wrong. However, if the system becomes irretrievably corrupt (in other words, you cannot find, fix, or replace the corrupted files, programs, or settings), the only option is to reinstall. Unfortunately, Windows NT 4.0 does not have the capability to install over itself or any other operating environment. Windows 2000 is supposed to provide this capability. However, we have not confirmed this to our complete satisfaction. In fact, all of the data on the drive to which Windows NT is installed will be lost because the NT installation begins by configuring and formatting the drive. What an incentive to keep up-to-date backups!

Never fear. The troubles with installing Windows NT on our example computer were not over yet. Windows NT is not particularly fond of Plug-and-Play (PnP) adapters. However, when you have old, new, and nonstandard PnP devices in the same system, Windows NT has more than fits. We almost spent money on a new CD-ROM drive. We thought a 6x speed CD-ROM drive that is not more than a couple of years old would have no problems. It gave us some minor problems under Windows 95 and 98, with the hard drive and CD-ROM haggling over grabbing the primary Integrated Device Electronics (IDE) port. But, at first, Windows NT did not even want to deal with the problem. The problem? Windows NT installs by booting from a disk, loads some files to your hard drive, and then it enables the CD-ROM to complete the rest of the installation. Apparently, all of the conflicting PnP, nonstandard PnP, and pre-ATAPI devices were not cooperating. The BIOS identified some of the devices (the motherboard's BIOS date is July 20, 1998) but not the nonstandard ones. The solution? The CD-ROM is now using the secondary IDE connection under Windows NT. The hard drive and CD-ROM are on different cables, so there is little chance of a conflict.

NOWindows NT/2000 does not support all the hardware devices you can install on older systems. Because of the lack of support in running older software (Windows, as well as DOS!) under Windows NT, you cannot assume that you will be able to use your legacy hardware. The NTHQ bootable disk and the report it creates refer to the "HCL," which is Microsoft's Hardware Compatibility List. If a device is not on the HCL, chances are you will not be able to use it. Or if you can use it, the device may not have full functionality. From this point on, no more problems arose during the installation.

However, Windows 2000 offered an entirely new challenge. The program run by the installation procedure did not detect that the BIOS was one version too old, and this was not discovered until Windows 2000 had already taken control of the computer. It would boot, it but could not complete the installation. At least not until the BIOS was upgraded. Thank goodness for FLASH ROM and for the BIOS manufacturer's Web site (Intel), where files were available to create a bootable diskette that we used to save the old BIOS (just in case the new BIOS didn't work either) and then upgrade the BIOS that was in place. From that point on, the Windows 2000 installation completed smoothly.

Microsoft Windows NT and 2000 Servers

With Windows NT, Microsoft brought networking and sharing of computing resources out of huge, cold computer rooms and into the closets and under the desks of many small offices, even into our homes. Good or bad, for various reasons, not the least of which are availability and ease of use, Windows NT is typically the first server for most people interested in taking their computing work beyond a few desktop systems. More people probably begin their first Internet Web site presence with a Windows NT server than with Linux, though that is changing.

Setting up a Windows NT or 2000 server begins with roughly the same system requirements as any Windows PC, as listed here.

The basic NT 4.0 Server system requirements are the following:

✦ 486/33 Pentium or Pentium PRO

✦ 16MB of memory; 32MB recommended

✦ 125MB of disk space

The basic 2000 Server system, additional requirements are as follows:

✦ 133 MHz or higher Pentium-compatible CPU. Windows 2000 Server supports up to four CPUs on one machine. Advanced Server supports up to eight CPUs.

✦ 256MB of RAM recommended minimum. 128MB minimum supported. 4GB maximum supported.

✦ 2GB hard disk with a minimum 1GB of free space.

Note   Additional free hard disk space is required if you install over a network.

Microsoft assumes that you know your hardware should include a VGA video and a mouse, and you probably want to include a network card, otherwise a server has no way to act as a server. Windows NT and 2000 use memory very well—much of it. As with Windows NT and 2000 workstations, you will quickly find that the minimum requirements seem to barely boot up and run the operating system. The minimums leave little CPU, memory, or disk space available for applications. Servers should have at least a 233 MHz CPU, 64MB of RAM, and a gigabyte or two of free space for minimal file- and printer-sharing performance for a few (10–20) users. Add more users, more resources shared, more server-based applications or file storage, and you will want more RAM and free disk space for the system as soon as possible.

I don't think we've ever tried running Windows NT 4.0 on anything less than a 150 MHz Pentium and 32MB of RAM—a 486 and 16MB seems so inadequate. In fact, just such a system runs a couple of our low-traffic Web and mail servers, and that's about it. If miraculously we begin to get more Internet traffic, we'll have an excuse to upgrade the hardware — probably to 300 MHz or faster, 128MB of RAM. We can then retire the old, slow disk drives in favor of newer models.

If an office grows beyond 20 people and edges up to 100, shared services will need to be moved to different servers — printers on one server, file sharing on another. Internet connection always should be totally separate. The office should also consider fast CPUs and 128–256MB of RAM — typically with a system designed to be a server, such as a Compaq ProLiant, a Dell PowerEdge, and so on. Anything less and the office risks reliability and performance — and the tempers and wrath of its employees.

Setting up Windows NT servers

Windows NT may not be the best choice of server operating system for hosting an Internet presence, but it is easy. And it makes even more sense for a small- or medium-sized office, Internet-connection or not, because in many ways Windows NT and 2000 resemble the familiar Windows 9x desktop environment. As with NT Workstation and 2000 Professional, resemblance is where Windows 9x desktops and Windows NT/2000 part ways.

Servers rapidly begin to handle the bulk of most businesses — e-mails, shared files, accounting data, Web sites, and so on. As such, servers must be considered with the weight and impact of your entire business in mind. So if we haven't yet mentioned it, or if you've forgotten backups, it is time to get serious — add a fast and adequately sized tape, CD-ROM, or DVD backup device to your minimum system requirements.

By all means, do not neglect considerations for securing your servers, especially if any of the servers are connected to the Internet. Install hardware or software firewall products, properly configure the servers according to Microsoft's recommendations (www.microsoft.com/technet/security/iischk.asp), apply all recommended security patches, and monitor the systems regularly for possible intrusions.

While we have a few pointers, our scope here does not lend itself to complete server system installation. For the bulk of Windows NT and 2000 server considerations, we heartily recommend IDG Books' *Windows NT Server 4.0 Secrets* and *Windows 2000 Server Secrets* for their scope, depth, and experienced coverage of planning for, installing, and maintaining these systems.

NT workgroups and domains

A possibly confusing aspect of networking Windows systems, now that the Internet is so commonly equated with networking, is that of Windows workgroups and domains. These terms and features came about with respect to Windows NT in its early days. They are still relevant today when configuring a LAN or a wide area network (WAN) connection between systems that must interact, but with a few new precautions due to the release of Windows 2000 and its Active Directory service.

Windows workgroups

Workgroups are typically set up for small networks with one or a few Windows NT servers. For example, you may establish the accounting department as one workgroup and the engineering department as another workgroup. The respective workstations and servers set up for these separate workgroups cannot share file or print resources across the network with each other. If you want to share resources, the disadvantage to using discrete workgroups should be obvious. In other words, printers and other network resources you may want to share, should not be "hidden" in a Workgroup.

In a small network, it is better to stick with one workgroup and establish distinct user groups on the server, which provides access only to specific shared resources. You have to set up each user on each server you add to the network, creating more maintenance work.

Instead, you could establish separate Windows NT domains that can be set to trust each other and share some security information. You could then maintain different user groups with specific resource access rights. This makes the process of controlling access to shared resources more manageable.

Windows NT domains

Workgroups are still workgroups, but until Windows 2000 came along, Windows NT domains had nothing to do with Internet domains — the familiar .net, .org, .gov, .edu, and .com domain names associated with Web sites and e-mail servers.

With Windows NT, NT domains are a term associated with breaking a network into secure zones with different, but possibly shared, security exchanges as a way to control and manage access to resources. Windows NT domains are in a sense superworkgroups. Windows NT domains enable users to establish a hierarchy of global and local workgroup entities.

A network can have one or more domains, depending upon how a user wants to break apart workgroups, resources, and network security. You can have a master domain for all users, and subdomains for specific areas and workgroups. You can elect to have one or more domains trust each other so that they can share security information and resources. Domains can become complex in a large enterprise, but for most of users, a single domain works fine.

Windows 2000 domains

The Windows 2000 server sets the entire Windows NT architecture on its ear and introduces Internet-centric architectures and issues on your network scheme. With Windows 2000, Microsoft has embraced (although some may call it a stranglehold) merging Windows NT domains with Internet domains on local networks. While this sounds like a great advantage, Microsoft has built in the need to be the controller of the network, which, of course, conflicts with many non-Windows 2000 network controllers, capabilities, and devices.

This shift in Windows NT network architecture is meant to address a couple of Microsoft's concerns and to address the reality of the way people network today. Specifically, Microsoft needed to compete in the large enterprise market where Unix has held the top spot for large server-based data systems. Furthermore, as business has embraced the Internet for interoffice and global communications, it seems logical that Windows NT should shift to work more like the Internet infrastructure.

Unfortunately, the new Windows 2000 server domain scheme goes a step or two beyond just Internet-level compatibility. It imposes itself on existing Unix-based, Internet-centric network designs. Windows 2000 now wants to be top dog in network design, which probably has Unix system administrators and network engineers throwing fits in their back rooms and staff meetings.

To use domain-level network segregation and security under Windows 2000, you must plan around TCP/IP networking, Internet domain names, Domain Name Services, and the Internet at large. All of this is to suit Microsoft's new Active Directory services for improved, though perhaps more complex than necessary, network management tasks.

Active Directory

Directory services are not new to computing or networking. Unix and Novell NetWare systems have benefited from the Lightweight Directory Access Protocol (LDAP) for years, and NetWare, since version 4, has used some form of directory-service-like management. With the Internet Engineering Task Force's (IETF's) LDAP standard, directory services provide a centralized repository or database that contains sets of network properties, available shared resources, secure access lists, and more. This is a good service for large network environments, but it is prohibitively complex for small- and medium-sized networks.

The alternative for a small network is to configure its Windows2000 servers as standalone servers under one or more workgroups and to manage each server separately. This is less efficient than Windows NT domains, but much less complicated than becoming involved with Active Directory. Of course, a couple of standalone servers may be all that you need, and concerns about Active Directory in this context may be superfluous. If you decide to upgrade from Windows NT to 2000 under these conditions, you will do fine.

Caution   We should mention one last caution about Windows 2000's Active Directory. If you implement it, be aware that you will no longer be able to use any of the directory-type services you have set up in Windows NT. Also, Windows 2000's Active Directory will not cooperate with the directory services in either a Unix or a NetWare network. With Windows 2000 Active Directory, you either give total control over to Windows 2000, or it does not work. It will not work with your Unix systems, anyway.

Troubleshooting Windows NT and 2000

Here are some things to look for when you are faced with server or workstation problems.

Symptoms

▶ Your Windows NT/2000 server or workstation will not boot or work properly.

Suspects

▶ You have already tried the following:

- Reviewing your system for IRQ and memory port conflicts

- Restoring the Registry

- Scanning your system for virus infection

- Removing suspect hardware

- Uninstalling hardware and software added to your system since it last worked correctly

- Reinstalling programs

- Booting from your Emergency Startup disk created when you installed Windows NT (and which you have been updating as you have added new hardware and software!)

- And, if you have the ability, editing the Registry and other configuration files

Solutions

▶ Reinstall Windows NT/2000. Hopefully, you have backups of everything you cannot install because Windows NT/2000 will format your drive before continuing the installation. However, you can try the new installation recovery feature in Windows 2000. We have not tested it under enough conditions to state that it will work every time. If you have more than one drive, installing Windows NT/2000 on the boot drive and installing everything else (programs and data) on the second and subsequent drives makes reinstallation easier. You will still have to reinstall all of your software (especially software that stores important parts in the Windows NT directories), but your data and some of your configuration will be preserved on the other drives. Just make sure you have a current backup of your Windows registry!

▶ One way to make sure your system is ready for a Windows NT/2000 installation is to create the NTHQ disk by using the MAKEDISK.BAT program in the Support\HQTOOLS directory on your Windows NT/2000 installation CD-ROM. The NTHQ disk is a DOS disk that boots your computer, collects information about the installed hardware, and checks your system for potential installation problems. See the README.TXT file in the Support\HQTOOLS directory. It will confirm the steps to create the disk, and it supplies information about how to interpret the information it reports. Just make sure you have the latest possible BIOS for your PC—*before* you attempt the upgrade!

Summary

We've just scratched the surface about systems and considerations for advanced workstations and servers for larger more secure network requirements. Networking and the Internet are covered in the next two chapters.

You may want to read IDG's *Windows 2000 Secrets* and *Windows 2000 Server Secrets* in order to better appreciate the complexities and nuances of deploying Windows 2000 as a desktop or as a server platform.

The good news is that once you have a good installation of Windows NT/2000 and have completed all of your software installations and configuration, you should encounter few problems. Of course, all of this depends upon having a good hardware base on which to perform that installation and for that hardware base to meet all of the requirements that your software expects from your PC. Keeping your new technology system up to date with the all-too-frequent Service Release updates is also important.

The next two chapters examine the reasons for connecting PCs via Networks. The chapters delve into networks in general and the Internet, specifically.

✦　　✦　　✦

Networking

A network may be as small as two PCs connected with a serial or parallel cable, or a dial-up network connection via modems. Two or more PCs may be connected using network adapters, cables, and appropriate software to enable sharing of files and printers as a small workgroup. Many more PCs and other computer systems may be added to the workgroup with more cabling and network hubs and routers. Remote-control software may be installed to enable using software from one PC on another. A server may be added to the workgroup providing a common shared resource for file and application storage and printer sharing. Routers and additional connectivity equipment may be added to connect a home or office with another, or to the Internet. We cover the Internet options and common problems in Chapter 11. Connecting your office network to the Internet is a way to become a part of the largest network in the world. Unfortunately, networks are just as subject to trouble and the need for troubleshooting as any other combination of hardware and software.

Networking Basics

We can trace the development of networking back to the early 1960s and the use of terminals to large, time-share computer systems. In the early days of the PC, the 1980s, we used terminal or communication programs to emulate terminals to connect our PCs to mainframe and mini-computers. We used the file capture and send capabilities of the PC to get more work done in a shorter time — saving a lot of typing time.

Let us consider *networking* to be nearly any connection that enables users to share files or services between two or more computer systems. We cover other ways for making the connections in Chapters 11, 21, and 22; our coverage here begins with general file sharing and access rights, since these are the primary reasons for connecting multiple computers.

Once we have covered the essence of file sharing and security, we can begin to tie these elements together with networking hardware and software to build workgroups and larger network systems. Then the troubleshooting begins.

Legacy file sharing

In the early 1980s, we used various communication tools on our PCs to access files on other PC systems. These initial tools were DOS-based applications such as PC-TALK, ProComm, COM-AND, and LapLink. These applications and others like them provided hosting for connections from other PCs with similar connection software installed to enable copying files between systems using file transfer protocols such as XMODEM and ZMODEM. Bulletin board systems (BBSs) are related to this type of software, too.

In the mid 1980s we began to use products with remote control functionality such as pcAnywhere, Reachout, Carbon Copy, and CoSession. These programs, and others like them, enabled one PC to provide keyboard input to, and view screen output from, another PC, as well as supporting file sharing and program access.

Typically, these tools used a serial port connection, either through a direct null modem cable connection or over phone lines via modem. To transfer files directly between systems, you were limited to between 1,200 and 19,200 bps data transfers over a serial cable connection or about five to ten times faster if the tool supported special parallel port interconnections. Although quite useful, these capabilities did not satisfy everyone's need for the fast connections supported only by true networking.

Network capabilities were developed for PCs very shortly after the PC was introduced (by about 1983), but few PCs had network interfaces or were connected to a network until a couple of years later. The early software tools, mentioned previously, did not recognize or support network connections. Networking was typically used for single offices carrying data for specific applications.

As technology advanced, the remote control applications began to support system-to-system connections via the Novell/NetWare protocol known as IPX/SPX. This was still quite short of true networking capabilities. You would have to copy files first to a commonly accessible network drive from the non-networked source system, and then copy the files to the networked target system (or the reverse to copy a file in the other direction). Merging file transfer and remote control tools with networking capabilities provided benefits but was nothing like the built-in network and file-sharing features supported by Windows 95, 98, NT, and 2000 that we take for granted today. While it took years for the Internet Protocol (TCP/IP — Transfer Control Program/Internet Protocol) to expand beyond its start in the academic and defense communities in the late 1960s, once the World Wide Web took hold in the early 1990s, networking began its unbelievable growth.

Today, networking, personal computing, and the Internet seem synonymous. By far, the most often used capabilities of networking are electronic mail, file sharing, file transfers, and browsing the Internet for interesting sites — other computers or Web pages. Increasing in popularity and usefulness are capabilities such as electronic commerce: marketing, banking, selling, and shopping. Business-to-business use of the Internet for expanding commerce, managing supply chains, and cutting the costs and time for developing and delivering new products is the latest and largest use of the Internet today.

Security

Protecting our systems and files has always been important and becomes more so as we consider exposing our PCs to more users by connecting to more systems with local area networks, wide area networks, and the Internet.

File transfer and remote-control host systems usually provided some form of logon — user name and password-based access security — and the capability to configure them to allow, deny, or limit access to a select group of files, disk drives, or programs. The level of security provided was adequate for most limited access systems, especially since just a few people knew the phone numbers or system names. Security has become a much greater concern since these individual host systems also have access to local networks and the Internet and due to the tremendous increase in the number of personal connections to the Internet.

With increased workgroup and Internet connectivity between systems, finding a specific system or any system at random, connected to the network, is relatively simple. Thus, tighter security must be implemented, monitored, and maintained on all systems. In purely network server-oriented systems, we usually trust that the local area network and server administrators will handle security and access rights for us, protecting individual and global information. As the pervasiveness of connections increases, this is surely not enough security.

We are, and should be, responsible for the security of our own PCs. Many companies prohibit dial-up remote access and the running of any kind of file transfer, remote control host, FTP host, or Web-server software on individual PCs from inside the company's network. This policy helps protect users and the company from information theft and other forms of unauthorized attacks. The deterrent is simple — employees lose their jobs if they violate security policies.

At home, the deterrent is not quite as harsh, but the potential for loss of data and damage can be just as significant. Although it may not seem like a big deal if your PC has a disk drive or printer setup that is freely shared with other trusted users, you should realize that systems can be penetrated and manipulated through weaknesses in operating system, networking, and host access software, things over which you have little control. You should not be paranoid about unauthorized access to your PC, but you should make security a deliberate part of the ways you use your computer and connect to other systems.

Simple Security Tips

In the absence of company (or even home) security guidelines, follow these basic rules for system access security under any circumstances:

✦ Pick a cryptic user name, especially for remote access systems — use a mix of alphabetical, numerical, and special symbol characters that is not in a dictionary (if allowed by the system to which you are connecting).

✦ *Always* pick a cryptic password — again, use a mix of alphabetical, numerical, and special symbol characters that is not in a dictionary or made up of common names, words, or numbers familiar to you that others might recognize.

✦ Change passwords often — every 30 to 90 days at least. Do not share your password with anyone, but if you must, change it as soon as possible afterward. Never use the same password twice or on different systems.

✦ Don't leave remote access, file sharing, or host access software running when it is not needed.

✦ Don't leave Windows 95/98/Me file and print sharing enabled on your system when it is not needed, especially if your system is ever connected to the Internet.

✦ Don't use Microsoft's NetBEUI protocol on systems connected to the Internet if you do not need it, or unless the firewall at your company or ISP blocks this protocol from outside access. NetBEUI is not carried on the Internet and using it can cause dial-up networking and routers to connect needlessly to service providers.

✦ If you regularly connect to the Internet with Windows 95, obtain and install the Dial-Up Networking version 1.3 with Winsock 2.0 update files from the Microsoft Web site to protect your system against common denial-of-service attacks across the Internet. Hackers target random and known IP addresses to see what happens just for fun — do not give them extra pleasure. Along the same lines, if you get a notification that a security problem has been discovered in operating system or other software you are using (make sure it is a valid notice), you should get the fix or update offered by the responsible company.

✦ If you must set up file and print sharing, host or remote access, carefully configure your system to provide the least amount of visibility and access to system resources. Providing full privileges to the root directories of your disk drives is asking for trouble, even through innocent mistakes. Assign a specific subdirectory (folder) to hold only those files that must be shared and leave the rest of the system inaccessible. Any file or print sharing makes your system vulnerable to access violations from outside systems through Windows' NetBIOS interface.

✦ Use virus protection software. Files transferred to your system by others may not be checked by the originator to be free of viruses.

✦ If you have an always-on Internet connection — via cable modem, xDSL, ISDN or other media — obtain, install, and keep up to date a personal/desktop firewall security product such as NetworkICE' BlackICE Defender, Sybergen's Secure Desktop, or ZoneLabs' free product, ZoneAlarm. Use this protection even if you only dial in to the Internet for your connection. Hackers know the IP address ranges used by dialup providers and can use that information to access your system whenever you are connected.

✦ If in doubt, don't allow *any* connections to your system. Turn it off or disconnect it from all external systems if you are not sure it will be secure.

Cross-Reference We cover security issues in the context of Internet connectivity, hackers, denial of service attacks, and more in Chapter 11.

Note Visit www.grc.com and follow the ShieldsUp! links to check your system's vulnerability, and follow the advice given for hiding your PC from Internet lurkers.

A few simple rules and some clear planning about what you need to do with interconnected systems can make for a very productive network experience.

Network layers

To better support network troubleshooting, networks may be viewed as being built using very different layers. It is the definite segregation of these layers and their components that has enabled us to make so many advances with network technology and enabled the building of the World Wide Web on the Internet. Knowing about these layers will help you focus on where the problem may exist. The layers we will present here are as follows:

✦ The Physical Layer, which includes the network adapters, modems, plugs, wiring, hubs, switches, and routers that make up the pieces of the network you can install, configure, touch, and repair. Twisted pair, coaxial cable, and fiber optic are some of the types of wiring. ARCnet, Ethernet, ISDN, FDDI, ATM, and Gigabit Ethernet are some of the types of networks that have both physical (special wiring components and characteristics) and protocol aspects.

✦ The Network Protocol Layer, which includes network-enabling protocols such as IPX, SPX, ODI, DLC, NetBEUI, TCP/IP, PPP, PAP, CHAP, and PPTP. It is these protocols that enable different computer systems and networks to work with each other. Essentially, these are languages that the hardware speaks and understands.

✦ The Network Operating System Layer, which includes networking systems such as Novell NetWare, Windows Networking, and Unix. This is the software that is installed in a computer operating system or is part of the operating system itself, and provides capabilities to control access to all of the capabilities of the computer system and interface with the network. Operational software such as server software to support specific capabilities is included in this layer.

✦ The Internet Protocol Layer, which includes the protocols that enable disparate networks to interact and support the Internet. Protocols such as HTTP, SMTP, HTML, SHTML, DHTML, FTP, IMAP, CTI, DNS, LDAP, MIME, SHTTP, SSL, and XML are device, operating system, and language independent so that they enable communication over networks and computers with very different hardware and software components. TCP/IP belongs both here and in the Network Protocol Layer because many Local Area Networks (LANs) are now using the Internet Protocols as the basis for the internal as well as the external network. This is not a problem. The Internet Domain Name System and other features have been designed to support this dual existence.

Figure 10-1 is a visual representation of the layers.

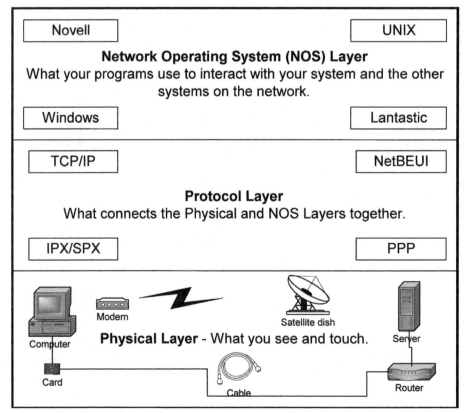

Figure 10-1: Network Layers

Network Physical Layer

Every network has the Physical Layer, Network Protocol Layer, and Network Operating System Layer. It may be difficult to see all these pieces, but they are always there. When you use your notebook computer and a PCMCIA modem via Windows Dial-Up Networking to call your computer at home and connect to its network, you have all of these pieces at work. The PCMCIA modem on your portable and the modem at home are taking the place of the network adapters. The telephone connection is taking the place of the plugs, wires, hubs, and routers. These are your Physical Layer. You are probably using (or should be) the TCP/IP network protocol, which is the Network Protocol Layer. And Windows' built-in network capabilities are providing the Network Operating System Layer.

In your office at work or, as in my home, with seven computers capable of plugging into a self-wired Ethernet (which supports both 10BaseT and 100BaseT transport), the Physical Layer is easy to see. If you did not build it yourself, it may be difficult to maintain or understand. However, someone decided what type of wiring to install, made sure the wiring was installed correctly and all of the connections were correct, and that the wiring was electrically sound. If, as in the case of my own network, the wiring is provided to each computer outlet over a separate line (called home-run cabling), all of the wiring is connected to a central hub and/or switch that provides the highest possible network speed to each computer. At this point, the physical layer is completed for each computer on the network by proper installation of the network adapter. Every device on the network (some of the printers have their own network adapters) is using the TCP/IP network protocol, so our network starts out being Internet-friendly before connecting to anything in the outside world.

The typical network is a combination of network adapters or communications devices, cabling, and connection hardware. These are discussed later in the chapter.

The Physical Layer does not concern itself with the protocols, type, origin or destination of network traffic; it is simply a medium to get signals from one place to another. The Physical Layer may be shared equally by IP, NetWare, Vines, Windows, Unix, or other network system traffic types.

Network Addresses

We are not trying to provide a prescription for designing and building your LAN, but we should point out here that the above network uses valid IP addresses authorized in RFC 1597. Available from the Internet Engineering Task Force (IETF) at http://www.ietf.org, RFC 1597 specifies Internet addresses that may be used for private Internets that are *not* to be transmitted over the Internet. It also uses Network Address Translation (NAT) processes, detailed in RFC 1631, which specifies how Internet packets to be directed to and from the Internet and a specific LAN device using the private Internets addresses may be used to isolate your network from the Internet and still allow interaction with the Internet. Security must be provided by a firewall or firewall software, but your entire network can be IP-based from end to end.

Once the Physical Layer of the network is installed correctly and has been tested, you are ready to go on to dealing with other layers.

> **Tip**   There is no sense trying to deal with Network Protocol Layer or Network Operating System Layer problems if there is a problem in the Physical Layer of your network.

Information about designing, building, and installing a physical network is beyond the scope of this book. We must assume that you started with a physical network that was working at one point. This means that a problem in your physical network has been introduced by physical damage, a loose or broken connection, or an incompatible device or connection you have added, or that time and use have taken their toll and your network has died of old age.

Coaxial network cabling

Coaxial or 10Base2 Ethernet networks are somewhat simpler to install than other types of cabling. However, 10Base2 networks are a little more challenging to plan, configure, and troubleshoot if there are problems. For two to thirty or so systems in a small office coaxial cabling may make sense — you simply run a coaxial cable from one end of the office to the other, looping the cable near each PC system. At each system you cut the cable, install BNC connectors on the cable ends, and connect them to a T-connector, which then connects to the network card. At the far ends of the cable, you install a BNC connector, connect it to one side of a T-connector, connect a special terminating resistor connector to the other side of the T-connector, and connect the T-connector to the PCs network adapter. See Figure 10-2 for a basic layout. However, prepare for some frustrations. In a 10Base2 network, any broken connection brings down the entire network!

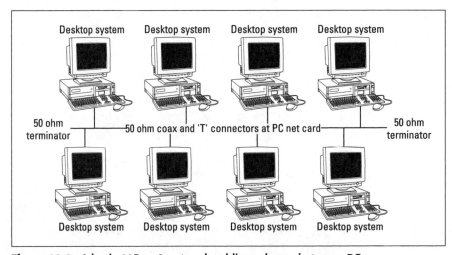

Figure 10-2: A basic 10Base2 network cabling scheme between PCs

Coaxial cable networks present a few problems and are so irritating that many people have opted to switch to simpler and less troublesome network architectures. Proper network-quality coaxial cable can cost up to 50 cents per foot. Proper BNC connectors can cost up to $3.50 each and each workstation connection requires a T-connector—another $1.50 or so. A crimping tool for installing the BNC connectors costs about $60. Cable lengths are also critical. You should not use a cable any shorter than 1.5 meters (5 feet) between PC systems and the total end-to-end length of the cable segment cannot exceed 100 meters. Some 10Base2 adapter cards will support a maximum total cable length of 180 meters. If you need a longer cable total length for your network, you have to provide a server, workstation, or repeater that can route the signals to another cable section. This adds complexity and dependence on expensive hardware.

Disconnecting the cable from one workstation can open the network, leaving some of the workstations on part of the network stranded without connectivity. Opening the cable also removes the proper termination resistor at the far end, causing signal corruption on the cable. This disconnection can happen all too easily when someone moves office furniture or catches their feet on the cabling.

Another problem is that one single coaxial cable carries all of the network traffic all of the time. If the network adapter in one workstation goes bad, sending erroneous signals onto the cable, the entire network is corrupted and will not pass data. If one workstation is doing a lot of file transfers, it can take up an excessive amount of the network bandwidth, leaving other workstations without data for long periods of time.

Unfortunately, the only way to find and fix a problem in a coaxial cable network is to find the place where the break has occurred and fix it. That can be done by physical inspection or by sending a signal over the cable and determining where it is lost. Neither option is easy or straightforward.

Note We suspect that there is little or no 10Base2 coaxial cabling left in use, as it is somewhat troublesome to localize and identify cabling problems, and is generally incompatible with most network systems these days.

Twisted-pair network cabling

Twisted-pair networking requires more cable than a coaxial network, but it is easier for technicians already familiar with telephone-type cabling practices to install and maintain. Twisted-pair, 10BaseT, or 100BaseT Ethernet cabling is now the most popular network cabling type. Each workstation is provided with a single cable. All cabling is typically routed to a central connection point where it is connected (often first to a patch panel and then "patched") to a network interconnection device known as a hub. At the workstation end of the cable, a telephone-style RJ-45 connector is installed, which then plugs into the network interface card directly. There are no special T-connectors or terminators, as the termination is provided by the interface cards or hub at respective ends. Figure 10-3 shows a typical small 10BaseT network with a simple hub.

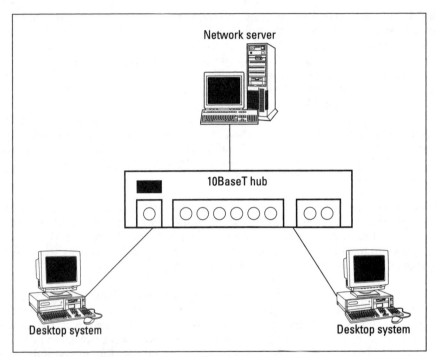

Figure 10-3: A basic 10BaseT network cabling scheme between PCs

Twisted-pair cabling comes in several grades or categories. Category 3 is the minimum specification for 10 megabit-per-second 10BaseT networks; Category 5 is the minimum specification for 100-megabit-per-second 100BaseT networks. It is only slightly (on the order of pennies) more expensive to use Category 5 (or Cat5) cabling for all networks, in the event your network equipment is upgraded from 10BaseT to 100BaseT speeds. A 1,000-foot roll of Cat5 cable costs less than $100. Crimp-on RJ-45 connectors cost about $5 for a bag of 100 and the crimping tool costs about $60.

Tip   When you use Cat5 twisted-pair cabling, the maximum cable length from end to end (not the total network cable as in 10Base2 but from one point to another within the network) can be up to 100 meters, but 90 meters is recommended to allow 10 meters of combined cabling for connectors, hubs, patch cables, and so on.

Note   If you have Cat3 cabling left in your network system, its presence and use may explain network performance problems or unusual failures. Although this cable is rated for 10BaseT use, most network cards are tested with Cat5 cable.

A single cable, properly configured as a crossover cable, may be used between two systems (to plug one system's network adapter directly into the other) for a very small network. To connect more than two systems, a non-crossed cable must be connected from each system to a special network *hub* device. The hub mixes the transmitted data signals from the workstations and distributes data separately to each workstation. Simple 4- to 8-port hubs cost between $50 and $150. Larger capacity hubs and those that can be managed and configured by network management software or used as routers may cost $500 or more.

The good news about 10BaseT cabling is that if one workstation becomes disconnected, the remaining systems are not affected, other than not being able to connect to the disconnected system. Detecting a bad connection is made simpler by the use of LED indicators on network cards and hubs. At least one LED is available as the LINK indicator lamp, showing that a proper connection exists. Another LED may be used or the Link LED may be blinked on and off or changed in color to indicate proper data flow on the circuit.

Network interfaces

To connect to the network cabling, we use Network Interface Cards, commonly called *NIC*s, or network adapters to interconnect computer systems, network devices, and servers. The NIC acts somewhat like a modem, although the connection is active all of the time. The NIC converts data from your PC's internal bus into signals that can be transported over the network cables at high speeds. Typical network data transfer speed over an Ethernet is 10 megabits per second (Mbps). Newer network hardware provides up to 100 Mbps. Compared with serial ports that transfer data at 115,200 bits per second (.1 Mbps) or parallel ports that can move data at about 500,000 bits per second (.5 Mbps), a network is lightning-fast. Compared to the faster PC's CPU speed, a network is still pretty slow, but not too much slower than the average disk drive, making network applications and data storage feasible. Compared to a T-1 connection to the Internet, your 10BaseT, internal local network is 7 times faster. A 100BaseT network is 66 times faster.

Some systems have a network adapter built into the system board, although most are in the form of ISA or PCI add-in cards. For portable and laptop systems you can get network adapters that connect to the parallel port or plug in as PCMCIA/PC Card devices. We will address only the most common interfaces, cabling, and protocols as we flow through this chapter and into the next.

The most common network adapter today is probably a 3Com 3C905 or similar Intel, D-Link or LinkSys NIC. These are produced and sold by many manufacturers under various brand and non-brand names.

Occasionally, you will see cards that support both BNC/coax and twisted-pair wiring, and rarely cards that also support Thick Ethernet connections using special 15-pin D-connectors.

You can now purchase usable generic network cards for about $20 to $40 each, or the 3Com or Intel name brands for around $100 each.

Note   Each network adapter has a unique hardware address, known as the Media Access Control address, or MAC, associated with it. The MAC address is a series of six hexadecimal numbers similar to 0A:1C:03:DB:07:AE. Typically this address is not used for any network or system addressing that we can configure or use to communicate between systems, but you may see the address appear in Windows error messages when there is a conflict between two different systems on the same network. To see your network adapter's MAC address, use the WINIPCFG program provided with Windows 9x/Me, or the IPCONFIG program from Windows NT/2000.

There have been and are still other types of network cabling schemes, including ArcNet, DECnet, and Token Ring, although the hardware, configurations, and applications are beyond the scope of this book, and their use is declining.

Network drivers

Your network adapter card or modem requires configuration and management software that also packages its data into the proper type of network communication protocol necessary for the type of network you are using. Drivers for the specific card and support for various protocols are usually provided by the network card manufacturer, and may be supplemented by network software vendors.

Hubs, bridges, routers, and switches

When you start getting serious about networking, you have to get serious about the equipment required to interconnect systems and different networks, direct traffic, and provide security for the overall network. We discuss each of these items briefly as they pertain to the user's perspective of a network system. Remember, using the right equipment and making sure it is of good quality can reduce your troubleshooting challenges.

Hubs

A hub is a device used to merge and distribute the transmit and receive data signals from different networked devices. The incoming data from each connection port is conditioned and sent back out to every other port, except the one it came from. A small hub for home and small office use may have 4, 6, or 8 ports to provide connections for PCs and servers. The basic hub serves many purposes:

✦ It enables each networked system to communicate with other systems.

✦ It keeps each transmitting station from sending data back to itself.

✦ The signals from each system are isolated from the others, which prevents a bad cable on one system from interfering with the entire network.

✦ The signals are reconditioned by the circuitry in the hub so that the signals do not degrade further with long cable lengths.

For larger or more complex networks, medium-sized hubs will typically provide 12, 16, 24, or 32 discrete data ports. These may also provide the capability to segment or separate various network connections into multiple smaller networks. Large hubs, providing 64, 128, or 256 ports, may be used in very large network environments and offer a variety of network management features to enable troubleshooting individual port and network problems, or provide more control over network segments.

Note In most hub configurations, all data to and from all networked devices appears on the network cables, which can cause network congestion. Switched hubs are becoming more popular as they can provide on-the-fly data traffic routing between network segments, keeping data away from other parts of the network to avoid congestion. Switching hubs can take the place of more expensive *routers* in many large network situations.

Bridges

Bridges are devices that interconnect two or more network segments, often networks of different types, much like a hub, but with some capability to control which segments get to communicate with each other. Bridging is most often used to connect networks with different transport protocols. For networks using the same protocols, the preference is to use switched hubs or routers to control data flow between networks. A bridge will perform network protocol translations. Today, bridging between networks is most often handled in the network servers so the existence of bridging equipment is declining.

Routers

Routers control the traffic flow between different network segments. Routing can be configured to allow or prevent all traffic from flowing between segments, or fine-tuned to control specifically which traffic can and cannot flow between segments.

Routing of data traffic can happen at different levels. Your PC can act as a very simple router through the software that provides dial-up networking support. The routing in this case is very simple: TCP/IP traffic through your modem is routed through software to enable it to flow to and from your PC. Windows NT and Unix servers can also act as routers, especially when two or more network adapters are installed. They also support using a modem to establish one connection while others are connected to the network adapter.

Routers can be as small and minimally functional as ISDN or Frame Relay connection devices with limited traffic control capabilities, or as large and complex as network control systems mixing and directing traffic between fiber optic, T-1, and other high-speed connection types to a 10BaseT or 100BaseT network.

A specific piece of router hardware (a Cisco, Ascend, 3Com, or other brand-name device) is typically one of the first lines of defense or points of traffic control between the Internet or interoffice networks and the local area network in your office. A small office or home environment may use a router to establish a connection with another office or an Internet service provider. Although there may be routers at the other end of the connection as well, a local router can prevent unwanted traffic from flowing, or from causing unnecessary ISDN connection charges.

For large networks, a larger router can provide traffic direction between an ATM, T-1, T-3, OC-3, or other high-speed circuit and the internal network, and filter what kind of traffic can go to which part of your internal network. Large offices will typically use multiple routers, providing discrete routing of interoffice traffic only through one router and data circuit, and separate e-mail and Web traffic through other routers. This type of configuration can provide significant levels of security, too.

Routers connected to the Internet are used to provide basic firewall services, blocking or allowing specific types of traffic or traffic from specific sites. Internal office routers are typically configured to work at the network address and port levels, and should be left to do their job of traffic routing, not performing a lot of policing.

Tip   If you find you cannot access a particular network segment or address or use a specific network port number to connect to a specific host, chances are the router needs to be reconfigured.

Switches

Recently, the combination of a network hub to bring connections together and network switching technology has become very popular as a way to make internal networks more efficient. Where a hub combines all network traffic together to go to/from a common routing point, a switch is somewhat like a dynamic router — directing traffic between specific hub connections depending on the address the data needs to go to or from. Traffic is still intermixed, but only the traffic between specific hosts/devices goes where it needs to. This avoids traffic congestion across the entire network and reduces the need for routers to control internal network traffic.

Connectivity

Although 10BaseT network connections may be used in your home or office to interconnect PCs and servers, you cannot use them to connect your network to systems in other locations, such as the Internet. We would all love to have a 10 Mbps Internet connection, versus our typical 28.8K, 56K, 64K, or even 128K ISDN, DSL or T-1 connections, but it is a little more difficult getting really high-speed communication across average phone lines. Cable-TV Internet connections have the potential for transfers of 10 megabits per second (Mbps), but the bandwidth of the cable connection is shared with everyone who is connected to your cable segment and that could be a large number of users. The next step up in traditional Internet access speeds is a 45 Mbps T-3 line — a bit of overkill for 10 megabits.

When your local network has to extend beyond the walls of your building, or certainly beyond the property lines of your office or campus, you will need to employ communications services from an outside service provider of one form or another. This provider is most commonly your local phone company, but other network communications providers are beginning to provide significant, and less costly, services.

There are many types of telephone or alternate data circuits that can be used to connect your local network to other locations, most commonly the Internet, but otherwise your remote offices, creating a wide area network, or WAN. Often now the WAN circuit may use the public Internet routes but it generally uses a secure a point-to-point route with Virtual Private Network (VPN) software to encrypt the data going between two recognized points. This saves many companies a lot of money by leveraging the ever-present Internet.

Frame Relay

One of the least expensive circuits for continuous use has been the Frame Relay circuit, typically available at 64, 128, 256, 384, and 512 kilobits per second (Kbps) data rates. A Frame Relay circuit requires an interconnection device called a CSU/DSU at both ends. Frame Relay circuit costs range from $150 to $500 per month and the equipment costs approximately $350 to $500 per end. The CSU/DSU connection piece may be combined with a router in one package or require an external router.

You can request a Frame Relay circuit and Internet connectivity from most phone companies, or the Frame Relay circuit must have a specific destination at your ISP or other office location.

Note   Frame Relay is being displaced by commercial DSL service providers and VPN applications.

ISDN

An alternative, for sporadic use such as a home or light office Web browsing and e-mail traffic, is the Integrated Services Data Network (ISDN) circuit. ISDN equipment comes in the form of both "modems" and routers. Which type you employ depends on the type of unit used by the hardware at the place your ISDN unit would dial up. ISDN is capable of basic uncompressed data transfer rates of either 64 Kbps or 128 Kbps. ISDN "modems" interface and interact with your PC system very similarly to analog modems. ISDN routers are designed for known point-to-point connections. Either offers dial-on-demand connections and most units also provide access to standard analog connectivity for analog fax or data modem use or voice calls, which makes them very handy as a second phone line.

ISDN units cost between $200 to $350 for "modems" and from $500 to $1,200 for routers. ISDN lines cost about $120 to install and require approximately a $30 monthly charge; usage charges may apply depending on time of day and whether the line is in a home or business. Generally you should expect total monthly ISDN charges in the range of $80 to $800 per month in some locations.

Note   ISDN is also being displaced by xDSL services due to cost and complexity, although some areas of the U.S. and many areas outside of the U.S. provide ISDN for very reasonable fixed rates.

xDSL

Digital Subscriber Line circuits are becoming the economic alternative to Frame Relay and ISDN. DSL can be offered over Frame Relay circuits or specially conditioned lines and provide from 114 Kbps to 1 Mbps data rates in various combinations of upload and download speeds. They are less expensive than ISDN and Frame Relay in terms of telephone company line preparation and maintenance, with end-user equipment costs coming down into the $150 to $250 range, if not provided free or leased with your DSL service subscription, which costs anywhere from $30 to $50 per month for a single-user IP address. DSL circuits must have a specific destination point, such as a like-equipped office or ISP equipment in a local phone company office.

Soon we will have nearly universal DSL service that enables us to order over the Internet or go to our local computer store to pick up a DSL kit — and order service and hook up much like we do normal analog phone/modem services. Take the kit home, plug it in just like a modem, hook up your PC and presto — you are on the Internet. Unfortunately, this is not available yet.

T-1

Most of us have heard about or envy those with T-1 Internet connections. A T-1 circuit supports up to 1.54 Mbps. A T-1 circuit costs anywhere from $1,200 to $2,500 per month and requires data connection equipment, usually combined with a router, costing between $500 and several thousand dollars.

A T-1 circuit is similar to Frame Relay in that there must be a specific "other end" for the circuit to connect to — your ISP, the phone company, or another known office location. T-1 circuits may be configured as a single circuit, such as to carry Frame Relay traffic, or to provide 24 channels of voice or data.

Cable modems

Cable (TV) modems essentially bring Ethernet connectivity to the Internet across specifically conditioned digital-capable cable television circuits. An Ethernet connection is brought to your PC system, you are assigned one IP address and host name, and you can surf the Web to your heart's content at up to 10 Mbps. However, be aware that you are sharing this connection with everyone on your cable segment. That means you have security issues (since your packets are passing through everyone else's hardware on your same network segment) and also that others on that segment are "using up" your bandwidth when they are using their connections.

Wireless connectivity

As phone circuit cabling gets more expensive or difficult to come by in certain areas, we find more and more applications using point-to-point wireless (radio) systems to carry data from place to place.

A very early and still popular wireless service known as Ricochet has been available from Metricom of Los Gatos, California, for a number of years. They recently advertised 128 Kbps service for around $30 per month. So it's not a T-1, but it does go anywhere with your laptop!

Some wireless products work in the no-license-required 2.4 GHz microwave radio band and have a distance range of up to 10 to 30 miles depending on elevation and location. One of us has been enjoying a new "wireless T-1" Internet access service for over a year, and although there are some unusual early-development issues and some latency in making the first Internet connection, it is *a lot* cheaper than a wire-based T-1.

Fiber optics, SONET, and ATM

Fiber optic networks are among the fastest and most reliable, but they are very expensive in terms of installation and connection equipment. They can deliver data rates in excess of 45 Mbps, and offer many options in terms of redundancy and traffic routing. We leave further discussion of these "big pipes" to books focused on just networking. You should find references to the Gigabit Ethernet that supports transport speeds measured in gigabytes per second. Just when we thought the speeds were heading out the roof, we find research references to developing technology that provides network speeds measured in terabytes per second. If you are not happy with the speed of your connection, look around, there are new solutions popping up every day!

Frame types

The frame type used by a network adapter refers to the organization of the data transmitted on the network communication line. Novell NetWare 3.*x* typically uses the IEEE 802.3 frame; NetWare 4.*x* typically uses 802.2, and TCP/IP networks use Ethernet_II. For Windows this is usually configured for you automatically. For DOS and special situations, the frame type is configured in a NET.CFG text file.

Network Protocol Layer

Between applications and the protocols that communicate with networks are program or driver layers known as Network Basic Input/Output System (NetBIOS) and Windows Sockets (Winsock for short). NetBIOS was originally developed by a company named Sytek for IBM, and came bundled in some network cards. Winsock was developed by Microsoft, using the UC Berkeley Sockets API, for Windows program developers to develop network interfaces. NetBIOS and Winsock essentially remove the need for applications to "know" how to communicate with the different transport or communications protocols, except in certain cases of IP-specific or NetWare-specific applications. Applications will obtain and use network resources through the common NetBIOS or Winsock programming interfaces, whichever is most suitable for the resource and data communications at the moment, instead of each application having to build in specific network protocol support.

A protocol defines the structure and articulation of communications between networked devices. Novell NetWare typically uses IPX/SPX, whereas the Internet and most current LANs use TCP/IP. Microsoft Networking uses NetBEUI by default, but can use IPX/SPX or TCP/IP when configured to communicate with Microsoft's NetBIOS services.

Of these, TCP/IP is among the most efficient, using a minimum amount of frame and data packets to transfer information, with robust retry timing and delivery guarantee features. TCP/IP was developed for inter-networking and can carry information for other protocols or be used by itself. It is also the preferred protocol on many LANs because it uses the available bandwidth efficiently and is relatively easy to troubleshoot and control with common software tools.

Note   Using TCP/IP for both internal networks and external network connectivity simplifies the overall design, traffic control, bridging, routing, and troubleshooting of all networking operations.

One common extension of or addition to protocols such as TCP/IP is called Point-to-Point Protocol, or PPP, used for establishing network connections over relatively slow Dial-Up Networking connections such as modems and ISDN circuits. PPP adapts the modem's serial data stream into TCP/IP (or other protocol) data and routes it into the system as if a normal network connection existed.

NetBEUI was originally developed by IBM for small (20- to 200-user) networks. Microsoft also adopted it for its first networking implementations. It used to be the default for almost all of Microsoft's network products unless another protocol was installed. If you install another protocol, you can leave or remove NetBEUI and let your Microsoft Networking use NetBIOS services conveyed through TCP/IP. This is what you will see displayed in the NetBIOS tab under the Windows 95/98/Me TCP/IP Properties dialog box. Under Windows NT/2000, you can readily disable both NetBEUI and NetBIOS communications over your network, but doing so under Windows 95/98/Me takes some manual Registry editing. If you disable NetBIOS services you will no longer have Microsoft Networking capabilities between workstations or servers. Without it, you would only have use of basic IP functionality with services such as Telnet, FTP, HTTP (Web), and so on.

Note   NetBEUI, which is not carried or routable across the Internet, is still highly recommended for small internal networks using it to carry NetBIOS inter-system traffic instead of TCP/IP, which you use for Internet communications. Removing the connection between NetBIOS and TCP/IP adds a significant layer of protection from hackers to your home network.

Network Operating System Layer

In order to make use of a network, your PC needs a variety of software, from the network card drivers to protocols and services, to establish the connection between other hosts on the network. These may be provided by your operating system if it is designed in that way. Windows 95/98/Me, NT, 2000, and Unix are such operating systems. If your computer's operating system does not provide complete network support, the Network Operating System Layer software installed on your computer must make the connection between the network and your file system and applications.

In the "good old days" of DOS and with Windows 3.*x*, we had to install and run the network card and protocol drivers in our AUTOEXEC.BAT or perhaps with another convenient batch file to initialize the connection. These commands started with the configuration of the Physical Layer, continued with the installation and setup of the Network Protocol Layer, and ended with loading the control program for the Network Operating System Layer.

For a NetWare network, your AUTOEXEC.BAT file might contain lines similar to the following:

```
NE2000.COM
LSL.COM
IPXODI.COM
NETX.EXE
```

NE2000.COM would be the network card driver used to claim system resources (an address and IRQ assignment) and make the network card available to the next series of drivers. LSL.COM is known as the Link Support Layer, a bridge between the network card and the protocols to be loaded next. IPXODI.COM is the IPX protocol driver for NetWare connectivity. NETX.EXE establishes a connection between your system and a designated server, or supports connections to peers on a peer-to-peer network.

Each of these files is internally configured to look for a file named NET.CFG and read its contents for specific information pertaining to the driver's configuration and use. A NET.CFG file has contents similar to the following:

```
Link Support
  Buffers 8 1514
  MemPool 8192

Link Driver NE2000
  PORT 280
  INT 9
  Frame Ethernet_802.3
  Frame Ethernet_II
  Protocol IPX 0 Ethernet_802.3
```

```
     Protocol TCPIP 8137 Ethernet_II

Protocol TCPIP
  bind ne2000
  ip_address     192.123.45.67
  ip_router          192.123.45.1
  ip_netmask     255.255.255.0
  tcp_sockets    24
  udp_sockets    12
  raw_sockets    4
  nb_sessions    8
  nb_commands    16
  nb_adapter     0
  nb_domain

SPX CONNECTIONS = 60
PREFERRED SERVER = GRAPES
SHOW DOTS = ON
CACHE BUFFERS = 32
FILE HANDLES = 80
```

This particular NET.CFG file contains configurations for both IPX and TCP/IP networking. The Link Support section configures the LSL driver resources. The Link Driver section specifies which protocols and frame types to use. The Protocol TCPIP section sets up the TCP/IP address and basic routing information. The remaining lines, from SPX CONNECTIONS down, are specific to NetWare and NetWare applications configuration, and indicate which server NETX.EXE should try to establish a login connection with first.

If you are connecting to NetWare, Unix, or other network services with Windows 3.x you probably also have configuration information for the specific connection software that works under Windows. Novell, FTP Software, NetManage, Distinct, and Hummingbird Communications all provide some set of Windows-specific features, enabling your system to use network server disk drives and printers as though they were part of your local operating system (either Unix or other Network File System [NFS] enabled services or NetWare directories).

The after-market vendors also provide FTP, electronic mail, and other common IP-related file access and communications features, for internal and external network services. Sun, MCD, and Hummingbird Communications are among a few companies that also offer X-Window interfaces for connecting your PC to and running graphical applications on Unix or other hosts. The X-Window means of sharing computing power and system resources, although a bit hoggish in terms of resources and performance, is what some think "Windows" really ought to be.

Microsoft Windows for Workgroups (WfWG) provided Microsoft proprietary network drivers and connectivity through the NetBEUI protocol. WfWG networking can be used with other network drivers and protocols, at the expense of using up precious system memory and time.

With Windows 95, 98, Me, NT, and 2000, the network card and protocol drivers are installed with the operating system, with considerable advantages, not the least of which are speed, memory conservation, and long filename features.

The basic features and capabilities of all Network Operating System Layer software are quite similar: mapping drives to your local system, support for running programs, security features to protect your own work areas, multiple layers to protect the network resources, and so forth. The way these capabilities are supported, configuration capabilities, navigation methods and commands, sets of keywords or reserved words, and so forth, are quite different on even different versions of the same networking software.

Internet Protocol Layer

If you want to find the origins of the Internet Protocols, just take a peek under the covers of the Unix operating system. Because the Internet has been in development for about 30 years (the first four systems were linked in 1968 to create the ARPANET — Advanced Research Projects Network for the U.S. Department of Defense and universities to share research information), and until the last four or five years Unix was just about the only major operating system in use in the communities doing the development, this makes a lot of sense.

IP, which stands for Internet Protocol, concerns the addressing and routing of data across networked systems (meaning that you are able to communicate with systems on other networks). TCP, short for Transport Control Protocol, is the mechanism that actually transports the data and ensures the accuracy and completeness of the data transport. IP networks also carry User Datagram Protocol, or UDP, packets. TCP and UDP, among others, may be considered as peers or on the same level as each other when carried over an IP network. TCP/IP is the networking protocol that has encircled the globe. TCP/IP is also built into the major LAN networks (Novell and Windows) and has literally enabled the interconnection of networks around the world.

Unix is based on public domain standards. So is the Internet. Unix and Internet protocols are constantly being augmented, updated, and advanced to keep pace with technology and, in some cases, set the pace for technology. Since Unix uses ports to provide connection to just about anything, it is natural that the Internet would start at about the same place.

Ports

TCP/IP networks establish communications through specific ports. These are not physical ports, as with hardware connections, but internal allocations of network, host, and node resources and address specifics to support the actual data transport.

The most common TCP ports are 80 for HTTP/Web browsing, 23 for Telnet terminal sessions, 21 for FTP file transfers, 53 for DNS table lookups, 25 for POP3 mail collection, and 110 for SMTP mail transfers. Several other ports are used for inter-process and inter-application communications, network games, and so forth.

Tip Knowing that these ports exist and knowing some of the data types is essential for filtering or blocking network traffic and troubleshooting some network problems. The firewall software is given the port and protocol information for enabling or disabling those specific items to enable and protect your network.

IP addresses

Most network environments provide a method of providing unique names and numbers to devices that communicate with each other. For IP networks, each active host — a system that can request and deliver data traffic — is given an IP address. An IP address is another cryptic set of four numbers separated by decimal points, such as 192.123.45.67, for example. Each of the numbers has relative significance in the routing of data to a specific host device. The IETF has designated a series of IP addresses that may only be used for private LANs (the NAT addresses referred to above), which enables network designers to create private IP networks that can still interact with the public Internet.

IP addresses are assigned and distributed by a central, recognized Internet name and numbering authority. For non-government, non-military IP networks, this authority has been the InterNIC in Virginia, but this has changed significantly in the past year when the United States government relinquished control of the Internet for good; other Internet domain registrars have been certified to assist with domain name registrations.

Tip Where do you get an IP address? Your local area network administrator, corporate hostmaster, or Internet service provider will tell you how to configure your system and, if applicable, assign your IP address.

Caution Do *not* pick an IP address at random unless it is within the private address ranges of 10.0.0.0–10.255.255.255 or 192.0.0.0–192.255.255.255. Picking someone else's IP address could have a significant impact on other networks. Primarily, it will ensure that you cannot communicate over the Internet.

Corporate/office networks vary as to whether they preassign IP addresses to specific host systems or use an automatic IP address distribution system. Internet service providers will automatically assign an IP address and other applicable network information when you log on to a dial-up session, and may preassign an address range for multiple users connected via ISDN or other connectivity types.

Your IP address could change between active connections, as it does when you use Dial-Up Networking. In Dial-Up Networking to an Internet service provider or many office networks, IP addresses can be assigned as needed and only when needed by a Dynamic Host Configuration Protocol (DHCP) server on the network. This is necessary for the proper management of the limited number of IP addresses available, especially in an ISP situation in which many hundreds of users must share a specific address range but only for relatively short periods of time. After all, there are only about 4,162,314,256 IP addresses that may be used to support connections in our entire galaxy. At least until IPv6 is accepted by the Internet on the whole.

Tip   Your IP address and other information are configured in the Windows Network Properties dialog boxes, and may also be viewed with the WINIPCFG program. If you are not using Windows 95, 98, Me, NT, or 2000 you may have TCP/IP software and drivers from FTP Software, Distinct, or another company, that provides for your TCP/IP configuration and connection to the network card or modem.

IP addresses are divided up among various domains. Groups of numbers are allocated to corporations, networks, and Internet service providers. The groupings of numbers are arranged into classes that define the number of addresses available to whomever they are assigned. Related to the groupings of the numbers in the address, the classes are identified as A.B.C.0: Class A includes all IP numbers starting with the number assigned to the A license. These numbers are actually HEX digits that allow each letter to represent 1 of 256 possible values. These numbers may be referred to as octets. A Class B license is a subgrouping within a Class A license that includes all of the Class C licenses starting with the A.B numbers for that license, and so forth.

✦ A Class A address group, such as 192.0.0.0, provides the assignee with control over 16 million IP addresses — from 192.0.0.0 to 192.255.255.255. Someone assigned a Class A range, typically only very large Internet service providers or whole countries, will usually parcel out Class B and/or Class C address groups.

✦ A Class B address range would appear as 192.45.0.0, for example, providing use of about 64,000 addresses from 192.45.0.0 to 192.45.255.255. One or more Class B address ranges are typically assigned to ISPs, very large corporations, or small countries.

✦ Class C addresses, such as 192.45.23.0, provide 256 addresses from 192.45.23.0 to 192.45.23.255 (only 254 are usable), and are distributed to small-sized companies for implementation across various internal network plans.

Class C addresses may be further divided into smaller address and routing groups, called *subnets*, to help define workgroups and traffic routing. With each class of IP addresses is another set of numbers, called the *subnet mask*, that provides a method for routers to help refine and filter network traffic control. For full Class A addresses, the mask is 255.0.0.0, for Class B the mask is 255.255.0.0, and for Class C the mask is 255.255.255.0. As you can probably tell, the *255* means to match only the number for the current subnet, and the *0* is used as a wildcard to match any address in that group.

The mask defines how many bits of the address must be passed or decoded to identify a specific host device. The mask may be further refined to filter data into smaller subnets, such as 255.255.255.192, which breaks up a Class C address range into four discrete subnets of 64 hosts each.

The four subnets are then grouped into IP addresses of 0–63, 64–127, 128–191, and 192–255. The first and last address in each subnet are unusable as device addresses since they are used for network control. In the greater scheme of things, data routes and flows "downhill" through Class A, Class B, Class C, and then specific subnets to discrete addresses in increasing levels of address and routing refinements.

But those strange numeric addresses are so complicated. . . .

Domain and host names

To make life easier for the people involved in IP networking, IP addresses are allocated to various types of Internet users, called domains, and further qualified by specific host names within the domains. Currently, there are four non-government domain types in the United States: COM, EDU, NET, and ORG. Government domain types include GOV and MIL. States and cities have their own domain names. Domains for Internet users outside of the United States are designated by a two-character country code, such as CA for Canada. Educational institutions are assigned to the EDU (EDUcation) domain, and non-profit interests are assigned to the ORG (ORGanization) domain. If you run a business or have any commercial traffic, you are assigned to the COM (COMmercial) domain. Network service providers are assigned to the NET domain. Additional new domains have been proposed by Internet and government entities to expand the number of possible domain names and may be available whenever the politics of every imaginable faction and big business interests can quit trying to make sure their special positions are protected.

Within each domain are the domain names. Domain names are the source of much contention and debate between individuals, companies, and within the courts and government agencies. Many of us have our own personalized domain names that have specific significance to us — such as the one for our publisher, IDG Books Worldwide, whose domain name is "idgbooks". IDG Books is assigned to the COM domain — thus it is known as "idgbooks.com" on the Internet. Today you just aren't hip unless you have your very own Internet domain.

For each specific Internet domain and domain name there must be a unique host name and IP address assigned to the network equipment or service provided by each network address. Thus there is usually a one-to-one correlation between IP addresses and host names. Often one network address can be used for several host services — such as using one server, given one IP address, for both WWW and FTP services.

Your host name can be almost anything you want it to be, within agreed-upon Internet limits. Typically we choose a name that is representative of the system, workgroup, or some derivative of domain and IP address. In a small office or home environment we would probably use the name of the primary user of the system involved. Host names are not too important for personal use or general Internet activities, but they are important to find and help keep track of the servers or services that provide users with mail, news, and Web pages.

You are probably familiar with names such as `www.idgbooks.com` or `ftp.cdrom.com`, which may indicate the actual host name, but more than likely refer only to the actual service being provided, which is translated by the domain name server into a specific IP address. In reality, you could encounter a server in `mydomain.com` that has been given the host name `theserver`, which becomes qualified as `theserver.mydomain.com`. This server could provide Web, FTP, and mail services combined or on separate machines, but in common use it would be addressed as `www.mydomain.com`, `ftp.mydomain.com`, or `mail.mydomain.com`—where the same host and IP address can instead be addressed by the services it provides.

Even if your local network is not connected to the Internet, most network administrators follow good Internet discipline in designing, numbering, and naming their internal host systems.

Note   Not all local host names are registered in any domain name server, so if you name your home PC connected to an @Home cable-modem Internet connection "jack," don't expect that host to officially be known as jack.home.com. Chances are the @Home provider knows your host by some obscure subscriber code number followed by their domain name—and even that may not be listed in their DNS table.

How do you tell the difference? How does the Internet know which IP address to use for which service?

Domain name server

We have come to depend on using a friendly name for locating Web and FTP sites on the Internet. However, the routing of our Internet traffic from one place to another relies strictly on the IP addresses. This leads us to the domain name system, which is a cross-reference service provided by Internet service providers and large Internet hosts to translate host and domain names into IP addresses. This service, called the DNS, must be located on a server somewhere on the network to which you are connected.

You might also rely on a local HOSTS table, an ASCII file on your local system that contains the "friendly name" to IP address mapping, but to do so would involve a very difficult and inefficient process to update and maintain the HOSTS table. Even if you do not have to worry about your own system's IP address, at the very least you do need to know the address of at least one domain name server and manually configure it into your system. Once you have established an Internet connection and can access a DNS server, finding almost anything else on the Internet will be relatively easy—just let the DNS do the work.

Note

Don't think that the DNS can do the job of a search engine. You need to know either the IP address or the actual name in order to use the DNS to make a connection.

Within and part of the DNS application are rules and configuration files that indicate specific host names and addresses for local systems and other systems the DNS service gets addresses from and can give addresses to. This is a dynamic, ongoing process running across the Internet and many large local area networks every minute of every day. A recognized DNS service provider can issue or obtain updates about the IP address for any advertised host name on the Internet within hours of a change being made.

Tip

If you experience a host name lookup failure in your Web browser or e-mail application, wait a few minutes and try again—chances are that somewhere on your local network or your path to the Internet, a DNS update is occurring and things will settle down shortly.

Cross-Reference

We cover much more about the Internet in Chapter 11.

Firewalls

A firewall is a device with specific software used to control the types of network traffic that flows from one network connection to another. Most of this control is implemented by denying or permitting packets to be passed in one direction or the other through the firewall. The basis for the decisions the firewall makes are usually based on IP addresses, subnetworks, ports, and content of the data packets being evaluated. Some firewall functions can be and are performed in a router, but most routers are usually too busy directing large volumes of network traffic and do not provide detailed reporting or ease of configuration. Many firewalls can be used in conjunction with network access security tools, such as RADIUS and SecurID, to act as the centurion for your network security.

Tip

Together, firewall services and routers can make a network very secure.

Proxy servers

A *proxy server* is used to step in between network users and an outside network connection in order to isolate, reduce, and more easily monitor certain types of network traffic. Proxy servers are most commonly used in medium-to-large network environments to act as a controlled isolation gateway for WWW and FTP traffic.

Proxy servers, also known loosely as *gateways*, are very commonly used for sharing a single Internet connection between several different PCs at home. WinGate (http://wingate.deerfield.com/) and WinProxy (http://www.winproxy.com/) are two very popular Internet connection sharing programs you can get from the Internet file sites. Microsoft recently included an Internet Connection Sharing service in Windows 98 SE and 2000 and will in Windows Me.

A proxy server can sometimes, but does not always, cache the contents of commonly accessed Web sites, reducing the volume of traffic for outside connections by delivering the cached pages to the users much faster than regathering them from the Internet. Proxy servers can also be used as security gateways, requiring a user ID and password, or limiting use to only specific workstations — in cases in which a company does not want to provide access to outside WWW and FTP services to everyone in the company.

Note When a connection is made through a proxy server to an outside server, the connection appears to come from the proxy server's IP address rather than internal hosts or workstations, thus adding a degree of isolation from exposing the design of the internal network to others.

Network address translation

One of the things a proxy server often does in separating internal host systems from direct contact with the Internet is provide translation between internal addresses and the Internet address for your single connection point. Thus, you could be using 10.x.x.x internal network addresses but you appear to the Internet to have 222.33.44.55 as your host system address.

Dynamic Host Configuration Protocol

One way to manage, or not to have to manage, a group of host system addresses and configuration is to employ a Dynamic Host Configuration Protocol (DHCP) server to assign and set host IP, gateway, and DNS addresses automatically when they first come onto the network. A network administrator preconfigures critical network information at the server and each workstation obtains their configuration from that server. The result is a central point to control some otherwise confusing technical information.

This is, in fact, how most ISPs run their dial-up networks and enable you to simply "borrow" an IP address for the duration of your connection. With DHCP they do not have to pre-assign an IP address for every dial-up customer — and there simply are not that many addresses available for all dial-up ISPs to provide fixed addresses to subscribers anyway.

Check the Specs Before Buying

Our caveat: Check the specifications for any home network product that you want to buy. Be sure it supports Internet connection sharing. Be sure it includes all the components you need and that you can easily get additional components should you experience failures or want to hook up more systems. While your phone wiring can be old-style Red-Green-Yellow-Black "station" wire, performance and reliability will be better if you have up-to-date twisted pair phone cabling—similar to that which a real 10BaseT connection would use. Our preference, of course, is to go to the expense of having your entire phone cable system rewired and add 10BaseT network cabling.

Home network alternatives

There are a handful of alternatives to installing conventional 10BaseT network wiring and hub connection schemes such as Intel's AnyPoint home network. This and similar products use existing home phone line wiring to interconnect PCs equipped with AnyPoint (or similar) interconnection gear. There are also wireless products with similar no-new-wiring connection advantages.

These are great alternatives for simple PC-to-PC data and printer sharing, and some of these products even enable multiple computers to share a single Internet connection through another computer—meaning they support, allow, or will use the TCP/IP protocol.

The performance of these products varies slightly, but is roughly one-tenth the speed of a normal 10BaseT network connection between systems, so don't expect "office quality" blazing speed for printing or large file sharing.

Wrap-up for networking basics

Although the preceding discussion of the primary components of networks and our division of networks into layers will not make you a networking expert, it should give you a conceptual view of your particular network and the basis for delving into common network problems.

The type of network software and protocols (the language or format used in network communications) is perhaps the biggest difference between network types. Fortunately, the physical or cabling layer of most networks is becoming standardized on one cable and connection type, the twisted pair Ethernet, which is similar to telephone cable. This provides economy and flexibility, but there are still a lot of networks that use vastly different cable and connection types, such as the IBM-specific Token Ring cabling and hardware. Certainly, several thousand computers and networks still communicate via IBM Token Ring, Digital DECnet, Banyan Vines, Novell NetWare, and other networks, but the Internet or TCP/IP-style networks seem to be taking over the vast majority of the systems we encounter.

Since Windows and Internet networks are literally everywhere, we provide specific examples using these networks and address problems in other networks in general and through specific examples where necessary.

Windows Networking

Beginning with the release of Windows for Workgroups, Microsoft began providing basic intersystem networking services on the desktop. These services support basic file and printer sharing between systems, access to Windows NT services, and basic but proprietary Microsoft Mail services. Many of these services have been enhanced and replaced by the current versions of Microsoft Exchange, Outlook, and other communications and presentation services built around Windows 9x/Me and NT/2000 networking features.

If you are not connecting your office to the Internet and just want contained resource sharing services, using only Microsoft Networking's NetBEUI protocol is more than adequate to keep your business or home running. You can easily add NetWare or TCP/IP Internet communications to any of your systems and keep them separate from other internal resources, if you desire. However, as feature-capable as NetBEUI is for internal networks, you do not want to expose or let NetBEUI be routed or tunneled (sending another protocol's information, such as NetBEUI) out over the public Internet; you would be leaving yourself open to hackers if you did. The NetBIOS interface part of Windows systems is rich with hacker holes, but that can also be easily tamed with proper routing and filtering within your internal network at the expense of some Windows-related services for those accessing your network from the outside (such as traveling employees).

Windows networking can be almost as simple as "tossing" a few systems together through a hub, establishing a workgroup, and sharing necessary disk and file resources among coworkers. Windows networking can also be as complex as connecting together several distant offices, having multiple separate workgroups, and introducing the concept of Windows domains to isolate and contain groups of workgroups. Toss in a few Internet-related services, either an intranet or access to the Internet, and you have quite a collection of systems, users, security, and other issues to manage. Here again, we need to provide some basic information related what you will see and what you can do from your desktop system.

Workgroups

Workgroup is the term Microsoft uses to define small networks of systems used with a particular group of people, functional area, or department. Establishing a workgroup identity on your PC is a simple matter of configuration of your Windows for Workgroups or Microsoft Networking setup within the operating system. WfWG and the newer versions of Windows make these configuration tools available within their specific network control panels.

Choosing a workgroup may be pretty simple—if you work in Finance, your system is probably going to be configured for a workgroup named "Finance." Once established in the "Finance" workgroup, you will not have much to do with the "Personnel" or "Sales" workgroups unless you change your system configuration and reboot your system—an obviously cumbersome process, but of course their workgroups will not have direct contact with yours, either.

Workgroup configuration is fine within a small company, and with few users, everyone in the office probably belongs to just one workgroup. Of course, each resource that is shared and used from each workstation affects that system's performance, which can be a bit of a drag. Workstations running Windows for Workgroups, Windows 95, or Windows 98 are not as secure as other server-based systems.

Tip   When you need to branch out, share resources with other workgroups, and minimize the performance impact on other workers, it is time to consider an NT, Unix, Novell, or other type of network.

Windows NT and NT Networking

Windows NT takes us to a new level of sharing resources within our own workgroups, between other workgroups, and across an entire company or multi-office enterprise. NT is still a relative newcomer to networking, running up against Unix and Novell NetWare as the network operating system and infrastructure of choice.

Although Unix is one of the original network-based operating systems and is the ultimate network backbone of choice for overall speed, power, and security, for many situations, Novell NetWare provides a level of increased simplicity more suitable for a lot of business users. NetWare is still the backbone of many large corporations today and should not be disregarded for its features and security,if only because so many have so much invested in it and it simply works.

NT is growing up to be an enterprise-wide solution, but it's not quite there yet. You will still find the powerhouse business applications and databases, Oracle, SyBase, and SAP preferably run on Unix-based systems simply for the power, security, familiarity, and prior existence of so many Unix machines in large enterprises. As the platforms that NT runs on become powerful enough to match large Unix systems, and as Microsoft or others pitch in and debug and provide more security for the environment, NT may begin to become a significant player in this area that has always been occupied by Unix.

Still, Windows NT offers an economy of scale, resources, and relative simplicity that give it increasing popularity for small- to medium-sized network environments. (And, some will say, even for large enterprises, but perhaps only for those with considerable expertise and a business or technological reason underlying their decisions.)

For small- to medium-sized workgroups and businesses, NT is typically the network operating environment of choice. Most intermediate to advanced PC users can buy a decent PC capable of handling multiple users and running a few applications, install NT, and have folks up and running in a day or even less.

The same can be said for LINUX and Solaris x86, *if* a Unix-savvy person is around to do the work, which is the real case in favor of NT. There simply are not as many good Unix people around as we would like, and the ones that are around are getting paid a lot of money elsewhere. So, many of us do NT. It is a matter of economics and resources that no doubt Microsoft and others are exploiting to their advantage. Half of us are fairly good at Unix, but NT is so much easier to learn. (But never fear; Unix has been around a lot longer and is not going away! If there is any operating system that has a chance of slowing or preventing the dominance of Windows, it is Unix and its cousin, Linux. Novell is not going away either!)

This build-it-in-a-day free-for-all many people have with Windows NT can leave systems improperly planned and vulnerable to security and denial-of-service risks, especially when so many NT systems are deployed in conjunction with Internet connectivity. Barring that, very adequate and well-serving NT systems can easily be deployed to meet the needs of basic office environments with a little time, knowledge, and planning.

If you come to understand little else about Windows NT/2000, soon you will soon see that it is *not* Windows 3.*x*, 95, or 98. OK, some say it is much better, and it is in a lot of ways, but it will not run all DOS programs under its command prompt, nor will it run all Windows 3.*x* and 95/98 programs. If you elect to partition the system so that you may boot under DOS or an older version of Windows, you can get the best of both worlds, just not at the same time.

NT-based networking versus workgroups

Windows NT gives its operators a much higher degree of control over security, access to services, division of functions and work, and greater performance than a simple workgroup environment.

In its simplest form, NT can eliminate the need for workgroups or augment them. NT introduces the concept of domains (or, rather, borrows the concept from Unix/Internet), or groups of workgroups and/or servers. NT and domains are used to segment and provide security and global services rather than dependency on individual workstations. Workgroups and local resource sharing can still be accommodated while using NT networks. Individual members and nonmembers of the workgroups can be allowed access to NT server resources, or they may be configured to allow no small workgroups to exist apart from NT, with all groups being authenticated by and using the NT resources.

There is also considerable economy in setting up an NT server for a group as small as 10 to 20 users. Above 5 users or so, with a lot of printing or file sharing demands, normal office workloads could slow a shared workstation to a crawl, and its users would never get any work done. If you elect the "bargain system" route of buying a basic Pentium system to set up a server for about $1,500, and add an NT server license for about $800, your additional cost per user in a 20-user system is only about $115.

Note   NT printing and file sharing services are much faster, more reliable, and more secure than exposing individual workstation sharing to the entire network.

Several "bargain systems" make up the NT domain, Web, and e-mail presence that have been some of the basis for this chapter. They are Pentium-class systems running at 120 to 150 MHz, all using only 32 megabytes of RAM, with an assortment of "average" disk drives. These systems are used more for central file storage, security, print services, and Internet presence than they are to serve a group of employees, and they perform reasonably well. These servers are not adequate for a lot of daily office activity; they cannot support an accounting or central contact management system of any size, nor can more than four to five regular users and applications run on them. The systems should be upgraded to 200+ MHz systems and at least 128MB of RAM to be considered as even marginally serious servers if they were to be used for true commercial applications.

As you add more users and get to at least 50 to 100, you will probably determine that you want to use a high-reliability, higher-performance server system from COMPAQ, Dell, Gateway, H-P, or Micron, costing $6,000 and up. Even with the higher server expense, the per-user economics get even better. We recommend buying systems specifically designed for server applications for a number of reasons:

✦ **Warranty.** Unless you want to be in the business of doing all of the technical work on your own servers and can afford the down time and frustration, let the vendor support you! This also gives you an excellent excuse to get the users off your back. Waiting for a vendor to provide free parts is better than 100 people waiting for you and having to ask your boss for a fresh $200 or so to fix that haphazard pile of bits you constructed and just crashed!

✦ **Expandability.** Server systems are designed with more memory slots, disk drive bays, and power supply capacity than standard desktop and tower systems. There's almost nothing worse than running out of space to add more RAM or disk drives, or not having enough power supply capacity to run them.

✦ **BIOS and O/S Support.** Server systems have BIOS that supports RAID and other advanced storage systems as well as multiple processors and internal server-optimized functions.

Setting up an NT server is no small task — something not recommended for the novice or even intermediate Windows 95/98 user — but it does not have to be a particularly complex one, either. If you do some homework, you can develop a good grasp on what you are trying to accomplish. There are several books on the subject, and anyone interested should scour Microsoft's Web site and other NT-related sites to get more information about performance improvements, security concerns, setup, and general problem-solving hints. Setting up an NT server is as much about what you need and want to install as it is about what you do not need or should not install — for the best performance, security, and overall system management.

Windows NT 3.x and 4 domains

A Windows NT server may be set up as a stand-alone server or as part of a "workgroup" of servers known as a domain. Windows NT 3.x and 4 domains are not to be confused with Internet domains but may be thought of in a similar fashion: a collection of like or functional systems under the control of one or more responsible servers.

Note   Domains differ from Windows workgroups in that they offer centralized server-based rather than individual workstation-based security and control.

Windows 2000 changes this perspective of NT domains and now follows (or rather forces) Internet domain conventions in network design, doing away with the prior NT-domain scheme altogether.

If you elect to establish NT domains, one server becomes the primary domain controller, and other systems may become part of that domain or serve also as backup domain controllers. Domain controllers are responsible for providing and sharing domain security, user groups, group profiles, login scripts, and other domain administration functions. Changes to any of the domain parameters may be done through any one of the domain controllers and the changes are replicated across all domain controllers.

Domain controllers may be located proximate to each other for local redundancy practices or distributed to different locations to provide domain access and features regardless of connectivity or the status of other domain controllers. Using domains enables like workgroups of users to share resources across multiple locations. Without domains, you could have same-named workgroups on different servers, but those groups would not necessarily have access to or share the same resources. In fact, it is possible to have different or conflicting groups on different servers, leading to user and administrative confusion.

Multiple domains may share some groups and users in common through trust relationships established between domains. Domains may have mutual, bidirectional trust, or trust in only one direction.

User groups

With or without NT domains and their controllers, groups of users may be created, like workgroups, with different privileges and access to different system resources. User or group access to resources may be controlled by time and/or based on policies set at the server.

By default, new users are placed in an "Everyone" group under NT, but they can be added to other groups, taken out of default groups and put in others, and put in groups specifically denied access.

Again, think of NT user groups as workgroups, with the security and access control determined at the NT server rather than at individual desktops. Users do not have control over their NT groups; only the system administrators do. So if you are about to migrate from peer-to-peer network workgroups to NT-based groups, you will probably want to disable all local file and print sharing on the workstations and configure specific user groups on the NT server.

One or more users can belong to multiple groups; thus Finance and Personnel may have discrete user groups, but the heads of each of those departments may belong to each other's groups and to a common Management group, for example.

Windows NT with TCP/IP

As we discussed earlier, Windows networking typically uses NetBEUI as its protocol of choice for transporting NetBIOS and thus application information, between interconnected systems. Unfortunately, both NetBIOS and NetBEUI are very open and vulnerable communications methods; if they are connected to the outside world, almost any similarly equipped system can easily infiltrate your networked systems. For that reason NetBEUI is very seldom, if ever, carried outside of local area networks, being blocked from the outside world by data filters configured into traffic-routing equipment. NetBIOS can also be, and usually is, blocked, not just for security and anti-hacking reasons, but because other methods are typically used to share system resources across both private and public networks.

It is also more efficient in terms of CPU resources, memory, and network bandwidth to run only one communications protocol, and since most networked systems are also using the Internet on a regular basis, TCP/IP is the protocol used in most networks.

It is possible to leave two or more protocols installed and running on networked systems, either NetBEUI and TCP/IP or IPX/SPX and TCP/IP, to facilitate internal networked applications, in which case TCP/IP might only be used for selective Internet communications. Again, it is easier to design and plan around only one network protocol, and TCP/IP seems to be it for most networks these days.

Tip

Using TCP/IP with NT enables you to use NT and Windows 95/98 systems to provide the typical Internet and Web services, and internetwork more easily with other systems, such as Unix, H-P, Tandem, Cray, DEC, and IBM servers and mainframes.

Windows NT routing, DNS, and proxy services

Since Microsoft realized the importance of being able to inter-network systems, it jumped into some of the territory occupied by Unix systems. NT can provide inter-network routing services for TCP/IP, which is useful for mixed-environment and Internet-connected systems, as well as strictly NT-only environments.

Although an NT server is not an excellent router because it usually exists to provide file, print, and applications services more than anything else, it can perform basic IP routing functions. It also has capabilities to perform domain name services and can step in as a proxy server for various types of Internet traffic. Microsoft would like us to believe it can at least supplement many Internet and IP services, if not replace other systems that provide them.

Tip

For a small network, an NT server in conjunction with Internet connectivity services (through ISDN, DSL, T-1, or an analog modem) can easily provide most of the basic connectivity features we need to connect a few people to the Internet with relative ease. Installation, configuration, and management of these services is considered to be at the advanced user level, but to know they exist can give you some indications of how to identify problems you may be having in other parts of your network.

Remote access server

Last on our list of prominent NT networking services is the capability to provide access to the server, if not an entire network, through remote access such as ISDN and dial-up (modem), and establishing private internal-to-remote user network connections over the Internet.

Windows NT Remote Access Service (RAS) makes dial-in access to your network possible by connecting a modem to the server and configuring some internal NT software without having to add terminal servers or other high-end networking equipment to the network. This same service feature is also what enables you to use one modem or ISDN connection as an on-demand connection to the Internet or other remote offices (WAN) without expensive, full-time, public-service-provided data circuits.

This two-way (but may also be configured as in-bound or out-bound only), on-demand, as-needed connectivity provides a number of benefits. If your internal network system is already connected to the Internet, users can dial in to an NT server running RAS and use the Internet (if enabled by configuration). Between other offices or Internet-connected telecommuters, RAS also lets you establish a privatized network connection, either via the Point-to-Point Tunneling Protocol (PPTP) or Virtual Private Network (VPN) configurations, so your internal network resources (file and print sharing) can be available outside of the office.

Similarly, internal users may access the Internet by routing specific IP addresses and traffic through an NT server and RAS to dial out to an Internet provider.

Windows 2000 Server and Active Directory

Windows 2000 Server and Advanced Server, along with Windows 2000 Professional, are probably among the most significant advances in "personal" and business computing to come our way in many years. While a great many things have been done with Windows NT, we probably reached the limit of tolerance for the capacity, marginal performance, and reliability of NT two to three years ago. With "2000," Microsoft hopes to provide an environment that will compete with the prevalent Sun/Unix presence in high-end business and Internet computing.

Many chuckle at the notion that 2000 is 13 to 18 times more reliable than Windows NT, when Unix aficionados believe that Sun OS/Solaris, FreeBSD, and Linux have always been at least 100 times more reliable than any Microsoft product. Makes you wonder what we've been missing all these years, and why Microsoft is now admitting that NT is unreliable. Have we paid way too much in lost time and lost business and for tools and workarounds up to this point, and will we get any of that investment back through 2000? The truth is that we really don't know what the "truth" is, and may not for at least a year or so. 2000 is just too new despite the Microsoft case studies of secret year-long 2000 deployments in specially selected corporations.

The Windows 2000 release event is significant — based on and around enterprise-level computing — a market segment that Microsoft had not penetrated to its satisfaction against Sun and IBM products. It seems that 2000 is aimed at really big networks. So where does that leave those of us small-network folks?

To understand that question, we have to look at Microsoft's big selling point for Windows 2000 — Active Directory. For the network that uses only one or a few NT servers, changing to 2000 will of course give you any benefits of increased reliability and the capability to grow and still manage your network. 2000 changes a lot of things — not the least of which is that of course Microsoft had to change the user interface so much that finding familiar configuration and feature items in 2000 is a challenge at first. When you get to the level of working with configurations and applications, the features are as familiar as they were under NT.

If you've got just one or a few NT servers, are using workgroups instead of NT domains, and are considering 2000 — go for it! Prepare yourself by thinking about reconfiguring for workgroups only instead of NT domains, unless you want to dive into Active Directory (be wary, there be complications ahead). 2000 Server takes a bit longer to set up but is certainly more robust and, we think, just plain more fun to watch it install and go through the configuration steps. If it is as robust as it is pretty, Microsoft may have a winner here.

Active Directory

Active Directory is Microsoft's implementation of the Internet Engineering Task Force's (IETF) Lightweight Directory Access Protocol (LDAP) standard. LDAP defines inter-server and inter-application authentication and data sharing communications. Directory services are essentially single-centralized or multiple-distributed databases that contain information about network resources, access control, users, services, and so on, that can be used as a single point of network management.

Directory services enable network administrators to manage the users and resources of multiple network components through one reference point without having to constantly reconfigure and cross-check several individual servers.

Small- to medium-sized NT networks may have only stand-alone servers without domain association, or just a single NT domain. Most current medium- to large-sized Windows NT networks run under one or a few NT domains that are linked together and may or may not have trust relationships between separate domains. These configurations may not be likely beneficiaries of a directory service implementation. Large- to enterprise-size networks probably use some form of directory services.

Until Windows 2000 and Active Directory were available, directory services were only available with products from iPlanet (Netscape/Sun) or Novell. These are standard cross-platform (Windows, NetWare and Unix) implementations of LDAP that helped integrate network management in mixed environments. So far, Active Directory is a Windows 2000-only product.

Note   Active Directory eliminates the notion of prior NT-domains and forces network design into partial conformance with Internet domain standards. As such, you can no longer have a Windows server that acts as an NT domain server separate from a specific Internet domain.

With Windows NT, a small office may for some reason combine or attach its Internet Web and mail server with its office print and file server(s). In this case the NT domain may be named *ACME* and have 10 to 20 office workers logging on to that domain to gain access to file shares and printers. Additionally, there may be a server connected to this network and set up as part of the NT domain, perhaps their Web server, having an Internet domain of *acme.com*. The NT domain and the Internet domain have no relationship except that they share a physical network connection and have similar "domain names." Public access to the *acme.com* Web domain does not mean that the public has access to the *ACME* NT domain, and vice versa.

With Windows 2000, this separate domain configuration would have to change to a single or subdivided Internet domain—*acme.com*—with the internal worker network access managed under a sub-domain, say *office.acme.com* or *internal.acme.com*, while the public Internet sees *www.acme.com*. In this case, as with the separate NT domain/ Internet domain scenario, the public Internet may still never "see" the internal domain and resources and the internal people may not have Internet access, but the concept and setup changes drastically. While this makes sense in some cases and may not seem like a big deal, obviously the notion of separate NT domains and Internet domains disappears when the Internet domain naming scheme is forced into the picture.

Forcing this new concept and redesign onto NT network administrators in NT-only environments is one thing. In mixed-platform environments in which the Internet part of the operation is run under Unix, significant arguments can and will arise as to who manages which part of which domain or sub-domain. It is possible and probably preferable to have the NT portion of the network function as a sub-domain under the Unix-level Internet domain, especially if Internet presence is involved. It is highly unlikely that Unix systems would be managed in a sub-domain under a Windows 2000 Active Directory domain scheme—for several reasons.

The most significant reason for the complications with introducing Windows 2000 Active Directory into an existing Internet domain, especially with Unix systems at the top-level, is that Active Directory uses and provides Dynamic DNS (DDNS) features. DDNS enables participating servers and network components to be added and updated into the DNS tables automatically—so the network can change and grow without having to be managed down to every printer or workstation and back up to manually updating every DNS server in the environment. For a few servers, printers, and many workstations this is not a big deal. For thousands of network components, the domain management task is non-stop—to the point that most networks are never completely up-to-date.

The upside

While there is a down side to Active Directory in the changes it will force upon many networks, there is an up side as well. Part of the up side is that Microsoft now provides a standards-driven method for their network management services. Since most enterprises now participate in the Internet and use it in some form to communicate locally, nationally, and globally, it makes sense that they would base at least some of their implementation on proven Internet methods. Directory services integrated with or designed for the operating system also provide a competitive (or is that non-competitive?) single-source advantage in selecting and deploying such a scheme—you no longer have to be too worried about competitors not cooperating on creating the best possible solution. (Didn't IBM have a similar issue with mainframes quite a few years ago—our solution or none?)

By Microsoft's own admission, Active Directory is not something to be taken lightly. They recommend spending a significant amount of time (3 to 12 months) planning for and beginning to deploy Active Directory. This means considering all of the aspects of converting from existing NT network designs, converting or working around any Unix or Novell systems within the network, changing or creating an Internet or Internet-like system architecture, and just plain learning the system as you go.

With that in mind, Windows 2000 and Active Directory are much too new to even touch on troubleshooting tips at this point.

An excellent book by Harry M. Brelsford, *Windows 2000 Server Secrets* (IDG Books Worldwide, Inc.), provides pre-release glimpses of this new server operating system and Microsoft case-study implementations in large network environments. This book is full of details, tips, and solutions for all sorts of 2000 server-related issues.

We believe that certainly Windows 2000 is not an easy upgrade for those who are just now becoming familiar or have even had years with Windows NT. We believe it will be quite some time before 2000 replaces a majority of the NT 4 systems now in service. However, we are sure that the experts and others will agree that when it comes to any operating system or application environment, the hardware that it is installed on must be top-notch, solid, reliable, and set up and functioning correctly. When we begin to see the real-life problems and practical solutions for Windows 2000, they will be documented for a revision of this book.

NT summary

It might seem as though we are making a sales pitch for various versions and features of Windows NT but barring that appearance, our point is to illustrate that end users can get involved with implementation of networks. Windows NT and, by extension, Windows 2000, is more familiar to most of us who use Windows as our preferred desktop environment. It is readily accessible and affordable from computer store shelves (as are a few Unix variants), and it is relatively easy to install and set up, all of which makes it very popular.

As with other types of network and server environments, many things are possible with Windows networked systems, and it takes a lot of different devices, software, and configuration to make them happen. One piece can be broken and others will still work, or a single piece can make it appear that everything is broken. Knowing what's what in your NT or 2000 environment can make your life a little easier.

Basic Network Troubleshooting

The following are some typical and basic networking problems that you may have or probably will encounter. We use examples of problems related to TCP/IP networking as some of the simplest means to illustrate network problems and the tools and indicators to help you fix them.

Remember the various layers we talked about near the beginning of this chapter? Start with the Physical Layer. If your plugs are loose or not connected, your network simply will not be connected. If your Network Interface Card is not installed properly and does not pass the simple tests provided with most installation programs, you will not be able to connect to your network, no matter how much neat software you install.

After you verify that your physical network is able to pass signals from one station to another, check your Network Protocol Layer. You do this by checking the configuration of each of your network devices — computers, printers, and so forth. They all need to be using the same protocol or set of protocols and with similar parameter settings.

Checking your network operating system is the biggest job. It involves reviewing your installation and, in the case of systems in which the network operating system is part of the computer's operating system, involves the most basic installation, your operating system and its configuration. If networking never worked in your systems and this is an initial installation, your best course may be to start the installation process over again. You may have learned some things about your computers or your network that will help you make a more complete installation. If your network used to work, you need to investigate anything new to your system that could be the cause of current network problems. It may be the new section of the network you just installed. It may be the new computer you just installed in your network as a server. If nothing is new, you need to start searching for something that has recently broken. By the time you get to this point, you are ready for a learning experience. We hope to help.

Symptoms

▶ DOS or Windows does not recognize my network card.

▶ Network driver or Windows indicates an IP address conflict with another interface.

▶ Network driver indicates an invalid hardware address.

Suspects

▶ Nonstandard network interface card.

▶ Improper card type detected.

▶ Improper device driver installed.

▶ Conflict with other system resources.

▶ Defective network interface card.

Solutions

▶ Configure card to NE2000 standard values using the manufacturer's provided setup software.

▶ Using the configuration program for the network card, manually disable Plug-and-Play operation and, instead, configure the card with a known address and IRQ setting.

▶ In your system BIOS, reset the Plug and Play or NVRAM auto-configuration value so that at next-boot the Plug-and-Play BIOS resets each device and lets them resolve any resource conflicts.

▶ Install the driver provided by the card's manufacturer.

▶ Replace the network card.

While there are dozens of industry standard and well-known network card types and manufacturers in the market, there are also a handful or more manufacturers who make clone, or "compatible," cards with various features. The most commonly cloned or imitated network interface card is the Novell, Novell/Eagle, or Novell/Anthem NE2000-style card.

With the right driver, the one designed and shipped with that card, these clones appear to mimic the original card in functionality. Unfortunately, the internal electronics and the methods of configuring these cards, as well as copyright issues and other laws, do not allow these cards to be identical to the originals in terms of how other drivers and Windows identify them. Truly NE2000-compatible cards enable card resource and driver configurations within the limited range of NE2000-compatible addresses and IRQs. Some address and IRQ combinations are not supported by NE2000 standards. A card configured to settings other than the original NE2000 limitations may not appear to be an NE2000 card at all.

As we have indicated in prior chapters, many cards may claim some variation of "plug-and-play" compatibility but do not truly conform to the real Plug-and-Play specification. Although Plug and Play itself is not perfect, not conforming to any of it and trying to fool you, the user, is much worse. Some DOS-based network card drivers, such as those for early Windows Networking, cannot detect the presence of nonstandard or Plug and Play-only cards because DOS itself does not support Plug and Play.

The card may not appear to use any resources until after Windows is active, and then those resources may conflict with previously assigned ones. Some 3COM cards and various systems' Plug-and-Play BIOS do not work well together, warranting manual configuration of these cards. Network cards are not a high-priority device in the Plug-and-Play resource negotiation scheme and may lose out on resource assignments. Sometimes you are as well off setting the configuration manually and/or installing a DOS-level driver to make the card visible for Windows detection.

Typical Addresses

A typically safe bet for configuring non-NE2000-compatible cards is address 280h or 340h and IRQ 9 or 10. Addresses 280h and 340h have no known conflicts, are not normally used for other devices, and have seldom, if ever, been a problem for use by a network card. Addresses 210, 320, and 360 may conflict with other devices (SCSI, sound, LPT, and IRQ 9 while shared with IRQ 2). IRQ 10 is commonly assigned to or needed by SCSI, sound, or video adapters. Address 300h was used for an old IBM network card and is otherwise assigned for an essentially nonexistent prototype card.

If your system BIOS supports manual configuration or reservation of IRQ assignments, set the IRQ used by your network card to Legacy/ISA instead of PCI/PNP in the BIOS setup so that the Plug-and-Play processes do not claim that IRQ.

Symptoms

▶ No LINK light on network card.

▶ Workstation can ping itself but not the rest of the networked devices.

▶ Workstation cannot see other systems on the network.

▶ Workstation cannot log on to server.

▶ "No domain server available" message appears at logon.

▶ Network functions erratically.

Suspects

▶ Improper cabling.

▶ Bad connector or no terminators on cable.

▶ No hub connection.

▶ Network card configured for the wrong cable/connection type.

▶ Network card not fully enabled after configuration.

▶ Unflagged hardware resource conflict (no yellow "!" in Windows device manager, but inspection of individual device resources shows two devices on same IRQ).

Solutions

▶ 10Base2/Coax Networks:

• Ensure you are using the proper coax, T-connectors, and cable lengths, and that you terminate each end of the coaxial cable at the last T's in the string.

• Check or replace the BNC connectors on hand-made cables, and ensure there are no shorts in the cable after connector attachment.

• Ensure that you have a connection all the way through between workstations— a single bad or disconnected cable can bring down the entire network.

▶ 10BaseT/Twisted Pair Networks:

- Ensure you are using proper network cables, not phone cables — the pairs of wires are configured differently between network and phone cables.

- If you are configuring only two systems without a network hub, use a proper network crossover cable between the two systems.

- If you are using a network hub, be sure you are not using crossover cables except in the few cases in which one may be needed (only between two hub-like or two workstation-like devices).

- Check for continuity and no shorts in cable connectors — a simple cable test box is available specifically for network cables.

▶ Be sure the hub has proper power.

▶ Shut down, power down, and restart the workstation after reconfiguring the network card; these network cards often need a cold reset before the reconfiguration takes effect.

▶ Verify resources for each device and reset Plug-and-Play BIOS or manually configure conflicting device(s).

▶ No account on server or shared system — see next scenario.

▶ Improper Gateway, IP address, DNS, or HOSTS table configuration — see the next scenario.

Symptoms

▶ Workstation can ping itself but not the rest of the networked devices.

▶ Workstation cannot see other systems on the network.

▶ Workstation cannot log on to server.

▶ "No domain server available" message appears at logon.

▶ "No DHCP server" message appears after startup.

▶ Network driver or Windows indicates an IP address conflict with another interface.

Suspects

▶ Wrong network card driver or protocol.

▶ Improper hardware settings for your network adapter.

▶ Network card settings have not taken effect yet.

▶ Missing protocol for your network type.

▶ Network configuration wrong or incomplete.

▶ Server or network connection is down.

▶ Configured for DHCP when no DHCP server is available or all addresses are taken.

Solutions

▶ Ensure that you have selected and installed the right drivers for your specific network card. After configuration of all network parameters, shut down your system completely, power off, restore power, and reboot. Some network cards require a complete internal reset before cable connections, hardware addresses, and IRQs take effect.

▶ Check for errors related to your network card:

   • For non-Windows systems you may expect to see errors appearing onscreen as network drivers are loaded, and you may need to test each network device and protocol driver manually rather than have them flash by during batch file loading.

   • For Windows 95/98/Me systems, click the System icon in the Control Panel and select the Device Manager tab. Scroll down and verify if there are any yellow-highlighted exclamation points next to any devices, especially the Network Adapter listing. If there are, double-click the specific network adapter that is indicated and view the dialog boxes for troubleshooting information. Most often you will find an address or an IRQ conflict between your network adapter and another device. Check the first troubleshooting example earlier for more information.

▶ Ensure you have installed the TCP/IP protocol:

   • Click the Network icon in the Control Panel or right-click the Network Neighborhood icon on your desktop and select Properties. If TCP/IP is not listed with your network adapter or Dial-Up adapter, select Add ➪ Protocol ➪ Microsoft and double-click TCP/IP in the right pane.

▶ Ensure that TCP/IP is set up correctly for your network type:

   • Double-clicking, or right-clicking and selecting Properties for the TCP/IP protocol in Windows' Network dialog box ,brings up the IP Address page.

   • If you are pre-assigned an IP address, you must select "Specify an IP address" and key in the IP address and subnet mask information provided to you by your network administrator. Using the wrong IP address can make your system invisible to the network and the network invisible to your system.

   • If your network uses DHCP, you will select "Obtain an IP address automatically" and let the network connection and DHCP server do the work of configuring your system.

   • The subnet mask must be appropriate for your network design. For testing purposes you can use either 255.255.0.0 or 255.255.255.0 and you should be able to see other networked devices.

- Select the Gateway tab in the TCP/IP Properties dialog box to see the IP address settings for various gateways or the next network in the path to other networked systems. If you do not have any or select the wrong gateway address, you will not be able to communicate with other systems.

- Be extremely careful with IP addressing. The entry fields in some dialog boxes automatically separate the four IP address numbers with the requisite decimal points for you; others require that you enter each decimal point between the numbers.

Symptoms

▶ Network Neighborhood does not show all servers/workstations.

Suspects

▶ Wrong or missing workgroup in Network Neighborhood Properties.

▶ Wrong or missing gateway in Network Neighborhood Properties.

▶ Inadequate rights to access network resources.

▶ You are not a member of a workgroup or NT domain.

▶ Improper IP address or subnet mask.

▶ Bad cable, adapter, or hub connection.

Solutions

▶ Provide the correct workgroup name: The workgroup name is configured by selecting Properties in the Network Neighborhood and clicking the Identification tab to bring up the appropriate dialog box. The name inserted here is not case-sensitive. The workgroup is typically not the same as the NT domain name used under "Client for Microsoft Networking."

▶ Verify and correct your IP address and subnet mask.

Symptoms

▶ Network resources are visible when browsing the network, but you are unable to access and use them.

▶ Messages indicate that your user name or password is incorrect or that you do not have rights to the server, domain, or resources.

Suspects

▶ For workgroups:

- Resources must be online and usable from the host system.

- Resources of the systems you need to access must be shared.

- You must be specifically allowed to access, via your user name and password, the resources on a specific system.

- You must be using the local PC with a logon that has access to the shared resource(s).

▶ For server-based resources:

- Resources must be online and usable from the host system.

- Resources of the systems you need to access must be shared.

- You must be specifically allowed, via your user name and password, to access the resources on a specific system, either by individual user ID or server groups.

- You must be a member of the resource's domain.

- You must be logged on to the providing domain.

Solutions

▶ Contact the network administrator or host system user to obtain access rights to the shared resources.

▶ Restart the system you are using and log on as an authorized user.

Summary

Networking requires some understanding of how people work, how their work is organized, with whom they work, and the resources they need. Planning and coordination are the keys for any deployment of new resources that extends to and certainly beyond the individual desktop user. Chapter 10 made the following main points:

✦ A small network may appear to be a "no-brainer" to implement. However, if implemented without keeping in mind that you may have to grow a network to handle more users, groups, or locations, you may have to do and redo the planning and implementation work many times over, until you get it right.

✦ Expanding into a medium-to-large-sized network brings on considerable complexity at the server implementation level and, with any luck, very little complexity at the user-level. If you have done the planning and migration from peer-to-peer workgroups to a server-based scheme correctly, growing the network is basically "more of the same."

✦ Troubleshooting network problems is also, basically, "more of the same" — you have to work your way from the workstation level, through the network connectivity, to the servers in a logical fashion, and you will find solutions along the way.

Since we believe that it is becoming more difficult to distinguish local networks from Internet connectivity, we'll see what may be more common and practical networking concerns in Chapter 11.

If you are interested in learning more about networking, especially about the Internet and its addressing, naming, and routing methods, try the *Internet Bible* from IDG Books Worldwide (`http://www.idgbooks.com`). And, of course, the ultimate involvement with networks will be to get involved with the Internet Society and some of its related organizations, such as the Internet Engineering Task Force, and help build the network protocols for the future!

✦　　✦　　✦

The Internet

"**W**hat a tangled web we weave . . ." has never seemed more appropriate to technology than when it is applied to the Internet. The apparent simplicity of surfing the Internet can indeed be deceiving if you get stuck in myriad parameters, acronyms, addresses, HTTP, FTP, SMTP, POP3, PPTP, VPN, and all those other Ps.

We believe we will be able to get you connected and keep you connected, browsing to your heart's content with few complications. When you connect to the Internet, and collect and install all the right applications and features, you will be rewarded and perhaps bombarded with all that the Internet has to offer. You will acquire ability to find and hear that special audio snippet, catch that perfect graphic for your own Web site, amass reams of travel information for your family vacation, check those investments, do research for your own dot-com business proposal, and chat with friends around the World. Surf's up!

The latest developments on the Internet are taking us much further than we had ever expected — *and* we're realizing that we've just begun to scratch the surface. Business-to-business use of the Internet is blossoming — it's expected to be more than a trillion-dollar part of the Internet industry by 2003! Within the next few years we may be receiving all of our home entertainment over the Internet. Who knows what else the future holds!

Internet Basics

The Internet exists for the purpose of sharing information between host systems and users worldwide. This sharing of information is made possible by several means once connectivity is established between your PC system and the rest of the Internet. From there you can request a connection with and get information from almost any of over 17 million host systems that are also connected to the Internet.

What the Internet is

The Internet was originally called a "network of networks." This description is probably as true as any could be considering the state of today's Internet. In the 1960s, 70s, and 80s, "networks" were clusters of computers located in but a few university and government research sites. Those were the decades when the Internet was conceived, born, reared, and fostered into a nearly mature, defined, contributing member of scientific society. Most everything we do with the Internet today is firmly based on the principles of intercommunication between many different types of computer hardware that were developed in the Internet's defining early years. During those times the Internet was known to relatively few in our global population. Internet access and use in the United States, much less worldwide, has not been common for most of the Internet's total lifetime.

The World Wide Web was actually introduced by Tim Berners-Lee at CERN (Conseil Européen pour la Recherche Nucléaire — European Organization for Nuclear Research) in 1991. However, it was not until 1995, a mere five years ago, that the general public became aware of and began to make full use of the Internet. The Vatican Web site was first introduced in 1995, which indicates just how pervasive the Internet has become, in a very short time! This after more than 20 years of government and private funding and a select few commercial interests began to fund the continued existence and growth of the Internet by offering low-cost access. For a modest fee — about $20 per month in most cases — now anyone close to an Internet service provider's point-of-presence can begin to explore a new means of communicating with others. Internet access is perhaps one of the few things that has not inflated in price one penny, and certainly not as much as it has inflated in use, value, and traffic. In fact, like the cost of home computers, average access costs have gone down in the last five years.

Online Service Providers

Prior to the widespread use of the Internet, *electronic communications* that was not voice, telephone, or radio communications, consisted of a variety of online services such as CompuServe and America Online (AOL). These services, which have since adopted and converted to being primarily Internet-based, were mostly private, contained communities of users within the relatively familiar safety and comfort of a single online environment. While providers such as AOL still support the more private community, the Internet extends that community environment to include the entire world — not all of it secure or comfortable all of the time. The basic communication features enjoyed with the previous incarnations of online services have also been expanded. Now users not only enjoy the familiar e-mail, chat and forum groups, and file transfers, but a whole new genre of multimedia offerings, ranging from doing the family grocery shopping to enjoying online music and video entertainment — often live.

The Internet is not bound to a proprietary set of communications programs and methods like the online services of old. Instead it is based on, grows from, and is somewhat limited by dozens of internationally agreed-upon standards for establishing connections, requesting information, transferring data, and making sure everything all runs smoothly. Opening up online communications by using universal methods has brought a lot of good information, interaction, and a greater sense of community to the wired world. This open methodology also brings with it certain risks, responsibilities, and new challenges. The challenges are primarily the capability of the Internet to contain and carry millions of times more information than anyone ever believed possible, and protecting the rights and security of the Internet's users.

These challenges are tremendous. Imagine a global network that has been allowed to grow in relative proportion to the technology we use to access and enjoy it — exponential growth in numbers of users, amount of information, opportunities for commerce, and, unfortunately, the impact of crimes. The technology has changed dramatically in recent years. Remember when . . .

✦ A 32 megabyte hard drive was a big deal, and now you're using a 40 *giga*byte hard drive!

✦ 256 kilobytes of RAM memory was a lot, and now 256 megabytes is not uncommon!

✦ A 2400 or 9600 bits-per-second modem was fast, and today, we're not satisfied with anything less than a million-bits-per-second!

In the early 1980s, 100,000 users made CompuServe the world's largest single online service provider. In mid 1990s, AOL purchased CompuServe, raising the single online service subscriber bar well above 20 million.

In 1995 the typical connection to the Internet was a plain old character-based 2400-baud terminal session, similar to the way we connected on CompuServe. The Internet backbone consisted of a handful of T-1 data circuits spanning a few dozen major cities. HTTP and the World Wide Web barely existed, and File Transfer Protocol (FTP) was as foreign to computer users then as CPU pipeline cache timing is to users today. We access the Internet, today, with the equivalent of T-1 data circuit performance (using DSL or cable modems). The backbone consists of dozens of extremely high-speed fiber-optic connections between each major node of the Internet. Further, if you do not have your own Web page, or a few of them by now, you must have just come back from a ten-year meditation session on Mt. Everest. Now the picture should be firmly etched in your imagination. The Internet is BIG.

Not too many years ago we had to worry about a few programs floating around the local computer club bulletin board system with a virus attached to them. We still do. Now the impact of a few files is like the impact of the Internet, multiplied by thousands, even millions, not just because more people get those files, but because the further distribution of those files happens thousands of times more frequently and faster than it did just five years ago. The open standards of communication that make the Internet possible are also part of the Internet's "dark side." Thus, as much as we focus on getting and staying connected to the Internet, we also emphasize your online security.

Connecting to the Internet

Connecting to the Internet requires very little actual work. Your PC, or Macintosh, Unix, Linux or other suitable computer system, must be equipped with hardware, software, and communications tools to establish an Internet Protocol (IP) connection. This connection goes to the Internet-at-large, usually via an Internet service provider (ISP), that then spans the earth — perhaps even the universe as we know it, as someone is sure to assign a host name and IP address to a system in a space station or satellite, too. Think that's science fiction? Vint Cerf, one of the inventors of IP, is working with the Jet Propulsion Laboratory (JPL) to develop the Interplanetary Network Protocol for immediate use in NASA Mars missions and then in all of the space programs. The Internet is everywhere, and it is for everyone!

Meanwhile, back here on earth, the work you have to do to establish an Internet connection, though minimal, does involve a handful of specific technical details and conditions. These details and the conditions surrounding them must be correct in order to access the Internet.

If you are using the Internet from home, you probably subscribe to the services of an ISP. This is usually a company that provides access through an ISDN, xDSL, or cable modem, or a standard analog modem dial-up connection. This connection receives and stores, provides access to, and transmits your e-mail for you. It also passes through your requests for and enables you to view specific Web pages, send and receive files, and participate in online forums and chats, as well as transmit and receive audio and video. As a subscriber of an ISP, you are dependent on the ISP for all routing, connections, and protection from unwanted traffic. With this account or subscription type you are usually limited to one IP address assignment (whether "permanent" or temporary), one e-mail address, and perhaps a personal Web page hosted on the ISP's server.

Larger ISPs provide multiple Points-of-Presence (a *POP*, not to be confused with the Post Office Protocol [POP3] services of an e-mail system) in different cities throughout the country and even overseas. Small ISPs may only provide local POP access in the region or city they serve. America Online, CompuServe, and Prodigy are large online services that also provide Internet access, whereas AT&T, GTE, Netcom, MCI, IBM, Earthlink, and others have provided Internet access, e-mail, and some Web services, with little or no online content (forums, chat rooms, and so on) other than their own Web sites. If you travel you will appreciate having an account with one of these large ISPs so you can access your mail and use the Internet from nearly anywhere in the world via a local connection.

You are dependant upon your ISP for your connection to and protection from the Internet. To help you understand this connection, we'll expand a bit on what the Internet is, and what being connected to it means. From this discussion you will gain some perspective on what being protected from the Internet means as well.

While connected to the Internet

Steve Gibson, a well-respected software author and investigator of many things good and bad about working with computers, once said that "when you are connected to the Internet, the Internet is connected to you." Let's explore this statement a little bit. Two things are apparent:

✦ Connecting to the Internet implies that you want something.

✦ The Internet being connected to you implies that it can give you what you want or get what it wants.

By its intent and design, the Internet is an open medium for the transfer of information. Within specific technical bounds, very little information cannot be conveyed across the network. It is the closest thing we have seen in history that could be described as universal:

✦ How you connect to and communicate via the Internet is openly published, well known, equally available, and readily accomplished with nearly any type of computer equipment available and, lately, even noncomputer equipment. The information used to command, contribute, and accept data transfer across the Internet is the same at the connection point of an Apple Macintosh as it is at an old Digital (DEC) mainframe as it is at an IBM PC or compatible system. And information can move across the Internet in many ways.

✦ The Internet knows no political, economical, or geographical boundaries — it literally reaches every corner of the earth, and into outer space, too.

✦ The Internet is democratic, completely neutral in terms of gender, race, color, creed, politics, and economics. Anyone and everyone with a computer can participate in it — contributing to or merely partaking of the Internet's vast amount of information.

Perhaps the only real barriers the Internet may have are language differences and access limitations. The Internet as a medium does not (yet) translate across all languages, and access is limited because the presence of the Internet does not preclude economic or political issues barring people from participating, even though the Internet itself is, by its nature, politically and economically neutral. Otherwise, nothing is stopping the Internet from letting anyone do anything with his or her Internet access.

How or why is this possible? The Internet is simply a medium. It is a medium that, as it stands, can and must allow all forms and types of data traffic flow across it. It cannot bias, alter, or preclude any data that flows through it. So what is "it"? Who is "it"? As indicated before, the Internet is a network of networks. It's a consortium of cooperative groups, entities, institutions, corporations, and people who have interconnected their communications systems and system users to each other. This has been done through various types of equipment and data transportation methods (electrical cabling, fiber optics, and radio waves) that speak, interpret, and convey the same types of commands and data uniformly.

By design, the data could be specific to a proprietary type of IBM equipment, it could be specific to communications between Apple computers and printers, it could be pictures from a camera mounted on a satellite in orbit. That the data can get somewhere, and how it gets there, is the purest value of the transparency and cooperation that makes the Internet work. As long as everyone follows the Internet's rules, they are allowed to use it.

The rules of the Internet are not the rules of any government, religion, or economic power. The rules of the Internet apply only to its existence and function — not to what it conveys. As long as the Internet does not limit, alter, add to, deny, give preference to, or take away from anything specific beyond purely technical considerations, it is a free and open access communications system. In some ways, and in the United States, just as an example, you could say that the Internet is the epitome of what the First Amendment of the Constitution stands for. The responsibility for the protection of this capability, for individual protection of what is placed on or taken from it, lies upon each user.

The Internet is a Tool, a Vehicle, for Expression

The Internet itself is no more or less responsible for what someone sends through it, or for what someone feels or does because of what is sent across it, than air is for letting bullets pass through or around it. The Internet, as with air, does not create "bullets," it does not propel or direct them, and it is not affected by their impact.

In that vein, the providers of the Internet — those who conduct the flow of the "air" that is the Internet — are likewise neutral carriers. The phrase "do not shoot the messenger" definitely applies to the Internet.

We may extend this understanding to the creators of content that appears on the Internet. With certain exceptions the content itself is not responsible for the impact it has on others. The single most important responsible party on the Internet is the *user*. Only an Internet user can deliberately target, abuse, or seek to take advantage of the medium of the Internet and its content. A bullet is a thoughtless, inert object without deliberation or intent. When propelled at a bale of hay it harms no one. When propelled at a person it can kill. The one who controls, aims, and with deliberation intends for and propels a bullet to do harm is the responsible party.

Limiting any one of the capabilities of the Internet denies someone the advantage of it — and if that could be done to someone else by your preference, then someone else may decide that what you want to do with the Internet is unacceptable to them, and they could try to turn your specific use of it off also. Think about it. The Internet is an open global medium belonging to everyone and to no one in particular.

As Internet users, we must be responsible for how we use the Internet. We should also avoid circumstances that can put us in harm's way, and defend ourselves if we are an available target. Let's make sure we can use this technically sophisticated "air" that is the Internet, and learn how we can enjoy it safely — by whatever definition and extent "safe" is for you.

Dial-Up Internet access

Accessing the Internet requires that your PC be equipped with a modem or network interface card, and that it has a properly configured set of drivers and protocols. The simplest connection is to have a dial-up adapter and the TCP/IP protocol associated with the dial-up adapter (as listed in the Network Neighborhood properties page in Windows). A dial-up adapter using TCP/IP enables you to establish a Point-to-Point Protocol (PPP) connection between an Internet service provider and your PC. In this case you need only set up a few details (we discuss these in a bit) for the specific dial-up networking connection type your ISP supports. When you dial in to the ISP, your system is automatically provided an IP address, and then the ISP's equipment then routes all network packets to and from your PC based on that network address.

Cross-Reference   For more information about drivers and protocols, see Chapter 10.

The dial-up adapter and TCP/IP functions are typically those provided within Windows 95, 98, 98SE, Me, NT, or 2000, or from third-party software such as Trumpet Winsock at `www.trumpet.com`, FTP Software's OnNet package at `www.ftp.com`, or from other software developers specializing in Internet connection software.

If you are using Windows 95 or 98, you will typically use the Dial-Up Networking (DUN) and Make New Connection wizard to set up a connection through a modem to an ISP. By default, if Windows 95/98 detects that a modem is installed in your system, some basic DUN entries will be made in the Network dialog box under the Control Panel. You will want to check this dialog box to be sure a dial-up adapter and the TCP/IP protocol are installed for you to be able to connect your system to the Internet. Figure 11-1 shows a typical Network dialog box. We also have a generic NE2000 network adapter installed on this system. Notice that TCP/IP is associated with both the dial-up adapter and the NE2000 adapter, and that no other protocols are installed.

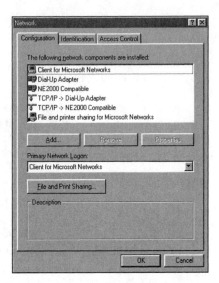

Figure 11-1: Typical networking properties within the Control Panel

Dial-Up Networking can be used with standard analog modems, ISDN "modems," and wireless modems such as those provided by the Ricochet ISP, available in some metropolitan areas. An ISP may not be the only place to which you will be setting up DUN configurations. Many corporations provide dial-up services exclusively to enable their employees to access their internal networks, and the principles are basically the same as the ones presented here. The only exceptions may be if you are also logging in to a Windows NT or Novell NetWare network requiring additional protocols and network access parameters.

Once you have created a new Dial-Up Networking shortcut for a specific ISP, you will need to configure specific network-related settings. The following three figures, Figures 11-2 through 11-4, show the Dial-Up Networking properties/dialog boxes you will need to configure. To access these dialog boxes, navigate from your desktop to My Computer, then Dial-Up Networking, and then right-click the shortcut for your ISP. Select Properties from the pop-up menu.

 Note   The process for Dial-Up Networking is similar when working with other versions of Windows, Unix, Linux, or other operating systems. Just some of the names of the items are different.

The General tab of DUN properties shown in Figure 11-2 provides edit boxes for changing the phone number and the selected modem for dialing out to your ISP.

The Server Types tab in the dialog box shown in Figure 11-3 enables you to change the configuration of the networking parameters specific to the system you are dialing. Notice that "Log on to network" is selected for all the installed protocols. This parameter is incorrect for most ISP connections, but may be required for dialing in to your office network.

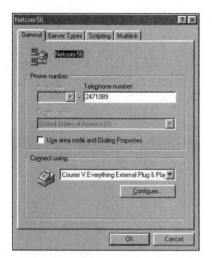

Figure 11-2: Typical Dial-Up Networking properties

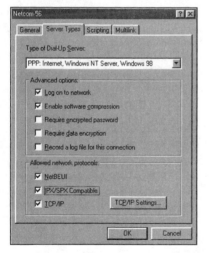

Figure 11-3: Typical Dial-Up Networking server type settings *before* Internet configuration

Figure 11-4 shows the typical server settings for most ISPs. Most ISP connections do not allow logging on to their network directly; instead, they allow simply dialing in and establishing a connection that authenticates you and enables you to use the network for Internet activities. So you probably want to deselect "Log on to network." Also, the Internet does not use the NetBEUI or IPX/SPX protocols, so these are also deselected. From this dialog box you may also need to select TCP/IP Settings to add a couple of critical IP addresses.

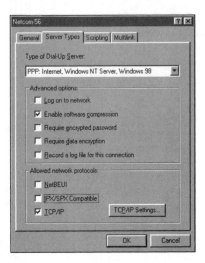

Figure 11-4: Typical Dial-Up Networking server type settings *after* Internet configuration

As most ISP connections provide DHCP (Dynamic Host Configuration Protocol) services, meaning that its server assigns you an IP address when you connect, and you can leave the first selection in the TCP/IP settings dialog box alone, per Figure 11-5. However, your ISP may require that you configure at least one name server (DNS) address, unless they have full DHCP capability that also provides name server addresses when you make your dial-up connection.

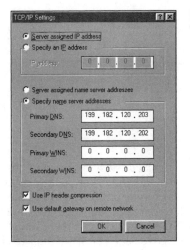

Figure 11-5: Typical Dial-Up Networking TCP/IP settings for Netcom

The dialog boxes we have presented represent typical settings for one location with access to the Netcom ISP. The phone number and DNS settings for your location and ISP will be different, but the Web site or written documentation for your ISP should provide instructions similar to these.

The next step is activating a DUN connection for the first time. Figure 11-6 shows an incomplete DUN dialog box. You will have to enter your own user name and password to make a successful connection. By default, Windows 95 and 98 insert the current Windows user name into this dialog box, but your ISP account name will probably be much different.

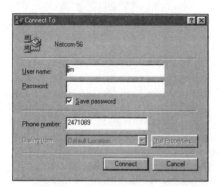

Figure 11-6: Starting a Dial-Up Networking session

Figure 11-7 shows a DUN connect dialog box with a user name and password for a Netcom "NetComplete" or "ix" account. Note that the user name is the e-mail address with a # symbol in front of it, which instructs the Netcom system to look you up as a full Internet access user rather than as a terminal access session user. We have also checked the "Save password" box so that our system remembers our DUN password every time. This is a mild security issue that you should consider *not* using if others have access to your computer.

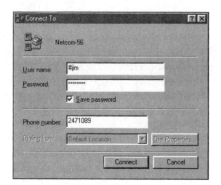

Figure 11-7: A working Dial-Up Networking configuration

Fixing a Corrupt Password File

If the Save password checkbox in the DUN connect dialog box is grayed out, meaning that you cannot select or deselect this item, it is an indication that your local password file is corrupt. This is a known flaw with the first version of Windows 95 and the first Service Pack for Windows 95. Microsoft provides a fix for this, currently as the full OSR2 service pack available from its Web site. A quick fix for this is to use Explorer to look in your C:\WINDOWS folder, locate your specific .PWL file (JIM.PWL or MIKE.PWL, for example), delete this file, and then restart Windows. You will have to reenter all of the passwords you use on your system as you encounter them, but this will rebuild a new password file, which will be good until the next time Windows corrupts it. Windows 98 can suffer a similar fate if the .PWL file becomes corrupt.

When you select Connect in your DUN dialog box, your system should activate your modem, dial out to your ISP, negotiate a modem connection, and then begin negotiating a PPP-type TCP/IP connection with your ISP. Once you have a PPP connection, you are assigned an IP and gateway address, and then your user name and password will be checked. If all is well, the dialog boxes will minimize and you will be "on the Internet." If you have a problem negotiating a connection with your modem, establishing the proper network protocols, or authenticating your name and password, you will be shown one or more pop-up dialog boxes to that effect. Double-check your settings, per the previous descriptions and figures, against the instructions for your specific ISP to make sure you have everything filled in correctly.

Corporate Internet access

If you are on a local area network (LAN), your company may already provide Internet access through one or more of several types of connections. Corporate networks typically get their Internet access from an Internet access provider (IAP) — a service that merely provides connectivity without dial-up, e-mail, or other services that individuals might subscribe to.

Your company may have two or more IAP connections — one for Web and Internet news services and one for inbound mail and company Web-site traffic, or a combination of these. Typical corporate IAPs are UUNET, the local telephone company, Sprint, MCI, or one of several other larger-capacity Internet traffic carriers. The connection capacity may be as low as a 64Kbps Frame Relay circuit, up to a T-1, T-3, OC-3, or ATM circuit, which is hundreds or thousands of times faster than you will get by using a modem.

Connecting Workstations to the Internet

How the connection between workstations on your local area network (LAN) and the Internet-at-large is made can vary significantly. A small office may use a simple router configuration and depend significantly on the ISP's router to filter most of the traffic. A large corporation will likely dedicate an access or firewall type router to inbound and outbound traffic to protect the company and its users and to monitor all traffic flowing in and out. Connection from your local desktop workstation to the Internet uses existing protocols and IP connections within your existing LAN design. If you telecommute or must access company network services on the road, your company may also provide dial-up access, limited to accessing local area network traffic or possibly providing full Internet access. Some companies are even venturing into the super-secure world of tunneling protocols to provide secure access to the company internal network to individual users. These are called Virtual Private Networks or VPNs.

Within a corporate network, your network or system administrator will have assigned the IP configuration parameters, or provided a means to do so automatically, over the internal network. This process may also involve configuring installed Web browsers, FTP, and news clients to use one or more proxy servers in order to protect the identity and structure of the internal network from being viewed or determined from the outside. A proxy server sits between the internal network and the Internet, acting much like a firewall. It accepts the requests from all workstations, processes them, and sends them on to the requested Internet sites as if any and all of the requests came from the same single host system. Returned data comes back to the proxy server and is then distributed to the respective workstations.

Note

One advantage of some proxy servers is that they may also cache frequently accessed Internet sites and be able to deliver their content without actually making an external connection. This can deliver faster apparent Internet performance and save on data communications and network traffic costs. If you defeat or ignore the proxy server configuration you may not be able to gain access to any external Internet traffic.

Corporate e-mail systems operate in much the same way. A single inbound SMTP server sits on the Internet and accepts all e-mail coming in to your company's domain, and then distributes it to the desktops with a POP3 server running on the same hardware, or to other e-mail distribution servers providing POP3 services to deliver your e-mail. Outbound e-mail is usually sent to a central SMTP transmission server, and then out to the Internet. More secure organizations may actually have the mail handled by systems located outside of the company network and physical location, and then transport mail into the company network on a private dedicated circuit. Either method can screen all mail messages for viruses, and potentially for confidential information leaks coming into or going out of the facility.

Virtual Private Networks

New with Windows 98SE is the addition of easy setup for a Virtual Private Network (VPN) connection for secure access, typically into a corporate LAN. A VPN connection uses your existing ISP connection to the Internet for communications to the VPN host system (your corporate office, for example), and then secures that connection with data encryption so that it cannot be monitored or corrupted. This type of connection makes your PC think it is connected directly to the VPN host while that connection is actually "sneaking" across the public Internet.

VPN can use a standard dial-up or one of the many always-on high-speed connections. It will not be as fast as you may be accustomed to at the office, but you can use most applications and gain access to shared resources if you need them.

To use VPN, you must first add "Microsoft Virtual Private Network Adapter" in the Network properties list. Adding the VPN adapter should also automatically add "Dial-Up Adapter #2 (VPN Support)" and "NDISWAN-> Microsoft Virtual Private Network Adapter" entries, as well as associate network protocols with the new "Dial-Up Adapter #2 (VPN Support)" entry.

Depending on your required office network configuration, you may have to include a WINS Server IP address. Your office network administrator, if needed, should provide this address. It is entered into the TCP/IP properties, WINS Configuration page for your dial-up adapter (not #2) or your network interface card, so you can access specific office resources through the VPN connection.

To set up for the connection, open My Computer, choose Dial-Up Networking, and then Add New Connection. Give it a name associated with your office VPN so you can remember it. Select the VPN adapter from the list of modems that appears. Click Next. You will then need to provide the IP address or host name for the system that will be receiving the VPN connection from you — perhaps vpn.yourcompany.com. Your office network administrator may provide you with additional details for setting up VPN properties. Be sure to include those settings so your connection works smoothly.

Once this is done, close the dialog box, establish your regular dial-up or high-speed connection to the Internet, and then select the new VPN "connectoid" you just created. Enter your office user name and password, and then click the Connect button. You will see a status dialog box like the one that appears when you connect to your ISP with a modem. After checking your credentials and authorizing you to use the VPN system, the dialog box goes away and you're "in."

At this point your PC is part of your office network and you may not be able to connect to Internet sites unless your office provides Internet access through the VPN connection. When you are done using the office network/VPN connection, simply disconnect as you would for Dial-Up Networking, and continue to use your Internet connection as you like or disconnect from it, too.

Intranets and extranets

An *intranet* is essentially a mini-Internet presence that exists within the bounds of corporate LANs and WANs (wide area networks). Intranets typically do not provide access via the public Internet. They are employed to provide commonly used information such as job opening postings, company news, and help desk tools as well as workgroup- or mission-specific corporate information to groups of users within a company or enterprise.

An *extranet* is an extension of or a specific "intranet-like" presence designed for the sharing of information between trusted entities, such as your company's vendors and customers. You might access the vendors for your company through their extranet connection to place and track orders with them, and your customers might access your company's extranet to place orders and get support information for your products.

 Note   An extranet is protected from Internet "intrusion" in much the same way as an intranet.

Internet Applications

Windows 95, 98, 98SE, Me, NT, and 2000, have been designed for networking — covering LANs, the Internet and intranets. The built-in networking, Web-browser support, and related tools and applications all lead to an Internet-aware PC system.

Before there was a Web there was the Internet. The Internet began with the first four computers connected to the ARPANET in 1968. From this small beginning, which supported the capability to transfer files and broadcast messages (neither looking or acting anything like the stable capabilities we take for granted today), we have witnessed the development of the capability to communicate with just about anyone in the world. Well, we are not quite there, yet, but the percentage of people in the world who have not even heard of the Internet is smaller than the percent that have. That is quite a statement for a world full of such diverse peoples, cultures, and interests.

To make the Internet really useful to everyday people, the very technical and, sometimes, cryptic specifications that enable the myriad of computer hardware and software to talk to each other had to be incorporated into simpler-to-use programs. To identify one event that brought the Internet to regular people (as opposed to scientists and technologists) is really unfair to the hundreds and thousands of talented people who have made so many contributions that have enabled the Internet. However, it is difficult to argue with the impact that Mosaic (by Marc Andreessen, best known as the founder of Netscape) has had on this industry.

Because of its success, many of the previously difficult protocols have been incorporated into the newest browsers, and we all have the ability to use the power of the Internet.

The most common means of sharing information over the Internet is through the Hypertext Transfer Protocol (HTTP) used between Web servers and browsers; the File Transfer Protocol (FTP); and electronic mail sent via the Post Office Protocol (POP3) and Simple Mail Transfer Protocol (SMTP). Common application programs such as Netscape, Microsoft Internet Explorer, and Microsoft Outlook Express support these high-level, data-transfer protocols. Internet electronic mail is also supported by separate applications such as Qualcomm's Eudora, Pegasus, and embedded in enterprise applications such as Lotus Notes and cc:Mail.

WWW, HTTP, and Web browsers

We might as well state this now — a Web browser is, or was, developed simply to be a passive viewer or reader tool for accessing and viewing specifically formatted text documents. These documents use a special text formatting and layout control language known as the Hypertext Markup Language (HTML), a derivative of the Standard Graphical Markup Language (SGML). A Web browser application, Mosaic, was developed to interpret and present HTML files so that a content author could create and share with other users on the Internet documents that had better appearance and navigational control than a bland ASCII file.

Special server software was created to deliver HTML through the File Transfer Protocol known as HTTP that browsers and servers used to communicate with each other. Before Mosaic and the implementation of HTTP, you could get HTML-formatted documents transmitted from one computer to another by any number of file transfer methods, but most likely through FTP or as an e-mail attachment. HTTP is used to do this in concert between the user side (using HTML viewing software) and the source of the information (a system on the Internet running HTTP server software). That means the HTML-formatted files could be delivered from the source and viewed immediately, online, with all of the presentation or layout arriving intact, just as the author intended.

Basically, a Web browser application simply connects to a Web-host site on a network and requests that a specific document be displayed (such as index.html). The document is transmitted across the network to the requesting user's system, and the browser presents that document as formatted by the author.

Between its inception and the present day, HTML and Web browsers have had many enhancements. The original browser and formatting language have been reworked significantly. Some of the best of the added features and functionality are the capability to view graphics of different formats, as well as content selection and data entry facilities. We are now able to share much more information between many more people through the Web than we were with the conventional text-based online services and bulletin board systems of yesteryear, when many of us started enjoying computing.

Web browsers and the tremendous number of tools available to help with the creation of Web-based applications have expedited our access to all types of information, without the hassle of conventional software creation and distribution methods. Yes, careful and professional development skills and techniques are still strongly advised, but they are not always applied. It is easier to create various applications and presentations of information, and it is also just that much easier to create bad applications and have them distributed more quickly to thousands of unaware Web surfers.

Although Web browsers today have many nice and compelling features, the Web and its tools are not always the ideal solution for every interaction humans have with computers. When you add ActiveX, JavaScript, Java applets and applications, helper applications, and external viewers, the otherwise simple Web browsing functionality becomes much more complex than a mere window on the world beyond our desktops, offices, cities, and countries. Many of these add-ons to the simple browser allow for a much more powerful and, unfortunately, more risky interaction with other users and computer systems.

Without still more tools and features lumped into an otherwise simple file-viewing utility, using a Web browser can expose you and your system to the risk of crashing, invasion of privacy, and general concerns about the suitability of various types of content shared on the Internet.

Choosing a Browser

As for HTML file viewers, or Web browser software programs as they are more commonly known, the two obvious products that come to mind are Microsoft's Internet Explorer and Netscape's Navigator. These are very feature-rich, sometimes complex, often system-resource-hogging applications that enable us to enjoy anything and everything the World Wide Web has to offer. Microsoft's Internet Explorer is designed for use on Windows 9x, Me, NT (on both x86 and DEC Alpha), and some Apple Macintosh platforms, whereas Netscape Navigator is available for a wider variety of platforms, including most of the variations of Unix. These applications are capable of displaying a variety of text and graphic file formats as files come across the Internet, and provide for the addition of helper applications to support enhanced audio and visual content, such as RealAudio programming and Vivo streaming video. Additionally, current browsers also support Java applets and applications, and inline JavaScript to enhance Web site interaction. Microsoft's Internet Explorer is also tied closely to ActiveX-executable content, all making possible the use of browsers as front-ends for server-based applications.

Your choice of browser depends on your needs, or the dictates of your company, and, often as not, on the type of content or server interactions you expect to encounter. It is possible to design Web hosts or sites that deliver content specific to one type of browser or the other. Neither Explorer nor Navigator represent or set a clear and unquestionable standard for being a universal, works-with-all-sites browser application. Many of us believe there should be complete equity, compliance, and uniformity between all browsers. HTTP, HTML, and various other standards exist to help make the Internet a globally viable communications medium. Unfortunately, each of these vendors continues to fight, "innovate," and alienate themselves from what should be a universally accepted and implemented information-sharing medium.

Note   Much more information about browsers, HTML, and various Web applications and services can be found in the *Internet Bible, HTML in Plain English,* and similar books from IDG Books Worldwide. But remember, the main purpose of a browser is, or was, to do just that, browse through a selected document that provides links to other related documents.

POP3/SMTP

If you have ever received or sent e-mail via the Internet, chances are you have used POP3 and SMTP to get and send your messages. POP is the Post Office Protocol, and POP3 is the third version of this Internet e-mail retrieval protocol. SMTP is the Simple Mail Transfer Protocol that is used to transmit e-mail from your client application or a mail server to another mail server. These two protocols typically go hand in hand on the Internet. IMAP4 is a newer protocol that supports new features such as being able to scan messages before downloading them from the mail server — useful for folks using hand-held PCs and small notebooks to read their mail while away from the office or home.

Electronic mail programs such as Qualcomm's Eudora, Microsoft Outlook Express, and Netscape's Messenger Mailbox (part of Navigator) are capable of retrieving e-mail from POP3 servers. These programs use SMTP to transmit mail you originate to an SMTP server that distributes your mail to the SMTP servers for the message's recipients. Most Internet service providers operate Unix-based servers that provide POP3 services so you can pick up your mail, and they use SENDMAIL and SMTP services for accepting and transmitting mail delivery from you.

FTP

The File Transfer Protocol is one of the first protocols used to transfer files, but now probably ranks third in popularity and typical use of the Internet. With FTP you may access file directories on other systems to copy files between systems. Typically, FTP is used for downloading information from other systems, such as Internet file libraries, to your personal system, but it is also the method of preference for submitting your personal Web pages to an offsite Web server. For file library use, you access a distant FTP server as an anonymous or generic public user with read-only access to the server's specific directory(s). For sending your Web content to an offsite hosting server, you are usually required to provide a specific user name and password to gain write-access to your Web directory. FTP is supported in Microsoft Internet Explorer, Netscape Navigator, general communication programs such as Procomm Plus, and as an MS-DOS/Windows/Unix prompt command-line driven application that is part of the operating system.

NNTP

Network News Transfer Protocol (NNTP) is used to communicate with Internet/USENET newsgroup servers that store and forward archives of messages in an open forum format. You can find newsgroups on many different subjects, from technical issues through alternative personal issues. You can read and post items to newsgroups using Microsoft Outlook and Netscape Navigator among other applications. Typically your ISP or the company can provide you with details about how to configure your application to connect to their news server so you can both read and post messages in the groups.

SNTP

SNTP stands for the Simple Network Time Protocol, a standard data transfer format used between servers and client systems to share date and time information in order to synchronize systems with each other. A good Windows-based application to experience SNTP time services with is Tradis95, which you can find by searching the popular software listing sites such as www.shareware.com or www.download.com.

Telnet

Telnet is probably not as descriptive as it could be. It is basically a terminal or plain-text Teletype-like session established between a terminal program (much as you might have used ProComm Plus or Windows' HyperTerminal to connect to bulletin board systems) and a server that provides access to a command-line session. For Unix this would be a shell session, and for DOS systems it would be using the DOS prompt, but on another machine. This is the old-fashioned but classic way system administrators communicate with the routers and servers on their networks. Some corporations still have Unix, VAX, and other systems that can only be used through a Telnet session.

X-Windows

If you have used a recent vintage Unix system where you work, you are probably familiar with some variation of the MIT X-Window user-interface. The X-Window interface is a method of conveying the graphical properties of one or more dialog boxes, similar to but predating the Apple Macintosh and Microsoft Windows schemes. In its ideal implementation, X enables applications designed for like systems to share processing resources across multiple machines. We do not see too many of these applications in commercial use, but they do exist. Sun Microsystems, Hewlett-Packard, Digital Equipment Corp., and Silicon Graphics provide their own versions of X-Window-like user-interfaces on their platforms and operating systems.

Because X-Window provides for similar GUI behavior and the capability to share processing across systems, it requires that a lot of data be transferred back and forth across the network. Unlike Windows, entire graphic screens are not transferred, just the graphic commands. The volume of data makes it unsuitable for most dial-up connections because the performance and behavior is a bit clunky, but over ISDN and faster circuits X is quite usable.

For PC systems to share in an X-Window environment you must use an X-terminal software package such as the Exceed package from Hummingbird Communications, which runs under Windows. If you can find a copy, Quarterdeck's DESQview/X package enables multitasking DOS sessions, running Windows 3.x sessions, and communicating with other X-systems.

Chat and forum systems

For those of us who came from the classic text-based, online systems, such as The Source, PeopleLink, UNISON, and even the early days of CompuServe, one of the things we missed about the growth of and moving to the Internet were chat sessions and forums. Thanks to a lot of different innovations these features are available on the Internet in many forms.

One of the most popular one-on-one and group chat applications is ICQ (an adaptation from the phrase "I seek you") from Mirabilis Ltd., which can be found at www.mirabilis.com. Other chat programs exist, but ICQ seems to have won the popularity contest hands-down. It is easy to configure, and Mirabilis provides central servers through which chat participants can look up who is online and decide what kind of topic to join, or to find another specific ICQ-enabled person. ICQ is great for those long distant, nonvoice interchanges between friends and family. ICQ also supports voice and video conferences.

Forums come in a variety of flavors and presentations. The Internet has had newsgroups, large archives of notes covering various topics, for years. These are a little daunting to navigate and keep under any form of discipline, and you have to put up with a lot of people playing "Net cop." To avoid the more public newsgroups and their issues, various vendors such as Forum Enterprises, at www.foruminc.com, have created forum software for Web sites. Forums can be as simple as a listing of questions and answers submitted by users, or as complex as sorted, searchable, moderated groups of topic-specific text.

Audio, video, and telephony delivery

It was only a matter of time before someone figured out how to get more than just a bunch of text and a few static pictures across the Internet in reasonably usable form. Enter Intel and, early in the game, CU-SeeMe from Cornell University (www.cuseeme.com), with its video-conferencing software, and now RealAudio (www.realaudio.com), for a variety of live and archived radio and television programming. Kick in RealVideo, VivoActive, and other inline content players for the delivery of video programming content, some complete with audio. RealAudio and programming from AudioNet.com and other companies is exceptionally handy for computer-side listening of various events you might miss otherwise, because you can go back to the site and listen to archives of previously recorded streams.

If video-conferencing is not on your to-do list, but keeping in touch with people and hearing their voices is, search the Web for a copy of VocalTec's Internet Phone application. Trial versions are available from a number of places, but the best place to try is www.vocaltec.com. Using your PC's sound card with speakers and microphone and a connection to the Internet, you can connect to VocalTec's servers or directly to other users and find various open or private conversations to join. Even with just a 28.8 connection, voice quality is quite clear, and the price is right! In addition, if you are a licensed amateur radio operator, you can obtain add-on software for Internet Phone that enables you to connect one-on-one, over the Internet, to various live radio stations that are on the air.

Many of these applications are said to *stream* their content, which means that the program is usable as it is delivered, often live, from the source, as opposed to fixed file content that must be fully downloaded to your system first. Of course, digitizing pictures and audio has been around for a long time — the phone companies have been converting our phone calls to and from digitized formats for years. Unfortunately, it took until the mid-1990s before we had adequate computing power and data transfer pipes to be able to enjoy these features at home. These enhanced content applications have certainly changed the way people interact over the Internet, compared to the old days of chat rooms and forums.

For the voyeur in you, try connecting to various sites that feature Web cams — video cameras mounted on hilltops, buildings, bridges, and other places offering scenic views of popular tourist attractions and local features. For instance, Surf City, USA (Huntington Beach, California), has a number of sites that have cameras pointed at surfer's favorite locations (such as next to the Huntington Beach Pier where national and international surfing contests are held every summer). You do not have to drive to the beach to find out if the surf's up — just check the Web! Go to http://wavetrak.surfline.com/hbcam.asp.

Using CompuServe, AOL, or Prodigy

If you use CompuServe, AOL, or Prodigy as your online service provider, you are no longer limited to using the software provided by these special online services for all of your Internet activity.

Their dial-up connections create and use standard PPP and TCP/IP communications. Once you establish a dial-up connection with any of these services, you are free to launch and use Internet Explorer, Netscape Navigator or other Internet-related programs to access other sites and e-mail accounts, as you wish.

You must still use their respective software packages to send e-mail through and receive e-mail from your mailboxes on these specific services, and they will translate and convert Internet mail messages between their special formats and those of the rest of the Internet at their servers. However, because these are conversions, you may not get the message in exactly the same format or with the same content as was sent.

Internet application configurations

For the most part the technicalities of the applications you will use can remain hidden within the configuration screens for the application. You should be able to install the application, provide a few personalization parameters — such as an e-mail address and details about your e-mail servers — and go on to enjoy the application and the Internet without too much fuss.

For each site or system to which you wish to connect, you must provide some form of address, and perhaps, also, some form of authentication to gain access to remote resources. Most browsers and Internet applications do not require you to enter the full Uniform Resource Locator (URL) that includes the protocol specification (for example, `http://`) as well as the fully qualified host and domain names.

Addresses you are probably most familiar with are those common "www" prefixed names such as `www.yahoo.com` (which specifies a host name, `www`, and the domain name, `yahoo.com`, with or without the full qualification of protocol, as with `http://www.yahoo.com`. You may also use `ftp.cdrom.com` to directly access the file directories at the Walnut Creek CD-ROM archives site.

Your e-mail applications likely require that you configure your e-mail address, such as "jim@raisin.com;" the address of the POP3 server you get mail from, perhaps "popd.ix.netcom.com;" and the address of the SMTP server you send mail out through, perhaps "smtp.ix.netcom.com." If your ISP provides Domain Name Service (DNS), you do not have to worry about specific IP addresses, except for those of the DNS servers. In fact, using specific IP addresses to access some sites can cause a desired connection to fail because large ISPs have many, many servers performing the same functions in parallel, and rotate in round-robin fashion which server will handle requests to balance the load between systems. This also enables the ISP to take a system offline for maintenance as required, so never expect to connect to the same IP address or host name twice—just let the ISP and DNS do the addressing and routing work for you.

News services require you to browse a lengthy list of available newsgroups and select or subscribe to specific groups. Subscription does not obligate you in any way, it merely enables your client application to collect content from a specific group and post information to that group. Be aware that thousands of groups and categories exist; some, just as with many Web sites, are not suitable for younger or sensitive individuals.

Internet Security

Security is one of the fastest growing concerns as an increasing number of people spend more time and expect to do more with the Internet. You have much to be worried about, due to the many unscrupulous users out there with nothing but time and curiosity (or even larceny) on their hands, who somehow find pleasure in causing trouble for others.

New discoveries of security holes in Microsoft's and other companies' products are made and verified every week. We'll do our best to bring you up to date, but you are strongly encouraged to keep up with the latest security updates and patches routinely posted on Microsoft's Web site. You can also keep up with the many Internet security issues by visiting the BugNet Web site at www.bugnet.com, and the Web sites for virus-protection product providers—Network Associates/McAfee at www.mcafee.com, Symantec at www.symantec.com, and others.

In general, you have three types of protection to be concerned with:

✦ Virus protection to prevent programs, e-mail and Web content containing viruses or other types of malicious program code from ruining your day

✦ Content filtering to prevent specifically recognized and known "adult content," violence, and other personally controversial material from reaching users

✦ Traffic filtering to be sure that your systems are handling only the necessary traffic, and blocking unsuitable or unauthorized access

You have numerous means to accomplish one or all of these protective functions, and we must recommend that you choose one of each kind of protection, even if you are not using one of those fancy broadband cable modems and sharing download time with your neighbors.

Viruses

Our first concerns have been about viruses, little snippets of program code that attach themselves to files, either executable files or even documents and spreadsheets, and cause damage to or restrict the use of computer systems. Virus-protection software has been one of the fastest growing sectors of the software business in recent years. Previously we used DOS and then Windows-based programs to scan our files to detect viruses in them, and also to monitor systems looking for virus-like activities that might cause file damage.

More recent virus-protection software automatically monitors Web site and e-mail traffic to detect inbound virus code as it moves across the network. Such advanced protection is highly recommended. Network Associates' (formerly McAfee Associates) VirusScan program, and Symantec's Norton AntiVirus, are among the most well known, popular, and up-to-date virus-protection products on the market. Get one of these products, install it, use it, and keep it updated.

Unauthorized file access

Our second-level concern, now that we are establishing true network connections with other systems, are whether or not people on the Internet can gain access to the files on our hard disks. The answer to this is, it can happen, although it probably won't, depending how we configure our PCs and network connections. However, it is a valid concern. If you have followed us through Chapter 10, or visited Steve Gibson's Web site at www.grc.com, you know that we disable/remove Microsoft's NetBEUI protocol on every system connected to the Internet. Although NetBEUI is not carried over the Internet, data packets can come across to your PC and affect your local NetBEUI driver, crashing your system or creating unwanted device sharing. We also recommend disabling the File and Print Sharing services of Windows 95 and 98 while connected to the Internet, because it is possible for someone to attack your system and create hidden connections to gain access to your files.

Tip   If you will not disable File and Print Sharing in Windows, at least use a good password; at best, use a personal firewall that can separate local network from Internet traffic and block the latter. If you need to share files across the Internet, more secure ways exist that don't involve letting the world have access to your local file system.

Denial-of-service attacks

Another issue is the increased frequency of denial-of-service attacks on networks and even individual users. A number of Web sites specialize in providing details about how to create programs (and may even make available those complete programs) designed to send erroneous data to a desired IP address, causing system crashes or routing failures.

These attacks by themselves have not destroyed data or caused system damage, but the events are at the least very annoying. The usual motive for launching a denial-of-service data attack on another user is as basic and childish as trying to knock an opponent offline and out of Internet-based interactive games. The same old story — if you cannot win, take the ball away from your opponent. Without a few updates, Windows 95 will crash into the "blue screen of death" and require a complete restart. Windows 98 can survive some attacks but is known to reboot under others.

Because most games work in extended DOS modes, the symptom is typically just a system halt or interruption in game play. To avoid most attacks, your ISP should be able to apply various filters and blocks in its routers, but few actually do. You should apply the Dial-Up Networking and Winsock 2 updates on your PC, even if you have installed Microsoft's OSR2 update for Windows 95. No known avoidance patches exist yet for Windows 98, but it does use Winsock 2 and has an enhanced DUN component. The best you can do is find a copy of NukeNabber at `www.dynamsol.com/puppet` or at other online file libraries, install it, and then use it whenever you are connected to the Internet, or look into one of the other personal firewalls that can block this activity.

E-mail attacks

Very recently, we have seen the vulnerability of various e-mail applications that can allow inbound messages carrying executable code to affect our systems. Because e-mail is now more than just text messages, local e-mail applications must interpret, recognize, and respond appropriately to various types of content — from containing simple Word .DOC file attachments to displaying HTML in the e-mail viewing window to playing voice messages.

Because it is possible for the client to pre-read the inbound message files and act on them before we see them, any ability for program code to be executed by the e-mail client during this process leaves us open for new types of attacks (though it is likely this problem will be solved by the time this book gets into print). One problem that Microsoft has fixed, for now, deals with an e-mail message with an attached file that has a filename too long to be handled properly. The biggest vulnerabilities come from e-mail programs that can display mail sent in HTML format, which means they may also be able to invoke Java or ActiveX applications and penetrate your system. This is one overlooked issue in the Microsoft lawsuits — the integration of Web features with the operating system weakens the entire system.

We used to get prank e-mails and false virus alerts from friends telling us not to open or read specific types of e-mail or those with certain subject lines — all hoaxes — but now, we may not even have the chance to cover ourselves before we read our mail. Call them high-tech electronic letter bombs, perhaps, but some of these things unfortunately go with the territory of being on the Net and of people feeling that they have something to share with everyone. These are current problems, but knowing about them is the first step to providing general fixes that protect us all.

Tip Make sure you keep up to date with the current version of your software. This provides protection because the current version includes the software vendor's latest security fixes.

Cookies

Despite the hubbub over cookies, these tidbits of information related to Web site visitations are really about as innocent as they sound. It all depends on who uses them and who can get them. Because a Web browser was, and still is, a passive method (IP is a "connectionless" protocol), in order to read a file from a server at some distant location, the server you visited had no way of knowing if you had seen that content before. In much the same way that crumbs were left behind to mark the way through the woods in that old Grimm Brothers fairy tale, cookies create an electronic "trail": cookies work from the server side, leaving a file with "bookmark" information about your visit to a specific Web site. This bookmark, or cookie, differs from the bookmarks you set in your browser, though the idea is about the same.

Cookies could theoretically be left by any site and be read by any other site, which lead to the cookie scare — worries about a potential Big Brother watching over us, knowing where we have surfed, and so on. At least Netscape has made it possible to configure Navigator so that it will not allow cookies to be read by any site except the one that issued that specific cookie. No reputable firm that you would give your credit card number to over the Internet would ever be foolish enough to apply a cookie to your system with your credit card number in it, and a cookie does not have the room to store any personal information of significance.

Personally, we don't care. Our ISPs can trace every Web site visited and file we have ever downloaded. And with all the spam, or junk e-mail, you might get that is addressed to a list of consecutive user names at xyz.com ISP, you might understand that your privacy is as much or more at risk from the people who work inside your ISP than anyone else on the Internet.

Also, the not-so-obvious NETSCAPE.HST and PREFS.JS files, as well as the local browser cache directory contents, will reveal more about your Web travels than any number of cookies would.

Again, cookies are just cryptic bookmarks that a Web site can use to acknowledge your prior visit, authenticate your access, or let you continue on through the site from where you last left off — rather ingenious little bits of data. Cookies are probably the least of your worries, but to avoid, decline, or accept them is your preference.

The alternatives — including a variety of active client programs and Registry entries that applications and Web-based programs would use — may be worse yet. This approach would put your system in real danger. Cookies are better.

ActiveX, Java, and helper applications

As we continue with Internet advances and the desire to do more things using Web browsers, the mere file viewer that a browser used to be has turned into an amazing tool. You can use your browser for interacting with server-based data records and running local programs on your PC for various purposes. However, it may leave you open to some Web site sending you an ActiveX (Visual Basic or other program) or a Java applet or an application that has complete access to your local PC system, including file and network resources. Just as various helper applications such as RealAudio work with data streams that come across the Internet and get written to your local hard drive, ActiveX and Java programs have the same capabilities and may be less predictable than programs from reputable companies.

Not all ActiveX or Java programs should be considered threats, as many of them are designed to help you maintain and get support for your PC system, but they should not all be trusted either. A simple, small helper application you've downloaded could well destroy your hard drive, gather up and then transmit your private data files, or simply annoy you with a bunch of nonstop screen animations. These are certainly reasons for you to use a good virus-protection program and perhaps even some of the newer Internet personal security software packages on the market today.

Tip   If in doubt, disable the capability to launch ActiveX and Java programs in your browser. However, keep in mind that disabling these will, most likely, disable some really neat packages you may enjoy.

In addition, many good JavaScripts are floating around, along with quite a few annoying ones. JavaScripts are provided "inline" with Web site HTML pages, and they are usually included to enhance site navigation and appearance; however, a few are used to create annoying pop-up boxes, launch new browser windows, and generally make visiting some sites a dizzying experience. JavaScripts *do not* have the ability to manipulate, copy, scramble, or destroy your local files, take information, or crash your system — unless they cause so much browser and graphics activity that your system runs out of Windows resources or CPU time.

SSL and encryption

The privacy of information conveyed between Web clients and servers is of sufficient importance that most browsers provide built-in encryption capabilities for selective data transfers. If you use Netscape, you may have wondered about the little broken key or padlock icon in the corner of the window. This is an indicator of a secure link between your browser and a Web server. Most Web browsing is not secure — that is, all requests for pages and links, data submitted in online forms, and pages sent back are transmitted as clear text that can be intercepted and easily read with common network monitoring equipment. When a secure link is to be made, your browser and the server establish a unique encrypted data path between them, and all data is scrambled. Theoretically, the scrambling and encryption used differs from session to session so that if someone happens to break the code of one session, they will not be able to use it to decrypt messages of other sessions. The level and type of security is determined by the version of browser you have and the encryption license or standard used by the site's server.

Third-party security "certificate" providers also exist; their purpose is to establish the authenticity of secure connection requests as a method of guaranteeing that a secure connection is indeed made with the site you requested. This is an additional level of protection that helps ensure that someone, pretending to be someone else, did not intercept the communications.

PPTP and VPN

The Point-to-Point Tunneling Protocol (PPTP) is a method of establishing a unique, private connection between two systems with encrypted data flowing over data circuits. Virtual Private Networks (VPN) can operate within the PPTP or other protocols to establish similar unique, private sessions between two systems. Either or both are methods of providing connectivity to a corporate or other unique network system over otherwise public circuits. These connections enable corporations to take advantage of the Internet for telecommuter or other remote-access needs without building a separate dial-up or private network communications path.

Policing content

As you may have heard or discovered, the Internet carries a little bit of everything, and sometimes too much of some things that may be unsuitable for certain audiences. Whether or not you concern yourself with the privacy of the information on your own systems at any given moment, you may be concerned about the type of content you feel is acceptable to your children or other family members. Preventing children from accessing pornography or participating in online forums or newsgroups with content you deem unsuitable for them, as well as discouraging others who would exploit children in any of several unacceptable ways are major concerns.

Self-policing has worked for Internet users for years, and you should continue to do this. To help control access to the sites or content that you may find unsuitable, a few companies have created software products that can intercept and restrict access to these sites.

Cyber Patrol and NetNanny are two products that fit into this category. They are to be installed on your system and configured to work with your browser and Internet connection. When running, they evaluate the requests for connections to Internet sites, compare these requests to a reference list of known sites and stop the connection, or make the connection, screen the data that comes back for unsuitable content and stop the data from reaching the browser. The publishers of these tools also provide regular updates to the reference list of sites so that ever-changing and newer sites do not sneak by the filtering process.

Likewise, Symantec recently introduced its Norton Internet Security product and Network Associates/McAfee offers its Personal Firewall. The latter is a relabeled version of the ConSeal Private Desktop product. These are very rich products that enable you to configure a variety of security levels — both in terms of content and types of Internet connections that will be allowed.

These tools are highly recommended for those who hesitate to bring the Internet into their homes or schools, but would like to provide access to the available resources of the Internet for student and family benefit. They are probably not effective or fool-proof against the increasing computer awareness and knowledge of the average 14-year-old, but they are effective for less-technically-skilled, younger children.

Personal firewalls

We've mentioned them by name and in general in various places throughout this chapter — ConSeal Private Desktop, Network ICE's BlackICE Defender, ZoneAlarm (included on the CD-ROM distributed with this version), Sybergen's Secure Desktop, and NukeNabber — and they are worth investing a little time, some money where necessary, and certainly the CPU and memory resources needed to run them.

When you do install one of these programs, especially if you subscribe to an always-on cable modem or xDSL service, you will quickly discover how often and how many different people elsewhere on the Internet have nothing better to do than scan your system for vulnerabilities, try to make connections on obscure ports, and so on.

The problem is far worse on cable modem systems because most of them use a well-known series of IP addresses. However, the series of IP addresses used by the ISPs to support modem users are also becoming known. All some smart-aleck kid needs to do is download and launch a port scanning utility, set the address range to scan into the screen, and launch what amounts to a few million packets of inquiry across an entire network. These are easily traced, and stupid is the person who uses such a program from his or her own xDSL or cable connection, because it is easy to identify and report it to their ISP. In time the IP address ranges for xDSL and other large-scale, fixed-address networks will become well known, and they will be vulnerable too.

So what if someone scans your IP address for open ports? This is the first step to launching a serious attack to see if attaching to a set of shared files or a printer is possible, if you are running a personal Web server, FTP server, and so on. The best way to defend yourself against the second and subsequent waves of possible attacks is to use one of these firewall products to make your system appear invisible — actually, to not appear at all! Hackers cannot attack a system they cannot see.

Your passwords

Passwords are your keys to all sorts of network resources at work or on the Internet. You should treat them as you do credit card numbers, banking PINs, and other bits of information you hold in deepest secrecy. Just as you would no more leave your keys with a note indicating your car license number and home address on a bulletin board in a seedy bar on the wrong side of town, simply *do not share your passwords with others*. We are repeating this set of tips from Chapter 10 because it is a very important topic to remember. These tips are a medley of suggestions from various corporate and Internet security practices.

Simple Security Tips

In the absence of company security guidelines, follow these basic rules for system access security under all circumstances:

✦ Pick a cryptic user name, especially for remote-access systems, if the system lets you pick your own name. Use an alphabetic/numeric/special character mix that is not in a dictionary.

✦ *Always* pick a cryptic password. Use an alphabetic/numeric/special character mix that is not in a dictionary or made up of common names, words, or numbers familiar to you that others would easily recognize.

✦ Change passwords often — every 30 to 90 days is recommended. Do not share your password with anyone, but if you must, change it as soon as possible. Never use the same password twice or on different systems.

✦ Do not leave remote-access, file sharing, or host access software running when it is not needed.

✦ Do not leave Windows 95/98/SE/Me/2000 File and Print Sharing enabled on your system when it is not needed, especially if your system is ever connected to the Internet.

✦ Do not use Microsoft's NetBEUI protocol on systems connected to the Internet if you do not need it, or unless the firewall at your company or ISP blocks this protocol from outside access. NetBEUI itself is not carried on the Internet, but it is a point of vulnerability to workstation security, and using it can cause Dial-Up Networking and routers to connect to service providers needlessly.

✦ If you regularly connect to the Internet with Windows 95, obtain and install the Dial-Up Networking version 1.2 and Winsock update files from the Microsoft Web site to protect your system against common denial-of-service attacks across the Internet. Hackers target random and known IP addresses to see what happens just for fun — do not give them any extra pleasure.

✦ Frequently check for, download, and apply each and every security patch your operating system and applications offer to you. While exploits against such vulnerabilities tend to be seasonal, meaning that old hacking opportunities are soon abandoned and new ones are discovered, because they are exploited, never skip an update that covers a past vulnerability.

✦ If you must set up File and Print Sharing, host or remote access, carefully configure the system to provide the least amount of visibility and access to system resources. Providing full privileges to the root directories of your disk drives is asking for trouble, even through innocent mistakes. Assign a specific subdirectory (folder) to hold only those files that must be shared, and leave the rest of the system inaccessible. Any File or Print Sharing exposes your system to access violations from outside systems through Windows' NetBIOS interface.

✦ Use virus-protection software. Files transferred to your system by others may not have been checked for viruses. You never know what can come across in e-mail or by browsing Web sites these days. Just do it.

✦ Obtain, install, and use a personal firewall product. Again, just do it.

✦ If in doubt, do not allow *any* connections to your system. Turn it off or disconnect it from all external connectivity if you are not sure the system will be secure.

A few simple rules and some clear planning about what you need to do with interconnected systems can make your computing experience a lot more productive and safe.

Security hardware

An excellent way to protect your entire local network of PCs, Macintosh, or Unix systems is with a firewall. Traditionally, firewalls have been large, expensive, complex pieces of hardware deployed in network server rooms. Recently, a few companies have made personal firewalls available that are ideally suited for the home or small office network with an always-on cable or xDSL connection — and even for your dial-up modem connection!

Three personal firewalls we've looked at, the UGate-3000 from UMAX, the WebRamp 700s from Ramp Networks, and WatchGuard's SOHO Firebox, are reasonably priced ($300–400) and very easy to set up and use. They also have a four-port Ethernet hub on the LAN side so you can connect multiple systems to one device for a really small network, or connect another hub for a larger network.

These devices all provide a critical function in protecting any device connected to the Internet — *stateful inspection*. This feature examines every data packet coming into it from the Internet and determines if the data matches the type of connection requested. That is, they determine if it really is e-mail-type data on the TCP/IP ports for e-mail — 25 and 110, or FTP traffic on ports 20 and 21, Web traffic in port 80, and so on. If the examined data does not match the requested connection, the connection request is denied.

They also provide DHCP and NAT (Network Address Translation) functions so that your presence on the Internet appears as one IP address on the outside while having entirely different IP addresses on the inside of your network — typically "net 10" or "net 192" addresses that are not routed across the Internet. This feature makes your internal network system invisible to the Internet so it cannot be hacked.

Of course no firewall would be complete without controlling which IP protocols and TCP ports are actually allowed to pass through, so the common TCP ports — 20, 21, 25, 80, 110, 443, and only a handful of others — are allowed by default. You have to do some special configuration to allow special ports used by some games and common applications such as AOL Instant Messenger to pass.

You can also configure one or a few IP addresses of choice to be exposed to the Internet behind the firewall for special purposes — say a personal Web or mail server. However none of these products fills the midrange need of allowing multiple servers to be protected by these devices; for this type of service you need a midlevel 3Com or high-end Cisco product.

The WatchGuard and Ramp devices support up to five or ten users on the LAN side, with incremental price increases to enable more user capacity. WatchGuard also comes with built-in content examination and filtering that can prevent unwanted adult content, violence, or hate-related content to pass through to the user workstations. The UGate-3000 supports up to 253 users; however, this is a lot of users for such a small unit, so Internet data throughput may suffer with a lot of users accessing the Internet at the same time.

Basic Internet Troubleshooting

The following are some typical challenges you may have had or probably will encounter when working with the Internet.

Symptoms

▶ Dial-Up Networking reports that the modem is in use or not available.

▶ Dial-Up Networking reports no dial tone.

▶ Rapid-busy error signal when dialing.

Suspects

▶ Another program has taken exclusive control of the modem or COM port.

▶ The port configuration for the modem is incorrect.

▶ The modem is turned off or is defective.

▶ Cabling between the PC and the modem is not correct.

▶ The modem is improperly connected or not connected to the phone line, or is connected through another device.

▶ The COM port is defective.

▶ Dialing properties are not correct for your telephone system.

Solutions

▶ Disable fax or other programs that use the same COM port. Older programs may not be Windows-port-sharing friendly and will take over a port. Upgrade these programs to newer Windows versions.

▶ Be sure the port is set correctly for hardware flow control, rather than software or X-on/X-off control, and for the proper baud rate. Setting the baud rate too high can cause some modems not to respond.

▶ Be sure that the cabling between the COM port and the modem is correct, including any adapter cables between system board ports and rear panel connections. Many ten-pin header connector cables to D-connector cables look alike but are not wired the same, and must be installed on the board correctly. This is a common problem with home-built systems.

▶ Use a diagnostic program with a loop-back or test connector to check the ports. A reversed cable on the system board indicates only partial test success on the wrong cable type, and no test success on reversed cables. All tests must pass for the port connection to be good.

▶ Check to be sure that another device is not in-series with the phone line connection to the modem, or deactivate that device. You may have multiple modems, or modems and fax machines using the same line, and one of them may have taken over the circuit.

▶ Check to be sure that the phone line is connected to the proper jack on the modem. Many modems open the circuit marked for the phone when attempting to establish a line connection for the modem only. (The phone jack on the modem marked with the small telephone icon is for connecting a local telephone through the modem. This jack should not go to the phone line or wall jack. The phone jack on the modem marked with a rectangular box is for connecting the modem to the phone line or wall jack. This jack should not be used for connection to a local telephone.)

▶ Check the dialing properties for your location and the number you are calling. Call waiting, prefixes, and area codes may or may not be needed. If you are dialing out through a PBX that requires an 8 or a 9 to access an outside line, add a comma before and after this access digit to give the PBX time to respond between numbers.

Symptoms

▶ Unable to negotiate a proper set of protocols with the server.

▶ Unable to authenticate with server.

▶ A connection is established but drops suddenly.

Suspects

▶ Improper Dial-Up Networking configuration.

▶ Wrong protocols are set for dial-up adapter or connection shortcut.

▶ Excessively noisy phone lines.

▶ Someone else may have picked up a phone on the same line.

▶ Defective modem or power-supply causing data errors; a modem that overheats or is fed bad power may fail intermittently.

▶ Network congestion or equipment problem at the service provider.

Solutions

▶ Review Figures 11-2 through 11-7 and consult your ISP for proper settings. TCP/IP must be used for ISP connections. The presence of IPX/SPX or NetBEUI, if enabled, can confuse some ISP connections. If your company network only supports IPX/SPX (this is rare), disable the other protocols.

▶ Alternatively, try disabling Software Compression and/or IP Header Compression in DUN settings.

▶ If you must log on to an NT server, be sure "Log on to network" is selected. For most ISPs this is not required, but for some corporate remote-access systems it is.

▶ Ensure that you can use the phone line uninterrupted.

▶ Have your phone company check phone lines. Install the "Modem Condom" circuit as described in Appendix G to protect your modem connection from phone line voltage spikes and other problems.

▶ Move obstructions from around the modem case (external unit).

▶ Replace the power supply.

▶ Some ISPs limit the duration of dial-up connections and time-out connections to enable others to use the lines. Contact your ISP for details.

Symptoms

▶ Browser, e-mail, or other Internet applications indicate an inability to find the host name/address in DNS lookup.

▶ Unable to connect to server/site, or you get "host not responding" messages.

▶ Data requests go out and host connections appear to be made, but no data returns or you get "invalid host/destination" messages.

Suspects

▶ Improper or no DNS addresses in TCP/IP configuration.

▶ Improper gateway address in TCP/IP configuration.

▶ Wrong IP address in TCP/IP configuration.

▶ DNS server is down or busy.

▶ Your hostname, domain name, or IP address is not back-traceable through the DNS system.

▶ Your ISP or network does not allow reverse lookups to validate your host.

Solutions

▶ Try the connection again. DNS should retry with subsequent upstream servers to locate the desired host system, even though the first or second DNS lookup times out or does not roll over to the next DNS server properly.

▶ Ensure DNS addresses and domain search orders are correct. Often, a domain search order is not required nor advisable because DNS lookup timeouts may occur. You can change DNS server addresses in Windows TCP/IP settings for your Dial-Up Adapter or Network Adapter and apply them without restarting your computer, even though Windows will prompt you to do so. However, you should close and reopen your application (e-mail, browser, and so on) for it to establish a new connection with the Winsock or other services of Windows in order to apply the new settings.

Symptoms

▶ A VPN connection dialog box appears when you try to access a Web page or use another Internet connection.

Suspects

▶ A VPN connection is set as the preferred connection method.

Solutions

▶ From the Windows desktop, open My Computer, and select Dial-Up Networking. Right-click the VPN connection icon and then select Properties. Select the Dialing tab. Clear the "This is the default Internet connection" checkbox. Click OK and close the dialog boxes.

▶ From the Windows desktop, right-click the Internet Explorer icon and then select Properties. Select the Connections tab. Be sure that your ISP dial-up connection or None, rather than the VPN connection, is shown as the "Current default" (about two-thirds of the way down the dialog box). If it is not, highlight it in the listing and then click the Set Default button. You may also wish to select the "Never dial a connection" radio button so that dial-up connections do not happen from Internet applications automatically (a security preference).

Symptoms

▶ Dial-up connection does not happen automatically as it used to.

▶ Dial-up connection happens automatically but is not desired.

Suspects

▶ The configuration of Dial-Up Networking is not as you like it.

▶ The configuration of Internet Explorer is not as you like it.

Solutions

▶ **Check Dial-Up Networking settings:** From the Windows desktop, open My Computer, and select Dial-Up Networking. Right-click the Dial-Up Networking icon for your ISP connection. Select the dialing. Set "This is the default Internet connection" to your preference — to dial or not to dial automatically.

▶ **Check Internet Explorer settings:**

To automatically dial: From the Windows desktop, right-click the Internet Explorer icon and then select Properties. Select the Connections tab. Be sure that your ISP dial-up connection is shown as the "Current default" (about two-thirds of the way down the dialog box). If it is not, highlight it in the listing and then click the Set Default button. Then select either the "Dial whenever a network connection is not present" or "Always dial my default connection" radio button so that a dial-up connection happens when Internet connections are needed from within applications.

Not to automatically dial: From the Windows desktop, right-click the Internet Explorer icon and then select Properties. Select the Connections tab. Select the "Never dial a connection" radio button so that dial-up connections do not happen from Internet applications automatically.

Symptoms

▶ Tearing, distorted, incomplete graphics display on Web pages. A reload or refresh of the page may not clear up the display.

Suspects

▶ The host, ISP, or Internet system is likely congested and cannot send data streams consistently enough for proper transfer to your browser.

Solutions

▶ Because the distorted data is already stored in your browser's local memory or disk cache, a refresh only recalls the existing data from the cache. Use the "clear memory cache now" and "clear disk cache now" features of your browser configuration, and then refresh the desired page to try to get a fresh data transfer to your system.

▶ Try accessing the page at a later time, when the Internet or host system may not be as congested.

Symptoms

▶ Unusual or blotchy color on Web pages that are clear and crisp on other systems.

Suspects

▶ Insufficient video color depth.

▶ The Web page is using non-HTML standard color mappings requiring greater than 256-color depth.

Solutions

▶ Set the Control Panel ⇨ Display settings tab for at least 256 colors to suit the HTML-standard 256-color range. The standard VGA adapter and display of 640×480×16, meaning 16-color depth, is inadequate for most pages.

▶ If the Web page designer used colors outside the HTML standard ranges, you may need to increase color depth to 64K colors. Advise the Webmaster of this concern.

Symptoms

▶ You see JavaScript errors after a Web page appears to load correctly.

Suspects

▶ Insufficient memory and/or disk cache setup in browser.

Solutions

▶ Set memory cache to between 1,024 and 2,048K.

▶ Set disk cache to between 2,048 and 8,192K.

▶ JavaScripts load within the HTML page being viewed are processed after the entire page loads. If the cache settings are too low, some or all of the page content will remain onscreen, but the JavaScript will have scrolled out of cache and will no longer be available to be processed.

Symptoms

▶ Data in HTML forms disappears after the screen-saver/blanker activates, and then the display is restored.

Suspects

▶ Some data placed in HTML forms is dynamic and not embedded in the actual displayed HTML form. When a screen saver activates, it takes the current screen image and saves it to another page of video memory, or to diskette. When the screen saver is deactivated, the previous screen is put back onto the display. Because the missing data was not part of the actual form content, it is not retained.

Solutions

▶ Right-click in the form dialog box and select "refresh" or "reload" to replace the data.

▶ This is not a specific hardware or software problem per se. Notify the designer of this situation to determine if the form can be redesigned.

Symptoms

▶ Errors occur when trying to view graphics files from Web pages.

▶ You get a browser message indicating that no viewer or helper application is associated with the file type you are trying to view.

▶ The wrong application opens when you're trying to view graphics files from File Manager/Explorer or selecting links to them from Web pages or e-mail.

Suspects

▶ No application has been associated with a particular file type, or the application cannot be found.

▶ A recently installed or used application has replaced the prior, expected file associations with another application.

Solutions

▶ Download and install the appropriate application for the file type you are trying to view. By default GIF, BMP, and JPEG files become associated within the current browser and require no external or add-in helper application. Often a browser will be associated with a particular application type—though it does not need to be, if you prefer to use another external program to view graphics files in Windows without a browser present or active. Windows Media Player will display most AVI and MOV files, but you may prefer to use Apple's QuickTime viewer or another application for these file types. MPEG files typically require a software or in-hardware MPEG decoder to display them properly. An MPEG player is often bundled on a video card driver disk but must be installed separately. Vivo (VIV) movie files require a viewer from Vivo Software (www.vivo.com).

▶ Adobe Photoshop and similar applications may "take over" many graphics file type associations, requiring you to reinstall your preferred application. You may also change file associations by selecting View ⇨ Options from any Explorer dialog box, and then select the File Types tab. All known file associations are listed and available for edit/change or you may add new associations manually. You may also manually edit Registry entries to restore the desired association, but this is a tedious task.

Summary

Exploring and enjoying the Internet with Windows or any other environment has become a basically straightforward, everyday activity for hundreds of millions of people around the world. However, at each step a number of things must be in place and configured properly. Add various complications and parameters with different applications, servers, IP addresses, and such, and the Internet can seem to be impossible to get to at times.

Once you have a connection to the Internet, navigating and keeping up with the tremendous volume of content can be daunting. With the detailed content about networking in Chapter 10, help with serial communications and modems in Chapter 22, and the examples in this chapter, establishing a connection from your PC to the Internet should be quite simple. If you encounter problems, the information presented here, in addition to the help and examples from your ISP, should result in unlimited hours of successful Net surfing and other productive online activities.

The next part of this book is aimed at your PC hardware. Remember, no matter which operating system you are using — DOS, Windows, Unix, Linux, BeOS, or whatever — it will not work unless you have installed it into a well-functioning and up-to-date hardware environment!

✦ ✦ ✦

The Hard Side of Your PC

Part III dives directly into the base hardware of your PC's system. Where to start? At the point where you turn on the power, of course. The chapters in Part III are devoted to the process of booting your PC and to everything required for starting your computer.

Because your computer's operating system is involved with configuring your hardware and in providing all of your hardware's capabilities, Part III relies on some of the information discussed in Parts I and II.

Now get started with the hardware by turning on the power in Chapter 12.

Power and Startup Problems

◆ ◆ ◆ ◆

In This Chapter

What should happen
when you turn on
the power

Solving AC and DC
power problems

System problems
encountered
during startup

◆ ◆ ◆ ◆

What if you turn on your computer and nothing happens? The most frustrating thing is not being able to start the system, making it impossible to use its diagnostic tools to find out what is wrong. The system might beep, groan, or flash, if it does anything at all. You may be left with a cold, dead pile of hardware with your work trapped inside. You want to get some level of things working right. What do you do?

Because starting your system involves applying power to the circuits in the PC system, most of this chapter refers to power problems. Such problems can occur in the system unit or video monitor of typical stationary PCs, or within the internal batteries of laptop and notebook systems. With power issues, whether the concern is the power from an AC wall socket, the PC's internal power supply, or battery-related, there can be one or multiple symptoms and one or multiple solutions to those symptoms. Because of this multiplicity, this chapter lists symptoms and solutions in logical groupings, rather than separately.

Here you will find methods for performing some of the more detailed troubleshooting steps to help you arrive at various solutions for hardware-related startup problems. Once we get past hardware and some basic bootup issues, we address various operating system configuration issues in Chapter 13. But enough of our rambling—you want to get your PC up and running!

Order, Please

Computers are orderly devices when they are working. When you first turn on your system, it is designed to perform certain steps in a specific sequence. As with a string of typical Christmas tree lights, if one event in the sequence is not receiving or responding to the power you are sending it, the entire string of startup events might not work at all. Activating your power switch should set in motion the following string of events:

✦ The computer and monitor power supplies start, supplying power to the motherboard (CPU, memory, and I/O devices) and to the display circuits.

✦ When the CPU receives the proper power, it also receives an internal signal called Power Good that enables the internal clock to synchronize CPU, memory, and I/O operations.

✦ The CPU immediately looks for a specific memory location to find the startup program that tells it what to do. This is where the computer chip begins to take on its identity as an IBM-compatible PC because of the Intel microprocessor architecture and what happens as the basic input/output system (BIOS) software loads.

✦ The BIOS checks the system for the type of video display you have (color or monochrome), the amount of memory, the number and type of disk drives, presence or absence of a keyboard, and what external devices are connected to the system (parallel and serial ports). This process is known as the bootup and includes the power-on self-test (POST).

✦ The PlugandPlay BIOS extensions work within the realm of the normal BIOS device detection to detect any changes in device configuration and start the resource negotiation process so that Plug and Play and legacy devices can get along.

✦ If faulty or improperly configured hardware items exist in the system, POST issues a beep or displays an error message, indicating the basic problem area.

Beeps and other error messages are detailed later in this chapter and in Appendix F at the end of the book.

✦ If all is well through the bootup and POST processes, the BIOS instructs the CPU to load the operating system from either a floppy disk (drive A:), a hard drive (drive C:), or a bootable CD-ROM. If the BIOS finds the proper files on a disk drive, these files are loaded as extensions and supplements to the internal BIOS.

✦ These disk files make up the first distinctions between different versions and features of DOS and other operating systems and system capabilities. For DOS and Windows 95/98/Me, they are the hidden files on a system disk, named either IBMBIO.COM and IBMDOS.COM, or IO.SYS and MSDOS.SYS.

If the preceding files are missing from a disk, one of the following events can happen:

1. In original IBM systems, the BIOS will give up on the disk bootup process and change to loading a small version of the BASIC programming language system from another area of the BIOS chips.

2. In non-IBM systems, the BIOS issues a "nonsystem disk" error and instructs you to insert a bootable floppy disk. The wording of this error message will vary, depending on the manufacturer and version of the BIOS and the version of DOS. (Alternatively, if you have placed a nonsystem floppy disk in drive A: but have system files on drive C:, you can simply open the latch on the floppy disk door, press a key, and let the system boot from drive C:.)

3. For Windows 95/98/Me systems, IO.SYS contains both the boot and initial command processing programming. MSDOS.SYS is a text file containing special bootup commands and parameters required by Windows. The absence of this file or a valid boot record yields a message indicating the presence of a nonsystem disk or nonbootable disk.

✦ For MS-DOS versions 6.0 and above including Windows 95/98/Me, the BIOS also loads a disk compression driver (DBLSPACE.BIN or DRVSPACE.BIN) to enable the boot sequence to continue using files off the compressed drive. This occurs at the "Starting MS-DOS" message. If you have non-Microsoft disk compression, these drivers may load before, during, or after CONFIG.SYS is processed.

✦ After the disk BIOS files and any boot sector or special drivers are loaded (drive compression or BIOS translation/partition drivers for special disk drives), the disk is searched for a CONFIG.SYS file. CONFIG.SYS provides parameters and device driver information to be loaded and used even before the visible part of DOS (COMMAND.COM) is loaded. CONFIG.SYS may also specify what program is to be used as the main command processor — which most users are familiar with as DOS. This program is typically COMMAND.COM, but can be any program that provides interface and file services to the application programs you will use.

For DOS 6.x systems, when the "Starting MS-DOS" or "Starting PC-DOS" message appears, you should be able to press F5 to bypass further boot file processing or F8 to step through each line of CONFIG.SYS and AUTOEXEC.BAT. This way, you can watch, for troubleshooting purposes, as drivers and programs load.

For Windows 95/98/Me and 2000, pressing F8 presents an internal boot menu that enables you to select various startup modes, including normal Windows operation, Safe Modes with or without networking, command-prompt only (DOS), or a prior operating system (if set up for dual boot). For better backward compatibility, Windows 98 provides two ways to go to the DOS prompt. One leaves a Windows tag in memory so you may return to Windows 98 by typing EXIT at a DOS prompt.

The other, which is more DOS-compatible, requires that you reboot your computer to return to Windows 98. Left to its own, Windows 95/98/Me will also verify its own system files and, if it detects a problem, you will be presented with a special boot menu from which to select a variety of options for normal or troubleshooting functions. Normally you will see only "Starting Windows 95" or "Starting Windows 98" and then see the Windows startup logo screen (a presentation of the graphics file C:\WINDOWS\LOGOW.SYS or LOGO.SYS for most prebuilt systems).

✦ For Windows 95/98/Me, the MSDOS.SYS file, normally set with Read-Only, System, and Hidden file attributes, performs the function of a special bootup configuration file. It is a plain ASCII text file that can be edited with Notepad or a similar editor (once you use Explorer ⇨ Properties to remove the attributes mentioned). This file indicates the Windows boot disk and environment path, and has parameters that control the loading of various bootup drivers, menu, and logo display characteristics. (Windows NT and 2000 have only a close equivalent for multiboot type selection, C:\BOOT.INI.)

✦ For versions of DOS since 3.0 and Windows 95/98/Me, CONFIG.SYS is a text file that you create or modify, or that may be created or modified by an installation process. Interpretation of the contents and how the actions are taken, depends on the version of DOS and type of system you have. It is at this point that boot menu options would be displayed, enabling you to select from any number of options you have created in CONFIG.SYS. You will find details about CONFIG.SYS later in this chapter.

✦ For versions of DOS since 3.0 and Windows 95/98/Me, if you have an AUTOEXEC.BAT file, the system reads it after CONFIG.SYS is processed and the command processor loads. Then the system follows its instructions to load terminate-and-stay-resident (TSR) programs, set screen colors, set the PATH used by DOS and applications to search for programs, and arrange your PC as you would like it every time you start your system. AUTOEXEC.BAT is another text file you can create and modify, or that may be created or modified by a software installation process. Details about this file also appear in Chapter 13.

Note   Windows 95/98 and Me do not need either the CONFIG.SYS or AUTOEXEC.BAT file to control the loading of necessary drivers for its operation. In the absence of CON-FIG.SYS, Windows 95/98/Me automatically loads the HIMEM.SYS memory driver, which is the only "DOS" driver Windows requires to run. Similarly, for best system performance you should not load DOS-level CD-ROM, sound card, or PCMCIA drivers in the CONFIG.SYS file sections used for Windows 95/98/Me.

Depending on your preferences or the configuration of your system, the CONFIG.SYS file might do the following:

✦ Present you with a customized boot menu

✦ Load drivers for CD-ROM drives or other system devices

Also depending on your preferences or the configuration of your system, the AUTOEXEC.BAT file might do the following:

✦ Process the choices made with a custom boot menu per CONFIG.SYS

✦ Leave you with a DOS prompt awaiting your input

✦ Execute the programs you will be using most of the time

✦ Load and run a menu program or other user interface (Windows 3.*x*, Windows 95, Windows 98, Windows Me, or some other application)

If one of these processes fails or nothing happens at all, you may have encountered what we classify as a startup problem. These problems can be caused by a number of components or files within your system.

Resolving startup problems, which is covered later in this chapter and in the chapters for the specific operating systems, begins with identifying what does or does not happen, how far the system gets into the process, and what error indications you are provided with. Obviously, the first place the problem could be lurking is in what happens when the power switch is turned on.

Power to the PC

The potential trouble spots here are relatively few. The culprits, if not the external or AC power, are unfortunately major parts of your system — the power supply or motherboard.

If you turn on your computer and nothing happens, yet you know you have AC power to the system, the problem could be one listed in the "Order, Please" section earlier in the chapter.

Further investigation will determine which of these parts needs attention or repair, and some good clues will help you in this area. After you figure out where the problem lies, the most time-consuming aspect of repair probably will be getting the replacement part.

A power supply can cost anywhere from $40 to $250, depending on its capacity and source (manufacturer or dealer). A motherboard or disk drive can be the most expensive item in your PC. XT, AT, 386, and 486 motherboards are no longer available. Pentium system boards range from $100 to $450. A CPU and RAM are typically optional when you put together a system — but you need them. Please note that these prices may vary widely, depending on your location and whether you are willing to risk ordering components by mail or the Internet.

Even though PCs use low internal voltages , the primary source of this power is a potentially dangerous high-voltage outlet (unless the unit is battery operated). In most cases even battery-operated units require AC power for recharging or have high-voltage sections for power conversion and displays.

Caution Use extreme caution when you work with the AC power from a wall outlet, outlet strip, or extension cord, or voltages inside the PC power supply. Working with the power cords, plugs, and sockets is not usually dangerous as long as you do not touch the metal parts and do not come in contact with a grounded wire or chassis component. If you are in doubt or concerned at all about electrical shock, ask for help from someone who is trained in this area.

With the preceding precautions in mind, let's follow the first set of problems to a workable solution.

AC power

Most PCs require two kinds of power: AC and DC. For office or home systems, or recharging portables, AC power from a wall outlet connects to the back of the PC, printer, and other peripherals.

A converter lies between the point where the AC power enters your computer or laptop charger and where it connects to the motherboard, disk drives, add-on cards, or internal battery. This is the PC power supply that changes your AC voltage to a variety of DC voltages used by the computer circuits. If the PC power supply has a problem starting up or will not work at all, you probably have a defective power supply.

Identifying which part of the power system is wrong and fixing it is relatively simple in most cases. If you have access to a voltmeter and some tools, you can get into some of these details much more quickly, but we recommend that level of troubleshooting only for those with technical skills. If you do not have a voltmeter and are not a technician, you can rely on the basic indications in the following section.

AC power problems

These Symptoms, Suspects, and Solutions focus on AC power problems.

Symptoms

▶ Error messages 01x or 02x

▶ Intermittent system operation/failure

▶ Printer, CRT, or accessory problems

Suspects

▶ AC power outlets

▶ Power cords

▶ Outlet strip

▶ Breaker or fuse in the outlet strip

▶ PC supply voltage setting

▶ Power supply

▶ Faulty on/off switch

Solutions

▶ Fix or replace the wall socket.

▶ Replace power cords.

▶ Replace the outlet strip.

▶ Reset the breaker or replace the fuse in the outlet strip.

▶ Replace the power supply.

▶ Replace the on/off switch.

▶ Verify that the 110/220-volt selection switch on the power supply is set properly (usually to 110).

Power outlets and cords

Most people plug their systems into some form of multiple-outlet strip so that everything related to the computer is operating from one source of electricity, or for convenience due to placement of their AC wall outlets.

Finding out whether AC power is getting to your PC is as simple as plugging in a lamp. If the outlet strip has a power on light, it may or may not properly indicate that power is available to your computer. Plugging in a lamp or some other electrical appliance is a sure-fire method of testing the strip. If the appliance or isolated parts of your system have power, your problem is probably not in the outlet strip. Just in case, though, swap plugs around to different sockets in the strip to make sure you don't have a bad receptacle in the strip itself.

Some outlet strips provide either fuse or circuit breaker protection. The circuit breaker might be the actual on/off switch for the power outlet strip, a separate button that pops out if the circuit is bad, or a small black breaker unit that resembles a very small rocker switch that toggles opposite the shape of the switch to indicate when it has opened the circuit. Outlet strips that use fuses have either twist-and-turn or screw-in fuse-holder caps. The fuse inside should pull out when you remove the cap. If the fuse is a clear glass cylinder, you can see the internal fuse wire. If the wire is continuous from one end of the fuse to the other, the fuse is probably good. Any obvious breaks or burn marks indicate the fuse is bad. Some fuses are made of a white ceramic cylinder that you cannot see through. You must use a continuity tester or an ohmmeter to determine if this type of fuse is bad. It may be easier to simply replace the fuse with one of the same value, preferably with a see-through glass cylinder.

If the outlet strip provides surge protection and has been running your system just fine up to the point of your present problems, one possible suspect is that a voltage surge occurred on the AC line, causing the surge protector to operate and the fuse or circuit breaker to open the circuit. If you notice the lights flickering or the CRT image changing occasionally, a voltage surge or unstable power is the likely problem.

Beyond the outlet strip are the power cords, most with molded-on plugs and sockets. If the cord's outer covering appears to be cracked or compressed, the wires inside may be broken. The same may be true for the cable on the outlet strip. If in doubt, find a new strip or power cord and try again.

Caution   Don't run your power cord through door jambs, under carpeting, under the legs of your desk, along the floor where people can trip, or where people put or move heavy objects. Aside from the fact that doing this may break your connection, you may be creating an opportunity for you or your equipment to receive a dangerous shock!

The computer or printer end of the cable typically has an ISO or IEC connector — one with three small parallel sockets, the center one offset from the others. (ISO and IEC are abbreviations for International and European electrical standards groups, respectively. It is easy to insert these pins into their coordinating connectors on the PC without achieving full contact. Generally these connectors should insert a full ⅜ of an inch, up to where the pin shell meets the rectangular shoulder of the cable socket. If any strain exists on the cable, it is very easy for this connection to become loose and fail.

After the AC power is fed successfully to your computer, you may still have a bad on/off switch at the PC's power supply. If you have a tower-style PC case and have to replace the DC power supply, be mindful of the way connections are made to the power switch when reconnecting the wires, because many tower cases have the on/off switch on the front of the tower and the power supply near the back. This means that wires connect the on/off switch to the power supply. Checking the 110/220-volt power line selector, as mentioned previously, is also a good idea.

As equipment suppliers in this market change quickly, you might find many differences in the way wiring is colored or connected. It never hurts to ask for help from your dealer, service shop, the manufacturer, or a technically skilled friend if you have any doubts.

Voltage-selection switch

The most obvious items, such as power cords and switches, can be checked quite easily. Your computer's 110/220-volt switch should be located at the rear of your supply, on the side near the on/off switch, or inside, as a switch or jumper wire. Most systems in the U.S. and Canada should be operated on 110 volts, so that is how the switch should be set.

Testing the AC voltage

Three possible voltage measurements can be taken of the AC line supplying power to your system under each of two conditions. You can take these measurements both at the wall outlet and at the outlet strip to help determine whether the problem is with the wall circuits or with the outlet strip.

 Caution Do not test the AC voltage unless you are familiar with the process because of the potential for personal injury or fire.

The three measurements and voltages are as follows:

✦ Hot-to-neutral voltage = 120 volts AC +/– 10 volts

✦ Hot-to-ground voltage = 120 volts AC +/– 10 volts

✦ Neutral-to-ground voltage = 0 volts AC +/– 0 volts

Figure 12-1 shows the expected positions of the hot, neutral, and ground connections and the voltmeter connections for the measurements. A digital voltmeter (one that displays with numbers on a panel rather than a needle across a dial) provides a more accurate reading.

Your actual hot-to-neutral and hot-to-ground voltage can measure from 110 to 130 volts AC, and should not change while you are measuring it. A small fluctuation (1 volt or so) in the meter reading is probably just a function of the meter itself. If the fluctuation is large or obvious (greater than 2 volts), your problem is probably in the wiring or the source of AC power, and repairs may be required.

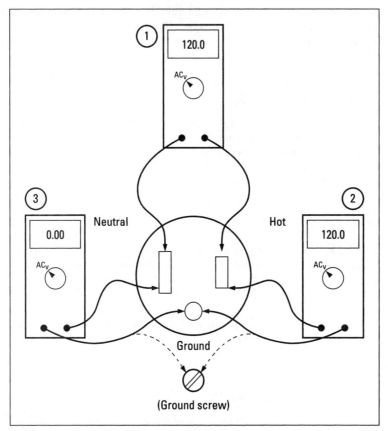

Figure 12-1: Typical positions of the hot, neutral, and ground connections and the voltmeter connections for the measurements

The neutral-to-ground voltage can actually show a slight measurement, but less than 1 volt. If this measurement is greater than 1 volt, you probably have a ground circuit problem that should be repaired by an electrician or investigated by someone with technical skills to see if you can add a ground wire to the PC without affecting other circuits.

These are the two conditions:

✦ No-load voltage (PC system and accessories turned off)

✦ Under-load voltage (PC system and accessories turned on)

There might be a slight (1- to 2-volt) difference between the no-load and under-load voltage due to some power loss in the wiring. If this voltage is higher than 2 volts, however, have a qualified electrician repair or increase the circuit capacity.

DC Power Supply Problems

If the system appears dead — no fans, no lights, and no beeps — but you know you have AC power to the system, your problem may lie with the power supply and its connections. Some systems have a power on indicator built into their on/off switch, but this indicator may only show that AC power is switched on, not that the PC has the internal DC voltages needed to run things. Fortunately, your system provides you with error messages or other symptoms as well.

DC power supply problems

This section discusses DC Power supply problems and how to solve them.

Symptoms

▶ Power-on indication but no operation; flickering LEDs

▶ Fan starts and stops

▶ Error messages 01x or 02x

▶ Nonspecific or intermittent system failures or lockups

▶ After successful startup or seemingly successful startup attempt, computer turns off automatically

Suspects

▶ Power supply

▶ Power connections

▶ PC power supply 110/220-volt selector

Solutions

▶ Check AC power connections.

▶ Check or set the voltage selector to the proper voltage.

▶ Replace the power supply.

▶ Ensure that the system is not overheating.

In most cases of PC power supply failure, you will get an indication of a short flicker of one or more LEDs on the keyboard, power switch, or disk drive. If you take the cover off or can see the internal fan blades from the rear grille, you might see the fan jerk a little and then stop. These are indications of any one of the following problems:

✦ The power supply tried to start but encountered an internal failure.

✦ A major overload occurred in the motherboard, add-in card, or disk drive.

✦ There is overheating.

A more unusual problem is a PC that will not start but used to, or one that starts only sometimes. Many PC power supplies are designed to operate on standard American 110-volt AC wall power, with an optional selection to operate on 220-volt main outlet voltages, such as those standard in Europe and Asia. Sometimes a system that is set for 220-volt operation starts okay when operated on the lower 110 volts, but operation is not reliable, nor does it provide full supply capacity for all the options in your system.

Older, original IBM PC systems with add-in cards that use a lot of power might indicate this problem by making an internal clicking sound. This indicates that either too much power is being drawn through the motherboard or the power supply is not adequate to handle the load. (The clicking sound is from a relay that controls the systems' cassette tape data storage unit.)

Original IBM PC systems were manufactured with 63-watt power supplies. That is enough power to handle one or two floppy disk drives and the five add-on cards that could be installed. Removing one add-on card at a time and trying the system again is one way of determining whether excess loading is the problem. The best thing to do in this case, especially if you have a hard disk, is to change to a new 135-watt or larger power supply. If your system is newer but you are having similar problems, changing the power supply from, for instance, 200 watts to 250 watts may solve the problem.

Get the Right Power Supply

Your PC power supply may be one of several common models that differ mostly by the wires and connectors that plug into the motherboard, the size and shape of the power supply unit itself, power ratings, number of power connections, and so forth. If you need to replace the power supply, make sure you get the right model. Some of the more common models are usually labeled ATX, AT, Mini-AT, XT, Mini-Redundant, N+1 Redundant, Redundant, NLX, Micro-ATX, or PS/2. Make sure you replace your old power supply with one that fits into your PC and plugs into the motherboard and devices you have installed.

Testing the DC supply voltages

The power supply in your PC is a type of power conditioner itself. It is needed to convert the AC wall power into regulated, specific voltages the computer and drive circuits require for proper operation.

Most of these supplies work quite well with line voltages from 95 to 140 volts AC (for 120-volt circuits) or from 180 to 250 volts (for 220-volt circuits). Supplies come with either an internal jumper or switch, or an obvious external voltage-selection switch. This switch must be set for the nominal line voltage from which you will power the system.

 Note If your power supply's AC voltage selection switch or jumper is inside the power supply itself, you will need a qualified technician to change its setting.

If your fan is running fine, the best way to test a suspicious power supply is to leave it in the PC system, connected to all the devices it should be connected to, and measure the various voltages with a voltmeter.

If the fan is not running, the supply is probably defective. The same is true if the fan starts and then stops immediately. If any of the voltages are missing, the supply is bad. It is rare to find a voltage that is simply too low as opposed to missing altogether.

The power supply provides four voltages to your PC (as illustrated in Figure 12-2):

✦ +5 volts DC to the motherboard, add-in cards, and disk drives

✦ –5 volts DC to the motherboard and some memory systems

✦ +12 volts DC to the motherboard, add-in cards, and disk drives

✦ –12 volts DC to the motherboard, add-in cards, and disk drives

A fifth signal line from the supply, called Power Good, is the reset indication to the computer. If the power supply fails for any reason, this line is changed to tell the CPU to stop everything no matter what.

The common or ground for all these supplies is usually the black wires in the wiring bundle. A +5 is usually red, –5 is usually white, +12 is usually yellow, –12 is usually blue, and the Power Good signal (which should read at or near +5 volts if all is well) is usually green.

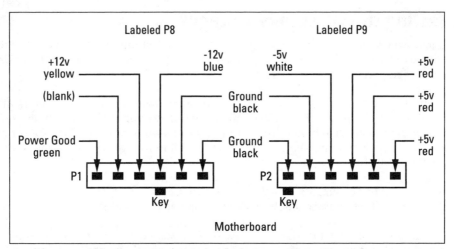

Figure 12-2: A view from the back end of PC motherboard power connections; wires go up and out to the power supply (P8 and P9)

Within some supplies there may be two different sources for the +5 and the +12 volts so that the disk drives and other internal add-in components are powered separately from the motherboard and add-on cards.

Figure 12-3 shows the disk drive connections.

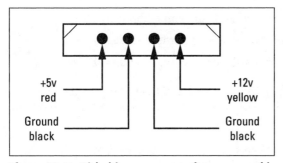

Figure 12-3: Disk drives are most often powered by cables coming out of the power supply.

Battery Problems

It seems that nearly everything we use today has a battery — alarm clocks, remote controls, cordless and cellular phones, pagers, PDAs, and, of course, portable PCs. In a PC, as with many other devices, batteries keep the internal circuits running and maintain small amounts of data when the main part of a piece of electronic equipment is turned off. Of course, for a portable computer, the battery is the only way your portable gets its power so you can use the system when it is not directly plugged into a wall outlet. In this section you will see how batteries can affect what happens in various PC systems.

286, 386, 486, and Pentium systems and CMOS setup

All 286 and higher systems use a special memory chip (CMOS RAM) to store information about the system's memory, disk drives, date and time, and other settings. The CMOS RAM chip and the PC's clock chip require a small amount of power to hold this information when the power is turned off, which comes from a small battery inside the system. The most common CMOS-related failure is the battery, but it is also possible for either chip to fail or for another component in the system to be defective and scramble the CMOS information.

Without properly stored and maintained information, the system might assume a set of default values about memory size and disk drives, begin each session with a date of January 1, 1980 (or another old date that you see each time you boot your computer) and/or a time of midnight, or give you an error at startup.

If your AT 286, 386, 486, or Pentium-class system boots up erratically, fails to recognize the proper amount of memory, cannot determine the presence of the hard drive, loses track of the date and time, or has any combination of these problems, the battery that keeps the CMOS RAM and clock circuits alive is likely defective.

The CMOS RAM and clock chip require a small amount of electricity to keep these functions running. When your system is turned on, the power comes from the main power supply. When the system is turned off, an internal or external battery maintains the CMOS data. External batteries may be small lithium "coin" cells mounted on the system board, small sealed packages containing lithium or alkaline cells, open containers to hold three to four AA-size alkaline cells, or NiCad cells soldered to the system board. No matter what type of battery you have, you should replace it every two to three years.

Since the introduction of 80386 systems, Dallas Semiconductor has combined the clock chip, CMOS RAM, and battery functions into a single module. These appear in systems as small black rectangular blocks, with obvious markings such as DS1287, Dallas Time, BenchMarq, and other brands. Most of these are soldered into the system board and require the services of a technician to replace them. Replacement units cost about $12 from various electronic mail-order sources.

When a CMOS error occurs due to any configuration or hardware error that causes a mismatch between setup and what POST determines at startup, you will be notified by a screen message that advises you of the condition and instructs you to press F1 or F2 to continue. Many of the common CMOS setup parameters are covered later in this chapter and in Chapter 14. Some typical symptoms, suspects, and solutions are as follows.

CMOS setup problems

The following Symptoms, Suspects, and Solutions pinpoint and solve some CMOS setup problems.

Symptoms

▶ Loss of date/time, memory, disk ,or system information

▶ Error messages 01x, 02x, 102, 103, 161, 162, 163, 164, 199, or 17xx

▶ Long beep at startup, followed by the preceding messages

▶ CMOS RAM error

▶ Memory size error

▶ Disk drive configuration error

Suspects

▶ Internal battery on clock card or motherboard

▶ CMOS RAM chip

Solutions

▶ Replace or recharge battery.

▶ Replace CMOS RAM chip.

Figure 12-4 shows how to locate the CMOS battery inside your system. Systems may use one of four types of batteries for retaining setup information:

✦ A sealed battery that plugs into the motherboard — probably containing alkaline cells or possibly a NiCad battery. The label should indicate what type of battery to use as a replacement.

✦ A cell holder for two to four AA-size alkaline or NiCad cells (alkaline cells are usually labeled with a manufacturer and battery type; NiCads might be unlabeled, plastic-encased cylinders).

✦ A lithium battery in a black coin socket with a contact across the top.

✦ A lithium battery in a small rectangular box soldered to the motherboard or mounted on the chassis and wired to the motherboard.

Most users can replace the first three types without any problems. Replacing the fourth type requires someone with technical skills if the battery unit is permanently attached to the motherboard.

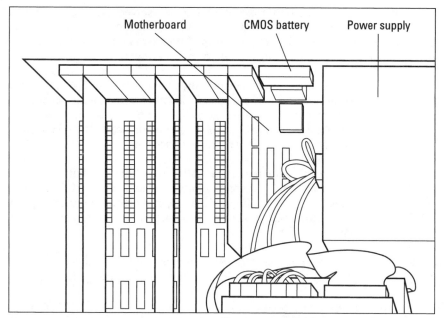

Figure 12-4: This is where you will probably find the CMOS battery inside your system, if and when you need to replace it.

An integrated CMOS RAM and clock system is now quite common on many system boards. The Dallas Semiconductor Company has developed a CMOS RAM device with a built-in battery. This device looks like a memory chip with a box on top. These CMOS RAM devices are said to have a life of six to nine years in normal use. Because this chip is likely to be soldered to the motherboard, a qualified technician should perform replacement. Many different types of this device may be in use, so you will have to check your module's part number carefully so you can match it to a replacement device.

Laptops, notebooks, and pocket PCs

As with desktop and server systems, many laptop systems also have a small battery inside to maintain memory and configuration if the main battery loses charge or is removed. Symptoms of internal battery failures are similar to those listed previously. Replacement typically requires a factory-authorized technician to service the unit.

Main laptop batteries might need to be replaced as frequently as twice a year or they might last as long as three years before needing replacement, depending on how you use your system, how many accessories it has, and the original battery capacity.

Laptops used to use NiCad batteries, which have a use/recharge life of about 1,000 cycles or three years if used within the limits set by the laptop manufacturer. Keeping a laptop on charge for long periods of time can be as detrimental to battery life as not charging it long enough or often enough.

Tip   There has been controversy for years over the memory effects of NiCad batteries — some say they last longer if they are used for a short time and then recharged; others claim they last longer if they are used until they do not work at all and are then fully recharged. The best advice is to follow the manufacturer's directions for the type of charger and battery provided with your system.

Today's laptops use nickel-metal-hydride (NiMH) or Lithium-Ion batteries, which do not exhibit the same "memory" or capacity-impairing symptoms of NiCad batteries. Lithium-Ion batteries have greater life or capacity, and also weigh more than NiCad or NiMH batteries. In either case, you should expect to have to replace these batteries every three years or so.

Note   Lithium-Ion batteries pose an extreme fire and explosion hazard when overheated or when exposed to sparks or flame when they are being charged or used.

Generally, if a laptop does not run for 75 percent of its rated battery operation time after a full charge (as indicated by the manufacturer's specifications), the battery is malfunctioning. Your use habits and the laptop's features (such as automatic disk or system power-down) will affect how long you can expect the system to last on a full charge.

Most handheld personal computers (HHPCs) have batteries that you can replace just as you would replace a battery in your watch or personal organizer. Most also have two battery systems, one that has a longer life and backs up the main configuration and setup and the other that keeps the memory and other features running. Never remove batteries from both battery systems at the same time. The reason is that you lose all of the configuration, setup, and data on your handheld computer (or personal digital assistant [PDA], as some are called) if both battery systems are dead or absent. Usually, the two systems back up each other long enough for battery replacement of the other battery system.

Some handheld computers provide rechargeable batteries. You should make sure to check your handheld computer regularly, as alarms, flashing indicators, and other features of your PDA may run down both battery systems. Luckily, most PDAs support connection to your office and/or home PC for backup and coordination purposes. If you maintain these links regularly, information lost in your PDA may be as simple to restore as replacing or recharging the batteries, connecting to your home or office PC, and restoring a previously saved backup. The operative word is *backup*. This means you should back up the data in your handheld PC just as often as you back up a regular PC. Because people carry handheld devices on trips and to places you would never think of taking a regular PC, you may even want to consider backing up, or at least synchronizing your handheld to your PC, even more often than you back up your regular computer!

Finally, PCMCIA cards plugged into your PDA (HHPC) will use battery power *very* quickly. Most often, you are cautioned to use PCMCIA cards when you have plugged-in power available. Of course, that is not always the case. For these occasions, you should make sure you have plenty of extra batteries available so you do not lose your work or run out of power before your important jobs are done.

Proper battery charging

You cannot get more out of a battery than is put into it. Generally speaking, you must put 1.6 times as much energy into a battery (over time and depending on the charging rate) than you get from it. Keeping the system and battery as cool as possible (but not frozen) will reduce power consumption and prevent battery damage.

Newer systems claim to prevent overcharging and some have battery warnings when the battery is discharged to a critical point, and may shut down at a predetermined voltage to prevent damage.

Note   Follow the directions that come with your system, charger, or, finally, the actual battery pack (replacement units might not be the same as the original equipment).

Full charge of a NiCad battery is determined by voltage. While the battery is being charged, a NiCad reads 1.45 volts per cell. When not charging, a fully charged battery should read 1.2 to 1.3 volts per cell. While in use, the voltage decreases from 1.2 to 1.0 volts per cell over time. Stop using the battery when the voltage reaches 1.0 volts per cell.

If you discharge a NiCad battery below 1.0 volts per cell, the battery might suffer internal physical damage and never work properly again. A damaged or bad battery may exhibit a higher voltage under charge (indicating the existence of an open or low-capacity cell), or never reach proper voltage (indicating a shorted or ineffective cell).

The number of cells might be determined from the rated voltage of the battery unit and 1.2 volts per cell. A four-cell battery will be rated for 4.8 volts, six cells for 7.2 volts, eight cells for 9.6 volts, and so on. If the voltage equals the number of cells, the battery needs to be charged. If it equals 1.5 times the number of cells, the battery is charged. If you test the battery voltage while it is charging and the voltage exceeds 1.5 times the number of cells, one or more cells is defective and not accepting a charge, and this condition is also preventing other cells in the pack from charging properly.

Short battery life

If your system is running properly but just not for as long as you think it should, check the accessories, reduce the screen lighting intensity, and set up the system for automatic screen dimming and disk or modem shutoff (if the unit has this provision)—and, if all else fails, get a new battery.

If your system is not running properly but you have taken care of the battery with proper charging and use, it might have an internal circuit problem that needs the attention of a service technician.

If the battery gets to be warm or excessively hot, it might have an internal short or the charger may be defective and applying too much charging current. *Warm* in this case is generally a little higher than body or skin temperature—the battery surface shouldn't feel hotter than you are at normal room temperature. *Hot* is definitely anything that is too warm for you to leave your hand on comfortably for any period of time.

To get the most life out of your batteries, use the power-saving or energy management features of your laptop and operating system. (Windows 95 and 98 both support power-saving features, and Windows/2000 and Windows/Me do as well.)

It is best to employ a trained technician if you need to replace the internal battery in small units. The numerous small wires, delicate circuit cards, and mechanical pieces inside most laptops make it inadvisable for users to open them; you also risk voiding your warranty or causing more problems than you started with.

Video Problems

You will find most of the common video problems covered in Chapter 20, but the following two are evident at system startup, or caused by power problems.

The first problem is commonly indicated by an audible beep and no display. The second set of problems can be caused by system location, poor (noisy or erratic) power, or a conflict between cards in the system.

Video display errors

Here are some common video display errors.

Symptoms

▶ One long and two short beeps

▶ Error messages in 4xx, 5xx, 24xx, or 74xx ranges

Suspects

▶ Improper video CMOS RAM setup

▶ Improper motherboard video switch setting

▶ Missing or defective video card

Solutions

▶ Run the CMOS setup program and correct the video setting.

▶ Set switches for the proper display type (color, monochrome, or none).

▶ Check the installation of the video card or replace it.

▶ Replace the motherboard (if video adapter is built in).

The most common problem is an improper switch, jumper, or CMOS setup setting for the type of video display card installed in the system. If you have changed from monochrome to color, or vice versa, you need to change the switch settings. Even some AT or higher systems have a video-selection switch on the motherboard in addition to a CMOS setting. This is because the CPU needs to know where to display startup information even before it reads the CMOS RAM settings. Because color and monochrome adapter cards have different addresses, this must be configured at the hardware level rather than be determined by software.

For most PC and XT systems, switches 5 and 6 on Switch Block 1 set the type of display adapter installed. Table 12-1 shows how to set these switches.

Table 12-1
Settings for Switches 5 and 6

Type of Adapter	Switch 5	Switch 6
None	On	On
Color (40×25)	Off	On
Color (80×25)	On	Off
Mono or both	Off	Off

AT and higher systems have one switch for either color or monochrome display adapters.

If the switches are set properly and the CPU and POST operation cannot address the video card and the preceding error occurs, this indicates that the video card or motherboard is malfunctioning. If so, it may be a simple matter of removing and reinserting the video card because a loose or badly connected card is most often the cause of the failure. If you replace the video card and the problem persists, your motherboard is defective.

Also check the settings in your system's CMOS setup program. Often the type of display will be automatically selected and set for your BIOS, but you should be sure that the correct value is entered and stored in the CMOS RAM.

Display problems

You may encounter some of the following display problems.

Symptoms

▶ Screen flickers or shrinks

▶ Display is wiggly, pulsing, blurred, too large, or too small

Suspects

▶ Varying AC power

▶ Unstable power supply in the monitor

▶ Defective or misadjusted internal monitor circuits

▶ Video adapter is getting interference from other PC cards or nearby electrical equipment

▶ Monitor is experiencing interference from nearby equipment

▶ Defective monitor

▶ Loose connection between the monitor and computer

Solutions

▶ Move the computer or nearby electronic equipment to see if the screen disturbance stops.

▶ Fix the power wiring or voltage selection, or apply power conditioning.

▶ Replace the monitor or have it repaired.

▶ Check and change video card placement.

▶ Replace the video card.

▶ Check the connections.

▶ Replace the motherboard (if video adapter is built in).

Screen flickering or shifting are indications that the AC power to your system might be unstable, you have inadequate wiring or excessive loads on the same power line (such as air conditioners, clothes washer, or clothes dryer), or the internal circuitry or power supply in the monitor is malfunctioning.

Because the screen (CRT/monitor) has its own internal power supply separate from the PC/CPU hardware, a problem internal to the display might appear to be an AC power problem. Many systems connect the monitor through the outlets on the PC supply. These outlets provide only a convenient pass-through source of AC power and do not supply voltage for the monitor's internal circuits from the same PC power supply that powers the disk drives and motherboard.

In some cases, unstable AC power or other devices within your PC can influence the video interface card. If you have just installed a new monitor or add-in card and find that the display wiggles or flickers, you might have to rearrange the location of cards inside your PC to avoid signals that radiate between cards and affect the display system. Moving the power and video signal cable that attaches to your monitor may also avoid sources of interference.

Tip   Keep all PC data cables (such as serial, parallel, mouse, keyboard, and video) away from motorized devices, magnets, and fluorescent lamps to avoid possible signal interference.

Use a voltmeter to measure the AC line to see if voltage fluctuations occur. You might also notice that the fluctuations coincide with another device nearby being turned on (if your monitor flickers or dims when your refrigerator, washing machine, or other appliance comes on, your house wiring may be defective.) The only cures for this type of problem are to have an electrician check and repair faulty wiring, find another more adequate circuit to plug the PC into, or get a power-conditioning system to stabilize the AC voltage.

Note   Power conditioning comes in many forms. The purpose for using one form or another is to provide a stable or limited voltage to your PC system to prevent possible damage or the annoyance of system crashes or display flickering.

Note   The issues of AC power problems are far too complex to cover in any detail here. Consult an electrician or other vendor who specializes in troubleshooting and solving AC power problems. Look under *Electricians* or *Power* in the yellow pages listings of your telephone book.

Memory Errors

The most common memory problem you might encounter is having more memory in your system than is indicated at startup. That is, you know you have 8MB of RAM, but POST shows less than that. While POST is testing memory, it usually displays the amount it finds and the progress of the test.

As indicated previously under CMOS setup, AT/386/486 systems stop and wait for a key to be pressed before continuing with the startup process. PC and XT systems might not give you an error indication; instead they might simply list the amount of memory as it is tested during startup and show less memory than you know you have in your system. You might still be able to use your system, but not have enough memory to run some of your programs.

Aside from differences in the amount of memory found, any true errors found during memory testing will give a very definite indication of the error itself, and perhaps an indication of which chip is bad.

Cross-Reference   Further details on memory size, types, and configuration are provided in Chapter 15.

Common memory errors

Here are some common memory errors, many of which you might already have seen, and how to troubleshoot and solve them.

Symptoms

▶ Memory size error (AT and higher systems)

▶ Not enough memory (PC, XT)

▶ Two short beeps and/or error message 2xx (PC, XT, AT)

▶ Parity check 1 or 2, or ????? message

▶ System hangs up

Suspects

▶ Loose memory chip(s) or card

▶ CMOS setup (AT and higher systems)

▶ Improper switch setting

▶ Bad memory chip(s) or card

▶ Add-on memory card

Solutions

▶ Reset memory chip(s) in their sockets.

▶ Remove and reseat memory card(s) or modules.

▶ Check the CMOS setup (AT and higher systems).

▶ Check the switch settings.

▶ Run a memory diagnostic test to identify any bad memory chips and then replace bad memory.

Watch the system display during startup and note the amount of memory found or being tested. If this differs from the amount you know is in the system or from the switch or CMOS settings, you will not have access to all of the memory in your system.

AT and higher systems (286, 386, 486, and Pentium)

Many AT and AT-clone systems have a memory-size switch for either 256K or 512K of base memory. Check your motherboard or manual for the presence of this switch, its location, and its proper setting. Newer systems may use jumper pins or DIP switches, or rely on the CMOS setup parameters for the memory settings. Still others simply automatically detect and set the amount of memory in the system.

> **Note**   The method used internally by the system BIOS to detect and report the amount of extended memory above 16MB differs significantly in various systems, especially older ones. This usually does not affect your operating system or applications but system information and diagnostic software may report the wrong amount of memory or test it improperly.

AT systems provide a CMOS setup configuration for the amount of memory in the system. If you have a true IBM-AT system, you will need the diagnostic floppy disks to access this information. IBM indicates different memory types between the 640K region of base or DOS memory and the size of the expansion memory above the 1MB address range. If you have 2MB (2,048K) of total memory, typically 640K of it will be assigned to base memory and the remaining 1,408K will be expansion memory. Figure 12-5 shows a typical CMOS setup program.

Although IBM uses the term *expansion* for the additional memory in AT systems, this is actually extended memory, not expanded, or LIMS-EMS, memory. The LIMS-EMS memory is not configurable in CMOS setup; it requires a device driver in CONFIG.SYS. See Chapter 15 for more information about memory.

Most clone and 386 systems do not differentiate between base/DOS memory and expansion or extended memory. In these systems, it is generally assumed that the first 640K will be DOS memory and the rest will be extended memory.

If you have an 80286 system, you can use extended memory as simulated expanded memory with some types of special driver software (loaded with CONFIG.SYS), but you cannot use this extended memory for multitasking as you can with an 80386 system.

Numbered error messages in the 200 range indicate actual failure of one or more chips or memory modules. Different BIOS versions and systems have different ways of indicating which memory bit or address range is defective and requires replacement.

```
CMOS SETUP UTILITY                          Page 2

Base memory size:                   640KB
Extended memory size:               1,408KB
Floppy drive A:                     1.2MB, 5-1/4
Floppy drive B:                     1.44MB, 3-1/2
Hard disk C:                        Type 14
Hard disk D:                        Not installed
Primary display:                    EGA/VGA
Keyboard:                           Installed
Math coprocessor:                   Not installed
Date:                               11-11-91
Time:                               13:30:00
Parallel port interrupt select:     IRQ7
Parallel port select:               378th (LPT1)
Serial port 1:                      3F8h (COM1)
Serial port 2:                      3F8h (COM2)
Default speed:                      HI


        ↑ ↓ ↵ moves between items, ←→ select values
        F10-Record Changes, F2-Next Page, F1-Exit
```

Figure 12-5: A typical CMOS setup program

Add-on card memory

If you have installed an add-on card to increase the system memory to more than the motherboard will hold, be sure that the switch settings for the starting and total memory are correct. If your motherboard has 256K of RAM but you set the add-on card to start adding memory below 256K, you will have a memory conflict and likely a system lockup. Check the documentation for your motherboard and memory card for the proper values. The switch settings may be a trial-and-error process, as many add-in card manuals do not adequately describe what some switches mean or give examples of various configurations.

Additional system board memory

You add memory to PC systems by installing memory modules directly on the motherboard. These modules, called SIMMs (single inline memory modules) or DIMMs (dual inline memory modules) have been available in sizes ranging from 1 to 256MB per module. Depending on your motherboard configuration, these modules must be added in groups of two, four, or eight. Adding an incorrect number of modules can cause problems, ranging from the system not finding the memory on startup to a complete failure of the computer. Check the manual that came with your mother-board for memory upgrade requirements.

Disk Problems

After the POST process checks the system video, device, and memory resources, the system looks to either the floppy disk drive (A:), the hard disk (C:), or a bootable CD-ROM for operating system information. Although we are primarily addressing DOS here, your system might be trying to load Windows NT, OS/2, UNIX, or some other operating system instead. The system will either start up with the operating system or yield one of three basic types of errors. If you have an IBM system that cannot boot from a disk, you might see an error indicating that the system could not load an operating system. It will then run a small version of the BASIC language that is built into the ROM-BIOS chips. For detailed information about disk drive problems, see Part IV.

Floppy disk errors

Let's take a look at some floppy disk errors you might encounter.

Symptoms

▶ Error messages in the 6xx or 73xx range

Suspects

▶ Floppy disk drives

▶ Floppy disk drive adapter card or system board (if the floppy disk controller is built in)

Solutions

▶ Check the floppy disk drive power and data cables.

▶ Swap or replace drive(s).

▶ Check the adapter card connection to the motherboard.

▶ Replace the floppy disk adapter card or system board (if the floppy disk controller is built in).

Hard disk errors

This section explores hard disk errors and how to solve them.

Symptoms

▶ Error messages in the 17xx or 104xx ranges

Suspects

▶ Hard disk drive(s)

▶ Hard disk drive format

▶ Hard disk adapter or system board (if drive adapter is built in)

▶ Bad CMOS backup battery might be a suspect as well

Solutions

▶ Check hard drive power and data cables.

▶ Swap or replace drive(s).

▶ Check adapter card connection to the motherboard.

▶ Replace adapter card or system board (if the drive adapter is built in).

▶ Check CMOS settings and backup battery.

DOS disk errors

These Symptoms, Suspects, and Solutions focus on DOS disk errors.

Symptoms

▶ Nonsystem disk or disk error

Suspects

▶ Nonsystem disk in floppy disk drive (A:)

▶ Missing DOS system files from hard disk

Solutions

▶ Remove disk from drive A: to allow boot from the C: drive or CD-ROM.

▶ Run SYS program on disk to make it bootable if it is not already used as a data floppy disk.

▶ If the drive is secured by a security/password program, reinstall the security program's driver software from INSTALL disk.

General disk errors

These Symptoms, Suspects, and Solutions focus on general disk errors.

Symptoms

▶ General failure reading drive x

▶ Invalid drive specification

▶ Drive not ready

Suspects

▶ Drive failure

▶ Disk not formatted

▶ Floppy disk drive door open

Solutions

▶ Format or replace disk or drive.

▶ Close the floppy disk drive door.

Depending on the drive where you intend to boot, and the condition of the disk or drive, any one of the preceding messages could appear, indicating the general nature of the corrective action to be taken. The third set of symptoms is fairly common if you use the floppy disk drive a lot and have left a data-only (nonsystem) floppy disk in the drive during startup. All other messages indicate a failure of the disk or drive.

A slow-starting hard disk drive can provide "not ready" or "invalid drive" messages during a cold-boot (power up) sequence, which may rectify itself if you do a warm boot (pressing the Ctrl+Alt+Del keys) after the drive has had time to come up to operating speed.

Summary

As you can see by now, it is not difficult to resolve problems with PCs when they are reduced to their basic elements of cause and effect, what should happen when, and what could happen if something is not working just right.

Granted, there are obviously more complex startup problems than those you can check by plugging in a lamp or listening to a speaker beep.

If you do get stuck with a particularly difficult or unusual startup problem and need extra help, use the examples in this chapter to gather enough details to explain the situation quickly and accurately to someone with technical expertise. With the right information at hand, a call to a friend, technical support, or an e-mail should bring swift results.

Once your system gets through the startup steps — from the power supply through POST and into loading the operating system (see Chapter 13) — the behavior and problems with your system are dictated not only by DOS or other operating systems, but by the device drivers and other programs you configure or load into the system through the older CONFIG.SYS and AUTOEXEC.BAT files.

Beyond getting the hardware running, once you can get an operating system loading, many problems should be easier to diagnose because the system should be running to some extent, giving you access to various diagnostic tools.

Chapter 13 discusses configuration problems, starting with a system that has power and is loading the operating system.

✦   ✦   ✦

Configuration Problems

In Chapter 12 we answered "What if you turn on your computer and nothing happens?"

Now we are ready to examine some of the more detailed troubleshooting steps to help you arrive at various solutions for hardware-related startup problems. In this chapter we address various operating system configuration issues. Now is the time to get your PC up and running.

Operating System Configurations

Configuration may be the most troubling aspect of PC systems. You may encounter problems with missing device drivers (devices are there but not working); the ability to use one piece of the hardware but not another, or not use both at the same time (possible hardware conflicts); or application problems that cause the system to crash unpredictably (hardware and/or software configuration conflicts).

Thus configuration of the system, from the basics through the complexities of hardware to the installation of the operating system and use of the applications programs, will receive much attention as we progress through this book.

Beyond the hardware aspects of system configuration, you have to consider the configuration for system bootup and establish the environment in which you will work. That is the focus of this section.

Cross-Reference Configuration of Windows 95, Windows 98, and Windows Me is covered in Chapter 8. Windows NT and Windows 2000 are covered in Chapter 9.

Your PC may use a variety of hardware, operating environments, and applications software. Your choices blend in various ways to make up the overall configuration of your PC system. Unless you work in a rigid, managed PC environment, one in which a system administrator or desktop support group is responsible for establishing and maintaining the PC(s) you use, you have many choices for your PC's configuration.

The Intel x86-based computing platforms can run many operating systems and environments, typically plain-old DOS, Caldera (formerly Digital Research) DOS, DOS plus Windows 3.x, Windows 95/98/Me, Windows NT/2000, OS/2, Linux, FreeBSD, SCO Unix, or Solaris. Admittedly and unfortunately, we cannot cover every operating system and environment in detail, and we made choices based on space, time, and reader focus. Thus without prejudices or preferences, we drew the line at the DOS and Windows environments. Indeed, Linux and the UNIX derivatives are desirable and preferred for many situations, just as reduced-instruction-set-computing (RISC) systems as well as the Apple Macintosh and the various operating systems for it, have been good choices for many people. Where appropriate, we do provide information regarding some UNIX-related systems, but the focus is DOS and Windows because they represent the mainstream of PC systems. (Well, we think more than 50 million systems and growing daily is a good indicator of mainstream!)

For the choices we do cover in this book, the basic difference between these environments is where or when, various memory management and device drivers need to be installed so that you can take advantage of all that your chosen environment offers. If you've reached this point in the book — that is, through the system being able to boot up and function to some degree — we have to assume that at least some of the hardware and software in your system does or did work together at one time. This is by no means an indication or assumption that all is well with your PC. This book, of course, covers troubleshooting of specific operating system and hardware problems in the chapters ahead.

DOS and Windows 3.x Systems

Although DOS and Windows 3.x systems are based in the previous generation, we still receive e-mail from users of DOS and Windows 3.x who find that these environments suit them just fine. Indeed, DOS is the foundation from which most computer systems are built, until you move on to NT-, 2000-, or Unix-derived operating systems (and yes, DOS is a knock-off of many features of CP/M and Unix.) Understanding what DOS does reveals insights into how starting up a PC with any other operating system works. Of course, you have to wonder how much faster some things would work if you ran plain old DOS and another user interface, such as DESQview or DESQview/X without all of the seemingly excessive device driver and graphical overhead that Windows takes up. Enough of showing our age; it's time to boot up!

Whether you boot your computer from a diskette, hard disk, or by other means, the system must load the two hidden files that are the basis for your version of DOS. Because the files are hidden, you will not see them in the directory of your diskette or hard disk when using the DOS DIR command, but the computer will not boot if these files are not present. They are usually named IBMBIO.COM and IBMDOS.COM for PC-DOS, or IO.SYS and MSDOS.SYS for MS-DOS. Preparing diskettes or your hard disk to contain these system files is a matter of using the FORMAT command with the /S option, or using the SYS command on an already formatted drive and specifying the drive letter, as in issuing the SYS A: command at the DOS prompt as follows:

```
SYS A: [Enter]
```

If these system files exist on the boot drive, they are loaded and your system looks for two additional files, CONFIG.SYS and AUTOEXEC.BAT, and your DOS command interpreter, COMMAND.COM. The two configuration files differ from DOS and other programs or system files you might install. You or a data processing professional can prepare these two files based on the hardware and software installed on your PC. If DOS finds a CONFIG.SYS file, DOS processes it before the AUTOEXEC.BAT file. After CONFIG.SYS is loaded, DOS looks for COMMAND.COM or the program installed as the SHELL, described later in this chapter. COMMAND.COM or the SHELL you have installed for DOS loads and executes the AUTOEXEC.BAT file if it exists.

The CONFIG.SYS file allocates your system's memory in ways that improve its performance and it installs devices such as expanded memory and tape drives. You may even use it to install a user interface that is different from the normal DOS prompt.

AUTOEXEC.BAT sets your DOS environment and performs tasks that you want completed every time you boot your computer. These tasks might include optimizing your disk drives, checking for viruses, loading terminate-and-stay-resident (TSR) programs, and executing programs that you will use right away.

Modifying Configuration Files

Many of the programs installed on your computer either provide a sample CONFIG.SYS and AUTOEXEC.BAT file, or the programs' install programs might take the steps necessary to modify your present files. Other programs may come with documentation of their requirements and instructions for making or modifying your configuration files. To modify CONFIG.SYS and AUTOEXEC.BAT files, use a DOS-compatible text editor that creates and saves plain ASCII text files. This means that the edited file will be stored on your disk without special characters that DOS cannot handle. If you use a word processing program such as Microsoft Word for Windows, WordPerfect, or WordStar, save your file in DOS (text or ASCII) format after you make any changes. The items in your CONFIG.SYS and AUTOEXEC.BAT files may be in uppercase, lowercase, or mixed case.

The CONFIG.SYS file

Although the best CONFIG.SYS file for your computer depends on the hardware and software installed, a couple of examples may help to identify the types of data it may contain.

One of the simplest CONFIG.SYS files enables DOS to open at least 30 files and provides 20 buffers to speed disk access. If you use the DOS TYPE command to show the CONFIG.SYS file on the screen (assuming you use drive C to start your computer), your screen might look like this:

```
C:\>type config.sys
FILES=30
BUFFERS=20
C:\>_
```

A simple CONFIG.SYS file such as this seldom causes problems. Problems arise from too much hardware and software to install in your PC.

If you have extended memory, expanded memory, or both, it becomes more complicated to use multiple programs, installable hard disks, a mouse or other pointing device, a tape backup drive, an alternate user interface (shell), or other items.

A typical CONFIG.SYS file created by an installation of MS-DOS, with a device driver or two added in, may be enhanced from the simple configuration as follows:

```
DEVICE=C:\DOS\HIMEM.SYS
DEVICE=C:\DOS\EMM386.EXE
FILES=30
BUFFERS=20
SHELL=C:\DOS\COMMAND.COM
```

If you have installed Microsoft Windows 3.x after the DOS installation just represented, the references to C:\DOS for HIMEM and EMM386 change to reflect the Windows subdirectory, typically C:\WINDOWS; this is based on the premise that to get the latest versions of these memory drivers, the version of Windows being installed would be later than the version of DOS that exists already. That may or may not be the case, but for a basic DOS and Windows 3.x system, these changes are acceptable.

The CONFIG.SYS file used to create this chapter originally, one that is a bit more customized, is as follows:

```
DEVICE=C:\WINDOWS\HIMEM.SYS
DEVICE=C:\WINDOWS\EMM386.EXE X=A000-BFFF
DOS=HIGH,UMB
STACKS=0,0
```

```
FILES=50
BUFFERS=3
DEVICE=C:\DOS\SMARTDRV.EXE /DOUBLE_BUFFER
DEVICE=C:\SCSI\ASPI4DOS.SYS
DEVICEHIGH=C:\SCSI\ASPICD.SYS /D:MSCD001
Rem DEVICE=C:\CDROM\CDROM.SYS /D:MSCD001
DEVICEHIGH=C:\SOUND\SOUND.SYS /I:5 /P:220
SHELL=C:\DOS\COMMAND.COM C:DOS /E:1024 /P
```

It looks rather complicated, but each entry has a specific purpose, and each was added either manually or by an installation or optimizing program.

The first line installs HIMEM.SYS, the extended memory manager required by the EMM386 driver in the second line and Windows 3.*x*, so the PC then can make better use of memory and perform multitasking with operating environments such as Microsoft Windows and Windows 95 and 98.

The third line instructs the operating system to load portions of itself into high memory at the beginning of the Extended Memory range above one megabyte; it also makes Upper Memory Blocks available between the 640K DOS limit and the 1MB mark in order to enable device drivers and resident programs to load into this memory space in locations not used by adapter ROM. These two attributes leave you with more lower DOS memory for programs and data files.

STACKS, FILES, and BUFFERS are valid CONFIG.SYS commands. STACKS=0,0 prevents DOS from using memory for stacks (temporary memory storage locations used by a PC to keep track of what it is doing). This system does not need DOS STACKS. FILES=50 enables the system to open and keep track of up to 50 files at a time. One of our database applications requires that many files be opened at the same time. BUFFERS=3 sets up three buffers for speeding disk drive activities, which we will augment by loading the SMARTDRV disk cache program in the AUTOEXEC.BAT file.

If you have any SCSI-type disk drives, as the example does, proper configuration rules for DOS and SMARTDRIVE might call for you to add the following line anywhere after DOS=HIGH, UMB for performance and compatibility between DOS and SCSI devices:

```
DEVICE=C:\DOS\SMARTDRV.EXE /DOUBLE_BUFFER
```

This configuration has a SCSI host adapter that connects to the CD-ROM drive. Thus you have to load the Advanced SCSI Programming Interface (ASPI) driver for the Small Computer System Interface (SCSI) host adapter and then load the appropriate ASPI CD-ROM driver. The presence of a CD-ROM drive also requires that another driver, Microsoft CD-ROM Extensions (MSCDEX), be loaded with the AUTOEXEC.BAT file. If you do not have SCSI devices installed, you will not need the previous three lines.

Note that we use DEVICEHIGH= instead of simply DEVICE= for some of the drivers. This causes the qualified devices to load into high or upper memory instead of using up lower DOS memory. The ASPI4DOS driver should not be given the DEVICE-HIGH prefix because of how and where various programs look for this driver.

If you have a CD-ROM drive, typically connected as either an extra drive along with your Integrated Drive Electronics (IDE) hard drive or connected to your sound card, you will need a line similar to the one shown beginning with "Rem." This driver enables the system to be aware that a CD-ROM drive is installed, as with the SCSI drivers previously mentioned, but the driver does not convert the CD-ROM drive into an active DOS disk drive. In the previous example, the line is inactive, due to the REM (REMark) that appears at the beginning of the line. That part is also handled by MSCDEX later.

The system also has a sound card and for DOS to be aware of and make use of it, as in for games, you need to include a sound card driver, generically shown as SOUND.SYS in this example. We chose to load this driver high with the DEVICEHIGH statement. Three parameters are also shown for SOUND.SYS: /I:5 specifies that the sound card is or should be configured to use IRQ line 5; /D:1 specifies that the sound card is or should be configured to use DMA line 1; and /P:220 specifies that the sound card is or should be configured to use address 220. We say "is or should be" because most I/O devices, especially non–Plug and Play ones, must be manually configured with switches or jumpers and then the software has to be set up with parameters that match the hardware. In other words, the software really has no idea what the hardware is set for unless we specify it as we have, and the hardware has no idea nor can it be told by software what it should be configured for unless the hardware was designed with this capability.

The last line of this customized CONFIG.SYS file tells DOS to use the DOS COMMAND.COM for its user interface.

This CONFIG.SYS file would not work in your system unless you have the same hardware as our test computer and install the software in the same directories. It is presented as an example that will describe what to consider when creating or modifying the system configuration.

Tip   As a general rule, your CONFIG.SYS file should contain only those items required to enable your system to use the devices that are already installed in, that you install in, or that you attach to your PC. FILES, BUFFERS, FCBS, and STACKS should be set to provide just enough of these resources for your system or software needs, as installing more than is required merely wastes memory.

Table 13-1 shows the commands that the CONFIG.SYS file may use. It may contain none, one, or any of these commands.

	Table 13-1 CONFIG.SYS Commands	
Command	*Description*
BREAK=	Specifies enhanced Ctrl+C/Ctrl+Break check setting (ON or OFF)
BUFFERS=	Indicates number of file sector buffers (1 to 99, or up to 1,000 if /x is used with DOS 5.0+; 1 to 8 secondary buffers only for DOS 5.0)
COUNTRY=	Specifies international time, date, currency, capitalization, collating sequence, and decimal separator
DEVICE=	Installs a device (file specification plus parameters)
DEVICEHIGH=	Installs a device in upper memory
DOS=	Indicates DOS is to maintain a link to or is to load itself into the upper memory area (HIGH, LOW; UMB, NOUMB) (5.0+)
DRIVEPARM=	Specifies parameters for block devices (drives, tapes, and so on) (4.0+)
FCBS=	Indicates number of file control blocks (1 to 255; default is 4)
FILES=	Indicates number of files that may be opened at one time (8 to 255)
INSTALL=	Loads memory resident program (4.0+)
LASTDRIVE=	Specifies maximum number of drives in your system (A to Z)
SHELL=	Specifies the command processor program to use
STACKS=	Indicates dynamic use of stacks for hardware interrupts (number, size, 0 to 64 number of stacks; 0 to 512 bytes each)

Table 13-2 shows the standard device drivers provided with MS-DOS and PC-DOS. Other drivers may be provided with DOS extenders, memory enhancers, special printers, fax boards, plotters, sound and other high-speed data transfer devices, network systems, graphic systems, and so forth. Your version of DOS may provide the device drivers listed in Table 13-2. The device drivers provided with other hardware and software should have different names.

Table 13-2
DOS CONFIG.SYS Device Drivers

Device Driver	Description
ANSI.SYS	Supports screen and keyboard device for the ANSI standard
COUNTRY.SYS	Supports code page switching for displaying international characters (Refer also to DISPLAY.SYS or KEYBOARD.SYS in different versions of DOS.)
DRIVER.SYS	Creates a logical drive that you may use to refer to a physical diskette drive
EMM386.EXE	Simulates expanded memory using your system's extended memory (5.0 +)
HIMEM.SYS	Manages your system's use of extended memory and high RAM (5.0 +)
PRINTER.SYS	Supports code page switching for parallel ports (international characters)
RAMDRIVE.SYS	Creates a simulated hard disk in your system's RAM, extended, or expanded memory (See VDISK.SYS.)

Memory management

Although other methods exist, the industry standard and by far the most commonly used method of expanding the memory on your PC under DOS has been the Lotus/Intel/Microsoft Expanded Memory Specification Standard (LIMS EMS). The Enhanced Expanded Memory Specification (EEMS) specification by AST Research was incorporated into the current version of the standard, and it is referred to as EEMS version 3.2 or EMS version 4.0.

Unfortunately, there was some confusion in the industry regarding expanded memory, especially among memory board manufacturers. The confusion is not so much a misunderstanding of the standard as it is the manufacturers taking advantage of the difference in the names of the standard. The earlierEMS 3.2 standard, when applied to the hardware (memory boards), cannot use the current standard software.

Tip

When you encounter an extended or expanded memory board (they are no longer manufactured), make sure it is compatible with the EMS 4.0 or EEMS 3.2 standard. If you have extended memory and use a driver such as Quarterdeck's QEMM386, don't worry about the standard because QEMM (and other advanced memory drivers) can use extended memory as either extended or expanded memory.

Extended memory is addressed as one continuous addressing area from the bottom to the top of memory. Expanded memory uses a scheme to map sections of the expanded memory into a page frame in the upper memory area (above 640K and below the DOS 1MB limit). Because you decide which type of memory to use, it is important to have the ability to access both types. QEMM386 uses the upper memory area on your computer much more efficiently than DOS 5.0 or higher and most of the other extended and expanded memory managers available. However, based on the software you use, another memory manager may be more suited to your system, especially if a particular program, network, or device requires the installation of a particular memory management system.

You may find similar reasons to use 386MAX, NETROOM, Headroom, or some other memory manager in your system. The specific parameters used to install these and other drivers again depends on the hardware and software installed in your system. These products are mentioned because they are the ones most commonly used to extend the capabilities of PCs using DOS.

Chapter 15 provides more details about memory and memory management issues.

Device drivers

Many SCSI, CD-ROM, tape drives, fax boards, and document scanners require a driver in your CONFIG.SYS file. Others may be installed via a program in your AUTOEXEC.BAT file or may be installed as needed by executing a batch file or program after your system is already in use. Some may have conflicts with other software and devices in your system. This does not mean that they may not be used — they just cannot be used at the same time. For a historical example, the Complete PC FAX board is incompatible with DESQview. One solution is to copy in a different CONFIG.SYS and AUTOEXEC.BAT file and to reboot the system with the fax board operating. It is a little inconvenient, but it may satisfy your occasional need to send and receive faxes on a particular PC.

ANSI drivers

The ANSI.SYS driver provided with DOS is installed in the CONFIG.SYS file. It lets your computer use programs and communicate with some other systems that require an ANSI-compatible terminal. FCONSOLE (FANSI), VANSI, NANSI, and other ANSI drivers that may have been provided with your CGA, EGA, VGA, MCGA, and other screen drivers may be installed in your CONFIG.SYS, AUTOEXEC.BAT, or other program setup files. FCONSOLE is installed via your CONFIG.SYS file and provides an extended keyboard buffer, the ability to scroll back through previous screens, and so forth. Other ANSI drivers may be provided with a particular monitor or video adapter or with a program that has special requirements beyond those provided by the standard ANSI driver.

Security drivers

A special class of hard disk drivers provides some level of system security. The simplest uses a password that must be entered during the boot process. You can bypass some of these simpler security drivers by booting the system using a diskette. A more secure driver does not allow access to the hard disk, no matter what method is used to boot the computer, unless the proper password is provided.

Security drivers can be both secure and dangerous. If you forget the password, you cannot access your system until you get the company that provided the security driver to provide an override. Some of the more secure drivers supply a special boot disk that provides access to the hard disk without using a password. This is convenient, but the special diskette itself must be protected, never lost, and kept in a secure place.

Configuration drivers

Another class of driver or program (used at the DOS prompt) provides an easy way to boot your computer with different configurations. BOOTCFG.COM, a user-supported program, is an example of such a program. This type of program maintains copies of separate CONFIG.SYS and AUTOEXEC.BAT files and merely copies the selected set to replace your current CONFIG.SYS and AUTOEXEC.BAT files and reboots your system. DOS 6.*x* provided multiconfiguration capability with new CONFIG.SYS parameters.

The SHELL= command

The SHELL= command in your CONFIG.SYS file may be used to provide you with an alternate user interface. COMMAND.COM, with its DOS prompt and set of utilities that provide access to programs, files, and the DOS batch language, may be enhanced or replaced by the alternate shell. The DOS SHELL provided by Microsoft with DOS 4.0 is an example of such systems. It is called the Microsoft MS-DOS Shell and is a text-based system that supplies the capabilities of DOS via windows and menus, rather than via commands entered at the DOS prompt.

NDOS, from Symantec Corporation's line of Norton products, is a commercial version of the user-supported 4DOS program, and it is another example. It provides the familiar capabilities of COMMAND.COM, but it adds commands and Batch language capabilities, makes the DOS command line twice as long (the number of characters that may be included on the command line), and provides easy access to the DOS environment. It also uses less DOS memory than COMMAND.COM.

Problems with Mixing 8-Bit and 16-Bit Adapter Cards and Their BIOS ROMs

Another source of configuration problems, especially those affecting upper memory, is the installation of devices with both 8-bit and 16-bit ROMs within the same 128K block of memory in your PC. A confusing factor is that many adapters, such as VGA cards, state in their documentation that they are 16-bit devices. They may use a 16-bit data-transfer path, but they may or may not use a 16-bit address path. The 16-bit transfer channel makes the board display faster on your screen. However, if it uses 8-bit addressing, it requires that addressing within the 64K block of memory in which it resides to be set to use 8-bit addressing. If there is ROM in that same 64K block of memory or in the 64K shared with a 128K block and the memory block was set to 16-bit addressing, your system will lock up when one or the other ROM is accessed using the "wrong" addressing scheme.

The real problem will occur when you have a mixture of 8-bit, 16-bit, and 32-bit ROM extensions that could be installed in the same system. Thirty-two-bit ROM requires every device within a megabyte (or larger) boundary in your system to use the same addressing scheme. This is a problem that requires the cooperation of many system operating system developers. One solution is to use device drivers rather than ROM for controlling the hardware extensions on your system, but some companies do not provide device drivers as an alternative to using ROM extensions. Device drivers may or may not fit into upper memory by trying to "load them high." Therefore, there is a risk of using up more DOS memory to work around this ROM addressing problem.

Note   The C000-CFFF and D000-DFFF ranges of memory are each 64K blocks. Each resides in the same 128K block of memory and are the locations normally used for video, hard disk, and other ROM extensions.

The AUTOEXEC.BAT file

AUTOEXEC.BAT may contain any valid DOS command, program name with parameters, and the DOS batch language commands. It enables DOS to perform the steps necessary to make your system ready for regular use. It is a special DOS batch file that runs automatically when you start your system. It must be located in the root directory of the drive you use to boot your system.

Assume your system has its own internal clock and that the date and time are already set. You have your DOS program files on the C: drive in a directory named DOS and your utility programs on that same drive in a directory named UTILITY. A simple AUTOEXEC.BAT file that provides your system with a more informative prompt (one containing the disk drive and the current directory—the default for

DOS 6.*x* and above), as well as access to DOS and your utility programs from any subdirectory on your system, would look like the following:

```
PROMPT=$p$g
PATH C:\DOS;C:\UTILITY
```

Such a simple AUTOEXEC.BAT file would seldom be the cause of system problems. The AUTOEXEC.BAT file on the system used to create this chapter is the following:

```
ECHO OFF
PATH D:\U;C:\dvx;E:\D;D:\E;C:\DOS;...(Continued below)...
     G:\TP;G\TA;G:\td;G:\c5\bin;G:\ng;...(Continued below)...
     F:\U;G:\H;E:\W;G:\N;E:\WP;E:\pm
SET COM-AND=F:\U
SET UNISIG=F:\U
SET BBS=F:\BBS
SET MEDIR=F:\EM
SET TEMP=E:\W\TEMP
SET INCLUDE=g:\c5\include;
SET LIB=g:\c5\lib
SET OBJ=g:\c5\obj
SET PLL=g:\c5\pll
set clipper=f:30
PROMPT $P$G
chkdsk c: /f > startup
chkdsk d: /f >> startup
chkdsk e: /f >> startup
chkdsk f: /f >> startup
chkdsk g: /f >> startup
chkdsk h: /f >> startup
FR C: /SAVE >> startup
FR D: /SAVE >> startup
NUMOFF
```

Looks complicated, right? It is really a simple startup program. It could contain commands to perform an automatic backup or just about anything else you might like your system to do before it starts. This one sets up the computer for access to many directories, sets DOS environment variables for some programs that work more easily if the variables contain the right information, and sets the DOS prompt so that it shows the current drive and directory. It also performs some disk drive diagnostics and turns off the NumLock key. More specifically

✦ ECHO OFF starts the AUTOEXEC.BAT file so that it does not print the commands onscreen. The "interesting stuff," the results of the commands, is still printed onscreen. DOS 3.3 and later enable you to use the command @ECHO OFF so that even the ECHO command is not printed onscreen.

✦ PATH is too long to print on one line, but the thing to notice is that it gives DOS access to 17 directories. DOS is limited to 128 characters for a command line with arguments. NDOS increases this to 255 characters, but this AUTOEXEC.BAT file will boot with COMMAND.COM or NDOS.COM. Shortening the directory names makes this possible.

✦ U is the Utility program directory and gets used most often; therefore, it is the first PATH entry.

✦ DVX is the directory containing Quarterdeck's DESQview/X, the X Window System development environment.

✦ D is the DESQview directory – still installed but no longer being used.

✦ E is the directory containing the Turbo Power Editor, which is used most often for programming and editing DOS-compatible files. DOS is the directory containing the standard DOS programs for the version of DOS installed on this system.

✦ TP, TA, and TD are the directories for the Turbo Pascal, Turbo Assembler, and Turbo Debugger programming systems, respectively.

✦ C5\BIN contains the Clipper Compiler to be used for compiling dBASE-compatible programs.

✦ NG contains Norton's Guides system, which in this case provides instant access to Clipper online documentation.

✦ The U directory on drive F: contains a system named UNISIG that uses the COM-AND communication program.

✦ W is the Windows system.

✦ N is the directory in which the current version of Norton Utilities and most other Norton programs reside.

✦ WP contains WordPerfect, and PM holds PageMaker.

These are not all of the directories in this system, but they are the ones used most often on this obsolete system. Note that the PATH statement provides reference to the directories, with a drive letter for each one. This ensures that the proper directory on the proper drive is referenced. DOS can find these directories regardless of the current default drive. In addition:

✦ The list of SET commands creates DOS environment variables and gives them values. These are used by programs to determine the location of their files, modify program options, and so forth.

✦ SET COM-AND=F:\U and SET UNISIG=F:\U identify the drive and directory where the COM-AND communication program and the UNISIG system files are located.

✦ SET BBS=F:\BBS is used by a COM-AND script that provides a full-featured BBS. This is the directory containing the BBS files.

✦ SET MEDIR=F:\EM provides access to a powerful but little-known text editor, MicroEmacs.

✦ The E:\W\TEMP setting is used by Windows and some other programs for a temporary work space.

✦ INCLUDE, LIB, OBJ, PLL, and CLIPPER variables are used by the Clipper compiler and the programs it creates.

✦ PROMPT=PG is used often so that DOS will display the current drive and directory as the prompt that accepts DOS commands. The prompt may contain messages, date, time, set colors, and many other useful and fun option. DOS 6.*x* and Windows 95 default the DOS prompt to this setting.

The long series of CHKDSK commands, redirected to a file named STARTUP, ensures that there are no minor problems on any disk drive each time this system boots. The /F parameter for each one instructs DOS to fix a problem it finds on the drive. The STARTUP file may be viewed to see whether any problems were found and fixed, and also to see a display of the space on the drive and how it is used.

The two FR *<drive letter>* /SAVE commands use Norton's Format Recover command to save information about drives C: and D: that may be used to restore the disk if it is accidentally formatted. The results of these two commands are also echoed to the startup file. Note that the first redirection to STARTUP uses the > redirection character and the remainder use the >> characters. This is so that a new STARTUP file is created each time the system boots. The > character creates a new file and the >> characters append to the file.

Note   NUMOFF is a tiny program that turns off the NumLock key. It is handy if you seldom use the number keypad to enter numbers.

The above file is an old AUTOEXEC.BAT file on the computer used to write an earlier version of this chapter. The computer is as obsolete as DOS, and most of the programs it contains would not be found in a new system. However, it does show a good deal of what has been and may still be done using DOS on a computer. The AUTOEXEC.BAT file is just one of ten AUTOEXEC files used on that old computer on a regular basis. The other AUTOEXEC files have extension names representative of their purpose. To reboot this system and have it execute a different startup sequence, it is simple to copy the desired AUTOEXEC.xxx file to AUTOEXEC.BAT and press Ctrl+Alt+Delete to reboot.

Multiple Configuration Options

Microsoft introduced a menu-driven, selective configuration option during bootup with version 6.0 of DOS. It is available with equivalent versions of IBM's PC-DOS as well. These services have been offered in at least six public-domain and shareware utilities, available on BBSs and online services for a number of years. Implementing them with the operating system allows them better use of memory and guarantees compatibility, and it reduces their generation and maintenance into one or two files.

The ability to select a configuration at bootup within a single set of CONFIG.SYS and AUTOEXEC.BAT files, rather than keeping different copies of CONFIG.SYS and AUTOEXEC.BAT files for each type of configuration, simplifies your setup and use of your system.

A CONFIG.SYS file with multiple configuration options uses the same commands and structure as a regular CONFIG.SYS file, with a few modifiers or labels for organizing and directing what happens when you boot up. Following is an example of a CONFIG.SYS file with two configuration options. Remarks defining each line are shown on the right.

CONFIG.SYS Command	Description
[menu]	Label defining start of menu.
menuitem=EMM386, Run EMM386	Defined menu item, menu text.
menuitem=PLAIN, Just DOS	Defined menu item, menu text.
menudefault=EMM386, 5	Default menu item and time-out period.
[common]	Label indicating common items for all configurations; the CONFIG.SYS commands follow the label.
DOS=HIGH,UMB	Loads DOS into High Memory and creates Upper Memory Blocks.
BREAK=ON	Allows the user to use the BREAK key
STACKS=0,0	Affects DOS' use of memory stacks
FILES=30	Sets number of files DOS may have open
BUFFERS=10	Sets the number of Buffers DOS can use
LASTDRIVE=M	Sets the highest drive letter DOS can use

Continued

CONFIG.SYS Command	Description
FCBS=1,0	Affects the number of File Control Blocks
[EMM386]	Label indicating the start of commands to be run for the EMM386 menu selection
DEVICE=C:\DOS\HIMEM.SYS	Provides a device driver file for DOS to be able to use High Memory
DEVICE=C:\DOS\EMM386.EXE C:\DOS/E:1024 /PRAM NOEMS	Enables the use of Expanded Memory
DEVICEHIGH=C:\DOS\SETVER.EXE	Loads the SETVER driver into high memory
INCLUDE=Plain	A multiple configuration command indicating that menu item Plain should be used after the preceding commands.
[Plain]	Label indicating start of commands to be run for Plain menu selection (that is, no EMM386).
SHELL=C:\DOS\COMMAND.COM C:\DOS/E:1024 /P	Indicates which command processor to load. At bootup, a new screen showing two menu selections appears, one for Run EMM386 and the other for Plain, as well as a countdown indicator. After the new screen appears, the default configuration, EMM386, executes. You may select the Plain configuration by selecting the number 2 or by using the cursor keys to highlight a different menu item from the default and then pressing Enter. Because multiple configuration operation also extends to the AUTOEXEC.BAT file, you can control what happens during the execution of AUTOEXEC.BAT by using standard batch file labels (text preceded by a colon) and an additional variable line, goto %config%, which directs DOS to advance to the batch file label indicated by the same label name chosen in CONFIG.SYS. A simple AUTOEXEC.BAT file to complement the preceding CONFIG.SYS file might look like this: Production: Again, please maintain blank cells. Please use a Bible Table with the following column headings:
AUTOEXEC.BAT command	Description

CONFIG.SYS Command	*Description*
@ECHO OFF	Some typical AUTOEXEC.BAT commands. Turns off echo of commands to the screen.
@CLS	Clear the screen.
@VERIFY OFF	Turn off Verify, to speed disk usage.
Goto %config%	Special multiconfiguration command directs processing of AUTOEXEC.BAT to follow label chosen in CONFIG.SYS at boot up.
:EMM386	Label for EMM386 configuration selection, not executed if Plain configuration is selected at bootup.
LH C:\DOS\SMARTDRV C+ D+ /V 1024 1024	QEMM version of LOADHIGH to load the SMARTDRV driver into high memory.
LH C:\dos\doskey/insert	Load High the DOSKEY driver
LH c:\dos\mouse.exe	Load High the Mouse driver
:plain	Label for Plain menu selection, also run in sequence after EMM386 section.
SET PATH=C:\B;C:\T;C:\DOS; C:\;	Set the search path for DOS
VERIFY OFF	Speed disk access by disabling VERIFY
PROMPT pg	Set the familiar C:\path\ prompt
SET COM-AND=C:\CA	Set a DOS variable named COM-AND to C:\CA
SET DIRCMD=/a	Continue setting DOS variables
SET TEMP=C:\TEMP	
SET TMP=C:\TEMP	
SET WIN$=C:\WINDOWS	
call c:\b\ask_net.bat	Execute another BAT file and return.
c:	Change to the C: drive.
cd\	Change directory to the root.

As you can imagine, there are as many possible variations to configure in your system's setup—with and without device drivers, memory managers, TSRs, network options, and so on. Your creativity and your grasp of DOS, CONFIG.SYS, and batch file commands can provide you with many convenient ways to run your system.

Troubleshooting multiple configuration setups is aided by the common DOS error messages and during bootup by use of F5 to bypass CONFIG.SYS and AUTOEXEC.BAT entirely, or by use of F8 to step through each line of these bootup files to watch the operation and stop where you think there may be trouble.

Tip   Placing ECHO and REM statements at various points in your AUTOEXEC.BAT file helps isolate the location of troublesome commands that may not provide an onscreen message when they execute.

Windows 95/98/Me

Windows 95/98/Me is configured using some of the same concepts as DOS and the previous versions of Windows. The graphical interfaces do less for your basic DOS configuration issues than they do to provide you with an easier way to get to your work. You must still attend to certain parameters, device drivers, and especially memory management issues to provide the enhanced graphical environments the appropriate resources.

Note   Windows 98 and Me do not support alternate memory manager software.

The magic in these newer versions of Windows is that they have smarter installation routines that detect existing and new hardware and configure accordingly. These features depend on the continuation of three other advances in the PC industry: the Microsoft Plug-and-Play hardware configuration standard, new system BIOS programs that conform to Plug and Play, and new hardware devices that conform to Plug and Play. Eventually, you will be able to buy a PC system that knows what hardware is installed and how to configure itself when new hardware is added. We are not quite there yet, but Windows 95/98/Me helps you avoid many of the common and confusing address, IRQ, and DMA conflicts that plague present and older systems.

Although Windows 95/98/Me needs neither a CONFIG.SYS nor AUTOEXEC.BAT file, it uses configurations similar to those with which you may already be familiar — the basic HIMEM.SYS and other parameters in CONFIG.SYS. HIMEM.SYS is loaded automatically, and the FILES, BUFFERS, STACKS,and similar commands are set to their defaults. These parameters typically apply only to DOS sessions, and will carry over to DOS sessions running under Windows 95/98/Me. The common PROMPT, PATH, and SET commands in AUTOEXEC.BAT, as well as exposure to a command-line prompt, will be limited because Windows normally starts right away at boot up. The next two sections explore what may or may not work best for your Windows 95/98/Me configuration.

CONFIG.SYS and Windows 95/98/Me

If you upgrade from DOS or an older version of Windows (which requires DOS installation) or you have devices that may only be installable under DOS, you will have a CONFIG.SYS file that Windows 95/98/Me will use in the bootup process. Windows 98/Me actually makes better use of the CONFIG.SYS file than does Windows 95.

During bootup all of the CONFIG.SYS commands and drivers are loaded, and if Windows 95/98/Me requires or has 32-bit support for the installed devices, the older drivers will be removed from memory. Any drivers remaining will most likely be ignored by Windows 95, and Windows 98/Me will attempt to use them.

It is important for you to work with the contents of your CONFIG.SYS file for those occasions when you need DOS (for using hardware or programs that will not run under Windows 95/98/Me) or when you need to make sure that Windows 98/Me has the old drivers to use. Fortunately, most hardware manufacturers and software producers provide updates for their drivers to either Microsoft or Microsoft's product distributors so that they can include the information in releases of Windows operating environment or make the information available on the Internet.

Tip You should always have a DOS-mode device driver for your CD-ROM and a CONFIG.SYS and AUTOEXEC.BAT file somewhere on your emergency disk that loads this driver and runs MSCDEX.EXE. Otherwise, you will never be able to reload Windows 9x/Me.

You may run into situations in which the defaults that Windows 95/98/Me uses in place of the commands normally found in the CONFIG.SYS file are not adequate for the programs you may have to run in a DOS window. Again, the need for the items in the CONFIG.SYS file are dwindling, but they have not disappeared completely.

AUTOEXEC.BAT and Windows 95/98/Me

Windows 95/98/Me does not require the AUTOEXEC.BAT file. However, Windows 95 will process the AUTOEXEC.BAT file if you press F8 during a RESTART. You may then choose the Step option to execute each command in both the CONFIG.SYS and AUTOEXEC.BAT files to boot to MS-DOS. You may also choose to bypass the process and go directly to the MS-DOS prompt, but none of your configuration files will be loaded.

Windows 98 and Me process both the CONFIG.SYS and AUTOEXEC.BAT files, if present, during bootup. To maintain better compatibility with DOS, Windows 98 and Me use all the drivers and configuration data in order to better prepare your system for DOS. If a 32-bit driver that does the same job or conflicts with the 32-bit operating environment is available, the older driver that had been loaded during the processing of the CONFIG.SYS and AUTOEXEC.BAT files is removed from memory.

The Best of Both Worlds

Your reaction to reading about CONFIG.SYS and AUTOEXEC.BAT files may have been, "Oh, no! I thought we were getting rid of DOS!" However, because neither Windows 95/98 nor Me requires that these files be present, and Windows 98 and Me actually provide better support for the older applications, you end up with the best of both worlds. If you need to use older DOS programs or have had problems running older programs under Windows 95/98, Windows Me may provide the kind of support you need. Windows 98 and Me provide a second way to run DOS that does not retain the ability to return to Windows 98 and Me. In that case, you have to reboot your system to run Windows 98 and Me.

Because Windows 98 and Me provide a much more robust environment than Windows 95 (in the case of DOS, it actually starts a Virtual Machine (VM) in which DOS programs will run), it provides the capability to run older applications in a much more stable environment. When you exit from a DOS program, the VM does not shut down until the DOS program's activity actually ends. Then all of the resources that had been used by the DOS program are returned to your system.

Windows 95/98/Me MSDOS.SYS file

Beginning with Windows 95, Microsoft replaced the original DOS IO.SYS and MSDOS.SYS with different versions and gave them new functions. IO.SYS became a much larger and more complex bootup/BIOS extension file, and MSDOS.SYS became a bootup configuration text file. Both files were given read-only, system, and hidden file attributes to protect them from being tampered with. The attributes for MSDOS.SYS must be changed to remove the read-only, system, and hidden attributes using the Windows Explorer program in order to allow a text editor, such as Notepad or WordPad, to modify it.

Once the file is modified and accessible for viewing and editing, note some obvious and some not-so-obvious configuration abbreviations. By studying various works describing the file and the parameters, you can learn and change much about them. However, for purposes of this book, your concern will be those parameters that control multiboot configurations. Here is a typical original Windows 95/98/Me MSDOS.SYS file:

```
[Paths]
WinDir=C:\WINDOWS
WinBootDir=C:\WINDOWS
HostWinBootDrv=C

[Options]
BootGUI=1
```

```
Network=1
DoubleBuffer=1
;The following lines are required for compatibility with other programs.
;Do not remove them (MSDOS.SYS needs to be >1024 bytes).
;xxxxxxxxxxxxxxxxxxxxxxxxxxxxxxxxxxxxxxxxxxxxxxxxxxxxxxxxxxxxxxxxxxa
;xxxxxxxxxxxxxxxxxxxxxxxxxxxxxxxxxxxxxxxxxxxxxxxxxxxxxxxxxxxxxxxxxxb
;xxxxxxxxxxxxxxxxxxxxxxxxxxxxxxxxxxxxxxxxxxxxxxxxxxxxxxxxxxxxxxxxxxc
;xxxxxxxxxxxxxxxxxxxxxxxxxxxxxxxxxxxxxxxxxxxxxxxxxxxxxxxxxxxxxxxxxxd
;xxxxxxxxxxxxxxxxxxxxxxxxxxxxxxxxxxxxxxxxxxxxxxxxxxxxxxxxxxxxxxxxxxe
;xxxxxxxxxxxxxxxxxxxxxxxxxxxxxxxxxxxxxxxxxxxxxxxxxxxxxxxxxxxxxxxxxxf
;xxxxxxxxxxxxxxxxxxxxxxxxxxxxxxxxxxxxxxxxxxxxxxxxxxxxxxxxxxxxxxxxxxg
;xxxxxxxxxxxxxxxxxxxxxxxxxxxxxxxxxxxxxxxxxxxxxxxxxxxxxxxxxxxxxxxxxxh
;xxxxxxxxxxxxxxxxxxxxxxxxxxxxxxxxxxxxxxxxxxxxxxxxxxxxxxxxxxxxxxxxxxi
;xxxxxxxxxxxxxxxxxxxxxxxxxxxxxxxxxxxxxxxxxxxxxxxxxxxxxxxxxxxxxxxxxxj
;xxxxxxxxxxxxxxxxxxxxxxxxxxxxxxxxxxxxxxxxxxxxxxxxxxxxxxxxxxxxxxxxxxk
;xxxxxxxxxxxxxxxxxxxxxxxxxxxxxxxxxxxxxxxxxxxxxxxxxxxxxxxxxxxxxxxxxxl
;xxxxxxxxxxxxxxxxxxxxxxxxxxxxxxxxxxxxxxxxxxxxxxxxxxxxxxxxxxxxxxxxxxm
;xxxxxxxxxxxxxxxxxxxxxxxxxxxxxxxxxxxxxxxxxxxxxxxxxxxxxxxxxxxxxxxxxxn
;xxxxxxxxxxxxxxxxxxxxxxxxxxxxxxxxxxxxxxxxxxxxxxxxxxxxxxxxxxxxxxxxxxo
;xxxxxxxxxxxxxxxxxxxxxxxxxxxxxxxxxxxxxxxxxxxxxxxxxxxxxxxxxxxxxxxxxxp
;xxxxxxxxxxxxxxxxxxxxxxxxxxxxxxxxxxxxxxxxxxxxxxxxxxxxxxxxxxxxxxxxxxq
;xxxxxxxxxxxxxxxxxxxxxxxxxxxxxxxxxxxxxxxxxxxxxxxxxxxxxxxxxxxxxxxxxxr
;xxxxxxxxxxxxxxxxxxxxxxxxxxxxxxxxxxxxxxxxxxxxxxxxxxxxxxxxxxxxxxxxxxs
```

The following parameters and bootup behaviors exist within this file:

✦ WinDir=C:\WINDOWS indicates that Windows is installed on the C: drive in the \WINDOWS subdirectory (folder).

✦ WinBootDir=C:\WINDOWS indicates that the Windows operating system files are installed on the C: drive in the \WINDOWS subdirectory (folder) structure (tree).

✦ HostWinBootDrv=C indicates where the system boot files are located.

✦ BootGUI=1 indicates that the Windows 95/98/Me graphical interface will run after the configuration files are processed. As with prior versions of DOS, device drivers and resident programs from CONFIG.SYS and AUTOEXEC.BAT will load. The default without specifying this is 1, which loads the Windows environment. With a 0, the system will stop at a DOS prompt after loading drivers and processing the CONFIG.SYS and AUTOEXEC.BAT files.

✦ Network=1 indicates that networking support is to be loaded when Windows 95, 98, or Me starts. The default without specifying this is 1, which loads the network drivers and logon sequences.

✦ DoubleBuffer=1 indicates that double buffering for a SCSI hard disk is to be set. The default without specifying this depends on the detection of a known SCSI host adapter. With a 0, you can tell it not to load DoubleBuffer for the presence of a SCSI adapter. With a 1, you can force the loading of DoubleBuffer, even in the absence of a SCSI adapter

Other parameters may exist by default, depending on your system configuration. Networking and double-buffering are not common on most off-the-shelf, stand-alone systems and would not be present in most MSDOS.SYS files. The above configuration file contains no provision for multiboot or other special options. You must add them or let Windows 95/98/Me add them by making changes in its configuration within Control Panel when making hardware or software changes. As indicated, do not shorten this file to less than 1,024 bytes or else some software or system functions may not work properly later on. This may happen because some older or legacy programs look to see if an MS-DOS.SYS file is present.

Here is a modified Windows 95/98/Me MSDOS.SYS file:

```
[Paths]
WinDir=C:\WINDOWS
WinBootDir=C:\WINDOWS
HostWinBootDrv=C

[Options]
BootGUI=1
Network=1
DoubleBuffer=1
DblSpace=0
DrvSpace=0
BootDelay=3
LoadTop=1
BootWarn=1
BootMulti=1
BootKeys=1
BootMenu=1
BootMenuDelay=5
Logo=0
;
;The following lines are required for compatibility with other programs.
;Do not remove them (MSDOS.SYS needs to be >1024 bytes).
;xxxxxxxxxxxxxxxxxxxxxxxxxxxxxxxxxxxxxxxxxxxxxxxxxxxxxxxxxxxxxxa
;xxxxxxxxxxxxxxxxxxxxxxxxxxxxxxxxxxxxxxxxxxxxxxxxxxxxxxxxxxxxxxb
;xxxxxxxxxxxxxxxxxxxxxxxxxxxxxxxxxxxxxxxxxxxxxxxxxxxxxxxxxxxxxxc
;xxxxxxxxxxxxxxxxxxxxxxxxxxxxxxxxxxxxxxxxxxxxxxxxxxxxxxxxxxxxxxd
;xxxxxxxxxxxxxxxxxxxxxxxxxxxxxxxxxxxxxxxxxxxxxxxxxxxxxxxxxxxxxxe
;xxxxxxxxxxxxxxxxxxxxxxxxxxxxxxxxxxxxxxxxxxxxxxxxxxxxxxxxxxxxxxf
;xxxxxxxxxxxxxxxxxxxxxxxxxxxxxxxxxxxxxxxxxxxxxxxxxxxxxxxxxxxxxxg
;xxxxxxxxxxxxxxxxxxxxxxxxxxxxxxxxxxxxxxxxxxxxxxxxxxxxxxxxxxxxxxh
;xxxxxxxxxxxxxxxxxxxxxxxxxxxxxxxxxxxxxxxxxxxxxxxxxxxxxxxxxxxxxxi
;xxxxxxxxxxxxxxxxxxxxxxxxxxxxxxxxxxxxxxxxxxxxxxxxxxxxxxxxxxxxxxj
;xxxxxxxxxxxxxxxxxxxxxxxxxxxxxxxxxxxxxxxxxxxxxxxxxxxxxxxxxxxxxxk
;xxxxxxxxxxxxxxxxxxxxxxxxxxxxxxxxxxxxxxxxxxxxxxxxxxxxxxxxxxxxxxl
;xxxxxxxxxxxxxxxxxxxxxxxxxxxxxxxxxxxxxxxxxxxxxxxxxxxxxxxxxxxxxxm
;xxxxxxxxxxxxxxxxxxxxxxxxxxxxxxxxxxxxxxxxxxxxxxxxxxxxxxxxxxxxxxn
;xxxxxxxxxxxxxxxxxxxxxxxxxxxxxxxxxxxxxxxxxxxxxxxxxxxxxxxxxxxxxxo
;xxxxxxxxxxxxxxxxxxxxxxxxxxxxxxxxxxxxxxxxxxxxxxxxxxxxxxxxxxxxxxp
;xxxxxxxxxxxxxxxxxxxxxxxxxxxxxxxxxxxxxxxxxxxxxxxxxxxxxxxxxxxxxxq
;xxxxxxxxxxxxxxxxxxxxxxxxxxxxxxxxxxxxxxxxxxxxxxxxxxxxxxxxxxxxxxr
; xxxxxxxxxxxxxxxxxxxxxxxxxxxxxxxxxxxxxxxxxxxxxxxxxxxxxxxxxxxxxxs
```

With this modified file you will see the following behaviors available at bootup:

✦ F4 will enable you to boot to the original DOS configuration when the "Starting Windows 95" or "Starting Windows 98" message appears.

✦ No Windows background graphic and starting message logo will display.

✦ A Windows boot options menu appears.

✦ A legend describing the bootup option keys will be shown on the last line of the display.

The changes made by editing this file are indicated by the following parameters:

✦ LoadTop=1 causes the system to load into the top of available memory.

✦ DblSpace=0 indicates that the DoubleSpace (DOS 6.0–6.2) disk-compression driver should not be loaded. The default without specifying this is 1, which loads the driver, if found.

✦ DrvSpace=0 indicates that the DriveSpace disk-compression driver should not be loaded. The default without specifying this is 1, which loads the driver, if found.

✦ BootDelay=3 sets the delay in seconds. Windows waits after the "Starting Windows" message before booting. You have that much time in which to press F4, F5, or F8.

✦ BootMulti=1 indicates that the system should provide multiboot options to another operating system (earlier version of DOS).

✦ BootKeys=1 indicates that the bootup Function keys should be available and displayed at bootup.

✦ BootMenu=1 indicates that the system should provide the boot menu, just as if you pressed F8 after seeing the "Starting Windows" message.

✦ BootMenuDelay=5 tells the boot menu to wait and count down five seconds before executing the default boot option (typically normal Windows protected/multitasking mode).

✦ Logo=0 tells the system not to display the Windows logo.

Having set at least the BootMulti parameter to 1, you can now use F4 to boot with your prior version of DOS as long as BootKeys is not set to 0. The other parameters merely show some of the other available options. Less technical users may prefer not to have all the menus and boot progressions shown onscreen.

Windows F4 bootup key

Windows 95 includes a new magical button option at bootup — the F4 key. With Windows 95/98/Me installed, if you elected to preserve your existing DOS configuration — by not selecting the "Save your old version of Windows and DOS" option during the installation process and reconfiguring a new MSDOS.SYS text file as described earlier — pressing F4 will enable you to load your prior version of MS-DOS after the "Starting Windows" message appears.

Upon detecting F4 at bootup, the Windows multiboot configuration reconfigures the system files on your boot drive, renaming some of the Windows files and the prior DOS files in order to restore the prior DOS environment.

Windows NT and Dual-Boot Installations

Windows NT provides an easy means to support not just dual boot but also the capability to boot to literally any operating system on any device available to your system during bootup. It is implemented by using the BOOT.INI file, a read-only file in the root directory of the boot drive.

BOOT.INI is a text file and may be edited using any text editor, such as Word Pad, or even a word processing program, as long as you save the file in "text only" format. You will have to remove the read-only attribute of the file before editing. You may do that by using Windows Explorer, navigating to the BOOT.INI file, highlighting it, selecting File ➪ Properties, and clicking off the Read-only check box.

Windows NT Help (accessed from the Windows Explorer) provides the following information:

To define an alternate startup operating system for an x86-based computer

1   Open the Boot.ini file in the root folder of your C: drive with a text editor program, such as Notepad.

2   Add the name and location of the alternate system in the [operating systems] section.

3   Save and close the Boot.ini file.

Locating Source Files in BOOT.INI

There are no rules for how to refer to each kind of operating system listed in Boot.ini except that you must include the path for the drive and directory where the source files for the operating system are stored. For example:

```
[operating systems]
C:\Winnt="Windows NT 4.00"
C:\="Microsoft Windows"
```

The descriptive text after the equals sign (=) appears in the Startup box on the Startup/Shutdown tab of the System option in Control Panel.

To save BOOT.INI, you need to first open its properties in Explorer or My Computer and then click to clear the Read-only check box under Attributes. Once you've saved the file, go back and select the Read-only box to turn it back on."

Here's a typical BOOT.INI file on one of our systems:

```
[boot loader]
timeout=30
default=multi(0)disk(0)rdisk(1)partition(1)\WINNT
[operating systems]
multi(0)disk(0)rdisk(1)partition(1)\WINNT="Windows NT Workstation Version 4.00"
multi(0)disk(0)rdisk(1)partition(1)\WINNT=
"Windows NT Workstation Version 4.00 [VGA mode]" /basevideo /sos
C:\ = "MS-DOS"
```

This file was created by Windows NT by installing NT over a Windows 3.1 system and by selecting the option that retains the ability to boot from MS-DOS.

Guidelines for Handling Configuration Conflicts

General guidelines for the construction of a CONFIG.SYS or an AUTOEXEC.BAT file are not easy to define. Some programs state in their documentation that they must be the first or last entry in your AUTOEXEC.BAT file. What should you do if you have two programs that claim the right to be the first or last? Simple — try them each way and see which way works best.

What about the order of commands and programs in a CONFIG.SYS, AUTOEXEC.BAT, or other batch file?

✦ If you have used the DOS batch language to perform commands based on the values of environment variables or the existence of certain files, the sequence of commands will be dictated by the job that needs to be done.

✦ Otherwise, those items that set environment variables (SET, PATH, and PROMPT) should be executed before programs. The reason is that DOS continues to expand the default environment space until the first program is run.

✦ Programs that set up capabilities used by other programs should be run before those programs. Examples include installation of your mouse and other auxiliary devices, if they are activated by AUTOEXEC commands.

✦ TSR programs, such as SideKick, screen grabbers, and so forth, should be installed before you run other programs.

Start simple

It is possible to install devices and run programs that perform similar functions, use the same interrupts, access the same ports, or attempt to use the same memory locations. However, it is also quite possible that using these programs in your system at the same time will result in a system crash or a locked-up system. Well-behaved programs may use any of your system's resources without harm to any other driver, program, or TSR. These programs act on an interrupt and pass that interrupt on to another program that also needs to monitor that interrupt. The program also steps out of the way of other programs that need the resources it is using. On the other hand, a program that is not well-behaved does not pass along an interrupt it is monitoring, does not step out of the way of other programs, and is the culprit that causes your system to crash.

Finding conflicting drivers, programs, and TSRs is not easy. You should start with a "plain-vanilla" system. If you can boot your system with just a DOS disk and no device drivers or programs, this provides the best starting point. Using programs such as MAPMEM, DVECT, SYSID, MANIFEST, MSD, and other programs that can report on memory use can give you accurate system information, and you should document the use of interrupts and memory locations of your basic system.

Document changes

As you add each new driver and program, document the changes to your system. Compare the memory use information from a selected utility program. Through the sequence of adding each new driver or program, you will find that some interrupts change to the control of the new program. This means that the new program must pass the interrupt action to the previous program, which needs to receive the interrupt information for your system to remain stable. The utility programs should also provide the memory addresses of the drivers and programs that are loaded. The programs should also provide analysis of available program memory, file handles, file control blocks, the DOS environment, extended and expanded memory, and the status of many system settings. They may even provide warning messages or suggestions for improvement of the configuration of your system.

Track program status

With DOS Version 6.*x* and higher, using F8 at bootup is highly recommended for catching program status and error messages as they load. If during the process of loading each driver, program, and TSR into your system, you run into a situation that locks up or disables your system, you will have complete information available for making decisions about which programs to eliminate, load in a different sequence, reinstall, or reconfigure. The conflict may not be caused by the latest driver or program loaded. It is possible that a driver or program loaded earlier is the culprit. Changing the sequence of loading drivers and programs may emphasize or eliminate the problem. Finding system conflicts is not an exact science, but the more information you collect for further analysis, the better your chance of finding and curing a system conflict.

These guidelines are not strict. The proof of the pudding is a CONFIG.SYS file, an AUTOEXEC.BAT file, and a suite of programs in your system that accomplish the job you want done and do not leave your system in such a state that it fails under certain circumstances. The order in which you execute commands and programs may or may not be important. Unfortunately, about the only way to be certain that the order you use is best is to try the various combinations. Some optimizer programs perform this task for you.

Beware of memory-optimizing programs, however, as they may be too aggressive in trying to squeeze every last byte of free RAM out of a configuration. The optimization may result in a wonderful configuration for DOS, but it could result in disaster for Windows, which is where you are likely to run more complex programs and devices.

If a memory-optimizing program makes your system work well with DOS but not with Windows, removing all of the fancy parameters that the optimization program added to your DEVICEHIGH and LOADHIGH lines in CONFIG.SYS and AUTOEXEC.BAT may be the best thing to do.

Configuration Troubleshooting

The following sections of this chapter deal with the problems associated with the AUTOEXEC.BAT file, the CONFIG.SYS file, and specific versions of DOS, and offer helpful information related to installing DOS Versions 5.0 and above.

With the release of DOS Version 6.x and higher (or DR-/Novell/Caldera DOS 7.0), you can control or eliminate the loading of your CONFIG.SYS and AUTOEXEC.BAT files, and step through their commands one line at a time in order to help isolate problems.

At bootup, after the "Starting MS-DOS" or a similar message appears, pressing F5 prevents your CONFIG.SYS and AUTOEXEC.BAT files from running, leaving you instead at a DOS prompt and your DOS PATH set to C:\DOS.

Create a System Diskette

Before trying to optimize your CONFIG.SYS and AUTOEXEC.BAT files, create a system diskette that you can use to boot your computer. Invariably, you will try some combinations that will not have the desired result. If you cannot boot your computer using the hard disk, the system diskette will be the only way to get you back to the starting point. Otherwise you will have to install your operating system again.

Pressing F8 at the initial DOS title causes the system to present you with each line of your CONFIG.SYS file followed by a [Y/N]? prompt, to which you may respond by pressing Y to execute that line or N to bypass that line.

These features are powerful and they can be the key to isolating improper command lines or specific programs that may be causing problems, and you don't need to use a boot diskette and repeatedly edit these files in order to find the problem.

For the multiple configuration menu schemes that you must build and maintain manually with a text editor, it is up to you to ensure that the titles, labels, and features you want are organized and matched properly. This is not a process intended for the new user, unless you like a challenge and want to spend time tinkering with DOS.

Problems in CONFIG.SYS

The following Symptoms, Suspects, and Solutions sections explore common CONFIG.SYS problems.

Symptoms

Bad or missing commands or drivers in CONFIG.SYS indicated by one or more of the following messages:

▶ System Message: "Unrecognized command in CONFIG.SYS."

▶ System Message: "Bad or missing d:\subdir\driver.sys" ("*drive:\path\driver filename*" of a driver supposedly installed in your system).

▶ System message: "Label not found."

▶ System boots okay, but some things may not be just right, such as an inability to open enough files, the system runs slow, or a device (printer, network connection, plotter, expanded or extended memory, or other system extension) does not function.

Suspects

▶ Misspelled command word in the CONFIG.SYS file.

▶ CONFIG.SYS file has been corrupted.

▶ CONFIG.SYS file is missing or in the wrong directory.

▶ A menu item label is missing or improperly specified.

▶ Improper driver filename or location.

Solutions

▶ Check the spelling of CONFIG.SYS command words (use the lists earlier in this chapter).

▶ Check the spelling and proper location (drive) of your device drivers.

▶ Restore your old CONFIG.SYS file from your backup.

▶ Check the values assigned to the BUFFERS, COUNTRY, DRIVEPARM, FCBS, FILES, LASTDRIVE, and STACKS commands.

▶ Check device driver parameters for valid and optimum settings.

▶ Check to be sure your menu items match labels and that the labels exist.

▶ Make sure device drivers referenced in the CONFIG.SYS file actually exist in your system.

These problems may not prevent you from booting your system, but your system will not work as expected. If you cannot boot your system, you will have to use your boot diskette to boot the system so that you can work on its configuration and then boot normally.

Symptoms

▶ System locks up in CONFIG.SYS.

▶ System stops before executing the AUTOEXEC.BAT file.

▶ Some CONFIG.SYS command results (messages) may be onscreen, but your system does not respond.

▶ Ctrl+Break, Break, Ctrl+C, Esc, Ctrl+Alt+Delete, and other keys normally used to get out of problem situations do not have the expected effect. Your system is locked up.

▶ You may see a message containing "System Halted."

Suspects

▶ The filename in DEVICE= filename is not a valid device driver file.

▶ Device driver is not compatible with your system, either your version of DOS or your hardware, or the device parameters are incorrect.

▶ A device driver file has become corrupted.

▶ CONFIG.SYS commands and parameters use more memory than is available in your system.

Solutions

▶ Use your boot diskette to get your systems running.

▶ Compare your device driver files with the backup copies. Replace driver files as necessary.

▶ Check your CONFIG.SYS command parameters and device driver parameters to ensure they are compatible with your version of DOS and your hardware.

▶ You may need to make DOS version or hardware changes in order to bring your system up to the requirements of the new software and configuration it requires.

There is no such thing as "the best" CONFIG.SYS file for every system. Each of the commands and parameters in your CONFIG.SYS file uses some of your system's memory and may use other devices. The memory used by your CONFIG.SYS file will not be available for DOS or other programs. Therefore, your aim is to configure your system with the minimum number of files, stacks, buffers, and so forth that will accommodate your applications.

The CONFIG.SYS file is also used by extended and expanded memory managers, such as QEMM386 and HIMEM.SYS. These programs use a small part of your system's memory to give you access to the extended or expanded memory installed in your system. Each of these memory expander systems has its own requirements for installation and operation in your system.

Problems in AUTOEXEC.BAT

Learn how to identify and resolve common AUTOEXEC.BAT problems:

Symptoms

▶ Bad, missing, or wrong COMMAND.COM indicated by one of the following:

- "Invalid COMMAND.COM, system not loaded"
- "Bad or missing command interpreter"
- "Cannot load COMMAND.COM, system halted"
- "Incorrect DOS version"

▶ System message: "Label not found".

▶ Your version of DOS may display a different message than the preceding message, but it will have a similar meaning.

Suspects

▶ COMMAND.COM or the program identified by the SHELL= command in your CONFIG.SYS file is not compatible with the version of DOS installed on your system.

▶ The correct version of DOS is not installed on your computer.

▶ A CONFIG.SYS menu-item label is missing or improperly specified.

Solutions

▶ Boot with your system diskette and check the hidden system files on your hard disk (IBMDOS.COM and IBMBIO.COM or IO.SYS, and MSDOS.SYS) and the COMMAND.COM or the program identified by your SHELL= command in the CONFIG.SYS file on your hard disk. Make sure they are all in the correct locations (as referenced in your CONFIG.SYS file) or that the system files are identified as System, Hidden, Read-only files, and have the same date as the original files on the installation disks.

▶ You may have to copy new files (COMMAND.COM or the program identified by the SHELL= command in your CONFIG.SYS file) to your hard disk or use the SYS.COM program to install the system files. If you have to reinstall the DOS system files using the SYS command, make sure you have booted with the system diskette that has the correct version of DOS for your hard disk.

▶ If you do not have the utility programs to check the system files (such as SD.COM, SDIR.COM, ATTRIB.COM), or you do not feel comfortable working directly with the files on your hard disk, it may be easier and safer to install DOS again, just as if it had never been installed.

▶ Check to be sure your menu items match labels and that the labels exist.

In the preceding situation, there may be nothing wrong with your CONFIG.SYS or AUTOEXEC.BAT files, but the command interpreter (COMMAND.COM or the program installed by the SHELL= command in your CONFIG.SYS file) is either missing, located in the wrong directory, or has been corrupted. It could also be that the version of DOS installed on your hard disk is not compatible with or is a different version from the COMMAND.COM or other SHELL program. DOS and your configuration files and command interpreter must "get along," or your system will not boot.

Symptoms

▶ Missing or wrong AUTOEXEC.BAT file (wrong in the sense that it is not doing what you expect and assuming you may have more than one).

▶ Your system asks for the date and time before displaying the DOS prompt.

▶ Your system boots, but the system setup you expect to use does not appear.

Suspects

▶ AUTOEXEC.BAT file has been erased, named incorrectly, or is damaged in some way.

▶ AUTOEXEC.BAT file was replaced by a new software installation that is misbehaving.

▶ AUTOEXEC.BAT file has been damaged.

Solutions

▶ Replace your AUTOEXEC.BAT file from your backup and then reboot.

▶ Check your system for a file with the AUTOEXEC name and an odd extension, probably created by a new software package during its installation. This may be your old AUTOEXEC.BAT file that you will want to rename so that your system will use it when you reboot.

▶ Make a new AUTOEXEC.BAT file and then reboot.

DOS asks for the date and time if there is no AUTOEXEC.BAT file or if you have included these commands in your AUTOEXEC.BAT file. If you expected your system to boot and perform certain tasks and they were not done, it could be that your AUTOEXEC.BAT file is either missing or was replaced by another file. If you have recently installed new programs on your computer, the installation could have modified or replaced your AUTOEXEC.BAT file. On the other hand, the AUTOEXEC.BAT file could have been erased by mistake or renamed so that it no longer has an effect.

Because your system was successfully booted, you may enter the PATH and other commands that would have been in your AUTOEXEC.BAT file and use your system as you would normally. However, first find the backup copy of your old AUTOEXEC.BAT file and copy it back to the root directory of the drive used to boot your system. You may also create a new AUTOEXEC.BAT file.

Symptoms

▶ Bad commands, or missing files or programs in AUTOEXEC.BAT.

▶ Onscreen message: "Bad command or filename."

▶ Onscreen message containing the following:

   • "file not found"

   • "missing"

   • "not installed"

▶ Your system boots, but the system setup you expect does not appear.

▶ Your system might become locked up, but only after it gets past loading the devices and parameters in CONFIG.SYS and you see some of the results of your AUTOEXEC.BAT file.

Suspects

▶ Invalid command, program name, or command and/or invalid parameters in your AUTOEXEC.BAT file.

▶ A file or program specified in the AUTOEXEC.BAT file does not exist in the specified directory.

▶ AUTOEXEC.BAT file has been corrupted.

▶ A device, such as a mouse, has not been installed in CONFIG.SYS or AUTOEXEC.BAT, or the device is not connected.

Solutions

▶ Review your AUTOEXEC.BAT file for proper DOS command names and parameters.

▶ Check your AUTOEXEC.BAT file for proper names and locations (drive and subdirectory) of all programs to be executed.

▶ Check the programs you are trying to load for proper parameters and switches (the forward slash (/) and hyphen (-) options) on the command line.

▶ If you are loading a program into upper memory, make sure the program can be loaded there and that enough upper (high) memory is available to load and run the program.

Symptoms

▶ Onscreen message containing "insufficient memory"

Suspects

▶ System does not have enough memory to execute the batch file or program indicated.

▶ Memory manager may not be configured properly.

▶ You have loaded too many device drivers, TSR programs, or both.

▶ You may be trying to run the program from within the SHELL of another program and do not have adequate memory to continue.

▶ A previously run program has failed to release the memory it used after it finished.

Solutions

▶ Install more memory in your system (seldom a problem with anything greater than a 386, but not uncommon with XT or 286 systems).

▶ Use a memory manager, such as EMM386 or Quarterdeck's QEMM, to create and manage upper memory.

▶ Reconfigure your memory manager. For EMM386, this may be as simple as adding RAM to the DEVICE=EMM386.EXE command line in CONFIG.SYS. Another option is to run the MEMMAKER program with DOS or OPTIMIZE with QEMM to gain more upper memory space so that you can load device drivers and TSR programs into upper memory.

▶ Check the amount of RAM required by your programs in their documentation versus the amount of RAM available to DOS programs after you boot up (the DOS MEM program will indicate this). If you are trying to run your program from within a menu or shell program (such as DOSSHELL), this program may not leave enough RAM for your other programs.

▶ Try booting up your system with a clean CONFIG.SYS and AUTOEXEC.BAT file, and not loading unnecessary device drivers or TSR programs in order to see if the problem goes away. This solution set applies to programs you run on your computer as well as to the configuration files in this chapter. Application programs may provide a message indicating insufficient memory.

Symptoms

▶ Some device or accessory is not running or available after booting up your system.

▶ Message onscreen containing one or more of the following:

- "device not found"
- "device not installed"
- "unable to access"
- "unavailable"

Suspects

▶ The program or .BAT file just executed expected to find a device in your system that was not installed or incorrectly installed, or the memory containing the computer instructions for using the device has become corrupted.

▶ The program or .BAT file just executed is not configured correctly for your system.

▶ These error messages could be referring to a mouse or other pointing device, a hard disk or other data storage device, a printer or other output device, or even a memory driver.

Solutions

▶ Install the device required by the program being executed.

▶ Review the installation and configuration of the device required by the program being executed.

▶ Check cables and power switches, and reseat the I/O card for the device.

▶ Review the installation of the program being executed to ensure it is accessing the correct device installed in your system.

Symptoms

▶ "Infinite loop" problem. (The computer keeps doing the same thing over and over again):

- Repeating messages onscreen
- Executing the same program repeatedly
- Initializing one or more devices repeatedly

▶ The computer may continue indefinitely or, eventually, crash or lock up.

Suspects

▶ A batch file or program contains instructions to the computer that cause it to repeat a section of the batch file or program, therefore preventing the batch file or program from ending.

▶ A batch file or program contains a CALL statement or executes another batch file or program, which in turn contains a CALL statement or executes the batch file or program that caused it to run.

▶ A new batch file or program has been installed in your system. It does not know where to find what it needs or it may have replaced a batch file or program that you had used in the past because it has the same name, but it does not do the job you expected.

Solutions

▶ Press Ctrl+C or Ctrl+Break in order to try to stop the repeating sequence. If neither of these work, try entering the command or commands that normally end the program that is running. If BREAK has been turned off in your system, you may have to press Ctrl+Alt+Delete to reboot your computer, or you may need to turn off the power switch for a cold reboot. Try everything you can before you reboot because your system may contain information important for solving the problem, or information that you must save before turning off the power.

▶ If you or your computer executed a batch file that led to the infinite loop, try running each of the programs referenced in the batch file to make sure that each one works independently. If not, replace the offending program with a backup copy or eliminate it from your system. If all the programs work, review the batch file to see if it contains GOTO or CALL statements. GOTO statements cause the execution of the batch file to begin at a different location. If the repeated commands follow a LABEL, which is used by a GOTO command, you may have found the loop that needs to be fixed. If you find a CALL statement, the batch file or program it calls may contain a command that executes the batch file or program that you or your computer executed.

▶ Unless you wrote the batch file or program that caused the problem, you may not be able to fix it. However, because you have found the cause, you may know who can fix it.

Symptoms

▶ Your batch file never ran.

▶ You have a batch file that contains the commands needed to do a particular job, but the job does not get done.

▶ A program is executed by your batch file, but the batch file should be doing more.

Suspects

▶ The batch file you are using contains a GOTO statement that bypasses the commands to do the job you expected.

▶ The batch file executes another batch file or program that does not return to complete the remainder of commands.

Solutions

▶ Read your batch file to find GOTO commands that either go to a LABEL in the file that bypasses some of the commands or that goes to a LABEL that does not exist. You may be able to remove the GOTO statement or insert the proper LABEL in the correct location.

▶ If your batch file needs to execute another batch file and return, use the CALL command. This command allows the other batch file to be executed and, when it is complete, returns to the original batch file so that it may complete its job.

▶ If your batch file uses the SHIFT command to cycle command-line parameters through a sequence of commands that processes each one, you may have an extra SHIFT command or the parameters may be in the wrong order.

Summary

In this chapter, after a general introduction to operating system configuration, we focused on the following:

✦ AUTOEXEC.BAT and CONFIG.SYS configuration files used with DOS and also with Windows through Windows Millennium. Windows NT and 2000 do not use these files.

✦ Dual-boot setup for Windows, including NT and 2000.

✦ General guidelines for configuration files.

✦ Configuration troubleshooting.

Chapter 14 gets right down to the system board, that part of your PC to which everything else is connected and that actually contains the central processing unit (CPU), or the "real computer."

✦   ✦   ✦

System Boards

The system board, also known as the motherboard, is the heart of your system. Its primary function is to provide a processing, memory, and hardware interface to the operating system and in turn, to the application software. This chapter covers the primary components and functions of the system board, in order of their relative significance to PC operation.

There are many different types of system boards, from the original IBM PC to the latest ATX-style boards and multiprocessor versions. The IBM PC system board provided only five add-in card slots, no built-in input/output (I/O) or disk drive ports, and the capacity to hold a whopping 256K of RAM. New boards may provide only three to five add-in card slots, but they include almost every I/O device you could imagine — from serial ports to speaker jacks and Universal Serial Bus (USB), along with disk and hard drive connections — and they have the capacity to hold between 16 and 256MB or more of RAM. Some boards may also contain Small Computer System Interface (SCSI) disk drive adapters, a built-in video adapter, and alternate video I/O bus types.

The system board has become more complex since the original IBM PC. Not only are more functions performed on the system board, but also there are several more options, and many of those features have been combined into fewer, separate integrated circuits. These integrated circuits constitute the "PC chip set." Those circuits are also no longer easily replaceable by unplugging them from sockets because they now are in the form of densely packed, surface-mounted (soldered to the board without pins or holes) multifunction chips. These chips are often referred to as application-specific integrated circuits (ASIC) or glue chips because several specialized functions are combined together in one chip.

In This Chapter

System board components, functions, and features

Proper care and handling of your CPU and support chips

BIOS, CMOS clock, and RAM, and supporting chip-set devices

System bus, I/O connections, keyboard and mouse connections

System clock and Year 2000

Plug and Play (Pray?)

System BIOS and setup

Flash ROM and special recovery procedures

System board problems

The system board has been evolving with a variety of significant enhancements in the past few years. Among these have been and will likely continue to be the following:

✦ New chip sets to accommodate faster CPUs, new I/O features, and new memory types

✦ Software-upgradeable BIOS stored in FLASH ROM

✦ New BIOS features to accommodate Plug and Play (PnP), larger hard drives, new I/O bus features, and energy conservation

✦ Smaller form to fit into smaller cases

✦ Faster disk drive interfaces and I/O ports

Despite the enhancements in system board designs and features, the functions, and thus, the problems are basically the same, no matter what vintage board you have. The problems you may encounter do not change significantly because these problems share the same circuit board space with the CPU and memory. However, the solution for a problem may differ significantly among dual in-line package (DIP) switches, jumpers, software settings, and add-in card changes.

Cross-Reference For those functions normally associated with separate ports or devices, refer to the chapters covering those specific items: keyboard (Chapter 4), memory (Chapter 15), disk controllers (Chapters 18 and 19), video (Chapter 20), and serial and parallel I/O (Chapter 22).

System Board Components and Functions

The major components and functions of the system board are common or similar to all systems, as discussed in this section. To be PC-compatible, apart from speed, memory capacity, and enhancements for greater performance, newer systems must provide at least the same functions as those provided in the original IBM PC.

Figure 14-1 shows a basic system board layout, complete with the following components: central processing unit (CPU), keyboard, add-in card slots (both ISA and local bus), memory, speaker, and connections for an outside power source.

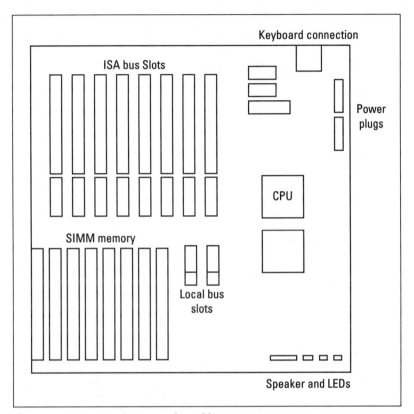

Figure 14-1: A generic system board layout

Figure 14-2 shows an ATX-style system board layout. Notable in this style of system board is the cluster of I/O connections in the upper right corner of the drawing. If you are counting, the cluster includes all the multimedia features: sound (microphone and speakers), gaming, video, serial and parallel I/O, keyboard, mouse, and USB connections. You wonder why 16-bit Industry Standard Architecture (ISA), Peripheral Component Interconnect (PCI), and Accelerated Graphics Port (AGP) connections are also on the board — for expansion or upgrade, of course! The power connection on an ATX-style board also is different than previous system boards — it conveys the usual power requirement to the board, as well as on/off control. If you build an ATX-style system, the power switch now connects to the system board, not the power supply. This enables software-controlled, power-on-and-off control.

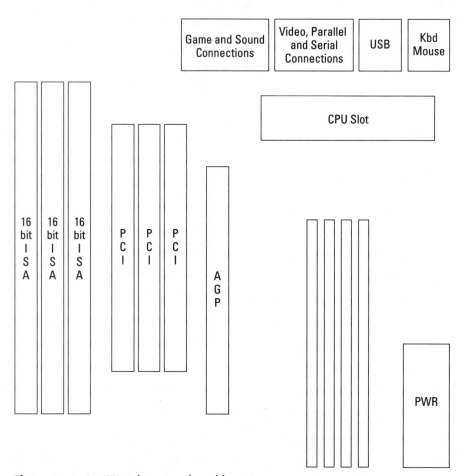

Figure 14-2: An ATX-style system board layout

CPU chips

In the 1970s and 1980s, when microprocessors were first implemented, they were intended for use more as microcontrollers or terminals in dedicated systems than for use as powerful computers for the multiple application tasks of today. This original design limited the ways programs could use the CPU. Furthermore, when 64K of memory was considered extravagant and when it was expensive, the designers of these CPUs thought they were building in plenty of capability by allowing for 1MB of RAM space. In the 1970s, anything that was computerized could be perceived as tremendously fast and impressive in capabilities. No one expected that we would all own computers or use them in the course of our daily work.

Until the introduction of the Intel Pentium CPU, the microprocessors used in PC systems operated in a sequential process. The common PC CPU (8088–80486) contained the internal circuitry to accept and process only one instruction and its various support functions, in a specific sequential order.

To operate on the available CPU chips, typical DOS programs and the tools that create them are produced using the sequential, single-instruction mode. Most of the common PC CPU chips are listed in Table 14-1. All of these CPUs share the basic functions of the original 8086 chip but with increased speed, memory, and processing capability. Note that the 8088, 80286, 80386, and 80486 chips are no longer manufactured.

<table>
<tr><td colspan="4" align="center">Table 14-1
Common PC Microprocessors</td></tr>
<tr><td>*Microprocessor Types*</td><td>*CPU Chips*</td><td>*Math Chips*</td><td>*CPU Speeds*</td></tr>
<tr><td>8-bit CPU and
8-bit I/O</td><td>Intel i8088
NEC V20</td><td>Intel i8087</td><td>5 MHz*
8 and 10 MHz</td></tr>
<tr><td>16-bit CPU and
8-bit I/O</td><td>Intel i8086
NEC V30</td><td>Intel i8087</td><td>8 MHz 8-bit I/O
8 and 10 MHz</td></tr>
<tr><td>16-bit CPU and
16-bit I/O</td><td>Intel i80286
AMD 80286</td><td>Intel i80287
IIT and Cyrix
versions</td><td>6–12 MHz 16-bit I/O
10–16 MHz</td></tr>
<tr><td>32-bit CPU and
16-bit I/O</td><td>Intel i80386SX</td><td>Intel i80387SX</td><td>16–25 MHz</td></tr>
<tr><td>32-bit CPU and
32-bit I/O</td><td>Intel i80386DX;
i80486SX2;
i80386SLC
Intel i80486SX;
i80486SLC
Intel i80486DX
Intel i80486DX2
Intel i80486DX4
AMD 80386-40
IBM 80486SLC
IBM 80486SLC2
TI486SXLC2
TI486DX2
TI486DX4</td><td>Except for the
80386DX and
80486SX parts,
math chip functions are included
in the CPU</td><td>16–33 MHz; 20–33
MHz; 33–50 MHz
50–66 MHz;
100 MHz
60–66 MHz
33–66 MHz
100 MHz
40 MHz
33 MHz
66 MHz
50–66 MHz
66–80 MHz
100 MHz</td></tr>
</table>

Continued

Table 14-1 (continued)			
Microprocessor Types	CPU Chips	Math Chips	CPU Speeds
64-bit CPU and 64-bit I/O	Intel Pentium		60–166 MHz
	Intel Pentium Pro		150–200 MHz
	Intel Pentium II		200–450 MHz
	Intel Celeron		300–433 MHz
	Intel Pentium III		500–1,000 MHz
	AMD/NexGen 586	N/A	75–120 MHz
	AMD/NexGen 686/[PLO1]K6	N/A	150–266 MHz
	AMD K6-2		300–550 MHz
	AMD K6-III		400–450 MHz
	AMD Athlon		600–1,000 MHz
	Cyrix Cx486DX		33–40 MHz
	Cyrix 5x86		100–120 MHz
	Cyrix 6x86		100–300 MHz

* Megahertz

The 8088 and 8086 CPUs are limited to a 1MB memory addressing range using 20 bits. The very foundations of the PC and DOS were designed within this limitation. The 80286 increased memory capabilities to 16MB, while maintaining certain limitations based on the 8086. The 80286 can exceed the capabilities of the 8086 with the ability to change its operating mode, but a design flaw made it impossible to shift between real- and virtual-machine modes easily. Even with Pentium processors, DOS never changed to take advantage of the enhancement because so much was invested in the original 8086-compatible software, some of which is still in use today.

The 80386 maintains both an 8086-compatible mode and an 80286-compatible mode, as well as further enhanced memory and processing capabilities that allow users the advantages of multitasking with environments such as Microsoft Windows, Windows 95, Windows NT, and IBM's OS/2. In what is commonly referred to as 386 Enhanced Mode, or Protected Mode, the processor can swap, move, and restore various parts of memory (in essence, entire programs, data, and operating system functions) to give the impression that the computer is performing many functions at one time. However, the computer is in fact switching among, or rotating, different tasks fast enough to keep the programs running smoothly — much as a juggler moves around to various spinning plates, giving them a spin to keep them moving. Operating systems, discussed in Part II, are responsible for controlling the switching between processor jobs.

Table 14-1 lists common PC microprocessors, their companion math processors (where applicable), and the CPU speeds of operation, from the earliest to more recent PCs. This list is as complete as the manufacturers' technical information available would allow at the time. Expect higher speeds or newer designations for the same or similar class chips to be introduced frequently as technology progresses.

The Intel DX and Pentium-class chips, as well as many non-Intel CPU chips, contain an internal instruction cache for faster performance, and a math coprocessor for complex (floating point) math functions. A *cache* is a dedicated area of very fast memory where data can be loaded for immediate access or for faster access than having to go to the primary RAM or I/O operations for each byte of data.

The Intel-compatible CPUs and math chips from other companies offer some performance advantages, typically in multiplication speeds or optimized instruction processing, and they operate at the same speed as the original Intel parts that they can replace. The SLC (a model number used to indicate a low power consumption version of the standard CPU chips) parts provide a variety of power management options for automatic shutdown, allowing power conservation in portable and desktop units. Automatic shutdown conserves overall energy consumption when a system sits idle (no input or specific processing operations) for a specified period of time.

Intel Overdrive, SX2, DX2, DX4, and similar CPUs, internally multiply the CPU clock speed by two or four times for performance of up to 120 MHz.

Pentium-class chips (as well as the aftermarket and future processors) provide tremendous benefits in performance because they can process instructions and their support operations more efficiently. One part of the CPU handles certain parts of the instruction execution, while other parts of the CPU handle other functions at the same time. This is not parallel processing (the simultaneous processing of multiple instructions), but the processor can split the required tasks that make up a single instruction. Different parts of the CPU execute different pieces of the instruction, enabling the instruction to finish much faster — at times even operating at the same clock speed as non-Pentium processors.

Note Applications are being created and updated using new programming tools (programming languages and compilers) to take advantage of these benefits in the Pentium-class processors. These benefits are being built into new operating systems, further enhancing the performance of PCs.

CPU chips have gained another feature set over the past couple of years — having optimized graphics instructions built into them. For Intel's Pentium CPUs, this comes in the form of the Multimedia Extension (MMX) instruction set. AMD CPUs call their graphics support 3DNow, which enhances OpenGL-based graphics programming. To take advantage of either type of this feature requires graphics, game, and multimedia software programmers to include programming extensions in their projects that can use the new instructions in the CPU. Having commonly used, complex graphics instruction execution features in the CPU helps reduce the amount of complex program code that must be put into a software program, and it enables graphics to function much faster because the CPU already "knows" what to do for these graphics functions.

CPU identification

The Pentium CPUs introduced a new internal register, or ID byte, so that software can interrogate the CPU and determine which CPU is running in the system. This ID byte is also found in newer (1993 and more recent) 80486DX and higher series CPUs. You may notice that some system information and diagnostic software packages might not correctly identify the chip in your system. Without the ID byte, or a program's awareness of it, processor identification requires a series of logical tests, and sometimes guessing on the part of the programmer, in order to identify the processor. The significance of this to the software you are running can be minimal, but note it in case you question what the actual CPU is inside your system. If the CPU chip has a heat sink glued to the top, there may not be another way to identify the CPU except through "CPU-aware" software.

Note   In fact, Windows 95 and 98 do not correctly identify the Pentium III and some later non-Intel CPUs. It is unknown whether this affects Windows installation or not, but it can fool many folks when it comes to identifying the system. Of course, Windows 2000 and Millennium (Me) have no problems identifying the newer chips.

Over-clocking

People always seem to want more than what they already have, and getting more performance out of CPU chips is one more manifestation of this desire. *Over-clocking* is the practice of increasing the speed of the master clock signal, or "heart beat," of a CPU chip. Techie PC users have been playing with ways to increase the speed of their CPU chips almost since Day One of the PC. If the process works, the result can be a 10–50 percent increase in the performance of systems and programs. If the process fails, the result can be loss of data or hardware damage.

In earlier PC days, increasing the speed of the CPU meant finding and changing the main system clock crystal that provided the heartbeat for the CPU and surrounding chips, and it possibly meant getting a slightly faster CPU chip as well. Sometimes this involved de-soldering the old crystal (a small, rectangular metal can with two wires), removing it from the system board, and replacing it with a faster crystal — messy and not without a little risk. Today, over-clocking consists of changing jumpers on a system board or altering BIOS SETUP parameters to affect the base CPU clock frequency and the multiplication factor, which together establish the final CPU clock frequency.

The resulting speed depends on the type of CPU involved and what combinations of base frequency and multiplication the CPU will support. Some CPU chips require that the multiplication factor be an even number (2, 4, or 6), some require an odd number (1, 3, or 5), and some require a fractional value (1.5, 2.5, or 3.5). The maximum base clock frequency depends not only on the CPU chip but also on the capacity of the system bus and plugged-in I/O cards — whether or not they can handle 60, 66, 75, 83, 95, 100 MHz, or higher.

Users who play many games or use many multimedia applications commonly over-clock. There are some noticeable performance improvements because many games work outside of Windows, have their program code loaded in specially managed memory configuration, and do not use disk files much. Thus, the systems run program code from memory and displays it as fast as possible. However, over-clocking is not always that effective.

 Note

If you over-clock your system, will Windows load faster? Will you be able to surf the Web better? Not likely.

Before over-clocking your CPU, in addition to any CPU and I/O limitations, as well as potential damage to the CPU chip or data loss because the I/O system could not properly handle faster disk and memory reads and writes, you have to consider whether or not your system and applications really will work faster after you are done. If you take a system originally built with between a 300 to 400 MHz CPU, Windows will not load significantly faster. Therefore, your e-mail or Internet browsing will not be faster or better.

Not a Significant Speed Improvement

Making a CPU run faster does not speed up the keyboard, mouse, or disk drives, and it does not significantly affect video display. Another way to look at system performance is that it is largely "I/O bound" — disk drives spin and transfer data only as fast as their design, and they are not as fast as CPUs. The same is true for any other I/O device. Even CPU-to-memory data transfers do not happen as fast as the CPU works — it is not yet possible. Add to this the overhead of all of the timing and operations that DOS, Windows, LINUX, or any operating system must do to monitor and control file transfers, video display, and so on (so that users can see what is occurring), and operations are not going to move significantly faster.

Most PC functions involve many I/O operations to and from a number of different devices hooked to the PC. It would be nice if the operating system and display tasks could be set aside for a few moments while data transfers between devices, but because users like to see and interact with what is occurring, a single PC operation will never be as fast as might be possible.

Over-clocking is perhaps the cheapest performance upgrade for a system. Cheapest, that is, if you do not lose data or burn up the CPU chip in the process. If your memory or system board chip set cannot handle the increased speed, then program execution and data transfer can become confused. Windows setup, typically the Registry, can become corrupt, and your applications and data files can also be destroyed.

If your CPU chip is protected by only a heat sink with no fan, or by a clunky, dusty old fan, you then need to think of improving the cooling of your CPU before you over-clock — because with speed comes heat. If the heat sink on your CPU is too hot to keep your hand on, now, or after you over-clock, you need better cooling!

After considering all of this, should you over-clock? We do, within limits. However, if increasing the CPU speed 10–20 percent doesn't yield a noticeable improvement in Windows' loading performance, running of applications, or saving files to disk, then there is no reason to over-clock. Now, you probably won't break a disk drive or a video adapter by over-clocking your CPU, but these are the other two items you can upgrade in order to gain performance benefits. On the other hand, it's probably more fun to buy a new system with all new, fast components instead of trying to milk an extra 10 percent more performance out of an old system by over-clocking or making other upgrades.

Proper care and handling of CPUs and chips

The CPU chip is one of the most complex and delicate components of a PC system. There are 168 pins on the 486 chip. Fewer pins appear on the 386, and many more appear on Pentium chips and modules. System board manufacturers use many different types of sockets to hold the CPU. DIPs and sockets are used for the 8088, 8086, and 80286 processors. Pin grid array (PGA) is used for 80386 and 80486 CPUs. Zero-insertion-force (ZIF) sockets are used for some 80486 and all Pentium CPUs. Finally, Intel has employed a proprietary Slot-1 module and system board connector arrangement for the Pentium II, Celeron, and Pentium III. Each of these socket types provide for different handling and cooling options.

Insertion and removal

DIP-mounted parts did not necessarily require, nor were there available, special tools to remove them from their sockets. It is common practice, but not recommended, to use a small screwdriver to pry CPU chips from their DIP sockets.

For PGA-style parts, using a screwdriver can apply excessive stress on the chip and pins, and cause pin breakage, which can ruin a chip. Intel and other manufacturers provide a special crowbar, or pry tool, that looks like a bent comb and fits in between the CPU chip pins to reduce the possibility of pin damage and stresses on the chip.

For convenience, and on those system boards that are designed for upgrades, from SX to DX parts, or SX/DX/DX2 to Pentium parts, there is a special mechanical socket, often referred to as a ZIF socket. The ZIF socket, labeled either Socket 5 or Socket 7, provides a pin-release mechanism to disconnect and release the CPU pins, allowing the CPU to sit freely in the socket for insertion and removal.

With Pentium II processors, Intel has repackaged the chip and its supporting circuits onto a plug-in module with a complex-looking support structure. Whether or not other CPU manufacturers will be able to take advantage of Intel's new packaging is a legal issue at this point.

Handling and storage

CPU chips, as with all other integrated circuits, are extremely static sensitive. Even the slightest, unseen, unfelt static buildup or discharge can destroy integrated circuits. Ideally, you should wear a special antistatic strap when handling integrated circuits (ICs) and store them in antistatic foam or component carriers. Do not carry them around without antistatic and mechanical protection.

Cooling

Your CPU chip might have a heat sink (a black- or gold-colored block of aluminum) attached on top. For proper operation above 33 MHz, the CPU should receive as much cooling advantage as possible, both from a heat sink and forced-air circulation. Intel Pentium chips require fan cooling. 80486DX parts are rated to operate at chip case temperatures up to 85 degrees centigrade (185 degrees Fahrenheit). DX2 chips are rated at 95 degrees centigrade (203 degrees Fahrenheit). These temperatures can contribute a significant amount of heat inside the case of your system. A CPU running at these temperatures can malfunction if allowed to overheat.

A number of cooling options are available for CPUs and heat sinks. As in most cases, you get what you pay for. A cheap fan costing $15 to $20 probably will not move enough air across the heat sink to do much good, and it might inhibit some of the free airflow around the heat sink by being in the way. The cheaper fans also have sleeve bearings versus the true ball bearings found in the $25 to $35 variety.

Check the fan you want to buy. Some are somewhat noisy, and you might find the high-pitched noise annoying. It may be better to add a slightly larger, extra fan that blows directly across the CPU inside your computer case, and be sure that cables and add-in boards do not block air flow across the system board components.

If your CPU gets too hot, you might experience intermittent failures or unexpected shutdown. Complete failure of the CPU, before you notice operational errors, is unlikely, but it is something to consider. Add-on heat sinks that use snap clips to hold them in place are adequate for DX-series parts. DX2-series parts should come with a permanently glued-on heat sink. If not, ask your computer dealer about adding one.

Caution   The glue used to attach heat sinks is a special high-temperature epoxy that must be applied carefully to avoid air bubbles and to allow maximum heat coupling from the chip to the heat sink. Don't use garden-variety epoxy, permanent glue, or anything other than specific compounds for permanently attaching heat sinks to processor chips. Go where "techies" shop to find the right glue, preferably a computer store that builds its own products.

If you are a technically oriented person, you may be attracted to the electronic CPU coolers, more properly known as Peltier-effect thermocouple packs. These units electronically transfer heat from one surface to another — quite ingenious, but also a little pricey at about $50 to $80 each.

CPU power regulation

Beginning with DX4 CPUs, manufacturers have been producing chips that operate at power supply voltages from 2.5 to 4 volts, versus the normal 5 volts for 486SX, DX, and DX2 CPU chips. Those that require lower voltages will be so marked on top of the chip. To put these upgrade processors into a standard 486 system board, you will need an additional power regulation adapter board to plug into the system board's CPU socket. You then plug the CPU into this device. Many newer system boards provide this power regulation on the main board, so you will need to check for CPU voltage jumpers when configuring some boards.

Tip   JDR Microdevices (www.jdr.com) in San Jose, California, is one of several technical mail-order firms that carry these special adapter/regulator sockets for the 3.3 volt 486DX4 chips.

CPU support and interfaces

The CPU requires several support functions to interconnect it with memory and I/O circuits. Among these are the following:

✦ **Main timer functions.** These circuits provide the CPU main clock at 4.77, 6, 8, 10, 12, 16, 20, 25, 33, 40, 50, 60, 66, 75 MHz, and so on. The timer also provides a 3.58 MHz reference clock for video and the 18 Hz/55msec timer tick used as a reference for most program timing. For Pentium boards, there is also a clock multiplier setting. Multiply the main clock by the multiplier setting to determine what the actual CPU clock speed should be.

✦ **Interrupt controller.** This circuit receives interrupt request (IRQ) signals from the timer, keyboard, and I/O devices, and then it sends the IRQ signals to the CPU to handle various software functions.

✦ **DMA controller.** This function handles requests for I/O direct memory access (DMA) activity that can transfer data without moving it through the CPU. This provides for faster data transfer functions. DMA transfers can occur at rates from 5–10MB per second, depending on the I/O card used and the PC bus in use. Non-DMA transfers are typically well under 1MB per second.

✦ **Memory addressing and interface.** These circuits provide access to all memory, from the DOS RAM area (0–640K), high memory and ROM BIOS (640–1,024K), and extended memory (greater than 1,024K). This circuitry also provides the RAM refresh and parity checking for RAM chips and SIMMs. Some manufacturers modify this and/or the timing circuitry that uses some CPU time for refresh so that they can gain marginally faster system performance.

✦ **I/O bus interface.** This circuitry provides access to and from input and output devices, and it synchronizes timing of signals with memory operations so that the right data is in the right place at the right time. This interface was designed to operate at the original and later IBM PC/AT bus speeds of 6 MHz and then 8 MHz. The I/O bus in many ISA systems runs at 10–12 MHz to increase I/O performance. For VESA local bus systems, the maximum I/O bus speed is 33 MHz. For PCI systems, the local I/O bus speed ranges from 33–266 MHz, 66 and 100 MHz being the most common today.

✦ **Internal cache.** 486DX and higher CPUs contain a moderate amount of internal cache memory to store information for faster access by the CPU to enhance CPU performance. This is also referred to as the level one, or L1 cache, and comes in sizes from 8–512K.

✦ **External cache.** 486DX and higher systems began providing cache memory external to the CPU to assist in providing information to the CPU to enhance overall performance. This is also referred to as the level two, or L2 cache, and has been offered in increments from 64–512K and at most 1MB.

Math chip

Most systems, from the early PC to 80486SX systems, provide a socket for holding an optional math chip. The math chip is also referred to as a Numeric Processing Unit (NPU), math coprocessor, floating-point unit (FPU), or numerical coprocessor. The 80486DX and Pentium processors have the FPU built in.

Math coprocessors are dedicated microprocessor chips separate from a main CPU chip. They work in cooperation with a main CPU to speed complex math operations. They are designed to perform floating-point and other complex math calculations that would otherwise be done by software routines run through the main CPU. Performing complex math calculations in software is relatively slow.

Math chips were once used only for drafting and drawing programs, as they involve complex shapes and angles that require excessive amounts of CPU time to define and redraw onscreen. Spreadsheet programs also take advantage of a math chip if one is present. Drawing and complex math are still the primary uses for the math coprocessor today, and you will find that your system already has these complex math capabilities if you have an 80486DX-, DX2-, or Pentium-class CPU chip.

Intel makes an 8087 math chip to accompany the 8088 and 8086 CPU chips. The 8087 math chip also works with the NEC V20 and V30 processors. The 80287 math chip complements the 80286 CPU chip, while the 80387 math chip complements the 80386DX CPU. You might also find 80386SX systems that accept the 80387SX math chip, and 80486SX systems that accept an additional upgrade processor. The upgrade processor is essentially an 80486DX chip, and its configuration into the system board disables the SX processor.

The math chip acts as a calculator for the main CPU, accepting commands from it and preparing answers for it, and then signaling the main CPU when it has completed the calculations. The results are then taken by the main CPU and passed on to your application program.

If you are installing a new math chip, as in Figure 14-3, in a PC or XT system, you will have to change a DIP switch setting on the motherboard before the CPU will recognize and use the chip. AT, 386, and other larger systems automatically recognize the presence of the coprocessor and should not require setup or other configuration changes. For these systems, you should see an indication of the presence or lack of a math chip appearing on a startup screen, or you can use the system's CMOS RAM setup program to check.

If a program requires a math chip, but the program does not find a math chip when it starts, the program should exit to DOS or Windows, or otherwise give you a message stating it does not have the necessary chip. In less fortunate cases, your system may lock up without telling you what is wrong and require a reboot to continue.

Math Chips Improve Performance

Adding a math chip in some of the following types of programs will significantly increase performance. Some programs require a math chip to run at all.

✦ Drawing programs, such as GenericCAD, AutoSketch, AutoCAD, Visio, and so on

✦ Rendering and morphing programs for special effect and multimedia graphics, such as Radiance (if you're using Linux or FreeBSD) or some of the high end Adobe applications in Windows

✦ Circuit design, simulation, and layout programs, such as OrCad and Tango

✦ Large spreadsheets in Lotus 1-2-3 or Microsoft Excel

✦ Some advanced games.

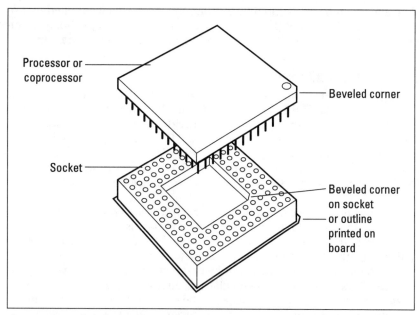

Figure 14-3: The math coprocessor chip must be seated properly in its socket on your motherboard.

Math chips should be afforded the same cooling and handling precautions as those listed for CPU chips. Adding an 8087 math chip to a PC or XT system provides a noticeable increase in heat at the system board of these systems. The math chips for 286 and 386 systems add a somewhat less noticeable increase in heat. In either case, adequate cooling and airflow clearance is recommended.

Math coprocessor speed

Because the math chip is a separate, dedicated CPU, it might run at speeds independent from, but generally no faster than, the main CPU chip in some non-8088/8086 systems. Whether this is the case for your system depends on the actual clock speed provided to the math chip. Your owner's manual should show what speed math chip your system requires.

If you install a math chip that is rated for slower operation than the clock signal supplied to it (again, this is subjective for each different system), the math chip might overheat or malfunction, causing a system or software lock up. Or, you might see error messages in your applications, misdrawn lines in CAD programs, miscalculations in spreadsheets, or the BIOS error message 700 or 701.

Installing a math chip that is rated faster than the clock signal supplied to it or faster than the CPU does not provide faster math performance, although it might be more reliable over a long period of time and be more expensive than necessary.

Math coprocessor alternatives

There have been at least two external software programs that emulate some math coprocessor functions: EMUL87 and FRANKE.387, for use with 80386 systems. Another program, Q87 from Quikware, will provide math chip emulation for 486SX and 486SLC CPUs, as well as for the NexGen 586 CPU. These programs have been available on many bulletin board systems (BBSs). These emulations are installed as device drivers or terminate-and-stay-resident (TSR) programs in CONFIG.SYS or AUTOEXEC.BAT files so that they are available to be used by applications.

If you are using one of these emulations, your applications program might "believe" that there is a physical chip in your system, and it may use the complex math functions provided in the emulation software. This enables you to run many programs that require a math chip, although rather slowly, without the expense of the actual integrated circuit. Slow operation might be better than none at all if you are patient and must get the work done. These emulations do not enhance applications that can use but do not require a math chip because the emulation, which is just another piece of software, might run slower than the program would run by itself.

The EMUL87 and FRANKE.387 emulation programs are not compatible with most of the advanced memory management programs (such as QEMM and 386Max) because both programs attempt to use the same software interrupts. This creates a conflict and system hang-up that is often resolved only by rebooting your system and removing one of the two programs to prevent the conflict. There are no error messages or signs specific to this problem, but QEMM will display Error 13 and give you a polite opportunity to prevent the conflict from locking up your system.

CMOS clock/calendar

The complimentary metal-oxide semiconductor (CMOS) clock is the perpetual clock and calendar that keeps time when your system is turned off. An internal clock circuit operates from a small battery. This battery is also used by the setup RAM to retain configuration information, such as the amount of RAM, the type of video adapter, and the number and type of disks and hard drives. This device also holds special settings required by the system board, such as wait states, bus clock speed, and I/O device configurations. In most recent systems, much of this function is contained within one or two plug-in modules, commonly of the type made by Dallas Semiconductor.

Early AT-type systems used discrete, wired-in components and an external or soldered-in battery to operate the clock and maintain configuration information.

PC and XT systems do not have a built-in clock/calendar or any CMOS setup functions. Instead, you might have an add-in clock/calendar function, perhaps on a multifunction card.

The year-2000 problem

Just in case you were wondering if, where, or when we would cover issues concerning PCs and the year 2000 — here it is — or was. We're happy to report that most of us got by Y2K without a glitch — even with supposedly non-Y2K-compliant PCs. Most of us are still finding small date problems related to the dreaded Y2K issue. On February 29, 2000, when many users looked at their digital watches, the clocks in their cars, or their VCR clocks, they saw March 1, 2000. Did this cause major problems? No! Was it difficult to fix? No! Was this a real Y2K problem? Yes.

Now that Y2K has passed, all we need to do is be attentive to date-related issues and continue to take the simple steps that have kept us from experiencing more intrusive problems. The more of these glitches that are immediately caught, the more likely that the cascade of failures that were predicted will be averted.

The concerns about Y2K began with the original Motorola clock chip that IBM used in the PC/AT system, and it carried forth for compatibility in other clock chips and modules.

The problem is that these chips, and thus in many cases the PC, can only accept, store, and increment years, months, days, hours, minutes and seconds. There is no support for accepting, storing, or incrementing century information.

The BIOS may know no better

Your system's BIOS may only know the century as "19" — in most cases of BIOS chips created before 1994, the century is hard-coded, bolted-down, sealed in bits, untouchable. The year to which your older PC system rolled over, upon passing December 31, 1999, may have been 1900, 1980, 1984, 1972 or some other non-logical "century transition". We have seen all of these dates and there may have been others because of the hard coded date in the PC's BIOS or clock support chips. As long as the system that exhibits this kind of problem does not perform critical and date sensitive processing upon boot up, and you set the date manually every time it is rebooted, it will not cause further problems. Many people using older PCs are using this method to avoid further date problems.

The operating system is a willing victim

The problem is further compounded by the system BIOS code, but could be patched with an update to that code or in the operating system. The incorrect century information from the BIOS will be applied to the operating system, which may or may not know the difference — but neither 1980 nor 1900 are valid dates to any PC operating system because, like the PC, these operating systems did not exist at that time. Although either the BIOS or the operating system should know that they could not possibly have been around or running prior to 1980, they still blindly accept the erroneous information and do nothing about it.

Tip   Microsoft has issued Year 2000 patches for both Windows 95 and Windows 98 — if you don't have them, get them.

Some applications are not safe either

Once the BIOS and operating system are running with an incorrect date, your application programs and the date/time data they create will be wrong. From here, your financial, retirement, entitlements, expirations, memberships, calendars, and all sorts of date-based programs and functions will be messed up.

The problem with applications is not limited to when the year 2000 rolls around, either. Many applications cannot support dates beyond 2017, 2025, 2038, or various other years that are now well within consideration for financial or retirement plans. Thus, even if you fix your clock or your BIOS, your applications may not be able to properly handle dates in the not-so-distant future.

Note   Many popular applications, such as Intuit's Quicken bookkeeping program, require patches or software upgrades to keep them compliant. But, hopefully, you already bought these patches. Right?

Testing your system for year-2000 compliance

A free year-2000 comprehensive test is available from OnTrack at `www.ontrack.com`. There are also another dozen or so sample, free, and commercial software programs available to test and report year-2000 compliance of PC systems. Simply browse to your favorite Web-based search engine, tell it to search for "Year 2000," and then follow the links!

Solutions to the year-2000 problem

There are four levels of compliance and solutions to the year-2000 (Y2K) problem with PCs. The solution available to you depends on the hardware and software used in your system, and your degree of or access to technical expertise.

Clock chip upgrades

The first level of solution is obviously with the PC clock circuit. If you have a system with the old Motorola clock chip, you will not be able to find a year-2000 replacement — there are none available. If there were, you would probably have to perform some precision soldering to remove and replace the chip, as most of these were permanently installed on the system board.

If your system uses one of the Dallas Semiconductor, BenchMarq, Odin, Twinhead, or similar clock modules, you may have an easier time. Dallas Semiconductor makes an inexpensive upgrade clock chip, which is available from Resource 800 at `www.resource800.com` or by calling 800-430-7030. You may also have to de-solder the old chip and re-solder a new one in place in order to execute this solution. A new clock chip will give you first-level hardware compliance, but you will still need to ensure that your BIOS is Y2K-compliant. The good news is that you may be able to fix the problem with just a BIOS upgrade, saving you this step, but you will not have full system compliance, as required by many companies.

BIOS upgrades

A system BIOS upgrade can give many benefits, not the least of which is year-2000 compliance. BIOS chips prior to 1994–1995 were generally not year-2000 aware or compliant, and they did not support hard drives larger than 512 megabytes. A post-1994–1995 -BIOS fixes the year-2000 support problem in itself by allowing the century data to be changed and incremented properly beyond "19." It also understands that the date for a PC system cannot possibly be valid before 1980, and it automatically assumes that the century is "20" for years less than 80. This is, perhaps, a little tricky, but a plausible solution, nevertheless.

The upgrade involves either of two options. The first is pretty simple — you download a BIOS upgrade file set from your system manufacturer. This option is not available for all BIOS chips. Only those capable of accepting a "BIOS flash update" are in this category. An example of performing the upgrade is covered later in this chapter in the section "System BIOS."

The second option is to purchase a new BIOS ROM chip from available BIOS resellers — BIOS upgrades can be obtained from a number of resellers. Do not call Award, Phoenix, or other BIOS vendors directly; they will merely refer you to one of these resellers. Micro Firmware (800-767-5465 or www.firmware.com), sells BIOS upgrades for many popular computer systems (Gateway2000, Micron, Packard Bell, and Dell) and motherboards (from Intel and Micronics) using Phoenix BIOS chips. Prices range from $69 to $79. Unicore Software (800-800-2467 or www.unicore.com) sells upgrades for Award, AMI, MR BIOS, and Phoenix chips, with prices ranging from $40 to $60. Unicore claims it can find either an exact match for your motherboard or an upgrade that should work. If Unicore does not have a specific Award BIOS version for your system, you will get a MR BIOS equivalent. And if that does not work, Unicore may offer to examine your motherboard and create a custom BIOS for the same fee or perhaps even for free.

Once you get a new chip, you have to open up your system, locate the BIOS chip, remove the old one, insert the new one, and reboot. Again, neither of these solutions will give you *full* Y2K compliance to the hardware level, but the resulting system improvement and date support is the same.

Software fixes for year-2000 problems

What if there is no hardware solution to your problem? What if you cannot replace your BIOS? Various software fixes that mimic the actions of the BIOS updates are starting to pop up on the Internet. Check www.slonet.org/~doren for Rosenthal Engineering's Year 2000 correction application. All of these programs are run from your AUTOEXEC.BAT file so that the date is correct for your environment and applications.

Operating systems and applications

So far as we have read, been told, and experienced, all of the operating systems we have been dealing with in the past few years, way back to DOS 2 and 3, are year-2000 compliant to one extent or another. The file manager application in Windows 3.*x* (and useable under Windows 95 and 98) is not year-2000 compliant, but Microsoft has a downloadable fix for it. Unfortunately, the operating systems do not do what can be done with BIOS, which is perform a smart guess about the century based on a range of years. However, the BIOS is the right place to correct the problem because many programs still use BIOS level functions to get date and time information, rather than using the operating system clock.

Your real challenge will be to research or otherwise determine if your applications are year-2000 compliant and then to discover just how far into the twenty-first century they will continue to work properly. Unfortunately, there is no single place on the Internet or elsewhere to look for this information. You have to check the individual Web sites of your software vendors.

Enhanced system board features

As CPUs improve in speed and performance, so must their supporting elements. For system boards with 8088–80386 CPU chips, the supporting circuits were often a large number of discrete circuit chips designed essentially to create the rest of the computer, excluding the actual I/O devices, which were plugged into add-in card sockets. Later models of 80386 systems and all higher-level systems began to benefit from combining these support circuits into fewer components with more internal functions. These became known as chip sets, specifically designed to make it easier to build smaller and faster PC systems. Major semiconductor companies such as Intel, LSI Logic, and Chips and Technologies are among the early leaders in this area, but many offshore, lesser-known brands also appear in numerous PC systems. Some of the enhanced features on a typical system board are detailed in the text that follows.

These new chip sets and features required improvements in the system BIOS, including providing access to the parameters of various features through the SETUP program. First, we cover the features and then discuss the BIOS.

More Than a Hardware Problem

The important concept to grasp is that the year-2000 problem is not just a hardware problem. Actually, that aspect of the problem is the easiest to identify and fix. It is not just a software application problem, either. Even though virtually all of the commercially available programs, programming languages, compilers, and utility programs have been fixed or replaced (a monumental undertaking in itself), the problem is not completely fixed. The data that has been collected for decades and longer, oblivious to the year 2000, will not change itself to be compatible. Beyond that, business methods and procedures that have become commonplace may have obscure vulnerabilities.

External cache and control

Most 386 and higher systems provide a special high-speed memory area between the CPU and its I/O to store retrieved memory data (programs and information) for faster access by the CPU so that the CPU can perform at optimum speed. This is called the level two, or L2, cache. Typical external cache sizes range from 64K to 256K, and lately, up to 1MB. The benefits of a larger cache depend heavily upon how memory is accessed and used.

Improved I/O bus support

The circuits that provide data connections between the CPU and the many I/O devices have evolved to support more and faster data flow, from plug-in video adapters to network cards. These are an integral part of and a basic purpose of a system board — to contain and care for the rest of the system's elements. For Plug and Play to work and for local bus, PCI, and AGP devices to deliver screaming I/O performance, the CPU-to-I/O device paths must have more and better support from chip-set components on the system board.

Disk drive interfaces

Integrated drive electronics (IDE) interfaces between the system board and IDE disk drives are little more than special electronic paths to the main system data bus. It is easy and efficient to place these circuits on the system board, leaving the add-in card slots for other uses and enabling faster data transfer speeds that can be better controlled by the system BIOS and user-accessible system setup parameters. Only a few (mostly more expensive) name-brand systems provide built-in SCSI adapters. These are more complex but certainly an excellent choice for placement on the system board to keep things close to the CPU and as fast as possible.

Input and output ports

People always seem to need a way to flow information between their CPUs and memory to destinations in the real world. I/O ports are the basic means of interfacing with these two. With the ability to put more things into smaller spaces, these basic functions might as well be built into the system board — you have to have them! Following is a list of I/O ports:

✦ **Serial I/O Ports.** Your modem and probably your mouse each need one of these. Perhaps you have more?

✦ **Parallel I/O Ports.** A relatively easy interface to provide directly from the main I/O bus.

✦ **Mouse Ports.** Typically uses an unused I/O port on the keyboard controller chip.

✦ **USB Ports.** As the need for more and faster external devices has developed, the Universal Serial Bus (USB) I/O port has started showing up on new systems. USB provides a true Plug-and-Play interface to support smarter I/O devices, such as advanced gaming tools — control sticks, virtual reality headsets, video cameras, sound systems, and so on.

✦ **IEEE-1394 Ports.** Just as USB is a significant improvement over the capabilities of the serial and parallel I/O ports, IEEE-1394 is a significant improvement over USB. IEEE-1394 is primarily used for the transfer of video data between camcorders and editing or storage systems but we expect to see it as a standard PC port in the future.

Power management

The purpose of power management in PCs is both to conserve energy and to enable the features of the PC to be available as quickly as possible. The energy-savings concept is to turn off or slow down PC features if they are not used over a period of time. The PC availability concept is to enable you to turn your PC "off" on demand and to return to work exactly where you left off. First introduced in laptop and notebook PCs to conserve battery life, power management is now standard in factory-built PC systems and off-the-shelf system boards and power supplies.

It seems like a waste of a perfectly good Pentium processor to make it decide when to turn the display or disk drive on or off. But actually, the supporting chip set and software perform some of this work. Power management in PCs is variously supported by industry standards, such as Advanced Power Mode (APM) and Advanced Computer Power Interface (ACPI), in the system BIOS and the Windows operating system.

Many items must work together in a PC — the system board, the BIOS, the operating system setup, and even applications. Unfortunately, even as far as technology has advanced, often these elements work together poorly, or not at all. Generally speaking, chip sets, BIOS, and most of the operating system work well together — though a manufacturer can make mistakes in how it designs and implements power control on the system board and in the BIOS.

The biggest and perhaps most familiar inconvenience occurs when attempting to shutdown a systems through Windows. Users often experience the system hanging up at the Windows shutdown screen. Then, you end up turning the system power off, only to be greeted by "improper shutdown" error messages and the running of the Scandisk utility when you start up again. This scenario is generally related to a computer program that will not release memory or that stops running properly when closed — which Windows tells all programs to do when you tell Windows to shutdown. There is no simple solution to this because the solution depends upon your system configuration and which applications are loaded or shutdown in what order. We keep hoping for a uniform solution, and you may see it if you make the transition out of the Windows 95 and 98 realm into Millennium and 2000 versions of Windows.

I/O connections

The system board also accepts power supply connections, as well as providing connection points for indicator lights, reset and CPU speed switches, the sockets for RAM memory, and the connectors for add-in cards. We discuss each of these briefly in this section, exploring some of the features, benefits, and things you should be aware of when working with these connections.

The original IBM PC system provided only modest accessory and feature capabilities. It contained only five add-in slots, and it did everything it was minimally required to do with the BASIC programming language support built-into the BIOS ROM. It had add-in cards to provide support for a monochrome or a color video display. Since 1981, the need and demand for more significant features and expandability encouraged the addition of more, faster, and significantly different add-in and I/O performance and feature benefits.

Throughout the life of PC-compatible systems to date, there have been six major I/O configurations. Each builds on and sometimes significantly alters the original connection schemes. As these changes have occurred, different ways of configuring systems and various aspects of system performance improvements have developed. Table 14-2 lists the various PC I/O bus system classes, their data bus width, and their maximum data transfer speeds.

Table 14-2
PC System I/O Bus Types and Performance

System	Data Bits	Bus Speed	Throughput
PC and PC-XT	8	4.77 MHz	4.77 MBps
PC-AT	16	8 MHz	16 MBps
EISA	32	8 MHz	33 MBps
Micro Channel	32	10 MHz	40 MBps
Micro Channel	64	10 MHz	80 MBps
Micro Channel	64	20 MHz	160 MBps
VESA local bus	64	33 MHz	132 MBps
VESA local bus	32	66 MHz	264 MBps
VESA local bus	64	66 MHz	528 MBps
PCI	32	0–33 MHz	132 MBps
PCI	64	0–133 MHz	264 MBps
AGP	64	0–133 MHz (see note below)	266–533 MBps

Note   PCI and AGP I/O bus speeds are advancing towards 200 and 266 MHz speeds.

Power connections

Most PC system boards use the original PC-style dual power connectors, supplying voltage to the system board and through the system board to the I/O connections. These are adequate to handle the current draw of most typical system boards, with up to eight I/O connections, the load of a 486 or Pentium processor, and several megabytes of RAM memory. Some systems that support more than eight add-in cards or have special I/O features might have additional or different power connections to handle heavier loads, thus making the system board incompatible with the layout of the original PC, XT, or AT systems. See Figure 14-4 for a view from the back of the PC motherboard. Wires go up and out to power supply (P8 and P9). Colors indicated are typical of the wires between the power supply and the connectors.

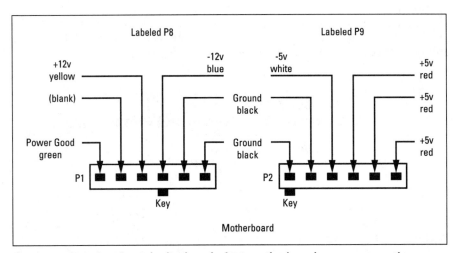

Figure 14-4: A view from the back end of PC motherboard power connections

Keyboard connector

Keyboards can be connected to the system through either a direct or indirect attachment to the system board. In most cases, the direct plug-in is a circular connection, either a 5-pin Deutsche Industrie Norm or DIN (about ½ inch in diameter) or a 6-pin mini-DIN (about ⅜ inch in diameter). On system boards that also provide a mouse connector, the keyboard and mouse connector are of the same style, making it confusing to tell which is which. You can misconnect the keyboard and mouse, usually without any damage, but you will likely receive a keyboard error message at startup.

The keyboard interface to the CPU may be viewed as an entire subsystem. The system board has a keyboard controller (a dedicated microprocessor) with its own BIOS that communicates with a similar microprocessor chip inside the keyboard.

In many systems, the keyboard BIOS must match the system BIOS, so if you upgrade one, you must upgrade the other. In other systems, the keyboard controller might share circuitry with other functions, and its BIOS is built into the system BIOS, so upgrading one BIOS usually upgrades the other automatically.

The CMOS SETUP and BIOS of a few systems enable you set the timing responses of the keyboard — the delay before a key repeats itself and the rate at which the repetition happens when you hold down a key. You might also find an option to set a system password, which might be supported in your system or keyboard BIOS.

Caution

Be careful of setting a system password because if you forget your password or there is a malfunction, you might not be able to use your system until you erase the stored CMOS settings.

Tip

If you cannot erase the CMOS (usually by disconnecting the battery and not using your system for 5–30 minutes), you might have to replace the CMOS RAM/clock unit, the keyboard BIOS chip, or both.

Mouse connector

IBM introduced the onboard mouse connection with the PS/2 series systems. This is a 6-pin, mini-DIN connection attached directly or indirectly to the system board. As indicated previously, this connection can be easily confused with the similar keyboard connection. This built-in feature saves you from having to use an add-in card slot or serial port to gain the use of a pointing device. Most mouse driver programs recognize this onboard connection and configure themselves automatically when the mouse driver program is included as a DEVICE= line in the CONFIG.SYS file or loaded in the AUTOEXEC.BAT file. Microsoft Windows, Windows NT, Linux, FreeBSD, and IBM OS/2 will recognize the onboard mouse connection at initial setup and will configure these environments to use your mouse accordingly.

Industry Standard Architecture

With the original PC began the evolution of the Industry Standard Architecture (ISA), also known as the ISA-bus. ISA is the original, functional and design compatibility standard for PC compatibility. The ISA-bus provides 8-bit parallel data I/O and 20 bits of memory addressing (will address 1MB of memory) capability, IRQ, DMA request and acknowledgment, and clock signals (which synchronize CPU and I/O operations). The ISA-bus was extended with the introduction of the IBM PC/AT, which added more signal, address (32-bit addressing), IRQ, and DMA circuits to accommodate greater memory (up to 4GB) and data throughput capabilities. The 16-bit ISA-bus is an extension of the original 8-bit ISA-bus, and it operates at a higher speed of 6 or 8 MHz versus the 4.77 MHz of the PC and XT systems. Some AT-bus systems operate as fast as 16 MHz. Newer systems provide 66 MHz and up to 266 MHz bus speeds, but not from systems providing only ISA or EISA slots. The original 8-bit ISA I/O connections are contained on a 62-pin (31 pins on each side) edge connector. The 16-bit ISA I/O uses the original 8-bit connector and adds a 36-pin connector to accommodate the additional lines for 16-bit capability (see Figure 4-5 in Chapter 4).

Micro Channel

After the successful life cycles of the PC, XT, and AT series computers, and enhancements clone manufacturers made to processing and I/O speeds and system features, IBM departed from its own hardware standards and introduced the Micro Channel Architecture (MCA) in the IBM PS/2-series systems (models 25–95, in 8086, 80286, 80386, and 80486 versions). Micro Channel was intended to reduce the system add-on setup and configuration confusion by providing a form of serialization of I/O devices, and a reference or setup program facility to better merge the functions of various add-in devices and the base system. Micro Channel I/O cards are not physically or electrically compatible with the original ISA I/O devices. This major concern, considering all of the original and cloned XT and AT systems on the market, and the significant investment users had made in ISA devices, made Micro Channel systems less than successful and allowed many other once-small competitors to take over the PC market.

Enhanced Industry Standard Architecture

With the introduction of the first 386 systems came the need to use the 386's 32-bit data and extended addressing capabilities. Compaq Computer Corporation, along with others, developed Enhanced Industry Standard Architecture (EISA). EISA uses dual-purpose I/O connectors to accommodate both the 8- and 16-bit ISA conventions, plus an additional row of pins to accommodate the extra signals for 32-bit operations.

Along with support for 32-bit operations, EISA was designed with an intelligent add-in card identification and configuration facility for hardware items, plus system ROM-BIOS extensions and an I/O device configuration program so that you can set up your system to handle 32-bit devices and take advantage of the larger and faster I/O operations. EISA has been considered the high-end system architecture for the past few years. Although its capabilities are significant, EISA did not make PCs more economical, easier to build, set up, or use, and it requires a special BIOS and setup software. EISA is also not fast enough to support the extremely fast processor and I/O speeds of 486 and Pentium systems or the demanding applications and environments within which systems are operating more and more.

PCMCIA/PC Card

The PCMCIA, or PC Card, interface is designed for portable and laptop systems and is a means to connect memory cards, disk drive, sound, modems, network, and other interface devices to these systems without opening the case or using external cables. PCMCIA can be added to standard desktop systems as an add-in card and/or an extra disk drive bay.

VESA local bus

Changing part of the physical PC architecture, the VL-bus, or local bus, places faster I/O devices in closer contact with the processor. Local bus video cards, using the Video BIOS Extensions (VBE) from the Video Electronics Standards Association (VESA) provided incredible video display speeds, clarity, and color resolutions. Local bus added another connector to the original ISA connection scheme. Each local bus-capable add-in slot can act as an ISA slot. Local bus was implemented for disk controllers and other high-data-volume add-on devices. The local bus exists only on PC systems and for systems using the 80486 and higher processors.

Peripheral Component Interconnect

Intel and other major vendors are credited with developing Peripheral Component Interconnect (PCI), which changed the way people look at PC I/O systems, much as the Micro Channel did, by using a completely different I/O connector. A PCI slot does not have a companion or associated ISA connection. The PCI connection scheme differs by shifting the connector in relation to the normal ISA slot guides so that neither ISA nor EISA cards can be accidentally connected. The components on a PCI card are on the reverse side of the board as compared to ISA and EISA cards. Components face to the left or down in relation to the front or top of the case.

PCI has several advantages over other previous I/O bus designs. It is also a local bus, as it is connected more directly to the CPU I/O circuits than ISA, EISA, or Micro-Channel. As with VESA local bus I/O, the data transfer speeds between CPU and I/O devices are tremendously faster for improved performance, from 33 to 133 megabits per second. PCI is designed with and for PnP support, saving considerable time and hassle in configuring I/O devices into a system.

Typical uses for PCI are with disk drive interfaces, video adapters, and network cards. As new I/O devices are developed and implemented, many more PCI devices will be available. PCI devices have been somewhat more expensive than other I/O devices, as were EISA cards, but this higher cost may be offset because more of the other basic I/O functions are typically built into the system board.

PCI has other benefits. It is processor and system independent, so I/O devices can be designed once and used in many different types of systems, including the Power PC, Silicon Graphics, and Sun workstation platforms. This means that as more PCI devices are developed for PCs and other systems, costs will come down. It also means you can swap I/O devices among other system types to upgrade or shift your computing platform. The PCI bus also handles IRQs differently and can sh are IRQs with other PCI devices.

Advanced Graphics Port

Advanced Graphics Port (AGP) is an extension of PCI dedicated to providing the extremely high-speed data transfer rates for video display information. Basic data transfer rates are up to 266 megabits per second, with 2× mode achieving up to

533 megabits per second. These speeds accommodate the fast screen paints and refreshes required by very graphics-intense programs, such as games and multimedia content. AGP appears as an extra connector in-line with a PCI socket on the system board. As with PCI, AGP is PnP compliant.

Universal Serial Bus

The Universal Serial Bus (and the faster FireWire) is the PnP, quick-connect, smart, and fast external PC interface people have been expecting for years. With Universal Serial Bus (USB) you can attach up to 256 devices to your system and not have to worry about I/O addresses, or IRQ or DMA configurations. When a USB device is attached to the system, it identifies itself to the PnP handling scheme of the system or operating system, allowing drivers to be installed and started, or stopped and removed, from memory as necessary (hot swappable). Devices can transfer data at up to 12 megabits per second. USB can also provide a small amount of power to low-power devices (joysticks, keyboards, and so on) but larger devices (printers, modems, and so on) must provide their own power source. As a matter of fact, both the bandwidth and power supply may be serious considerations when connecting multiple devices.

Like PCI, USB is system independent — it can be implemented equally well on Apple Macintosh or other system platforms, so you can swap and share devices easily between these systems. You can obtain system boards with USB built in, thus taking up no additional I/O slots, or you may purchase PCI add-in cards to provide the USB interface for your system. USB is supported by Microsoft Windows 98/Me and Windows 2000.

System BIOS

Basic input/output system (BIOS) exists on every system board, but it evolves with and must support all of the integrated functions listed previously. The BIOS usually contains the setup program that lets you configure almost every aspect of the features and timing of the system board. The BIOS provides support for the features listed and access to the setup parameters needed to configure their features.

These advanced system board configuration features were unavailable until around 1991, or they were provided only through a handful of different I/O cards. In terms of functionality, problems, and solutions, you can look to the chapters on particular hardware for more details on these items. In terms of the system board, this chapter addresses these items as it works past basic system board functions and moves into the system setup program where these items are controlled.

The BIOS is the second program your PC runs when the power is turned on. The first is a small bit of code built into the CPU chip that tells the CPU to look for bootup instructions at a specific memory location—that being the starting location of the BIOS. We have already covered the BIOS functionality in Chapter 4—it is responsible for determining some basic system configuration and status information, and finding a bootable device.

IBM created the first PC system BIOS back in 1980. Since then the majority of BIOS implementations have been functional "clones" and enhancements upon the original idea. Today at least four firms are creating PC-compatible BIOS—IBM Corporation, American Megatrends (AMI), Phoenix Technologies, and Award BIOS. Award BIOS now also owns Microid Research, the creators of MR-BIOS. Most PC-system manufacturers invariably use BIOS building block kits from either AMI, Award, or Phoenix.

It is because system board manufacturers start with a basic BIOS building block kit and customize it to suit their chip sets or other design options, that every BIOS and setup program can be expected to be quite different from system to system. Thus, the different terminology, parameters, and support for different systems are not universal. Despite these customizations, the system BIOS must support a basic feature and function set, compatible with the original IBM-PC through the AT. Similarly, accessing the setup program can differ significantly from system to system.

Now that we have covered many functional aspects of the BIOS and support on the system board, we will move on to various setup parameters.

BIOS in standard ROM

The original and many other system BIOS implementations are done the good old-fashioned way—using a read-only (write-once) memory chip, or ROM. A ROM chip requires a special piece of hardware designed specifically for programming binary data into the chip. Some ROM chips are erasable by ultraviolet light, but since there is not much need to consider these chips reusable, some manufacturers use non-erasable chips. These chips are typically 24-pin DIP or DIP parts that plug into a socket on the system board. They are easily replaced for upgrade purposes. This style of BIOS storage is relatively reliable because the chips are preprogrammed and tested at the factory, and there is little chance of a failure in this type of memory device.

BIOS in flash memory

The fast pace of technology and economics of PC support today justifies using a slightly more expensive, but certainly more versatile, FLASH memory chip as the way to go in providing PC BIOS. FLASH itself does not stand for anything other than being able to change the contents of the chip "in a flash"—versus the time it takes to erase and reprogram the older style ROM chips.

The contents of a FLASH chip can be read from the chip and saved to disk, or read from disk and written to the chip with a program developed specifically to modify the contents of the BIOS. This makes the process relatively fast and economical, but it also involves some risk. If your system has electrical or logical problems, or the FLASH chip is defective, you could experience a hardware failure in the middle of writing data into the FLASH chip, and this could leave your system useless.

BIOS upgrades

Because of customizations and differences in BIOS between different system board vendors, it is always advisable to first check with your system or board manufacturer for updates and support. AMI requires this because it provides and supports BIOS strictly for system board manufacturers (although Award and Phoenix provide various levels of support to end users). If you think that the BIOS is not supporting all of the features you think it should or if your system acts buggy, you may need to consider a BIOS upgrade.

There are a few reasons to consider updating the BIOS in your PC system:

✦ Even though year 2000 has begun, year-2000 compliance issues may still occur.

✦ Large disk support (greater than 512MB).

✦ Improved performance or functionality.

✦ New features, timing, or bug fixes.

Earlier in this chapter we gave a little direction and mentioned current resources for BIOS upgrades on year-2000 issues. Supporting larger disk drives became an issue a few years ago when users realized what was well-known in technical circles but seldom encountered by users — the BIOS was not designed to handle disk drives with more than 1,024 cylinders, 16 heads, or 63 sectors per track. This limitation in combination with limitations in earlier versions of DOS left users having to deal with drives larger than 512MB with various aftermarket disk drivers, as well as with aftermarket formatting and partitioning software. A new BIOS that can handle larger numbers of cylinders and heads, is the first step to overcoming this problem. Upgrades to the operating system take care of the rest.

Universal Serial Bus and faster IDE hard drives are now industry standards that people buy and use. A system board and its BIOS that was designed and sold before the rest of the hardware was ready could probably use a BIOS update to support current features. As system boards go from design through production to use, it is not uncommon for a manufacturer to encounter problems with various memory or CPU chips, new I/O boards, or new software that comes on the market. For this reason the manufacturers may offer upgrades to accommodate changes that are not under their control.

Some vendors will only sell you the upgrade in chip form because it is easier to support, and, thus, better for their business, even if that chip is just another FLASH-type ROM chip. There is less risk involved in doing the upgrade through this process.

If you only have the option to replace the BIOS chip, rather than using the FLASH ROM method, the replacement procedure is relatively easy. Open the case, locate the chip, remove the old one, insert the new one, reboot and test the system, and then close things up and go on your merry way.

The methods for performing the Flash ROM upgrade are just about as simple, but could involve a little more risk of losing your BIOS in the process, so we cover that in detail next.

BIOS updates in a flash

Historically, if you required a BIOS upgrade to support IDE drives or to fix a bug in the system, you had to replace the BIOS chips, which cost anywhere from $50 to $100. This can become expensive and time-consuming if your motherboard manufacturer is adding new features or redeveloping things, as often happens with new systems and designs. If you are upgrading to Windows 2000, you most likely will need to replace the BIOS chip.

Flash ROM is a new type of memory chip that stores the BIOS program in a chip that allows the data within it to be rewritten using a special program. Although this technically means that the chip is not read-only, the intention is to use the device mostly in read-only mode, and only at startup. Using a Flash ROM instead of a conventional ROM chip is slightly more expensive at first, but it saves a great deal of time, money, and technical hassle if you need to update the BIOS in your system because you can perform the upgrade by running a downloaded program.

BIOS updates and their implementation programs are available on technical-support BBSs, online forums, and Web sites of many computer companies. Many manufacturers are using these support tools with great success.

BIOS updates also enable you to change the personality of your system. For instance, you may have a generic system board that provides basic features, but you might have noticed an extra connector or two. Calling the board manufacturer's BBS or looking up the manufacturer on a Web site and downloading a set of new files may provide you with the clues and the new BIOS you need to use the new features. Here, we present an example of one of many Flash ROM update procedures.

One popular system board has two IDE drive connectors, but only one is used or mentioned in the documentation and CMOS setup. Checking the BBS or Web site for the board's original manufacturer, and those of system integrators (one of those popular magazine and catalog advertisers), we found that one of the integrators has a BIOS and documentation that enables us to make use of the additional connector and new CMOS setup routines. Now we can have up to four IDE drives connected to a system originally limited to two. After using the Flash BIOS update program to load a new BIOS file, this system now boots up with a new message, indicating that it is a system from a particular company (it is not, but the BIOS tells us it is) and that four IDE drives are running nicely under the hood.

Except for adding the drives, we did not have to take the cover off, worry about anti-static protection when removing and replacing chips, change jumpers, or use a single tool to add extra drive support and get the latest BIOS updates. Except for the BBS or Web site calls and file download, which took about 30 minutes, the entire process of using the update program and checking things took 10 to 15 minutes. We have no complaints about getting a free update.

The Flash ROM BIOS tool set in our case consists of at least four files — the Flash control program (usually FSH.EXE), the Flash ROM BIOS code file (usually file-name.BIN), an emergency Flash-ROM–code floppy-disk utility program (in our case, WRDISK12.EXE), and a README (helpful text) file describing the use of the files and the position of a special jumper on the system board. Read the information file and follow the directions closely.

Getting the BIOS update

Follow these steps to update the BIOS:

1. Follow the directions for making a backup floppy disk of your existing (and hopefully, working) BIOS code. You do this with the WRDISK12.EXE (write to disk) program. This requires a floppy disk for drive A, preferably a 1.44MB disk for a 1.44MB drive, or 1.2MB disk for a 1.2MB drive. This disk does not need to be DOS formatted, and it will not be useful for anything but restoring the BIOS once you finish this process. Run the backup program, writing the BIOS code to disk and labeling it Flash BIOS BINARY Backup File Only.

2. Create a DOS-formatted and bootable disk for drive A and copy all of the downloaded Flash BIOS files to it. You may need this later to restore one BIOS version or the other. Do not copy your original CONFIG.SYS or AUTOEXEC.BAT files from your hard drive to this disk unless you need special files to access your disk drive. If you do need these files, make them short and simple so that you do not load any memory managers, device drivers, or other parameters that are not essential to using your system for this process.

3. Reboot your system using the bootable floppy disk. Before your system boots up, run the CMOS setup program. Once in CMOS setup, write down the configuration items for disk drives, disk controllers, caching, wait states, shadow ROMs, and so on. If the new BIOS offers new features or changes your existing CMOS information in any way, you will need this record to restore the CMOS values after the BIOS update.

4. Follow the instructions to use the FSH.EXE program to read your existing BIOS code from the Flash ROM and save it to a file, which you might call ORIGBIOS.BIN (the BIN extension will indicate that this is a binary file, or

data readable only by the CPU). This process should involve using the DOS disk that you created earlier to boot your system and then should involve executing the FSH program from the command line. Choose the option in the FSH.EXE program to save your existing BIOS to a disk file.

5. Use the FSH.EXE program to load in the new BIOS (BIN) file into the Flash ROM chip. The process takes a few seconds, and it verifies itself after it is done. Onscreen instructions should then indicate when you should reboot your system for the changes to take effect.

6. Reboot your system using this bootable disk to avoid possible complications between the new BIOS and your original system configuration and to make sure things are okay. At bootup, you will likely see a slightly different onscreen message about the BIOS version or an indication that you should use the CMOS setup to reconfigure the settings. That is why you wrote these items down in step three. Reenter the CMOS setup information before rebooting.

7. If all appears well, reboot from your hard drive instead of the disk. We suggest you try running different programs, especially memory-intensive environments such as Windows, OS/2, UNIX, or Linux, without writing any new or old data files to disk to make sure that the new BIOS version does not create any conflicts or errors with these complex environments. If everything checks out, try reading and writing different files to be sure that disk operations are okay and then go on about your business with the new update.

Caution Be aware that some Flash ROM programs only write new BIOS data files into Flash ROM and do allow you to copy the existing BIOS to a disk file. Be sure you really want to use the Flash update, and preferably only after consulting technical-support people for your system board or BIOS.

Reviving the system in a flash

Along with the benefits of Flash ROM BIOS, there are also a couple of problems you might encounter. The first concerns a set of one of those obscure little jumper sets on the system board. A basic rule is, if you do not know what a jumper does, do not change it. If you change the wrong jumper and turn on the power to your system, you could be greeted with a strange message (such as "Erasing Flash ROM. Use BIOS update disk to restore") or a dead system — no beeps, blinks, flashes, or messages of any kind. A completely dead system that "worked just a minute ago" could be an indication that the BIOS code has been damaged.

Most Flash ROM BIOS systems provide a service jumper that is used to erase the chip completely in case the system starts acting strange, and the only alternative is to refresh the BIOS. Make this determination with the help of technical support, experienced users, or technical users.

Restoring the Flash BIOS requires the backup disk you made in the first step of the procedure previously outlined. If you can download all the necessary files described, the WRDISK or similar program may provide a feature that will create this backup disk from the downloaded BIN file. If you do not have or cannot make this disk with the WRDISK program, making the disk may be complicated; it is not a task for the novice user. However, it is necessary and may be the only way to recover your system.

With the backup BIN disk and the instructions for your system handy, locate the Flash ROM service jumper and make the change necessary to reset the Flash chip. This should also cause a special Flash ROM bootup program to run when you turn on the power to your system. This program prompts you to press a key appropriate to the disk drive that you will put the BIN disk into. When you press this key, the program will read the special binary file, write the data to the Flash ROM, and verify the results. If everything is successful, you will receive an instruction prompt to turn off the power, move the service jumper back to its original position, and then reboot your computer. If there is an error or failure message shown in this process, you may have a bad Flash ROM chip, or something else is wrong with your system board, requiring complete replacement or service.

After the Flash ROM code is restored, your system should boot up normally. If you do not have the required BIN backup disk, but you do have access to another PC and new Flash ROM files, you can create the BIN disk by following the steps in the next section.

Creating a Flash ROM BIOS binary backup floppy disk

If you have blown up the Flash ROM (BIOS) in your new system, and you do not have the utility to create a backup disk (a non-DOS floppy disk with just the BIOS code written in the first few sectors) from the existing or running BIOS (performed using a special utility for your specific system board), you have a problem. There is no way to reboot the system, even if you exercise the special Flash ROM disk load utility built into some system boards by moving a jumper you should not normally touch.

The technical support department for your system board or BIOS may try to help, but the usual solution is to wait until a new Flash ROM chip is mailed to you. With a new chip, you have to find the old chip, remove it, and insert the new one.

Basically, your PC was dead in the water . . . until now. The solution is really no secret — you just have to be technical and creative, and you have the right tools at hand. Here are the right tools:

✦ The appropriate Flash ROM BIOS file, usually a 64 or 128K file (a file name with a BIN extension).

✦ The Norton DiskEdit program or a similar raw file utility program, configured and run in "Write and Maintenance mode" to use on the drive where the Flash ROM file exists.

The process is as follows:

1. With the Norton DiskEdit (DE.EXE or DISKEDIT.EXE) program available and the Flash ROM Binary file at hand, start the DiskEdit program:

```
DE C:\ /M /W
```

2. Select Hex under the View menu item. Leave the cursor at the start of the file (offset 0).

3. From the Object menu, select File and then read the file that has a BIN extension.

4. From the Edit menu, select Mark and page down to the end of the file. (A 65536 byte file will indicate 65520 for the Offset.)

5. From the Tool menu, select "Write To."

6. Select a drive of the same type as the A (first/boot) drive in the dead system.

7. Select Physical Sector as the destination type. You are going to "carve" these new bits in "raw" form onto a blank disk. This will not be a DOS-formatted disk after you are done.

8. Let DiskEdit write the marked 64K (or 128K) of the BIOS file to the disk.

9. Remove the disk. Label this disk as in the first step in the earlier section "Getting the BIOS update."

10. Follow the steps listed in the preceding "Reviving the System in a flash" section.

11. Be careful the next time you play with your system board.

Yes, we did wipe out our Flash ROM by attempting to modify a few simple bytes of a BIOS file and loading it into the Flash ROM. Booting resulted in a dead system — nothing worked. We thought we had a backup of the BIOS on a special disk, and we had no idea but guesswork about how to recover from this disaster. The backup disk was useless, but we did have a bootable recovery disk with the appropriate files on it. On another system, we had to copy the BIOS file from one disk (DOS file) to the Flash ROM special disk. It is not normal to have to do absolute or physical sector work on disks and files, but once again, the value of Norton's original file recovery work saved the day.

A recent innovation in the distribution of system BIOS updates has come from Microid Research, the makers of MR BIOS. You can download a variety of BIOS versions from its Web site (www.mrbios.com) to suit different system boards and chip sets as shareware. The same rules that apply to shareware applications apply to shareware BIOS — if you like it, you are expected to pay for it. The fees are surprisingly reasonable. The availability of downloadable BIOS has saved many users hours and days of frustration because something has caused a Flash BIOS to become corrupt with no other means of recovery than a complete replacement. Microid's BIOS packages come with programs to save and restore an existing BIOS to disk (a bootable disk preferably) as a safety feature and to allow loading of a new BIOS.

System Board Setup

With each successive development and enhancement since the ISA-bus, PC manufacturers and software creators have been working together in various groups in attempts to make building, configuring, supporting, and using PCs easier. The original ISA-bus and system BIOS provided no awareness of installed devices (beyond those that you set up with small DIP switches, as seen in Figure 14-5), jumpers, and CMOS setup routines. Today users still encounter several cards and devices that require them to learn a variety of technicalities. Starting anew or adding to your system requires you to set address and IRQ settings on add-in cards and cable configurations, and to check jumper settings on disk drives and other accessories.

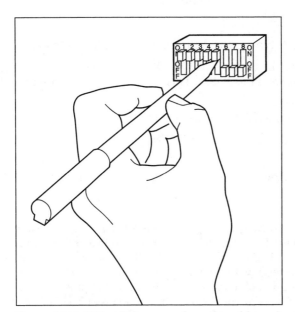

Figure 14-5: DIP switches are where the address, hardware interrupt, or operating conditions of various PC options are set.

Every system board sold today (and no one is manufacturing PC or XT-style boards anymore) uses some form of AT-style CMOS setup for at least minimal onboard feature configuration. Most of these provide access to the CMOS setup options directly from the system keyboard, as part of the system's ROM BIOS. The original IBM PC/AT and many early clone systems required the use of a system-specific, disk-based program to access the CMOS setup options. In many cases, these options can be accessed with a generic CMOS setup program, available from a variety of utility and diagnostic software companies.

The original AT CMOS setup provides the following basic configuration options:

✦ Date and time

✦ Base (DOS) memory size

✦ Extended memory size

✦ Floppy disk A and B type (360K or 1.2MB)

✦ Hard disk types (0–15)

Since the days of IBM-PC/AT, the CMOS setup program has typically been built into the BIOS chip. The setup program is accessed with various key or key combinations during bootup—Esc, Delete, F10, F2, Alt+S, Alt+F2, and Ctrl+Alt+Insert are some examples. Compaq and Hewlett Packard have set aside special, small disk partitions that hold the setup programs, diagnostic programs, and multiboot routine in the BIOS chip to enable selection of normal bootup or of the diagnostic mode and setup program.

CMOS setup options now offer additional options beyond those of the basic IBM-PC/AT settings with many different parameters. These include, depending on the system board and BIOS, some or all of the following:

✦ Leap-year calculations and corrections

✦ Automatic setting of base and extended memory sizes

✦ Shadow ROM and memory cache settings

✦ Additional floppy disk drive types (720K, 1.44MB, and 2.88MB)

✦ Additional hard disk types in the CMOS setup (numbered from 15 to over 40, customizable entries, and automatic determinations)

✦ Onboard floppy disk and hard drive controller enable/disable

✦ Boot drive preferences (floppy first, hard disk first, CD-ROM, and exclusions)

✦ Local system access passwords

✦ CPU speed selections

✦ I/O bus speed selections

✦ Memory timing factors (wait states)

✦ Internal (CPU) and external cache enable/disable

✦ Onboard I/O port selections (COM and LPT port configurations, and mouse ports)

✦ System board specific features

The original AT BIOS or CMOS configuration designs did not support these enhancements, but later enhancements must and obviously do coexist with the original specification for compatibility. Quite often these features vary between different system board and BIOS vendors. Access to these enhanced features is rarely if ever available with generic, disk-based AT-style CMOS setup programs.

None of these AT-style configuration provisions encompass the variety and complexity involved in either the Micro Channel or EISA systems, which have their own system-specific configuration utility programs that are run from DOS. I/O devices designed for these systems are sold with device-specific setup information on disks that contain information about the features and functions of that specific device relevant to the Micro Channel or EISA architectures. You must use the configuration programs and information files provided with your system and add-in cards for configuration.

In each of these cases, you are required to keep track of the devices, addresses, and other settings that are currently in your system. Adding a new device requires you to make any necessary changes to one or more devices, with switches and jumpers, so that all the devices can work together without conflicts and system hang-ups. These resources, devices, and their configuration, as well as potential conflicts, are covered in later chapters.

Every generation of system board has some method to either detect or specify the amount of RAM installed in the system. For PC, XT, and some AT systems the amount of installed RAM and how it was to be addressed was specified by a set of DIP switches on the system board. Additionally, for AT systems the system setup program had to be used to configure the amount and type (either base, extended, or a combination of both types) of memory in the system.

Early 386 systems also provided a combination of both switches and CMOS settings for memory. When 486 systems came along, almost all of the memory detection and configuration was done automatically within the power-on self test (POST) process — you got 640K of base or DOS memory, and everything else became extended memory.

Date and time

Setting date and time may be done in the CMOS setup, at the DOS prompt, or within commands or programs provided by your operating system. Most systems today have a battery backed-up clock. If you notice that your system date is set to an old date, such as January 1, 1980, or July 7, 1997 (or some other old date), it is probably an indication that your CMOS battery has died and you have lost your system clock and other configuration information. The old date is just the date that the manufacturer of your BIOS or CMOS memory chose as the default.

When you set the time, remember to use the 24-hour clock hour settings or to indicate a.m. or p.m. so that your system has the right time of day.

If you are connected to a corporate network, you may find your clock is set by the network.

If you are using a portable computer and do much time-zone hopping in your travels, you may get tired of setting your clock, so just leave it set to "home" time.

Whatever the case, it is important to set your clock so that you or your system will be able to tell when files were last saved or when something is really old and may be a candidate for removal from your system. In this regard, some automatic backup systems remove files older than a particular time designation. In such a case, a poorly set system clock can result in data loss.

PC and XT system board memory setup

For PC and XT systems (and most clones), you might need to verify the setting of switches 3 and 4 on switch block 1. This switch is located near the right rear corner of the system board, near the CPU chip. The typical settings for these are shown in Table 14-3.

Table 14-3 Typical Settings for PC and XT Systems		
Amount of Memory Installed	**Switch 3**	**Switch 4**
128K	Off	On
192K	On	Off
256K or more	Off	Off

AT system board memory setup

Many old AT systems have a memory-size switch for either 256K or 512K of base memory. Check your motherboard or manual for the presence of this switch, its location, and its proper setting.

AT systems provide a CMOS setup configuration for the amount of memory in the system. If you have a true IBM AT system, you will need the diagnostic floppy disks to access this information. IBM indicates different memory types in the 0–640K region of base or DOS memory and in the size of the expansion memory above the

1MB address range. If you have 2MB (2,048K) of total memory, typically 640K of it is assigned to base memory and the remaining 1,408K is expansion memory.

Although IBM uses the term expansion for the additional memory in AT systems, it is actually extended memory, not expanded, or LIMS-EMS, memory. The latter is not configurable at setup; it requires an EMS driver program to be operational.

In an 80286 system, you can use extended memory as simulated expanded memory with some types of special driver software (loaded with CONFIG.SYS), but you cannot use this memory for multitasking, as you can with an 80386 system, because the 80286 has internal bugs that keep the CPU from working correctly in some cases. Multitasking software, such as Windows, requires hardware-compatible expanded memory for multitasking on 80286 and higher systems. Microsoft Windows, Windows NT, and IBM OS/2 use extended memory on 386 and higher systems for multitasking purposes.

386, 486 and Pentium system board memory setup

Your 386 or 486 system board might contain jumpers for configuring the type and amount of memory you have installed. Other systems will automatically determine the amount of RAM installed and simply display it during the POST at bootup, and in a listing in the CMOS setup.

Most clone and 386 systems do not differentiate between base or DOS memory, and expansion or extended memory for the amount of total RAM in the system, although DOS does. In these systems it is generally assumed that the first 640K of memory is DOS memory, and the rest is extended memory.

Disk drive setup

Of all the features you should know about in your system setup, the parameters for your disk drive can be among the most significant, and possibly a little confusing. What are all of these modes and strange numbers anyway? Disk drives will be covered in greater detail in Part IV, but the setup issues are important at this point.

Iterations of setup drive parameters

Unless you have a SCSI hard drive, and some CMOS setup programs even have an option for that, there are five basic disk drive configuration methods to be concerned about in setting up your system. The first goes back to the legacy days of the PC-AT, when you could only specify the type number of your disk drive, and the parameters for a given type number had to match or closely approximate those of your disk drive. If the type or the parameters did not correctly match, either you would not be able to use all of your disk drive, or you could not use your drive at all. (For PC-XT systems, you had to depend on the disk drive controller to provide support for your disk drive.) Most users almost take it for granted now that they can bring home a new disk drive, set a jumper, connect the cables, and triple or quadruple their storage capacity in a few minutes. But it wasn't always this way, as we show you in the following sections.

Disk drive type tables

IBM set up the first disk drive type number tables, with other BIOS vendors following suit and expanding IBM's original list of 15 types to more than 45 drive types. This was, of course, well before the days of the high-capacity, high-speed, automatically configured systems and drives enjoy today. A drive type was assigned with a certain set of disk drive parameters and included the number of cylinders, heads, sectors per track, a write precompensation number, and a landing or head parking track number. Mismatch any of these first three parameters and your system may not recognize your drive. If you incorrectly set the write-precompensation number, your system may be incapable of saving data beyond a certain part of the drive. Thus, you could not use your drive if it could not be typecast into a role dictated by IBM or the other BIOS made available to you.

Custom drive types

Anticipating that new disk drives would come along faster than BIOS could be updated and dispersed, BIOS vendors decided to add the facility of providing a user-customizable drive type — one in which you could enter the specific number of cylinders, heads, sectors, and other parameters of your specific drive. This method was okay for a few years, but it still could not keep up with larger drives. It also had users just as confused as before, if not more so, because the name of one parameter or the other did not match what the setup called it, or users could not remember if there was supposed to be more heads than cylinders or the other way around. Still, the custom drive type is useful, despite some limitations.

BIOS limits on drive size

The limitations encountered are that BIOS could not support more than 1,024 cylinders, or more than 16 heads, or more than 63 sectors per track. Thus, a drive with 1,201cylinders, or more than 16 heads, left users wondering what to do next. (Doing the arithmetic, 1,024 cylinders × 16 heads × 63 sectors × 512 bytes per sector results in 512MB.) Most of users just used the maximum of 1,024 cylinders at the expense of wasting a good portion of our drives to useless magnetic real estate. Additionally, early DOS versions could not handle larger drives either — so users were in a squeeze. After users had just overcome the 32MB partition limit with DOS Versions 3.x and less, with improved DOS 5.0, they were still stuck with the hardware limits.

Sometime in 1995 or 1996, manufacturers got wise and decided to expand the capabilities of the BIOS. BIOS vendors extended the maximum number of cylinders to at least 2,048, and the maximum number of heads to 63. Terrific — 2,048 cylinders × 63 heads × 63 sectors × 512 bytes per sector equals 4GB of capacity. Too bad DOS 5 and above, until Windows 95 (revision B) and NT came along, limited users to 2GB partitions.

Automatic drive detection

Although BIOS capabilities had improved for larger drives, users were still struggling to manually enter all of this information. Fortunately, the advances in disk drives had resulted in the IDE drive, which had much more smarts than previous drives, so the BIOS could also extend itself into doing automatic detection of disk drive parameters, saving users from much work and from many headaches. Computer users were truly coming into the age in which they could simply plug in a drive and almost be on their way without fooling around too much with numbers and system limitations.

Now BIOS can be set to auto-detect drives on any of four IDE interfaces and to set their parameters properly, even indicating the make and model of a drive, and what mode it could operate in along the way (thanks to the Read Drive ID command that returned all of this valuable information, and then some). But wait, there is more. Indeed, the BIOS would also present the method in which the drive parameters were being used. You could have Normal, Large, and Logical Block Addressing (LBA) modes for your drives. Most new disk drives with greater than 512MB capacity ended up in LBA mode. Older drives, but still larger than 512MB, ended up using Large mode.

Drive modes?

Yes, disk drives now have different modes of operation, actually two different types of modes. One mode relates to the way drives are addressed (how they finds different sectors on the disks), and the other mode relates to the maximum speed at which they are capable of transferring data.

As far as addressing, in addition to the numerical limitations of Normal mode's 1,024-cylinder-×-16-head-×-63-sector (CHS) configuration scheme, disks and BIOS waste a much time if they have to plow through the convolutions of figuring out which cylinder, head, and sector a block of data lives in. If you could address a block of data in one swoop without all the new math, things would be faster, so along came LBA mode. One big number and there you are—data. The BIOS and the drive handle the block or sector numbers between themselves, translating them and, thus, keeping DOS and such out of the picture. Large mode is used when a drive does not support the LBA process, but the drive has more cylinders, heads, or sectors than has a drive in Normal mode.

Now we come to a parameter we rarely see, data transfer mode, except on disk drive advertising or data sheets, but that we could select for ourselves as part of the disk drive interface parameters in setup. Normally, we let the BIOS automatically determine the data transfer mode selection when it discovers the other details about the disk drive at bootup. Letting the BIOS handle this automatically also reduces grief when configuring the system. Data transfer modes range from PIO modes 0 to 4, to DMA modes 0 to 2.

PIO stands for Programmed I/O mode, a mode in which the CPU has to handle each and every disk drive read or write operation, pretty much keeping system performance in the dark ages and slowing down operation. DMA stands for Direct Memory Access mode, where the drive interface and memory are allowed to talk freely among themselves without requiring time from the CPU, which is much more efficient.

Data transfer rates in PIO Mode 0 are equivalent to the old XT and AT hard drive — about 3.3 megabytes per second (MBps), which is fast, but not blazing. Mode 1 ups the transfer rate to 5.2 MBps, Mode 2 to 8.3 MBps, Mode 3 to 11.1 MBps, and Mode 4 to 16.6 MBps. In DMA Mode 0 the rate is a paltry 2.1 MBps, Mode 1 is 4.2 MBps, and Mode 2 is 8.3 MBps. In multiword DMA modes the rates are doubled. A new mode, UltraDMA33, has the capability to transfer data at a screaming 33 MBps. All these modes require that both the disk drive and the system board support the same modes. You cannot force a PIO Mode 2 drive to run at Mode 4 — the BIOS and drive intercommunications prevent this. If you could force the system to run faster than the drive, the transfers would be unreliable, and you would lose much data in the process.

Unfortunately, under DOS, Windows 3.*x*, 95, and 98 (and unlike Windows NT and most UNIX variants), the DMA modes are not significantly faster than the PIO modes because the operating system is still closely tied to the various file I/O operations in order to maintain file system compatibility. In reality, you will be lucky to see drive transfer rates exceed the Mode 2 rate with either a Mode 3, 4, or UltraDMA 33 drive running under Windows. Your best bet is to use a drive with the fastest average access or seek time available — with any time under 9–10 milliseconds usually being fast enough. These days, a 10–12 millisecond drive is considered slow.

Let the system do the work

All that said and done, once you figure out the correct combination of drive jumper settings that the system board and the BIOS need in order to recognize your drive (see Chapter 18), let the BIOS automatically do the drive detection and the setup. This is why it's there!

Enhanced features setup

To support all of the CPU, memory, I/O, and chip-set functions, the creators of the system BIOS have to keep up with a variety of new memory and I/O parameters to configure the PC system.

You may have found the documentation or built-in help for the enhanced setup features to be less than useful in helping you decide which settings are best or apply to your particular situation. Thus, we present in the following text information about these settings. All system boards do not have the same features or parameters, or equal access to features and parameters, so you should not be surprised if your system setup is missing one or more of these parameters.

Some system board manufacturers optimize these settings internally and do not let you access them. This allows the manufacturer some flexibility in limiting or providing different features based on who their customer (a PC system factory) is and how the customer wants some features set. To reduce technical support problems, some PC manufacturers might choose to limit the options available to end users.

Tip   Because of the wide variation among system, BIOS, system board, and chip-set manufacturers, you should assume the safest approach and not change settings that you are unfamiliar with or that do not pertain to the advice of a particular document or vendor's support representative. Although changing parameters may not damage components, trying to speed up the system data bus or memory operations too much may result in data and time loss, which is what you are trying to prevent in this context. If in doubt, use the BIOS and/or factory default settings.

Load BIOS defaults. This is a typical hot-key or menu selection that allows you to reset the parameters to those that the manufacturer has built into the BIOS. This would return the settings to those you would find if the system board was brand new. This option may get you out of serious trouble if you suspect that your configuration is messed up.

Load setup defaults. This is a typical hot-key or menu selection that enables you to reset the parameters to those that are optimum for the chip set on the system board. These may be the settings originally provided by the BIOS or settings modified and placed into the BIOS by the system board manufacturer. As with the load BIOS defaults, this setting may get you out of serious setup trouble.

IDE HDD automatic detection. This is a typical main menu selection that enables you to let the BIOS identify and set the parameters for IDE hard disk drives. This option can keep you from having to guess what your drive parameters should be. If you do not have the technical details indicating the number of cylinders, heads, or sectors per track for your hard drive, this is a helpful feature. If you have a SCSI hard drive, this selection will not work for your SCSI drive.

HDD low-level format. This is a typical main menu selection that enables you to low-level format your hard disk. This feature will erase all data from your hard disk and may make it unusable. Use this selection only if you really want to nuke the contents of your hard disk so that you can possibly repair or bypass bad sectors on your drive. This is not for SCSI drives.

Daylight savings time. This is a typical CMOS setup selection that lets the system clock automatically correct the system time when daylight savings time changes.

Error halt. This selection allows you to specify under what types of system errors you want to stop the system from booting up or from continuing to work any further without rebooting or correcting the problem.

Password setting. This selection allows you to configure a password that would be required to allow the system to boot up. Use this selection with care. If you forget your password, you will have to erase the CMOS memory or the system BIOS and reload it with a fresh, unconfigured version.

The next set of parameters applies to the Intel Triton chip set, but it may also apply to other chip sets with similar parameters.

DRAM precharge time. The number of CPU cycles the memory row address strobe (RAS) signal is allowed to charge before dynamic random access memory (DRAM) refreshes. The default setting is four clocks. Three may improve memory reliability but also slow the system slightly.

DRAM r/w timing. The number of CPU cycles allowed before DRAM may be read or written. The default setting is 8/7. 7/5 may improve memory transfers but also slow the CPU's processing slightly.

DRAM RAS to CAS delay. The delay time, in CPU cycles, between row address and column address signaling. The default setting is 3. A setting of 2 may improve memory speed at some risk to memory reliability.

DRAM read burst timing. Sets the timing of memory to CPU operations. Usually indicated as values of x2222, x3333, and x4444, representing the cycles allowed for each CPU/memory operation. The lower number allows faster memory addressing at some risk to memory operation reliability. x2222 is the default.

DRAM write burst timing. Sets the timing of memory to CPU operations. Usually indicated as values of x2222, x3333, and x4444, representing the cycles allowed for each CPU/memory operation. The lower number allows faster memory addressing at some risk to memory operation reliability. x3333 is the default.

System BIOS cached. Sets whether or not access to the system BIOS is cached or not. Can only be cached if the cache controller is enabled. This option speeds up system booting and some basic operations.

Video BIOS cached. Sets whether or not access to the video BIOS is cached or not. Can only be cached if the cache controller is enabled. This option can speed up video operations for DOS.

The next set of parameters covers some chip-set, PCI bus, and IDE disk drive interface features.

8-bit I/O recovery. Sets the number of CPU cycles that the CPU waits after the completion of an 8-bit I/O operation for data to be stable. Range is from 1–8 clocks. Default is 1.

16 bit I/O recovery. Sets the number of CPU cycles that the CPU waits after the completion of a 16-bit I/O operation for data to be stable. Range is from 1–4. Default is 1.

Memory hole at 15M-16M. Sets whether or not specific memory space can be reserved for ISA I/O devices. If enabled, it can improve performance if your system contains ISA I/O devices. The default is disabled.

IDE block mode. Sets whether or not fast block mode data transfers are allowed for IDE drives. The default enables this. The BIOS will negotiate the use of this mode with your disk drive.

IDE 32-bit transfer mode. Sets whether or not 32-bit transfer mode is enabled for IDE drives. The default enables this. The BIOS will also negotiate the use of this mode with your disk drive.

IDE PIO mode. Sets the programmed I/O mode for IDE drives, Modes 1–4. Not all drives support all modes, and this mode is selected for each drive in the system. Default is AUTO, which allows the BIOS to detect which mode a drive supports.

The next set of parameters covers system power-management features:

Power management. One of four power-management methods may be selected. Within each method are timings related to which modes (Doze, Standby, Suspend, and HDD power down) are implemented.

- ✦ **Disabled.** The default.
- ✦ **Minimum.** The timings for which devices are shut down are system dependent.
- ✦ **Maximum.** The timings for which devices are shut down are system dependent (for SL CPUs only).
- ✦ **User defined.** The timings for which devices are shut down. This is set by the user, as indicated in the following text.

These parameters control various power management features:

PM control APM. Allows for power management to stop the CPU clock. Default is No. Many CPUs in current use do not support this feature.

Video off mode. Selects the method used to reduce power consumption in the video system by either turning off the video sync lines or blanking the screen after a predetermined or set amount of time.

Doze mode. Enables the power management feature to slow down the CPU clock to reduce power drain after a predetermined or set amount of time.

Standby mode. Enables the power-management feature to shut off the hard drive and blank the video to reduce power drain after a predetermined or set amount of time.

Suspend mode. Enables the power management feature to shut off all devices, except the CPU, after a predetermined or set amount of time.

HDD power down. Enables the power management feature to shut off the hard drive after a predetermined or set amount of time.

Power down activities. Enables you to select which activities are monitored to prevent system power management from disabling various system features if the system is in use.

The next set of parameters is specific to the PCI bus and PCI devices:

PCI concurrency. Sets whether or not more than one PCI device can be active at a time. Default enables this. Overall PCI operations for the entire system will be faster with this on.

PCI streaming. Sets whether or not PCI data transfers occur in small or large blocks, either without bothering the CPU. Default enables this. Individual PCI data transfer will be faster, but other devices may not be able to use the PCI bus as efficiently.

PCI bursting. Sets whether or not a PCI device can transfer large blocks of data in short bursts. Default enables this. This speeds PCI data transfers.

Slot *x* using Int #. This parameter exists for each PCI slot and is used to select which PCI interrupt is being used by the slot. The range for this setting is A–D, and the default setting is AUTO for all slots, unless a particular slot needs more than one PCI interrupt. Note that PCI interrupts are different from ISA IRQ lines, but a PCI device may also use an ISA IRQ line for compatibility.

Available IRQ. This parameter exists for each listed ISA IRQ and is used to select which PCI interrupt is matched to ISA IRQs. The default setting is NA (not available) for all IRQs, which means that the interrupt is not available to the PCI bus. Note that PCI interrupts are different from ISA IRQ lines, but a PCI device may also use an ISA IRQ line for compatibility, as needed.

PCI IRQ activated by. PCI interrupts may be triggered by ISA-type interrupt signals (called Edge, indicating that they may be detected for only a short time) or EISA-type interrupt signals (called Level, indicating that they are present until cleared by the system or the device). The default is Level.

PCI IDE IRQ map to. This parameter enables you to configure the type of IDE adapter you are using. By default, the setting is PCI Auto to let the system determine this automatically. You may select a specific IRQ for a primary or secondary IDE adapter. Typically, this is IRQ14 for the primary adapter and IRQ15 for the secondary adapter.

Depending on your system or BIOS brand, or version of BIOS, a variety of other settings may be available to you. These include the following, listed in generic names:

Memory wait states. This parameter allows you to configure the number of wait states the CPU holds off before accepting RAM data as valid for reading or writing data into RAM. This has to do with the RAM timing specifications and speed of the system. If you are using marginal, 80-nanosecond RAM chips in a system that should have 70-nanosecond chips, you may find the system operates faster or more reliably with a setting of 1 or 2 wait states. The same applies for a system with 70-nanosecond RAM but should have 60-nanosecond RAM installed.

Memory parity checking. This parameter enables you to set whether or not the system checks for memory parity errors. Most systems and chip sets are designed for memory parity checking. Turning it off in setup may not completely disable the parity circuitry, yielding false parity errors when you know you have nonparity RAM installed. The Intel Triton chip set does not provide parity checking. If in doubt, always use RAM with the parity bit and do not mix parity and nonparity RAM, unless the system board documentation specifically states that you may.

Memory refresh. This parameter may not be shown exactly as indicated here, but it relates to the period of time between memory refresh cycles. The standard refresh time for most DRAM is 15 microseconds. Some RAM need not be refreshed more often than every 125 microseconds, enabling higher performance in some systems. Setting this for the longer time can cause memory reliability problems if your RAM does not support the longer refresh timing. Memory refresh is absolutely necessary, but it occupies critical (but nearly invisible) CPU time.

####-#### ROM cacheable region. A parameter such as this may be present and apply to specific regions of memory between 640K and 1,024K (the upper memory region) that are used for video and disk adapter ROM-BIOS and the system BIOS. This means that an adapter's BIOS contents can be cached into faster DRAM for higher performance. This provides a similar but different performance advantage to features provided by memory managers that move, stealth, or otherwise place BIOS ROM contents into DRAM. Usually, this caching feature provides the best performance advantage. Stealthing of ROM contents is more effective at making more upper memory available for loading device drivers and TSRs into high memory.

ISA bus speed. In many systems it is possible to set the relative speed of the I/O bus proportionate to the CPU speed. The ISA bus is specified with a standard 8 MHz speed, but if you are using newer I/O devices, you may be able to increase this speed to 10, 12, 16 MHz, or higher. I/O (and thus, often disk data integrity, if using a plug-in disk adapter) may be less reliable at higher speeds. You can experiment with this setting to see what works best or worst for your system and its components. But be aware that data may be lost, or your system may lock up at higher speeds.

8/16-bit DMA wait states. These parameters, one for 8-bit DMA and one for 16-bit DMA, set the number of cycles that data read or write operations are delayed after addressing a location in RAM for DMA operations so that the data is ready and stable for the transfer. Fewer wait states can result in less reliable DMA operations because the memory may not be ready when data is to be read or written. More wait states can slow performance.

Security features. There may be any number of options available that provide user security at system bootup or that provide recovery after power management turns off a particular device. If you set up password protection on your system, be aware that you may only be able to recover from a forgotten password by completely resetting the system parameters to their factory default values, losing valuable time and possibly losing data if you set one or more parameters improperly.

Software or semiautomatic I/O device configurations

New I/O and setup options resolve much of the legendary technical complexity with jumpers, switches, and setup programs. There have been several attempts to produce what are called, for lack of a better term, soft configured I/O devices, or I/O devices that do not have DIP switches and jumper settings to configure I/O addresses and IRQ settings. These devices use setup programs that are shipped with and specific to the I/O card, and they provide menu-driven or automatic detection and setup routines to help you get them to work.

Intel, 3Com, National Semiconductor, and various offshore manufacturers of network cards, modems, and I/O ports have attempted, with varying degrees of success, to simplify the addition of new hardware into legacy PC systems (that is, PC systems that do not have fully integrated I/O devices on the system board or that do not support current PnP specifications). In most cases, the automatic configuration program works well, and you end up with no conflicts between these devices and the ones that were already in your system. Still, there are times when you have to forget the automatic process and delve into manual settings, this time from a menu of I/O settings, rather than from a handful of microscopic address switches or pins.

VESA local bus and PCI systems do not provide the same configuration difficulties as other devices because these I/O devices should be supported in the bus systems and the system BIOS. However, you may still have to configure some PCI information in comparison to similar ISA information for some ports.

The familiar complexities of switch and jumper settings are being addressed in several ways. Many vendors are developing add-in cards that are software configurable. These cards are shipped with a default and hopefully with nonconflicting preconfiguration, as well as with a device-specific installation and setup program. These specific setup programs will attempt to determine what addresses and settings are already in use in your system, and they automatically reprogram the new device with nonconflicting settings.

Plug and Play

Plug and Play (PnP) is an industry-wide development to detect and configure PC system components with no user intervention required. It is a global effort to keep the technical details of a PC system out of sight and make the technical details easier to manage. It is a considerable advancement from EISA, Micro Channel, and interim soft-configured (items configured by programs rather than switch or jumper settings) devices. PnP takes into account old and new devices, it is better designed in new chip sets, new I/O features, and system boards, and it is critical to the success of advanced operating systems, such as Windows 95/98/Me, Windows NT/2000, and OS/2. PnP is also an integral part of PCI systems and devices because PowerPCs and other systems that are designed to use PCI-compatible devices already have some form of "Plug-and-Play" BIOS or operating system. Often fondly referred to as "Plug and Pray" because in the early phases of implementation PnP did not always work completely for all systems and all devices. In other words, the goals have not yet been met.

PnP is a multilevel standard. It encompasses the PC system BIOS, all hardware devices, and the operating system. For PnP to work as designed (that is, to save users from the hassles of myriad technical details when changing add-in devices), all pieces of a system must be capable of communicating with and responding to PnP operations. The BIOS must help support the gathering of all existing peripheral configuration data, as well as allow an operating system or configuration utility to change the system's peripheral configuration as necessary so that new plug-in devices can be fit into the system to avoid configuration conflicts.

As PnP is introduced, as more systems begin to support it, and until all legacy or ISA devices disappear, PnP must maintain backward compatibility with ISA devices. No one intends for you to throw away all of your existing peripherals and I/O cards, at least not right away. Although this might be good for the profits of many PC companies, it is impractical and unrealistic. Thus, for now, you may keep your multi-I/O cards, favorite internal modems, video cards, and disk controllers, and you may rely on PnP to be aware of and continue to support most of these devices, at least until they are a minor segment of the PC market.

This means that implementing PnP is no small task for programmers and hardware designers. Everyone has to be aware of the numerous devices that cannot be changed electronically through software, and they also must be aware that many devices cannot be configured outside of a limited range of addresses, IRQ assignments, and DMA assignments.

PnP can be confused by some of the early soft-configured devices, and they in turn may be confused by PnP operations. In some cases, you will find it best to disable PnP support for a particular device and configure it the old-fashioned way, by the numbers, even if those numbers appear in a program's menu instead of being represented in the form of switches and jumpers. Here is where being familiar with the original standards of PC device configuration can be a great help because most software still uses only normal, everyday DOS devices and configurations, which PnP should strive to maintain, as well.

When Plug and Play Really Isn't

Beware, many hardware and software vendors abuse the term *Plug and Play* and disguise that their products are not truly PnP compatible by burying the term in marketing and sales dialog. Anything not specifically labeled "Plug and Play" is probably *not* truly a PnP compatible device.

Here are examples of phrases that abuse the PnP concept and mislead buyers:

✦ Features plug and play

✦ A Plug-and-Play Flatbed Scanner

✦ Plug-and-play simplicity

✦ Plug & Play

✦ Plug'n Play

Note that few, if any, instances of misuse specifically use either PnP or Plug and Play. There are no standards for print advertisement or for what is called *box copy* on product packaging. Thus the appearance of the phrasing is subtle. If a device has Microsoft's "Designed for Windows *xx*" logo on it, and it claims "Plug and Play," it must truly be a compliant device. Even the press can get it wrong, as you can see by following some of the links that show up after searching for "Plug and Play" at www.yahoo.com.

A true PnP-compatible device will almost never run you through a hardware parameter or port setup program, refer you to switch settings, or do much of anything but show you a "Windows has found a new device and is installing the software for it" message when you restart Windows 95/98/Me.

Note   When the PC's operating software identifies its own devices, rather than having you take the cover off and check switches and jumpers, the installation of new operating systems and applications software will be significantly easier. You will have to know less about the technical details of your system, and you will be better able to enjoy the functions and features of the system and its application programs. We all look forward to that day (meaning it has not quite yet arrived).

How Plug and Play works . . . or does not

PnP is one of many half-fulfilled promises of technological advancement. PnP is a good idea, and works reasonably well, if initially you know how to make it work right and if you know how to make it work right again, if you need to change something later on. For PnP to be of value you need PnP hardware, a PnP-compatible PC system BIOS, and a PnP-compatible operating system, such as Windows 95/98/Me/NT/2000 or OS/2.

In our discussion of PnP we will focus on Windows 95/98/Me/NT/2000 because OS/2 has made it a little easier to deal with some of the hardware device settings than has the Windows Registry.

The concept behind PnP is that the PnP code in BIOS can detect which devices are installed and the resources they use. Devices designed for it can report the system resources (IRQ, DMA, I/O, and BIOS address ranges) that they can use when they are to be installed. The BIOS then determines a set of available resource settings that the new devices can use, and it sets up the devices with the determined settings.

This is a relatively sound process, especially if you plan ahead. First, add your non-PnP devices. Hold off installing PnP devices until you have the old devices working correctly, if possible. Adding your PnP devices after this process should produce working results without much hassle. Unfortunately, if you need to go back into the system and add a legacy, non-PnP device, or even a PnP device that would normally use ISA assignments, the PnP detection and configuration process may make erroneous assignments. On the other hand, devices on your motherboard or adapter cards that are not used, such as a secondary IDE interface, may occupy resources that they will not use. Even if you disable the interface in the BIOS setup, PnP may detect the interface, not determine if there are devices attached to the interface, and assign resources that you may need for another device.

Worse, you generally cannot intervene in this process and reconfigure a device after it is installed. Whether or not you can change the settings on a PnP device depends on how the device is designed, how the driver is loaded, and what Windows 95/98/Me make available for configuration options in the Control Panel ⇨ System ⇨ Device Manager resource settings dialog box for the device.

IRQ assignments are probably the biggest headaches in arranging a combined ISA/PnP system configuration. There are so few IRQ signals available and so many devices that want them. You should establish proper legacy/ISA assignments for COM, LPT, and built-in disk drive adapters before working on other devices.

Because having a video display is one of the prerequisites to doing almost anything with your PC (in other words being able to see what is going on is a prerequisite to being able to setup your PC), PnP logic allows some preference for the types of devices that can or will be configured first. Otherwise, devices are left to fight for first position in a random race of "who gets the resources." Some video adapters aggressively rob IRQ assignments that they may not actually need, except for a few, unique programs. This can complicate establishing the assignments you might want or need for other devices.

How you can make Plug and Play work

The only sure way to configure a combined ISA and PnP system is to follow these guidelines:

1. Remove all PnP devices that are not required to boot your system. You may have to leave in your PnP-compatible video card, but if you have had conflicts with it and you have an old ISA video adapter, use the old non-PnP ISA card until everything else is configured. (The object here is to let the aggressive cards worry about whatever resources are left as the last steps. They will hopefully find other resources already taken and avoid them.)

2. Properly configure and install all legacy/ISA devices first, including devices built onto the system board and configured in system setup.

3. If you are already in system setup (if not, get there), you should invoke the one-time selection for PCI/PnP options to reset PnP configuration settings. This will clear the system's memory of prior PnP reserved settings so that you can establish a new configuration.

4. Restart your system to let it adjust to the proper legacy device settings. (After you start installing PnP devices, you may have to repeat this PnP reset and restart process a few times as you add PnP devices, in case you have to make manual changes to non-PnP devices to accommodate a newly added PnP device. However, do not invoke the PnP reset feature after you have invoked it on the most finicky device, or you may have to start over.)

5. Install any common non-PnP ISA or PnP devices, such as sound cards, that have relatively standard (de facto) IRQ and DMA settings. Reboot your system after each card is installed and then repeat Step 4 until you have no more legacy and standard cards to install.

6. Install any common non-PnP ISA or PnP devices that may have particular legacy significance, such as NE2000-compatible network cards.

 Note Truly NE2000-compatible (or really old) cards do not allow you to use just any address/IRQ combination. Repeat Steps 4 and 5, and then skip to Step 7.

7. Install either your PnP-compatible SCSI or video card (you may have to start this process with a non-PnP video adapter). Go to Steps 4 and 5, and then finish or come back to this step and install more PnP devices. Heed Step 8.

8. Do not reset the PnP configuration in system setup once you have a particular device set the way you want it. Instead, let the devices and the operating system work out the remaining resource assignments as best they are able.

Each time you reset the PnP configuration, Windows 95/98/Me will rediscover and reinstall many devices, leaving you with a messy trail of devices in the Registry. You may not see that trail in the Device Manager under normal operation unless you dig around with the Windows RegEdit program or view the device tree when running in Safe Mode. (This, and any driver files left behind, is where some system information and driver update profiling information programs get their erroneous lists of installed devices.)

If this sounds like the old trial-and-error, switch-or-jumper-setting game you have grown to hate, you have seen the point. COM ports 1–4, LPT ports 1–3, and the primary and secondary disk drive adapters should almost never end up with assignments out of the ordinary. Beyond these devices, PnP ignores almost all of the de facto and classic device setup resources, except for the originally specified legacy/ISA devices from IBM. Network cards, sound cards, SCSI host adapters, and anything newer than known IBM-PC/AT devices seem to be left to fend for themselves, despite the huge quantities of common devices, such as NE2000 network cards and Sound Blaster-compatible cards in use before PnP came about. When you change one of your adapters for a newer model, you will find yourself in this same reconfiguration battle.

We look forward to a future in which PnP really works. This would make technical support and inventory management (for companies and network supervisors) more effective, and less invasive of your time and productivity. Utility and diagnostic software would help you more, and your software should encounter fewer problems with various hardware devices. These developments will save everyone precious time and money. Your local PC technician and your PC-expert friends might feel like the proverbial Maytag repairman.

Further developments are placing more of this automation directly on the hardware devices. With these new boards and, eventually, more support in the system BIOS and programs that use the devices, you will be able to unwrap a new device, install it, turn on the system, and then watch the device configure itself, report through the system BIOS what it is, what it is set for, or what settings it has changed to work properly alongside other devices. PnP is but one such effort. Smarter, faster, and simpler serial port connections and devices are under development. Hardware and software vendors, in order to support many easier methods of installing and upgrading systems, are adopting new standards.

System management features

System management, or managed PC systems, are becoming more important to organizations supporting a few hundred to many thousands of systems. System management can involve the simplest collection and reporting of system information for inventory or basic support purposes, for verification, for remote configuration, and even for software auditing and upgrading. While not specifically a feature provided by a system board, the system board, as the heart of and a significant piece of the system, is one place where system management support must begin, and it does so as part of the BIOS.

This support is relatively simple to provide — add a bit of additional software code to the BIOS to enable it to report, if not also accept, configuration information from a system management tool. These tools involve at least one program or part of the operating system at the user's desktop that can communicate with one or more master control centers throughout a network.

To many users, this can appear to be an implementation of Big Brother keeping an eye on you. And in some ways, it is. But the system management capability itself is not as intrusive or devious as you might think. If you had invested several millions of dollars on the 5,000–10,000 PCs in a company, you would probably want to know that they were all accounted for and working properly. There are far worse things undesirables can do than just learn what type of hard drive you have, whether or not your system is in sleep mode, or what type of video card is in your system.

The real desire and value in managed systems is in the time and cost saving possible with improved help-desk or technical-support performance. With a well-designed and implemented system management program, someone can immediately identify your PC system, determine its configuration and health, and dispatch the proper parts and tools to keep it running correctly — often without you being there and certainly without bothering you with all sorts of technical details. Although system management functionality is not yet deployed widely for the general public or by all those vendors from whom you may eventually need technical support, many have tried and still work with it. The benefits are available, and eventually will save everyone time and money. We discuss more about networking and remotely communicating between systems in Chapters 10 and 11, but for now we want to just mention two essential pieces to the overall supportability of your system — Desktop Management Interface and Enhanced system configuration data.

Desktop Management Interface

Desktop Management Interface (DMI) is an emerging standard for detecting, recording, and sharing computer system configuration information. The DMI specification calls for methods of detecting hardware installed in the system, specifies how the information will be stored and formatted for transmission, specifies the development or programming interface tools for reading or writing this information, and determines whether the system is to update particular programs and configurations.

A DMI-compliant system, typically by virtue of DMI features in the BIOS, accepts information requests from DMI applications, and it reports system configurations in the DMI format back to the requesting application. Without DMI specific tools, minimal DMI data is stored only temporarily in system memory.

Enhanced system configuration data

Many new system boards, PnP, DMI, and other system management features, may be supported by *Enhanced System Configuration Data* (ESCD). ESCD is a small record of the current system configuration extracted from the standard system setup and PnP information. It is stored in a small portion of upper memory (typically in a region between disk and system BIOS) and may also be stored to a disk file or the CMOS RAM, if the system tools support it. The presence of ESCD is dependent on support for it in the system BIOS. There is typically no user interaction with or visibility to this data without advanced development tools for use in the process of creating system management software.

System Board Problems

As system boards include more I/O functions, PC systems actually begin to exist on a single board. Because few, if any, components, except the CPU, cache RAM, and SIMMs, can be moved from one board to another, complete replacement of a defective system board is usually the most economical and time-saving solution, and it is an opportunity to upgrade your system, as well. Having covered system board and CPU basics, we now take a look at their related problems.

Bootup and lock-up problems

Here is how to recognize and resolve bootup and lock-up problems:

Symptoms

▶ System does nothing at startup.

▶ System suddenly hangs up.

▶ Windows will not run.

▶ System reboots when you try to run or exit from Windows.

Suspects

▶ CPU clock speed is set too fast for the CPU.

▶ Temperature is too high.

▶ Defective CPU chip.

▶ Defective CPU support chips/chip set.

▶ Defective external cache chips.

▶ Defective RAM chips/SIMMs.

▶ Defective system board.

▶ Defective power supply.

Solutions

▶ Run diagnostics to verify CPU, memory, and other components.

▶ Reduce the clock speed by deactivating turbo mode and then replace the CPU clock with a slower unit (change from 66 to 60 MHz, 66 to 50 MHz, 50 to 40 or 33 MHz, and so on).

▶ Check additional CMOS setup parameters for possible increases in wait state settings or for reduction in bus or CPU speed settings.

▶ If you cannot find temperature problems with the system case open, run diagnostics with test logging on, starting from a cold system until it warms up or until a failure occurs.

▶ Remove add-in cards that are not essential to system bootup (leave in the disk and video adapters) and retest the system.

▶ Be sure that the air vents are not blocked.

▶ Remove excessive dust from the chassis and power supply.

▶ Replace the CPU.

▶ Replace memory chips.

▶ Replace or upgrade the system BIOS.

▶ Replace the system board.

Some Intel 80386DX and early Pentium chips have bugs that affect multiplication functions. Many bulletin board systems have a small program that identifies this problem, and some diagnostic programs identify it, as well

Tip   Look for keywords "386" and "multiply" when searching for these files.

If you encounter difficulty when trying to run Windows or other multitasking programs, and you have an Intel 80486DX-33 or DX-50 CPU, your CPU chip might be defective. Remove the CPU chip, note all numbers on the top and underside of the CPU, and contact Intel customer service for a possible replacement. Decreasing the system to a speed of 25-MHz for the DX-33 or 40 MHz for the DX-50 may enable the CPU to function, if you cannot get a replacement CPU chip.

System and application speed problems

Let us take a look at some common speed problems with your system and application.

Symptoms

▶ Games and programs run too fast.

▶ Time-out errors from applications.

▶ Divide-by-zero errors.

Suspects

▶ Program was designed before the 8 MHz IBM PC-AT.

▶ Program uses CPU/software timing versus hardware timing methods.

▶ Program configuration settings are wrong.

▶ You have an enhanced CPU or math chip.

▶ You have a fast CPU that may be too fast for some situations.

Solutions

▶ Check the program configuration.

▶ Disable system turbo mode in CMOS setup or with the turbo button.

▶ Use a slow-down program (such as SLOWDOWN or SLOWAT) before running the application.

▶ Get an upgrade for the application program.

Note

Programmers often use software calculations to affect timing of events. If a programmer does not take into account higher-speed CPUs and faster instruction execution, and if the programmer compensates for this with internal corrections in the software, the calculations will execute faster and the program will run too fast (for example, animated characters run instead of walk, or in a video game you cannot fire a weapon at the characters quickly enough) or you will get a fatal divide-by-zero error that will crash your program. Enhanced CPUs (such as those from AMD and Cyrix) also execute some functions faster and can cause a similar problem.

System board-related memory problems

This section focuses on memory problems related to the system board.

Symptoms

▶ Memory size error (AT).

▶ Not enough memory (PC and XT).

▶ Two short beeps, error message 2xx, or both (PC, XT, and AT).

▶ "Parity Check 1 or 2," or "Parity Check ?????" message.

▶ System hangs up.

Suspects

▶ Loose memory chips or card (PC, XT, and AT)

▶ Improper CMOS setup (AT)

▶ Improper switch setting (PC, XT, and AT)

▶ Bad memory chip(s) or card (PC, XT, and AT)

▶ Defective add-on memory card

▶ Improper mix of memory chip types or speeds

Solutions

▶ Reseat the memory chips in their sockets.

▶ Remove and reseat the memory cards.

▶ Check the CMOS setup (AT).

▶ Check the switch settings (PC, XT, and AT).

▶ Replace the memory chips or card.

▶ Replace dissimilar chip types.

Math chip problems

This section focuses on problems with your math chip.

Symptoms

▶ Error message "Coprocessor not found."

▶ Application failure.

▶ Hardware lock up.

▶ Diagnostics fail or do not show math coprocessor interrupt.

Suspects

▶ Software does not recognize the coprocessor.

▶ System does not recognize the coprocessor.

▶ Coprocessor is not seated properly in the socket on the motherboard or is in the wrong position.

▶ Coprocessor socket is short-circuiting with the motherboard, or the socket itself is bad.

▶ Coprocessor has a broken pin.

▶ System board does not support or provide a hardware interrupt line for the NPU.

Solutions

▶ Check system setup. (Refer to your owner's manual for CMOS or DIP switch settings.)

▶ Check your application software setup to see if it provides a math-chip selection.

▶ Make sure the coprocessor is aligned with the socket properly. (Refer to the owner's manual.)

▶ Turn off system to let the coprocessor chip cool down. (Check system ventilation, fans, and cable routing for possible causes of poor cooling.)

Some manufacturers do not provide circuitry to support the interrupt request line between the math chip and the system board because the circuitry is not required. As a result, any tests for the NPU interrupt will fail. However, if other aspects of your system are running fine and there are no other math problems, your system is okay.

If you have a Weitek math chip instead of an Intel-compatible chip, some software will not recognize or use it. Conversely, if your software requires or is configured for a Weitek chip and you have an Intel chip, change the chip or software configuration, if possible.

Clock problems

The following are indicators that you have clock problems, and ways to resolve them.

Symptoms

▶ Date and time are wrong, fast, or slow.

▶ CMOS/clock battery does not last more than a few days or weeks (expected life is one to five years).

▶ Error messages 01x, 02x, 102, 103, 161, 162, 163, 164, 199, or 17xx occur.

▶ Long beep at startup, followed by previous messages.

▶ CMOS RAM error.

▶ Memory size error.

▶ Disk drive configuration error (drive not found, no boot device available, or similar messages).

Suspects

▶ CMOS/clock battery.

▶ Defective CMOS RAM device.

▶ Amount of memory has changed.

▶ Disk drive changed or disconnected.

Solutions

▶ Replace CMOS clock battery (available at most electronic and computer stores).

▶ Replace system board battery circuit (refer to a technician).

▶ Replace defective clock or CMOS RAM chip (replacement is easy if these are in a plug-in Dallas module).

In many systems the CMOS and clock operate from the main power supply when the system is turned on, instead of just a battery. In these cases the battery and the main power supply are isolated from each other with a small diode component. Often a technician can find, check, and replace this part quickly. See Figure 14-6 for the location of the CMOS battery.

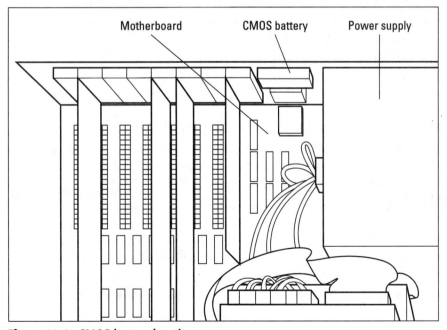

Figure 14-6: CMOS battery location

System board-related keyboard problems

The following Symptoms, Suspects, and Solutions section discusses keyboard problems related to the system board.

Symptoms

▶ Keyboard is locked or inactive.

▶ System prompts for a password.

▶ Keyboard error message at startup.

▶ Keyboard errors during testing.

Suspects

▶ CMOS setup

▶ Old or wrong keyboard BIOS

▶ Bad keyboard cable or connections

Solutions

▶ Check and set proper parameters for the keyboard in the CMOS setup.

▶ If unable to access CMOS setup, disable the CMOS battery or replace the CMOS chip.

▶ Update the keyboard BIOS chip (an Intel 8042 chip, often labeled AMI) to match your system BIOS and system board.

▶ Replace the keyboard BIOS, the keyboard, or both.

▶ Replace the keyboard cable.

System board-configuration problems

New system board and I/O card designs bring about the potential for a few newer problems than we have experienced with simpler PCs and ISA devices. Some problems may seem more obscure, until you identify what bus and I/O device types your system has so that you can work through either plain ISA or enhanced-system type problems.

Symptoms

▶ System or software does not recognize an I/O or add-in device.

▶ Unable to configure or use network card, modem, or disk adapter.

▶ System locks up when network or disk drivers are loaded.

▶ System locks up when a communications or mouse program is loaded.

▶ PCI devices are not detected or will not configure properly.

▶ PnP devices are not detected or will not configure properly.

Suspects

▶ PCI configuration in setup allowing PCI devices to use the same resources as an ISA device.

▶ A PnP device exists that does not fully support PnP version 1.0A or higher.

▶ System BIOS version is not compliant with the PnP version 1.0A or higher specification.

▶ A soft-configured device is conflicting with PnP functions.

▶ A PnP device is conflicting with other soft-configuration program functions.

Solutions

▶ Upgrade system BIOS to one that supports PnP 1.0A or higher specification.

▶ Replace non-PnP, soft-configured devices with a PnP device.

▶ Upgrade PnP device to one that supports PnP 1.0A or higher specification.

▶ Disable PnP support for older PnP device, and configure it manually.

▶ Disable PCI configuration and disable use of one or more ISA IRQ assignments.

Watch the system display during startup and note the amount of memory found or being tested. If it differs from the amount you know is in the system or from the switch or CMOS settings, you will not have access to all of the memory in your system.

System board troubleshooting and diagnostics

The solutions presented in the previous section should cover the common problems you may encounter with a system board. Some problems might not be as obvious as the items indicate. You might instead see unpredictable errors or lock ups at random times, and you might need to dig deeper than the BIOS or common applications allow. For the less-obvious problems, you will probably have to invest some time and perhaps a modest amount of money to buy and to use a set of diagnostic software that enables you to test the system board under known conditions.

The troubleshooting guidelines provided in Chapter 1 should help you understand and perform the typical trial-and-error and process-of-elimination methods necessary to isolate certain problems. Combined with a proper set of diagnostic tests, you can further qualify your efforts and arrive at a solution more economically in terms of both time and money. Do not forget to check related functions and the I/O boards because their operation directly or indirectly affects the CPU and support circuits, as well.

If you need to test your system board, there are many functions that a diagnostic software package should test and reveal. Some software packages merely indicate that they are either testing the system board as a whole unit or that they are testing various functions without giving you technical specifics.

The PC-Doctor program provided with the CD-ROM included with this book will give you most of the tests and information you need.

Even if you are not a technically oriented PC user, you still might want to know that everything possible is being tested. Then, you will know what to fix or what to ask a service person to fix (and you can be sure that the right repairs were done). Without much technical detail, the following list shows the functions that should be tested and reported for your system board, without consideration for the extra functions that are covered in other chapters.

✦ **CPU test**. To be sure all modes of operation are working correctly.

   1. Flags and registers: 8-bit functions (8088, 8086, v20, and v30), 16-bit functions (80286), and 32-bit functions (80386, 80486SX, DX, DX2, Pentium).

   2. Integer mathematics.

   3. Internal cache (80486DX and Pentium).

   4. External cache (80486DX and Pentium), if supported for your chip set.

✦ **CPU interface data paths**. To be sure that I/O and support signals reach the CPU properly.

✦ **Interrupt controller**. To ensure that this CPU interface receives correct clock and I/O signals.

✦ **Interval timer (18Hz/55mSec timer tick)**. To ensure that this "heartbeat" clock is operating correctly.

✦ **Refresh interval (30uSec standard.** To verify that memory is refreshed properly.

Some manufacturers "steal" a small amount of time from this function in an attempt to increase CPU performance. If this test fails, you might experience data loss in your memory with some combinations of memory chips and system speeds.

✦ **CMOS setup RAM**. To ensure that your CMOS setup data is stored safely.

✦ **Clock/Calendar**. A check of the stability of the DOS clock versus the CMOS clock. They should match within tenths of a second and not drift off faster or slower. Drift, or instability, means your system date and time settings could change unpredictably during the day.

✦ **DMA transfer**. A check of the data transfer between I/O devices and memory, without the CPU's help.

✦ **Math chip**. To verify this microprocessor's complex math calculations.

✦ **PC speaker**. Makes sure that your speaker beeps when it is supposed to and tests other timers in the same chip that make the beep.

✦ **Bus tests (EISA, MicroChannel, and PCI)**. These I/O interfaces provide special functions that must work properly in order for data to transfer correctly.

Summary

Even without knowing a tremendous amount of detail about how computers work, you should still be able to appreciate the significance of how much your system board does for your PC. As you look beyond the system board to the various devices attached to your system, you will begin to see how almost everything in a computer links to everything else through the system board and its functions.

At one time, the system board was the second or third most expensive part of a computer. Now, one chip or a single-function add-in card, such as a video card or disk controller, costs much more and does almost as much as a system board.

In Chapter 15, we'll cover Memory.

✦　　✦　　✦

System Memory

Your computer cannot work without sufficient functioning memory. Your CPU uses memory to get its instructions. Programs loaded into the memory from your hard drive or other resource also use memory to store temporary data; device adapters use memory for their control programs; and the operating system and other programs (remember, they are also occupying memory) use memory to hold data while displaying information, sending information to your printer, receiving keystrokes, and working with your mouse. Memory is also used by the video display system to store images on their way to your display screen and it appears on the system board and some add-in cards to hold specific control programs. Memory also buffers data on its way to and from your disk drives, acting as a disk cache and acting as a virtual or emulated disk drive, holding inbound or outbound serial communication data, and much more. Your computer makes use of a lot of different types of memory.

If you are using Windows 9x , NT/2000, OS/2 or Unix, you may find this chapter interesting more from a historical perspective than to help with your memory configuration. These newer operating systems perform the majority of memory configuration and management without much user interaction. However, understanding the history of the installation, configuration, and use of memory in your PC may come in handy. It may help you to understand that a problem might have a simple solution in the way you use your system or to identify the need to increase memory or allocate your virtual memory.

If you are using DOS, Windows 3.*x,* or one of the newer operating systems with some old programs using these older operating systems in a different partition, you should continue reading this chapter to get to the heart of configuring and managing your computer's memory.

Programs and data are available to your PC's CPU only if contained in memory. It takes several kinds of memory to make a working system, including read-only memory (ROM) and random access memory (RAM).

The first memory your computer encounters when you turn on your system is the ROM BIOS (read-only memory, basic input/output system) that contains the Power-On Self-Test (POST). The POST is described in Chapter 8 and in Appendix A. One of its tasks is to determine how much memory is installed in your computer. Then the system encounters the RAM memory used for the operating system and applications. As your system continues to start and you begin to work with it, many other types and configurations of memory are used, created, and managed. We will first define the different types of memory chips, then discuss different types of memory uses, memory addressing, adding memory, then configuring and using memory for different purposes.

Memory Types

There are many kinds of memory or data storage on your PC system. These include the well-known system random access memory (or RAM) that DOS and Windows use, the CMOS RAM that your system setup parameters use, and the read-only memory (or ROM) that stores your system, disk, and video BIOS to the disk drives. Your system RAM is and can be configured and used for a multitude of different purposes, which we will explore. Your disk drive serves virtual memory functions beyond being just a repository for programs and data.

Read-only memory

Read-only memory is memory, as the name implies, that the system can only read. Using special devices at a factory, data is put into a ROM chip and is not meant to be changed. The data is stored in a matrix of cells that respond to electrical impulses to program, or put data into, the chip, and there it stays. Some types of ROM can be erased with ultraviolet light, and then have new data written to them. For our purpose, the data in ROM chips is permanent — that is, when you turn off your PC, the ROM will not lose its contents.

Note

In other chapters, you probably noticed terms such as ROM BIOS (the basic input/output system, which gives your PC the capability to communicate with the outside world) and Adapter ROM (such as that on a video or disk adapter card, which holds program information that lets your PC work with that device). The ROM in your system contains both programs and data, which are permanently installed and required by the system when the power is turned on. The Power-On Self-Test (POST) is one of the programs stored in ROM.

Except for some special types of memory, such as the battery backed-up CMOS RAM memory used to store your computer's configuration, ROM is not used for storing your data permanently. It exists to serve the device it is built onto.

EGA and VGA video adapter cards contain ROM to hold the BIOS program that controls the functions of the display. Most disk drive adapters contain ROM holding the BIOS program that controls disk drive parameters and data I/O to allow your computer to boot up and run programs. Some network cards may also contain a ROM chip that holds a small program to allow the network to boot up the operating system from a network server. Other cards in your system, such as CD-ROM adapters or sound cards, may also contain their own ROM to provide special-purpose functions.

ROM comes in chips and packages under many different names. *Programmable read-only memory* (PROM) means that the company that provided the ROM wrote their own program into the ROM before they installed it in your computer. The *erasable programmable read-only memory* (EPROM) program can be changed but most likely not by you or the equipment in your system. *Electrically erasable programmable read-only memory* (EEPROM) and FLASH ROM may be used to retain a program or configuration information that your system or an application might be able to change. This is a type of ROM found in some modems, network adapters, sound cards, or even on your system board to contain the system BIOS so that you may store your own settings, even after the power to the system is turned off. FLASH ROM is very popular in system boards and modems and facilitates easy upgrading of the BIOS.

Random access memory

The definition of *random access memory* describes how it is used, rather than its characteristics or limitations. RAM loses its contents when you turn off your PC. Most RAM can be accessed or addressed and read from or written to randomly. The important characteristic or limitation of most RAM is that the data it contains is or can be dynamic — ever changing — and that in order to hold its data it must be provided with power and, in some cases, the internal circuits must be refreshed on a regular basis. Except for the CMOS RAM that holds your system configuration data, which is always given power from a small battery, the contents of RAM go away when the power is removed or the refresh signals fail. Therefore, it is not used as a permanent storage place for data or applications; it is only used when your PC is running.

RAM comes in several forms, each with different advantages and disadvantages. It is known by many names, such as Dynamic RAM (DRAM), CMOS or Static RAM (SRAM), Extended Data Out (EDO) DRAM, Synchronous DRAM (SDRAM), RAMBus DRAM (RDRAM), and Video RAM (VRAM), and comes packaged in Dual Inline Packages (DIPs), Single Inline Memory Modules (SIMMs), and Single Inline Packages (SIPs).

Of the types of RAM found in your PC, we must know the differences between them, what they are used for, which ones we have control over or can configure, how to configure them, and how to tell if one or the other is defective.

There are differences in speed, the sockets where they are plugged in, and the manner in which they are controlled by the hardware in your system. Because the speed of CPUs is always increasing, new and faster memory is also being produced. Currently popular memory packages run at 60- and 70-nanosecond speeds. SDRAM is already operating at 4 to 12 nanoseconds. The physical format or configuration of the RAM to install in your PC is dependent on the hardware sockets it has available.

Caution   Your PC's motherboard and memory adapters will work only with the specific kind of memory for which they were designed. Installing memory that is too slow or of the wrong type causes a number of problems.

Dynamic RAM has historically been one of the most significant bottlenecks in PC performance because of its design and the technology that is used to manufacture and address it. DRAM's biggest problems are its speed of operation because it requires a portion of the system's processing time to refresh its contents, and it must be addressed in at least two different steps. Most DRAM must be refreshed every 15 microseconds, which is pretty frequent. Some DRAM types may be refreshed less frequently (every 125 microseconds), which leaves more time for actual data processing. Conventional or standard DRAM has been used in every PC system from the 8088 through 80386 systems.

Fast Page Mode RAM or *FP RAM* allows more of the RAM to be addressed or refreshed at a time, saving some CPU time, and is the preferred RAM technology for fast 386, 486, and early Pentium systems.

Extended Data Output RAM or *EDO RAM* is an incremental step in RAM performance, reducing the time to address a portion of the memory, making data available to the CPU faster. EDO RAM can be found in later 486 and most Pentium processor systems.

Synchronous DRAM or *SDRAM* (not to be confused with Static RAM SRAM), used in faster systems, combines addressing, cache, and refresh operations to speed up memory performance greatly, which is generally required by processors operating above 150 MHz, to ensure full effectiveness. Not all systems will support newer RAM types, but systems that do support the newer RAM types generally support at least one prior generation of memory type.

Memory parity and testing

The memory in your system may be implemented with a parity check bit. This is an extra bit associated with each memory address. It is used for error-checking. When data is written to a memory address, the parity bit is set to 1 or 0, based on the content (the number of 1's or 0's) in the data. When data is read from a memory location, the parity is recalculated from the data read, and this parity result is compared against the parity bit stored with the data. If they match, the data is considered good. If the two parity results do not match, a signal is sent to the CPU indicating an error, and the system stops.

Memory checking is usually performed when you first turn on your computer, and then continuously while you use your computer. When you cold boot your computer (when the power has been turned off and then turned back on) the Power-On Self-Test (POST), among other tests, checks your system's memory. If a memory parity error occurs during the POST, your system will display a 201 error followed by information about the bad memory location. The POST generally prevents your system from booting completely if it finds an error.

IBM and compatible PCs are among the few types of computer systems that use parity checking as a means of error detection. Recently, because of the cost of providing the extra storage for the parity bit and because memory components have proven to be more reliable, many manufacturers are eliminating the need for parity checking, and RAM components (SIMMs) are available without the extra parity bit.

Some ROM BIOS programs allow you to disable memory parity checking by a setting in the CMOS memory so that you may continue to use your computer. There have been some 486 and early Pentium systems that claimed not to need "parity RAM," but would also use non-parity RAM. These are actually systems that can and do check for parity errors, but the error circuitry is ignored or the error-checking part of BIOS is turned off by a parameter in the system setup program. Sometimes this worked and sometimes it did not, because the chipset and CPU parity circuits were still active, and the CPU could still get a parity error signal from electrical noise. Later systems, such as those using the Intel Triton chip set, have no parity checking circuits at all, so parity RAM and non-parity RAM work equally well without settings changes.

However, you should follow up on any parity check errors, since they are a symptom of a bad memory chip or package that needs to be replaced, or a system board problem.

If in doubt, use parity-RAM unless your system is specifically designed with non-parity support.

Parity errors have also been known to appear in Microsoft Windows because a disk system error resulted in the virtual memory or swap file being corrupted or read improperly. When parity errors occur in Windows, check both the disk system (with CHKDSK, SCANDISK, or a utility such as SpinRite, the Rosenthal Utilities, or Norton Disk Doctor) and run a diagnostic test on the system RAM.

System RAM

System RAM is that which is counted and tested as the total amount of DOS and extended memory in your system. It is implemented as DRAM, FPRAM, EDO, or SDRAM. Which type you use depends on what is supported or required by your system board, both physically (the type of sockets) and electrically (the speed and interconnections to be used).

Cache RAM

Cache RAM, which is used within your CPU chip (internal or L1 cache) and on the system board (external or L2 cache), is an implementation of SRAM. It is typically available soldered onto the system board, as discrete plug-in chips, or as DIMM modules to suit your particular system board.

CMOS RAM

CMOS RAM is a significantly different variation of RAM. It uses very low-power circuits that enable us to maintain its contents using only a small battery. It is usually built in to the system clock chip.

Video RAM

Video RAM, found on the video adapter, is a special implementation of DRAM, FPRAM, EDO, or SDRAM, depending on the vintage of your video adapter. Most video RAM today is dual-ported, which means that the system can be writing data into one side of the video RAM bank at the same time that the video card is reading out and displaying data on the other side.

Memory Addressing

As we use and refer to the different types of memory in our systems, we need to know how it is addressed. We need to know how to accurately refer to various physical portions of memory so we can configure various hardware and programs. We need to know where to put it when we want to add more or replace it if it is bad, and how the system accesses it.

The Intel-compatible processors use a method of addressing memory referred to as Segment:Offset. The technical reason for using this method is that the original Intel CPU registers hold 16 bits (meaning that the computer was a 16-bit computer). The CPU would not have been able to address one megabyte of memory without using more than one register to represent the memory address. A 16-bit binary number is limited to representing 65,535 addresses (64K). 20 bits are required in order to address one megabyte. Since a one-megabyte memory space was considered to be "all the memory anyone could ever hope to use in a small computer," Intel designed the Segment:Offset method to address one megabyte. What foresight!

The method selected to address one megabyte of memory was to use two registers (32 bits), but since only 20 were required, the two registers were added by offsetting one by 4 bits and adding the other. Four bits are used to represent a hexadecimal number. The maximum hexadecimal digit is F, which is the same as 15 in decimal notation. Hexadecimal digits range from 0 to F (0,1,2,3,4,5,6,7,8,9,A,B,C,D,E,F), as decimal digits range from 0 to 9. The highest address that a 16-bit register can represent in hexadecimal notation is FFFF, which is the same as 65,536. If you think of the

Segment register as being an index into 65,536 16-byte blocks of memory and that the Offset provides 4 bits (another hexadecimal number) to point to the particular byte in that block, you understand Segment:Offset memory addressing. Luckily, we really do not need to use Segment:Offset addresses unless writing programs that have to address memory directly. We presented this discussion to give you enough information to understand that memory is allocated by assigning segments of memory to particular uses and devices.

The last byte of memory DOS can address is expressed in Segment:Offset terms as 9FFF:000F. The first hex number, 9FFF, is the address of the last 16-byte block of DOS's 640K of memory. The second hex number, 000F, addresses the last byte in the block. The whole number is 9FFFF. The next hexadecimal number (in other words, you add 1 to 9FFFF) is A0000. As shown in Figure 15-1, DOS is located below the A0000 memory address. Also, the first 64K of memory just above DOS is referred to as the A-range of memory. Again, as you can see in Figure 15-1, the reason for this is that its addresses start at A0000 and end at AFFFF.

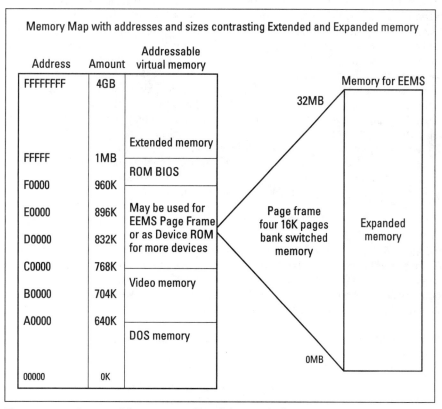

Figure 15-1: A map of the memory (RAM) in a typical PC

You usually use segment address references to set the memory address for things such as your hard disk ROM. One of the most common locations for hard disk ROM is at segment C8000, which indicates that it is located in the C-range of memory, starting at 768K. C8000 is the start of the third 16K block of memory in the C-range. It is also the start of the second 32K block in the C-range. Hardware manufacturers refer to memory addresses and settings in several ways.

We will refer back to Figure 15-1 later in the chapter when we discuss extended versus expanded memory and for other memory addressing discussions.

System Memory

System memory is the bulk of the memory in your system. You see how much total system memory you have when you boot up your system. It consists of all of the memory: the base 640K of RAM used for DOS, Windows or OS/2 and programs; the 384K of upper memory used for video, device ROM, and ROM BIOS; and all of the extended memory (above the 1 megabyte address). Expanded memory, discussed later, is not counted when your system boots. It comes in many different and evolving technologies to meet the speed and requirements of the processor and system board. DOS or base RAM, extended, expanded, high memory, and upper memory are all different in the way the overall total System RAM may be configured and put to use. System RAM is available in different physical types or technologies (DRAM, FPRAM, EDO, BEDO, SRAM, and SDRAM) and it is important to understand these when selecting memory to put into your system, and as a part of the overall system selection and performance. However, in some systems, such as portable computers, your only choices are the specially designed memory modules provided by the portable's manufacturer or from an after-market developer. Check your computer's documentation or the documentation for your motherboard for limitations on the types of memory and specific part numbers it may use.

DOS can only use the first 640K of this memory for the operating system and programs. Special programs called *memory managers* can create dedicated RAM areas or functions using the memory area between 640K and 1 megabyte. Device ROMs are installed in these special areas. This memory above 640K and below the 1MB threshold is also the location for the upper memory and page frame for expanded memory. The high memory area is the first 64K above 1MB. Beyond the 1MB threshold are extended and expanded memory.

These special types of memory are discussed in subsequent sections.

DOS memory

One portion of system memory, the first 640K, is sometimes called DOS or program memory and is used by the system to load and run device drivers, batch files, terminate-and-stay-resident programs (TSRs), caches, and your application programs. The operating system also uses it to store environment variables and the status of the many devices attached to your system. Without special memory managers and newer versions of DOS and Windows, this 640K of memory is all of the memory DOS programs and their data can use. Refer to Figure 15-1 for visualizing the following memory locations.

Low DOS and BIOS memory areas

This is a small region of DOS or base memory at the lowest addresses of the system. It contains system information from the BIOS and DOS bootup processes and is where the running DOS clock information is kept. The locations of the disk drive, and serial, parallel, and other basic PC device ports are also in this region.

Program memory

This is the memory area where all or portions of the operating system are loaded, followed by any device drivers and resident programs that are loaded. Beyond this area is the memory where application programs and data are loaded.

Memory size

Most PCs purchased today have 16 to 32 MB of RAM. Memory in the range of 64 to 128 MB is becoming common, too. Each kilobyte (K) of memory contains 1,024 bytes. Each megabyte contains 1,024 kilobytes. Each byte can hold a character, a number, or a single-byte machine instruction. Older PCs had much smaller memories, such as 64K, 256K, or 512K.

If you have the need and the funds, you can purchase PCs with 32, 64, 256, or more megabytes of main memory. Database servers and other high-performance systems are available with multiple processors and gigabytes of main memory. The amount of memory installed in your system should be dictated by the work you and your computer need to do, the maximum memory capacity of your computer's design, and the capacity of your bank account. Most Windows 3.x users will do well with 8 to 16 megabytes of RAM in their systems. For today's operating systems, Windows 9x/Me, NT or OS/2, 16MBof RAM is a bare minimum to realize reasonable performance. Windows 2000 requires a minimum of 32MB of memory, but this is only the minimum. Unless your system is a network file or application server or you are working with advanced graphics applications, 32 to 128 megabytes of RAM is usually more than adequate for most end-user application needs. Again, this is RAM—the memory generally used to describe how much memory your system provides for your use.

Performance considerations

It is actually possible to slow down the performance of your system by having too much memory installed—it's a matter of diminishing returns. To avoid or reduce the amount of virtual memory or disk swapping with Windows, you need to add RAM, which is a good thing, to a point. Windows automatically allows a virtual memory swap file that is at least half as large as the amount of RAM memory in the system and can be as big as the entire available free space on your disk drive. The more RAM in the system, the larger the swap file. The larger the swap file, the more time Windows spends working with the disk drive, which is slower than RAM. The solution to this is to adjust the Windows swap file to a fixed size no larger than the total amount of RAM in your system or as best suits your multitasking needs.

Also, the more RAM in the system, the more time Windows HIMEM.SYS and other memory management tools in the system have to spend managing the use of the memory. Beyond even a lowly 32 megabytes of RAM, and certainly beyond 64 megabytes, you are making the processor spend more and more time doing memory housekeeping, which means less CPU time for your applications. Granted, this is a relatively small amount of time, but there are some performance considerations here. Nevertheless, you should install the fastest affordable memory available for your system to get the most out of it. If your system accepts SRAM, use SRAM; if EDO, use EDO; and so on. Using mere DRAM or FPRAM in an EDO system handicaps the chip set and the system from working at its best.

CPU speed, memory speed, and bus speed

The CPU speed of a computer is one of its primary attributes. Manufacturers find this so important that it is often included in the promotion for a particular PC model. The memory speed is a bit more elusive and may be expressed in terms of wait states. A *wait state* is a period in which the CPU does nothing except wait for the requested memory contents. A 500 MHz CPU would require memory rated at 2 nanoseconds and a bus able to handle that same speed (500 MHz). This would ensure that the memory contents requested by a particular operation are allowed the time to get to the place where the CPU can access them without having to wait. Since current bus speeds are just now reaching 150 MHz and memory faster than 10 nanoseconds is very expensive, it may be a while before a 500-MHz CPU is able to run at full speed when accessing widely distributed data. Table 15-1 shows the speed required for both memory and bus to avoid wait states for selected CPU speeds:

Table 15-1
Avoiding Wait States with Proper Memory and Speeds

CPU Speed (in MHz)	RAM Speed (in nanoseconds; required for no wait states)	Memory Speed to Use (in nanoseconds; limited by what is available)	Processor
4.77	209	200	8088/8086 (PC/XT)
6	167	150	80286 (PC AT)
8	125	100–150	
10	100	100	80386 (PC-compatible)
12	83	80–100	
16	63	80–100	
20	50	80–100	
25	40	80–100	
33	30	70–80	
40	25	60–80	80386/80486
50	20	60–80	
100	10	60–70	80486/80586/Pentium
133	7.5	15–25	80586/Pentium (EDO)
150	6.6	15–25	Pentium (EDO)
200	5	10	Pentium/Pentium II (SDRAM)
233	4.3	10	Pentium/Pentium II (SDRAM)
300	3.3	10	Pentium II (SDRAM)
400	2.5	10	Pentium II (SDRAM)
500	2	4	Pentium III (SDRAM)
			AMD K6/K7/Athlon
1000	1		PC 100 Intel Coppermine
			AMD K7 Athlon

In reality, memory chips today do not operate at speeds faster than 4 to 12 nanoseconds. Processors really do not interface to memory and I/O systems as fast as they process internally. Thus, special memory I/O circuits, caching, and other timing and addressing techniques — Fast Page Mode (FPM), Extended DataOut (EDO) and Synchronous DRAM (SDRAM) and variations of these such as Burst EDO (BEDO) and RAMBus DRAM (RDRAM) — are used to keep data flowing to and from the CPU while the physical memory works at slower speeds.

If any memory chips or the bus speed are slower than that required by the CPU's memory interface, wait states or cache circuitry are required to hold off the reading or writing of data to memory until the memory addressing is stable, so that memory is written reliably into the right location. It is not uncommon for systems to have 1 to 2 wait states set in the system setup (if this parameter is visible at all) to allow it to run more reliably with slower RAM. Having memory that runs at a speed that is too slow for the CPU means that your PC is not operating at the speed you expect. A PC with proper RAM speed that requires zero wait states will operate at the speed you expect.

Caution   If you reduce the number of wait states below that required for the RAM speed you have, your system may encounter undesirable delays or data errors if those wait states are actually required.

Adding memory

Today's computers provide sockets on the motherboard for installing 30, 72, and/or 168-pin memory modules. The most important information about memory for your motherboard, once you know the number of pins for the available memory module sockets, is what kind of memory your mother board will support. Some 486 and most newer computers can use memory with or without the parity bit. It is important to know whether your computer requires it or not so you purchase the right kind. Older computers must be provided memory with the parity bit. Some motherboards will only support memory up to certain speeds and built with chips on just one side of the memory module. Other motherboards may accommodate just about any memory module as long as it has the right number of pins to plug into the memory socket. Generally, as long as the mother board will accept it, faster memory is better than slower and will work better with your CPU. One of the reasons memory is most often installed on the motherboard is to provide the best possible environment to take full advantage of chip speeds.

To install memory on adapter boards (for some older computers, the only way to add memory) and configure it for the use of programs and utilities, you need to know how much memory is already installed and something about memory addressing. Your PC gives a little help with determining the amount of memory already installed. If your PC has an 8088 or 8086 CPU (PC- and XT-class computers), it tests the first megabyte of memory and tells you how much is installed. For PCs with 286-, 386-, 486-, and

Pentium-level CPUs, the memory test includes extended memory (covered in detail, following), but may or may not tell you how much expanded memory has been installed.

For your system to test its expanded memory or show you how much is installed, you may have to install an expanded memory manager program. You might have to refer to the documentation for your expanded memory adapter boards and the switch and jumper settings on the boards to determine how much expanded memory they provide. You may also use the free MAPMEM program from Turbo Power Software (if you are using DOS or Windows versions prior to Windows 95 and Windows NT), available for download from many bulletin board systems and online services, to display the amount of conventional and expanded memory installed in your system. For instance, you can find it today at `http://www.ctyme.com/doc/doc0082.htm`.

If you are installing more memory in your PC and run out of sockets into which to plug new memory on your motherboard or existing memory adapters, you may be able to install a new memory adapter board into one or more of the SIMM slots so that it will accept more SIMM blocks. Otherwise, you will have to change your entire memory scheme and use SIMM components with more RAM per SIMM. Older memory boards usually have switch or jumper settings that you must use to indicate the amount of memory already installed in your system, or the starting memory address for the new memory. In this case, the information you collected while determining how much memory your system has installed will come in handy. Most often, you set the switches or jumpers to the value of memory you found. If you have 16MB of memory installed, you might find a setting for 16,384K or 16MB (these are the same). You might also have to make a setting for how much memory is provided by the new adapter card. This setting is usually related to the number of rows, or banks, or packages that contain memory chips on the board.

Using a memory address to set the switches or jumpers can be a bit tricky. In standard mode, the PC uses segments and offsets to address memory. For the PC, the segment part and offset part of the address are groups of 4-digit hexadecimal numbers. Because a kilobyte of memory is 1,024 bytes, 640K of memory is 655,360 bytes. The hex number for 640K (the maximum DOS can use) is A0000.

If you have a lot of older 30-pin SIMMs and a new system that uses 72-pin SIMMs, you might also try to combine multiple 30-pin SIMMs on a 30-to-72-pin SIMM converter card. There are also 72-pin to-72-pin converter cards that enable you to install multiple small capacity SIMMs to free up a couple of slots for more RAM; however, these devices are only effective on moderate to slow 486 and Pentium systems because they lengthen the signal and connection paths between the board and the SIMMs. Such extra length can limit the high-speed transfer of information and render the system unreliable or useless.

Note The safest way to put memory in your machine is to look at the number on the memory module, call a memory supply house, and order the identical part. Most machines require you add memory in specific increments (8/16/32). Also, the module types must match, even if it means you toss out two old 8MB modules and replace them with two new16MB modules to upgrade to 32MB.

Non-System Memory

We don't have much cause to deal with memory that is not used by programs and data, except as a matter of system configuration or performance considerations. The following memory types — CMOS, video RAM, cache, and virtual — are indeed necessary parts of your system, depending on your application, but they are not visible nor part of system memory as discussed above, nor of extended or expanded memory features. We must be aware of them as we configure our systems, and we must understand how they fit within other memory areas.

CMOS memory

A special type of RAM found in PCs since IBM released the AT class of computers is referred to as CMOS (CMOS stands for complementary metal oxide semiconductor) RAM or static RAM. This memory depends on a small amount of battery power to retain its contents. This type of RAM does not require the refreshes that DRAM does, but it is slower than DRAM. It contains data about the configuration of your system such as the current date and time for your system clock, the number and types of floppy and hard disks installed, the amount and types of memory installed, your system's display type, the type of keyboard attached, whether there is a math coprocessor (to speed your system), the current CPU speed (if your system can switch speeds), whether shadow RAM is used to speed your display, and other configuration information.

The content, format, and whether you may make changes to this data depends on the type of BIOS installed in your system. Some CMOS RAM configurations even allow you to specify the hardware configuration of your hard disk so that you are not restricted to using only the predefined types.

The CMOS RAM is not counted with the rest of your RAM when describing how much memory your system has installed.

If the battery that provides the power to your CMOS RAM loses its charge, you also lose the setup information for your system (another good reason to keep a record of your computer's setup).

The data stored in the CMOS RAM is accompanied by a checksum that is calculated when the data is stored in the memory. When you reboot your computer (either a cold or warm boot) this checksum is used to compare with a new checksum calculated by the program that starts your computer. If the checksums do not match, you are informed that there is an invalid checksum and you are offered an opportunity to correct the problem, which involves checking and modifying the setup information about your computer.

Video memory

No matter if you have a simple monochrome display adapter (anyone else remember those?) or the latest in high-resolution video adapters, the video system has RAM on the adapter card that is used to store and switch the images you see on your display screen. This RAM is not accessible to DOS or other operating systems for data storage other than for the data required to create a screen image. Video RAM, or VRAM, is usually DRAM or EDO RAM although high-speed graphics systems are using SDRAM today, with circuitry optimized for the access requirements of video applications.

Note

The video RAM on an EGA or VGA display adapter is located just above the 640K DOS memory boundary, and is sometimes referred to as occupying the A-range of memory. The A-range starts at the 640K boundary and extends for 64K to the beginning of the B-range, or A0000–AFFFF. The video BIOS ROM occupies 32K of the B-range (B0000–B7FFF) and some video adapters also use the remaining 32K area of the B-range, B8000–BFFFF, for special functions. This is important to know as you configure your memory manager and want to avoid conflicts between programs and Windows.

Cache memory

A cache is typically a small, very specific storage area known or accessible to few. In the case of computers, a cache is a specifically assigned type of memory, dedicated to storing data that is accessed by only a single device or two. There are two common applications of cache memory in most computers today.

In most cases, we may think of caching or cache memory in terms of a disk cache — memory dedicated to temporarily pre-storing data on its way between disk drives and main system memory. Memory for disk caching is usually allocated from DOS base, extended, or expanded memory. Microsoft's SMARTDRV disk caching program supports caching of both hard drives and CD-ROM drives. For DOS and Windows 3.x systems, SMARTDRV is loaded as a resident utility in the AUTOEXEC.BAT file. For Windows 9x/Me systems, SMARTDRV is loaded as part of and under control of the operating system.

More recently, with most 486 systems and all Pentium and higher class systems, external cache memory support is also found in the microprocessor support circuitry. CPU cache memory is made up of very high-speed RAM.

In 486DX and higher CPUs, a small amount of cache RAM is provided within the CPU chip itself. This is called L1 or Level-1 cache. This cache is under complete control of the CPU, but may be disabled if the option to do so is provided in your system setup program. It is used to store instructions and a small amount of data en route to and from the CPU. You would disable the L1 cache only if the main application your computer is running is so poorly written that it takes more time to search the cache and then go get the next instruction every time because the cache never contains the next instruction. This should be so rare that you should not have to make this kind of decision.

Many 486 systems and all but the cheapest Pentium-class systems provide external, L2, or Level-2 cache on the system board. This is very high-speed RAM, typically from as little as 64K up to 1MB, that is under control of the CPU and the supporting chip set. External cache may be disabled or controlled if the option to do so is provided in your system setup program. L2 cache provides even more instruction and data storage in route to and from the main CPU. An external cache of 64K may be adequate for slower 486 systems, but faster 486s and Pentiums perform much better if they have at least 256K (or up to 1MB) of L2 cache RAM.

Virtual memory

This term refers to a method of temporarily swapping RAM memory contents to a special file on your disk drive in such a way that your computer thinks that it has a lot more memory than is really installed. The memory freed up by swapping the data to disk is then made available for other uses. This can be very economical and convenient, but remember that RAM and ROM speeds are normally measured in nanoseconds (billionths of a second) and hard disk speeds are measured in milliseconds (thousandths of a second). This means that virtual memory is a *lot* slower than actual memory.

A program that uses overlay modules is using a form of virtual memory. The program is loaded into the computer's memory, but some of it is left on disk until needed. Almost all multitasking operating systems or environments such as Unix, OS/2, or Windows may swap an application to disk, but normally the application does not continue to run while in that condition. If the application does not continue running, then it is not considered to be a true virtual memory implementation.

Extended and Expanded Memory

Extended and expanded memory refer to two different memory configuration and management technologies that have helped to provide and improve applications and utilization of evolving PC systems.

The CPU chips used in the PC, XT, and AT class of computers (the Intel 8088 and 8086 chips) and the 80286 chip used in the AT in Real Mode can address 1MB of memory. DOS can access only up to 640K of this memory. The remainder of the 1MB of memory is dedicated to space for video RAM, video ROM, hard disk ROM, the ROM BIOS, and the ROM for other installed devices (refer to Figure 15-1 earlier in the chapter). The memory above the 1 megabyte address available on 80286 and higher systems is called *extended memory.*

Expanded memory came about as an improvement to the limitations of the 8088 and 8086 CPUs (PC and XT systems) and DOS's inability to address more than 1 megabyte of memory or use more than 640K of RAM. Various implementations of expanded memory were used to suit these older systems until things settled down and we had better memory capabilities with the 80386 CPU and systems.

To understand the differences between expanded and extended memory, consider this analogy. Suppose you have 8MB of memory in your system. You could compare it with an eight-story building with 1MB of memory on each floor. If the floors of your building were made of extended memory, you would get in the elevator and go to the floor that contains the program or data you need. If the building was constructed of expanded memory, you would stay on the first floor and the rest of the building would go up or down so you could access the program or information on the correct floor without your having to go anywhere. The first floor would not move with the rest of the building,

Lots of arguments were made about which of these methods was the best. The driving factor was the need to get beyond DOS's 1MB limit for program memory. Both expanded and extended memory satisfy this need — mostly. Extended memory requires the use of memory addresses with larger address numbers. Expanded memory requires keeping track of what memory block is to be mapped into the area DOS can access using its normal addressing methods. However, if you are using a very old CPU or applications that require the use of expanded memory, you have no choice.

Executing a memory access instruction (extended memory) and changing the mapping context for memory access (expanded memory) are both very fast. However, if a single program must be larger than the 640K limit imposed by DOS, it must be written to use extended memory and should use DPMI for DOS and older versions of Windows or the Win32 API for Windows 9x/Me and NT/2000. Alternatively, the program could be broken into logical units to be run under a multitasking system that uses expanded memory and can communicate between the separate modules. This latter requirement is satisfied by Windows and its Dynamic Data Exchange (DDE).

The overriding consideration for you in choosing whether to install expanded or extended memory is the type of programs you are going to run and whether you are installing the memory on an old PC. New applications are not being developed to use expanded memory. If any of the programs you are running require extended memory or you have an 80386 or newer PC, then install extended memory in your system. If you never plan to run a program that requires extended memory, then expanded memory should work. If you have a computer with an 80286 or older CPU, expanded memory is the only kind of memory you can use to get past DOS's memory limit. If you have an 80386 or newer computer, install extended memory because a memory manager such as QEMM can use the extended memory to provide any kind of memory a particular program needs. For the newest computers and the latest versions of Windows (9x/Me and NT/2000), there is no dispute: Extended memory is the only way to go.

Extended memory

The following discussion applies mainly to DOS and early versions of Windows. Windows 95 uses extended memory and does not require but will work with some alternate memory manager systems. Windows NT uses extended memory and does not work with any alternate memory manager systems.

The memory above the 1-megabyte address is called *extended memory*. Extended memory is implemented in the PC as contiguous blocks of memory, starting with the first megabyte and extending to the maximum memory installed that your CPU can address. Microsoft's Virtual Disk (VDISK) program was one of the first to use extended memory on a PC. VDISK used a small amount of conventional memory (in the first 640K of DOS memory) to manage a larger amount of extended memory used to create a RAM disk.

The use of extended memory has come a long way since then. Windows NT/2000 supports up to 4 gigabytes (GB) of system memory — 2GB addressable by the system and 2GB addressable by applications. Microsoft's extended memory specification (XMS) for DOS and Windows allows high memory area (HMA), upper memory block (UMB), and extended memory block (EMB) methods of interfacing between DOS programs and extended memory. Windows requires the presence of its extended memory manager, HIMEM.SYS, or an equivalent memory manager such as Quarterdeck's QEMM, to provide XMS support.

 Note   Windows NT/2000 neither requires nor uses an alternate memory manager other than its own built-in memory manager.

Quarterdeck and Phar Lap developed and published a specification named Virtual Control Program Interface (VCPI), which specifies how 80386 control programs and DOS extenders communicate with each other. A large group of companies cooperatively developed the DOS Protected Mode Interface (DPMI), which manages application use of extended memory. Wide acceptance of these specifications has resulted in the production of many programs and multitasking systems for the benefit of those using PCs.

Quarterdeck's QEMM (now available from Symantec) provides management functions for both expanded and extended memory by providing programs with the kinds of memory they want to use at the time of their request. QEMM is the extended/expanded memory manager most often used in PCs that are running DOS or Windows 3.*x* or WfW.

Since DOS 6.*x*, portions of DOS can be loaded into the high memory area (HMA) created by an XMS driver (HIMEM.SYS or QEMM) using a special DOS=HIGH parameter in the CONFIG.SYS file after the XMS driver is loaded.

Expanded memory

Prior to the 80386 and later CPU chips that can access much more memory, industry leaders developed a scheme to expand the memory available to PC programs. Lotus, Intel, and Microsoft developed one method termed Lotus/Intel/Microsoft-Expanded Memory Specification (LIM-EMS). AST developed another called Extended Expanded Memory Specification (EEMS). These specifications involved both hardware and software, and competed until October 1987 when they were merged into the still current LIM-EMS Version 4.0 specification that does not require special hardware for 386 and higher systems. The combined standard provides access to more expanded memory and better memory management capabilities.

Although the hardware technology method is outdated, we mention LIM-EMS here because it is still being used in older computers and some manufacturers of computer memory had advertised boards compatible with LIM-EMS, Version 3.2. You might find expanded memory at a computer swap meet or installed in a used computer. There are hardware differences between these boards and those that support EEMS 3.2 or LIM-EMS 4.0, the current standard for expanded memory. If you depend on your hardware to provide expanded memory, make sure you get memory that conforms to LIM-EMS 4.0. Expanded memory, implemented in hardware is required on 80286 and earlier processors. Expanded memory on 80386 and newer systems is most often implemented in software by conversion of extended memory.

Expanded memory gives your PC access to more than 640K (up to 32MB) by dividing the additional memory into 16K logical pages. Any logical page can be mapped into the page frame, which can contain from 0 to 12 logical pages of expanded memory at any one time. The page frame is located within the 384K of memory above DOS's 640K. An expanded memory manager (EMM) program is loaded either as a device driver or as a TSR program that manages the page frame and may do a lot more. All of this memory and its use occurs within the 1MB memory limit imposed by DOS.

Upper Memory Blocks

Upper memory is the area of memory between 640K and 1MB. It is primarily occupied by video memory, video BIOS, disk drive BIOS, SCSI adapter BIOS, any expanded memory page frame assignment, and the system BIOS.

The unused areas of upper memory are known as upper memory blocks. With an expanded memory manager driver such as EMM386 or QEMM, these areas can have portions of extended memory RAM re-allocated into the empty upper memory spaces so they may be used for loading DOS device drivers and resident programs. This leaves more of the main DOS memory area below 640K available for larger programs and data.

QEMM can also reassign portions of extended memory RAM and load the contents of slower ROM BIOS chips into this RAM so that ROM BIOS code can be read and executed faster. This is also referred to as shadow RAM or stealth ROM.

Unless otherwise configured or excluded from memory manager or Windows use, conflicts in the range of B8000 to BFFFF may occur with use of this area by various video cards and drivers. If you have the option, specifically exclude this region from your memory manager. The exclusions are usually done by specifying only the *segment* part of the memory address.

For EMM386, this exclusion is specified when you load the memory manager in CONFIG.SYS as:

```
DEVICE=C:\WINDOWS\EMM386.EXE X=B800-BFFF
```

For QEMM, this exclusion is specified when you load the memory manager in CONFIG.SYS as:

```
DEVICE=C:\QEMM\QEMM386.EXE X=B800-BFFF
```

Memory Problems

Memory problems typically manifest themselves in one of three ways — insufficient memory for an application or data set, data or parity errors and messages, or incompatibilities with system hardware or other memory devices. These are covered in the sections below. A fourth class of memory problems, conflicts with device drivers or applications, is covered in Chapter 4.

Bad chips and hardware conflicts

This section focuses on the symptoms, suspects, and solutions for bad chips and hardware conflicts.

Symptoms

▶ 201 error upon booting your computer. Your computer will not complete booting.

▶ Memory Parity Check error message. This can occur upon booting your computer or after you have been using it for a while. Your computer will not complete booting. (Older computers may display a Parity Check 1 message to indicate a memory error on the motherboard and a Parity Check 2 message to indicate a memory error on an expansion card.)

▶ Running a memory diagnostic program (such as Norton Utilities) reports bad memory chips, parity errors, or read/write errors.

Suspects

▶ If the memory location associated with the 201 error message, parity check message, or memory test program report is consistent (meaning that it reports the same memory address or the same block of memory every time you boot the computer) there is a strong possibility that memory chips or packages need to be replaced. Memory cannot be repaired.

▶ If the memory location changes each time you get an error report, the problem might be due to conflicting hardware installed in your system, faulty memory control circuitry, or other problems on your PC's motherboard or adapters.

Solutions

▶ Find and replace the bad memory chips or packages.

▶ Determine whether the memory problem is due to hardware conflicts and if so, remove the offending hardware.

You will need to determine if the bad memory is located on the motherboard or a memory expansion card, if you have one. The memory address reported in the message you receive from your system or the memory test software should lead you to this information. For instance, if your system has 4MB of memory on the motherboard and the address of the bad memory is at a memory location beyond 4MB, then the bad memory is on an add-in card. You will have to determine how much memory is on which part of the system, which one of multiple adapters is accessed first (usually by jumper or switch settings on the add-in card), and so forth, in order to determine which memory adapter contains the bad memory.

Memory on older adapter cards, like the one shown in Figure 15-2, is usually provided in rows of nine chips. Each chip in a row contributes 1 bit for a memory byte or the parity bit. The amount of memory in each row depends on the number of bits per chip. Memory chips and packages generally come in 16K bits — 32 megabits per chip. Newer memory comes in packages with different numbers of chips, on small circuit boards plugged into the motherboard and identified as Bank 0 (1, 2, and so on) or Slot 1 (2, 3, and so on), and other configurations. To determine which row of memory chips or packages contains an error, you will need to determine how much memory is in each row.

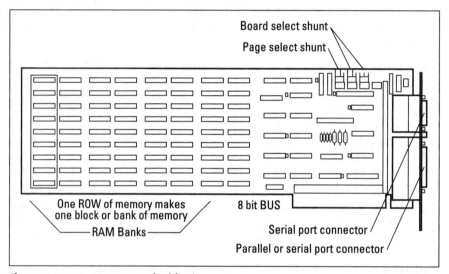

Figure 15-2: A memory card with I/O ports

Some systems and boards enable you to put different sizes of chips or packages in different rows as long as all of the chips in that same row are of the same size, speed, and type. Some memory packages provide an entire row of chips (block of memory) in a single package. If you cannot determine the size of the memory for each row, contact the distributor or manufacturer of your computer and ask. (The alternative is to have an entire library of technical specifications for memory chips and packages or access to the World Wide Web and the address for the memory manufacturer and their technical library.) An additional wrinkle in this problem is that some distributors of memory chips stamp their own numbers on the chips or packages so that you need their interpretation of what that number means. Most computer stores can look this up for you.

Chips and boards that may give your computer more memory includes ISA adapter boards (meaning they are destined for installation in the PC/AT type of computer) that allow memory expansion using the newer SIMM (Single In-line Memory Module) boards. Newer portable or small computers can use PCMCIA cards, among other memory boards and chips.

The 9-chip and 3-chip, 30-pin SIMMs and 72-pin SIMMs are now the most common memory modules. The predominant method of adding memory to newer PCs is through 168-pin SIMMS. SIMMs are commonly provided with 1, 2, 4, 8, 16, 32, 64, 128, and 256 MB of memory. Figure 15-3 shows an older ISA memory board with individual chips and a three-piece memory module. Most likely, the memory module contains a lot more memory than the adapter card.

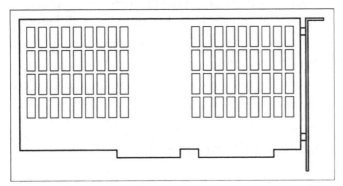

Figure 15-3: A memory card with rows and columns of chips and a three-chip memory module

Before you replace the bad memory chips or package, try moving the chips or package in the same block of memory (swapping chips in the same row, if possible or not soldered) to see if the location of the bad memory is changed. This will help you to determine if only one chip or the whole package needs to be replaced. You might also try swapping the chips or packages to different blocks of memory (different rows) to see if the memory error relocates to the other memory block when you reboot.

After you identify the bad chip, row of chips, or package, the only alternative is to replace it. Memory chips and SIMMs cannot be fixed. If you cannot identify the bad chip or package, the socket itself may be defective, requiring you to replace the motherboard or adapter board where the bad memory is located. If the memory error is the result of hardware conflicts in your system, replacing the bad or conflicting adapter board with a new one may or may not cure the problem.

Determining which adapter board is the cause of the problem is not easy. The best way to attack this problem is to remove all adapter boards from your system and only install the minimum boards necessary to boot your computer. Before you start, you might try cleaning the contacts on the adapter boards and re-installing them—this sometimes works. (You will need at least the video display adapter and the interface to your disk drives, if it is on a separate board, so you can boot your system to be able to run test programs.) Some systems have the CPU, main memory, and keyboard attached to adapter boards that are needed to boot your computer.

Tip   The problem may often be resolved by just removing and reseating the board, module, or a chip. This action can clean the electrical contact pins as the board is moved in and out of its socket.

Arrange the boards not necessary for booting your PC in order of their importance to your PC use. For instance, your hard disk might be the most important to you. Others may include:

✦ Memory expansion adapters

✦ SCSI controllers

✦ Additional hard disk controllers

✦ Additional serial/parallel ports

✦ A universal serial bus (USB) or FireWire adapter

✦ Internal modems

✦ Fax or scanner adapters

✦ Network interface cards

✦ CD-ROM adapters

✦ Sound cards

Install each of these boards separately, in your priority order, and boot your computer after each card installation. Continue this process until you receive the memory error again. This should indicate which situation causes the error condition.

There is a good chance that the last board installed is the one that has the conflict. However, before going on to the next board for installation, try moving the boards you have installed into different slots and reboot. You might have an adapter board that prefers to be in a particular slot or that must be closer to the CPU because it borders on being too slow for your system. If moving the boards around and rebooting cures the problem, install the next board in your priority sequence. If the problem persists, remove the last board installed and reboot your system to ensure that the boards left in are still working together correctly.

Continue adding each board in sequence and running through the test-and-move process until all the boards are installed or until you have removed any that have caused problems. The ones that are not installed in your working system are the ones that need to be fixed or replaced.

Parity checking or bad memory problems

Some motherboards and memory adapters enable you to disable memory parity checking through a jumper, switch, or the settings in the setup program. Some ROM BIOS programs enable you to turn off memory parity checking after a parity check error has occurred so you can continue working. This can be a viable alternative to resolving a hardware conflict in your system that has no other resolution. Before you run your PC with memory parity checking turned off, perform the tests of your memory and the potential hardware conflict and try to resolve it before giving up and using this risky procedure. Running without memory parity checking is risky; it can mask a real problem that could affect the validity of your data.

Symptoms

▶ You or your computer has disabled memory parity checking due to the occurrence of a parity error, or the parity checking was disabled during installation of your computer's memory. Everything seems to be working okay until some strange result or action occurs such as:

- Data loaded into memory gets changed or corrupted.

- A program locks up or performs seemingly impossible actions.

- Data stored to disk does not retain the same values that were observed while in memory.

- TSRs and installed devices may exhibit some of the same problems.

Suspects

▶ There really is bad memory in your system.

▶ You might also suspect hardware conflicts or nonfunctional programs. However, if the hardware and programs worked together previously, the memory should be considered a valid candidate.

Solutions

▶ Refer to the previous procedure in "Bad chips and hardware conflicts."

Symptoms

▶ Microsoft Windows indicates memory parity errors and stops running.

Suspects

▶ There really is bad memory in your system.

▶ The virtual memory or Windows swap file on your disk drive is corrupt.

▶ There was a disk read or write error that caused an error in swap-file operations.

Solutions

▶ Run a memory diagnostic test on your system RAM. Do this from DOS if you are using an old version of Windows (3.11 or earlier). Identify and replace any bad RAM indicated by address or bank location.

▶ Run a disk file test (CHKDSK, SCANDISK, SpinRite, Rosenthal Utilities, or Norton's Disk Doctor) to verify the disk/file systems. For Windows 9x/Me, boot up in Safe Mode (press the F8 key immediately after your system says it is starting Windows and then select Safe Mode) and use the SCANDISK program to repair your hard disk system. For Windows NT/2000, use the CHKDSK program with the /R switch — it will run the next time you reboot.

▶ Run a disk drive diagnostic test to prove that your controller and drive hardware are okay.

▶ For Windows 3.x, close all open programs, go to the 386 Enhanced settings in the Windows Control Panel, change or delete the current swap file, restart Windows, and then reinstate the virtual memory settings and restart Windows to create a new swap file.

▶ For Windows 9x/Me, close all open programs, go to the Performance tab on the System Properties icon in the Windows Control Panel, select "Let me specify my own virtual memory settings," and disable virtual memory. Restart Windows, and then reinstate the previous virtual memory settings and restart Windows to create a new virtual memory file. This may be the only way to get rid of a bad one.

▶ For Windows NT, if the CHKDSK did not fix the virtual memory problem, create the NTHQ program disk. (Unfortunately, the HQtool is not available on the Windows 2000 CD.) Close all open programs, insert the Windows NT CD ROM, go to the Support\ Hqtool directory and use the MAKEDISK.BAT file to make a 3.5-inch, 1.44MB floppy that will boot your system under MS-DOS and collect information about your system and to identify hardware that may be causing problems. The procedure will also create a Readme.txt file that contains instructions to use the information collected and reported from your system.

Caution

Windows 9x/Me users should boot into Command Prompt (DOS) mode after pressing <F8> at the "Starting Windows 9x . . . " message rather than trying to run any DOS-based utilities in a DOS window under Windows, but if disk testing is necessary, only disk utilities specific to Windows 9x/Me should be used to preserve long file and directory names.

Insufficient memory problems

The following set of problems indicates that you have insufficient memory installed correctly in your system. Please see Chapter 8 for complementary Symptoms, Suspects, and Solutions.

Symptoms

▶ The message on your screen contains the words "insufficient memory."

▶ A program fails to run or load configuration or data files.

▶ A program quits running and locks up your machine, returns to the DOS prompt, or the application's window closes.

▶ The program you are running displays a message that expanded or extended memory is required or that not enough of either is available.

▶ A program displays a message that your machine is running low on virtual memory.

Suspects

▶ Insufficient DOS memory is installed in your PC.

▶ Insufficient expanded memory is installed in your PC.

▶ Insufficient extended memory is installed in your PC.

▶ You have too many open program groups or too many icons open and displayed under Windows.

▶ Expanded memory manager or extended memory manager is not installed or configured correctly.

▶ Corrupted swap file or incorrectly set swap file parameters.

Solutions

▶ If you know you have sufficient memory in your system, check to make sure that it is installed correctly, that your programs are complete and configured correctly, and that your expanded and/or extended memory manager program is installed correctly.

▶ If you have memory that operates at different speeds installed in your system, make sure that the slowest memory is fast enough for your CPU and the number of wait states that your system implements.

▶ Run a comprehensive memory test. Most memory management software includes diagnostic programs, such as Windows NT's NTHQ program, mentioned previously, and Norton's NDIAGS for identifying memory problems and hardware and software conflicts in your system.

▶ If you need to install more memory, make sure that you purchase memory that is correct for your system. Both the type (such as DRAM, SRAM, SIMM, or SIP) and speed must be correct. Check first to see if there is room to install more memory on your system's motherboard. For older PCs, you might find that your expanded or extended memory manager makes better use of its own memory for "backfilling" the motherboard memory.

▶ If you need to select a memory manager, make sure it matches your system. QRAM is for the 80286 CPUs. HIMEM/EMM386, QEMM386 and others are used for 80386 and newer CPUs. DOS 5.0 and newer versions provide some minimal memory manager capabilities such as use of the upper memory block and expanded memory for task switching (as opposed to multitasking) and EMM386.SYS for multitasking. Your choice of memory manager may dictate the type of memory to install in your system in addition to matching your CPU's class and speed. (Windows NT and 98 provide their own memory management.)

▶ Under Microsoft Windows — close unneeded applications and program groups.

▶ Delete the swap file and reboot. See the section "Performance Considerations" earlier in this chapter for the correct and safest procedure to create a new swap file.

Memory Configuration Problems

Any DOS-based PC allows programs to use the memory in real mode. This refers to the 640K of DOS memory in your computer's first megabyte of memory. Using other memory modes and kinds of memory requires the use of a memory manager. Extended memory, expanded memory, 16-bit DOS extenders, and 32-bit DOS extenders all require a memory manager. Windows NT and 98 simply have the memory manager functions built in. Memory management functions include creating specific types of memory from the available memory hardware, allocating and deallocating memory, writing and reading values, moving and copying values, and reallocating memory.

Because your computer may contain programs that use or require different types of memory, it is necessary for multiple memory managers to cooperate. This is the purpose of a Virtual Control Program Interface (VCPI) memory management feature. If applications use the DOS Protected Mode Interface memory management scheme, it is also necessary to use a DPMI driver. Having all of these capabilities and all of this cooperation can lead to conflicts. This does not apply to Windows 9x/Me/NT/2000, which provide its own memory management.

Symptoms

▶ Error messages about insufficient or no memory of a specific type

▶ Error messages containing the letters DPMI, VCPI, DOSX, or another name that refers to a DOS extender

Suspects

▶ Unless there is a real lack of a specific kind of memory, the problem is probably memory management.

▶ Some programs are memory hogs and use memory they don't need.

Solutions

▶ Check your CONFIG.SYS and AUTOEXEC.BAT files for driver and program parameters and settings that affect memory. Look for terms such as SWAPFILE, EXTMAX, MAXMEM, DPMI, and VCPI, or numbers that set memory sizes.

▶ Check for programs that use extended, expanded, or protected mode, and other types of memory to determine if any can access unlimited amounts of memory. If a program can grab all available memory, sometimes it will do so just in case it needs more later. These programs are not very friendly and should be told that there is only the amount of memory they actually require. Some programs allow you to use DOS environment settings or program command line options to limit their memory use.

If your memory management problems continue to occur, you may want to get a new memory manager. If you already have one, call the producer of the memory manager for technical support. There might be a specific hardware driver or a piece of software in your system that is known to cause memory manager problems and there may be an easy fix. If the offending program or device is one that you really need, contact the producer of that software or hardware for assistance.

Summary

After memory is installed and working correctly in your system, it seldom gives you problems. It is possible for memory to fail, especially if some external event such as an electrical storm or power surge affects your computer. However, the best time to find bad memory is when you first install it. At that point, you should perform as many tests of the memory as you can. Finding any conflicts or other problems will save you from future problems.

You might also find problems with the memory in your system when you make hardware or software changes. Adding or removing hardware can introduce a memory conflict with ROM or other memory on the new board, or can result in faulty connections or improperly seated memory modules or adapter boards if you have moved the boards in your system. Adding a new memory module or adapter can result in a conflict if the switch or jumper settings on the mother-board or the new adapter board are incorrect. Adding new software can introduce conflicts between device drivers, TSRs (common in DOS systems), or programs in your system.

Be sure you install memory that is the proper type for your system and that operates at a speed fast enough for your CPU and its bus.

Environments such as Microsoft Windows 3.x have raised the awareness of memory management both in DOS and Windows and with application programs. Hardware and software conflicts within Windows will be covered in greater detail in later chapters.

Finally, your computer's memory is primarily a hardware issue. If you are going to use your computer to install Windows, Linux, FreeBSD, or another operating system, it will still need a sufficient quantity and speed of memory. Linux and FreeBSD generally make better use of memory and will run on systems having less memory than required by Windows 9x/Me/NT/2000. However, all operating systems require that you provide a system without memory problems.

In Part IV, Disk Drives, we cover the more permanent data storage system. Some people confuse Memory and Disk Storage, since they are often identified by so many bytes of space. Memory is fast and usually for temporary storage (the contents go away when you turn off the computer). Disk space is usually for more permanent storage and retains its content when the power is turned off.

✦   ✦   ✦

Disk Drives

The disk drive is your computer's long-term memory. It never forgets — well, almost never, and sometimes it is hard to find things that you know are "on there." Disks — diskettes, hard drives, removable disks — are the medium to which you save data. Like the tires and brakes on your car, you want them working properly. You want them to be in top condition. And you want them fixed quickly if they break, with as little loss of "road time" as possible.

By reading Part IV, you will realize that understanding disk drives and their configurations is essential to troubleshooting your PC. Considering that computer users expect disk drives to keep spinning endlessly at high speeds, their read/write heads hovering precariously over platters and shuffling about each time information is read or saved to a file, you must take the time and expend the effort to keep them in good working order.

Part IV shows you how to check your drive configurations, set up and optimize their file systems, and how to survive the most common failures. For disk drive failures that can occur, and from which you cannot recover, we have just three suggestions:

1. BACKUP!
2. BACKUP!!
3. BACKUP!!!

Disk Drive Basics

A disk drive is one of the few truly mechanical devices commonly found in PCs. Disk drives provide a place to store programs, files, data, and other information we use. We view the disk drive in our operating system and user interface as simply a drive letter or icon that contains directories or folders and individual data files. A lot of technology is behind the drive letter and folders that help keep track of files. Between the software that connects the disk drive to the operating system, and the plugs and wires used to connect a disk drive to our PCs, are a lot of details, bits, bytes, modes, interfaces, and jargon. The sooner we sort all of these things out, the better.

Disk Drive Types and References

The first hard disk drive was a fixed-platter, fixed-head device in which the read/write heads made light contact with the disk surface and did not hold much data. Considerable research led to advancements that brought us both the Winchester (heads were lifted to float above the disk surface) and Bernoulli (heads were held down to float or fly above the disk surface) hard drives. Along the way also came the invention of the flexible diskette drive for IBM. These basic technologies are still with us in one form or another today, in addition to the newer technologies of compact disc (CD-ROM) and digital video disc (DVD) drives, and various portable and removable drive and media offerings.

Although our primary focus in this chapter is hard or fixed disk drives, we also discuss diskette drives and higher-density cartridge drives (IOMEGA/Bernoulli, Zip, Jaz, Syquest, Avatar, and LS-120 products such as the SuperDrive from Imation). We also discuss the CD-ROM drives, including DVD, and magneto-optical drives. All of these devices are different in both their physical and software characteristics and in their connections to the system. They can show up on your system as a logical disk drive letter (at least in DOS, Windows, and OS/2) or as a drive icon. What we mean by this is that many different methods or layers refer to and define the presence of a disk drive.

The following is a list of different ways a disk drive may be identified:

✦ Type of bus used by the drive's adapter, including Industry Standard Architecture (ISA), Peripheral Component Interconnect (PCI), Small Computer System interface (SCSI), and others

✦ The ISA, local bus, SCSI, Extended ISA (EISA), or PCI add-in slots or system board ports used by the disk drive adapter

✦ Address, interrupt request (IRQ), and direct memory access (DMA) assignment of the adapter

✦ Type of drive adapter and its interface to the drive

✦ Diskette, hard drive — ST506, Enhanced Small Device Interface (ESDI), Integrated Drive Electronics (IDE) — SCSI, or drive specific

✦ Drive hierarchy or device number as seen by the adapter

✦ Master, Slave, Drive 0, Drive 1, SCSI Device ID #

✦ Basic input/output system (BIOS) and DOS device numbers assigned to the drive

✦ The specific file system partition on a hard drive

✦ Drive letter assigned to a logical drive as or within a partition

✦ Volume label given to a drive by the user

We discuss each of these briefly, although a bit out of order, for reasons that should become obvious as we go along.

Drive interface bus

The type of bus used by the disk drive's interface is not terribly important in terms of the drive's preparation and use, unless you have special drivers or memory constraints as discussed in Part III of this book, which covers configuration, startup, and memory problems. It is important to know that disk drive interfaces built onto the system board may be considered either ISA or PCI types, although some systems also provide SCSI adapters, depending on the system board. Diskette adapters and interfaces are almost always ISA-bus devices, as they do not require the higher speed performance or special BIOS handling required by new IDE and Enhanced IDE (EIDE) hard drives.

Except in the case of SCSI adapters, which can accept 6 to 15 devices, each disk drive adapter or interface will accommodate up to two drives per interface.

PC, XT, AT, and subsequent systems natively only provide for diskette and non-SCSI hard drive interfaces in their BIOS and DOS. By default, the BIOS will attempt to boot up from a diskette and then a standard hard drive interface, in that order. If your PC does not have a bootable diskette or a standard hard drive interface (either ISA, ESDI, or IDE) or hard drive BIOS in memory, the system BIOS may detect and use an appropriate SCSI BIOS, adapter, and hard drive as if they were a standard hard drive. It may be used for boot up and logical drive assignment purposes. Because SCSI drives were not included in the original PC standard, you will not see a standard or reserved address or IRQ assignment for SCSI adapters.

The address and IRQ assignments for standard disk drive interfaces are given in Table 16-1.

Table 16-1 **Address and IRQ Assignments for Standard Disk Drive Interfaces**			
Drive Interface	*Address*	*IRQ*	*Drive Letters*
First diskette interface	3F0–3F7	6	A and B (are reserved for the diskette adapter. If none exists, there is no drive A or drive B.)
Second diskette interface	370–377	6	C and D (or the next letter after the last hard drive letter if one or more hard drives are installed)
First hard drive interface	1F0–1F7	14	C and D and up*
Second hard drive interface	170–177	15	E and F and up*

* There are exceptions to drive letter assignments for hard drives depending on the number of drives and how they are partitioned and formatted, as discussed later in this chapter.

Typically there is a drive interface at the first expected address location. If no drive interface is detected at the first interface's address, the BIOS and DOS will skip over it and use the second interface as though it were the first. Drive lettering will begin according to the logical assignment rules for the first disk found on the first interface found. As with COM and LPT ports, this is a dynamic assignment process performed at bootup. If the first interface is found to exist, by replacement or enabling the interface in setup, the logical drive letter assignments will begin on the first interface as usual. This is not the case, however, if a diskette interface is missing: DOS will not assign drive letter A to the first hard drive if there are no diskette drives.

Note   Drive designations A and B are reserved for diskette drives only.

Device numbers

The BIOS and DOS assign and share drive device identification numbers. These numbers are assigned in a logical order, based on the interface to which a drive is connected. Diskette drives are assigned numbers 0, 1, 2, and 3. Fixed or hard disk drives are assigned device or drive numbers 80, 81, 82, and 83. Appropriate SCSI drives with proper BIOS support can be assigned hard drive device numbers in sequence as well.

You are not likely to encounter these device numbers unless you are doing very low-level programming in assembly language, or are involved with disk interface hardware design. Device numbers are used to specify a particular physical hard drive, without reference to drive letters, partitions, and so on. You may see the hard drive number assignments displayed during the bootup process with some BIOS; otherwise, you won't see the assignments unless you are working with program code that uses the BIOS or addresses the hardware directly. Such references are necessary when building disk utility software or creating new BIOS or operating systems.

Logical drive letter assignments

DOS, Windows, Linux, Unix, and OS/2 are kind enough to shield us from the lower-level details of how disk drives are actually detected and assigned drive letters. Well, that's true in most cases in which we have one or two diskette drives and one or two hard drives, and the hard drives only have one partition each. Linux and Unix do not even use drive letters. Linux and Unix deal with "devices" that become volumes or parts of volumes and file systems.

Drive letter assignments get a little more confusing depending on how you partition and format your hard drives. The first DOS-formatted partition on the first or only hard drive detected is always drive C. If you have more than one DOS-formatted partition on this single hard drive, the drive letters then increment from D and up. If you were to add a second hard drive to the existing multiple-partitioned drive, the first DOS-formatted partition on the second drive would become drive D, and all the other drive letters on the first drive would be bumped up a notch (becoming E, F, and so on.) When you run out of DOS partitions on the first drive, drive lettering would continue on the DOS partitions on the second hard drive, and so on.

Any additional CD-ROM, Zip, or Jaz drives, or other storage media installed in the system will be assigned letters in sequence after all the floppy and hard drives are handled. Network and RAM or virtual hard drive letters should be assigned after other media is addressed. Windows 95, 98, Me, NT, and 2000 do allow some latitude and additional configuration options for manually reassigning drive letters after these environments are loaded and running correctly.

The example becomes more complicated if you add a third and fourth hard drive. These drives will attach to the second hard drive interface. Introduce hard drives on SCSI adapters before you add more to a second interface, and then watch all of the drive letters shift around until you lose track of which physical hard drive actually hosts which logical drive letter's data. Understanding the concepts and methods of disassociating logical, conveniently named or referenced devices from their physical and programmed characteristics can be quite challenging. We include several real-world examples in the sections ahead.

Early hard drive systems

Small hard disk systems were first introduced using the ST506/ST412 electronic interface designed by Seagate Technology in the early 1980s. Since hard drives became available and affordable, we have seen the introduction of the SCSI, ESDI, and IDE drive interfaces. Each has advantages in features suitable to a variety of systems and applications. The type of drive and interface you choose can make a significant difference in system capacity, performance, and reliability.

You have two choices:

✦ The original ST506 (the original hard disk interface type), which includes both modified frequency modulation (MFM) and run-length limited (RLL) data schemes (no longer available except in floppy disk drives)

✦ ESDI, SCSI, or IDE interfaces and drive types

Note You may also select a simple controller, or one with built-in caching or advanced error-correction schemes to improve the drive-to-system data transfer performance.

ST506 (MFM and RLL) and ESDI drives and interfaces are effectively obsolete, having been replaced by less expensive and more efficient IDE or SCSI drives. ST506 and ESDI disk drive controllers are not always interchangeable. Unless you are replacing the disk controller in your system for one identical in make, model, and revision level, you may find that the disk drive is unusable because of differences in the controllers. Most controller cards are configured for that model or revision of controller, and this information may be written on the disk drive.

You cannot reliably connect a drive formatted and used on a Western Digital controller to an Adaptec or Seagate controller and expect to use it without reformatting. A more common scenario would be replacing the original IBM XT or AT Xebec controller with one from Western Digital, Adaptec, or another vendor. You will have to reformat the drive at the low level, repartition with FDISK, and then DOS format the drive, losing all of the existing data on the drive.

Controllers and Interfaces

There is a difference between a disk controller and an interface or host adapter card. With ST506 and ESDI drives, a disk controller is required to provide not only the interface to the system board's input/output (I/O) bus, but also basic drive control and data read and write functions (meaning there will be more than one cable connecting the drive). A disk controller may also contain its own BIOS to interpret and process drive control and data operations. This BIOS would also likely provide low-level format and some error-correcting functions because they are not performed by the PC's BIOS.

For SCSI and IDE drives, the interface between the system board I/O bus is more of an adapter, possibly with some data-handling functions in an on-board BIOS program. For SCSI systems, this interface is commonly called a *host adapter*. Interfaces or adapters are typically less complex than complete disk controllers. They do not need to provide a lot of support for hard drive control functions because these are supported within the hard drive electronics.

In the progression of the PC's development, we have seen a lot of disk drive types come and go. We will not dwell on the earlier ones because they are no longer available or supported through any vendors; however, if you still have one running, most diagnostic and utility software will still work with them, and the principles of partitioning, formatting, and such still apply. The point in mentioning these items is to help you identify the drive, interface, and controller type you have now, and the options you have, or do not have, for correction or replacement if trouble arises.

ST506/ST412 types

The ST506/ST412-type drives commonly available for PCs were in add-in drive and controller kits, providing a storage capacity of 20MB. These drive types are still in use in many old systems, but they are out of production and can only be found used or refurbished in surplus electronics and computer supply outlets.

Commonly recognized manufacturers of ST506/ST412-type disk drives for PCs are Seagate, Maxtor, Miniscribe, Micropolis, Rodime, and Quantum.

The maximum data transfer rate for this interface is specified by standards as 5 megabits per second (Mbps), or 625,000 bytes per second. This is much faster than a diskette system and suits the performance of PC, XT, and slower AT systems.

ST506/ST412-type disk drives require a hard disk controller card to create a hard disk control interface for the system BIOS, and also to interconnect the system board bus with the disk drive. The hard disk controller card may or may not contain other interface circuits, such as those for diskette drives, serial and parallel ports, and so on. The most commonly found hard disk controller cards, for standard MFM data recording drives, are from Everex, Omti, and Western Digital. Western Digital and Adaptec made controllers that supported RLL data recording.

Note In most cases, RLL-type controllers cannot be used on MFM-type drives because MFM drives do not support the data formatting used by RLL data recording techniques (26 sectors per track versus 17, for higher data density and storage capacity).

Figure 16-1 shows the ST506 interface connectors. The ST506 interface on a hard drive has two adjacent rows of gold-colored pads that extend from the connector on the bottom rear of the drive. As you face the back of the drive, the leftmost row contains 10 pads on each side (20-pin connector) and the right row contains 17 pads on each side (34-pin connector). The space between the two rows distinguishes the connectors of the ST506 interface from those of the ESDI interface.

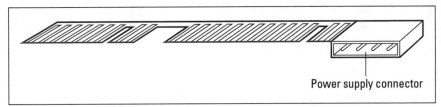

Power supply connector

Figure 16-1: The ST506 interface connectors

The ST506/ST412 electronic, or cabling, interface appears on both MFM- and RLL-type drives, so the interface type alone is not an absolute reference to performance, disk capacity, or the type of adapter you will use with the drive. This interface supports two disk drives. Two cables are required per drive.

One cable is a 34-pin ribbon cable between the controller card and the one or two drives. This cable carries drive-addressing information, and has four wires twisted in the middle of the cable between the first and second drive connectors — much like the diskette drive cable, the first drive goes on the far end. The four twisted wires for a hard drive cable begin four wires in from the 34th wire (the non-striped edge). For a diskette drive cable, the twisted wires begin with the 10th wire in from the striped edge. The second connector cable is a 20-pin straight-through cable, one for each drive, between the controller and the drive to carry the data.

ST506 drives require low-level formatting or initialization to establish the type of data areas required by the operating system. A low-level formatting program is usually contained within the hard disk controller card, but an external DOS program may also be used.

Actual performance or data transfer drops to between 400,000 and 600,000 bytes per second, depending on the sector interleave formatted on the drive, the computer bus speed, and the performance of the controller card.

> **Tip**   The ST506 interface has been a reliable standard for years. You should not encounter any problems switching between vendors for ST506, except that the controller might create unique data signatures on the disk drive, which may not be compatible with other controllers.

ESDI

The Enhanced Small Disk Interface (ESDI) is a step up from ST506 (see Figure 16-2). You can identify the ESDI interface on a hard drive by the two adjacent rows of gold-colored finger-like projections that extend from the bottom rear of the drive. This spacing is less than that of ST506 drives. It offers high-performance data transfer capacity and can handle larger disk sizes defined for PC systems. These drives use a two-cable interface that is similar to the ST506 drives, but the drive connections are typically much closer together. ESDI drives, like ST506/ST412 drives, are no longer in production. Seagate and Maxtor were two of the most common makers of ESDI drives.

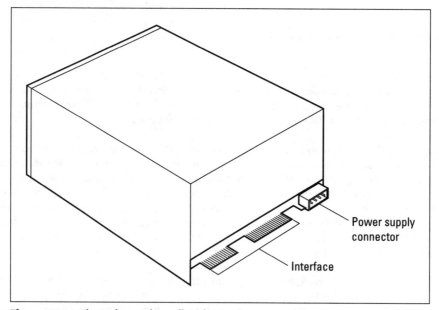

Figure 16-2: The Enhanced Small Disk Interface

The data transfer capability can be as high as 20MB per second. Early ESDI units were only capable of 10MB per second. Actual performance depends on the adapter card and your system I/O bus speed.

ESDI drives are not merely old drives with new wheels. Most were designed as high-performance drives from the inside out, commonly providing 34 sectors per track versus 17 for MFM drives or 26 for RLL drives. They also move the heads between tracks faster, often by using voice-coil positioning instead of stepping motors.

 Note ESDI drives require an ESDI-specific, add-in disk controller card that often provides formatting and high-capacity translation functions between DOS, BIOS, and the drive. Western Digital and DPT are the most common makers of ESDI controllers.

There have been several ESDI controllers available with various caching and advanced features, which are especially useful for demanding applications or network servers. Only one known standards problem exists among ESDI devices from different vendors. As with ST506 controllers and drives, you may not be able to replace a controller from one manufacturer with that of another without reformatting the drive. To provide larger drive capacities, ESDI controllers can perform a translation of a drive's head, sector, and cylinder values to match those available or within the limits of the system board BIOS drive types. These translations are necessary due to the BIOS and DOS limitations discussed earlier.

SCSI

The Small Computer Systems Interface (SCSI) is a general-purpose interface that may be used for hard disk drives, tape drives, CD-ROM drives, or nearly any other high-speed device of interest. SCSI is one of two drive types of choice for high-performance applications, competing with the lower-cost and, until recently, the limited IDE interface. SCSI devices are more universally supported in networking and other non-DOS applications and systems. You will commonly see SCSI hard drives from Quantum, Seagate (which also produces drives known formerly as Imprimis and CDC), Conner, IBM, Micropolis, Maxtor, and Western Digital.

SCSI is the interface of choice for Apple Macintosh computers and many workstations. With little trouble, an SCSI device can be attached and used in minutes. SCSI host adapter cards for PCs are slightly more expensive than other drive interface types because their performance (the speed and methods with which data can be transferred) is extremely fast and the complexity for handling different types of storage devices is increased.

 Note One advantage that comes with the higher cost of SCSI is that an SCSI host adapter card can be used for many different types of storage devices, and you can use more than the DOS limit of two physical hard drives with special driver software support.

The host adapter is much more than an interface between the system data bus and the drives. Host adapters usually provide a BIOS to translate PC BIOS and other program operations into SCSI device commands, and to eliminate the need for worrying about drive parameters and setting drive types. SCSI host adapters are available from a number of companies, the most common being Adaptec, Buslogic, and Always Technologies. Adaptec, NCR, and others also make their host adapter circuits available to system board manufacturers, enabling them to provide built-in SCSI support without an add-in card. Integrating the SCSI interface directly on the system board can greatly improve data transfer performance.

The SCSI interface standard provides for up to seven (or fifteen for the newer, 32-bit bus cards) attached devices, although not all host adapters support more than one or two devices, such as the SCSI interface for CD-ROM drives provided on some PC sound cards. The attached devices may be disk, tape, CD-ROM drives, or document scanners. You may have multiple host adapters installed in your system, enabling you to have more than seven (or fifteen for most 16-bit cards) attached SCSI devices.

The standard electrical interface between SCSI devices is a single 50-pin ribbon cable. SCSI devices are connected in parallel, and there may be up to eight connectors on a single cable. Alternative SCSI cabling may be available from a 25-pin, D-style connector, a miniature 50-pin parallel connector, or a miniature 68-pin parallel connector for the Fast-Wide SCSI-III specification. See Figure 16-3 for an illustration of the 50-pin connection.

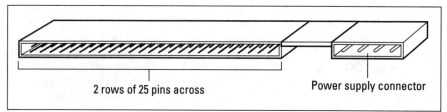

2 rows of 25 pins across   Power supply connector

Figure 16-3: The 50-pin connection

Tip   You can identify the SCSI interface on a hard drive or other storage device by the two rows of 25 pin-like projections extending from the connector on the bottom rear of the drive. The rows are often surrounded by a black- or blue-colored plastic shell or collar that guides the female SCSI connector onto the pins properly.

Devices are addressed uniquely with jumpers or switches on each drive. The host adapter is addressed most often as device ID 7. The first and second hard drives are usually addressed as devices 0 and 1, respectively. The first hard drive is usually device 0, and it must be device 0 in order to use it for booting up the system. Additional disk drives should be numbered in succession from the first and second just to keep it simple, unless the adapter, BIOS, or driver software imposes another requirement. CD-ROM and tape drives may use any device ID from 2 to 6 (or to 15) that is not in use by another device.

The SCSI connections must also be electrically terminated with a set of plug-in resistors at the host adapter and at the last device connected to the cable. These resistors help make sure that the electrical signals do not pick up interference and that they properly transfer the ones and zeros of digital data between devices.

Advanced SCSI programming interface

Support for and access to some SCSI devices, such as CD-ROM and tape drives, require the use of device drivers or special software to interpret and adapt the non-DOS/non-disk data formats of these devices for BIOS and DOS functions. The most common device driver for this purpose is called an ASPI driver. Advanced SCSI Programming Interface (ASPI) provides a standard software interface between programs and the host adapter. This enables access to standard SCSI device functions for DOS and other programs that need to communicate with SCSI devices but may be unable to talk to the host adapter directly through software. ASPI drivers must be provided by the host adapter manufacturer because, typically, only they know the specifics about their hardware, and can create the translations necessary to provide ASPI program services to other applications.

In DOS and Windows 3.x systems, the ASPI driver, or manager, as it is often called, is loaded into memory by the CONFIG.SYS file at boot time. Windows 95/98/Me and NT/2000 provide this driver internally. It must be loaded before any other drivers or programs that require the ASPI interface. These may be CD-ROM drivers, which should be loaded before the CD-ROM interface to the operating system (such as MSCDEX, provided for MS-DOS). Appropriate example line entries in a typical CONFIG.SYS file are shown here:

```
DEVICE=ASPI4DOS.SYS   (Adaptec ASPI driver)
DEVICE=ASPICD.SYS /D:ASPICD0    (Adaptec CD-ROM driver)
```

SCSI performance

The performance of the SCSI interface enables data transfers of 10MB per second and higher (40MB per second for the Fast-Wide SCSI-III interface). The actual performance achieved depends on the drive specifications, the system board, whether the SCSI host adapter supports DMA data transfers (which pass through the CPU), or Programmed I/O (standard CPU-controlled data reads and writes), and the operating system. DOS, Windows 3.x, and Windows 95/98/Me are not capable of taking full advantage of SCSI performance capabilities, unlike Windows NT/2000, Unix, and OS/2.

SCSI is a standard, but it may only be a standard within specific system architectures (such as PC or Mac) and hopefully, a consistent standard among vendors.

In most cases, it is easy to interchange adapters and drives of different manufacture, but you must be aware of whether the drive you are using is an SCSI-1 or an SCSI-II device, because these types of drives require an adapter that supports these types. You can connect an SCSI-I device to an SCSI-II adapter, but you may not be able to use an SCSI-II device on an SCSI-I adapter. Today, Fast SCSI, Wide SCSI, and SCSI-III standards have evolved to further enhance performance and capabilities and are also not compatible with the older SCSI adapters.

Tip   The main symptom of incompatible device types is that the device will simply not be recognized or available to BIOS and the operating system. The solution typically involves upgrading to host adapters or drives with mutually compatible support levels — typically to SCSI-II or SCSI-III standards. To identify attached SCSI devices or diagnose them, you typically use software provided with the device, host adapter card, or ASPI driver software.

Integrated Drive Electronics

The Integrated Drive Electronics (IDE) drives define the connections between the system and the drive, and the common and required internal operation of the drive. The drive contains all of the circuitry normally found on a disk drive for motor and head control, and reading and writing data, plus a PC bus interface that replaces an add-in controller card (such as those used for ST506 and ESDI drives). Providing the interface electronics together with the drive electronics at the drive allows for smaller and faster drives. Advanced electronics and disk media in the drive allow a higher concentration of data and greater reliability through advanced data writing and error-correction schemes.

All IDE drives are not created equal. A set of technical standards exists for IDE drives, but these standards did not necessarily apply to early drives. Also, manufacturers of IDE drives have not universally or fully implemented all the standards, and the existing standards left some features open to wide interpretation, and thus are handled differently in different drives.

IDE drives, interfaces, and adapters have continued to improve. IDE drives used to provide only basic data transfer functions. Now they include on-board data-caching, faster programmed I/O (requires time from the system CPU) transfer modes, and Direct Memory Access transfers (direct reads from and writes to memory without involving the PC's CPU). IDE drives with capacities larger than 6GB are now quite common.

Installing an IDE drive is a matter of drive selection jumpers, the mechanical placement of the drive in the box, and running a single data cable, along with a power cable. The drive selection jumpers tell a drive if it is the only drive or if it is the first or second drive in a two-drive system. The implementation of drive selections is not the same for all drive manufacturers. Sometimes, a drive must be the first or must be the second drive or may not work at all with a drive from another manufacturer in a two-drive system. Because of the number of different drives and methods of selection, it is impossible for us to provide much help for this situation. If this information is not clearly available in the owner's manual for your drives, you will have to contact the manufacturer's technical support office to get the information you need.

Electrical connection of IDE drives consists of a 40-pin ribbon cable, as pictured in Figure 16-4.

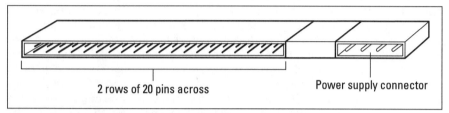

2 rows of 20 pins across   Power supply connector

Figure 16-4: 40-pin ribbon cable electrical connection of IDE

Tip

You can identify the IDE interface on a hard drive by the two rows of pins extending from the connector on the bottom rear of the drive. Pin 1, the striped edge of the cabling, is typically located near the DC power connector. Because of electrical restrictions, this cable should be limited to 18 inches in total length.

The connections from the drive to the system are essentially direct to the PC system data bus, with an adapter card or chip to isolate and protect various signals. These connections may be provided by an add-in card or through a connector on the system board.

Based on the early PC hard drive system specification, we are limited to two drive interfaces with only two drives each. The computer and operating system has to do a lot of work to perform disk operations unless the BIOS, chip set, interface, and drive all support the new UltraDMA33 mode of operation. IDE still lags behind the best SCSI devices as far as performance, but its use has been expanded to include CD-ROM and other media, such as Zip and tape drives, making it possible to choose between SCSI and electronic data interface (EDI) for most common storage devices.

Primary and secondary interfaces

Most system boards and IDE interfaces provide two hard drive ports — a primary port at address 1F0h using IRQ 14, and a secondary port at address 170h using IRQ 15. Each interface supports a maximum of two drives. The drives connected to each interface may be either hard drives, CD-ROM drives, tape drives, or other IDE-interfaced devices. The system BIOS sorts out which drive is which by using the on-drive Master/Slave configuration jumpers, which relate to the BIOS assigned disk drive device numbers 80h and 81h on the primary interface and 82h and 83h on the secondary interface. The device numbers relate only to hard drives. Other devices are not natively recognized nor assigned BIOS device numbers.

Note   In most cases if you expect to be able to boot up from one of the drives, a hard drive with the boot files and operating system on it must be configured as a Master drive and connected to the first interface. Some system BIOS now have the option of being able to seek out and boot up from a bootable CD-ROM disk as well, but the convention is to have the boot drive on the first interface port as a Master drive.

There are two types of drive interface and selection cables. Most new IDE drives typically connect to the interface with a 40-pin flat ribbon cable that has a single connector at the interface port end that is wired straight through in parallel to two connectors spaced slightly apart at the other end, enabling a connection to either or both of two drives. Since all of the connectors in most configurations are hooked up in parallel, it does not matter which connector goes to which drive (Master or Slave). Very early and mostly obsolete systems use a similar 40-pin cable but, at the drive connectors, you will notice one of the wires is trimmed off so that its signal does not reach the drive. This means that the drives must be configured using Cable Select jumpers, rather than the Master/Slave jumpers, to determine which drive is which.

Master/Slave and Cable Select configurations

IDE drives provide configuration options to act as the Master or the Slave drive in a two-drive-per-interface configuration. The Master and Slave jumpers configure the routing of the drive addressing signal into, through/between, and out of the drives. In the simplest form, a drive needs to be told that it is a Master — whether or not a Slave drive is also attached is determined by the drive; the Slave drive needs only be told that it is the Slave. Some drives require that you also set an additional jumper to indicate that there is a Slave drive attached on the same cable.

Older drives used a Cable Select jumper that configures which drive gets the drive addressing signal to determine whether it is the first, or Master, drive versus the second, or Slave, drive.

Note   Because there are so many different drives available, it is recommended that you consult the drive documentation or each manufacturer's Web site to obtain the latest information about configuring drives from different manufacturers.

EIDE drives

Enhanced IDE, or EIDE, drives are generally those that provide greater than PIO Mode 2 data transfer performance, and are larger than 512MB. To take advantage of these features requires disk drive BIOS, in either the system or interface card, that supports these modes and larger drives. Today, EIDE drives typically support Mode 4 PIO and UDMA-33 or UDMA-66.

UDMA-33 and UDMA-66

Since 1995 or so, many IDE hard drives have had the capability to perform DMA transfers at speeds of up to 33 or 66 megabits per second — provided that the hard drive interface chip and the operating system also supported this operating mode. CD-ROM drives have acquired this capability also. As significant as this increase in data transfer rate is, it is barely noticeable under Windows 95, 98 or Me because these operating systems do not perform DMA transfers to full rate or efficiently without affecting other tasks.

IDE smarts

IDE drives are relatively flexible in terms of adapting themselves to the limitations of available drive types in the system board BIOS, selected and saved in the complimentary metal-oxide semiconductor (CMOS) setup process. Many drives can translate automatically and change their apparent or logical cylinder, head, and sector parameters to suit the drive types available in the PC's BIOS so that you do not lose functionality or capacity, which can occur when drives and system drive types do not match.

These drives are also self-correcting in that they have data space reserved to replace data areas that are bad or become bad during the drive's life. If one or more sectors go bad, that area is marked as bad by the drive's internal computer. The computer saves this information, and another good area of the drive is used in its place. This makes IDE drives virtually error free.

You should never see a data error due to a bad disk area with an IDE drive. There is a limit, relative to each drive and manufacturer, as to how much of the data area on a drive can be bad, and thus the data is reallocated to the spare sector area, before the spare area fills up. When this happens, you begin to see errors that can only be corrected, or more precisely, avoided, by repartitioning and DOS formatting (but not low-level formatting) the drive, or through the use of a disk utility program such as the Norton Disk Doctor or Gibson's SpinRite.

Many recent IDE drives are "SMART," that is, they are equipped with a new self-monitoring analysis and reporting technology system. The SMART system can be built into disk drives to monitor their reliability and performance, and to communicate this information back to the system or to software such as Symantec/Norton's System Doctor monitoring program. SMART takes advantage of years of disk drive technology and reliability and failure history. It monitors the mechanical, electronic, and data aspects of the disk drive, determines conditions or trends, and then reports these findings to the system, indicating potential problem areas. This gives you or your system administrator the opportunity to plan ahead for making a backup of data and drive replacement. Very "SMART" indeed.

Tip   Even without SMART, troubleshooting an IDE drive problem is simple. If you receive bad sector or general errors, the drive is probably defective or is going bad. Often, the failure is sudden and absolute. You lose all data, without using enhanced recovery processes done by specialists.

Older, conventional drive test and correction software, and reformatting or interleaving software, unless specifically designed to work with IDE drives, is generally useless. You can scan a disk for problems with CHKDSK or SCANDISK software, or older (pre-1992) diagnostics, but the built-in controller may mask most of them. It might correct the problems before you see them or prevent you from taking conventional steps to correct the data problems as you might for other drive types.

Forget that format

IDE drives do one of three things in response to commands that tell it to perform a low-level format, depending on whether the drive is new (1992+) and follows industry standards:

✦ Drives complying with current industry standards should simply accept the format command and do nothing but return an indication that the operation is complete, although no formatting will have been performed.

✦ Older drives may indicate an error in response to the format command because they do not support that function and cannot do anything with it.

✦ If neither of the first two responses occurs, and your drive is busy for a few minutes, chances are a format is occurring. This destroys the head-positioning data, erasing all data and otherwise making the drive useless.

IDE drives usually cannot and should not be low-level formatted in the traditional sense (as you would for ST506, ESDI, or SCSI drives). The internal track positioning for the read/write heads is determined by data written on the disk adjacent to the data. Most drives self-correct the head position during normal operation so that track-formatting is unnecessary.

Steve Gibson's SpinRite program performs very in-depth testing and rewriting of drive data areas to account for tolerance and mechanical changes, and to increase reliability. The only remedy for an improperly reformatted drive is to have it reworked by the original manufacturer or a data recovery service, which may still have the equipment available to repair your specific (older) drive.

Backing up an IDE drive

The need for regular backups has never been more obvious than for IDE drive systems. Granted, the drive systems as a whole are simpler and more reliable, but you have less control or ability to separate the electronics from the drive and repair single flaws. A defective IDE drive is often cheaper to replace than repair. As system components get more modular, you will replace entire drive systems, and perhaps entire PC systems, in the near future instead of having a technician replace a resistor or single IC chip. Bigger components mean higher prices for their replacement, but the repair will be quicker, and in all cases, time is money.

ATAPI

The AT-Attachment Programming Interface (ATAPI) is a standard specification for communicating with various devices, such as CD-ROM drives, which offer a wide range of multimedia and differing data formats, in addition to behaving like read-only removable media disk drives. Since there are many data formats and the capability for multimedia/mixed content CD-ROMs, ATAPI, like the ASPI for SCSI devices, offers a wider range of device control and information options for the support of features such as audio and recordable CD-ROMs.

ATAPI features are usually included within the CD-ROM device driver loaded from the CONFIG.SYS file for DOS and Windows 3.*x* systems, and within the operating system for Windows 95, 98, Me, NT, and 2000 systems.

How data is put on the platters

There are several methods for squeezing large amounts of data onto the relatively small disk platters. They all involve turning magnetic pulses on and off as the disk moves under the magnetic read/write head. The various characteristics depend on the preparation of those pulses before they get to the disk, how much information can be put in a given space, and the precision and quality of the read/write heads and the disk platters themselves. We'll discuss two terms that are not spoken of very much today, but they mattered a few years ago when disk drive technology was changing, and they provided us more complicated choices. Today we worry much less about how the data gets and stays on the platters and more about how much data we can write and how fast we can put it there.

MFM

The earliest method used is called modified frequency modulation (MFM). This is a low-density recording method that yields 17 sectors per track and the conventional 512 bytes per sector. Until 1987 or so, this was the only method of putting data on disks used in PCs, and it is still the method used for diskettes.

The technical details are not particularly important to MFM, and they are more appreciated when discussing RLL drives.

Run-Length-Limited

Run-Length-Limited (RLL) encoding is a much higher-density method of writing data on the disk surface. RLL takes less space to store the same amount of data than the MFM method.

An RLL-encoded disk typically has 26 sectors per track, increasing the capacity of the drive by 1.5 times that of MFM-written drives. Not all disk platters can accept this higher density. Drives that can accept higher densities specifically state that they are RLL-certified. RLL drives have platters made of finer materials, created with greater precision to support the higher data density more reliably.

Some higher quality (higher priced) hard drives that specify they are MFM-only drives might accept RLL-encoding, but there are no guarantees. RLL-certified drives have no problem accepting lower-density MFM data, but wasting an RLL platter on MFM cheats you out of 30 percent of your drive capacity.

In each case, the controller is specific to the recording method used and it requires absolute control over the drive, such as that provided by the ST506, or ESDI interface.

Note   SCSI and IDE drives use RLL and other advanced techniques to place more data on the drive. These may be similar to the method used for older ST506 and ESDI drives, or modified to concentrate more data in the smaller areas of 2.5-inch and 3.5-inch drives.

Diskettes and drives

Until the introduction of the small-format hard disk drives that we get with PCs, diskettes or cassette or paper tapes were the only way small computer users had to store data. The capacity of the first diskettes to appear for IBM PCs held all of 160,000 bytes of information — that's smaller than the size of this chapter.

We have seen 2.88MB diskette drives as standard equipment on new IBM systems, and 100 to 120MB diskette-like units are on the market and even found in portable computers.

The most common problems you may have with diskettes include the following:

✦ Data loss due to improper handling or careless placement (leaving them in extremely hot or cold places, or next to wires, CRTs, motors, or magnets; or exposing them to dust, static, or x-rays). Do not use a refrigerator magnet to hold a diskette in plain view.

✦ Excessive data errors on less-expensive bulk disks.

✦ Improper formatting of disks, which is quite easy to do when buying bulk disks that have no label stating their capacity.

✦ Formatting over a diskette that has data on it, which makes the data unrecoverable.

✦ Slippage in worn-out drives or because there is no added hub ring at the center hole to help hold the disk on the spindle.

✦ Data loss or errors due to dirty drive heads.

✦ Jamming or catching in cheap or broken drives.

✦ Improper placement in a drive, or forgetting to close the drive door or latch before use.

✦ Forgetting to open the drive door or latch.

✦ Spreading of data viruses from system to system.

✦ Attempting to increase the capacity of low or standard (referred to as double-density) disks (making 1.44MB diskettes from 720K disks by using a special hole punch or drill).

It's All in the Details

As you work with disk drives, you will see drive parameters referring to cylinders, tracks, heads, and sectors. Sectors are the individual data storage blocks. The basic data storage capacity of a sector is 512 bytes. This value holds true for most media types, and it is also known as a single block of data. Heads, or read/write heads, read data from and write data to individual sectors. Tracks are concentric rings of sectors aligned around a disk drive's platters. A cylinder represents the tracks, on both sides of all platters at a particular radius.

Cylinders and tracks are related but have an important distinction. A disk with 1,024 cylinders and four heads (one head for each side of two platters) has 4,096 total tracks (1,024 × 4). The heads are positioned by cylinders, which place them over the same track on different surfaces. Heads will move the range of the maximum number of cylinders. This is referred to as placing a head over a specific track.

Disk drives store data as magnetic strips of data bits in incremental areas, known as sectors, on a disk. A single sector is referenced by its location on one side of one of the disc-shaped platters inside the drive (or diskette) housing. The location of a sector is more or less two-dimensional. Sectors are located in the concentric rings known as tracks, which are spaced out across the diameter of the platter. These rings are subdivided by radial sections that cut the platter into pie-shaped slices, from the center to the outer circumference. "Sectors per track" refers to the number of pie-shaped subdivisions made around a data track.

Some disk parameters refer to the number of tracks per inch and differing numbers of sectors per track. This indicates the density with which data may be reliably stored on the disk medium. The quality of the magnetic oxide material used to store the data, the quality of the surface on which it is laid, and the precision of the movement of the read/write heads that place and detect the magnetic signals on the platter all determine how much data can be placed on a disk. Technology has advanced considerably from once-common 14-inch hard disk platters that held 2.5MB of data to 8-inch flexible (floppy) disk to 5.25-inch disk and hard disks to 3.5-inch diskettes and hard drives. Newer types of diskette-sized removable disks, either flexible media or hard media, that store 100MB to 2GB of data in a single cartridge are available. Portable computers have 2.5-inch hard disks that may hold more than 4GB of data. Technology has also given us 1.8-inch Personal Computer Memory Card International Association (PCMCIA) disk drives. (And some folks say the space program has done nothing for us. . . .) Figure 16-5 shows an interior view of a typical hard drive.

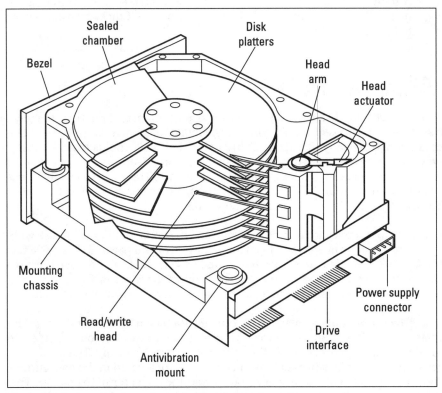

Figure 16-5: Interior view of a typical hard drive from the rear

Data sectors are read-from or written-to by placing a read/write head, which is similar to the needle on a phonograph, over the cylindrical division or track of interest. A magnetic impulse is sensed, or placed, on the platter by the read/write head. The position of the tracks is controlled by sensors attached to a mechanical arm that moves the read/write head over the disk surface, from outer edge to an inner limit. Individual sectors are found by timing the rotation of the disk from a reference mark (such as the little hole or index mark in a disk) or by reading the sector number information written on the disk.

Most disks use at least one side or surface of the disk for data storage. Early disk drives used only one side of the disk, much as a CD-ROM (for music or data) uses only one side of the plastic compact disc. Most hard disk drives contain at least two disc platters, and they store data on both sides of the platter, requiring four read/write heads inside the drive housing. In some drives, one side of one platter and one read/write head is dedicated to helping the drive locate the track and sector position information, at the expense of valuable data storage space. Others may use both sides of the disk platter for data and positional information interleaved together on the media.

Disk Space Defined

For the purpose of these discussions, and as it applies to PCs and DOS (and Windows and other operating systems), assume that all disks store 512 bytes of data per sector or as a 512-byte data block, and that this is the smallest possible data storage area to which you can assign files. This has been the case for most disk drives and diskettes used in mainframe, mini-, and micro-computers, including the PC and other popular computers and storage devices. Tape drives also usually store data in 512-byte increments or blocks.

You can calculate a disk drive's total data storage capacity by multiplying the total number of cylinders by the total number of heads (yielding the total number of tracks). Multiply that result by the total number of sectors per track and then by the data storage size of the sectors. For example, a 1,024 cylinder drive, with 4 heads, 17 sectors per track, and 512 byte sectors will have a disk capacity of 35,651,584 bytes (about 32 MB).

It might not be obvious, but since data storage units are measured in blocks, or sectors, the minimum size a data file may occupy is at least one sector. If the computer's file system keeps files separated so they do not run into each other and keeps track of them properly, any file that is 512 bytes or less in size occupies one 512-byte sector. Two separate files, each less than or equal to 512 bytes, occupy two separate sectors. Files larger than 512 bytes occupy multiple and, ideally, sequential sectors on the disk. Keeping the data in sequential order leads to better read/write performance times.

 Note   Data that is stored out of sequential order is considered fragmented.

There are many 512-byte data blocks on a disk's surface. On an original 160K disk there are 312 sectors. On a 1.44MB diskette there are 2880 sectors in which data can be stored. A 20MB hard disk contains over 39,000 sectors. A 6GB hard disk contains over 10 million sectors. In the old days, data records were tracked by the number of

512-byte blocks they occupied, from the start to the end of a file. In many cases you had to know how many files you were going to be storing and how big you expected them to be. This forced a lot of advanced planning, but was not very efficient or flexible.

Fast-forward in time to the good old days of DOS and the implementation of the hard drive. The early PC and DOS developers did not envision the need for hard disk drives, much less drives that could hold over 8 billion characters. It is unlikely that anyone imagined having as many as 312 files back in 1981, much less 312 diskettes. We thought it significant when the shareware collections we kept up with consumed more than several hundred 1.44MB diskettes. Today, some of us have over 300 CD-ROM disks, which if they were full of data would be storing about 200GB of data and program files. And that's just personal programs and files.

DOS Version 1.0 did not support hard disks at all. DOS versions 2.1–3.2 supported up to two hard disks of up to 32MB capacity each. Relatively few of us saw much of DOS Version 4.*x,* which let us use disk drives of up to 2,048MB (2GB) with some limitations. We really enjoyed it when DOS 5.*x* and 6.*x* came along, giving us easier access to a lot more disk space through the capability to compress the data on our drives. Now many of us have reached and exceeded the 2GB limit and hope for more capacity—enter Windows 95 (with OEM Release 2-OSR2), NT, and now Windows 98/Me and 2000, with the capacity to handle a single logical drive of up to 2 tera-bytes—that is 2,000 gigabytes, or 2 million megabytes.

To keep track of all this data on the new hard drives requires a tremendous number of numbers, or some form of data tracking system. The DOS designers decided early on that they did not want to force users to predict how they would use their drives or how much data of what size they would be storing where (yet we do it anyway). Also, they had to be sure that most of the tracking system used for hard drives was compatible with the existing system used on diskettes. The method used on much smaller disk was inadequate to the task. Individually referencing 64,000 data sectors on a 32MB drive to individual files could occupy too much disk space. Thus, they devised the File Allocation Table system (FAT)—one that would allow an indirect reference to the location of a data file, and would not consume too much valuable disk space in the process.

Note   The File Allocation Table system is a two-tier system. The first tier is the file direc-tory that refers to the second tier. The second tier is a linked list that refers the physical or sector location of the pieces of a file on the disk. This second tier is actually the FAT.

The File Allocation Table does not deal with individual sectors. Instead it deals with clusters, or groups of sectors, which leads us to the next section.

Sectors and Clusters

Keeping track of every sector requires a lot of sector-information storage area and a numbering system that is easy to manage and quick to calculate so that it does not slow access to information. The numbering scheme that was first developed used a 12-bit numerical range, allowing up to 4,096 different sectors to be managed. This limited initial disk capacities to just over 2MB (4,096 × 512 bytes). This was quite adequate for diskettes, but a 2MB hard disk seemed impractical — at least for a PC (although some early minicomputer hard drives had 2.5MB-capacity data platters).

For capacities exceeding 2MB, a bigger number or another scheme had to be used. The original DOS developers realized this, and compared other disk file tracking systems before arriving at the file tracking system used now. The FAT is a small area of disk space dedicated to storing information about the status of all sectors on the disk drive.

Combining four sectors provided a data storage unit, or cluster, of 2,048 bytes. This was the first incremental step in increased capacity. DOS, through the FAT, began to keep track of data storage areas in 2,048-byte pieces rather than 512-byte pieces. This meant that any file of 512 bytes or less occupied the same single sector, but just one sector, in one storage unit, or cluster. This left three quarters of that cluster vacant and unusable by other files. DOS could and would run out of data storage units four times faster than before, if you stored a lot of small files.

Having 4,096 clusters, each containing 2,048 bytes, allowed for a disk capacity of 8MB. Because some of the first PC hard drives had capacities of 10 to 20MB, obviously having 4,096 × 2,048 bytes (or 2K) clusters was inadequate to manage the disk capacity. Since the numbering system to track storage units was limited to keeping track of only 4,096 units, the cluster size had to be increased to keep up with capacity. The next cluster size increments were 4,096 and 8,192 bytes. A 4K cluster allowed disk capacities of 16MB, whereas an 8K cluster (16 sectors) allowed disk capacities of 32MB.

Be Careful When Using CHKDSK

Utilities such as CHKDSK should not be run in a DOS window under Windows or other multitasking environments (although one from an older version of DOS may be run under Windows 95). You could use them only in their nondestructive/non-write modes to merely check for data errors, but running them outside of Windows is recommended. For CHKDSK, this means you should not use the /F switch that would allow CHKDSK to fix errors it finds. If you insist on running disk utilities under Windows, use only those utilities designed for this. The SCANDISK program included with Windows 95 and other Windows 95 specific utilities, such as Norton Disk Doctor with the Norton Utilities for Windows 95, are preferred. CHKDSK /F, run under Windows NT, will give you an option to perform the operation, along with the capability to fix found errors, the next time you restart Windows NT.

You can see this on your own system, with either the DOS CHKDSK program or other utility programs that provide detailed information about your disk drive.

The size and resulting number of clusters on a disk is determined through the hard disk definition or partitioning utility called FDISK. For the 12-bit FAT-12 file systems FDISK automatically increments the number of sectors per cluster to keep the number of clusters within the limit of 4,096. While a 32MB drive was thought to be huge initially, it was not long before users accumulated more data and programs and needed more or larger drives. Buying one larger drive was cheaper than adding a second drive.

DOS and FDISK support multiple partitions on a single disk, so you can have more than one logical disk of up to 32MB each partitioned out of a larger physical drive — for example, a 40MB or 80MB drive. Unfortunately, before DOS Version 3.2, you could not access these other partitions without using FDISK to change which drive was active or visible to DOS. Needless to say, this limitation had to go away if we were to advance anywhere toward the world of today's PCs. DOS 3.2 allowed access to multiple partitions or logical drives within the same larger hard disk, but those drives were still limited to 32MB each. Table 16-2 indicates disk capacity by the number and size of clusters.

Table 16-2
Cluster Sizes Versus DOS FAT (Partition) Types

FAT Type	Maximum Number of Clusters	Sectors per Cluster	Disk/Partition Cluster Size	Capacity
12-bit	4,096	1	512 bytes	Up to 2MB
12-bit	4,096	1	2,048 bytes	2–8MB
12-bit	4,096	8	4,096 bytes	8–16MB
12-bit	4,096	16	8,192 bytes	16–32MB
16-bit	65,536	1	512 bytes	32–64MB
16-bit	65,536	4	2,048 bytes	64–128MB
16-bit	65,536	8	4,096 bytes	128–256MB
16-bit	65,536	16	8,192 bytes	256–512MB
16-bit	65,536	32	16,384 bytes	512–1,024MB
16-bit	65,536	64	32,768 bytes	1,024–2,048MB
32-bit	2,048,000	8	4,096 bytes	Up to 8,192MB

FAT Type	Maximum Number of Clusters	Sectors per Cluster	Disk/Partition Cluster Size	Capacity
32-bit	2,048,000	16	8,192 bytes	8–16GB
32-bit	2,048,000	32	16,384 bytes	16–32GB
32-bit	2,048,000	64	32,768 bytes	32–64GB
32-bit	2,048,000	128	65,536 bytes	64–128GB
32-bit	2,048,000	256	131,072 bytes	128–256GB
32-bit	2,048,000	512	262,144 bytes	256–512GB
32-bit	2,048,000	1,024	524,288 Bytes	512–1,024GB
32-bit	2,048,000	2,048	1,048,576 bytes	1,024–2,048GB

Original equipment manufacturer (OEM) releases of Microsoft's DOS Version 3.3 (by Compaq, Dell, and others) implemented a new file allocation system, expanding the 12-bit numerical range limit to 16 bits, and supporting up to 65,536 clusters and drive partitions larger than 32MB (up to 528MB). These new versions of DOS also recognized and supported the older 12-bit FAT scheme to maintain backward compatibility. The release of DOS Version 5.0 allowed us access to more than two physical hard disks, which is useful for Small Computer System Interface (SCSI) disk systems and new IDE drive systems that support up to four IDE drives.

You can see an illustration of this issue right on your own system by using the DOS CHKDSK program or another utility that provides detailed information about your disk drive. As we noted earlier, disk utilities should not be run under Windows or other multitasking environments unless they are specifically designed to do so.

BIOS and DOS Limitations and Features

DOS and standard system BIOS impose a few interesting and often conflicting limitations to drive capacities. These limitations involve the ranges of numbers allowed to represent the various parameters involved in figuring total hard drive capacity. Remember that DOS began with no support for hard drives and has provided only two major improvements to hard drive support. These allowed DOS to support hard drives (DOS 2.1 and later), and then allowed partitions larger than 32MB (DOS 3.3 and later).

Numerical limits inherent in both system BIOS and DOS can restrict the ultimate accessible capacity of large disk drives. Previously, 1,024 cylinders, 16 heads, and 63 sectors per track defined the maximum disk size that either BIOS or DOS could handle. At 512 bytes per sector, accessible drive capacities were limited to 512MB. Recently, enhanced system BIOS removed some of these limitations, allowing for more cylinders and heads. Unfortunately, DOS still has a limited capacity of 1,024 cylinders, or tracks. This method of specifying disk parameters and addressing drive access is known as Cylinder/Head/Sector (CHS) addressing.

Note   Cylinder/Head/Sector (CHS) addressing is done within the disk drive controller or integrated drive electronics, and is therefore invisible to the user, who may only see clusters as file directory entries.

Because most of today's newer and larger drives have more than 1,024 cylinders, the cylinders beyond 1,024 have been unrecognized by DOS. With this limitation in place, compensated somewhat by enhanced BIOS, the disk capacity DOS can access has been increased, allowing 1,024 cylinders, 64 heads, and 63 cylinders for a total DOS capacity of 2,048MB, or 2GB, of data.

This limitation applies only to ST506, ESDI, and IDE hard drives. Until recently, if you needed single drive storage capacity greater than 528MB, you had to invest in an SCSI device.

Enhanced system BIOS, used in system boards or on disk adapters, or a variety of software programs, can provide track and sector translation to maintain the cylinder count that DOS sees to 1,024 or less. Sector translation can take a typical drive with 1,580 cylinders, 16 heads, and 63 sectors per track (815MB), and make it appear to have drive parameters of 790 cylinders, 32 heads, and 63 sectors, to fit within the limits of most older system setup (CMOS) drive parameters, and thus DOS.

Enhanced BIOS, typically specified for system boards or drive adapters as EIDE BIOS, should also enhance the system SETUP function to provide two or three disk parameter type selections. These are NORMAL for the original drive type limitations we have seen, LARGE for the sector translation functions to maintain the DOS-apparent cylinder count below 1,024 cylinders; and Logical Block Addressing (LBA) mode.

LBA mode is internal to disk controllers and adapters and ignores the CHS addressing scheme, tracking data sectors by their native 512-byte data blocks. The LBA arithmetic and tracking scheme, also invisible to users, is more like the method used for disk sector addressing in SCSI drive systems.

Note   Many enhanced BIOS versions provide an internal utility that will automatically identify and suggest the drive type parameters to use with your configuration.

SCSI drives, host adapters, and device drivers (where required for certain host adapters) provide data storage in terms of data blocks, called Logical Block Addressing (LBA). The BIOS on the host adapter or a special device driver, loaded at boot-up time from the CONFIG.SYS file, adapts SCSI devices into hard drives that BIOS and DOS can support, with support for larger disk drive capacities. BIOS and DOS still relate to the cylinders, heads, and sectors, and the SCSI host adapter translates these into its block format.

Using a Device Driver

Without enhanced BIOS, in either the system board or disk drive adapter, you will have to use a device driver such as Ontrack's Disk Manager or one specifically provided by your disk drive manufacturer to condition the drive identification so your operating system can access all of your drive. These device drivers intercept the normal DOS boot process, loading themselves, and thus drive translation, prior to the BIOS or operating system's check of the drive. This device driver scheme puts all of your data at the risk of the reliability of this driver on your disk, and may prevent the use of certain disk or system utilities that work directly with disk drive sectors.

Even with the capability to access greater numbers of cylinders, heads, and sectors available through the BIOS, the DOS FAT-16 file system is still limited to maximum drive capacities of 2,048MB (2GB). Now that we have larger drive capacities and proper operating system support for them, we can investigate how the operating system uses these drives, which is essentially the same way it was with DOS 2.1.

The BIOS limitation of support for only two physical hard drives has been addressed as well. Western Digital and other companies have developed support for up to four IDE drives either with add-in cards or IDE interfaces built onto the system board.

Disk Partitioning and Formatting

Partitioning is the process of defining and establishing the type and size of logical drives that can become usable file system space on a hard drive. *Formatting* is the process of establishing the basic directory and data storage structure of a logical disk drive, specific to the operating system. Diskettes are automatically partitioned by the operating system's format process. CD-ROM drives have their own file system established by the CD-recording software. The CD-ROM file system is mated to the operating system by device drivers. Other removable media (such as the Iomega Zip and Jaz products, or Syquest's products) are partitioned and formatted by their own utilities or the operating system's formatting program, and linked to the operating system by specific device drivers.

A logical disk drive differs from the physical one. The term *logical* indicates that we refer to the drive by an alias, nickname, or some other abstraction from the technical hardware — port addresses, drive addresses, device numbers, and so on. A logical drive designation gives us access to the file system through all of the various device drivers and hardware between the DOS drive letter and the actual hardware of the disk drive. For diskettes, CD-ROMs, and other types of removable media, the logical and physical drives equate to each other. There can be multiple logical disk drives within a physical hard disk drive's space, with the logical designation translating to different partition spaces (drive letters) on the drive. The logical drive letter assignment process can get a bit confusing when you see what happens with multiple disk drives and multiple partitions.

For DOS/Windows 3.x and Windows 95/98/Me systems, the most common program for establishing or changing the file system on a hard drive is the DOS FDISK program. There are also third-party or after-market programs, such as Partition Magic, that can create and manage hard drive partitions. These programs do what FDISK does but with more automation and a friendlier user interface.

The primary job of FDISK is to determine the size of the disk drive, indicate how it can be divided into usable disk space according to the FAT and cluster-size rules it supports, and to create that space suitable for formatting by the operating system tools (usually the DOS FORMAT program). FDISK gives the options to establish a primary partition automatically or by specific partition size, establish extended partitions automatically or by specific partition size, create logical drives within those partitions, and set which partition will be the active partition or the one that will hold the boot-up information. The logical drives are then available to be formatted by the operating system. This information is written to the boot sector as a Master Boot Record, which typically resides on the first few sectors of the drive (beginning at and using Head 0, Cylinder 0, Sector 0). Most other operating systems are aware of, use, and can contribute their own information to the boot record as well.

For most DOS systems, the first partition is also the only partition, of a size up to the limit of the largest partition size that the operating system can support. It is possible to make this first partition smaller than either the entire drive's capacity or the operating system's capacity, which is 2GB for DOS. This is quite useful as evident by all the discussions about cluster sizes and wasting disk space due to excessive cluster sizes. If you elect to make the first partition smaller than the drive's capacity, this becomes the primary partition, and is automatically given the first logical drive assignment (typically drive C: for DOS systems). The drive C: designation is a logical drive identifier.

Caution   When partitioning your hard drive for multiple operating systems, such as Windows, Linux, FreeBSD, OS/2, and so forth, make sure you know the limitations of your computer's BIOS related to hard disk size. For instance, if you are using an IDE hard drive that does not use the LBA mode of addressing, an operating system must be loaded from a partition in the first 504MB partition of that drive. To accommodate multiple operating systems and be able to boot from either, each must have its own partition, at least for the files required to boot that operating system, in its own partition (slice) in that first 504MB. Other limitations apply for other BIOS/hard drive combinations at the 1-gigabyte, 2-gigabyte, 4-gigabyte, and 8-gigabyte limits imposed by the BIOS and hard drive combinations installed in your system. You may be able to install the additional operating system but not be able to use it because it will not boot.

Once the primary partition is established, for DOS or another operating system, you can then make other partitions for DOS or other operating systems (with only one other DOS partition, for a maximum of two per drive). The second partition for DOS becomes an extended partition. The extended partition can be no larger than the operating system's limit — typically also 2GB, for Windows 95 (OSR2)/98, 4GB for Windows NT and 2 terabytes for Windows Me and 2000. Within the extended partition you must then create logical DOS drives within this partition.

Tip　Logical drives can be as big or small as you want, up to the limit of the partition's size. If you do not complete assigning logical drives, FDISK will complain, and you will not have use of that available drive space.

FDISK has some funny quirks about calculating partition sizing and establishing the proper cluster sizes for a given logical drive size. For instance, according to the preceding tables and text, to maintain cluster sizes of 8,192 bytes, the partition can be no larger than 512MB. If you specify 512MB for the partition or logical drive size in FDISK, it creates 16,384-byte clusters. This also happens if you specify 511 or 510MB logical drive sizes, but not if you specify 509MB. If you do the arithmetic, specifying 512MB should work out to consuming no more than 65,536 clusters. Calculating on 509MB does not yield any logical numbers that give us a clue about how or why we get this unusual result, but apparently Microsoft uses some new math we do not know about.

Cross-Reference　We provide examples of multiple partitions and using multiple disk drives and organizing data types in Chapters 17 and 18.

Formatting a drive gives us access to the logical disk drives or volumes that we have created on our hard drive. The format process provides sector headers on the disk and establishes the root directory structure on which we build the rest of the file system.

For DOS systems, the formatted portion of a partition can also have a volume name or label. Saying that another way, you can give a name or label to a specific partition, independent of the logical drive letter. You can label a partition when a logical drive is formatted, or with the DOS LABEL program. This is a friendly name to help remind us of what the drive letter may contain or who owns it, such as "Jim's Disk," "Mike's Programming," and so on. Labels show up in directory listings and file manager programs to make it easier to identify the disk. The volume label is also used as a friendly reference for sharing the drive over a network because most network software deals with partitions and their labels rather than logical disk drive assignments.

Tip　Volume names or labels can be very handy and important because they stay with the particular formatted storage space — the partition — unless you add, remove, or change the label, whereas logical drive letters can change depending on the number of drives and how they are connected to the system.

The DOS File System and Disk Control

DOS uses two key data elements stored on a disk to refer to the storage capacity of a disk, keep track of files and subdirectories, and locate files and subdirectories. These data elements are limited by the numbering system used to define and record this information.

The two key elements are as follows:

✦ The FAT, as discussed earlier in this chapter. The FAT is established when you partition your drive with FDISK or a similar program. It is a crude reference system that records the status of every storage area on a disk. For diskettes, the partitioning and FAT creation is done as part of the DOS format process, and FDISK is not needed. The FAT is located at the start of the disk, just beyond the area reserved for the hidden DOS files (if the disk was formatted to reserve this space) used at bootup and the disk or volume label. It is essentially a map of the drive's clusters, and it indicates if a cluster is in use, if it is bad (cannot hold any information), or, if a file exceeds one cluster in length, it contains the number of the next cluster used to store the file.

✦ The file directory, a dedicated area just after the FAT. More specifically, this directory area is the root directory for the disk. The root directory area keeps track of up to 256 files for diskettes and 512 files for hard drives. These files can be actual files or entries identifying subdirectories on the disk. A subdirectory is effectively a file that lists the other files or subdirectories organized within it. A directory entry, either in the root or a subdirectory, contains the name of a file or subdirectory, the starting cluster number, and the length or size of the file.

To locate a file, DOS, or your programs, look to the FAT for information leading to the location of the file's first data storage cluster. The DOS path and/or a fully qualified path declaration (drive:\subdirectory\filename) used to identify a file and located in the File Directory also gives DOS access to files. The first file or subdirectory placed on the disk, theoretically occupies the first available data cluster and sector on the drive, after the dedicated FAT and root directory space. It is the first FAT cluster (and subsequently the first data sector on the disk) stored in the beginning of the FAT.

Among the file declarations, paths, directories, File Allocation Table, DOS, the system BIOS, and the disk drives are several translations and conversions of the FAT identification of a data cluster into sector information and positioning commands that a disk can understand and use.

These conversion functions are the responsibility of DOS, or another operating system, the BIOS, the disk controller, and the drive. We users have little control of this process, generally up to and including the disk controller's functions. We can, however, understand how these factors affect the types of disk drives and controllers we use, how we prepare, partition, and format the drives, and which disk device drivers or features we want or need to implement.

Summary

In this chapter, we presented some of the history, defined a lot of terms, and explained the basics of disk drives to help make the following chapters about disk drives a bit more understandable.

In this chapter we covered the following:

✦ Disk drive types and references

✦ How data is stored on disk drives

✦ Limitations imposed by the hardware

✦ Partitioning and formatting your disk drives

In Chapter 17 we move on to how you, your programs, and your PC's operating system use these disk drive basics to store and manipulate your data.

✦   ✦   ✦

Disk Drive Utilities and Diagnostics

The basics and details covered in Chapter 16 are important for a more complete understanding of material we will cover in this chapter. If you are not familiar with disk drive features and terminology, please read Chapter 16 before you proceed.

Now let's get started with making your drives work *for* you instead of against you.

Drive Copying Utilities

It seems that almost everyone is seeing ghosts around their PCs — well, the GHOST drive copying software, anyway. GHOST is an abbreviation for Global Host Operating System Transfer or General Hardware Oriented Software Transfer, developed by Binary Research International (now owned by Symantec). GHOST is the first and still the most innovative of a growing category of programs that copies the image of one disk drive onto another. These utilities make the migration from, say, a 540MB disk drive to a larger drive almost painless — your new drive will end up with a bootable mirror image of the smaller drive and provide all of the new storage space you bought.

There are several options in this category of GHOST (www. symantec.com/sabu/ghost/), and they include DriveImage from PowerQuest (www.powerquest.com) and ImageCast from MicroHouse (www.supportsource.com), among others. Each has its own particular features and functions, whether it works across a network or with other media types.

The benefit of these utilities is that they remove several time-consuming and potentially complicated steps from the process of adding a new disk drive to your system. Most of us started with a 540MB or 1.2GB hard drive and needed to upgrade to a new drive with more capacity. We also wanted the new drive to be our C:, or the primary boot and operational drive and the older, smaller drive drive D:.

Installing a new drive

The typical new drive installation process is as follows:

1. Configure and install the new drive as a Slave or second hard drive (D:).

2. Boot from the old C: drive, stopping at the DOS prompt.

3. Use FDISK to create one or more partitions on the new D: drive.

4. Use the DOS FORMAT command with the /S command parameter to format the new drive (this can take up to 20 minutes).

5. Use XCOPY to copy the C: drive files to the new D: drive (this takes 30 to 120 minutes). This is only partially effective because it does not make the new drive immediately bootable, nor does it necessarily copy over all of the critical hidden files of Windows 95/98/Me unless all the XCOPY options are set just right.

6. Swap the drives around (make the new drive C: and the old drive D:).

7. Boot from a disk.

8. Run FDISK to make the first partition on the new C: drive active.

9. Run the DOS SYS program to put the DOS boot files on the new drive.

10. Reinstall Windows to get it to work right (this can take 30 to 90 minutes).

11. Get back to work.

There are many variations on this theme and the process can be done successfully by these separate manual methods, but why bother when the following method works just as well?.

Using drive imaging software

Drive imaging software provides an alternative to the previous cumbersome multi-step process:

1. Prepare a bootable DOS disk with the disk copying program on it (this takes five minutes).

2. Configure and install the new disk drive as the Master or C: drive.

3. Reconfigure the old drive to be the Slave or D: drive.

4. Boot from the disk.

5. Run the disk copying program.

6. Copy what is now the old drive completely over to the new Master drive (this takes 20 to 30 minutes).

7. Remove the bootable disk.

8. Reboot the system.

9. Get back to work.

Notice the considerable time difference in executing the copy operation! The image copying utilities do not use the DOS or BIOS functions to perform the copy operation. Instead they are tailored to work at the most basic level of the drive operations, copying data sector-by-sector or track-by-track rather than with and according to the file system.

 Note   Using low-level read and write operations and avoiding the file system saves considerable overhead involved in waiting for the operating system's file routines.

Additionally, these utilities will adjust to different partition sizes, enabling you to allocate or specify that you are taking data from a smaller partition, but you want the resulting partition to be larger, yet otherwise appear the same as the smaller one. This is ideal for doing our migration from a small drive to a large one without partitioning hassles.

Depending on your level of comfort with the entire process, the value of your time, the potential frustration of not getting the manual process right and so on, it would appear that the initial cost of drive imaging software is offset by the overall savings of using it.

Creating Multiple Systems

Image copying utilities are ideal for creating many systems that are configured exactly the same, especially when you are upgrading an entire workgroup of systems. If you keep an image of the master system on a network drive or CD-ROM, you also have a very handy method of recovering, repairing, or replacing a broken drive. Some organizations refer to this process as "reimaging your workstation" or in similar words. There are additional savings in being able to create mirrored Web site servers or rescue a blown Windows NT server installation from a like system. It is *much* quicker to copy an image from one drive to another and change the server's attributes (IP addresses and so on) than to go through a full-blown NT installation.

Partitioning Utilities

PowerQuest's PartitionMagic is one of a few utilities that take some of the confusion out of the disk drive partitioning process. This class of utilities is used to determine how much disk space is wasted by files that are much smaller than the cluster size used in a disk partition. Once this determination is made, the utility may offer the option to repartition the drive into smaller partitions, which provides smaller clusters and as a result gives back more free disk space.

These utilities are also very useful when you want to install a new operating system (or keep an older version of Windows completely separate from a newer version you are installing) by allowing you to repartition the hard drive to accommodate the new system. You will find references to Partition Magic in Linux, FreeBSD, and other operating system installation guides.

When you install a drive, it is best to plan your disk space use and partitioning before you commit too many programs and too much data to a particular arrangement. If you elect to repartition a drive with one of these third-party utilities, you should perform a full backup of your hard drive beforehand. If the process fails or the system crashes or loses power in the middle of the process, you could lose all of your data.

Tip   You should check all your programs and data paths after repartitioning a drive because drive letters and thus the area where programs and data are stored may change. You may also have to reinstall or make adjustments to batch files, program shortcut properties, and program configurations to get everything running correctly.

Translation Drivers and Enhanced BIOS Adapters

If you are stuck with an old system whose BIOS drive support will not support a hard drive that is larger than 512MB, chances are you have or will run into one of two popular large-drive translation utilities — either EZ-Drive from MicroHouse or Disk Manager from OnTrack.

These two utilities, once installed onto your boot drive, insert a small driver utility that appends your BIOS' drive support with a translation between a basic drive type already supported in your BIOS (typically drive type 1) and the parameters of your larger hard drive. At bootup, your BIOS goes through the normal routine, accesses the disk drive, loads the new driver, and recognizes your large hard drive as if your system had known how to support it all along.

Both utilities are intended to be used on new hard drives or drives for which you have full data backups, because the setup process, like FDISK, must destroy and then re-create new partitions on the drive based on the options it presents or that you select yourself. The setup process will typically also handle the basic DOS formatting of the drive, making it ready to receive your data.

An alternative to the bootsector translation drivers is an add-in disk adapter that provides drive parameter translation in hardware. This interface provides its own EIDE BIOS and typically recommends that you set the drive type to 1 in system setup just to establish that there is a hard drive known to the system BIOS. The EIDE BIOS will do all of the work involved in making the full drive capacity available to the system.

Caution

There are inherent weaknesses in both of these options for large hard drives. Both rely on proprietary schemes to accommodate the differences between your system and your drive. The boot sector driver method cautions you to keep handy an emergency boot disk with the driver software. The chances of getting updates or support for various aftermarket specialty disk drive interface hardware are limited by the short life cycle of PC products. Maintain a frequent full backup of all of your data in case the driver fails or is overwritten by a utility or virus, the drive controller fails, or the drive crashes.

Disk Compression

There have been four popular disk compression utilities on the market — Stacker from Stac Electronics, SuperStor from AddStor, DoubleDisk from Vertisoft, and XtraDrive from Integrated Information Technology — as well as implementations (and complications) with Microsoft offering different versions of DoubleSpace and DriveSpace. Microsoft settled on DriveSpace with MS-DOS 6.22, offers DriveSpace Version 3 with the Windows 95 Plus! Package, and provides file-by-file compression with Windows NT Version 4.0 and Windows 2000.

Disk compression software has received a lot of publicity for both its benefits and certain specific situations that can cause data loss. This software actually does nothing to compress your disk or increase the capacity of the disk medium, which are physical rather than software properties. Disk compression utilities provide their benefit by creating a virtual disk made up of a single large file on your hard drive. Within this single large file your program and data files are compressed and managed by the disk compression software drive.

All these programs operate in essentially the same manner. A significant portion (typically 90 to 95 percent) of your physical hard drive becomes the host for this large file. The operating system boot files and the compression software driver reside in the remaining free 5 to 10 percent of the drive as usual, enabling you to boot up the system and provide access to and control of the compressed file system.

Disk compression software performs two separate and advantageous functions to gain more usable file storage space. One of these functions keeps track of file storage areas on the disk. The other uses mathematical rules to analyze data and represent it in encoded formats that do not occupy as many bytes as the original format.

Since the compression software manages almost the entire disk drive, the typical File Allocation Table partitioning scheme used by DOS has very little work to do. The compression software allocates and tracks the location and organization of files within the large compressed file. This also makes more efficient use of the available space than the FAT and cluster system.

The inherent weaknesses with this method of storing files are the reliance on proprietary disk compression drivers, file management and data recovery methods, and the vulnerability of a single large file versus disk drive reliability. File system performance is also decreased by 5 to 10 percent because of the extra processing work that has to be done with yet another level of software to compress, decompress, and manage the files.

 Tip   Although DriveSpace 3 is much more reliable than prior versions, disk drives are relatively inexpensive these days. Buying a new, larger hard drive is a much more effective and reliable means of achieving better performance and greater storage capacity.

We cover the specifics of compression next.

Rediscovering the 512-byte sector as a first step

One relatively simple function that compression (or more appropriately, capacity-increasing) software does is to intervene and effectively replace the FAT file tracking processes with special device driver software (such as DBLSPACE.BIN, DRVSPACE. BIN, SSTORDRV.SYS, or STACKER.BIN). The process of installing compression software creates one large file, called the host or volume file, and installs the special device driver software to manage this large file. DOS is made to think that its disk drive is now the device driver that controls this large file, which contains its own file structure.

This alternative file system can keep track of more than the DOS limit of 4,096 or 65,536 clusters and reduces the minimal file storage unit back down to 512 or in some cases 256 bytes. The file system internally manages the original DOS sectors and clusters and combines many small files into the space DOS would allocate for only one file.

In effect, the minimum allocation unit is returned to the original sector capacity of most drives — 512 bytes. Any file that is 512 bytes or smaller occupies only 512 bytes of disk space as a single cluster — effectively virtual disk sectors under software driver control, rather than a larger cluster of 2K, 4K, or 8K.

This function alone has limited value because most of the files we store today range from 32K to 256K, with some much larger. Those files larger than the FAT cluster of 8K keep us from gaining any real advantage from the smaller cluster sizes used in the compressed disk. Larger files still occupy large amounts of space. This is where using mathematical data compression techniques provide an additional advantage.

Compression — taking the repetition out of data

You are probably familiar with .ARC, .ARJ, .LZH, .PAK, .ZIP, and .ZOO files that contain multiple files in a single, compressed package to store on Web sites and bulletin boards, or squeeze larger files onto disks or store them in smaller spacse. These are the result of data compression techniques that analyze the data patterns in files and represent them in known or predictable patterns that occupy less space than the original readable/usable data format. Most data files are full of repeating patterns or noninformational characters (such as multiple spaces and carriage return/line feed sequences) or characters that do not need a full 8 bits to represent their value. The alphabet, numbers, and punctuation we use require less than 7 bits to convey their value or meaning, but PCs use 8-bit character sets to suit hardware and memory structures.

This aspect of data storage is where disk compression software provides an advantage. Most text and data files can be stored in less than 60 percent of their original space if the data pattern is reduced to the minimum number of bits to represent it or the repeating patterns are eliminated by representing them in fewer bytes. Compression routines use a combination of both aspects. Different compression routines apply different rules and formulas to create their resulting data files.

The disk compression software evaluates each data file being stored, attempts to represent it in the smallest form possible, and then stores it — not in 8K FAT clusters, but in 512-byte (or less) virtual clusters within the host disk file.

The compression software makes the large host disk file look like a disk drive to BIOS and DOS, and then it often swaps disk designations with the original drive. A host file such as DBLSPACE.000 or STACVOL.000 first becomes drive H: or D:, and then swaps designations with drive C: to give you a larger disk drive.

Compression caveats

If disk drives are fragile, then compressed drives are the precious family china in the path of a wild bull on the loose. There are several significant pieces of hardware and software including your keyboard, serial devices, network ports, and the disks to which you trust all the data and which could be the cause of accidental lost data.

Compressed drives are subject to all the potential threats your hardware poses plus the reliability of one or more device-driver programs, the proper execution of these programs, and all the other related software and drivers you may be using at any one time. Remember that a compressed drive is actually one big file on your disk. It is also a software-managed file system working in conjunction with other file managing software (such as BIOS, DOS, and applications).

You can probably afford to lose one or two files from your original hard drive. These You might have these backed up on a disk, have copied them to a coworker for review or use, or can recreate with a little bit of hard work. One file on a plain hard disk may be just a part of your data or an application. In the case of a compressed drive, this one file is all of your files — data, programs, drivers, batch files, subdirectories, and so on. For most of us, this represents several hundred or thousand files.

Tip   If your application and file-handling software is not compatible with every aspect of your compression software, the virtual drives created and managed by this software, and the accessory drivers (such as disk caches and deleted file monitoring utilities), you might suddenly find it would have been better to buy a newer, larger hard disk than to invest in the time and risk of disk compression utilities.

All of the work the compressed drive control or driver program must do requires processing in your CPU. This means that accessing and writing to data will be slowed somewhat while making file allocations and compressing or decompressing.

We have experienced various problems due to the use of, or incompatibility with, disk compression software. The worst of these is represented in the questionable implementation of the DoubleSpace facility with MS-DOS 6.00 and 6.20, and versions of disk caches, including Microsoft's SMARTDRV, and in DOS itself. Even the pronouncements of bug fixes and extra precautions taken in MS-DOS 6.20 were not entirely successful or reliable. Due to legal and technical implications, MS-DOS version 6.20 was replaced on the market with MS-DOS 6.21, which did not contain disk compression features. Once the legal implications were resolved, Microsoft was allowed to release a new compression utility, DriveSpace. DriveSpace now lives on in MS-DOS 6.22, Windows 95, and newer versions of Windows NT.

Other compression software packages have been developed with different perspectives, not as an integral part of DOS or BIOS development, and may implement more precautions and utilities to help manage the larger host files, and thus be more reliable. However, you must remember that your new, larger drive is nothing but a big DOS file. Also remember that it is a disk drive only by virtue of software and it cannot be treated exactly like a piece of hardware — there are no physical platters, heads, or sectors.

Note Disk caching software only enhances the performance of data transfers from the original hardware drive, which contains the software drive's file. The performance gain of a disk cache might not overcome the performance loss of the compression process.

It is likely that if compression and reallocation become trusted and common methods of increasing disk capacity, we will see them implemented within the hardware of the disk drives or adapter cards. We will not have to work with fragile drivers and files at the BIOS and operating system levels. Performance concerns would diminish if the hardware performed the functions now using precious CPU time and hardware-based disk caches far exceeded the performance gains of those we load from DOS. Some forms of compression or data encoding are already in use in many drives to create the increased disk capacities of IDE drives.

The symptoms, suspects, and solutions for disk compression are the same as for other drive operations, because the same hardware and functions are involved for disk access and data transfers. The only things you need to keep handy while working with disk compression systems are the utility programs specific for your compression software. These programs can analyze and repair the unique files that make up the compressed drives, and the file structures within them, within the limits of the original disk subsystem.

Disk Caching

Disk caching consists of storing frequently used information, or information in advance of its anticipated use, in memory allotted for the purpose. This makes it available to the CPU much faster than waiting for disk operations. It is especially useful for enhancing the performance of your system while running Windows or disk-intensive operations such as multimedia and database applications.

Disk caching software intercepts and handles a program's request to get information from a disk. The software executes the request for information, often faster than BIOS or DOS services, and provides it to the requesting program via the CPU. Some portion of the disk beyond the initial request may be read and stored in memory, so subsequent data requests are also delivered faster. Many disk drive controllers also have a small amount of on-board disk caching to improve the performance of the drive subsystem hardware.

The disk caching software may consist of a device driver to include in the CONFIG. SYS file or a memory-resident program you run from the DOS prompt or in your AUTOEXEC.BAT file. Depending on the vendor and version of the software you use, the disk caching program may require between 10K and 50K of memory to run. With advanced high memory management features available in EMM386 in DOS Versions

5.0 and higher, and memory enhancements such as QuarterDeck's QEMM, Helix's NetRoom, and Qualitas' 386MAX, these programs may be loaded into high memory so they do not take up limited DOS RAM.

Note   The memory used for disk caching can be DOS (or conventional) RAM memory, extended (AT, 386, 486) memory, or LIMS-EMS expanded memory, depending on the capabilities of the software you are using. Microsoft's SMARTDRV uses only extended or expanded memory.

There are subtle differences between the various caching programs. Some are very simple to install and set up, such as SMARTDRV. Recent versions of Microsoft's SMARTDRV also cache the data read from CD-ROM drives, significantly increasing their performance. Disk and file caching are inherent in Windows 95/98/Me with its VCACHE driver, and in Windows NT/2000.

The features of most disk caching software can be configured to suit your needs, the amount and type of memory in your system, or the types of applications you use. The more common parameters you might find include those listed here:

✦ Which drives you do or do not want cached

✦ Which drives use write caching

✦ The type or memory — conventional, extended, or expanded — for the cached data

✦ How much memory to use for caching while working in DOS

✦ How much memory to use for caching while working in Windows

✦ The amount of time the cache software waits before writing cached data to the disk

✦ If the cache software allows multiple applications to perform disk operations (such as when running multiple applications under Windows)

Disk Caching versus RAM Disks

Disk caching is an enhancement to existing, more permanent disk or hard drive storage. Do not confuse disk caching with RAM disks, which are temporary virtual disk drives created in a region of system memory. RAM disks, although as fast to respond to reads or writes as your system and memory allow, provide no permanent storage. The data in a RAM disk disappears when you reboot or turn off the system. RAM disks are good places to store temporary files while you are using your system.

Caching Precautions

Caching data to be written to the disk is somewhat risky. It leaves you susceptible to data loss if there are memory errors or small glitches in the system during the short time that information may be held in the cache but not yet written to disk. Use a very short cache-to-disk write interval if your cache software lets you set the value. Remember that there are several million CPU operations and quite possibly other software operating while the cache is running. Any interval greater than one or two seconds places your data at an increased risk of being lost.

If you believe or find that you are losing data that should be written to disk or that data read from disk is not complete or correct take the following steps:

✦ Disable all caching.

✦ Run a memory test to verify RAM integrity.

✦ Use the cache without write caching or shorten the cache-write time.

✦ Allow a few seconds for the cache to write all pending write-cached data to disk before rebooting or turning off your system.

✦ Select another caching program to use on your system. Check the documentation for your system, applications, and memory management software for notes about compatibility.

Many programs recommend that disk caching, especially write caching, should also be disabled during certain utility operations, including the following:

✦ Low-level formatting.

✦ Hard drive testing and troubleshooting.

✦ Hard drive interleave and reformatting tests.

✦ File and directory sorting and compression (defragmenting files).

✦ Certain backup or restore operations. These may establish their own data buffers, but may benefit from increasing the DOS BUFFERS parameter set in CONFIG.SYS to 99. Check the documentation for the software you use.

✦ Conventional, extended, or expanded memory tests.

Overall, disk caching is an effective method of gaining system performance, bypassing BIOS, DOS, or hardware-imposed delays in disk-read operations, and making your applications respond more quickly to your needs. Caching is especially helpful for large applications and files such as Microsoft Windows, and graphics, spreadsheet, and database software.

Tip

If you need temporary storage space, use a RAM disk. If you need enhanced disk or hard drive performance, a disk cache is an inexpensive upgrade to your system.

Overall Drive and File System Performance

Ultimately, with or without DOS buffers or disk caching, nothing beats the simple performance benefits of selecting a disk drive with the fastest performance specifications possible. When selecting a new disk drive, look for the following performance specifications:

+ **Average access or seek time**. This parameter indicates the average time it takes for the read/write heads to travel from one file area to another as measured by timing random seeks to various disk tracks. Select a drive with seek times of 12 milliseconds or less (8, 9, and 10 millisecond drives are readily available). You may be amazed at the significant performance benefits of using an 8-millisecond drive versus a 12-millisecond drive, especially when running Windows.

+ **Internal cache.** This parameter indicates the amount of internal data buffering provided by the drive. Typical sizes are 64- or 2 megabytes, and these are quite adequate. 32K is unacceptable. 512- or 2048K are much better.

+ **Disk rotation speed**. To improve the access time performance, getting desired data sectors under the read/write heads faster, the disk should spin as quickly as possible. Limitations in hard disk material and mechanical stability tend to restrict disk rotation speed to 7,200 RPM for 3.5-inch drives. The 5.25-inch drives spin at 3,600 to 4,500 RPM. Older drives typically spun no faster than 3,600 RPM.

File Fragmentation

The DOS file system is perhaps like no other when it comes to finding places to stick files on a hard disk. Normally a file will occupy consecutive or sequential sectors on a disk so that the file is contiguous or all in one space on a drive. This is how files were first stored on disks. In the case of hard drives, DOS will begin using the first available unused clusters (groups of sectors) to begin storing a file. If the file's total size exceeds that of this first available space, it will store the rest of the file in the next available space until the entire file is stored. This is fragmentation — the file is not stored as one continuous stream of data on the disk.

Fragmentation delays or prevents optimal access to the entire file because the disk drive heads must be moved to different tracks on the disk surface to write or read all of the file. In doing so, the heads have to also go back to the beginning of the disk to read more of the FAT to look up which clusters the rest of the file occupies. This all takes time. Using a faster drive reduces the effects of fragmentation on performance, but it does not cure it.

Use Defragmentation Software Regularly

Using defragmentation software should be a regular part of your system maintenance and housekeeping routine. Before you do your regular backups, run your favorite defrag program and clean up the clutter on your disks. You will be glad you did.

Perhaps you will even discover that this two-step defrag-and-backup process actually improves your system performance!

Executive Software, Symantec, and other software utility companies produce defragmentation software that rearranges data files on the disk or optimizes their locations for faster access. The defragmentation utility included in Windows' newest versions is a minimal version of Executive Software's Diskeeper.

Tip   Do not think that installing Windows NT or 2000 will eliminate the need for disk optimization. Diskeeper makes a BIG difference in system performance and if you have ever experienced running out of disk space in Windows NT, which scrambles your Master File Table (as we learned from personal experience!), you will insist on using Diskeeper's "set-it-and-forget-it" feature.

Summary

Disk drive utilities and diagnostics, along with some very reasonable common sense, can help you avoid many problems and in the case of disaster, help you on your path to recovery.

In this chapter we covered:

✦ Partitioning and copying your drives

✦ Disk compression and caching

✦ Drive and file system performance

✦ File fragmentation

In Chapter 18 we will continue to build on the information presented in Chapters 16 and 17 to help with installing drives, and then dive right into the troubleshooting experience.

✦   ✦   ✦

Hard Drives

In This Chapter

Installing, adding, or changing hard drives

IDE, SCSI, and mixed drive systems

Partitioning hard drives

Formatting hard drives

Hard drive problems

After covering the basics and details of disk drives in Chapters 16 and 17, we are now ready to discuss hard drives. Although we believe you will get much more out of your PC and disk drives by reading through this chapter from start to finish as usual, feel free to skip ahead to any section that is most relevant to your situation.

Installing, Adding, or Changing Hard Drives

Because of the tremendous number of system board, hard disk adapter, and disk drive combinations, it is impossible to give you exact directions for the addition of or conversion between specific or different hard disks and types. We can, however, give you adequate guidelines for the settings, jumpers, and basic configuration issues.

One of your most significant concerns will be selecting the proper disk drive or drive-type parameters for your setup. If you have a pre-1995 386 or 486 system board, your system BIOS may not support your drive's parameters, and it may not allow you to provide custom, or user, drive-type parameters. These systems will likely not support Integrated Device Electronics (IDE) drives larger than 512MB or IDE drives with more than 1,024 cylinders, 16 heads, or 63 sectors per track.

Cross-Reference For more information on drive types and parameters, see Chapter 16.

Since the implementation of customized BIOS and Enhanced BIOS that support automatic detection and setting of drive parameters or Logical Block Addressing (LBA) mode, drive installation can be much less of a hassle than it once was.

If your system board BIOS does not support "large" or LBA mode drives, you may consider purchasing a disk adapter card that provides Enhanced Integrated Device Electronics (EIDE) drive support. If your system board provides its own disk adapter circuits, using an add-in adapter may require you to disable the onboard disk adapter so that the add-in adapter can function properly. The cost for add-in IDE adapters is roughly $40 to $80. But beware: Once you commit to a particular brand of adapter card, you may not be able to use your drive as is if you later replace the card with one from another vendor, due to chip set and BIOS differences that handle the translations providing support for larger drives. Once again, the importance of backups cannot be overstated.

Tip

As a minimum backup policy, you should back up your data files, configurations, and special settings, those things that make your PC unique to your environment. You do not need to back up the programs and utilities that are installed on your PC. You can reinstall them from the original disks (which should bebacked up too!)

Many of these drive-type and parameter limitations can be avoided by upgrading to a Small Computer System Interface (SCSI) host adapter and by using SCSI drives. They are more expensive than IDE drives, but they offer flexibility and significantly better performance. Mode 4 PIO and either UDMA-33 or UDMA-66 are closing the gap between high-performance SCSI drives and the newest IDE drives available today.

Preparations

The first guideline is to prepare yourself with bootable formatted disks that contain any and all of the DOS and special utility programs you will need to run—FDISK, FORMAT, SYS, and the special programs (Disk Manager or EZ-Drive) needed to get your hard disks up and running. For newer systems, make sure you have your bootable Emergency Repair Disks available.

Note

If you plan to add a second hard disk or change drives, a full backup of the existing data is highly recommended. Changing configurations and using the formatting tools creates a risk of data loss.

Mixing different types of disk drives

It is usually not possible to mix ST506/Enhanced Small Device Interface (ESDI) and IDE (except in the case of SCSI and either IDE, ST506, or ESDI) drives. This is because of older system BIOS restrictions with limited support for only one controller or adapter card and one controller BIOS in the system. New system BIOS does not have this problem with two drive interfaces but if you have a newer system, it is unlikely that you would try to use an old ST506 or ESDI drive.

You do have to pay attention to the resulting device numbers, partitions, and logical drive assignments if you have multiple drives and if at least one drive has multiple partitions and logical drives. The logical drive assignments will change, and what they become depends on the arrangement and order of drives in the system.

ST506, ESDI, and IDE

If you have an ST506 (MFM or RLL) drive in your system now, you can add only one other ST506 type drive of the same subtype, MFM or RLL. If you have an Enhanced Small Device Interface (ESDI) drive, you can add only another ESDI drive. With older systems, you could have only two IDE drives, but new BIOS supports up to four devices. Theoretically, you can have your ST506/ESDI controller as the primary or secondary drive adapter and the IDE interface as the secondary or primary adapter — as primary and secondary adapters use different addresses and interrupt requests (IRQs).

Small Computer System Interface

Small Computer System Interface (SCSI) adapters and drives can coexist with the other drive types. However, if there are other drive types in the system, the SCSI device cannot be the boot device because the standard disk drive BIOS for the ST506/ESDI or IDE adapter will take precedence. Prior to Windows 95, 98, and NT, if your SCSI host adapter did not provide its own BIOS, you had to use a device driver loaded from the C:\CONFIG.SYS file on the boot drive in order to gain access to the SCSI devices. Using SCSI enables users to add more hard drives easily and to use CD-ROM and tape drives within an existing configuration.

AT, 386, 486, and higher systems

AT and higher systems require that specific hard drive parameters be configured in the setup (CMOS) for the system. The original IBM PC/AT could only support 15 predetermined drive types. If your disk drives do not match any of these original types, you may be unable to format and to use all of the drive's capacity. To work around this limitation, you must use partitioning software or late-model IDE drives that automatically configure themselves within the range of a preset CMOS drive type parameter.

Appendix E lists common drive type parameters.

Most 386 and higher systems now provide for either a customizable drive type that you can set, or the BIOS can automatically detect and set a drive type at bootup.

If you cannot set the parameters individually, selecting a drive type to match or approximate the actual drive will involve selecting a preset drive type that has an equal or lesser number of cylinders than your drive and, in some cases, an equal or lesser number of heads. By careful selection of drive types; you may lose little — or none — of the full capacity of your drive.

Enhanced IDE BIOS

Whether the BIOS that provides hard drive functions is on your system board or on an add-in card, the BIOS or installation software may provide a built-in utility that will automatically detect the drive parameters and enable you to choose the mode for the drive in your system.

The correct mode may be either normal, large, or LBA. Large and Logical Block Addressing (LBA) modes provide internal translations for the cylinder, head, and sector values needed to establish the CMOS drive type parameter. Large and LBA modes in an add-in adapter may require that you set the CMOS setup drive type to 1 or 2 in order to enable the BIOS translation to function properly. Large mode will translate a cylinder count greater than 1,024 cylinders to a value less than 1,024 (typically half the total number of cylinders) for compatibility. LBA mode will ignore the cylinder/head/sector (C/H/S) count and address the drive in the most efficient manner possible for the adapter and drive. Normal mode means that the system setup will see the drive in its native C/H/S count mode, as typical in earlier drives and systems.

For more details on Logical Block Addressing (LBA) mode, see chapter 16.

Translation software

OnTrack and various drive vendors provide driver software that can translate your larger drive's C/H/S values into ones that your system BIOS and DOS can handle. This software must be used to initially partition and possibly format your disk drive. In so doing, it places a hidden device driver on the drive for the operating system to read and use at startup. The advantage to this method is that it is relatively simple and inexpensive or free with the drive. The disadvantage is that if the boot sector is damaged, you will lose the translation driver and quite possibly all of the data on your drive. The driver installation program may be able to reinstall the driver without data loss, but we have never seen that work.

Installing IDE drives

Installation of an IDE drive system, or addition of a second drive, or even a third or fourth drive is relatively simple. As with ST506 and ESDI drive systems, you must select an interface card designed for your system (PC and XT, or AT, local bus, or PCI) or locate the IDE interface port on the system board. An interface card must be configured with the right address and IRQ, which is usually preset on most interface cards. If you have an Enhanced Industry Standard Interface (EISA), local bus, or Peripheral Component Interconnect (PCI) local bus system, you can probably use an Industry Standard Architecture (ISA) type disk interface card. However, you may want to choose an interface card designed for the higher performance bus interface (EISA, local bus, or PCI) to get the highest data transfer rates possible.

The cabling system is fairly obvious unless you have an older cable or drives that require use of the Cable Select line and jumpers. An IDE interface cable may have two or three connectors attached to it. Normally it does not matter which connector attaches to which drive because drive selection is done with jumpers on the drive and internal signals between drives. If you have a Cable Select drive system, then the cable should be clearly marked as to which connector must go to the Master and Slave drives, respectively.

Drive Selection Jumpers

If there is a trick to having two or more IDE drives, it is in resolving differences in drive selection methods between drives made by different companies. There are three jumpers for drive selection on most IDE drives. The three jumpers are usually defined as Master, Master with Slave, or Slave. The first means the jumper is the only drive in the system. The second means the jumper is the Master in a two-drive system. The third means the jumper is the Slave drive. Actually, this refers to the one or two drives on a single cable. The second cable could have its own Master or Master with Slave drive with the jumpers set in the same manner as the first.

A single drive usually has only one jumper connected. This jumper is typically marked "M" or "DM" for the Master drive. If this drive is also the first or boot drive in a two-drive system, it may have a second jumper connected. This jumper might be labeled "DS" or "SP," indicating that a Slave, or second, drive is present. The Slave drive usually has no jumpers connected.

When using drives from the same manufacturer, the documentation or a label on the drive indicates how the jumpers should be set for a particular configuration. This configuration may be — but is not always — standardized between different drive manufactures.

The industry standard ATA, or AT Attachment, specification defines interfaces and operating modes for devices that use the IDE interface. The IDE interface is an adaptation of signals directly from the AT bus, thus, the name AT Attachment. Initially defined for hard drive interfacing, the ATA specification includes many types of devices that can be attached to the IDE interface (for example, CD-ROMs and tape drives).

If your adapter or drive supports it, you will see references to the ATA modes that a drive or adapter supports, perhaps intermixed with references to EIDE. These modes define adapter and drive timing, and data transfer methods. Increasing ATA-specification numbers typically represent faster timing and transfer rates. ATA-1 is the first ATA specification, and it is only provided for backward compatibility where necessary. ATA-2 is the most common specification level supported. ATA-3 and ATA-4 provide quite significant improvements in performance. If you have an ATA-4 drive, you probably want an ATA-4 adapter card in order to gain the full performance benefits, although the drive should recognize and comply with ATA-1, ATA-2, and ATA-3 adapters, just as ATA-4 adapters should comply and work with earlier version devices.

 Tip Technical support and configuration information for IDE drives and system setup is readily available from drive manufacturers' technical support lines, bulletin board systems (BBSs), or Web sites.

Once a drive is installed, you must configure your system's CMOS setup (for AT and higher systems) and select a drive type that is equal or similar to your drive, or you must create a custom drive type or select AUTO if your BIOS supports these features. You can have different CMOS drive types for the first and second hard drives, even if they are both set to autoconfigure in the BIOS.

IDE drives rarely require special formatting or preparation, unless your system does not support the type parameters of the disk drive. This includes the variety of basic predefined or user-settable CMOS or system setup parameters for irregular IDE drives, or the ability of your system BIOS to support drives larger than 512MB.

You may need to use software provided by the drive manufacturer, which may be similar to or a special version of OnTrack's Disk Manager disk parameter translation device drivers. The directions provided with this software should be more than adequate to guide you through the setup process.

Tip   If you can avoid using translation software by upgrading your present system BIOS or by using a disk adapter card that provides the Enhanced IDE BIOS itself, do so. You will enjoy increased reliability and no reliance on software, which can affect the way you gain access to the data on the drive.

Boot up your system and proceed to the sections "Partitioning Hard Drives" and "Formatting Hard Drives" to verify that your system's BIOS recognizes your drives, then create the partitions and format the drives. Finally, copy your data and get to work!

Installing an SCSI system

The SCSI interface system is one of the most powerful and expandable available for your computer. Because of this, installing a SCSI system involves more planning of the various configuration items on both the host adapter and the SCSI devices. Table 18-1 summarizes the different possibilities.

When you purchase a SCSI host adapter, it usually is preconfigured to be the primary and only disk drive interface in your system. That means it should by default provide hard drive controller BIOS support, a unique hardware address for the adapter card, and unique IRQ and direct-memory-access (DMA) settings. Because you can have more than one SCSI host adapter in your system, the cards must be configured uniquely, and only one such card can be configured to provide the hard-drive BIOS interface to your system.

Table 18-1
SCSI Devices and Their Possible Configuration Items

SCSI Device	Configuration Items
System CMOS setup and possible jumpers	Hard drive type Onboard disk controller enable Onboard diskette controller enable
Host adapter cards	Adapter SCSI device number Termination on/off Hardware address BIOS memory address Hardware IRQ DMA channel Diskette controller on/off Data parity checking Synchronous transfer DMA or PIO transfer type
SCSI hard drive	SCSI device number Data parity Synchronous data transfer Spindle motor start Termination on/off
SCSI tape drive	SCSI device number Data parity check Termination on/off
SCSI CD-ROM drive	SCSI device number Data parity check Termination on/off

SCSI standards

Over the past few years, SCSI has gained much attention and improved its performance. Transfer rates and interface cabling improve with each new specification. SCSI-I devices were common and are usually still supported in most adapters, although performance is probably intolerably low for most applications.

SCSI-II is the most common specification, and it is comparable to most common IDE drives in terms of performance. These types of SCSI devices still only support 8-bit parallel data transfers. Fast-SCSI-II is an incremental performance step beyond SCSI-II. Wide-SCSI-II provides 16-bit data transfers, and Fast-Wide-SCSI-II is only an incremental improvement over Wide-SCSI-II. Fast-SCSI-II devices may not be supported for their full performance in SCSI-II adapters, but they will function. Wide-SCSI devices and adapters require that Wide-SCSI–compliant devices be attached to them.

Tip   If in doubt, double-check the specifications and compatibility of all devices before committing your data to an unreliable or unsupported setup.

Preparing SCSI host adapters and drives

SCSI controllers typically have their onboard BIOS at a different location than that of XT and AT drive BIOS, and they require more setup detail for card addressing, DMA channels, PC bus, IRQ number, and possibly other selections.

SCSI drives are normally low-level formatted, but if you change controllers, you will probably need to format the drive using the BIOS in the host adapter that you intend to use.

Adaptec usually places the default onboard BIOS at DC000h, with a program start address of DC00:6 (use this in place of the C800:5 and similar references for DEBUG control of the format process in older adapters). Most ISA and local bus Adaptec controllers also default to hardware address location 330h. Plug-and-Play–compliant adapters will adjust themselves according to the preexisting devices in your system. You may wish to disable Plug-and-Play (PnP) capabilities and set the parameters manually; you will have to do this if the adapter card's and system BIOS' PnP schemes are incompatible.

You can change the assignments for the adapter and BIOS or disable the onboard BIOS entirely. If you change the hardware address of the controller, you might automatically disable the onboard BIOS support provided. This may be desirable if you wish to use a software device driver or, if you already have another disk controller installed and are adding SCSI for expansion purposes.

If you have an existing IDE, ST506, or ESDI hard disk in your system and wish to add SCSI drives, you may have to disable the onboard SCSI BIOS, continue to boot from your existing drive, and use an adapter-specific device driver (typically an ASPI driver) to gain access to the SCSI devices.

Note   ASPI stands for Advanced SCSI Programming Interface. It is a published standard for developing device drivers and device-specific programs for SCSI adapters and devices. In most cases, it supersedes the older and less substantial Common Access Method (CAM) specification that provided similar features. The CAM specification is no longer used.

Software drivers for specific needs are available from Adaptec for many operating systems and controllers. Adaptec provides many files and online support through their bulletin board system at (408) 945-7727 or on its Web site at www.adaptec.com.

Western Digital provides support and information, including controller and drive-wiring instructions, through its bulletin board system at (714) 753-1234 or on its Web site at www.westerndigital.com/.

Most SCSI adapter cards provide four or more addressing, IRQ, and DMA options for configuration choices, so you can work around most constraints that prevent you from reconfiguring other devices in your system. Table 18-2 indicates the devices, addresses, IRQ, and DMA settings that could cause conflicts between various input/output (I/O) devices. You should consult the documentation for your adapter card to verify the default settings and determine if the BIOS, hardware address, IRQ, or DMA settings will conflict with any other devices installed in your system. In Table 18-2, obvious conflict potentials are set in bold type.

Table 18-2
Conflicts in Various Input/Output Devices

Device or Card	*Typical BIOS Address*	*Typical Hardware Address*	*Typical IRQ*	*Typical DMA*
Non-SCSI hard-disk controller — primary	C800h	1F0h	14	N/A
Non-SCSI hard-disk controller — secondary	Requires Primary BIOS	170h	**15**	N/A
Adaptec 154x SCSI host adapter	DC00h	330h (must use 330h if using adapter's BIOS)	**11**	5
Adaptec 29xx PCI SCSI host adapter	DC00h	N/A — PCI bus	**11**	5
Always Tech. IN-2000	SCSI host adapter	C800h 220h	**15**	N/A
PC sound cards	N/A	220h	**5**	3
Network interface cards	N/A	280h, 2A0h, 300h, 320h, 340h, 360h	**2, 3, 4, 5, 7,** 9, 10, **11**	3, 5
PC serial ports	N/A	3F8h, 2F8h, 3E8h, 2E8h	**4, 3**	N/A
PC parallel ports	N/A	3BCh, 378h, 278h	**7, 5**	3 if ECP
PS/2 Mouse Port	N/A	3E8h–3EEh	12	N/A

Tip   You must ensure that no two devices share the same BIOS, hardware, IRQ, or DMA settings if you plan to use any of them at the same time. This is usually a problem only in the case of serial ports sharing the same IRQ, such as COM1 and COM3, and COM2 and COM4.

After you configure the host adapter card, you need to check and, if necessary, properly set the disk drive configuration. SCSI systems use an ID number, set by jumpers or switches, much as ST506 and ESDI drives use the drive select jumpers and a cable with twisted leads. Each device attached to the SCSI cabling must have a unique ID number. Table 18-3 shows common ID configurations.

		Table 18-3
		Common SCSI ID Configurations
SCSI Device	**Device ID Number**	**Comment**
First hard drive	0	The hard drive you want to use as your boot drive must be 0.
Second hard drive	1	The second hard drive is usually 1.
Tape drive	2	To create a sense of order, a third hard drive should go in sequence and be added as 2.
CD-ROM	3	Additional hard disks or other devices are typically 2 and higher.
Any device	4	
Any device	5	One of two options for Iomega Zip drives.
Any device	6	Second of two options for Iomega Zip drives.
SCSI host adapter	7	The host adapter *must* be 7. This is usually recommended, even if the IDs range from 0 to 15.

Most drives use jumper pins to set the SCSI ID number, and the settings are selected by binary numbering, using only three sets of jumper pins. SCSI IDs are usually set by jumper positions on the device. Table 18-4 shows how ID numbers are usually assigned to devices. Your adapter may provide other ways or, to support up to 16 ID numbers for a Wide device, there may be other jumpers, switches, or software settings.

Table 18-4
ID Numbers to Set for a SCSI Device

Device ID Number	First ID Jumper; Jumper 1 or A0	Second ID Jumper; Jumper 2 or A1	Third ID Jumper; Jumper 4 or A2	Fourth ID Jumper (if the adapter has 16 IDs)
0	Off	Off	Off	Off
1	On	Off	Off	Off
2	Off	On	Off	Off
3	On	On	Off	Off
4	Off	Off	On	Off
5	On	Off	On	Off
6	Off	On	On	Off
7*	On	On	On	Off
8	Off	Off	Off	On
9	On	Off	Off	On
10	Off	On	Off	On
11	On	On	Off	On
12	Off	Off	On	On
13	On	Off	On	On
14	Off	On	On	On
15	On	On	On	On

* ID #7 is reserved for the host adapter. The jumper may have a switch lever instead than pins. Off and On or 1 and 0 may be reversed on some devices. Wide SCSI adapters may require the adapter to be set as 15 or may conform to the usual ID #7 assignment.

The default settings indicated in the device's manual are your best bet for success.

Starting the SCSI installation

It is best to begin your installation with the SCSI host adapter and the drives attached to it as the only drives in your system. Do this by removing or disabling existing disk and hard drive controllers, and by using the disk drive connections provided on the SCSI adapter. Using the disk interface on the SCSI adapter will save a slot on the system board. Disabling the other hard drives makes it easier to remember which drive you are working on and helps prevent data loss that would occur by accidentally repartitioning or reformatting your other hard drive(s).

All SCSI systems require that you properly terminate the data lines at both ends of the interconnecting cable. Host adapter cards typically provide their own onboard terminating resistors, or at least the sockets for them, and a set of terminating resistor packs to plug into the sockets. Some new host adapters automatically configure themselves as needed. If you have both internal and external SCSI devices, the devices at the far ends of each cable should contain the terminators, and there should be no terminator set on the host adapter, which is in the middle of the cable.

Most drives have their terminating resistor connections at the bottom rear of the device. A few drives, such as early Sony CD-ROM drives, provide a terminating connector block to be attached at the rear of the drive next to the cable plug. These terminations ensure that the data signals arrive at the drive and host adapter at the proper voltage levels for reliable data transfer.

Set the device ID numbers for each device, with the first hard drive as ID #0 and the second hard drive as ID #1. When the hardware is configured, you can boot your system and proceed to check or set the CMOS drive type parameters. The CMOS setup hard drive parameters for SCSI drive systems should be set for None or, if provided in the BIOS, as SCSI.

Note   The BIOS in some systems requires that the CMOS setup drive type be set to Type 1 to recognize the presence of the SCSI adapter and drives.

The next step is to boot from a diskette with the essential DOS disk utility programs (FDISK.EXE, FORMAT.COM, and SYS.COM) and check the system in this configuration. You can view a listing of the files on the first or second hard drive with the DOS DIR command. If you receive an error message, it will probably be either "Invalid Drive" or "Non-DOS disk." An error indicates that the drive does not have a DOS partition on it or that the disk is not yet DOS formatted.

Begin troubleshooting with the FDISK utility program. If FDISK indicates that it finds a hard drive (better put, if it does not indicate that it cannot locate a fixed disk), you can view any existing partition information or create a new partition.

Tip   If you receive a message indicating that FDISK "cannot locate a disk drive" or you receive a similar message, recheck the connections and settings between the host adapter and the drive.

If FDISK indicates that your drive already has a DOS partition, it is possible that all you may need to do is use DOS' FORMAT command to format the drive. After you have a partitioned drive, your SCSI drive system is well on its way to working. The next step would be to format the drive for the operating system.

Adding SCSI drives to an existing hard drive configuration

SCSI hard drives need not be the only hard drives in your system. They can be used with ST506, ESDI, and IDE drives, but not as the primary boot drive. If your SCSI adapter will not be the only hard drive adapter in your system, it cannot be the boot device. You must typically disable the SCSI host adapter's BIOS and load a device driver in your boot drive's CONFIG.SYS file to gain access to the SCSI devices. If you already have a diskette controller in your system, you must also disable any disk controller on your SCSI adapter or disable the other controller and use the one on your host adapter.

The hardware configuration is otherwise the same as indicated for SCSI-only systems, though you may need to add an ASPI or similar SCSI interface device driver entry to your CONFIG.SYS file so that DOS, booted from your existing hard drive, recognizes the SCSI host adapter and attached devices. If you have a CD-ROM drive or other non–hard-disk SCSI device attached to the host adapter, you need the device driver files or software specific to that device to use it.

In a Windows-only or other operating system environment (Linux, FreeBSD, OS/2, and so on), if you are able to boot from another device, use that operating system's utilities to access the new SCSI drive, format it, and prepare it for your use. If you must treat the new SCSI drive as the only drive in your system, you will need to perform your operating system installation. Most operating systems, including Windows 98/Me/NT/2000, Linux, and FreeBSD, will install to that drive as long as your system will recognize it as a bootable device. See the previous discussion for the related configuration information.

SCSI formatting

Rarely do you need to perform a SCSI (low level) format on a new SCSI hard drive. If you obtain a used drive or one that has been used in a different system type (such as an Apple Macintosh or Sun UNIX workstation), then performing the SCSI format using the programs that come with or are built into your SCSI host adapter is highly recommended. The SCSI format will establish the proper drive parameter translations and reinitialize the sectors on the hard drive. Without doing so, you may not be able to use the drive or may not be able to take advantage of its full capacity.

The onboard BIOS or external utility software for SCSI host adapters provides access to a variety of tools for identifying, testing, and low-level formatting SCSI devices.

Caution   As with drive formatting programs and functions, some of these utilities will destroy existing data on a drive. The only way to avoid the danger of losing important data is to *not* perform the low-level formatting or normal formatting unless you must.

Partitioning Hard Drives

We have discussed a number of items concerning, clusters, formatting, logical drives, and volume labels in the preceding text. Some of you may be wondering when we are going to discuss low-level formatting, other than to warn you not to do it to IDE drives.

The answer to this is pretty simple (except in the case of older, obsolete ST506 and ESDI drives, which we have finally dropped for this edition): The process of low-level formatting of a drive is also obsolete.

Because the drive controller is now built onto IDE drives, it is the responsibility of each drive manufacturer to establish and to maintain the lowest-level details within each drive. Similarly, SCSI formatting is an issue specific to each host adapter and drive rather than a commonplace requirement.

Your most significant tasks after the physical drive and possible required driver installation will be to establish the file system and directory spaces into which you store programs and data.

Partitioning a drive

A new drive has only head, cylinder (or track), and sector information on the drive. These serve as the "surveyor's marks" for the area into which you are going to place data. The operating system must stake claim to and establish the specific territory it will use on the disk. This process is called *partitioning*.

Partitioning a drive will create or amend the proper Master Boot Record at the beginning of the drive—akin to a landlord posting a sign that lists all the tenants at the door of an apartment building. The FDISK program (or Disk Manager from OnTrack or EZ-Drive from MicroHouse) establishes the logical drive information for use by DOS and Windows 3.*x*, or Windows 95/98/Me. The Windows NT/2000 setup program has the partitioning and formatting functions built in.

Logical drives and partitions may consume the entire disk surface or they may be limited to part of the drive area. How much space is available and how it is organized dictates cluster sizes (the smallest unit of disk space the operating system and file operations use) and type and size of the FAT, MFT, and other drive and file system support files.

When using FDISK to establish partitions, the first partition is defined as the first hard drive, C:. If you do not give this first partition all of the space on the drive, an extended partition may occupy the rest of the drive and can be one logical drive assigned as drive D:, or it can be subdivided into further logical drives within the extended partition.

Partitioning for Multiple Operating Systems

We alluded to possible problems with partitioning for multiple operating systems in a previous caution regarding multiple bootable operating systems and the limitation that may be imposed by your BIOS or hard drive. Today's PCs can accommodate *large* disk drives, 40GB or even larger. Check the documentation for the version of the operating systems you are installing.

Just as in Windows 2000, you may have to install the bootable partition within the first 2GB (or even smaller) partition. If both operating systems have that same requirement, they will have to share (for example, both partitions exist within that first *x* number of bytes of that hard drive).

If your PC's BIOS has even more restricting limitations, you will have to reduce the partition to an even smaller size. This documentation may not be available. In that case, you will just have to try what you feel is reasonable and if it does not work, remember this caution and try smaller partitions within a smaller combined first partition size.

To avoid this altogether, install your multiple operating systems on multiple drives!

In any case, for the operating system, the first drive or partition must be assigned as the primary/active/boot partition in order for the PC-system BIOS to seek the proper area of the disk to find the system files for bootup (always beginning at Head 0, Track 0, Sector 0).

You could assign subsequent partitions for use by Unix, Windows NT, or some other operating system, defining and creating one or more logical drives with the utilities from the other operating systems for this purpose.

If you make a mistake with FDISK, you can always back out, delete the information you established, and try again with other combinations of partition and logical drive sizes. Sometimes you have to recalculate sectors, tracks, and heads to determine the size of a logical drive or, as with DOS 5 and higher, simply enter a partition or drive size in megabytes (1MB = 1,048,576 bytes).

Caution   Aside from the benefits of using FDISK, it is otherwise a dangerous utility to keep on your system, just as FORMAT can be, because using FDISK to remove a partition (and all data and files) can render all files unrecoverable. If others have access to your system, you might consider renaming if not removing FDISK from your hard disk to limit the chances of it being used in a harmful manner.

Running FDISK is a simple process, but you must read the screens and prompts carefully as you proceed. With a completely blank or unpartitioned disk drive, you have the choices of making DOS or non-DOS partitions of any size you want, up to the maximum capacity of the disk drive. The typical and simplest choice is to accept the first set of options and use the entire drive as one large DOS drive. Depending upon the drive configuration and capacity, you may or may not gain full use of the drive. Refer to the discussions of BIOS and disk-size limitations in the Installing, Adding, or Changing Hard Drives section earlier in this chapter. Without enhanced BIOS or special device drivers, DOS will only be able to see 512MB drives.

Tip   If you use OnTrack's Disk Manager on a hard drive and then view the partition information with FDISK, the entire drive will be viewed as a single non-DOS partition and will not be manageable by FDISK unless you want to remove, delete, or destroy this partition. If this is the case with your system, quit FDISK and use the OnTrack Disk Manager program to manage the drive's partitions.

Other non-DOS partitions may exist on your drive such as Windows' FAT32 file system, Linux (or other Unix operating system) set up as Network File System (NFS), OS/2 with the High Performance File System (HPFS), or Windows NT/2000 NT File System (NTFS). You can eliminate or ignore these partitions and not handle them with FDISK, which is recommended if you want to preserve these existing file systems.

Typically, you will define a DOS partition of 512MB or larger, depending on your needs. If you elect the first FDISK choices and defaults, the entire drive will become one single DOS partition that will constitute drive C: (if you are working with only one disk drive or the first disk drive) or drive D: (if you are working with the second disk drive). Take a look at a single DOS drive with one partition and one logical drive in Table 18-5.

Table 18-5				
Single DOS Disk Partition on One Physical Disk Drive				
Drive Letter	*Physical Disk Drive*	*Partition Number*	*Partition Type*	*Note*
C:	First	First	DOS, primary	First drive, first partition; or first logical drive in DOS partition; or first logical drive on first physical drive

If you simply add a second drive with one primary DOS partition, the two drives appear as described in Table 18-6.

Table 18-6
Single DOS Disk Partitions on Each of Two Physical Disk Drives

Drive Letter	Physical Disk Drive	Partition Number	Partition Type	Note
C:	First	First	DOS	First drive, first partition; or first/only logical drive in only DOS partition
D:	Second	First	DOS	Second drive, first partition; or first/only logical drive in second drive's first/only DOS partition

If you have two disk drives and multiple partitions on drive C:, some interesting things begin to happen with the second and subsequent partitions on each drive. With two disk drives, DOS always assigns the next drive letter, D:, to the first partition on the second drive, regardless of other partitions on the first drive, as shown in Table 18-7.

Table 18-7
Multiple DOS Disk Partitions with Two Disk Drives

Drive Letter	Physical Disk Drive	Partition Number	Partition Type	Note
C:	First	First	DOS	First drive, first partition; or first logical drive in DOS partition; or first logical drive on first physical drive
D:	Second	First	DOS	Second drive, first partition; or first logical drive in DOS partition; or first logical drive on second physical drive
E:	First	Second	DOS extended	First drive, second partition; or first logical drive in extended DOS partition; or second logical drive on first physical drive

Continued

	Table 18-7 (continued)			
Drive Letter	Physical Disk Drive	Partition Number	Partition Type	Note
F:	Second	Second	DOS extended	Second drive, second partition; or first logical drive in extended DOS partition; or second logical drive on second physical drive

DOS keeps assigning drive letters in the order in which it finds partitions, beginning with any and all primary DOS partitions and then back to any extended DOS partitions. The drive letter designations zigzag through the partitions, initially to the first drive and partition, then to the next drive and its first partition, then back to the extended DOS partition on the first drive, and finally to the second extended DOS partition of the second drive. The primary and then extended DOS partition sequencing is more vivid in Table 18-8. We have created the primary DOS partition and an extended DOS partition on each drive. In the extended DOS partitions, we have created three logical drives. We will end up with eight logical drive designations total, four on each drive.

	Table 18-8 Multiple Logical Drives in Primary and Extended DOS Disk Partitions with Two Disk Drives			
Drive Letter	Physical Disk Drive	Partition Number	Partition Type	Note
C:	First	First	DOS, primary, active	First drive, first partition; or first logical drive in DOS partition; or first logical drive on first physical drive
D:	Second	First	DOS	Second drive, first partition; or first logical drive in DOS partition; or first logical drive on first physical drive
E:	First	Second	DOS extended	First drive, second partition; or first logical drive in extended DOS partition; or second logical drive on first physical drive

Drive Letter	Physical Disk Drive	Partition Number	Partition Type	Note
F:	First	Second	DOS extended	First drive, second partition; or second logical drive in extended DOS partition; or third logical drive on first physical disk drive
G:	First	Second	DOS extended	First drive, second partition; or first logical drive in extended DOS partition; or fourth logical drive on first physical drive
H:	Second	Second	DOS extended	Second drive, second partition; or first logical drive in extended DOS partition; or second logical drive on second physical drive
I:	Second	Second	DOS extended	Second drive, second partition; or first logical drive in extended DOS partition; or third logical drive on second physical drive
J:	Second	Second	DOS extended	Second drive, second partition; or first logical drive in extended DOS partition; or fourth logical drive on second physical drive

This sequence of drive assignments will become even more confusing if you have three, four, or more disk drives, as you can have with IDE or SCSI drive systems. If you have more than two drives, it will be easier to identify and to manage the logical assignments and partitions if you simply assign the entire drive to the primary and only DOS partition on each drive. This way the logical drive assignments track one-for-one with the existence of each physical drive.

Note

If you decide to use disk-compression software on any one of the preceding partitioning methods, the host or uncompressed drive letter will be assigned after any physical or logical partitions are assigned, as shown. Be careful of the DOS LASTDRIVE= parameter setting in CONFIG.SYS, as you could restrict access to one or more drives if the LASTDRIVE is set to a lower drive letter than you have logical drives.

Why make multiple partitions?

There are three reasons for making multiple disk partitions on a single disk drive:

✦ You are facing the cluster and minimal file-size concerns that we have detailed earlier in this chapter. To conserve valuable disk space so that small files do not chew up 16K or 32K worth of space each due to each file occupying at least one disk cluster, you may elect to create smaller disk partitions.

✦ You wish to organize your files by their respective types or applications on separate disk drives, which also helps with the cluster and file-size concerns.

✦ You are sharing a disk drive with other users on a network, and you only wish to allow access to specific data organized by certain drives on your system. With separate drive partitions, you can easily assign or deny the file sharing access rights to other users on your network. Under Windows 95/98/Me and NT/2000 (using the FAT file system), you can set up sharing in no finer depth than by drive designation. You cannot refine access controls by subdirectories or files unless you are using Windows NT/2000 and the NTFS, or OS/2 and the HPFS. Thus, partitioning also enables you to plan and define your file structure for your own security needs and purposes under the FAT file system.

Mixed operating systems

It is not uncommon to want to mix operating systems on a hard drive, especially if you are learning to use Windows NT/2000, Linux, FreeBSD, OS/2, and others while maintaining familiar DOS/Windows 95/98/Me access to your programs and files. The Unix operating systems and Windows NT NTFS file systems do not share file systems (that is, do not allow DOS-type file storage and access) within single disk partitions. Windows 95 maintains the DOS file system and can be booted as a DOS-only system for hardware-level maintenance, and it can return to the prior DOS environment as needed (this works even better in Windows 98/Me).

OS/2 provides two ways to share drive space with DOS and Windows: the Dual-Boot method, which is not especially obvious in planning an OS/2 installation, and the Boot Manager method.

The Dual Boot method

The Dual Boot method enables you to have a drive that can be booted into DOS/Windows or OS/2 as you choose after you have the system booted into one operating system or the other. We think this is the safest way to experiment with and learn OS/, or another operating system before making a commitment to switching to it.

The Dual Boot method requires that you perform a complete OS/2 installation without using OS/2's HPFS or the Boot Manager facility. You cannot mix the HPFS and

DOS FAT file system within the same partition on your drive. If you want to use the HPFS, which is not accessible from DOS, you must repartition your drive, reducing the size of the DOS partition, to make room for the HPFS partition. Use a utility such as Partition Magic for this process.

The Boot Manager method

The Boot Manager method requires a complete repartitioning of your hard disk, which requires a complete backup of the DOS or other operating system's files, if you want to retain use of them for later. Boot Manager installation, selectable when you begin your OS/2 installation, creates a small partition at the front of your drive for the sole purpose of holding files to support a menu and boot control system. Use it to select among DOS, Windows, and other operating systems and OS/2 bootup each time you start the system. Subsequent partitioning for OS/2 and DOS, or another operating system, occurs after the Boot Manager partition is established, and the OS/2 partition can be set up for the OS/2 HPFS or DOS FAT type file system.

For operating systems other than OS/2 and Windows NT, facilities within those operating systems or optional programs may provide their own access to DOS partitions and file systems. For instance, Linux and FreeBSD have facilities to access DOS and Windows file systems and, in some cases, even run DOS and Windows programs. This does not include Windows NT/2000.

In either case, for a caution about partition sizes and locations, see the sidebar "Partitioning for Multiple Operating Systems," earlier in this chapter.

Formatting Hard Drives

The formatting done under the DOS FORMAT program performs the following functions:

✦ Establishes the bootable system areas, if a system format is selected

✦ Establishes the root directory area for 512 entries (on a hard disk)

✦ Marks the clusters (tracks and sectors) of the disk for reference during reads and writes

✦ Provides space on the disk for a volume label (to give a plain text label to a partition)

A DOS or Windows 95/98/Me disk's boot area contains information about the drive, and if it is bootable, the system boot files (IBMBIO.COM and IBMDOS.COM, or IO.SYS and MSDOS.SYS for the respective DOS or Windows version, to match the version of COMMAND.COM and other version-specific DOS files). This is similar for Windows

95/98/Me, though this contains only one active "executable" boot file, IO.SYS. Under Windows 95/98/Me, the MSDOS.SYS is simply a text file, with read-only, hidden, and system-level attributes, that is used as a bootup configuration file for IO.SYS.

If for any reason Track 0 is bad on any cylinder, the drive will not accept a boot sector and it may not format at all because this area that must be usable for the startup information for DOS/Windows. Utilities such as the Symantec's Disk Doctor or Steve Gibson's SpinRite might be able to recover this track. If not, you can allow these programs to attempt to repair Track 0. If the drive will format but not accept boot information, you cannot use it as a primary or boot disk but it may still be useful as a data disk.

Tip   A disk that indicates many failures during formatting or under disk utility tests should be thoroughly checked with a disk diagnostic or simply discarded.

The format process marks any bad areas it finds on the disk. This marking is done in the FAT, cluster by cluster. DOS does not use areas marked as bad in the FAT.

After the FAT and cluster areas are marked by FORMAT, the disk is ready to accept files for use by DOS and DOS applications.

Hard Drive Problems

System capacity and performance may be measured as much by the hard drive system as by the processor and clock speed. A slow hard drive in a fast processor system creates performance bottlenecks in almost every application you use. If your drive system fails, the speed of your processor and applications will not matter because your system will be unusable.

Resolving hard drive problems and keeping the drive finely tuned are the goals of this section. Some of the problems related to your hard disk will also relate to the files section, your operating system's File System and Disk Control, so you may wish to check Chapters 16 and 17 for references to your hard drive's symptoms if you do not find them in this section.

This section also provides further discussion of disk diagnostic and utility programs. These are the special tools needed to optimize and maintain a proficient drive and file system. The utilities available today are more user-friendly and helpful than ever before. They are no longer just for the gurus.

The following list describes common hard drive problems and solutions. This section includes the BIOS and power-on self test (POST) error messages related to hard drive and controller errors. You will find a number of hints and tips to help you improve your system's performance through its disk subsystem.

Note Remember that the BIOS and POST are operating system-independent. They apply to any operating system installed on your PC!

 Cross-Reference For more information on BIOS disk status codes, see Chapter 19.

Symptoms

▶ Drive will not start spinning or it groans.

Suspects

▶ Drive motor or electronics problems

▶ Power supply inadequate or defective

Solutions

▶ Check all of the cables, connectors, jumpers, and switches to make sure they are correct.

▶ Replace the drive.

▶ Check or replace the power supply.

Symptoms

▶ Drive spins up and down erratically.

Suspects

▶ Drive motor or electronics problems

▶ Power supply connection problems

▶ Data cable connection problems

Solutions

▶ Check power connections.

▶ Check data cables.

▶ Repair or replace the drive.

Symptoms

▶ Drive makes high-pitched noise.

Suspects

▶ Antistatic wiper on spindle is defective.

▶ Heads have crashed (heads touched the platter while spinning).

Solutions

▶ Repair or replace the drive.

▶ Adjust the antistatic wiper.

Symptoms

▶ Any of the following numeric error messages appear, usually during the POST:

1701	Controller/cabling/drive/drive select jumper/CMOS
1702	Controller
1703	Controller/cabling/drive/jumpers
1704	Controller or drive
1780	First physical drive (0:) failure
1781	Second physical drive (1:) failure
1782	Controller
1790	First physical drive (0:) error
1791	Second physical drive (1:) error
10480	First physical drive (0:) failure (PS/2-ESDI)
10481	Second physical drive (1:) failure (PS/2-ESDI)
10482	PS/2 ESDI controller failure
10483	PS/2 ESDI controller failure
10490	First physical drive (0:) error (PS/2-ESDI)
10491	Second physical drive (1:) error (PS/2-ESDI)

Suspects

▶ The numeric error messages are fairly accurate in describing the cause of a failure. If the drive or controller is new, the jumper or switch settings, formatting, or cabling might be the problem.

Solutions

▶ Configure, format, and connect cable properly.

▶ Replace the drive or controller electronics boards.

Symptoms

▶ Slow performance

Suspects

▶ Sector interleave problems (usually found on old drives).

▶ Controller problems.

▶ Disk-caching problems.

▶ BUFFERS= setting in CONFIG.SYS is wrong.

▶ DOS VERIFY parameter is turned on.

▶ Disk or data errors.

▶ DR-DOS 5 is in use.

▶ Sector interleaving is incorrect.

Solutions

▶ Ensure that the BUFFERS= setting in CONFIG.SYS is set to at least 3, and typically no more than 12 for most systems. Many DOS manuals recommend one buffer for each megabyte of storage capacity of the drive, though tests we have run with a number of programs indicate that optimum performance comes with the number of buffers set between 3 and 8. If you use disk-caching software, 3 is typically the optimum value.

▶ If the VERIFY parameter is set to ON, it slows disk write operations slightly. It does not error check the data written against the source information. Instead, it simply checks the newly written drive contents against a memory image of what is supposed to be written. Set VERIFY OFF if you have no preference for its use or if you use disk-caching software and it performs its own VERIFY.

▶ Test the drive with a thorough read/write diagnostic program. Norton Utilities and similar programs can report more specific controller, drive, disk, or data errors (and they offer to, or automatically, remedy the errors). The Norton Utilities or Gibson's SpinRite disk diagnostic packages provide thorough drive and data area testing, and automatic repair, as well as sector interleave testing.

▶ Use a disk-caching program. SMARTDRV (with MS-DOS and Windows), HyperDisk (an excellent shareware program), and the Norton Cache (NCACHE) are proven choices for most applications. SMARTDRV will also cache CD-ROM data, if it is installed after the CD-ROM driver (MSCDEX or similar).

▶ DR-DOS 5 performs 10 percent to 20 percent slower for disk-read and write operations because it involves an extra verification process on files when they are accessed. This may not be apparent on systems faster than 16 MHz or on systems that use a disk-caching program.

▶ Except for IDE drive systems, the interleave pattern of the sectors on the disk can affect drive performance dramatically. A PC or XT-class system works best with an interleave of 3 to 4. AT-class systems (286, 386, 486), drives, and controllers may perform best with interleaves from 1 to 3. This is highly dependent on the controller and drive. Here again, Norton, SpinRite, or other diagnostics may be your best tools to determine and correct improper sector interleaving.

Symptoms

▶ Drive fills up too fast.

Suspects

▶ Large cluster sizes.

▶ Many small files (file sizes that are less than the cluster size of 2K, 4K, or 8K).

▶ DOS version and disk size are affecting cluster sizes.

▶ Drive partitioning.

▶ A cluttered hard disk, possibly from undeleted BAK or TMP files, multiple copies of files (especially from MS Office programs), Web browsers, and some e-mail programs.

Solutions

▶ Check for the accumulation of many BAK, TMP, or similar temporary or backup files, and for unnecessary DOC, TXT, READ.ME, and other files. Delete these files if you find any. Reduce the size of your Web browser's disk cache.

▶ Check for unresolved FILE000x.CHK or similar CHKDSK-generated recovered files. Identify and rename them for use or delete them.

▶ Upgrade or change your DOS to a Microsoft version (or original equipment manufacturer (OEM) version) or to DR-DOS (now owned by Caldera), if you do not need IBM PC-DOS or vendor/machine-specific DOS versions.

▶ Repartition the drive to smaller logical drive sizes. The Partition Magic disk utility software enables you to repartition a hard drive without FDISK and without losing existing data on the disk.

Symptoms

▶ Files are partially or improperly written.

▶ Files are not saved on the disk.

Suspects

▶ Program compatibility

▶ Improper BUFFERS= setting in CONFIG.SYS

▶ Early release (June 1990) of DR-DOS 5

▶ Intermittent disk controller, drive, cabling, and power supply problems

▶ Disk/controller errors

▶ Disk write-caching/program operation/cache RAM errors

Solutions

▶ Applications in general distribution, commercially or on BBS distribution, should generally be reliable unless they are new releases or have precautions or limitations.

Some programs use direct hardware control techniques and may not wait for or get proper drive or controller approval status before reading or writing further data. This should be a minimal, even nonexistent, problem with programs written and compiled under DOS 3.0 and later, unless they are designed for a specific machine or set of hardware. Direct binary writes to disks are not recommended without verification routines or proper I/O handling in the software.

It is unlikely that the DOS BUFFERS setting will affect disk writes, but this value should be set to between 3 and 12 for most systems. Less or more slow drive performance.

The June 1990 release of DR-DOS 5.0 had known problems with some binary device write operations. If you have this version, upgrade to the August 1990 or a later version — DR-DOS Version 6 or Novell DOS Version 7.

Diagnose the disk system with CHKDSK or a more specific utility package to verify and resolve bad areas on the disk or to identify a bad drive or controller.

If you use disk write caching to enhance the performance of your system, you could encounter incompatibilities with applications that try to bypass standard DOS/BIOS functions or you may have an intermittent or hard-to-find RAM chip error. An intermittent or slow RAM chip can cause mysterious file read and write errors. Thoroughly test the RAM in your system for an extended period of time.

Be sure your disk-caching program is compatible with the hardware and memory you have installed. Test all of your system RAM thoroughly — all of it — DOS, LIMS-EMS (expanded), and extended memory (high memory area (HMA) and extended memory specification (XMS)). If you use write caching and the delay time for writing the data can be disabled or changed, set the disk write time interval to a lower number so that files stored in the cache are written to disk more often or disable the write-caching/delayed-write feature.

Symptoms

▶ Increasing occurrences of data errors.

▶ Frequent retries or errors reading data from the drive.

▶ CHKDSK or SCANDISK (MS-DOS 6.x and higher) indicates several bad clusters.

Suspects

▶ Disk surface or read/write heads are damaged.

▶ Drive motor bearings or read/write head mechanisms are wearing out.

Solutions

▶ Use a utility program, such as SpinRite or Norton Disk Doctor, to recover good data and mark the bad areas so they cannot be used again.

▶ Back up all good data on the drive to disks or tape.

▶ Low-level format, repartition, and DOS format the drive. (This is for ST506/ST-412, ESDI, and SCSI only. Do not low-level format IDE drives. Refer to the "Installing IDE Drive" section earlier in this chapter, for more information.)

▶ You can repair the drive, but it is usually quicker and less expensive to replace it.

You might be able to survive for a short time by reformatting the drive, but recurring errors are a sign of a worn-out drive. Data errors that appear consistently in one area of the drive, such as the beginning or ending tracks, indicate a mechanical problem with the drive, and these errors will likely begin to appear more frequently as the drive continues to wear out. If you begin to see more errors in random places on the drive, either the disk itself or the drive head is going bad — possibly because of a severe mechanical shock to the drive. In either case, back up your data to tape or disk, and prepare to replace the drive. If you replace the drive, you can transfer the data between drives before the old one fails.

Summary

Chapter 18 covered the following points:

✦ Installing, adding, or changing hard drives

✦ IDE, SCSI, and mixed drive systems

✦ Partitioning hard drives

✦ Formatting hard drives

✦ Hard drive problems

Now that you are an expert on hard drives, you can move on to Chapter 19, which addresses removable media and other types of drives.

✦   ✦   ✦

Diskette, CD-ROM, and other Drives

Removable and alternate disk storage media are quite similar to hard drives and, as a matter of fact, you will find that parts of the Problems sections of this chapter relate to all types of disk storage devices. However, there are differences, and they are emphasized in this chapter.

If, while reading or using this chapter, you find you are getting confused or the terminology seems foreign, you may need to go to Chapters 16 through 18 for some of the basics, definitions, and details. Although we believe you will get a lot more out of your PC and disk drives by reading through Part IV from start to finish, feel free to skip ahead or go to the chapter or section that is most important to you right now.

Working with Diskettes

The only requirement for using a diskette is that it be formatted, by your system's FORMAT program, in a SYSTEM, DATA-only, or non-SYSTEM (data with space reserved for SYSTEM files) type.

The FORMAT program expects the disk in the drive to match the type of drive reported at boot up, unless you provide command line or check box parameters for size and recording density that instruct it otherwise. If you have a 1.44MB 3.5-inch drive and request a FORMAT A: for that drive without specific parameters, the disk must be a 1.44MB disk, or the format will fail.

Caution

Later, you may not be able to format the same diskette in the proper drive (for instance, an improperly formatted 720K diskette in a real 720K drive) or with the proper commands for the lower density. This can cause the error message "Track 0 Bad" or "Diskette Unusable", to be reported.

This happens because the first format attempt writes some data on the disk and makes the disk appear defective to the lower-density format attempt. The same problem will occur if you try to format the following:

✦ A 720K disk in a 1.44MB drive as a 1.44MB disk

✦ A 1.2MB (high-density) disk to 1.2MB, and then trying to format that same disk to a lower density

✦ A 1.44MB disk to 1.44MB, and then trying to format that same disk to 720K

The same is true for the 2.88MB drive.

The sure cure for this problem is to expose the disk to a bulk-eraser unit (such as those used for erasing VCR and other tapes) to eliminate all traces of formatting and data.

Other than formatting and handling differences (which are more frequent and often more casual than hard disk considerations) the expected errors and solutions are basically the same for diskette systems as they are for hard disk systems. The error messages described for hard disks also apply to diskette systems. The only difference is that you will see 6xx or 73xx series error messages instead of 17xx or 104xx series messages if there are hardware errors detected by the POST or during system use. Similar utility software routines restore diskettes as well as hard disks, making them bootable again, recovering files, and so on.

Ways to Ensure Reliable Diskettes

Some *do* and *do not* rules for diskette reliability (believe it or not):

✦ Do not wash a diskette to get a "clean diskette."

✦ Do not remove the circular (reddish-brown) media from the plastic enclosure before trying to use a diskette. The white paper or Tyvek envelope for 5¼" diskettes is the only outside covering you need to remove from the diskette. 3.5" diskettes are in sealed plastic containers and have moveable plastic tabs for the write protect mechanism.

✦ Do not fold, bend, spindle, crush, x-ray, or expose the disks to magnetic fields (airport security hand-inspects requested items, at least in the U.S.), and do not put them on the refrigerator with one of those cool souvenir magnets from Nebraska.

✦ Do use a disk mailer or reinforce an envelope with a stiff piece of cardboard when mailing disks because postal carriers curl or force an envelope into a mail slot if they can.

✦ Do use a disk drive cleaning kit regularly. The special alcohol-based cleaning solution and pad that acts like a disk can put a lot of use back into a drive.

✦ Do throw away diskettes that do not format. If the format program reveals many bad sectors on the disk, you are probably better off throwing the disk away than trusting the rest of it to hold the data you need for any period of time. At 20 cents or less per diskette, you can afford to throw a few away.

✦ Do keep disks away from heat and magnetic fields. Beware strong magnetic fields around your video monitor and speakers. The shelf above your system is great for books, but the magnetic fields surrounding the monitor can scramble data in a matter of hours. Similarly, fans and motors use strong magnetic fields that can erase data. Treat disks as you would a valuable record, tape, or CD collection.

Working with CD-ROM Drives

CD-ROM drives are about as foreign to the original PC systems and specifications as the alternative media we discuss in the next section, but they are a common requirement for most operating system and software installations. They are not natively supported by the PC system BIOS nor the operating system (under DOS and Windows 3.*x*)—they may or may not use any of the normal PC interface ports or adapters, and they require additional drivers to make them accessible by the operating system.

CD-ROM drives have been indirectly supported by the Microsoft and IBM operating systems for many years, although they require special device drivers to make the hardware visible to the operating system and the Microsoft CD Extensions (MSCDEX) driver to attach a logical DOS drive letter to a CD-ROM drive.

CD-ROMs are still not recognized by most system BIOS, but this is changing as Phoenix and Award both make accommodations in BIOS to treat IDE-interfaced CD-ROM drives as bootable devices. The CD-ROM hardware interface and MSCDEX drivers are now delivered as part of Windows 95, 98, Me, NT and 2000, but they are not part of the underlying DOS or command-prompt layer.

CD-ROM interfaces

The first CD-ROM drives used either a SCSI interface or a proprietary interface unique to the drive manufacturer. The SCSI interfaced drives were fairly simple to deal with — they used standard SCSI cables and terminators.

The proprietary interfaces used either 34-pin or 40-pin ribbon cables and custom device drivers. Mitsumi and Panasonic are among those who used the proprietary interfaces. They had to furnish an extra add-in card to plug into your system board, or depend on sound card makers to design the proprietary interface onto their sound cards. The cabling was confusing because you could mistakenly connect these cables to diskette or IDE interfaces, or try to attach your diskette or IDE drives to the CD-ROM interface card. No CD-ROM drive was ever designed to hook up to the diskette interface. Making the wrong connections could destroy the drive interface, the CD-ROM drive, the diskette drive, or the hard drive.

Caution   Misconnecting CD-ROM drives or interfaces could damage your system. Do not be fooled by CD-ROM drives, adapters, or sound cards with 34- or 40-pin connections! If it has 34-pins, you can be sure it is not a diskette-interface type connection. If it has 40-pins, it may or may not be an IDE-interface. Do not take chances. Always check the documentation or the drive manufacturer's Web site to verify the connection type according to the exact model number of the drive.

IDE CD-ROM drives use the same Master/Slave jumper settings as IDE hard drives. Typically the CD-ROM drive is a Slave drive on the primary hard drive interface port for single–hard drive systems. The CD-ROM can also be the Master or the Slave on the secondary IDE interface port.

CD-ROM drivers

Since CD-ROM drives are not supported directly by most system BIOS or the operating system, they require two drivers under DOS and older versions of Windows — a device driver to be installed in CONFIG.SYS and a special DOS program called MSCDEX.

CD-ROM drives that connect to proprietary CD-ROM interfaces on separate add-in cards or sound cards require the DOS-level device driver specific to that drive and interface type. CD-ROM drives that connect to SCSI host adapters often require an ASPI driver for the host adapter, and an ASPI CD driver to recognize and support CD-ROM drive functions.

For CD-ROM drives that connect to IDE interfaces, almost any IDE/ATAPI CD-ROM device driver will enable your system to locate and identify most IDE-interfaced CD-ROM drives.

The appearance of a typical CD-ROM drive device driver in your CONFIG.SYS file is similar to the following:

```
DEVICE=C:\CDROM\CDROMDRV.SYS /P:170 /I:15 /D:MSCD001
```

You may have the /P: and /I: parameters, or something similar to refer to the address and IRQ, or the interface port and Master/Slave configuration for the interface port to which the drive is connected. This is necessary if the driver cannot automatically detect it, but most ATAPI-compliant drivers can do autodetection. The /D: parameter gives this specific CD-ROM drive a name or label that you have to use with MSCDEX to know that this drive is to be handled by a specific instance of MSCDEX. You can have multiple or different CD-ROM drives and drivers. If this specific label is not used or does not match the name specified for MSCDEX, neither will know which drive to use.

Tip

Keep a copy of your CD-ROM device driver file and its appropriate DEVICE= line in the CONFIG.SYS file on your bootable emergency diskette in case you need to boot up your system from the diskette drive and reinstall your operating system!

MSCDEX

MSCDEX is a bridge between DOS and the CD-ROM device driver. It is used to support the multiple file formats and content types available on CD-ROMs. Many CD-ROMs are shipped with multiple operating system file formats, and may include audio CD and other multimedia data types. MSCDEX sorts this out for DOS and Windows, allowing access to audio/music CDs for play in the PC's CD-ROM drive, as well as providing DOS logical drive access to the data on CDs.

When you insert and play an audio CD, your PC is not actually reading the data and turning it into sound — instead you have merely given a "play" command to the CD-ROM drive. The digital-to-audio conversion is processed inside the CD-ROM drive and the audio is directed to a headset connector on the front and a special connector on the back of the drive, which may be connected to your sound card. The sound card is merely used as an amplifier and volume control for the CD-ROM sound.

When you insert and run a game CD, your PC is reading the drive as if it were any old DOS disk drive. The digital data is processed as digital information. The game CD may provide sounds in the form of WAV files, just like what you would play in Windows, or the multimedia graphics and sound could come from a non-data track on a mixed content or multisession CD-ROM.

MSCDEX is capable of discriminating between CD-ROM data types and send it to the right places. Windows' SmartDrive program is also aware of MSCDEX and will cache and speed-up CD-ROM data reading just as it does for hard drive data.

MSCDEX is loaded and configured in your AUTOEXEC.BAT file similar to the following:

```
C:\WINDOWS\MSCDEX /D:MSCD001
```

The /D: parameter gives this instance of MSCDEX specific reference to the CD-ROM drive name or label that you used with the driver in CONFIG.SYS. These two labels must match exactly. The name is not important, but by default most CD-ROM installation programs make this label MSCD001. For simplicity you could name this label "CD" in both command lines and things would be just fine.

If you wish to have the SmartDrive disk caching utility boost your CD-ROM performance, load it in AUTOEXEC.BAT after MSCDEX.

Tip

As in the preceding example, keep a copy of the MSCDEX file and its appropriate line in the AUTOEXEC.BAT file on your bootable emergency diskette in case you need to boot up your system from the diskette drive and reinstall your operating system!

Note

Windows NT/2000 does not use conventional drivers as DOS and Windows 95/98/Me do. If your drive is not recognized by Windows NT/2000 SETUP, you should check system (CMOS) setup to insure that the IDE interface the CD-ROM drive is connected to is enabled, and you may have to change the primary/secondary interface or Master/Slave configuration of the drive. Failing that, you may have an older drive that does not tell NT the information it needs to know when it is discovering storage devices, thus replacing the old drive with a newer model is recommended.

CD-ROM recorders

The more reasonable cost of CD-ROM recorders, blank writable CD-ROM media, along with the convenience and reliability of being able to permanently archive your own data, is attracting thousands of users to "burn their own CDs." CD-ROM media is certified to retain the written data for 30–100 years.

Most CD-ROM recorders use a SCSI host adapter and interface (though some are available that use UltraDMA33 IDE ports) because DMA mode operation is preferred, if not necessary, to keep a steady stream of data flowing to the drive during write operations. The write operation generally requires that you use a fast hard drive as the source. Those that perform periodic thermal or mechanical self-recalibration are not suitable as recorders because the self-recalibration interrupts the data stream during recording.

There are typically two modes of write operation:

- ✦ Creating a large, single file image of the content as it is to appear on the CD-ROM on your hard disk, which is then streamed onto the medium as fast as possible, or

- ✦ Writing on-the-fly, which accumulates all of the source content as the write is happening

The first is more efficient if you are going to write the data to more than one CD-ROM, but it requires that you have a hard drive with sufficient free space to hold the image.

If the source drive is a SCSI drive or an UltraDMA33 EIDE drive and can run the recorder at 2X or 4X writing speeds, the write operation will go rather quickly. It may not require that you store a single image file of all of the source content on the source drive. You can generally perform writes at 2X speeds without creating a CD-image file first. Otherwise, 1X writing speed and the image file are recommended if slow IDE-interfaced drives are used as the source.

Almost anything you would expect to find on a CD — music, multimedia, or data — can also be put on one with a typical CD recording installation. Music and multimedia content must be specially prepared to have the proper music image created and stored on your hard drive. You need to have an equal amount of free space on the source hard drive to hold the source content in normal format, or as an image of what will be placed on the CD-ROM, and enable it to be spooled to the CD-ROM drive.

CD-ROM data formats

CD-ROMs containing a wide variety of content and applications have been available for many different types of computers. The capabilities and applications of CD-ROMs are always being extended, with Digital Versatile Disk (DVD) being the most recent and quite compelling advancement in capacity, content, applications, and speed.

To the benefit of us all, CD-ROM data format and compatibility is established by the International Standards Organization (ISO), American National Standards Institute (ANSI), Sony, Phillips, Kodak, Microsoft, Intel, and other companies. These groups publish volumes of information relative to compatibility and features. Obtaining the documentation on the various aspects of CD-ROMs involves considerable expense or establishing development license agreements with the vendors involved in proprietary applications.

Rather than dive into the incredible amount of detail available concerning CD-ROMs, we will simply provide an overview of different data formats and their applications.

✦ ISO-9660 — Standard covering how CD-ROM and CD-R (recordable) discs handle directories and filenames to establish cross-platform compatibility. Strict conformity to ISO-9660 means that a CD-ROM can be read on DOS, Windows 3.*x*, Windows 95, 98, Me, NT, and 2000, OS/2, Apple Macintosh, UNIX, and other platforms that support ISO-9660. ISO-9660 allows 8.3 (eight-character filename, three-character extension) filename formats. Directory names may have eight characters. Subdirectories can be eight levels deep. The characters A to Z, 0 to 9, and underscore (_) are the only legitimate characters allowed in directory names.

✦ Joliet—Also known as High Sierra, encompasses ISO-9660, and supports UNI-CODE (international, double-byte character sets, which support languages such as Japanese and Chinese) and Windows 95/98/Me/NT/2000 long filenames.

✦ Mac HFS and Mac/ISO Hybrid for Macintosh and Macintosh/PC

✦ Mixed Mode—Features combination data/audio tracks.

✦ Red Book—The document or name for the Compact Disc Digital Audio Standard. This is the specification for music CDs.

✦ Yellow Book—The document or name for a typical data CD-ROM. Includes CD-DA and is a basis for CD-I and CD-XA (eXtended Architecture or multimedia/mixed-data CD-ROMs).

✦ Mode-1—This is for computer data.

✦ Mode-2—This is for compressed audio data and video/picture data.

✦ Green Book—The document or name for CD-I (Compact Disc-Interactive) media, for interactive multimedia applications. CD-I players are self-contained with drive, display and audio, and user-input features.

✦ Orange Book—The document or name for Phillips' and Sony's specification for recordable CD-ROMs.

✦ Part I covers CD-MO (Magneto Optical) including both read-only and rewritable areas.

✦ Part II—Covers CD-WO (Write Once) including both prewritten read-only and user-writable areas.

✦ Blue Book—The document or name for "Laser Disc" media.

✦ Photo-CD—A hybrid writing multiple/different sessions on the CD-ROM for accumulating digitized photographic images.

✦ Rock Ridge—Specifies compatibility with UNIX systems.

With so many competing formats and standards, it is amazing that today's operating systems, device drivers, and the drives themselves, are able to take almost any CD inserted for use. Right now, while working on this chapter, I am listening to a CD I picked up at a "Farmer's Market" in Long Beach because I like steel drum music. I was not concerned about the format the artist, who I met there at the market, used to record his music. I just inserted it into my CD-ROM reader/writer and am enjoying the tunes!

Working with Alternative Drives

Alternative data storage systems are popping up at the rate of one new device per year. These devices have storage capacities of from 100MB to 4GB, depending on the make and model. These devices may connect to your system using the parallel port, PC Card/PCMCIA socket, IDE interface, or a SCSI adapter.

Since these are not native BIOS or DOS devices, all of them need some form of device driver support so they can be handled as logical disk drives by the operating system. Drivers are available for plain DOS/Windows 3.x operation, Windows 95/98/Me/NT/2000, OS/2, and Linux/UNIX. Once identified by the system, these devices are assigned drive letters, or are associated with a device/volume name in the case of Linux/Unix, in sequence with the other drive letter assignments in the system.

 Note   Device drivers are essentially extensions to the system BIOS, providing software bridging between the new device type and the operating system's existing disk drive support functions.

There are increasing numbers of special drivers for nonstandard devices being included with new operating systems — Windows 95, 98, Me, NT, 2000, OS/2, and variations of Linux/UNIX all are being provided with more nonstandard device support. Still, many of these devices may never be known to the system BIOS, so the drivers are used instead of what could be in the BIOS. Microsoft has been diligently trying, with varied success, to work around the basics and requirements of BIOS, replacing BIOS support and functions with drivers and functions tied into the operating system. Working independently of BIOS makes sense in order to truly optimize the file and I/O system performance within the operating system. But, unlike the UNIX-variants (Linux, FreeBSD, SCO-Unix, and Solaris among them), a lot of old legacy DOS and Windows 3.x programs remain in use, and therefore we cannot escape the PC system's BIOS.

After these devices receive logical device letter assignments, they are treated basically like any other disk drive by the operating system, although their drivers may add optional features to disk management and file properties menus specific to the capabilities of the drive. For instance, the Iomega Zip drive and cartridges do not have a write-protect tab or slot like normal diskettes. Instead the medium has a read-only tag written on the media itself, which is under your control, and can be set or released by the driver software.

Zip, Shark, LS120, Quest, SyJet, and Jaz drives

Optical media drives are considered very similar to CD-ROM drives, except that these types of media are available double-sided, providing 2.3GB of storage capacity on each side, and use different standards than regular data CD-ROMs.

There are quite a few new high-density devices representing a class of advancing storage products that bridge the gap between diskettes and hard drives, offering portability with some security and performance. These new technologies have their benefits and their pitfalls, as we have seen with the Iomega drives.

For many years, Syquest has offered various versions of their 44- and 88MB cartridge drives, which have been quite popular in desktop publishing circles. Iomega brought us the Zip and Jaz cartridge drives. Avatar released their Shark drive in 1997. Imation originated the LS120 or SuperDrive, which performs double-duty as standard 1.44MB diskette drives and as 120MB cartridge drives using special media.

The LS-120 drives are great for systems with limited space for adding extra disk drives. Simply configure the LS120 drive for your IDE interface (Master or Slave), replace your old diskette drive with the LS-120 drive, connect the LS-120 to an available IDE port, and restart the system. The driver tells the system what medium is in the drive and handles it accordingly. If you have the space inside your PC, you can leave the existing 1.44MB diskette drive as drive A: and the LS-120 will show up as drive B:. If not, let the LS-120 drive be A:.

Don't Fall Victim to the "Click of Death"

Beware of the Zip and Jaz drive "click-of-death" syndrome! Occasionally Zip and Jaz media, drive electronics, or mechanics weaken to the point that the drive loses track of itself and where information is stored, allowing itself to overwrite and destroy existing data on the drive. The symptom of this problem is erratic clicking of the drive mechanism as it tries to figure out what to read from or where to write to on the disk. Since the media is essentially defective at this point, putting it into another drive will not help. Iomega will replace defective drives within their warranty period, but offers no data warranty or recovery services.

Help for the Zip-challenged is available through a free utility specifically provided for Zip drive users by Steve Gibson, author of the famous SpinRite hard drive utility. Version 5 of his SpinRite program also supports Zip and Jaz drives, and includes a wealth of new features for hard drive maintenance and diagnosis. Visit the Gibson Research Web site at http://www.grc.com for many more details. Steve's TIP.EXE (Trouble In Paradise) program is included on the CD-ROM you received with this book. TIP.EXE will test your Zip drive and let you know if trouble is brewing. Thanks, Steve!

Magneto-optical drives

Magneto-optical or 'MO' drives and media are, we believe, one of the most versatile yet seemingly unknown storage methods available. The term *magneto-optical* refers to a combined magnetic and optical read-write system where optics is used to affect a magnetic area, much like a laser-beam does when writing a CD-ROM, and data is stored and read in its magnetic form. The drives and platters are either single- or double-sided, providing 650 or 1300 megabytes of storage capacity. This is more than enough for performing an adequate data backup of almost any small system.

MO drives are meant to be used for archival or portable data storage, not as replacements for CD-ROM or standard hard drives, but many of them are fast enough that you would think they are hard drives. Typical interfaces for MO drives include IDE, SCSI, FireWire and USB.

If this sounds interesting to you, run out and buy one. As with most things in the PC industry, if they are not immediately successful, the chances that they will become a part of the mainstream diminish as time passes. MO drives are not new — they have been around for quite a few years — yet they are still somewhat obscure.

Disk Drive "Care and Feeding" and More

In this section we'll cover the things you need to do to take care of your drives, diskettes, and other media. We'll also discuss the things happening in the drive industry to make our data storage more reliable and better able to recover from disaster.

Taking Care of your Media

In most cases our tips for diskette drives apply to all media — and as some put it — disks like to be treated as well as humans.

- ✦ Provide them with a safe, dry, comfortable, place to live, not too cool and not too warm.
- ✦ Do not bump, jar, throw, or toss them around.
- ✦ Do not immerse them in water for extended periods of time — in this case *never.*
- ✦ Provide them with a clean, non-hazardous environment.

All disk drives rely on high-precision machined parts to turn the disks and position the heads. In effect a disk drive is a precise machine. If the mechanism gets dirty or suffers any damage, the resulting work will be imprecise. The motor, bearings, gears, wheels, and work surfaces must fit together perfectly and run smoothly. The tooling (read/write heads) that works with the raw material (the disk itself) must be "sharp" and clean, fit properly into the machine, and be able to meet precisely with the working piece.

The mechanical parts and controls are designed to work with very delicate raw materials — the disk platter and its surface coatings. If this raw material is flawed, no matter how good the machine, you will have a less than ideal product coming out of the machine.

The precision mechanics and their interface to the raw material are controlled and monitored by very stable, high-speed electronic systems. If they are subject to excess electrical noise or extreme temperatures, their accuracy will be impaired, the mechanics will not function correctly, and the work will be useless.

What happens between the machine, its tools, and the raw material while work is being done is equally critical. A different but interconnected and related set of electronic controls handles the tooling interface (reading and writing data) and tells the tool what to do and how to interface to the computer system.

The hardware and programming between the computer system's data stream and the read/write heads are extremely complex. At one time in the very early days of computer systems, you could almost read the data off of a disk platter, using an oscilloscope to see the patterns of 1's and 0's that made up your data. This information was communicated back and forth between the disk drive and its controller. Data comes in from the computer system and turns into magnetic 1's and 0's on the platter, or comes off the platter as those magnetic impulses and is turned back into usable data and given to the computer.

Today the data on the disk platter looks nothing like your word processing documents, in legible words or even simple 1's and 0's. Instead the information on the disk appears as you might imagine a scrambled radio signal coming from another galaxy would look if you could visualize it. In fact, the data on the platter is 'scrambled;' it is compressed and otherwise heavily processed so that we can get more data into a smaller space. The signal processing that makes useful data out of the patterns stored on the disk surface is done by a microprocessor on the disk drive itself. Disk drives have firmware and programming associated with them to make all of this happen. The same data comes from and goes back to the computer system as it did in the old days, but it is processed and stored quite differently.

Note   Remember that disk drives are delicate devices. The fact that manufacturers have made more and new portable varieties, and use them in more portable systems, should not mislead you into thinking that they are more rugged or tolerant of abuse than previous devices.

Some aspects of new drive technologies that have been overlooked are those of how "smart" disk drives and their supporting technologies are getting — that is, how the designers are trying to improve on the known weaknesses of prior technologies. Although it is difficult, if not impossible, to make the new smaller and more precise drives any more durable or tolerant of abuse than early models, we can make them "smarter" and better able to do perform their primary function — to store and make available our valuable data.

From our user-aspect of working with files, file systems, and data on disks, things are pretty simple. Diskettes are fairly basic in their file allocation and directory structures, and most disk utilities can recover data from mildly damaged diskettes — media that has been exposed to magnetic or temperature extremes or that contain damaged file systems because of electronic glitches, program errors, or system crashes. Files on hard drives, though the hardware is more complicated, but without the same degree of risk from external magnetic influences, generally have the same file system recoverability as diskettes. They have two File Allocation Tables and various utilities to record drive file system structures, maintain drive integrity, and recover data.

Data Storage Media Industry Activities

In the problem solving sections that follow we mention a lot of error messages, numbered error messages, and symptoms that you may never see again in a PC system, but they are possible and still exist. The reason you may "never see them again" will be covered below in the discussion of industry efforts to increase reliability and even provide self-fixing hardware.

The lack of visibility on these errors is partly because of the protection or isolation we have from the lower-level details of most of the hardware through Windows 95, 98, Me, NT, and 2000. If we do get errors they are often indirect, obscure, cryptic, and soft-peddled by the operating system and its device drivers. It is as if Microsoft is telling you, "If you get an error, replace the hardware" and leaves it at that. Microsoft is not in the business of hardware troubleshooting or repair — yet. Also, we have been asking for the software people to make this hardware less cryptic, less technical, and easier to use for years, and we got what we wished for — almost.

The "friendlier" messages we get through the software and the operating system are generated in the hardware, BIOS, and the more technical end of the operating system. If you see a message similar to "Cannot write to file XYZ" you can assume that the disk drive subsystem or the file system has produced a lower-level error code of some type. The operating system or software just put a prettier message on the same old problem.

Underneath the operating system, the drivers, the BIOS, and the interconnecting hardware is a new layer of helpful services provided within the disk drives themselves. We have touched on the S.M.A.R.T. technology within EIDE hard drives, with which a portion of the drive electronics monitors the electrical, mechanical, and data operations of the drive, and can provide drive "health" status messages to software programs that know how to ask the drive for them. The status is derived from the drive's internal computer, which compares what the drive is doing against information about tolerances, timing, and overall reliability that the manufacturer has programmed into it.

The drive manufacturers invest a tremendous amount of time and money in reliability tests and studies, which helps improve their designs and, ultimately, the benefits we get from the drives. The hardware laboratories at Quantum, Seagate, and other manufacturers use dozens, if not hundreds, of systems (PCs, Macs, UNIX workstations, and so on) and diagnostic instruments to perform tests on raw drives using various operating systems (DOS, Windows 95, 98, ME, NT, and 2000; IBM OS/2; Sun Solaris; Apple Macintosh; and Linux). Drives are repeatedly partitioned and formatted, have "zillions" of bytes of data files of all sizes transferred to and from them, are erased and recopied—all to learn more about failure modes, collect data, and verify reliability.

The data collected from all of this testing is then processed and used within the drive firmware. It affects the standards for performance, new disk drive interfaces, drive platter manufacturing, disk adapter and BIOS, as well as operating system and utility software. Nothing goes to waste in the process, and it all comes back into the labs for more testing and verification.

This kind of work also goes into the new technologies and types of drives we have touched on, and is used again to improve drive operation and performance. The Iomega Zip and Jaz drives are the result of applying information about older and existing technologies towards delivering something new. Steve Gibson has given us tremendous insight into what these new technologies do, and what we do not and may never know about them.

Z-tracks are an example—four different tracks of information on the media itself that are used only within the drive to keep track of good and bad sectors and the condition of the drive and media. This is not unlike similar technology used within S.M.A.R.T. hard drives, except that the media within hard drives is sealed in, not as subject to dirt, chemicals, or magnetic fields. Hard drives can store their status information in EEPROM or FLASH ROM chips far away from and not subject to the problems that it is tracking. There is no facility to store the information about a specific disk's status on anything but that vulnerable removable media itself. If the information that could save the media is stored on the media, and that media is damaged, it cannot be used to save itself. This is why Norton and other utility software provide the utilities for and recommend making special emergency diskettes separate from the hard drives they are intended to protect.

With the right tools and knowledge, the drive manufacturers can access this status information within the drive or on the media to better understand what is going on. Unfortunately, this information is not always accessible or available to the operating system, because the drive's internal computer is not something that is wired to or accessed through the same data port that is used to connect the drive to your PC. This is both good and bad — it keeps us from being able to access proprietary information that differentiates one drive maker from the other, and also from being able to "screw up" the drive by performing inappropriate operations, accidentally or intentionally.

It also means that the drive can be diagnosed and occasionally repaired by the manufacturer, independent of the normal disk drive interface and electronics, but it is still as fast and cheap today to do backups and simply replace defective drives as it is to repair them. It is also a lot cheaper than using a data recovery service.

The makers of drives and media that use this kind of inaccessible or internal-only drive status technology may have outsmarted themselves — since they do not allow external programs to access or use the data to help fix defects within the media.

No amount of reliability data, software, or computing power is going to be able to fix or work around broken or worn mechanical parts, weak or defective electronic parts, or clean dirt from read/write heads or the media. Another of the Iomega Zip and Jaz problems is that while they provide a self-cleaning mechanism within the drive, there is no way to remove the dirt from or replace the cleaning material. Once the cleaning material becomes contaminated from cleaning dirty cartridges, it could begin to contaminate other cartridges, making things worse instead of better. At least hard drives are sealed; cleaning diskettes can be used on diskette drives, removed, thrown away, and replaced with new ones; and CD-ROM disks and heads can be cleaned, as can tape drive heads. We do not have that feature with some of these other drive types.

At the end of the day, you and your system will be better off if you take good care of your disks and drives, clean them often, back up your data frequently, and respect them as you would anything of value. If they are going to break, they will break — this is part of life with a computer. With that, let us look into the errors and symptoms you might see and how you can successfully work around them.

Common Diskette and Hard Drive Errors

Your system BIOS may present error messages during operations that encounter problems. A numbered error message indicates a serious hardware-level failure or one that is not recognized or handled by software. Textual error messages are the result of operations in which the operating system and applications encounter errors.

If your system is an AT-type, you might have lost some of the CMOS RAM setup information, which might also show up as an error at boot up. Run the system's SETUP program to verify disk drive parameters if nothing else appears obvious.

Also check the battery used to retain CMOS RAM and use anti-virus software to scan your disks for the presence of a virus. A virus can also scramble CMOS information.

The following Symptoms/Suspects/Solutions sequences present DOS and Windows messages and references, but they are similar to the ones you may encounter when working with other operating systems such as Linux, FreeBSD, SCO-Unix, Solaris, OS/2 and so forth. We won't present every possible message and nuance of these different operating systems. Instead, look for messages and symptoms that are similar but refer to different devices, objects, filenames, and so forth. The hardware is the same and the concepts apply to all of these operating systems.

Symptoms

▶ On-screen message: "Track 0 Bad - Disk Unusable"

Suspects

▶ Bad diskette

▶ Improper diskette or format type

▶ Virus infection destroyed Track 0

This message normally occurs while you are formatting a disk. Whether you are formatting a diskette or hard disk for DOS/system files or simply for data use, Track 0 must be good on the drive in order to hold boot sector or label information.

This message also appears if you are trying to format or reformat a 360K diskette as a 1.2MB disk in a 1.2MB drive (or a 720K disk as a 1.44MB disk in a 1.44MB drive or a 1.44MB disk in a 2.88MB drive, and so on).

This message may occur during boot up on some systems that check Track 0 before or while trying to read the system files. A virus infection can destroy the Master Boot Record and other information on Track 0.

Solutions

▶ Change the diskette to the proper type for the format you need or change the FORMAT options to suit the diskette you are trying to format. After you try to format a lower-density disk to a density higher than it is capable of holding, this message appears until you erase the diskette. You may use a magnetic bulk erasing device (such as those used to erase recording tapes) to completely clean off a diskette's information.

▶ If the diskette you are trying to format is of the proper density for the format parameters you are using, it might be corrupt. If you are using 3.5-inch disks and a 1.44MB drive, you might have a problem with the diskette size sensor or switch in your disk drive. This switch is located just inside the drive at the right side of the diskette slot. The sensor or switch looks for a hole in the right-hand corner of the disk case to determine if the diskette is a high or low-density type. You may find debris or dust in the way of the mechanism or just have a sticky switch. If you are not comfortable about working on this part, have a technician clean, replace, or repair this switch. If the switch is not bad, the diskette probably is, and it should be discarded.

▶ Run a virus-checking utility on the drive after restoring the disk to usable condition.

Symptoms

▶ Onscreen message: "Non-System Disk," or "Disk Error - Replace and Strike Any Key When Ready"

Suspects

▶ Wrong disk in drive

▶ Defective or damaged disk

This message refers to an attempt to boot from a disk that does not contain the proper hidden/system files that the BIOS is looking for to continue loading BIOS and DOS. The disk may be damaged or simply was not formatted for the operating system files.

Solutions

▶ If you want this disk to be bootable (typically the disk in drive A: or the hard disk, drive C:), you must first boot from a DOS or other operating system diskette (one that is intended to be used to boot your PC). Then run the SYS program (or appropriate OS-specific program that makes a bootable disk) for the hard drive or diskette that caused the error message.

▶ If you use the DOS SYS program and that does not help, try SCANDISK, SpinRite, or the Norton Disk Doctor program to attempt repairing damaged boot disks. Otherwise, you may have left a non-system disk in drive A:. If so, open the drive latch, press a key, and continue.

▶ If the disk was bootable at one time, run a virus protection program to verify the disk after restoring it.

Symptoms

▶ Onscreen message or message from DOS 6.x and above: "Invalid or Missing COMMAND.COM," when it cannot find a valid command-processor program

Suspects

▶ COMMAND.COM erased or destroyed

▶ Improper SHELL, SET, or PATH to COMMAND.COM

This message occurs if you try to boot from a disk in which the DOS hidden/ system files were located, but COMMAND.COM could not be found. Simply copying COMMAND.COM from another hard drive or diskette will remedy this problem.

This message may also occur if you run a program that uses COMMAND.COM, perhaps by entering DOS to check or copy files, or on returning or exiting from that program.

Solutions

▶ The COMMAND.COM file is not where the system expected to find it before you ran this program. COMMAND.COM should be in the root directory, and/or in the PATH specified by "SHELL=" in CONFIG.SYS, or "SET COMSPEC=" in AUTOEXEC.BAT, or another batch file that set the path to where the command processor program should be located.

▶ Reboot the system, from a diskette if necessary, and check all of the references to COMMAND.COM in your AUTOEXEC.BAT or other .BAT files to ensure that COMMAND. COM is located where it is expected. This could be changed by batch files you have run since you last booted your system. Look for any lines in these batch files that issue the "SET COMSPEC=" command.

▶ Unless you have a specific reason to change the location or name of the command processor, at least the following lines should be in CONFIG.SYS and AUTOEXEC.BAT files, respectively. In CONFIG.SYS:

```
SHELL=d:\path\COMMAND.COM C:\ /P
```

In AUTOEXEC.BAT, no line or the following:

```
SET COMSPEC=d:\path\COMMAND.COM
```

Normally, the d:\path\ portion of these lines would specify only C:\ to indicate the root directory of drive C:. COMMAND.COM does not need to be in the root directory of your system. If it is not, then the portion of these lines that contains the drive and path must be changed to the location of COMMAND.COM. If nothing was intentionally changed on your system, check for the presence of a virus with McAfee's VirusScan or a similar virus detection program.

Symptoms

▶ Onscreen message: "Invalid Parameters"

This error indicates that you have entered unsuitable options for a DOS program. The most likely disk-related reason is likely due to typing improper values for the size or type of disk you are formatting.

Suspects

▶ This message appears if you are trying to issue FORMAT parameters for a 1.44MB diskette in a 360K, 1.2MB, or 720K drive. When you boot your system, DOS reads the drive information and knows whether certain operations are possible on certain drives.

Solutions

▶ Issue the correct parameters for the diskette you are formatting. These parameters follow the FORMAT command at the DOS prompt:

- /T:xx specifies the number of tracks for the diskette:
  360K diskette have 40 tracks (0–39)
  1.2MB diskettes have 80 tracks (0–79)
  720K diskettes have 40 tracks (0–39)
  1.44MB diskettes have 80 tracks (0–79)
  2.88MB diskettes have 80 tracks (0–79)

- /S:yy specifies the number of sectors per track:
  360K disks have 9 sectors per track
  1.2MB disks have 18 sectors per track
  720K disks have 9 sectors per track
  1.44MB disks have 18 sectors per track
  2.88MB disks have 36 sectors per track

▶ Some FORMAT programs allow you to specify more directly the capacity of the diskette with a /F:xxxx parameter, replacing xxxx with 160, 180, 320, 360, 720, 1200, 1440, or 2880.

/4 allows you to format a diskette to 360K capacity in a 1.2MB diskette drive.

/B reserves space on the diskette for the hidden/system files but does not copy them there.

/S creates a bootable DOS system hard disk or diskette and places the proper files on the disk.

/V causes the FORMAT program to prompt you for a volume label when the format process is complete.

▶ Hard drives do not need size parameters, and they may accept only the /B, /S, and /V parameters.

Symptoms

▶ Onscreen message: "Incorrect DOS version"

Suspects

▶ You are trying to execute DOS program files from a different version of DOS than the one you used to boot your computer.

▶ Trying to use the FORMAT program from DOS 5.0 when you have booted with DOS 6.22 is one example of an operation DOS does not allow.

Solutions

▶ Be sure you have only one version of DOS programs in your PATH, and do not try to use programs older or newer than the DOS version used to boot your computer. Exceptions to this include all of the programs that accompany DR-DOS. This product's programs will work on any system and with any DOS version. You may also bypass this problem by using the SETVER.EXE program, which enables most programs to run from earlier versions of DOS.

Symptoms

▶ Onscreen message: "Abort, Retry, Ignore?" or "Abort, Retry, Fail?" preceded by "Error Reading/Writing Drive *x*" or "Drive Not Ready"

Suspects

▶ The specified diskette drive door is not closed.

▶ The specified drive does not sense a disk in the drive.

▶ The disk is not formatted or is the wrong format.

▶ A program cannot read or write to a section of a disk, perhaps because the information was damaged or the drive or disk is defective.

Solutions

▶ Make sure you are using the drive that you specified.

▶ The disk should be the proper format for the drive into which it was inserted.

▶ Ensure there is a disk in the drive.

▶ Check that the drive door is properly closed.

▶ Diagnose or repair the defective disk or disk section with one of the following programs: Norton Disk Doctor, SCANDISK, SpinRite.

▶ Make sure there are no viruses on your system.

Cross-Reference

For information on how to ensure your machine is protected from Viruses, refer to Chapter 3.

Symptoms

▶ Onscreen message: "Invalid Drive Specification."

This message refers to a condition in which you or an application has tried to address, log to, or use a drive designation that does not exist on your system. If you have only drives A:, B:, and C:, and try to use a drive D: when there is no such drive designated, this message appears.

Suspects

▶ If you do have the drive you specified, this could mean that you have a partition or disk controller failure that has caused that drive to be invalid or not appear to DOS.

▶ Situations that could cause this include the following:

- A large disk drive that uses a special partitioning software driver that the CONFIG.SYS file might not be loading. Without the driver, the other disk partitions may not be available.

- A line in CONFIG.SYS specifies LASTDRIVE=c, preventing DOS from addressing drives beyond drive C:.

- Partition information is lost. This could be caused by a weak drive sector, defective controller, or some other error overwriting the partition or FAT information.

Solutions

▶ Edit the CONFIG.SYS file. Include the partitioning software driver somewhere at the top of the file before making any reference to the drives beyond C:.

▶ Check your CONFIG.SYS file for an entry of LASTDRIVE=x. If the letter specified is less than the last known or accessible drive in your system, either remove this line or change it to reflect the actual last-drive designation on your system.

▶ You may run the FDISK program to display the partition information for your drive to verify that the specific drive does exist. If FDISK shows that everything is okay, using Norton, SCANDISK, or SpinRite may further identify and actually resolve the problem in the boot sector, partitions, FAT, or directory structures.

Symptoms

▶ Onscreen message: "File Allocation Table Bad, Drive x:"

Suspects

▶ Defective diskette, drive, or controller

▶ Program error

▶ Disk cache, RAM memory, or CMOS RAM error

▶ Virus infection

A read or write operation found that the FAT contains an error and the operation cannot proceed. Fortunately, there are two copies of the FAT, and utility programs can usually repair the damage and make the disk usable again. A virus can destroy one or both copies of the FAT, which means that if you have a bad virus attack, you had better have a good backup of your system from before the infection.

If you use a disk caching utility, the RAM used by the cache might be defective or the program was installed or configured incorrectly. The CMOS RAM, used to hold the system configuration information, might also be defective or have a bad battery.

Solutions

▶ Use either Norton Disk Doctor (NDD) and the Diagnose Disk or Common Solutions selection; SCANDISK; or SpinRite.

There is no other way to repair a defective FAT and recover the data without these utilities or one you might find on a Web site, BBS, or online service. Prior to the existence of the Norton Utilities, you would have to run DOS FORMAT to recover use of the drive and lose all of your existing files in the process.

As a preventive measure, use Norton's utilities to save an image of the file information on your disks. The respective recovery utilities can greatly improve the chances for recovery from many types of disk problems when these image files are present. However, they are not a cure-all, especially if more than one critical area on your disk is destroyed.

Symptoms

▶ Onscreen message: "General Failure Reading/Writing Drive *x*"

This is the error message to top all disk drive–related error messages. It indicates that something serious is wrong with your system, and that your system BIOS, DOS or other operating system, and your disk controller know nothing about the problem.

Suspects

▶ Your disk drive, cables, or controller have become disconnected or have failed.

▶ Some of the information on your disk has become scrambled due to a hardware or software failure or virus infection.

▶ Drive, power supply, or system components have overheated.

▶ There is a disk cache or RAM memory failure.

▶ Typically, DOS or your system BIOS will be aware of certain hardware failures if the hardware is even partially operative and can provide some error information. A general error indicates that DOS cannot determine whether a disk controller or drive is bad or can read some, but not enough, of the disk information to give a more specific message. Numbered error messages 6xx for 5.25-inch disk drives, 17xx for hard drives, 73xx for 3.5-inch drives, and 104xx for PS/2 ESDI hard drives, if present, may lead you to at least the right drive.

▶ Some IDE drives might not provide the system BIOS or DOS with enough error information to determine the nature of a problem either. RAM failure, a disk cache, or special disk driver program may intercept or mask error information from the system.

▶ Diskette is not formatted.

Solutions

▶ If you can, cancel the requested operation (press Ctrl+C or Ctrl+Break), quit, or exit from all programs back to the operating system and turn off the system. Let it cool for one to five minutes and turn it on again. During this time you may want to remove the cover from the system to check whether the disk controller cards and cables are properly seated and that the cables are not pinched or disconnected.

▶ Format the diskette (but not until you are certain there is no hope of recovery).

Provided the system boots okay when you turn it back on again, run a disk diagnostic if you have one, or SCANDISK; otherwise, run CHKDSK (without the /F switch) and verify that the drive is okay. If you cannot reboot the system from the hard drive, try booting from a diskette and then access the drive in question with DIR or CHKDSK.

If errors occur in testing the drive with CHKDSK or other utilities, you may need a more advanced utility such as Watergate's PC-Doctor to further isolate the errors to the drive, controller, or some other part of your system. Use these advanced diagnostics or the ones that came with your system to test the system board, CPU, memory, and other adapters as well — ideally before spending a lot of time checking the disks. The diagnostics for IBM systems perform many of the basic checks and yield numbered error messages that can also help you isolate problems.

 Cross-Reference For more information and a complete list of numbered error messages, see Appendix F.

Run the diagnostics without disk caching. If the problem goes away, you may suspect the caching program or a RAM error. There are several RAM testing programs available on Web sites, BBSs, and online services, but they vary in their applicability to different systems and memory types tested. The RAM tests provided with the advanced diagnostics are among the most complete and thorough tests available.

The process of elimination (cooling the system to determine if heat is a problem, eliminating disk caching software, and testing the RAM) is the best step toward narrowing the problem. You will usually find cabling or card insertion causing these problems.

Symptoms

▶ CHKDSK reports "Invalid Clusters" or "Files Cross-Linked."

Such a message indicates that the FAT is defective on the disk in question. The solutions are the same as those for the "File Allocation Table Bad, Drive *x*" message.

Numerical disk status messages from BIOS

Your system BIOS provides the basic disk drive services for file reading and writing, known technically as Int13. When DOS and your applications need to read from or write to a file on a disk, they typically make a request through the BIOS, which keeps track of who needs what services of the disk subsystem. Certain applications deal with the drives directly at the hardware level. These applications are typically limited to special device drivers, disk caching or compression software, and utility programs. These types of programs, in general, will not work under Windows 95, 98, Me, NT, or 2000 unless written specifically for use with these systems.

Demands for normal Int13 disk services may be routed through or replaced by the routines provided in these special applications, sometimes making disk access safer or faster than using the BIOS. Normal applications that use direct hardware access to the disk drives rather than BIOS or alternative Int13 services are considered ill-behaved or a possible threat to the integrity of the file structures (partitions, directories, and files) on your drives.

To provide feedback about a disk drive or file operation, a common set of numbered messages are used to refer to the status of a drive and most of the types of problems you may encounter. Some of these numbered messages are responsible for the textual messages you might see from DOS (in the previous section) or the critical errors that might pop up in the middle of applications or utility and diagnostic software. Rather than present more cryptic numbers, most applications interpret the numbers and create more meaningful messages, giving you more information. Table 19-1 shows the basic numbers and their meanings.

Table 19-1
BIOS Int13h Disk Status Codes

Int 13h Status Number and Meaning	Symptoms	Suspects	Solutions
00h No error	Requested operation has completed successfully.	None	None needed
01h Invalid function request	A command sent to the drive is not valid.	Defective software program. Defective disk controller.	This error may only be the result of a bad controller or an improper function in a software program.
02h Address mark not found	The disk media, drive heads, or electronics are defective or could not read a proper identification for a data area on the disk.	Defective data area on disk. Dirty read/ write heads. (Only applies to diskettes and diskette drives.)	Clean diskette drive heads. Evaluate disk and drive with utility software to recover data, or backup good data and reformat disk.
03h Write protect error (diskette)	Request to write to a diskette encountered the write-protect tab and could not write the data.	Write protect tab on diskette is positioned wrong. Write protect sensor in drive is defective.	Check/correct the write protect tab. Clean or replace the drive.
04h Sector not found	The disk media, drive heads, or electronics are defective, or could not read a proper identification for a selected sector on the disk.	Defective data area on disk. Dirty read / write heads.	Clean drive heads. Evaluate disk and drive with utility software to recover data, or backup good data and reformat disk.

Continued

Table 19-1 *(continued)*			
Int 13h Status Number and Meaning	**Symptoms**	**Suspects**	**Solutions**
06h Diskette change line active	Drive detected that you changed the diskette. This is good if you were supposed to, bad if you were not.	None	None needed unless you really did not change diskettes. In that case, it may indicate a bad drive.
08h DMA overrun	A data transfer exceeded the time allotted for a DMA transfer.	Controller or drive is defective. DMA chip on system board is bad. (Usually associated with a diskette write operation.)	Replace controller or drive. Replace DMA chip or system board.
09h Data boundary error DMA transfer.	A data transfer exceeded the buffer allotted for a particular DMA transfer.	Controller or drive is defective. DMA chip on system board is bad. (Usually associated with a diskette write operation.)	Replace controller or drive. Replace DMA chip or system board.
0Ch Media type not found.	The diskette, drive, or setup values do not match or suit the operation requested.	Wrong diskette or drive. Improper CMOS setup.	Change to proper diskette size for drive. Correct setup values to match drive capacity.
10h Uncorrectable ECC or CRC error	Reading data from the disk failed attempts to retry error correction of the data read. Good data could not be provided. (Usually associated with the sound of the drive heads moving repeatedly trying to find or reread data.)	Defective data area on disk. Dirty read /write heads.	Clean drive heads. Evaluate disk and drive with diagnostic software to recover data, or backup good data and reformat disk.

Int 13h Status Number and Meaning	Symptoms	Suspects	Solutions
20h General controller failure	The controller or host adapter, rather than a drive, experienced an error.	Disk controller or host adapter. Disk drive (if IDE or SCSI). System board, if controller is built-in.	Replace disk controller. Replace disk drive. Replace system board or disable on-board controller and use an add-in controller card instead.
40h Seek operation failed	The drive was not Table to place the heads over or locate a specific track on the disk.	Bad disk/format. Defective drive.	Check disk and disk drive with utility software. Replace diskette or drive.
80h Time-out	The drive was not able to complete the head movement or read or write operation in a specified period of time. (Typically one second for finding sectors; up to five seconds for seeking a track.)	The drive was not connected or ready. Disk controller failed.	Check drive and controller for proper power and data connections. Replace controller or drive.

Interpreting BIOS Messages

Symptoms, Suspects, and Solutions for these BIOS messages closely match those indicated for the more common and documented DOS error messages related to disks and files. If you see these BIOS messages, with or without similar DOS messages, note the numbers for reference should you need to consult technical support for additional help in resolving problems.

Since these are system BIOS–related messages, they apply to every operating system that may be installed and used on your PC. The messages might be different coming from Linux or Windows, but the hardware and your system are the same. The problem you need to fix is the same too!

The fact that you saw a numerical error message can more closely identify the cause and possible solutions in some cases. Be aware that hardware-level diagnostics can indicate problems that exist with a drive, but you might not experience any DOS-level errors because a particular sector or track is removed from data use and is marked as a bad track in the DOS FAT. The FAT is the primary cross-reference between file directory entries and the actual location of a file on a disk. Any allocation unit marked as bad in the FAT, is not used by DOS for file reading or writing.

IDE and many new SCSI drives should not indicate any of these low-level errors at any time if they are designed and functioning properly. These drives have spare, good data areas on the disk that are substituted for any bad areas, so you should always have an error-free drive, provided any natural defects on the disk do not increase and cause the good spare areas to be totally consumed. New drives that indicate errors may be considered defective, and your data will be at risk if you continue to use them.

CD-ROM Drive Problems

There is not a lot that can go wrong with CD-ROM drives, but they require attention to proper configuration settings and proper device drivers.

Symptoms
▶ "Drive not found" messages

Suspects
▶ All operating systems: Improper drive configuration (primary/secondary, Master/Slave).

▶ DOS: Wrong or misconfigured device driver in CONFIG.SYS.

▶ DOS: Missing or misconfigured MSCDEX driver in AUTOEXEC.BAT.

▶ Windows 95/98/Me: Unsupported drive or requires drivers for initial detection.

▶ Windows NT/2000: Unsupported (old) CD-ROM drive. Older non-ATAPI-compliant CD-ROM drives may not be properly detected by NT/2000's setup process.

▶ No CD in drive.

Solutions
▶ Ensure that the interface connected to the CD-ROM drive is enabled.

▶ Check that the cable connections are correct.

▶ Ensure that the Master/Slave settings on any Master drive and the CD-ROM drive are correct for the interface to which they are connected.

▶ Reconfigure or reinstall the correct CD-ROM driver in CONFIG.SYS. Many of these have parameters for port addresses, IRQ, and so on, which must match the interface used for the drive.

▶ Be sure that the name of the CD-ROM is the same for the driver in CONFIG.SYS and MSCDEX in AUTOEXEC.BAT. This is specified with the /D: parameter and must match exactly.

▶ Windows 95/98/Me: In some cases Windows needs to have the CD-ROM driver and possibly MSCDEX installed in order to detect the CD-ROM drive with the Add New Hardware wizard. Once detected Windows will reconfigure CONFIG.SYS and AUTOEXEC.BAT to remove unnecessary drivers.

▶ Windows 95/98/Me and NT/2000: Install a newer model ATAPI-compliant CD-ROM drive.

Symptoms

▶ "Device not ready" messages

▶ "Error reading" messages

▶ "Damaged CAB file" messages

Suspects

▶ Device or drive letter conflict between CD-ROM drive and other drive

▶ Damaged CD-ROM

▶ Dirty or defective CD-ROM drive

▶ Older version of CD-ROM driver or MSCDEX

Solutions

▶ Check Windows 95/98/Me Device Manager for drive letter conflicts.

▶ Check MSCDEX for drive letter conflicts with other drives.

▶ Ensure the latest MSCDEX (version 2.23 or later) is used.

▶ Check CONFIG.SYS LASTDRIVE=x parameter for setting last drive letter needed.

▶ Clean disk.

▶ Clean CD-ROM drive.

▶ Replace CD-ROM drive.

Avoiding CD-ROM Problems

One way to avoid excessive CD-ROM use or intermittent CD-ROM read problems is to copy the CD's contents to your hard drive, as is done with the CAB files for reinstalled versions of Windows 95, 98 and Me. Make a \WINDOWS\OPTIONS\CABS subdirectory on your boot drive and copy the Windows CD's \WIN95 or \WIN98 or \WindowsMe subdirectory to that new directory. The copy process streams data off the CD rather than incrementally and repeatedly seeking data off the drive and can make for a cleaner copy operation. Install the operating system using SETUP from the hard drive, and your CD files will always be available for faster access later.

Symptoms

▶ CD-ROM drive sounds like it's spinning out of control.

Suspects

▶ Worn, dirty, or defective hub lock inside CD-ROM drive

▶ Worn hub hole in disk

Many CD-ROM drives repeatedly or excessively spin the CD-ROM to check to see if the disk has changed. The torque applied to the hub and CD to spin them may be excessive and cause the hub mechanism or the disk to wear out.

Solutions

▶ Replace CD-ROM drive.

▶ Replace CD-ROM disk.

Symptoms

▶ No audio when attempting to play audio CDs

Suspects

▶ Missing or defective audio cable between CD-ROM drive and sound card

▶ Missing or no audio CD player support in multimedia or sound card installation

Solutions

▶ Install or replace CD-audio cable to sound card.

▶ Install multimedia/CD-audio player software.

▶ Reinstall multimedia features software.

▶ Upgrade CD-ROM drive or sound card for current audio compatibility.

Summary

We have now concluded one of the most important parts of this book. After all, we started this trek to the ultimate PC with DOS – the *DISK* Operating System – important enough to be in the name of our original operating system!

We covered:

✦ Working with diskettes

✦ Working with CD-ROM drives

✦ Working with alternative drives

✦ Disk drive "care and feeding"

✦ Disk drive error messages

✦ Common diskette and hard drive problems

✦ CD-ROM drive problems

In Part V we will go on to the "other" parts of your PCs system (no lack of problems there) to continue to enable you to keep your PC running through the "dark and stormy night"...

✦　　✦　　✦

Other Parts of Your PC

For many people, it's those "other" parts of the PC that really make PCs interesting and useful. Maybe standard hardware and software doesn't excite you. But that headset that projects images directly into your retina or a sound system that shakes the foundations of your home (and may even move your chair!), along with other experimental gadgets that will appear over the next few years that hook directly into your senses, now these devices excite you. These are the "other" parts of PCs that Part V addresses.

You'll have to get into the Part V's chapters to see where PCs have been, where they are now, and where they're going. So jump into Chapter 20, where you'll see and hear your PC.

Sights and Sounds

Your PC's video and audio consist of your screen and speaker, right? That used to be all there was. Now an ophthalmologist can test your peripheral vision using a pair of virtual reality glasses connected to a PC. You can watch TV on your screen while working on that project due tomorrow morning. Overcoming a fear of heights or flying can be a personal computing experience. Even sound can be 3D! Who knows where the world of new media experiences will lead us?

In this chapter we focus (pun intended) on your interface with your PC through sight and sounds. We'll address the installation, configuration, upgrading, troubleshooting, and repairing these important features.

What You See Keeps Getting Better

The display system of your PC includes the following:

✦ The monitor or screen (maybe even a set of glasses or a flip-out panel on a headband).

✦ An adapter card that acts as an interface between your monitor and your computer. It might even use a Universal Serial Bus (USB) or some newer input/output (I/O) port.

✦ The connections between those subsystems.

In many cases, particularly with Microsoft Windows, certain pieces of software are also necessary for a properly functioning video subsystem.

Older video displays

Since the original PC became available in 1981, many video display/adapter specifications and several modes of displaying information from the CPU have been developed for IBM PCs and compatibles.

In 1981, the original IBM PC was equipped for text-only display with some special extended or linedrawing characters to accent the old-fashioned Teletype, characters-only output from computer programs. As an alternative to the text-only display, known as Monochrome Display Adapter (MDA) technology, IBM also provided Color Graphics Adapter (CGA) standards and displays, mostly for modest entertainment uses. The PCjr systems had unique display features, similar to those found on the Mac, not shared with any PC before or since. In 1984, IBM introduced the Enhanced Graphics Adapter (EGA), which improved significantly on the fuzzy appearance of CGA. A little-known, rarely seen, high-resolution Professional Graphics Adapter (PGA) subsystem was available for a short time before the Multi-Color Graphics Array (MCGA) and Video Graphics Array (VGA) evolved in the PS/2 series in 1987.

Non-IBM variants have also been popular, such as the Hercules Graphics Card (HGC), introduced in 1982. HGC provided higher resolution text and shaded monochrome displays. Leading Edge and Compaq systems provided different versions of shaded monochrome display methods, which enabled color-only programs to be viewed on the typical green or amber display monitors.

Table 20-1 shows IBM standard video modes: Monochrome, CGA, EGA, and VGA (00–13 Hexadecimal).

Newer video displays

Higher VGA resolutions, known as Super VGA (SVGA), of 800×600, 1024×768, and 1280×1024 (and even higher resolutions for a bit more $$$) add to today's variety of choices. IBM has been marketing its latest technology in its Extended Graphics Array (XGA), and you can get resolutions of 2,048×2,048 if you use enhanced video adapters with CPU chips designed for faster, higher resolution graphics. Table 20-2 shows extended VGA Modes (54–5Fh) found on many Western Digital/Paradise-compatible VGA adapters.

Table 20-1
IBM Standard Video Modes

Mode # (in Hexadecimal)	Mode Name	Type/Use	Text: Row × Column	Pixels: H × V	Number of Colors
0H	CGA	Monochrome text	40×25	320×200	2
1H	CGA	Color text	40×25	230×200	16
2H	CGA	Monochrome text	80×25	640×200	2
3H	CGA	Color text	80×25	640×200	16
4H	CGA	Color graphics	40×25	320×200	4
5H	CGA	Monochrome graphics		320×200	2
6H	CGA	Color graphics		320×200	2
7H	Monochrome	Monochrome text	80×25	720×350	2
8H	PCjr Only	Color graphics		160×200	16
9H	PCjr	Graphics		320×200	16
0AH	PCjr	Color graphics		640×200	4
0BH		N/A*			
0CH		N/A			
0DH	EGA	Color graphics		320×200	16
0EH	EGA	Color graphics		640×200	16
0FH	EGA	Monochrome text/graphics	80×25	640×350	2
10H	EGA	Color graphics	80×25	640×350	16
11H	MCGA/VGA	Monochrome graphics	80×25	640×480	2
12H	VGA	Color text/graphics	80×30	640×480	16
13H	MCGA/VGA	Color text/graphics	40×25	320×200	256

* The N/A items in the above table are modes that were never used publicly, or at least not commonly.

Table 20-2
Extended VGA Modes

Mode # (in Hexadecimal)	Mode Name	Type/Use ×Column	Text: Row	Pixels: H × V	Number of Colors
54h	Extended VGA	Color text	132×43	924×387	16
55h	Extended VGA	Color text	132×25	924×400	16
56h	Extended VGA	Monochrome text	132×43	924×387	16
57h	Extended VGA	Monochrome text	132×25	924×400	4
58h	Extended VGA	Color graphics	132×43	800×600	16
59h	Extended VGA	Monochrome graphics	100×75	800×600	2
5Eh	Extended VGA	Color graphics	80×25	640×400	256
5Fh	Extended VGA	Color graphics	80×30	800×600	256

In 1989, several PC hardware and software companies formed a PC industry group known as the Video Electronics Standards Association (VESA). VESA combined various interests and developments in order to standardize a variety of existing video features and to provide a predictable growth path for future video features.

VESA began its work with the original 640×480×16 color VGA standard that depicts both resolution and color depth, and now defines software and certain hardware attributes that provide a stable environment and display capabilities to 1,280×1,024 resolution with 16-, 24-, and 32-bit color definitions. The PC is no longer black and white, several shades of gray, or just four colors. Because of these advances, most PC video systems provide better quality images than the best television sets. Table 20-3 shows VESA Video BIOS Extensions (VESA VBE) modes found on VESA local buses (VL-Buses) and other VESA VBE–compatible video adapters.

Table 20-3 VESA VBE Modes			
Mode # (in Hex)	**Type/Use**	**Text: Row × Column**	**Pixels: H × V**	**Number of Colors**
100h	Graphics		640×480	256
101h	Graphics		640×480	256
102h	Graphics		800×600	16
103h	Graphics		800×600	256
104h	Graphics		1,024×768	16
105h	Graphics		1,024×768	256
106h	Graphics		1,280×1,024	16
107h	Graphics		1,280×1,024	256
108h	Text	80×60		
109h	Text	132×25		
10Ah	Text	132×43		
10Bh	Text	132×50		
10Ch	Text	132×60		
10Dh	Graphics		320×200	32,000
10Eh	Graphics		320×200	64,000
10Fh	Graphics		320×200	16.8 million
110h	Graphics		640×480	32,000
111h	Graphics		640×480	64,000
112h	Graphics		640×480	16.8 million
113h	Graphics		800×600	32,000
114h	Graphics		800×600	64,000
115h	Graphics		800×600	16.8 million
116h	Graphics		1,024×768	32,000

Continued

Table 20-3 *(continued)*				
Mode # **(in Hex)**	**Type/Use**	**Text: Row** **× Column**	**Pixels:** **H × V**	**Number** **of Colors**
117h	Graphics		1,024 × 768	64,000
118h	Graphics		1,024 × 768	16.8 million
119h	Graphics		1,280 × 1024	32,000
11Ah	Graphics		1,280 × 1,024	64,000
11Bh	Graphics		1,280 × 1,024	16.8 million

VESA should not be considered exclusive to local buses or to Peripheral Component Interconnect (PCI) local buses and Industry Standard Architecture (ISA) data buses. VESA VBE–compliant video may come in any bus structure, but the local bus was where the VESA-compliant video adapters first appeared. These modes also require monitors capable of a variety of horizontal and vertical video scanning frequencies. The terms used to describe these monitors include *Multi-Sync* ((c) NEC), *multiscan*, or *autoscan* monitors.

Note Television screen image are roughly equivalent to standard VGA for moving images, but they are no better than 40-character-wide CGA for text display.

VESA video features and local bus are supported with a new video BIOS defined by VESA, known as the VGA BIOS Extension. Without VBE-compliant software interfaces between the hardware and software, getting high-resolution applications software and operating environments to work properly would be guesswork at best.

In addition to enhanced resolution and color attributes, VESA-compliant video systems usually include display speed enhancements, not only in how fast the video-adapter card works to accept, process, smooth, and present an image, but also in the interface between the CPU and the video card. The first of these CPU video enhancements is, by virtue of the hardware interface, known as the local bus. Local bus interfaces circumvent the slower ISA PC I/O connections with faster circuitry that routes video data more directly from the CPU to the video adapter. This enhancement is also used for disk drives and other fast I/O adapters.

Non-VESA Super VGA modes

Various video chip and display manufacturers provide and support other modes in addition to the accepted industry standards. S3, STB, Western Digital, and others publish their video chip specifications and assist video card vendors in creating specific device-driver files so that you can take advantage of these modes. Resolutions of 1,152×896, 1,536×1,280, 1,600×1,200, and 1,640×1,280 are not uncommon. These modes require that the video adapter card have 2 to 8 MB of video RAM on board and that your monitor support the vertical and horizontal scan frequencies (56 to 120 Hz) necessary to display them. A 17-inch or larger monitor with .28mm or smaller dot pitch and noninterlaced scanning is recommended for resolutions above 1,024×768 for clarity and comfort.

The VESA local bus, though still available, has pretty much been replaced by the PCI bus for 32-bit bus implementations. The PCI bus is actually a 64-bit standard and is also found in the Macintosh computer. In other words, it is a more widely accepted industry standard and will be around for a good while (in computer development terms).

 Note Whether the video adapter you purchase to install in your computer is VESA local bus or PCI depends on the design of your computer's motherboard.

Intel's newest addition to the video race is the Accelerated Graphics Port (AGP), which provides a separate channel for direct access to a computer's main memory. Because this is a relatively new channel, there is little chance of hardware conflicts when using an AGP adapter. The bandwidths supported by this new channel are 266 and 533 megabytes per second (MBps) and 1.07 gigabytes per second (GBps) (that is *very fast*). Because AGP is fairly new, you need to make sure the manufacturer of the adapter card has implemented all of the following important features: texturing, throughput, sideband addressing, and pipelining. Just make sure these are all supported. You should also find that the AGP cards have pretty much taken over the video market. Thankfully, few problems specific to AGP video cards have been reported.

Another new and exciting area in video is the capability to drive multiple monitors from the same system — not all showing the same picture, but displaying parts of the whole so that two, four, eight, or more monitors, when viewed from a distance, are displaying a single, large display.

Finally, the video displays that convey a 3D image to the viewer are becoming more believable. These displays come as special glasses, small screens attached to a headband, or attachments to video screens. Again, these displays use serial ports and newer devices, such as USB. Therefore, they provide little challenge for system configuration problems.

Video and memory

To support many recent display enhancements, video cards need more memory for holding incoming image data and they have processing provided by a dedicated onboard microprocessor chip that does nothing but process and improve video images.

Standard VGA display modes require only 256K of RAM on the video card in order to hold multiple pages or portions of a 640×480-pixel image with 16 colors. As the resolution increases, the number of colors and/or additional memory is required to hold the image data also increases. In many cases, and depending on the display mode or application software you use, the 1MB or 2MB of video RAM your adapter can have is shared between image-storage and display-enhancement functions. For systems that will be doing much multimedia work, you really need 8MB or more of video RAM, although 4MB seems to be standard. Unfortunately, 256K and 512K are inadequate for most work. Therefore, look for an adapter that can be upgraded to 8MB or more for when you need it. Serious graphics development and 3D display can require 8, 16, 32, or more megabytes of video memory.

The Cost of Video Enhancements

Advanced video features come at a price. In terms of resolution (640×480) and color depth (x16), a basic 640×480×16 VGA adapter can cost anywhere from $15 to $40. A Super VGA adapter capable of 800×600×256 operation costs between $20 and $60. VESA VBE–compliant adapters, many also providing graphics acceleration for certain types of applications, can cost up to $500 (but look around—discount catalogs have some of these high-priced adapters for less than $200!). Some of the latest crop of 3D graphics adapters, although offering tremendous advantages in speed, resolution, and color, can cost several thousand dollars. But again, look around for bargains. Fortunately, the biggest shock may be the price, because installation of the cards and software is relatively simple—it usually involves nothing more than installing the card and attaching the plugs in the proper places.

Most VGA video adapters display a manufacturer's name, product name, copyright notice, and possibly the amount of video RAM on board when you start the PC. They do this through the use of a ROM chip, as described in Chapter 15. VGA adapters that support multisync monitors can detect the presence or absence of a multisync adapter, and they may report this capability as well. New adapters and operating systems can also detect if the monitor is Energy Star power management-compliant for automatic shutdown.

Problems with Sights and Sounds

Fortunately, the range of video and audio problems you might encounter is decreasing as quickly as new programs are written and users upgrade older systems. Many software installation routines detect the type of video display a system has based on tests during startup. This information is saved in a specific memory location so that software can check to see what video equipment you have. With most application programs, you can accept what is shown onscreen or you can reconfigure a video option in your software before discovering that it will not work because you cannot see the screen output.

We cover video problems in general and as they pertain to specific video adapters or displays in the Symptoms, Suspects, and Solutions sections in this chapter. Remember that video display is one subsystem of your entire PC system. This subsystem generally contains three parts:

✦ a monitor

✦ a video adapter (whether on the motherboard or as an add-in card)

✦ cabling (both power and video signal between the video adapter and the monitor)

Applications and a motherboard switch or CMOS RAM SETUP comprise other interrelated aspects of displaying applications information. Problems with video displays can typically be isolated to these items or to the video drivers needed to enable applications or Windows to take full advantage of a video adapter's features.

Tip Check Web sites, bulletin boards, and online support forums and be sure that you acquire and apply the latest drivers from your video adapter's manufacturer.

Note It is not unusual to find software that is limited to use with certain types of displays or that is configured improperly and will not display all the features it is designed to display (such as highlight characters and special attributes). For laptops with CGA-type liquid crystal display (LCD) and some laptops with gas-plasma displays, this can be a primary concern, usually remedied by setting up the software for monochrome-only (black-on-white or white-on-black), high-contrast use.

How you approach a display problem depends not only on the symptoms, but also on the type of display system and software that you have. The common denominator for all nongraphical interfaces and software should be the capability to display text in monochrome mode. Windows, GEM, ViewMax, GeoWorks Ensemble, X-Windows, Windows/NT, and OS/2 are graphical interfaces requiring at least Hercules monochrome graphics capability. Whether your monitor is amber- or green-character monochrome, gray-on-white or white-on-gray LCD, gas plasma (typically orange characters), or a color type, it should display some text onscreen.

Color displays or monochrome VGA displays with gray shading for colors usually display white text on a dark background. You should see something when your system starts. If nothing appears, the problem could be quite simple, and this is where you begin your problem solving — with displays.

For laptops and portable systems, many of the issues relating to the video adapter, cabling, and monitor do not apply, but the aspects of video-mode settings, brightness, contrast, and onscreen messages do apply.

Installing sound and video

Before CD-ROM adapters, graphics accelerators, and sound cards were available, installing a better video card or a monitor was almost as simple as removing the old item, plugging in new one, and turning on the power switch. However, if you use Windows, there is often a struggle with a flawed or incompatible video driver file or problems with one or two switches on the video card.

Previously, you could upgrade from CGA or EGA to VGA, or from VGA to Super VGA without having problems with addresses, IRQ and DMA settings, device drivers, and environment variables. Now, however, if you add a new sound card or change an adapter for a CD-ROM drive, the installation program may be complicated.

Most of these issues are discussed in the section about sound cards. A sound card may also include a CD-ROM interface. A few earlier combination sound and video cards were touted as complete multimedia kits, but these are rare today. Taken step by step, converting that old PC to a multimedia showplace may be a breeze — with help from either the adapter's installation program, a system information or diagnostic program, or the process of investigation and elimination with the existing devices in your system.

 Tip   Under Windows 95, many sound cards and their CD-ROM interfaces are automatically identified such that you may only need to identify and resolve any address, IRQ, or DMA conflicts with other devices in your system.

Problems are relatively few after a successful installation. By then you have probably resolved more than just sound card problems. Adding new devices will likely bring on more concerns about addresses and configurations but by reading this chapter, you will have learned enough about your system to avoid future problems.

Video-subsystem problems are often unrelated to the other complexities of multimedia enhancements and they typically affect more than just one application. This chapter covers the more familiar and simpler video problems first.

Common video problems

Here are some symptoms, suspects, and solutions for common video problems you might encounter.

Symptoms

▶ No display (assuming your PC system appears to power on, that it beeps during the power-on self test (POST), and that drives become active for bootup)

Suspects

▶ Power cords — unplugged, frayed, or poor connection

▶ Display cable to adapter card — unplugged, bad plugs, or poor connection

▶ Monitor circuits, power supply, or internal fuse possibly bad

▶ Improper video mode or switch setting (CMOS SETUP or motherboard)

▶ Video card not properly seated in socket or not in the correct socket

▶ Defective video adapter card

Solutions

▶ Reseat the video adapter in its socket.

▶ Make sure your motherboard switch, if your motherboard has such a switch or jumper, is set for monochome or color as suits your video adapter.

▶ If your monitor's power indicator light-emitting diode (LED) is not on, check your power cords and switch for problems.

▶ Replace defective cable between the video adapter and monitor.

▶ Try your old VGA card, if you have one to verify if video is okay, and then replace the suspect card with a newer one if you have confirmed that the old card is bad.

▶ If your PC beeps more than once (and your monitor's LED is lit), you might receive an error message that the PC video adapter setting is wrong or that the video card is defective. Check other possibilities, but replacing the video adapter may be required.

▶ If the power indicator is on but the PC does not beep when you turn it on, the motherboard might have a problem. The motherboard is relatively expensive, so check other subsystems before deciding to replace it.

If your PC beeps only once, but the monitor's power indicator LED is lit, check your monitor's brightness and contrast controls and adjust them if necessary. Also ensure that the cable between your monitor and PC is plugged into the adapter card. If these external items check out, suspect a bad video adapter card, especially if you receive error-code beeps from your PC's speaker.

If your system does not display bootup information and you hear only one beep signifying the proper completion of the POST at bootup, the monitor, cabling, or one portion of the video card may be defective. Think of the video card as consisting of two portions — the computer interface and the monitor interface. In most cases, the bootup and POST process can test only the computer-interface portion of the adapter. It may not know the condition of the signals to the monitor, and it may not tell you if the monitor is disconnected or if these circuits work.

If the system shows bootup information but some or all of your applications do not display onscreen, make sure your problem isn't a video or color-setting device driver or program blanking the display. Booting your system with a plain DOS-system floppy disk and checking the CONFIG.SYS and AUTOEXEC.BAT files (or the configuration files for your specific operating system) on your hard drive or other boot floppy disks might reveal an incompatible display program that you need to reconfigure or remove.

Make sure your programs are intended for use with the type of display system currently installed. Unless your applications software can determine by itself the type of video subsystem hardware you have, the following limitations between hardware and software will apply:

✦ CGA, EGA, or VGA-specific programs will not display on either of the monochrome (MDA or Hercules) displays or through these monochrome adapters.

✦ EGA- and VGA-specific programs will not display on CGA systems.

✦ VGA-specific programs will not display on EGA or CGA systems.

Text should display on any of the adapters and monitors, but some applications might lack reverse video, underlining, or highlighting.

Early Leading Edge and some Compaq computer systems have a hybrid video system that enables some graphics programs to work on their monochrome displays. These variations on standards generally show only Hercules or CGA-type graphics, and they cannot display EGA, VGA, or higher-resolution graphics. If you have a monochrome monitor you can use it for MDA, Hercules, or in some cases, CGA programs (if the card and monitor can simulate CGA by shading). SIMCGA and HGCIBM are two programs found on bulletin boards and Internet archives that enable a Hercules-compatible graphics system to display CGA programs in "shaded" colors.

If you have a program set up for Super VGA (800×600) or IBM's 8514 (1,024×768) high-resolution modes, it will not work on standard nonmultisync VGA (640×480) systems. This can be a limitation of either the VGA adapter card or the monitor. The higher-resolution modes require either a specific IBM 8514 monitor or a multisync/scanning/frequency monitor.

If you are sure power is going through your monitor's power cord, the problem with your display might be as simple as a bad fuse inside the monitor. What seems to be as simple as a bad internal fuse, however, also could indicate a more serious problem with the monitor circuits. You should leave this problem to a technician.

 Caution Do not open your monitor to look for fuses or bad components unless you have the appropriate technical skills. Monitors contain high voltages and you can get a severe electrical shock.

Common video display problems

This section addresses how to pinpoint and then solve common video problems.

Symptoms

▶ Diagonal or spotty display lines

▶ Erratic, improper, or fuzzy display

▶ Rolling or rotating display patterns

Suspects

▶ Improper vertical sync frequency setting on video adapter card (could be a hardware or software setting)

▶ Monitor cannot display the video mode selected

▶ Improper selection of display mode settings in software

▶ Improper horizontal or vertical control settings

▶ Defective video card or defective motherboard if video adapter is built into motherboard

▶ Defective PC power supply (other symptoms may be associated — see Chapter 12)

▶ Defective monitor

▶ Speaker or other magnetic device too close to the monitor

Solutions

▶ Adjust horizontal/vertical controls.

▶ Configure software or adapter card for proper monitor type.

▶ Replace PC power supply.

▶ Replace motherboard if video adapter is built in.

▶ Replace video adapter card or disable onboard (motherboard) video adapter and use an add-in video card.

▶ Move magnetic device away from the monitor.

Rapid scrolling or sideways tearing of a displayed image is an indication that the monitor or adapter is not properly synchronizing the display control signals. This might look like a television screen with poorly adjusted horizontal or vertical controls. If you can, adjust either the horizontal or vertical control on your monitor. Also, make sure that the program you are using is compatible with your display system. Rapid scrolling or tearing also could be a sign of a defective monitor circuit or adapter, in which case you may need to service or replace the defective unit.

If sparkles, dots, or the cursor appear to race across the screen, you probably have a CGA system, or your program is set to run faster than the display adapter can tolerate. This can be a problem with the original IBM and some early clone CGA adapter cards. Check to see if your program has a video setup parameter for synchronized display or "snow-checking." If it has the setup parameter, set it to Yes or On. If this setting does not eliminate the problem, your display adapter may be defective.

If the display shifts or dithers in a pattern or wave through the screen, or the brightness flickers, there might be a cord, adapter card, or some other appliance near the video system that is affecting the video signals on the card or inside the monitor. Because the monitor is controlled by small electrical signals that move a beam of electrons across the screen face, almost any electrical or magnetic device near the screen can affect the image you see. Your electrical power also might be fluctuating, causing the monitor to operate improperly.

Compare the technical specifications of your display monitor against those of your video-adapter card. All VGA cards and monitors must provide at least 640×480 display capabilities.

For other modes, adapter cards and monitors must be able to detect or set at least one of several possible combinations of horizontal and vertical sync or scanning frequencies. These numbers are typically 43 Hz, 56 Hz, 60 Hz, 72 Hz, 75 Hz, 80 Hz, 85 Hz, 90 Hz, 95 Hz, 100 Hz, 110 Hz, or 120 Hz for the vertical refresh frequency; and 35.1 kHz, 35.5 kHz, 37.8 kHz, 48.1 kHz, 48.9 kHz, 58.1 kHz, or 66 kHz for the horizontal scanning frequency.

If you cannot match these numbers for one or all modes of your software, adapter, and monitor, you might have to replace your monitor or adapter with a newer one that provides either noninterlaced operation or operation on a wider variety of scanning rates.

It is also possible that your monitor has a wiring problem or you have an improper cable between your monitor and video adapter.

Symptoms

▶ Clicking noises coming from display monitor

Suspects

▶ Electromechanical switches (relays) inside the monitor

▶ Improper video adapter settings

▶ Improper display-mode setting in application software

Solutions

▶ Do not be alarmed by a few clicking noises coming from your monitor when you first turn it on, start your system, or switch between text and graphics modes. Multisync monitors usually contain relays to switch different circuits on and off for the various scanning frequencies and modes of operation. It is normal for these relays to click three or four times between modes.

If the clicking noise is persistent, try one or more of the following:

• Use a lower or higher display resolution in your software settings.

• Reset the switches on your video adapter or adapter setup software.

• Check video cables and connections, or change video cables.

• Check if the monitor or video adapter card is defective, usually by replacing it with a new monitor or adapter card.

Symptoms

▶ Snapping or popping sound

▶ "Electrical" (bitter) smells

Suspects

▶ Monitor is dirty or dusty inside.

▶ Monitor high-voltage supply is defective.

Solutions

▶ Have the monitor cleaned, serviced, or both.

Display monitors use high voltages to display images onscreen. If your display is dirty or dusty inside, or the electrical circuits that make high voltage for the display are defective, the PC might experience arcing, much like large static discharges, coming from inside the monitor. The distinct smell generated by high-voltage arcing is from the ozone created in the arcing process. Have the monitor cleaned and serviced by a technician to eliminate the cause of these problems.

Note   These problems may occur more frequently when the system is cold or the air is dry.

Symptoms
▶ Invisible or hard-to-find cursor

Suspects
▶ Software is changing the cursor shape.

▶ Software is changing the cursor color to the same color as the screen.

▶ You are using a laptop with an LCD or gas-plasma display.

Solutions
▶ Use a cursor size-setting program.

▶ Configure software so that it does not alter the cursor.

Under DOS, a common problem with laptop computers and their high-contrast displays (LCD or gas plasma) is that the cursor is often hard to find. Some programs alter the display cursor (such as a blinking underline showing where text will appear when typed), and then the cursor disappears from the screen.

Microsoft Windows (all current versions) provides built-in settings for mouse pointers and screen cursors.

There programs enable you to change the rate at which the cursor blinks, from very slow to no blink at all. For Windows 3.x and Windows 95, many cursor-control programs add mouse trails and other effects to the plain old arrow pointer, making it easier to locate the cursor or simply making it more entertaining.

Symptoms
▶ Improper number of lines or missing text

Suspects
▶ DOS or software is set for the wrong number of display lines.

▶ Monitor is not capable of the desired display.

▶ DOS MODE is set improperly.

▶ Software or driver is incorrect for the adapter or monitor type.

▶ Display adapter or monitor is not changing modes.

Solutions
▶ Reconfigure the software or driver.

▶ Run the DOS MODE program (see the "Using DOS MODE" sidebar).

▶ Repair or replace the adapter or monitor.

A number of possibilities exist for this set of symptoms.

Using DOS MODE

Occasionally, a software program might conflict with other software or device drivers, or it may attempt to set an incorrect display mode or one that you do not want. One of the easiest corrections is to run the DOS MODE program to reset the display mode. There are three common command-line settings:

✦ MODE BW: Sets the system to display in monochrome with 80 columns × 25 rows of text.

✦ MODE CO40: Sets the system to display in low-resolution color (CGA) or monochrome text with 40 columns × 25 rows.

✦ MODE CO80: Sets the system to display in higher-resolution CGA or monochrome text with 80 columns × 25 rows.

Unless you have a multisync-type monitor and VGA adapter card, an EGA adapter and display, or are using graphics, a PC and DOS are limited to displaying either 40 or 80 characters across the screen and 25 lines down the screen.

Trying to force the 35-, 43-, or 50-line modes with a program, adapter, or monitor that does not support them can result in missing or overwritten lines of text. Depending on the application you are using, some enhanced modes with a variety of video cards require the use of display-adapter BIOS, replacement ANSI.SYS, or other special drivers.

A defective multisync adapter card or monitor might not be switching to the proper mode for the resolution of text or graphics you desire. Most multisync monitors issue a distinctive "click" sound when they change modes. If yours made this sound before but does not now, swapping the card or the monitor between another similarly equipped system can help determine which of the two elements is bad. A diagnostic program that tests various display modes can also indicate adapter card errors. If the adapter card passes the tests and the monitor still does not change, the monitor is bad or is not set to operate in a multisync mode.

Microsoft Windows, Autodesk AutoCAD, Digital Research ViewMax and GEM, and GeoWorks Ensemble are some of the applications that allow you to include special display adapter files in their configuration for enhanced displays. These can be used in addition to ANSI.SYS as the text and display mode-control device driver at the DOS level. Your display adapter might also include floppy disks with special driver software on it for use with specific applications.

Windows 9x/Me and NT/2000, and their hardware drivers for a wide range of video adapters and monitors, enable you to take advantage of most relevant features of your system's hardware. If a particular mode is not supported, complain to Microsoft and the manufacturer of your hardware. Chances are a solution is already available (on the Web) or may be made available, especially if it is for a popular product or capability. However, Microsoft Technical Support has stated in past tech support calls that even if a monitor or other hardware works with a driver under Windows 9x/Me, this does not mean that it will be supported under Windows NT/2000. One example is a Shamrock SRC1451P, a video monitor that works fine under Windows 9x but will only work in standard VGA mode under Windows NT/2000. NT/2000 does not provide the means to adjust the video refresh rates with this particular monitor.

Symptoms

▶ Windows or other graphical programs cannot or do not display properly

Suspects

▶ Improper graphics/driver configuration

▶ Monitor incapable of the display mode or scanning frequencies of the video adapter

▶ Memory manager/memory address conflicts between A000 and BFFF

▶ Adapter BIOS conflict at address C000

Solutions

▶ Verify proper graphics driver installation in the Install, Setup, or Control Panel programs.

▶ Check the monitor and video adapter documentation for compatible modes.

▶ Run the software that comes with your video adapter to help determine the modes that both the monitor and the adapter will support.

▶ Reconfigure your memory manager to exclude the video memory regions (typically A000–AFFF, B000–B7FF, B800–BFFF, or other, depending on the recommendation of the video card documentation or the findings of the memory manager's configuration program).

▶ Verify that there is no other adapter card using the same memory region as the video card and its BIOS. This is typically C000–C7FF.

▶ Reconfigure your video adapter for the proper mode, video memory configuration, or other advanced features. Many cards include a utility to check and reset default settings. Some provide for sharing of video RAM greater than 1MB.

▶ If your system has more than 16MB of system RAM (or depending upon your system, more than 124MB), you might need to reconfigure your video card to avoidspecial memory-mapping options that it has.

▶ Check the video card and other vendors' bulletin board systems or online services for updated driver software, video BIOS changes, or helpful technical notes.

▶ For Windows 3.x, install the MONOUMB2.386 (or MONOUMB.386) device in your Windows SYSTEM.INI file under the [386Enh] section. It should read as follows:

```
[386Enh]
device=monoumb2.386
```

▶ Obtain new drivers from the manufacturer (often available on its Web site).

Symptoms

▶ Cloudy, dark, or no display on laptop LCD displays

Suspects

▶ Temperature too hot or too cold

▶ Damaged LCD panel

Solutions

▶ Cool or warm the system to room temperature.

▶ Replace the LCD panel.

Liquid crystal laptop displays suffer because they are fluid systems. Therefore, they are susceptible to temperature changes and physical shock. To display properly, the fluid must respond quickly to the electrical impulses applied to darken an area onscreen. If the fluid is cold, the response will be slow. If it is very cold, there will be no response at all. The display should work properly above 50 degrees Fahrenheit.

If the fluid is frozen or extremely hot, the liquid crystal areas can be damaged and the display will show permanent dark or cloudy areas. The only remedy for this condition is replacement of the screen. Avoid temperatures below 40 degrees or above 120 degrees Fahrenheit when storing, transporting, or using your laptop. By the way, the luggage compartment on an airplane often drops to near freezing temperatures during flight.

 Caution Dropping or suddenly jarring a laptop can cause permanent damage to the LCD panel. Be careful when carrying laptops and make sure that you protect your laptop with a high-quality carrying case when you travel. .

Audible and Displayed Error Codes

Some of the most important tests done during the POST at bootup are those that test the status of the video system. Although these tests cannot give you detailed information about the monitor's status, the displayed message indicates a good monitor.

 Note The monitor might still fail as it warms up or as you change applications.

The video POST tests check for the presence and function of an adapter card. The system BIOS tracks display function during the tests and can issue an error warning any time it encounters a failure. If the BIOS determines that it cannot display the error information, it will send a series of beeps to the system speaker to indicate a video system error. If you hear these beeps, the first thing to suspect is a failed video adapter.

Symptoms

▶ One short beep and a wrong or no display

▶ One long beep and two short beeps

Suspects

▶ Motherboard switch settings or CMOS SETUP incorrect for video adapter

▶ Defective video adapter card

Solutions

▶ Check or set the system board switch or CMOS SETUP.

▶ Replace the video adapter card.

This audible message at bootup indicates an error in the video display system. If you do not see a display, refer to the Symptoms, Suspects, and Solutions headings in the "Common video display problems" section. If the display shows anything at all, you will probably also see one of the numeric error messages detailed in the remainder of this section.

Symptoms

▶ Error 4xx displayed

Suspects

▶ Monochrome video adapter card

Solutions

▶ Check the program display mode.

▶ Replace the video adapter card.

Error 401 indicates a defective monochrome video adapter card or failure of the motherboard (if the system is a PS/2 or the video interface is integrated on the motherboard). 401 may also be listed as a problem with adapter memory, horizontal synch frequency text, or it may be listed as a failed video test.

Errors 408, 416, and 424 indicate that the system is trying to display in a mode in which it is incapable of displaying. This is rare. Check your adapter card, motherboard switch settings, CONFIG.SYS, and AUTOEXEC.BAT for configurations not supported by your system. An IBM MDA system can display only text and no graphics. A Hercules monochrome card can display text and 768×420-resolution monochrome graphics. Attempting to run CGA, EGA, or VGA graphics on these systems may not result in an error but the display might go blank or work erratically.

Error 432 indicates a defective parallel port on monochrome display adapter cards.

Symptoms

▶ Error 5xx displayed

Suspects

▶ Defective CGA video adapter card

Solutions

▶ Replace the CGA video adapter card.

Error 501 indicates a defective CGA video-adapter card or failure of the motherboard (if the system is a PS/2 or the video interface is integrated on the motherboard). 501 may also be listed as color adapter memory failure, horizontal synch frequency test, or failed video test.

Errors 508, 516, 524, 532, 540, and 548 indicate that the system is trying to display in a mode in which it is incapable of displaying. Check your adapter card, motherboard switch settings, CONFIG.SYS, and AUTOEXEC.BAT for configurations not supported by your system.

Symptoms

▶ Error 24xx displayed

Suspects

▶ Defective EGA/VGA video adapter card

Solutions

▶ Replace the video adapter card.

Symptoms

▶ Error 39xx displayed

Suspects

▶ Defective Professional Graphics Controller (PGC) or Professional Graphics Adapter (PGA) video adapter card

Solutions

▶ Replace the PGC video-adapter card.

Symptoms

▶ Error 74xx displayed

Suspects

▶ Defective VGA adapter card or PS/2 motherboard

Solutions

▶ Replace the VGA video-adapter card or PS/2 motherboard.

Symptoms

▶ Error messages referring to ANSI.SYS

▶ Foreign or "→_[2J" type characters

Suspects

▶ DEVICE=ANSI.SYS statement is not in CONFIG.SYS file.

▶ ANSI.SYS file is not on disk.

▶ Software does not recognize the ANSI.SYS driver.

▶ Software is incapable of ANSI functions.

Solutions

▶ Include DEVICE=ANSI.SYS in the CONFIG.SYS file.

▶ Specify the proper PATH (drive:\directory) for ANSI.SYS.

▶ Be sure ANSI.SYS exists on the drive.

▶ Reconfigure software.

You can use many types of display control and keyboard commands to affect what you see onscreen. There are DOS commands that clear the display (with the CLS command), set foreground and background colors (with the PROMPT command or ECHO commands), or that move the cursor from place to place. For these commands to be effective, you must have the ANSI.SYS display driver loaded in your CONFIG.SYS file (as a separate line that reads the following: DEVICE=d:\path\ANSI.SYS).

ANSI stands for the American National Standards Institute. ANSI in PC terms refers to an accepted set of computer display commands that may be shared among programs, terminals, and computer systems. The commands used to control the display are known as ESCape sequences because the actual command information is preceded by the ASCII ESCape character (→) and a left bracket ([). If you see the ESC sequences onscreen, it typically means that ANSI.SYS or one of many workalike drivers is not loaded or that your program is set to display them when you may not want them displayed.

Some programs might not recognize or use any ANSI driver except for the DOS ANSI.SYS program. If you have the capability through memory management software to load device drivers into upper memory, the software you are using might not see the driver in upper memory and therefore, the software won't use the driver. If this is the case, try renaming the alternative driver to ANSI.SYS and loading it under that filename, or loading the driver into low memory.

For Windows, ANSI support is built into DOS windows run under Win9x/Me. Many SVGA video cards conflict with the older alternate ANSI drivers, which may be the cause of your problem and leave you doing without the features in order to use the adapter properly.

The PC Speaks and Listens

Many people who use their PC for presentations need rich, detailed sound capabilities. The PC has always provided for interfacing a multitude of devices to its I/O bus, but in the past many of those devices, including sound enhancements, have been expensive or too specialized for everyday use.

Sound is just another form of data to be collected, processed, stored, and read back through your system. High-quality sound, like high-quality video, requires considerable processing and storage capacity. This has always been possible, but not always economical or practical. Considerable advances in hardware and software tools had to reach acceptable costs before the technologies became something everyone wanted, felt a need for, or could put to practical use.

You might remember a time when an 8 MHz 80286 processor, a megabyte or two of RAM, and 40 megabytes of disk space were thought to be more than adequate, and were also quite expensive. The average PC program occupied 100K or so of disk space and required only 256K of RAM to function. Several industry experts may not want to be reminded of their "expert" opinions, tremendous investments in, and promises of support for these now obsolete system configurations.

Circa 1993, when about the only applications that supported sound cards were games, you probably had too much invested in your computer already and too much work to do in order to justify purchasing a sound card that would really only be used for video games. Sound cards were novelty items.

Today sound can make all the difference in sales presentations in business and in expanding the value of research and educational uses of a PC. Sound can improve your ability to monitor various standalone control processes — giving a variety of status messages with much more meaning than simple beeps. Combined with voice recognition features, entire applications can be sound-operated for persons with physical impairments. Being able to reach out with something as relatively simple as voice-driven electronic mail messages can remove isolation and enrich lives.

As with enhanced video appearance and performance, these capabilities have their price. For many people monetary cost is not as much an issue as is the potential expense of time and frustration with jumpers, switches, and command-line parameters. Early sound cards could be more difficult to configure than formatting a new hard disk or adding serial ports. Now, if your sound card does not come with an automatic installation and configuration program, you might consider another brand or model.

What is a sound card?

A sound card, generically, is a signal-processing device that enables your PC to act like an expensive tape recorder. With a few of the added bells and whistles that almost always come with sound cards, you have some of the features of a small recording studio — mixing and editing sounds with fraction-of-a-second precision.

Sound cards are often thought of as devices that enhance the sound effects of games, add warning sirens or voices to various activities in Windows applications, or play music CD-ROMs at your desk (a little more expensive than a Sony Discman, but a lot more fun to play with). Until now, people generally thought of computers as digital or logical devices. Data is either on or off, true or false; a file exists or it doesn't. Sound cards begin to connect outside world senses (essentially analog signals) into digital information and back again. Figure 20-1 shows a typical sound card and connection.

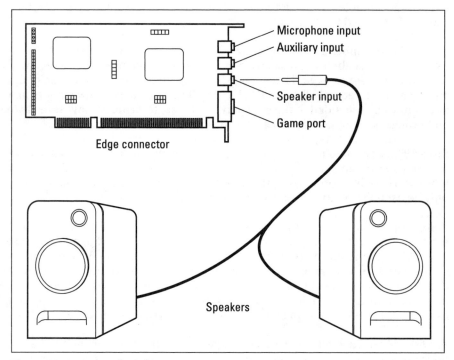

Figure 20-1: A sound card

Digital and analog signals

Sound cards can be used to record and play back much more than audio signals. With special signal adapters, they can collect, store, and play back real-life or analog information such as heartbeats, weather data, seismic activity, and just about anything that can be thought of as sensory, but just short of high-speed, high-volume digital data. Digital data is what becomes of these analog signals when the sound card processes them and converts them to bits and bytes for storage on your hard disk. Conversely, the digital data that is stored on your disks becomes analog data when you play it back.

Analog signals, such as "it's a little bit cooler now than it was a few minutes ago" or "the siren is getting louder as it gets closer," can be viewed as two-dimensional data elements. They have qualitative and quantitative values—recorded as particular intensities over a period of time.

Because a sound or sensory signal is so complex and must be recorded more or less one-dimensionally as a digital value on a hard disk, attempts to record additional dimensions require significant amounts of data space on disks. This comparison may be inadequate for the technically oriented reader, but we hope it serves the purpose of explaining some computer-related issues, such as why sound processing requires so much disk space and memory.

Sampling

A sound card takes many small samples of an incoming signal at regular intervals. The value of the signal's strength is recorded in a given data area for the period of time allowed for the sampling. The time and the signal levels can vary, but to be effective, the timing increments must be constant for the duration of the sampling.

Components on the sound card convert the signal levels to digital values for recording and then convert digital values to sound levels for playback. The software used for controlling the sound-card operation and the hardware that does the timing and the conversion must be synchronized and matched to allow for proper storage and reproduction of the signals. If the hardware and software do not work together properly, you might get playback that sounds like you're putting your finger on a record or slowing down a tape as it plays back.

For very accurate sound recordings and playback, the samplings are done more frequently—usually around 44,000 samples per second. It is possible to record and to play back usable audio signals as low as 10,000 to 12,000 samples per second. If the sampling occur less often than that, the recording begin to sound like the choppy voices of automatic message systems. If sampling rates are faster than 22,000 samples per second (or 22 kHz), your PC system, its CPU, and its disk-storage subsystem must be fast enough to keep up with the amount of data that is being presented.

Direct memory access

If you have not yet encountered the direct memory access (DMA) settings in your PC, as you might with a fast Small Computer System Interface (SCSI) disk controller, sound cards will introduce you to another technical setting in addition to addresses and IRQ settings. DMA is the I/O process of transferring data directly from a hardware device to RAM without intermediate processing by the CPU chip. Most data transfers, such as from the keyboard, serial ports, and disk drives, use the CPU to control the flow of information. It takes time to handle the software commands and the process keeps the CPU from doing other things.

Using DMA makes sense for high volumes of data that might otherwise be lost if they are not handled quickly.

Although DMA data transfers help smooth things out, you still need a fast enough system to handle information that is on the way to the CPU, I/O, and disk drive. Original multimedia Level 1 specifications for minimum multimedia systems allowed for as little as an 80386SX processor operating at 16 MHz with average I/O-bus and disk-drive speeds. If you want to achieve all of the quality possible in present technology sound cards and applications, a 100 MHz Pentium with a fast (10ms or less) hard disk and a 4x or even 40x CD-ROM drive is preferred.

Although this chapter has not addressed the issues of video recording and playback, the concerns of system capabilities for video are similar and (for system diagnostic reasons) more important than those for audio. Video images contain many times more data than do sound signals. Because of this, they must be processed on at least a 33 MHz 80486 system with maximum I/O and disk performance to have reasonable appearance. If you are considering both video and sound applications for your PC, a PCI or local bus motherboard with a 486DX4 or Pentium system with at least one gigabyte (1,000MB) of disk space is not too extravagant. Memory speed and cache are also important.

This section has shown just a snapshot of the workings inside a sound card and some of what you can expect for quality and performance, presented without comparative charts and many numbers and new terminology. What you probably need right now is to get a sound card installed and working properly.

Sound card installation and configuration

Your system has been running fine and you survived the installation of the new fax modem a few months ago. Now you feel pretty good about getting into this sound thing. Open the box and look at the new card. No dust, shiny bracket, glistening connector pins, and, *oh no* — extra wires and plugs, and yikes — jumpers!

If you need help with your fax modem, see Chapter 22.

There is much to technically discuss about sound cards—8-, 16-, and 32-bit conversion rates, dynamic range of frequencies and levels, and impedance and line levels. But to install, fix common problems, and simply enjoy the sound that accompanies the pictures on that encyclopedia CD-ROM or an audio CD by your favorite musician, or to make up your own sound effects and messages for Windows, you can simplify things to a few address, IRQ, and DMA settings, and the device-driver configurations required.

Fortunately, many of these technical details can be addressed with software. A robust installation program can detect the presence or activity of other devices in your system, and it knows the common rules for other device assignments. A quick software-driven "look" at your existing system before you remove the cover and plug in any cards or wires can tell you exactly what address, IRQ, and DMA assignment to use for the jumpers and switches, if there are any. If your motherboard can accommodate Plug-and-Play sound cards, about all you need to do is plug in the card, as shown in Figure 20-2.

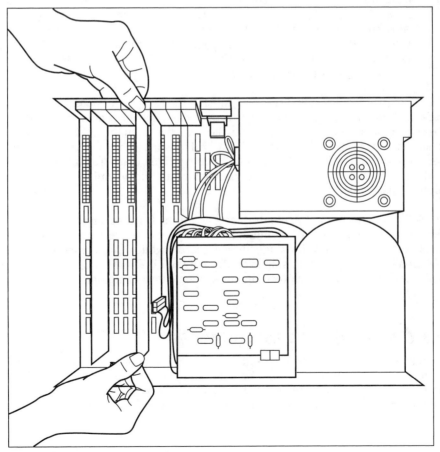

Figure 20-2: Installing your sound card

If the installation program is well-planned and customized for the card you are installing, it might even present you with a picture of the board and it might highlight where the jumpers are located and what their settings should be. Some cards, such as those from MediaVision, are automatically configured by the installation software to use only the unoccupied settings for your system — without using a single switch or hard-to-find jumper. This is one of the steps toward the Plug-and-Play cooperative hardware and software development work being done to make PCs less technical than they are now. This also constitutes a softset device, as covered in Chapters 5, 8, and 13. Plug and Play used to be referred to as "Plug and Pray" because there were so many problems. Happily, newer hardware and software are becoming a little more cooperative, and they work more often than not.

If you don't have a newer card with a "smart" installation program, you can get by combining the reference information in this book with and some of the system information and diagnostic programs available.

Tip   We strongly suggest that you determine and correct any possible conflicts with addresses, IRQs, and DMA settings before you attempt a sound card installation. Conflicts are typically found with serial (COM) ports, parallel (LPT) ports, network cards, and some disk and CD-ROM adapters. There are also potential device hardware address conflicts if you have a Personal Computer Memory Card International Association (PCMCIA) interface in your PC system because addresses in the 2xxh range have seen mixed uses.

IBM anticipated, defined, and reserved most of the assignments possible for a multitude of PC options and sound cards. However, most network cards, high-performance disk controllers, and PCMCIA interfaces did not exist when the PC, XT, and AT were designed. Developers of new devices have had to work within and around a limited set of opportunities, design issues, and "whatever's left over" from the original system designs. Sound cards generally allow for multiple but still only a few configuration possibilities.

Some PC systems are so full of interfaces, adapters, features, and functions that there is no place left to plug in, much less configure, a sound card. The same consideration may apply for some network cards, while other common adapters are usually accounted for in some variation of their original designs. In these cases, using newer PCI device adapters, if your system can accommodate them, is your best solution.

Hardware address assignments

Most sound cards are addressable at either 210h, 220h, or 230h. If other addressing options are available, they should be noted in the documentation or installation program that comes with the card. All of these addresses could create conflicts with either a network interface card or PCMCIA port. An automatic installation and configuration program (at least the newer ones) should be aware of these possibilities and should avoid them.

Hardware interrupt and DMA assignments

Although it might appear that some of the available IRQ settings are overused throughout this book, it is important to understand that we are doing much of this work on many different systems and have mixtures of 8-, 16-, and 32-bit I/O devices for our experiments. If you run out of IRQ and DMA assignments for 8-bit devices, consider changing one or more of your I/O cards to a 16-bit version. This adds to your available IRQ lines at least five choices and gives you four more DMA lines.

Note

At the risk of repeating ourselves, for the benefit of avoiding conflict with every subsystem and device, some IRQ assignments are best left as is, and some can be reused or reassigned, if conditions are right.

Table 20-4 shows the standard IRQ usage in most PCs. Since these are most often used by whatever device is the standard, they actually represent IRQs to try to avoid using for your new installation. Table 20-5 presents the common use of IRQ signals that are usually available.

Table 20-4	
Standard IRQ Assignments to Avoid	
Avoid This Assignment	**Because It Is Used Like This**
IRQ 0	System timer
IRQ 1	Keyboard
IRQ 2	Possibly available in PC, XT; used by IRQ 8-15 in AT and higher
IRQ 3	COM Port 2 (2F8h)/COM Port 4 (2E8h)
IRQ 4	COM Port 1 (3F8h)/COM Port 3 (3E8h).
IRQ 6	Floppy disk drive, all systems (though Mountain Tape and others have been successful doubling up the use of IRQ 6)
IRQ 8	Real-time clock in AT and higher
IRQ 9	Connected to IRQ 2
IRQ 13	If your system has a separate math chip, it is quite likely that this line is used on your system board
IRQ 14	AT Hard Disk controller, unless you have a SCSI adapter and it uses a different IRQ line

	Table 20-5
	Common Uses of "Available" IRQ Signals
This Assignment	***But May Be Used Like This***
IRQ 5	PC/XT hard disk; possibly available in AT and higher if no LPT Port 2; Novell server or OS/2 system; Sound Blaster cards.
IRQ 7	LPT Port 1 (3BCh and 378h) — available in all, if not a Novell server or OS/2 system, or if you do not print from them. Most printers do not actually use this IRQ.
IRQ 10	No predefined assignment.
IRQ 11	No predefined assignment. (IRQ 11 is often used as the default for Adaptec SCSI host adapters.)
IRQ 12	Available if you are not using a PS/2 (onboard) mouse port.
IRQ 14	Available if no MFM, RLL, ESDI, or IDE hard drive and a SCSI adapter are not assigned here.
IRQ 15	Available if your SCSI adapter is not using it.

For most DOS systems that do not have or use enhanced or bidirectional parallel ports, you can use either IRQ 5 or 7 for devices other than the printer ports. This is handy if you only have 8-bit I/O cards.

DMA channels 0 and 2 are the only ones reserved by DOS for the system and the floppy drives. DMA channels 1 and 3 are usually available for 8-bit cards, and channels 4, 5, 6, and 7 become available to 16-bit cards. DMA channel 5 is a popular default setting for many SCSI host adapters.

Tip

Relatively "safe" configurations for most sound cards commonly are hardware address 220h, IRQ 5 or 7, and DMA channel 1 or 3. For 16-bit sound cards, you gain the advantage of being able to use IRQs 10, 11, or 15 and DMA channels 5 to 7 if they not used by other hardware adapters.

Windows configurations for sound cards

Probably the most common or compelling reason to use a sound card is to enhance the presentation of applications running in Microsoft Windows. To use the features of your sound card, you must install drivers specific to your sound card from within Windows. This is usually done using a Setup program that comes with your sound card, unless the DOS installation program installed the Windows part for you. These drivers provide information to Windows and multimedia applications, telling them what types of sound services are available.

Some cards support only one or two types of sound services (such as the types of files they can play) and possibly no more than one service at a time. One of the more popular cards can be set up to emulate either an AdLib, Sound Blaster, or MIDI adapter, or an Aria synthesizer, depending on how you install and configure the software drivers. Until you select the type of service you want (most commonly Sound Blaster or a similar service that plays WAV audio files and is supported by most games), some of these cards take no identity and appear to not exist in your system.

After the drivers are installed, there should be an additional program group on the Windows desktop. This program group will include any audio-level controls or special configuration features for the card. You often have the option of playing audio CD-ROM sound directly from the CD-ROM drive either through the amplifier in the sound card or by reading and playing back digital sound files from a CD-ROM drive. Playing audio CD-ROMs through a sound card requires a special cable from the CD-ROM drive to the sound card. (If you need the CD-ROM drive only for data, a sound card is not necessary unless the audio card provides the simplest way to get the data portion of the CD-ROM interfaced as a disk drive on your system.)

Note Generally, sound cards do not support the CD-ROM drives that can write as well as read data. These CD-ROM drives are usually connected directly to an enhanced IDE or SCSI controller.

Common audio card problems and solutions

Unless you have no idea of what the switch, jumper, or software configuration settings are, or you have lost the special installation or driver floppy disk for your sound card, once it is installed there should be few problems. Except for outright failure or the need to reconfigure your sound card to accommodate a new device or software (as many games programs require), the common problems you may encounter usually show up first at installation. There are no common error messages or beep codes for sound cards as there are for video cards and some other features of your system.

Symptoms

▶ Sound card is not "seen" by the installation program or driver software.

▶ Sound card emits constant noises, "broken record" iterations of sounds, or pops and clicks when sounds are expected.

▶ Other devices fail, lose data, indicate errors, or otherwise appear to malfunction.

Suspects

▶ Improper hardware or software setup

▶ Conflicting device (PCMCIA, network, or SCSI cards are most often involved) configurations

Solutions

▶ Be sure that your hardware and software configurations match for all devices installed. Sometimes redoing the installation or configuration of one or two devices can solve the problem.

▶ Determine the hardware address, IRQ, and DMA settings for all the hardware devices installed in your system. This may involve using the installation program for these devices or a system information viewing utility. Windows 9x/Me provides this information in the System ➪ Device Manager icon in the Control Panel. This information is available from the Windows NT Diagnostics program accessed from the "Administrative Tools (Common)" menu for Windows NT and 2000.

▶ List all the devices and note all of the different combinations possible for each card, if they can be changed (some internal devices and PCMCIA adapters can't be changed).

▶ Select the best nonconflicting combination of addresses, IRQ, and DMA settings from all of the devices, and reconfigure them accordingly.

▶ Set up the device with the fewest possibilities for changes first, moving through successive devices, driver configurations, and the automatic installation programs, until all devices are working properly.

▶ If you run out of possibilities among the 8-bit cards in your AT or higher system, consider upgrading from 8-bit to 16-bit interfaces that have more configuration options.

▶ Check the Web site of the sound card vendor for updated driver files or for helpful technical notes for your situation.

Problems speaking to your computer (issuing commands, dictating letters, or recording sounds for special effects), if not attributable to speech pattern problems, may most often be attributed to background noise. A good noise-canceling or directional microphone usually removes the problem. If the problem persists, you may want to consider upgrading to one of the newer 3D sound systems. They are expensive, but they deliver much higher quality and capabilities.

Summary

The video subsystem serves as your "eyes" into your computer system and your applications software. Almost every other aspect of your use and problem solving with your PC depends on the visual clues you may get through error messages, diagnostics, or the results from your programs that appear onscreen. Luckily, basic video hardware seldom conflicts with anything else in your system. It is just the new, experimental, and high-demand applications that may bring video problems along with their fantastic new features.

Sound-card problems almost always require inspection of hardware settings, either those controlled by jumpers and switches, or from special configuration software provided with the card. Provided you have resolved any previously existing hardware conflicts, and no new ones are imposed by the addition of more hardware or changing old hardware, sound-card problems are usually limited to software compatibility and configuration, especially while multitasking. Just remember to clean your CDs and the lens, using only chemicals and devices designed for this purpose. A dirty CD or lens can act like a malfunctioning system.

Though accessibility features for PCs and their operating systems are increasing in capabilities and ease of use, the day when everyone has unrestricted access to the use of a computer is a long way off. Video, sound, and other forms of input and output (the subject of the next chapter) are both the challenges and the solutions for increased accessibility. Those of us who design hardware, software, and computer/information systems need to keep in mind that the people we are supporting are as varied in their abilities and interests as the applications that we design. Keeping our hardware and computer configurations in running order is a big part of accessibility issues.

✦　　✦　　✦

Basic Input and Output

Your computer would be useless without Input and Output (I/O). Networking, disk drives, audio, and video are covered in Chapters 10, 12, and 16 through 20. These are very important parts of I/O and provide not only some of the ways we use the computer but also some of the means to diagnose the parts that are not working.

Keyboards, pointers (mouse, trackball, light pen, pen pad, 3D spatial tracer), video adapters, monitors, alternate video devices, holographic chamber, scanners, speakers, sound systems, serial ports, Universal Serial Bus (USB), FireWire, modems (internal and external), parallel ports, printers, plotters, and scanners are all necessary or, at least, useful. Any of these may be a source of problems, but the most frequent problems occur while trying to print, scan, or while using a pointing device such as a mouse, trackball, or pen-pad. Other I/O problems may involve configuring the Small Computer System Interface (SCSI), Personal Computer Memory Card International Association (PCMCIA) / PC Card devices, or Universal Serial Bus/FireWire (USB and IEEE-1492) — all optional bus interfaces used for connecting I/O devices to your computer.

In all cases, as frequently mentioned throughout this book, proper system configuration, especially concerning the add-in I/O devices, and documenting their implementations in your system, is critical to having and maintaining a properly functioning system. If the configuration is wrong, the connected devices just will not work.

Printers

The first thing you need in order to get a good printout is good data. The next step is having the proper printer characteristics set up in your application for the available printer. You won't be able to print high-resolution graphics on a wheel-impact printer or even a simple dot-matrix printer — and none of these "speak" PostScript, if your application requires PostScript output. So, you must have the right devices connected to your PC, as selected in your application, and set up with the appropriate printer driver files.

For the applications, data, and drivers to work properly, the printer port must be connected and be set up properly to enable the data to get from the PC out to the printer. Printers come in various types and styles, from simple dot-matrix and text-only devices to high-speed, high-resolution, color, and graphics models.

Printers may connect to your system in one of four ways:

✦ Via serial port (COM1, COM2, COM3, or COM4).

✦ Via parallel port (LPT1, LPT2, or LPT3).

✦ Via the USB or FireWire.

✦ Via some form of network connection, typically at or near a server or as a standalone network device.

Table 21-1 shows the proper port configurations for the most common connections. USB and FireWire configuration is generally handled by the port/bus driver, is not accessible by the user, and most often does not use the standard PC interrupt request (IRQ) and memory port addresses. SCSI connections most often use one standard IRQ, memory port or basic input/output system (BIOS) address, and one or two direct memory access (DMA) channels.

Table 21-1 I/O Port Assignments				
Logical Port Name	Physical Port Address	Port IRQ	Notes	Potential Conflicts
COM1	3F8	4	Windows generically supports up to COM8. NT supports up to COM256. Special hardware and I/O channels are required.	Typically used for serial mouse or other pointing device.

Logical Port Name	Physical Port Address	Port IRQ	Notes	Potential Conflicts
COM2	2F8	3	Generally requires COM1 to be present.	Typically used for modem.
COM3	3E8	4*	Generally requires COM1 and 2 to be present.	Use of this port/IRQ at the same time as COM1 may conflict with COM1.
COM4	2E8	3*	Generally requires COM1, 2, and 3 to be present.	Use of this port/IRQ at the same time as COM2 may conflict with COM2.
LPT1	3BC or 378	7	LPT1 is typically 3BC if monochrome video; 378 if color video.	Printer may or may not require the use of IRQ7.
LPT2	378 or 278	5	LPT2 is 378 if LPT1 is 3BC; 278 if LPT1 is 378.	Beware of IRQ conflicts with network or sound cards.
LPT3	278	5*	278 is LPT3 if 3BC and 378 exist.	Beware of IRQ conflicts with network or sound cards.

* Without special hardware and drivers, two devices using the same IRQ may cause system problems.

A serial I/O (COM) port sends data out to the printer one bit of a character at a time, and usually no faster than 9,600 bits per second. Accounting for fancy page formatting and fonts sent to the printer, you will print one-tenth to one-hundredth slower to a serial printer connection than you would to a parallel printer connection. A parallel I/O (LPT) port sends data out an entire character (8 bits) at a time, and can do so 10 to 20 times faster than most serial printer interfaces — thus your printed output will be produced much faster. Networked printers are usually no faster than direct parallel connected printers because the network server usually has to process and re-send the data. A few high-speed, high-quality graphics printers will accept SCSI connections, enabling extremely large amounts of data to be transferred quite quickly. USB and FireWire printer connections may become common in the future.

Novell's NetWare, IBM's OS/2, Microsoft's Windows 9x/Me/NT/2000, and PC versions of Unix (Linux, FreeBSC, and so on) require that you have the proper printer driver installed so that the operating environment will know how to send data to the printer. The right "printer language" must also be installed and configured or you will end up printing garbage, wasting time and paper. Sending PostScript data to a character printer or HP PCL printer may result in lengthy, cryptic text outputs. Sending HP laser-configured printer data to a PostScript printer will cause an error. Sending bubble-jet or ink-jet formatted data to an HP laser printer will result in garbage output and wasted paper.

The printer in your office may be attached to the main network server. If you use Windows 9x/Me/NT/2000, the printer for your PC may actually be a shared resource on someone else's PC. Here again, the ports must be configured and function properly, and both PCs must use the right printer driver for the attached printer.

Note   If your printer is connected directly to a network, your network server software and printer driver will need to be configured for the network name and/or address of the printer (typically either an assigned TCP/IP) network address or a built-in Ethernet or Mac device address.)

Between the serial, parallel, or network port and the printer, the cabling must be correct and firmly connected. The printer must, of course, be turned on, have an adequate supply of paper and either toner, ink, or ribbon, and it must be "online" (ready to accept data). What could be simpler?

Common Printing Problems

Printer problems can range from very simple to very serious. A simple problem, such as incorrect cabling or using the wrong printer driver, can be just as aggravating as a defective printer port when you are stressed with an overdue report that needs to be printed.

Symptoms

▶ No output from printer

Suspects

▶ Printer is not turned on, is plugged into a nonworking outlet, or is not online.

▶ Try the printer's internal self-test mode. If it fails, the printer needs repair.

▶ Cables are improperly connected.

▶ Printer-port failure.

▶ Faulty software setup.

Solutions

▶ Make sure that the printer is turned on, plugged into a working outlet, and that it is online.

▶ Make sure the printer cable is connected to the printer, and that it is connected to the correct port on the computer.

▶ Turn off your computer and reconnect your printer cable (see the following discussion). Check your AC power for a voltage or power-spike problem; you may want to consider purchasing and installing a simple surge protection device.

▶ Make sure that the correct printer port and driver are selected for your printer.

▶ Have the printer repaired or replaced.

▶ Run the Windows 9x/Me/NT/2000 printer troubleshooter.

If your printer is turned on but its power-on light is not lit, check the most obvious potential problem first: Is it plugged into an electrical outlet? If the printer is plugged in and turned on, but is not working, test your outlet by plugging in something else, such as a small lamp. If this test indicates that your outlet is bad, and resetting the breaker for that outlet does not solve the problem, call a qualified electrician.

If your printer is plugged into a working outlet and turned on, but its online indicator is not lit, press the button closest to that indicator, usually on or below the indicator light. If the online indicator does not light up at this point, your printer has a problem that needs the attention of a service technician. It may be something as simple as a fuse inside the printer, but be cautious, as you may void the warranty if you open the case yourself.

Most printers attached to personal computers today use the parallel interface, also known as a Centronics parallel interface, which uses a cable that has a 25-pin connector on the computer end and a 36-pin connector on the printer end. This connector is usually snugly mated to its counterpart on the printer via a pair of spring clips attached to the printer, as shown in Figure 21-1. These clips are adequate for maintaining the connection under normal circumstances. If you move the printer, the spring clips can come loose and allow the connectors to separate. If you forget to use the clips when connecting the cable to the printer, it is possible for the vibration of the printer itself to break the connection. Always check the cable connection to the printer at the first sign of trouble.

Another cable-related problem is the connection of the printer cable at the computer. IBM established the 25-conductor D-shell socket as the standard for parallel interfaces on the personal computer when the IBM PC was introduced. This connector, also called a DB-25 socket, or designated as a DB-25S ("S" for socket), will be used on as many as three parallel printer ports on the computer. Many personal computers have only one parallel printer connector, and this makes identification of the correct port very simple. Look for a connector that looks like an elongated D with 25 holes arranged in two rows, one with 13 and the other with 12 holes. Use the screws on the cable connector to make sure everything is connected firmly.

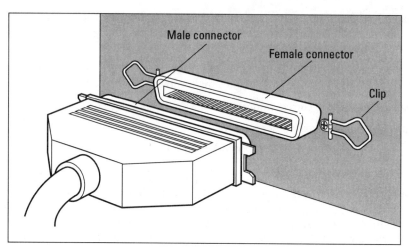

Figure 21-1: Printer cables usually connect to the printer via a 36-pin Centronics connector mated by spring clips to its counterpart at the back of the printer.

On many portable computers, the DB-25S connector may perform multiple duties such as being the connector for a printer, a floppy disk drive, or a CD-ROM or DVD drive.

If more than one DB-25S connector exists on the rear of your computer, then more than one printer port probably exists. If the ports are not labeled, it will take a bit of testing to determine which port is the proper one for your printer cable. This testing may be done from the DOS prompt, outside of Windows or other user-interface or operating environment. Attach the cable to your printer, and then to one of the printer ports on your computer. With the computer turned on and running, perform a print-screen operation by pressing PrintScrn or Print Screen. Under Windows 9x/ Me/NT/2000 you can send a test page to the printer from the Properties dialog box for the respective printer. Try this for each port that may be the right one for your printer by connecting the cable to each port and trying PrintScrn or Print Test Page.

You might have to hold down Shift along with the PrintScrn key, or press the PrintScrn key more than once to print the screen. Give it a few seconds to format and send the data before trying again. Consult your PC manual to see exactly how this should work on your computer. If your printer begins printing the contents of your screen, the cable is attached to the proper printer port. If the printer does not print, turn off the computer and change the cable to another of the DB-25S connectors.

Some SCSI adapter cards also provide a DB-25S connector, sometimes called an SCSI-I port. You should identify all cards inside the computer and label the connectors for them.

Repeat this process until you find the proper port. If none of the ports produces output, you probably have a printer port failure or a faulty cable. Try replacing the cable and repeating the tests. Cables are cheaper than I/O cards or motherboards.

If running the print-screen tests described previously resulted in failure, you probably have a faulty printer port. A printer port can fail for several reasons, but the most common cause of failure is plugging in the cable while the computer is running.

Caution

Always turn off your computer when plugging in or removing cables from any port on your computer because you might receive an electric shock if you do not. Newer "hot swap" technology may be implemented on your computer. If your computer documentation states that a particular device is "hot swappable," you may not have to turn off your computer. Without this assurance, you are much better off to turn it off.

Another cause of printer port failure is an AC power problem. If left undetected, an AC power problem such as high voltage, low voltage, or power spikes on the AC line can cause the failure of your computer system.

One more cause of printing failures is an incorrect printer setup of the application. Most DOS programs that perform enhanced printing functions, such as font changes or graphics printing, have a printer setup routine. This setup operation usually enables you to select from a list of support printers, and to declare the port that you have chosen for connecting the printer. Choosing the wrong printer setup or port can cause your system not to print.

Symptoms

▶ Printer output is not as expected.

Suspects

▶ Incorrect software setup

▶ Printer malfunction

▶ Printer cabling problem

▶ Port failure

Solutions

▶ Make sure the correct printer driver is selected.

▶ Try to pinpoint the problem by running a self-test on your printer. You may not be able to fix the problem yourself, but remember that discovering what is causing the problem is more than half the battle. The printer Self Test is usually started by holding down one or two keys while turning on the power to your printer. Check your printer documentation for the specific keys or other sequences to print a test page.

▶ Make sure your cable is connected properly, and check for damage to the cable itself. Rectifying either of these problems may return you to the land of proper output.

▶ If the POST (your computer's power-on self test) is not reporting a problem with the port when you start your computer, run an external, diagnostic program to test the printer port, such as the Rosenthal Utilities on the CD-ROM.

▶ If your software (or Windows) is trying to print, for instance, to an Epson LQ-1170 while you have a Hewlett-Packard LaserJet 5P attached, you will see some very strange results. Make sure you have selected the correct printer driver in your software setup (if you have plugged in a different printer without using the Add Printer option in the Control Panel). If your exact printer is not supported, you might be able to select an alternate that is emulated by your printer. For DOS users, another alternative is to configure your own driver if the software allows this.

Note   Building your own printer driver is a very difficult and tedious operation that involves careful study of the manuals for your printer and software. This is generally done by very technically qualified engineers with lots of experience programming the printer interfaces. Only attempt this when all else fails.

If your printer is working but not printing correctly, it might have an internal malfunction. Try executing the printer self-test described in your printer's manual.

✦ The self-test for **dot-matrix or daisy-wheel printers** checks the internal software that controls the printer, and also prints rows of letters and numbers or graphics on a sheet of paper. The printout, sometimes called a barber pole because of its appearance, shows every character that the printer can print. Examine the characters closely for deformities that indicate missing wires in the print head of a dot-matrix printer, or missing or misaligned characters for a daisy-wheel printer.

✦ **Laser printer** output might be fuzzy if the mirrors are out of focus, or streaked and splotchy if the image drum is damaged or dirty with toner. Graphic- or page-based printers usually print one or more test pages with sample fonts, graphic images, and a statistical report of the printer's use, and may include some diagnostic information.

✦ **Ink-jet printer** failure usually shows up with missing lines, colors, characters, or ink smudges and spots on the test page. Often, a bad cartridge just needs to be replaced.

If the printer passes the self-test, the next suspect is your printer's parallel or serial port. The port is checked in the self-test procedure, but it is possible for a port with a bad data line or intermittent problem to pass the test. A bad parallel or serial port is usually fixed by replacement.

If the connections to your printer or computer are loose, it is possible for one or more of the data lines to become disconnected. This causes very strange-looking output, if your printer prints anything at all.

A damaged cable presents the same symptoms as a loose cable. If data lines or control lines are cut, the results of your printing efforts will be erratic. Inspect the cable closely. Even if the outer jacket is not cut, internal damage still may have occurred if the cable is crushed, pulled sharply, or bent over a sharp corner. Look for flat spots in the cable, or places where the jacket does not feel "full." When in doubt, replace the cable.

Every time you start your computer, it runs a self-test procedure. This power-on self test (POST) usually detects a printer port with a major fault. If POST does not report a printer port failure and you suspect that the port is faulty, you might try running an external diagnostic program, such as the Rosenthal Utilities on the CD-ROM, to test the printer port.

For a more advanced checkout, use utilities such as Eurosoft or Watergate. Provided for you on this book's CD-ROM, demos of PC-Doctor and Rosenthal Utilities will perform thorough diagnostics and report failures.

You might also check the physical connections of the printer port. If the port is on an add-in card, make sure the card is secure in its slot and that any jumper settings are proper and secure.

Symptom

▶ Wrong number of pages, or pages missing.

Suspects

▶ A form feed was not sent to the printer to close out the document.

▶ Software and printed output with conflicting line counts.

▶ Software and printer with dissimilar line feeds.

Solutions

▶ Press your printer's Form Feed key to eject the last page.

▶ Make sure your software and printer are set up with the same page length or the same number of lines per page.

▶ Make sure that only your printer or your software — not both — is generating line feeds. If both are generating line feeds, disable one of them. The only way to discover that both your software and printer are generating line feeds is to check and, if necessary, change one. The printer settings may be changed through driver configuration, printer panel settings, or switch settings. The computer's software settings regarding extra line feeds may be found in the Page Setup for the document or in the printer Properties.

If your last page is missing, the cause is most likely a missing form feed at the end of the document. Try pressing the Form Feed key on your printer. You might have to take the printer offline to get the Form Feed key to work. If your last page is ejected from the printer, consider adding a form feed character to the end of your document. Older laser printers are especially notorious for failing to eject the last page of documents.

If pressing Form Feed does not eject the last page, or if other pages are missing, check the software to make sure you are selecting the entire document for printing. This is a problem in spreadsheets when you add data at the bottom of a worksheet and then fail to include the new lines in the output range.

If you want to see some really interesting things shoot out of your printer, just set your software and printer for different page lengths. You will get pages that appear to be full, followed by pages containing only a few lines, or page breaks that move up or down on each succeeding page of the printout.

The IBM PC standard is to include line feeds at the end of each line sent to the printer. Most printers give you the option to add line feeds to each line received from the computer. If your printer is set to add line feeds and you have not disabled the computer's generation of line feeds, you will see extra lines of white space after every line that the computer sends to the printer, and your document might be twice as long as you anticipated.

Symptoms

▶ Printer "offline" or "unavailable" error messages.

▶ Print out "never" happens.

Suspects

▶ Network printer server is down.

▶ Printer output is not "captured" to the network printer.

▶ "Work Offline" is set for this printer under Windows.

▶ Printer output is sent to a disk file rather than to a printer port.

Solutions

▶ Check the network server or contact the system administrator for network problems and get the server application started or the print queue cleared.

▶ Set Capture Port to a known-good network or workstation shared printer resource in the printer's Properties dialog box. The capture port creates a virtual connection to the identified printer, so that your output will go over the network to that printer instead of trying to print on a local printer, whether it exists or not.

▶ Deselect Work Offline under this printer's print status Properties dialog box.

▶ Set the port for the desired printer to a known-good printer port rather than to a default disk file output.

Pointing Device Problems

Your pointing device, which may start out as a welcome alternative to using key commands, can quickly become a habit and just as quickly become an enemy to productivity if you are not aware of certain signs and symptoms of a sick mouse or ailing trackball. Nothing is more embarrassing than screaming at your system for not responding to your mouse commands, only to have someone quietly point out that your mouse cable is not connected to your computer.

Pointing devices may connect to your system in one of several ways:

✦ Serial (COM) port

✦ Built-in PS/2-style mouse port

✦ Microsoft InPort or other special mouse adapter card (Logitech, or a video card mouse port)

✦ Infrared

✦ Included on your keyboard with no additional connector

✦ USB, FireWire, or other newer I/O bus

If you have a serial-port mouse connection, review the rules for proper port configuration, as shown previously in Table 21-1. Beware of conflicting IRQ activity between COM1 and COM3, or between COM2 and COM4 if you use these ports at the same time, because, as the default, they share the use of the same IRQs.

If you have a PS/2-style mouse port built into your system board, you cannot change its I/O address (this port is actually connected to a spare section of the internal keyboard interface chip; it does not have an I/O port assignment that you can change), and its IRQ assignment is fixed at IRQ 12, which may be in conflict with another I/O device.

If you have a Microsoft InPort mouse card, a Logitech mouse interface card, or a mouse port on your video card, you may not have any choice as to I/O addressing, but may be able to select an IRQ — typically 2, 3, 4, 5, or 7. Select an IRQ that is not in use by another device.

Improper operation of your mouse, trackball, or pen-pad can also cause unexpected trouble. If your mouse is not working, you might not be able to get a program to run correctly, or the program might not run at all. The problem might be something as simple as the mouse not being plugged in, or as serious as a conflict between your mouse and some other device. If you have the wrong driver software installed, moving the pointing device "up" may cause the onscreen pointer item to go left, right, or down, or the movement may act like a button push and select, move, or delete data highlighted onscreen.

Pointing devices have the same or similar function — to enable you to guide an onscreen "pointer" or marker of some style to an area of interest onscreen. Pointing devices perform this guidance by sending data to the mouse driver software that is running in DOS or Windows. This data is usually relative to the last position of the pointer. This data is translated into onscreen-pointer position information, and in turn is related to menu items, text lines, or columns, or to the placement of images. Different pointers may have different driver software, but the driver software must provide commonly known and expected information to the working environment and applications software.

Before assuming the worst when your system suddenly refuses to obey your commands, consider the following symptoms, suspects, and solutions regarding pointing devices. You might find your way out of the maze more quickly than you thought possible.

Symptoms

✦ Pointing device is not working.

Suspects

✦ Incorrect cable connection, incorrect driver, or conflicts with other devices.

Solutions

✦ Make sure that the cable connecting the device to your computer is firmly plugged into the proper port. If it is, check your CONFIG.SYS and AUTOEXEC.BAT files (under DOS), or your mouse and port setting under Windows, for presence of the correct driver as described in the manual that came with your pointing device. If you cannot trace the problem to the device driver, check for conflicts between your pointing device and serial devices installed on other ports in your computer (see the following discussion).

Several common interfaces exist for pointing devices such as mouse devices and trackballs: serial, bus, PS/2-compatible, and USB. All types of pointing devices must be connected to the computer through a cable to one of these interfaces. Even a cordless (infrared) mouse has a cable inside your computer between the receiver and the motherboard. The receiver is inside the box where the computer is located.

Tip

The first thing to check when your pointing device does not work is the connecting cable.

Every pointing device uses some form of device driver to tell the computer that it is installed, and what type of device it is. If the device is not installed, or is incorrectly configured, the pointing device will not function. Some pointing device drivers are installed in CONFIG.SYS; others can be installed with AUTOEXEC.BAT from your DOS command line. In Windows the mouse is installed in the Setup program. In Windows 9x/Me and NT/2000, you use the Control Panel to install the device drivers. Check these files and system icons for presence of the correct driver as described in your pointing device's manual, which also should describe the configuration options that will be included on the command line, in the file that loads the driver, or in the appropriate setting screen in Windows.

Still another problem that will keep your pointing device from working correctly is a conflict with other devices in your computer. A serial mouse or trackball normally uses either COM1 or COM2. These two ports are configured by convention to avoid conflicts with each other. If you have additional serial devices installed on either COM3 or COM4, you might experience conflicts between the IRQ lines for these ports and the IRQ lines for COM1 and COM2. A bus device might also use an IRQ line that conflicts with some other device installed in your computer. In all these cases, two devices that issue an interrupt request on the same IRQ line may cause either or both devices to malfunction.

Note   Pointing devices installed using the USB or FireWire connection do not usually experience device conflicts.

Symptoms
▶ Pointing device works sometimes, and then stops working.

Suspects
▶ You are using Windows, but running non-Windows software that uses a mouse, or running software with its own mouse driver. (This problem is especially notable when running Windows 3.0.)

Solutions
▶ Do not run such programs from within Windows. If possible, disable the program's pointing device driver, which will not support the mouse while using that program but will not affect your Windows' mouse, either, You may just want to restart your system, which will restore Window's mouse, after using the offending program..

Some vintage DOS programs, such as XTree Gold, provide their own pointing device driver that is loaded when the program is executed. These programs attempt to restore the default device driver when exiting. Windows also has its own device driver that is loaded at startup. If you load a pointing device driver at startup, load Windows, and then run the program that loads its own device driver from within Windows, Windows will probably work fine; the problem will occur if you attempt to use Windows during or after the time that the other program is loaded. While the program is in memory, Windows tries to use the other program's device driver. When the program is terminated, it removes its device driver from memory and tries to reload the original DOS-based device driver. In either case, Windows acts very confused, doing such things as opening files or starting to print, when all you are doing is trying to move your cursor.

Symptoms

▶ Pointing device used to work fine, now it behaves erratically.

Suspects

▶ The mechanism needs cleaning, your optical mouse surface is worn or damaged, or your connecting cable is damaged. (Remember, for an infrared mouse, an internal cable connects the infrared receiver to the system board.)

Solutions

▶ Periodic maintenance prevents the most common causes of erratic behavior in pointing devices. Inspect your pointing device frequently. Keep the mechanism of your mouse or trackball clean. Make sure that the optical sensors and grid surface of an optical mouse are clean and not worn. Inspect the cables for damage.

A device that once performed like a friend can turn against you for several reasons. Age and use are prime causes of component failure. Installation of new devices might cause conflicts. The most common causes, though, are dirt, wear, and damage. A cup of coffee dumped into a trackball or your child tripping the dog with your mouse cable will most assuredly liven up your computing hours in unanticipated ways. Protect your mouse from animals and children, keep liquids away from your computer and peripherals, and maintain clean working surfaces. And keep this book and your manuals handy.

Figure 21-2 shows how to clean your mouse. Simply unlock the bottom cover of the mouse, let the ball drop out, and clean the ball and socket with a nonabrasive cloth or brush and compressed air.

Tip   For best results, consult the manual that came with your particular mouse.

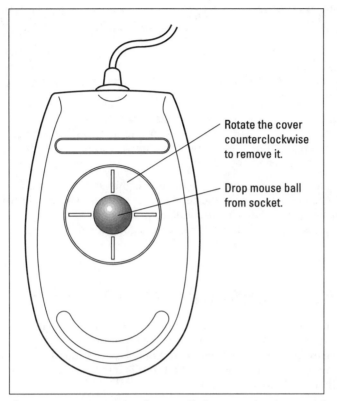

Figure 21-2: Mouse cleaning usually is a very simple operation.

Keyboards

You can usually trace a keyboard-related problem to either an unplugged cable or a bad key. If you press a key and nothing happens, check your cable connections first. If a bad key is the problem, you may need to open the keyboard by removing the necessary screws, and clean out the interior with compressed air.

 See the "Keyboards" section of Chapter 4 for complete coverage of the PC's keyboard.

You may encounter many styles of keyboards, and even older PC or XT keyboards in use on AT or higher systems, and attempts to use AT keyboards on PCs. PC and XT keyboards work okay on ATs. AT keyboards do not work on PCs or XTs. Check the bottom of your keyboard for PC/XT and AT switch settings and select the proper setting for your system.

Beware Advanced Keyboards

Some keyboards provide enhanced programmability functions, ranging from simply swapping the position or function of the Control and CapsLock keys to being able to reprogram single or combination keystrokes into full words or special program commands for your applications.

Be wary of your keyboard configuration switches or programmability features. Your worst computing nightmare may come true if you accidentally hit the Record Program key on your keyboard and later find that you reprogrammed the Enter key to send the Ctrl+Alt+Delete sequence to the system, causing frequent reboots.

The Gateway 2000 computer company produced one such frightening keyboard, which they have since discontinued, due no doubt to the support nightmare of having to instruct hundreds of customers in using the Ctrl+Alt+SuspendMacro sequence to deprogram an erroneously misprogrammed keyboard. Technology can be too good sometimes.

Small Computer System Interface Problems

An I/O interface now in wide use is the Small Computer System Interface (SCSI — sometimes pronounced "scuzzy"). This is not a specific input or output device, but an interface bus for easily attaching I/O devices. You may have a tape drive, CD-ROM drive, hard drive, scanner, or other device attached to this interface (if your computer is equipped with an SCSI host adapter).

Whether your SCSI host adapter is embedded, or a plug-in card, it must have a unique port address and IRQ. The documentation that comes with the motherboard or host adapter should explain the addressing requirements for your particular installation. Because an IRQ, BIOS address, DMA, and memory port address are involved, SCSI devices fall into the same category as other I/O devices; therefore, SCSI devices may conflict with other I/O devices in your system. Use the procedures for dealing with conflicts presented in Chapters 5 and 14 to make sure your SCSI devices have their own, unique resources.

An external SCSI host adapter, such as the Trantor T-338 or Adaptec Parallel Port SCSI Adapter, includes a device driver that enables the parallel port to serve as both an SCSI interface and as a printer port. An installation program eases the setup of the host adapter, and a diagnostic program tests the port and some of the devices on it.

The SCSI bus allows up to eight devices, one of which is the adapter itself, to be easily attached together. These connected devices are referred to as a *daisy chain*. The SCSI bus is controlled by either an embedded host adapter built into the motherboard, an SCSI interface card that is plugged in like any other expansion card, or an external interface that is plugged into the parallel port.

Using SCSI devices in a Daisy Chain

With special hardware and software, it is possible to daisy-chain SCSI adapters, each with its own daisy chain of devices. The practice does not seem to have reached the mainstream but one of this book's authors has seen one SCSI disk array supporting 45 disk drives on a single Wide-Fast SCSI bus, using the daisy-chained SCSI adapter method. The advantages of using this arrangement does not seem to be very great because all the data would be competing for the same limited SCSI bus bandwidth. It does, however, provide access to a very large store of data.

The SCSI bus must be terminated at each end. The host adapter card is usually at one end of the bus (but sometimes in the middle), and most adapters come with a terminator installed on the card. The last device on the bus, and only that last device, must also be terminated.

Note   Most SCSI devices are sold with a built-in terminator that can be removed if the device is placed in the middle of the SCSI bus.

If you have both internal and external devices on the same SCSI bus, the host adapter is now in the middle of the bus. The terminator must be removed from the interface card for things to work properly. Be sure, though, that the device at each end of the SCSI bus has a terminator. Some newer SCSI adapters have built-in software that detects the need for terminating internally or notifies the user that a terminator is required internally or externally or not at all. Some adapters even set the status of the SCSI board's terminator status automatically.

The devices on the SCSI bus must each have a unique address. The SCSI standard calls for up to eight devices, with addresses ranging from 0 to 7, to be placed on the bus. The host adapter (and therefore the computer) is usually on address 7, leaving seven other addresses for devices to be installed on the bus. The newer two-channel SCSI cards support the ability to accommodate up to 16 devices, one of which is the adapter itself.

Some SCSI host adapters treat addresses 0 and 1 differently than the other addresses. For example, the popular Adaptec 1540-compatible host adapters reserve the first two addresses for bootable devices such as hard drives or bootable CD-ROM drives.

The most common SCSI device problems are improper device addressing and termination problems. Two devices on the same address will cause both devices to fail to function, and may cause your SCSI bus to fail as well. Problems such as a missing terminator, or too many terminators on the bus, will cause erratic behavior from all the devices on the SCSI bus.

Symptoms

▶ Your SCSI adapter is installed correctly and has no IRQ, memory port address, or DMA channel conflicts, but still does not give access to the SCSI devices.

Suspects

▶ SCSI ID assignment conflicts between SCSI devices.

▶ Improper SCSI bus terminator inside your computer, on the SCSI adapter, or on an SCSI device outside your computer case.

Solutions

▶ Before you install a new SCSI device on your PC, use Steve Gibson's SCSI ID (ID.EXE) program to determine what SCSI adapters and SCSI devices are installed in your system. The program does not display IRQ, memory address port, or DMA channel assigned, if applicable, but it does tell you the SCSI IDs assigned to each adapter and device. This will help you determine what SCSI IDs are still available for assignment. The SCSI ID is usually set on the SCSI device by making switch, jumper, push button, or thumb wheel settings. Again, depending on your hardware, you may have 8 or 16 SCSI IDs available. The SCSI adapter is usually assigned SCSI ID 7.

▶ The best way to determine the SCSI bus terminator status in your system is to visually inspect each device and the adapter.

You need to determine the two ends of the SCSI bus daisy chain; make sure that those two locations, and no others, have an SCSI terminator.

If your SCSI adapter has two internal cable connectors, you may use both of them to connect internal devices *only* if no external devices are attached to that same adapter. If you have SCSI devices attached to both internal cables, the end device on each cable must be terminated. The end device is the one electrically furthest from the adapter on that same cable (or series of cables if an entrance and exit connector exists on a particular device). In this case, the termination on the adapter board must be disabled or off.

If you have both internal and external SCSI devices attached to your SCSI adapter, terminators must be placed at the ends of the internal and external cables. Again, the end device is the one that is electrically furthest from the adapter. With both internal and external devices, the termination on the SCSI adapter must be disabled or off.

If your SCSI bus has only internal or only external SCSI devices, the end device of the daisy chain of devices must have termination and the SCSI adapter card must have termination. This is true even if only one device exists on the cable.

The termination on your SCSI adapter card may be set in software, in your complementary metal-oxide semiconductor (CMOS) memory, in a special boot program such as Adaptec's Ctrl+A access during bootup, or may be automatic, detected by the board itself. It may also be a resistor bar, switch, jumper, push button, or thumb wheel setting that you must make manually. Check your SCSI adapter documentation.

> **Note** The total length of the SCSI cables connecting devices, both internally and externally, and between devices, must not exceed three to six feet. It is possible to have a longer cable if it is a very good, shielded, and electrically sound cable, but not much longer.

Scanners

Scanners are a much more varied product category than most people would assume. They started out as handheld devices that could scan a picture, drawing, or part of a page of text to load into your computer for printing, editing, or sending as a fax. Later, we encountered page feed scanners that work something like a fax machine but, instead of sending the document over the phone line, the scanner displayed it on your computer screen for sizing, editing, saving to a file, or cutting and pasting into other applications. Today, flat-bed scanners add the capability to scan pages from a book without having to cut the page from the book.

Connections and standards

The ways scanning devices connect to your computer vary as widely as scanners' size and capabilities. Most of them are sold with an adapter card you plug into one of the Industry Standard Architecture (ISA), Extended ISA (EISA), Video Electronics Standards Association local bus (VL-bus), or Peripheral Component Interconnect (PCI) slots on your computer's motherboard or even into a PCMCIA card plugged into your portable. Some scanners may be connected to your computer's serial or parallel port, SCSI port, or into one of the newer serial device ports such as USB or FireWire. While this variety gives us a lot of flexibility in making the computer connection, it also adds complexity.

Generally, scanners that connect to the computer via a serial connection are slower than those that use the SCSI or parallel port, but this is not always the case. Scanners may or may not support the capability to scan color images. If a scanner supports color image scanning, it may be limited in the resolution or the number of colors it may scan. High-speed and high-resolution and higher-color-capable scanners may have very demanding requirements in terms of your computer's speed, accessible memory, hard disk space, and type of connection.

Some scanners may not work with a connection other than the adapter board that was provided by the scanner's manufacturer. Even if the scanner supports an industry standard such as SCSI, it still may work only with the provided adapter or may be limited to a specific manufacturer's SCSI device and maybe even a specific model. The small SCSI adapter cards distributed with scanners are sometimes able to support only a single device and require their own memory port address, IRQ, DMA channel, and possibly adapter BIOS address.

Tip   If you already have an SCSI card in your system and cannot connect your scanner to that card, make sure no conflicts occur between the system's two SCSI cards.

A lot of scanners and scanning software support an industry standard called TWAIN (Technology Without An Interesting Name) or ISIS (Image and Scanner Interface Specification). Most scanners come with driver support for TWAIN or ISIS, unless they use a newer type of driver specification that is very specific to a particular scanner and provides direct scanner support.

Tip   Not all scanner software is TWAIN- or ISIS-compatible. Make sure that the software you want to use is supported by the scanner you purchase.

Most PC scanners use either Charge-Coupled Device (CCD) or Contact Image Sensor (CIS) technology, which uses tightly packed rows of receptors that can detect variations in light intensity and frequency. CCD is usually found in larger scanners because it provides the major components of the scanner (lens and sensors) as separate parts, whereas CIS incorporates the major components in a single, compact package. CIS is easier to produce and maintain but is more expensive to produce. The price is higher because the testing of these integrated components has a larger number of rejected parts.

Note   The major difference between CCD and CIS is that CCD is better suited to scanning pages from a book because CIS requires the lens and sensors to be very close to the scanned image.

As the image is scanned, a bitmapped array is created that the computer can interpret to present onscreen or save to a file. Black-and-white images have a 1-bit resolution, which means that a spot on the page—called a *pixel*—is either black or white. For grayscale or color, more bits are required to define each spot onscreen or page in order to set the amount of gray or color of the spot. For instance, a 24-bit color scanner can represent 16.7 million colors (2 to the power of 24) for each pixel in the image. From a user's standpoint, this means that higher resolution color images require a *lot* more memory and disk space than black-and-white or grayscale images. Color resolutions as high as 36-bit and 128-bit for "true color" are available in demanding and expensive products.

In addition to color resolution for each pixel in the image, an additional measure of scanner quality is the overall image resolution, which is the number of pixels that are used within a defined region on the "screen" to capture and display the image. Old dot-matrix printers provided about 80 pixels (or dots) per inch. High-resolution fax is defined as 200 pixels per inch. Common laser printers support 300 to 600 pixels per inch. The standard Video Graphics Array (VGA) screen presents 640×480 pixels onscreen. High-resolution screens today provide as much as 1,600×1,280 and even more pixels onscreen. This means that a full-screen image with just 1-bit resolution (black-and-white) requires 2,048,000 bits to display onscreen or save in a file (256,000 characters or bytes) without compression. A very-high-resolution color image could require 260MB or more memory for display and saving, again without compression. Thank goodness for Joint Photographic Experts Group (JPEG), a graphic file standard that provides significant compression, Tagged Image File Format (TIFF), which also provides compression, and other graphic standards aimed at speeding the transmission of graphic images for the Internet and for displaying and storing images in files.

These fairly large memory and file size requirements can also provide challenges to your system when you are editing and printing. If your system does not have enough memory, processing will be slowed down by being forced to use virtual memory, meaning a lot of disk file swapping. Not enough disk space means that you cannot work with a particular image unless you reduce the resolution so the saved image will fit your disk space. Too little memory on your printer may mean that the image fails to print after a very long time of trying to squeeze the image into available printer memory. Page printers seem to want the whole image in their own memory before they start printing.

Optical character recognition

One exciting feature of scanners is the option to scan and convert printed text into real characters (discrete symbols and words) in files your application programs may use. This capability is called optical character recognition (OCR). An image scanned into your computer is just a picture, so text scanned into your computer is a picture of text. Converting that picture to real characters, understandable and usable by your computer programs, requires that each character be recognized by the program that reads the picture and performs the conversion.

Most OCR programs require the scanned image to conform to some simple standards. The most common requirement is that the text characters in the scanned image be 10-point, plain characters, meaning that they are not fancy characters with fancy serifs and other enhancements. The computer must build each character based on the pixels scanned from the picture of the text. Really high-priced hardware and software may have the ability to scan and convert text pictures into character-based text at better than 98 percent effectiveness. On a PC with reasonably priced hardware and software, you may be pleased with achieving 90 percent effective conversion. Remember that these results assume perfect alignment of the text with the scanner array, not something easily achieved.

Note You will have to contact the manufacturer or distributor of your scanner for direct support. The device drivers for scanners are updated frequently and are specific to the brand and model of your scanning device. The capabilities supported, connection to your computer, software supported, and software distributed with your scanner are all very specific to the model you purchase.

Before you buy a scanner

Before you purchase a scanner, you should do some research:

✦ Have a pretty good idea of what you want to accomplish with your scanner. Because so many scanners are available and each provides different capabilities (and prices), you should make sure you start out with one that will do what you need.

✦ Review the scanning and graphics software available as freeware, shareware, and commercially, so you know what kinds of features to expect. In addition to helping you determine the capabilities you will want in your scanner, knowing what features are available will help you decide whether the software distributed with your scanner will meet your needs.

✦ Check the World Wide Web for online support for the scanners you are evaluating. Check the manufacturers' sites to determine what kinds of troubles are being reported and, especially, what kind of help is being provided. Just because a lot of activity occurs does not mean the scanner has a lot of problems. People need help getting started and, with new capabilities being developed continuously, an active Web site can show that a scanner manufacturer is keeping its customers on the leading edge.

✦ After you have made your decisions about capabilities and features, and completed your software and support research, you are ready to make your economic and system decisions. Remember that you may have to upgrade your computer with more memory, hard disk space, or connector features for the scanner and capabilities you need. You do not want to waste your resources and time on a solution that will not do the whole job.

✦ You will also need complete documentation of the system in which you will install the scanner. If you know what IRQs, DMA channels, memory ports, and connector-specific information, such as SCSI IDs and USB bandwidth and power are already used, you will be better prepared to choose the right hardware and software to match your system. You will also have a better understanding of what other changes may be required so you do not end up causing new or unusual problems in your system.

If you already have a scanner and some problems, the following will help you cure the problem or at least prepare to contact customer support for your specific hardware and software.

Symptoms

▶ The scanner software cannot find a scanner attached to the computer.

Suspects

▶ The hardware connection of your scanner to your computer is not correct or conflicts with another I/O device in your system.

Solutions

▶ Make sure your scanner is connected to your computer using the cable provided by the manufacturer or one that meets the manufacturer's specifications. Also make sure that the connections are good and tight. The length of the cable is very important. Most scanner cables are three to five feet long and should not be much longer even with special shielding and other signal enhancement capabilities. A cable that is too long may lose data and produce poor images. If the cable is not properly connected, your system will not be able to "see" the scanner or produce good images.

▶ If your scanner connects via a parallel port in your system, the parallel port may not be configured correctly—the possibilities include extended capabilities port (ECP), enhanced parallel port (EPP), bidirectional, or standard settings. Because each manufacturer and scanner model may be designed differently, you will have to refer to the documentation for your particular scanner to determine the correct parallel port configuration. The parallel port configuration may be corrected in your CMOS setup or in the hardware or driver settings if your parallel port is on an add-in adapter card.

✦ If your scanner connects via an SCSI port, check your scanner documentation to make sure it is able to use the particular SCSI adapter in your system. The brand, model, and driver version are very important. If the scanner supports a connection to your SCSI adapter, make sure you've used an available SCSI ID for the device ID setting and, if required, check to see that you've set the termination properly. If your SCSI scanner will only work with the SCSI card distributed with the scanner, make sure you have not created a conflict with another device over IRQ, DMA, memory port address, or adapter BIOS. You will discover the conflict when you run into another device on your PC that is not working right, even though it did just a while ago. If you want to avoid this conflict or at least narrow down the list of possible candidates, follow the recommendation to document your PCs in Chapter 23.

✦ If your scanner connects via a standard serial port, make sure that you have not used an IRQ or memory port address that conflicts with other devices or serial ports in your system. Again, if something else on your computer starts acting strange after you install a new serial port (or any other device that uses IRQs), you should suspect a hardware conflict.

✦ If your scanner connects via a USB bus, make sure your USB port is implemented and enabled correctly in your system and conforms to the real USB standard. If you have other USB devices attached, make sure you have sufficient bandwidth remaining to support your scanner. If your scanner requires power from the USB port, make sure you have sufficient power remaining or that you plug the scanner into a powered USB hub that conforms to the real USB standard.

✦ The final alternative for connecting your scanner to your computer is via the proprietary or non-SCSI adapter board provided with your scanner. Its installation, configuration, and use must be documented and supported by the manufacturer of your scanner. It may be faster or slower than the other possible ways to connect to your computer but, depending on the manufacturer, it may be the only supported or guaranteed way to connect your particular scanner. Again, this is another important reason to check on the amount of support provided by the scanner manufacturer before making your purchase.

Symptoms

▶ The scanner seems to be connected and the software will scan but does not produce a usable image.

Suspects

▶ The software connection or configuration of your scanner is not correct.

Solutions

▶ If your scanner uses the TWAIN driver, deinstall the driver and reinstall it or get an updated driver from the manufacturer. If the updated driver and reinstallation does not solve the problem, and you have eliminated the hardware connection problems identified previously, contact the manufacturer.

▶ If your scanner uses the ISIS driver, deinstall the driver and reinstall it or get an updated ISIS driver from the manufacturer. If the updated driver and reinstallation does not solve the problem, and you have eliminated the hardware connection problems identified previously, contact the manufacturer.

▶ If your scanner uses a direct driver, only the manufacturer of your scanner can provide support. Direct drivers provide much more specific scanner capabilities but are so different from one manufacturer to another, and even from one model to another, that the manufacturer is the only reasonable source for updates and help with specific problems.

Summary

This basic set of input and output devices for your PC is just a subset of the myriad devices you may encounter. We cover more in the chapters dealing with serial communication, disk drives, sight and sounds, and more. The fact is, most devices used with your PC will be there for the purpose of getting information into or out of your computer.

In this chapter we have covered:

✦ Printers and common printing problems

✦ Pointing device problems

✦ Keyboards

✦ Small Computer System Interface (SCSI)

✦ Scanners

In Chapter 22 we will spend more time on modems than anything else, but you will find that your serial port is quite flexible and may be used for many purposes.

✦   ✦   ✦

Serial Input and Output

Among the most versatile components of your PC is the serial communication port, called a COM port. You may use this port to connect your PC to other computers, modems, printers, plotters, lab equipment, manufacturing control devices, a mouse or other pointing device, home control and security devices, networks, and other I/O devices.

A serial port is used to connect to peripheral devices using a bit stream protocol. The term *serial port* refers to the actual physical hardware device that provides the interface between the PC's data bus and the device you use to connect to the world outside of your PC. The term *COM port* is the logical device name that software programs use to refer to the attached device.

In general, if a serial port is installed and configured correctly, you should not expect to have problems with a mouse, serial printer, or other serial device. If a problem does exist, and it is not due to an improperly installed or configured COM port, then the connections are so straight forward about all you can do is check the connections and make sure they are correct and connected completely. The use of multiple COM port devices, and modems in particular, are where most COM port problems occur. As a matter of fact, because modems are, by far, the most common serial communication problem, we might be tempted to call this chapter Modem Communications.

Because they are used with so many different devices, serial connections may be daunting. It is necessary to to deal with items such as the COM Port Base Memory Address (Port Address), Interrupt Request Line (IRQ), RS-232 (Electronic Industry Association standard for serial connections) wires and connectors, and the communication port's modem and software parameters. You may see these configuration parameters referenced in your PC's setup program, the port's documentation about switch or jumper settings, and in your communications software. Knowledge of these helps you to connect your computer to serial devices and get work done. Because modems use all of these parameters and are the source of most reported problems, we concentrate on using serial ports and modems.

Route: Your Personal Connection to the Information Age

It is no secret that the most common reason for using a modem is to get connected to the Internet. In Chapter 11, we addressed the Internet and discussed that modems are only one of many ways to get connected. Here, we are going to take care of the kinds of problems you might encounter while attempting to get your modem working correctly.

Connecting computers to other computers, and networks to other networks, is the primary purpose of the Internet. We have been connecting to various pieces of it for years (ARPANET, USENET, CompuServe, GOPHER, ARCHIE, and many more). Serial communication and modems have given millions of people and businesses access to information and capabilities outside of their own computers. Serial communications programs, serial ports, modems, local bulletin boards, and online services are the building blocks of the Internet.

The Information Superhighway has developed capabilities that go beyond the reach of modems. The connection speeds, the amount of information available, the number of people connected, and our own expectations may make it frustrating to continue using standard modems on the Web. The ways to connect are constantly changing and updating. Aside from modems, we now have the ability to connect to the Internet via our own networks, which may be connected to the Internet through DSL lines or very high speed modems, switches, or routers, attached to the same cables as our cable TV service.

 For more information on networks and DSL, see Chapter 10.

As noted in Chapter 4, the serial port or ports might be located on your system's motherboard or on adapter cards, and provide a 9-pin or 25-pin D-Shell connector, usually on the back of your PC. Some internal modems use a serial communication port address. Alternatively, they also provide a 9-pin or 25-pin connection that you may use to connect to another serial device, but they use a COM port address and may be the source of a hardware conflict.

Serial ports are quite versatile but, because of that, have several different physical presentations, and involve many complex parameters. The serial port hardware might provide either switches or jumpers for setting the COM port number, base address, or interrupt request line (IRQ), *or* it might rely on the ROM

BIOS or operating system to assign the proper port address (see Chapter 4). Serial ports are built into today's system boards. The plug-in serial port board is very rare today but, if you need one, they are still available. Some serial adapter cards provide chip sockets and cable connector blocks that might be empty. Each device you may attach to a COM port requires the use of specific communication parameters that identify the speed (bps rate) and character format (character bits, parity bit, and stop bits). These differences and options provide the major challenges to getting a serial connection working in your system.

COM Port Assignment and Selection

Each serial port useseight bytes of the PC's memory and a specific hardware interrupt. A hardware interrupt is an IRQ (Interrupt Request Line) provided by the CPU. These are translated into software interrupts that the operating system may pass on to programs to be used in their work with the serial port. These memory addresses and the hardware interrupt are important to programmers of communication programs and serial device drivers. However, they are also important to users, because they must be set correctly on the serial port hardware and in the communication program or device driver for your serial hardware.

Table 22-1 shows the memory addresses and hardware interrupts for the four standard serial (COM) ports for PC-compatible computers. The most important items here are the base address, which is the first memory address in each COM port column, (Transmit/Receive Buffer) and the interrupt request number (IRQ) for each of the ports.

Table 22-1 Standard COM Port Addresses and Interrupts				
COM1	COM2	COM3	COM4	Description
IRQ4	IRQ3	IRQ4	IRQ3	Interrupt Request Line
3F8	2F8	3E8	2E8	Transmit/Receive Buffer and LSB of the Divisor Latch
3F9	2F9	3E9	2E9	Interrupt Enable Register and MSB of the Divisor Latch
3FA	2FA	3EA	2EA	Interrupt Identification Registers
3FB	2FB	3EB	2EB	Line Control Register
3FC	2FC	3EC	2EC	Modem Control Register
3FD	2FD	3ED	2ED	Line Status Register
3FE	2FE	3EE	2EE	Modem Status Register

Some programs require information directly from this table in order to access a COM port. Likewise, some of the hardware needs to be set to use these parameters either through switches, jumpers, or software setup programs.

Tip   Only one serial device may use each COM port address. Besides improper settings, this restriction is one of the most frequent causes of problems with serial devices. This issue is covered further in the Symptoms, Suspects, and Solutions sections of this chapter.

COM port holes

Some versions of DOS and particular PCs do not tolerate having a "hole" in the COM port assignments. What this means, for instance, is that you cannot have a COM3 unless you already have a COM1 port and a COM2 port installed. Because so many different combinations of brands of PC compatibles and versions of DOS exist, the best policy is to install COM ports starting with COM1 and continuing in sequence with COM port assignments. Using COM ports is a different matter. You may choose which COM port is the most appropriate for the connected device. You do not need to use COM ports in sequence — just install them that way.

Adding a new COM port

If you install an internal modem in your PC (or any other device that uses the serial port structure for its interface), make sure that you set it to a COM port (base address and IRQ number) that is not already being used. For instance, if COM1 and COM2 ports are installed in your PC, even if they are not being used, they do exist, and you *must* set the internal modem's port address to COM3 (in this case).

If COM3 is already installed, the new device must be set to COM4. Even if a serial connector is not attached to a port (the UAR/T and supporting chips on the serial adapter interface) that is installed, it conflicts with another serial device installed using the same COM port number (base address and IRQ number).

Cross-Reference   See Chapter 5 for more information about how the device assignment process works.

Notice that COM1 and COM3 use the same IRQ (IRQ4) and that COM2 and COM4 use the same IRQ (IRQ3). It is a rule-of-thumb that you should not try to simultaneously use devices that occupy the same IRQ assignment. However, some programs or systems do claim to be able to separate one port's IRQ activity from another, so that, for instance, your mouse activity on COM1 does not interfere with your modem activity on COM3 even if they are using the same IRQ4. The only way this can be guaranteed or tested is by trying it in your system.

With this in mind, we normally put our serial pointing device on COM1/IRQ4 and our modem on COM2/IRQ3, and leave COM3 and COM4 for use by other devices that we may not be likely to use at the same time as our mouse or our modem.

Following these suggestions may prevent further problems and save you hours of frustration.

See the following Serial Port Problems section if you suspect problems with conflicting ports and IRQs.

COM Port Parameters

The COM ports on computers are devices that transmit one character at a time. For that reason, we need to start with the definition of a character on the PC and for computers and information systems in general.

The American Standard Code for Information Interchange (ASCII) defines the first 128 characters used in most personal computers. Computers store each ASCII character in a single byte of memory. Each byte is composed of eight bits, and each bit is like a switch that can be turned on or off. Bit status is referred to as being a one or zero for the on or off state. The 256 characters that can be represented by the eight bits in each byte are shown in the ASCII chart, Appendix C. This chart is specific to the IBM PC and compatible computers, because the ASCII standard defines 128 characters using just seven bits for each character. The additional 128 characters (to achieve the full 256 character set) are defined by the computer manufacturer or the programmer who develops a special screen font.

The ASCII Chart in Appendix C is much more than just the characters you can see onscreen, print on your printer, and transmit over the communication lines. It also contains characters defined for the antiquated punch cards as well as the EBCDIC codes used by large mainframe computers. While not a complete guide to every possible definition and use of the codes transmitted between computers, it is certainly one of the most comprehensive for use with PCs.

The 128 characters beyond those defined by the ASCII code and some language characters represented in computers using multiple bytes, such as Chinese characters, are another source of problems when connecting computers and other devices. Those who have engaged International connections via modem may have first-hand experience with these differences.

Communication parameters define the manner in which characters are packaged, to be sent to the other end of the serial connection. The parameters include the bps rate (speed of the connection usually described in bits per second). The newest transmission protocols include compression, error correction, and other options that do not relate directly to the phone line itself nor do they relate directly to the actual characters in the source of the data being sent. Also, the interpretation of the bits, the compression protocol, is transmitted between the two ends of the serial connection.

Note   The term *baud rate* is no longer accurate, because it is in reference to the phone line signal and not the data bit speed. The data bit speed is no longer tied directly to the speed of the phone signal itself.

When the PC sends a character to the serial port for transmission to the other end, the program that communicates with the COM port has already used the communication parameters to set the port so that it properly "packages" the character. For asynchronous serial communication (characters are sent whenever they are ready rather than being packaged in time-framed, synchronous packages), each package is 10 bits. The package begins with a start bit that informs the device on the other end that a character follows. The remaining bits are allocated to the character (seven or eight bits), with or without a parity bit, and the stop bit or bits. The speed is determined by the amount of time that a bit is turned on or off in the serial pipeline.

Common bits-per-second rates include 300, 1200, 2400, 4800, 9600, 14400, 19200, 28800, 38400, 57600, 115200, and 230400. Because these are bits per second and each character is sent in a 10-bit package, the speeds in characters per second are 30, 120, 240, 480, 960, 1400, 1920, 2880, 3840, 5760, 11520, and 23040, respectively. Current serial devices may use any or all of these settings.

56K modems are now common, and with data compression, are able to connect your PC to other systems at speeds over 57,600 bps. The V.90 standard for modems has been approved and enables modems to communicate with your PC at speeds up to 115,200 bps. Serial printers commonly use 9,600 bps. FAX programs and devices use 4,800, 9,600, 14,400, or even 28,800 bps. The bps setting you must use for your serial communication is determined by the device to which you are connecting. The settings you use must match the capabilities of the device you connect to your computer.

The most common asynchronous character package is 1 start bit, no parity bit, 8 data bits, and 1 stop bit. This uses all 10 bits of the character package and may be used to represent all 256 of the possible characters in the extended ASCII character set used in the IBM PC and compatible computers. Some serial devices or services to which you connect can only accept 7-bit characters (the standard ASCII character set) for compatibility with a larger community of computers and devices. The extra bit becomes a parity bit, which is the result of a bit-wise calculation of the other seven bits in the character.

The possible parity settings are None (used with 8-bit characters), Even, Odd, Mark, and Space. These last four parity settings are only used with 7-bit characters. The Even parity setting means that the parity bit is either a one or a zero to make it so that an even number of bits is turned on in the character, including the parity bit. Odd means that an odd number of bits is turned on. Mark means that the parity bit is always turned on. Space means that the parity bit is always turned off.

Tip   Just as for the bps setting, the character package must match the settings used for the device or service to which you are connecting.

Using DOS MODE

The DOS MODE command is often used to set up a COM port to be used with a serial printer. In this case, an additional communication parameter exists that is unique to the IBM PC and compatible computers. The last parameter on the DOS MODE command line should be ,P. It has nothing to do with the serial connection — it tells DOS that this serial port is being used by a printer and the amount of time it should wait for a response from the printer is much longer than it would be for other serial devices. In fact, with DOS 5.0 and later, the P parameter tells DOS to continue trying to print until the printer responds. DOS 5 and later can use other parameters, including the number of columns per line and the number of lines per inch; additionally DOS 5 has expanded the retry options to include:

✦ **E**—Return an error from a status check of a busy port.

✦ **B**—Return "busy" from a status check of a busy port (old P setting).

✦ **P**—Continue to retry until the printer accepts the output.

✦ **R**—Return "ready" from the status check of a busy port (the default).

✦ **N**—Take no retry action.

Using the DOS MODE command to set up your system for a serial printer requires two commands. For example, say your serial printer is attached to COM2 and you want DOS to redirect any printing that would normally go to the parallel port (LPT1, the DOS default printer). You would first use the MODE command to set up the serial port and again, to redirect the printer port to that COM port. The commands in your AUTOEXEC.BAT file would be:

```
MODE COM2:9600,N,8,1,P
MODE LPT1:=COM2:
```

Without these additional parameters for the DOS MODE command, DOS has no way of knowing that it has a printer on the other end of the serial connection that requires some special support actions.

Note   Windows requires no special commands when a serial port is used for printing. It takes care of the port connection and printer interaction itself.

Improper communication parameters

As we've pointed out, the COM parameters are dictated by the device or system to which you are connecting. If you cannot change the parameters on the other end, you must match the bps rate, parity type, character bits, and stop bits in the settings for your PC's hardware and software. If you can change the parameters used by the other end, you should choose the fastest bps rate that can be handled by every piece of equipment involved in the process, from your end to the other. You should also choose No Parity andeight Data bits because that enables you to use the full 256-character, extended ASCII character set.

Figure 22-1 shows the Control Panel under Windows NT 4.0. It is being used to set
the serial port named COM3 at 57.6 Kbps, and to useeight Data bits, No Parity, one
Stop bit, Hardware Flow Control, with 3E8 Hex as the Base I/O Port Address, and
IRQ 12 as the Interrupt Request Line. It also has FIFO enabled because this is a
port that has an NS16550 high speed UART (the Universal Asynchronous Receive/
Transmit chip).

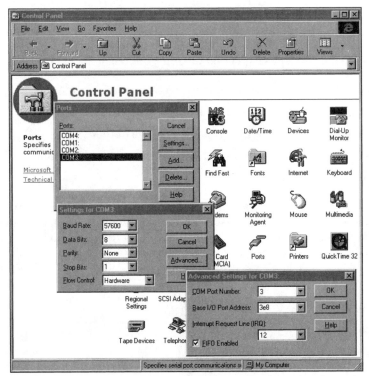

Figure 22-1: Setting COM port parameters using the Control Panel
under Windows NT 4.0

In the Windows 95/98/Me Control Panel, you select the System icon in the Control
Panel, select the Device Manager tab, and then select the Ports (COM and LPT) to
make changes to a particular port. Under Windows 3.*x* the COM Ports icon is in the
Control window, usually found in the Main window in the Program Manager. Under
DOS, COM port settings are usually made in the program that uses the COM port.
All of these must be set to match or use the hardware settings on the hardware
device providing the COM port.

Symptoms

▶ The right number of characters are transmitted or received but they look funny, wrap around the screen, and may even clear the screen.

▶ Too few or too many characters may be transmitted or received, in comparison to expectations, with lots of repeating characters of the same type or series of groups of similar characters.

▶ Connection to the device or system on the other end cannot be maintained or may not be completed at all.

Suspects

▶ Improper communication parameters.

▶ The DOS MODE command or the settings in your communication program, serial device driver, or Control Panel are set to a speed that the device you are using cannot accept.

▶ The information service or BBS to which you are connecting via modem states that a particular parity and data bit setting is required, but your communication software is set differently.

Solutions

▶ Change your communication parameters to match those required by the device or service to which you are connecting.

▶ Make sure your computer system has the capabilities to use the required communication parameter settings. If not, you may need to change the communication hardware device or settings.

If the device you are using is a serial printer and you are using the DOS MODE command to set up your serial port, remember to check the P parameter for versions of DOS prior to DOS 5.0 and the "cols" (columns), lines, and retry parameters for DOS 5 and later.

Newer modems enable the use of hardware flow control between your computer and the modem so that you can use a higher and constant speed setting. These modems adjust to the bps rate of the system you are calling, but do not require your computer to change the speed it uses to communicate with the modem. This is a real convenience, but it requires the communication software you are using to be able to use hardware flow control settings. Newer communication program software is able to support this setting.

Even though the vast majority of modem users today are connecting to the Internet, many reasons still exist to use direct modem-to-modem connections. For example, you might want to connect your home computer to a system at the office that has access to your company's network.. In these cases you still need to know how to configure and make the best use of your modem. Products such as pcANYWHERE 32, that work with all 32-bit Windows platforms, are quite useful.

Serial Port Problems

Before you install a serial device, you need to know what serial ports are already in your system in order to avoid using a COM port assignment that is already installed. This leads to our first serial problem.

One good indicator that you have COM ports is the existence of 9-pin or 25-pin D-Shell connectors, usually on the back of your PC. A cable may be connected to one or more of these ports leading to a serial printer, external modem, graphics plotter, voice synthesizer, or other device. However, even if no connectors exist, there might be a Universal Asynchronous Receive-Transmit (UART) chip on your motherboard or an adapter card that uses one or more of the COM port memory structures and hardware interrupts inside your system unit case. The numbers on the UART chip might include 8250, 82C50, 16450, 16550, or other numbers. No standard applies to stock or part numbers for chips.

One example of an adapter card that provides a serial port device structure is an internal modem that has a telephone jack on the back. The only sure way to determine what COM ports already exist is to run a program that can detect their presence and display information about them. ModemButler and ModemDiag are shareware programs that provide this capability. Some communication programs include scripts that detect and test your COM ports and tell you what type of UART is installed. One reason you may want to know for sure what type of UART is installed in your system is if you are trying to solve high-speed communication problems.

Windows 9x/Me and NT/2000 provide a good deal of information about the existence of serial ports and their settings.

For Windows 9x/Me the Control Panel//System Icon//Device Manager list shows you Communication Ports that Windows has found in your system. If the port plug icon is covered by an exclamation point in a yellow circle, the port has a problem. If it is covered by an X inside of a red circle, the port has been disabled. If the port is disabled, it should not interfere with another serial device using the same parameters. If the port has a problem (the exclamation point on the yellow circle) then the communication port parameters are wrong, unavailable, or are in conflict with another device.

Figure 22-1, shown previously, displays the manner of determining which COM ports are identified in a particular profile in Windows NT, through the process of selecting a port for setting the port's parameters. The Windows NT Diagnostics program, usually found in the Administrative Tools on the Programs menu, uses information generated from the Windows NT Registry to display IRQ's, DMA's, Port Addresses, and other resources associated with all of the devices in your system and recognized by Windows NT. Microsoft recommends that we use this as advisory information. It is quite comprehensive and may be just as helpful as buying a non-Microsoft diagnostic program to give you independent information and verification of port parameters.

Symptoms

▶ You are not sure you have serial (COM) ports installed in your PC.

▶ You need to install or attach to a serial device.

▶ You've already installed an internal modem or serial port adapter and it does not work.

Suspects

▶ An unknown or unused serial device in your computer.

Solutions

▶ If you already installed the new COM port (or internal modem) and it does not work, remove it before continuing.

▶ Record the current, working configuration parameters for each of your COM ports and serial devices. You use this information to help you determine the proper choices for additional ports and devices.

▶ If your information gathering discovered COM port problems, resolve the problems before you continue with installation of new hardware or configuration for additional serial devices.

▶ Under Windows, use the appropriate selections from the Control Panel (identified previously) or the Windows NT Diagnostics program under Windows NT/2000 to get information about your installed COM ports and devices.

▶ Following are the steps to use under DOS to install a new COM port. The same basic steps and information are involved to install a new COM port under Windows. You just get the information about your COM ports and serial devices from different places, as presented previously:

- Check your installation or setup programs for any serial devices already installed in your PC to determine which COM port each uses. This information might also be located in your CONFIG.SYS or AUTOEXEC.BAT files with specific reference to a port number. (Refer to Windows NT/2000 Diagnostics for Windows NT or the Device Manager in the System Icon of the Control Panel under Windows 9x/Me)

- Check the documentation for your PC to see if it has a serial mouse, a serial printer, or instructions to connect a modem or other serial device. This is only an indication that one or more COM ports may exist in your system.

- Check the back of your PC for the existence of 9-pin or 25-pin D-Shell connectors whether or not connected to another device. Also check for modular telephone connectors such as those used to plug your telephone into the wall.

- Run a serial or modem diagnostic program such as ModemDiag, Modem Butler, or the COM-AND communication program MDMDIAG and UARTTYPE scripts. These programs tell you what COM ports are in your system but do not work under Windows NT/2000 and may not give good information under Windows 9x/Me except in DOS mode.

These programs provide the only sure means of determining whether the UART has the 16550 FIFO buffering required by some high-speed, serial applications. These programs might not tell you which ports are already in use unless the connected device can respond to the modem type commands that these programs issue to the COM ports while they are being tested. Store the information you collect from this step so that you have a permanent record of what is in your system.

• Install your new serial device using a COM port that is not already in use. If the device is an internal modem or other type of adapter that also provides a new COM port, make sure that you set the jumpers and switches on the board so that it does not use a COM port number (base address) or interrupt that is already being used. Also, make sure that you do not leave a COM port hole by using a COM port assignment that skips over an unused COM port number. Some System BIOS do not work correctly with a set of COM ports that are not in sequence and use every COM port number from beginning to end. Refer to the tables at the beginning of this section to determine the proper settings for each COM port.

COM Port conflicts

The next set of problems you may encounter involves conflicts between COM ports in your system. If two or more COM ports in your system use the same COM port number (base address) and sometimes if they use the same interrupt number (IRQ), they produce erratic results.

Symptoms

▶ The modem dials out, but nothing else happens.

▶ The serial printer does not print or prints only pieces of what is expected.

▶ Your mouse gets lost or causes your cursor to move around the screen as your system locks up.

▶ Your voice synthesizer speaks with a garbled or unintelligible voice.

▶ Someone calls your computer's modem and gets connected to the modem, but your computer (communication program) does not respond or know that a connection exists.

Suspects

▶ Two or more COM ports in your system use the same COM port number (base address), and perhaps the same interrupt number.

▶ The IRQ for your COM port is used by another device.

Solutions

▶ Find the COM port assignments that conflict. This can be tricky, but you should start with the procedure to determine what COM ports exist in your system, detailed earlier.

▶ Under Windows 9x/Me just open the Control Panel, and then the System icon, select the Ports listing, and check for the yellow exclamation mark that indicates a port that is not working. Viewing the port's properties gives you the information you need to determine the exact conflict.

▶ Under Windows NT/2000, the Diagnostic program on the Administrative Tools menu provide the port conflict information and settings.

You already know one of the COM port numbers that could be conflicting from its assignment to the device that reported the error.

If you have trouble finding another serial port causing the conflict, keep in mind that there might be an adapter card in your system that has a UART chip but no cable connector attached. If you cannot remove that adapter card because it contains other devices your computer is using, try to remove the UART chip. If the chip is soldered in rather that plugged into a socket, you might not be able to remove it. However, there might be jumper or switch settings on the card that enable you to disable the UART chip or assign it to another unused COM port address.

Change the COM port assignment (hardware settings) for either one of the COM ports that is in conflict. The decision of which COM port to change depends on which COM port gives you the ability to make the change or which one has options that support the setting to which you want to make the change. Some older hardware and software enable you to choose only COM1 or COM2. This was the original specification for the IBM PC. Newer hardware and software usually allow you to choose between COM1, COM2, COM3, and COM4. Windows 9x/Me goes up to COM8. Windows NT/2000 supports up to 255 COM ports.

You must make sure that both your hardware and software can use the settings you choose. For instance, if you already have an older serial port adapter that has COM1 and COM2 ports, you may have to choose COM3 for your new internal modem. However, that requires that the communication program you use with the modem has the ability to use the COM3 port. Multi-port serial adapters (4 to 32 and more ports per adapter) and specialty software for configuring and using more COM ports than the "normal" standard four ports are quite varied, depending on the manufacturer and operating system supported, and are beyond the scope of this book. However, some of the same settings and data values apply with the exception that most multi-port adapters are designed to use just one IRQ per adapter no matter how many ports are being controlled.

If your computer is already using COM1 and COM2, there might be a conflict over the interrupt used. In Table 22-2, COM1 and COM3 both use IRQ4 as the default Interrupt. Also, COM2 and COM4 share the use of IRQ3. This should not be a problem if the software you are using performs these actions:

✦ uses that IRQ

✦ determines if it can do something

✦ passes on the IRQ to the next program in the "interrupt chain."

Table 22-2
Hardware Interrupts — Interrupt Request Lines.

IRQ Number/ Software Interrupt	Standard Use or Usual Use	Comment
0 08h	System Timer	18.5 clicks per second Not available
1 09h	Keyboard	System use only Not available
2 0Ah	Reserved / Multi-use	Sometimes available
3 0Bh	COM2 / COM4 / SDLC	May be available
4 0Ch	COM1 / COM3 / SDLC	May be available
5 0Dh	XT-Hard Disk / AT-LPT2 / Sound Card	May be available
6 0Eh	Floppy disk / Some Tape Drives	Not usually available
7 0Fh	Parallel Port (LPT 1)	Usually available
8 70h	Real-Time Clock	Not available
9 71h	IRQ2 re-direct	Not usually available
10 72h	None	Usually available
11 73h	None	Usually available.
12 74h	PS/2-Mouse	Available except PS/2
13 75h	Math Co-processor	Available if no Co-processor
14 76h	AT-Hard Disk	May be available
15 77h	None	Usually available

Use the information in the previous table to start your search for an available IRQ or software interrupt, to use for resolving the conflict you have encountered. Remember that other devices you or someone else has installed in your computer may be using some of the IRQs that are identified as "Usually available."

If your software does not support the use of a single IRQ by multiple programs, the only way to cure the interrupt conflict problem is to switch one of the COM ports to use another interrupt. By the way, most communication programs and drivers do not have this capability. It is generally available only when using specially designed hardware and software.

Choosing another interrupt requires that you know which interrupts are in use by other devices. Older PCs (those using the 8088 or 8086 CPU chips) have eight hardware interrupts (zero through seven), most of which are already in use (see Table 22-2). Interrupts two, five, and seven might be available due to differences in your system from the standard. For instance, most parallel printer ports do not use IRQ7, few hard disks actually use IRQ5, and IRQ2 is quite often shared between many programs and devices such as multi-tasking systems.

The 80286, 80386, 80486, and Pentium add eight more hardware interrupts (8 through 15) most of which are often available. The standard uses for these interrupts are shown in Table 22-2. Do not confuse these hardware interrupts with software interrupts having the same numbers. Software interrupts are generated within programs and DOS and used as signals for particular activities to be performed. Hardware interrupts are generated in the CPU and indicate that some hardware action has occurred.

16 hardware interrupts now exist. They duplicate the numbers for the first 16 software interrupts. They are not related except that some software interrupts are allocated for monitoring the hardware interrupts, and these are not the same interrupt numbers as their hardware counterparts. To help with the confusion over hardware interrupt numbers and software interrupt numbers, the software interrupts used in conjunction with the hardware interrupts are provided in the first column of Table 22-2.

Some programs may help you identify which interrupts are already in use, such as Watergate Software's PC Doctor, Quarterdeck's Manifest, and Microsoft's Control Panel features in Windows 9x/Me and the Windows NT Diagnostics program in Windows NT/2000. Generally, the program that is using the interrupt must be running at the time you run the program that determines the owner of the interrupt. As shown in Table 22-2, software interrupts 08 through 0F (Hexidecimal) relate to hardware interrupts zero through seven and software interrupts 70 through 77 (in Hexidecimal) relate to hardware interrupts 8 through 15. The Manifest program shows the current owner of each software interrupt. Windows NT Diagnostics displays information from the Windows NT Registry.

Cross-Reference

See Chapter 4 for instructions on how to open your system unit and pull the appropriate boards for checking the hardware assignments of COM ports and interrupts.

Modem Initialization and Flow Control

Modems are generally connected to a COM port on your system. When properly installed and configured, your modem allows you to use a telephone line to connect to other computers, other networks, and the World Wide Web. To take advantage of these features you must initialize your modem. This initialization process is performed by the communication program you are using, or by the Windows Phone and Modem panels in the Control Panel.

Most communication programs have a setup section where you specify items such as the type of modem connected to your system; the commands to send it when you first start the program; the commands to use to dial a number, hang up the phone, and reinitialize the modem after a call; the manner in which the modem or the communication program determines the speed of connection (bps rate); and so forth. The number and types of parameters and variables involved in this process can scare away the most stalwart individual. However, Windows x95/98/Me and NT/2000, along with a new modem, pretty much avoid this issue. Unless you run into problems, installation of a new modem under the newest versions of Windows is really a simple task.

Note Most modems use a command set generally referred to as Hayes compatible or the "AT command set" which is a de facto industry standard. Hayes is the company that first cornered the modem market for PCs. The AT stands for Attention!

Communication programs usually provide modem initialization strings (the commands required to get your modem ready to do its job) for the most common modems. Generally, the process of installing your communication program includes selecting your modem or a general-purpose initialization from a list. Some modems are delivered with a simple communication program, in the box, that is usually set up for that modem. See Figure 22-2 for an example of a vintage communications program setup screen in which the modem initialization string (and a lot of other program parameters) are set. In this example, COM-AND's setup screen shows a complex modem initialization string that is described using fly-out boxes. The rest of the screen shows other settings dealing with modem commands, control files, mouse, and other program settings. COM-AND is one of many communication programs that work with DOS and Windows, and under Windows 95/98/Me in a DOS window.

To optimize your modem you need to change the modem initialization string so that it does exactly what you want. You need to read some of the documentation related to the modem and communication program. You may also call a person who has the same hardware and software you use, such as a friend, business associate, user group "help" person, or the technical support people for the modem or communication program you are using to get the job done.

Note Once you get the modem initialization string and other modem settings correct, you most likely never have to deal with them again.

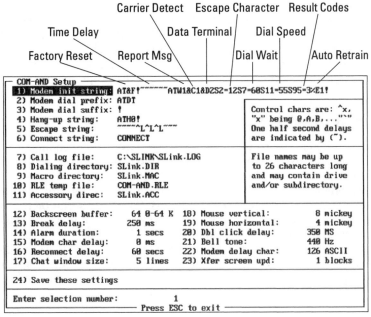

Figure 22-2: The COM-AND communication program's setup screen

Modem Initialization Strings

Modem manufacturers have a big job on their hands. They want to sell modems that are simple for any user to understand. However, this usually causes them to make the factory settings address the lowest common denominator. This means that no one gets the best performance from a modem if they use only the factory settings. Fortunately, because the majority of new modems are being used to connect to the Internet via one of the newer versions of Windows, the modems found on the Windows compatibility lists install and configure correctly.

Older and less capable communication programs and modems ignored a lot of the capabilities provided by the RS-232 signals. Some older programs cannot use a modem that is set to have its signals manipulated by the communication program. For instance, some older versions of BitCom (a program distributed with a lot of modems several years ago) suffer from this kind of problem. Also, some older modems and communication programs have the Data Terminal Ready (DTR) and Carrier Detect (CD) signals set to ON all the time. Newer communication programs expect these signals to be variable so that both the modem and the communication program know when they are connected to each other and to a system on the other end.

The following list of possible symptoms gives you a starting point for dealing with problems reported by your modem and communication program. Your modem may have many more or fewer settings than those listed here. We've included some fairly standard modem commands, but so many modems have provided variations and augmentations for these that you need to check the manual provided with your modem to determine the exact command to use to get the proper response.

Modem initialization problems

Because so many different interpretations of the standard modem commands and settings exist, as well as some differences in terminology used by the modem manufacturers and distributors, the following "Symptoms" section includes information about possible modem or communication program settings, along with suggestions on what may be the cause of many of the symptoms. Use the description to find the proper modem setting panel or menu in Windows or your communication program to make the changes. For older programs and operating systems, use the specific modem command letters for clues to find the settings for your particular modem in its documentation and the documentation of your communications program.

Symptoms

▶ Your communication program and modem are not working together.

▶ The communication program never knows when the modem is connected to the other end. (Modem CD control or communication program connect message setting. Check modem &C command.)

▶ You cannot make the modem hang up the phone or, if the phone is hung up, the program thinks it is still connected. (Modem CD control and DTR control or communication program hang-up string. Check modem &C and &D commands.)

▶ The speaker is too loud or too quiet. (Modem Speaker control and volume settings. Check modem L and M commands.)

▶ The communication program cannot communicate with your modem. You see numbers printed on your screen when the modem connects, resets, or hangs up, but the communication program does not realize the change in status. (Modem use of numeric or verbal command responses coupled with your communication program settings for the expected responses from your modem. Check modem V and W commands).

▶ The communication program cannot connect with your modem. You see commands such as CONNECT, RING, and NO CARRIER printed on your screen but the communication program does not realize the change in status. (Modem use of numeric or verbal command responses and the corresponding settings in your communication program. Check modem V command setting.)

▶ You expect your modem to make an error correcting connection (for example, MNP or V.42bis), but this does not happen. (Modem error correction protocol settings. Check modem &Q or \L or \O or other commands dealing with error correction.)

▶ Your modem does not dial, even when you know the communication parameters (COM port assignment, bps rate, parity, data bits, stop bit, and so forth) are all set correctly. (Dial command string in your communication program, usually ATD or ATDT coupled with a dialing command suffix that is usually a carriage return represented by a symbol such as ! or ^ or |.)

▶ Your modem does not answer the phone when you think it is supposed to. (Modem answer command and number of rings settings. Check the modem S0 (zero) register setting and/or an A command to answer the phone.)

▶ Your modem answers the phone when you think it should not. (Modem answer command and number of rings settings. Check the modem S0 (zero) register setting and/or an A command setting.)

▶ Your modem is supposed use pulse dialing, but it is not. (Modem dial mode command. Check for T or P command in your modem initialization string.)

▶ Your modem takes a long time to dial a number. The dialing tones are long and there seems to be a long delay between dialing tones. (Modem dial tone register setting. Check your modem S11 register setting.)

▶ Your modem dials so quickly that the phone cannot respond. (Modem dial tone register setting. Check your modem S11 register setting.)

▶ Your modem dials a number but hangs up the phone before a connection is made. (Modem and communication programs wait for connect time settings. Check your modem's S7 register setting.)

▶ Your modem is supposed to adjust to the communication speed of the computer you called or the computer that has called your system but it does not happen. (Check both the flow control and protocol mode selections in both your modem — usually &K and &Q or &B, &H, and &N commands — and your communication program.)

▶ You are trying to use your modem with hardware flow control but it is not working. (Modem and communication program hardware flow control commands and settings. Check your communication program settings and your modem initialization commands, usually &K and &Q or &B, &H, and &N commands.)

Your modem may have many more or fewer settings than these. Some fairly standard modem commands exist, but so many modems have provided variations and augmentations for these, as well as adding more, that we must refer you to the manual provided with your modem to determine the exact command to use to get the proper response. The previous list of possible symptoms gives you a starting point for problems reported by your modem and communication program.

Suspects

▶ Improper modem switch or jumper settings.

▶ Improper information in the communication program setup.

Solutions

▶ See Figure 22-3 for an example of settings in a DOS communication program that are not part of the Modem Initialization String but, nevertheless, affect the way the modem is used by your computer. In this example, the COM-AND communication program is set to use Software Flow Control (Item #13); Bi-directional Hardware Flow Control (Item #15); to drop the Data Terminal Ready (DTR) signal to cause the modem to hang up the phone; to reinitialize the modem after it has been hung up; to let the Carrier Detect (CD) signal affect the way the modem works; and to slow down the COM-AND program to keep it from working too fast with the modem on the other end. None of these makes a change in the way the modem works but does affect the way the communication program works with the modem.

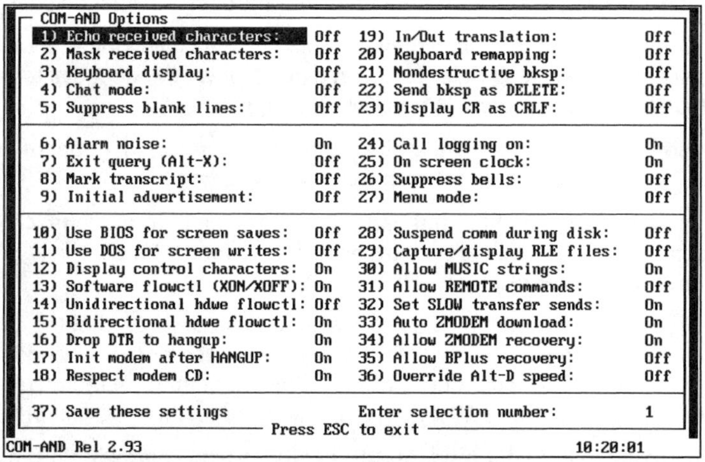

```
┌─ COM-AND Options ──────────────────────────────────────────────────┐
│  1) Echo received characters:  Off   19) In/Out translation:      Off │
│  2) Mask received characters:  Off   20) Keyboard remapping:      Off │
│  3) Keyboard display:          Off   21) Nondestructive bksp:     Off │
│  4) Chat mode:                 Off   22) Send bksp as DELETE:     Off │
│  5) Suppress blank lines:      Off   23) Display CR as CRLF:      Off │
│                                                                      │
│  6) Alarm noise:               On    24) Call logging on:         On  │
│  7) Exit query (Alt-X):        Off   25) On screen clock:         On  │
│  8) Mark transcript:           Off   26) Suppress bells:          Off │
│  9) Initial advertisement:     Off   27) Menu mode:               Off │
│                                                                      │
│ 10) Use BIOS for screen saves: Off   28) Suspend comm during disk: Off │
│ 11) Use DOS for screen writes: Off   29) Capture/display RLE files: Off │
│ 12) Display control characters: On   30) Allow MUSIC strings:     On  │
│ 13) Software flowctl (XON/XOFF): On  31) Allow REMOTE commands:    Off │
│ 14) Unidirectional hdwe flowctl: Off 32) Set SLOW transfer sends:  On  │
│ 15) Bidirectional hdwe flowctl: On   33) Auto ZMODEM download:     On  │
│ 16) Drop DTR to hangup:        On    34) Allow ZMODEM recovery:    On  │
│ 17) Init modem after HANGUP:   On    35) Allow BPlus recovery:     Off │
│ 18) Respect modem CD:          On    36) Override Alt-D speed:     Off │
│                                                                      │
│ 37) Save these settings              Enter selection number:      1   │
│ ──────────────────────── Press ESC to exit ───────────────────────── │
│COM-AND Rel 2.93                                        10:20:01       │
└──────────────────────────────────────────────────────────────────────┘
```

Figure 22-3: The screen where more communication options are set up in the COM-AND communication program

▶ Check the switches and jumper settings on your modem to ensure they are set to the factory settings or that differences from the factory settings are documented and logical.

▶ If you have Call Waiting on your telephone line, disable it before dialing by inserting the command to your phone company that turns it off. Most phone systems are using the *70 command, followed by a comma, then the rest of your modem dialing command (phone number). Check with your phone company for the exact method of disabling call waiting for a particular call. It is not standard among all phone systems around the world.

▶ If you have voice mail services that interrupt the dial tone, your modem may think it is not getting a valid dial tone. For most Hayes compatible modems, you can disable waiting for a (normal) dial tone with ATS6=0.

▶ Check the setup portion of your communication program to ensure that a proper modem initialization string (modem commands) has been entered. Also check to make sure the modem dialing command, modem hang-up command, modem auto-answer command, modem reset command, modem connect string, and other settings are correct.

▶ Check the documentation for your modem and communication program for the proper settings. Even different modem models and communication program versions from the same company may have differences in the proper commands and capabilities you should use.

▶ Sample modem initialization strings must only be thought of as a starting point due to the differences between the systems to which you may connect. However, here are a few examples to help you get started:

- Hayes compatible
- ZOOM/FAXMODEM 56K
- Practice Peripherals

Hayes compatible

Modem initialization string:

```
AT E1 S7=60 V1 X4 S11=55^M
```

These commands cause an echo of modem commands (E1), wait for call connect for 60 seconds (S7=60), use verbal command responses (V1), use extended connection response messages (X4), and dial the phone fast (S11=55).

Here, ^M is interpreted as a carriage return and can be different from one communication program to another. Some use the exclamation point (!), the caret (^), or the pipe/vertical bar symbol (|) as a carriage return character. A carriage return is required because it must be represented in the communication program's initialization string and it is not a modem command. Another example of a communication program character used in an initialization command string that is not a modem command is a character used to cause a delay between commands sent to the modem. For instance, the COM-AND communication program uses a tilde character (~) to delay between sending command characters. Most modems use the comma (,) character for a delay but, if your initialization string is too long (most modems are limited to 40 characters for the command string), then the communication program can help get around this limitation by inserting a delay without using up a character space in the command string.

ZOOM/FAXMODEM 56Kx

This is the initialization string provided by ZOOM for Windows installation:

```
AT&FE0V1&C1&D2S95=45S0=0<cr>
```

These commands, following the AT command, reset to the factory defaults (&F), do not echo commands (E0), use numeric responses (V0), set the modem to report the true state of DCD (&C1), set the modem to report the true state of DTR (&D2), set register 95 to 45 (S95=45), and do not answer the phone (S0=0). The <cr> is the way the carriage return is represented in the Windows setup for the Zoom modem.

Practical Peripherals

This is the setup for answering both data and fax calls and having the PC to modem speed set at 57K bps:

```
AT&F1!~ATH0L0M0&C1&D3&T5S0=1S95=3!~AT+FCR=1!~AT+FAA=1^M
```

These commands reset to the IBM PC compatible settings (&F1), pause for command settling (~), place the phone on hook (H0), set the modem speaker to low volume (L0), turn off the modem speaker (M0), set DCD to follow the true state (&C1), set DTR to follow the true state and hang-up on transition (&D3), prevent remote tests (&T5), set the modem to answer the phone on the first ring (S0=1), report modem-to-modem connect speed and show error correction protocol status (S95=3), tell modem it is able to receive a fax (+FCR=1), and use adaptive answering protocol to distinguish between data and fax calls (+FAA=1). This is not an ordinary initialization string but one that is quite useful if you want your modem to do all it is capable of doing.

US Robotics Sportster and Courier

This is the setup for both data and fax calls. In all cases, the US Robotics modems require RTS/CTS hardware flow control. For the Sportster and Courier 14.4 units, set the COM port speed at 38,400 bps. For the Sportster 28.8 and Courier V.EVERYTHING units, set the COM port speed to 115,200 bps. The initialization string:

```
AT&F1!
```

These commands reset to the IBM PC compatible settings (F1) for default hardware flow control.

Flow control

Serial connections over the telephone or carried over coaxial cables might use software flow control (X-ON/X-OFF — ASCII characters 17 and 19 or Ctrl-Q and Ctrl-S, respectively) to regulate the amount of data that may be sent or received at a particular time. Connections between your computer and a local device, using all of the RS-232 signal connections, might use both software flow control and hardware flow control. Hardware flow control uses the Clear to Send (CTS) and Ready to Send (RTS) signals to regulate the amount of data that can be transmitted or received by each end of the serial connection.

Note   Software flow control may be used over the phone line and simple serial cable connections. Hardware flow control may be used only when a full RS-232 connection exists (cable or other direct connection) or when it is used with buffering.

As modems and other serial devices increase in capabilities and speed, the need for hardware flow control has become more important. The PC hardware has always been able to accommodate hardware flow control but, without the need, the software (communication programs and drivers) has not implemented hardware flow control techniques. Both the device to which you are connecting *and* your PC software must have the ability to use hardware flow control or your connection will fail to work.

Software flow control settings must be the same on both ends of the serial connection, or the flow control does not function. Most modems and communication software that support hardware flow control provide settings to turn it on or off so that older modems or communication programs continue to work. However, in the interest of speeding your serial communications, consider upgrading to a communication program and modem that supports hardware flow control.

Flow control problems

Here are some ways to recognize and resolve flow control problems.

Symptoms

▶ Your PC does not make a connection to or does not continue to communicate with the serial device on the other end.

▶ Data is lost during a serial connection due to one side or the other continuing to transmit data when the opposite side is not ready.

Suspects

▶ There might be a problem with the software flow control settings in your software.

▶ There might be a problem with the hardware flow control settings.

Solutions

▶ Check the flow control requirements of the serial device to which you are connecting and make sure it is set the same as the software on your PC, and vice versa.

▶ If the software on your PC cannot use hardware flow control, make sure that the device to which you are connecting has hardware flow control disabled.

▶ If the device to which you are connecting requires hardware flow control and cannot be disabled, switch to software on your PC that does have hardware flow control capabilities.

▶ If you are using hardware flow control between your PC and other devices, make sure that you are using a serial cable that implements all of the signals (wires and connectors for each of the RS-232 signals identified in Table 22.1) required for a full serial connection.

▶ Windows 95/98/Me and NT/2000 provide access to these settings through the Modem icon in the Control Panel. The default settings are most often correct. If the system you are calling requires deviation from these standard settings, the documentation for making that connection usually has instructions for making the proper settings.

Line Noises and Line Attenuation

For a communication connection that is otherwise correct, line noise is one of the most frustrating and common disturbances.

You have probably encountered some form of line noise when you have used a telephone. Line noise includes static, hum, crackling, echoes, crosstalk, or other unwanted signals that can disrupt the sound path between callers. It can break the sound path intermittently so that nothing gets through, or it may be so loud or have such characteristics that it confuses your modem or other serial device and changes the data characters it receives.

The symptoms are:

✦ garbage or mistyped characters on your screen

✦ transmission errors

✦ retries during file transfers.

If you listen to the phone line without the modem tones present, you can actually hear the noise.

Many causes for line noise exist, from man-made sources such as motors, radios, or other appliances, to natural occurrences such as lightning or wind. Line noise can also be caused by poor connections along the miles of wires and dozens of phone company switches through which your data travels.

Noise is not the only cause of poor connections. Nearly the opposite of line noise or unwanted signals on the line is line attenuation, which is a reduction of the sound signal between callers' modems. A certain amount of attenuation is expected. It is introduced by the length and size of wires and the many connections it must pass through between points.

It is not unusual to have the signal decrease to one-tenth of its original level as it passes between one caller and another. This attenuation is acceptable.

An excessive amount of attenuation might be present in the lines because the phone company has placed filters or line adjustment devices in the lines. These devices are part of the phone company's efforts to equalize the lines so that they all work the same, or in some cases, work equally poorly.

Static, crackling, scratching sounds

If your telephone line sounds scratchy, the cause is most likely a bad connection. Sometimes you can tell if the noise is "closer" to you or from the other caller. One clue is whether you hear the same kinds of noise or have the same kinds of problems when calling some other locations but not all other locations.

You may be able to make the noises come and go by wiggling or gently pushing and pulling at the wires and connections. If you cannot keep a conversation or connection going while you inspect the wiring, you have to visually inspect and check without the benefit of knowing exactly where the noise begins.

If you see any wires that might be poorly connected (screw tightened down on insulation instead of the bare wires or crimp-on, twist or squeeze-type connections) repair or replace them.

Tip Make sure that your cables and lines are constructed using high-quality materials, and are of the appropriate types (twisted-pair and shielded cables). This applies to both phone system and direct cable connections.

Twisted-pair cable, made up of two wires twisted around each other, prevents unwanted signals from radiating into or out of the signal lines. The four-wire (with red, green, black and yellow wire colors) cable often used to make the connection between the telephone company lines at the outside box and your phone jacks, is intended to be used for one phone line only. A phone line uses only one pair of wires (typically red and green) and the other pair is used for an off-hook switch or the night-light in older phones. If you have multiple phone lines, use separate cables for each line.

The interconnection cables with modular (RJ-11) plugs and jacks are very reliable, but they can fail. The socket is designed so that the connections are supposed to be wiped clean every time you connect or disconnect these plugs. Most of the time this self-cleaning is not effective and you may have to use a cotton-tipped swap and some alcohol or contact cleaner to remove corrosion from the contacts.

Tip Applying a very thin layer of contact cleaner to all RJ-11 (modular) connections is recommended.

Many connection points use a very narrow V-shaped slot as shown in Figure 22-4, that you push the wire into — insulation and all (the drawing is a blow-up of the connector. It really is small). These are supposed to cut through the wire's insulation and make contact with the wire itself. Unfortunately, no V-shaped contact exists that is good for all the different sizes of wires and types of insulation available. A quick remedy for nonworking connections is to use real telephone grade wire or use a pair of narrow-nosed pliers to further squeeze the V-connection together. If that does not work, you might have to undo the connection, remove some of the insulation, and place the bare wire into the V.

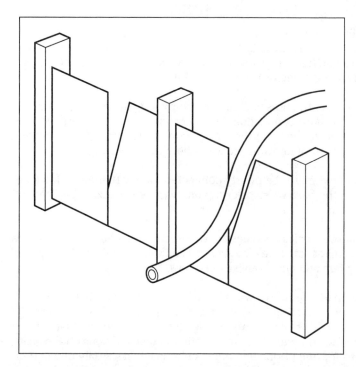

Figure 22-4: V-shaped connectors: Press the wire into the V so that the insulation is cut and the wire makes contact with the metal V.

If you have not found or corrected any obvious problems by the time you reach the outside connection box, this is the last place you can do anything before calling the phone company. Inside you find screw terminals or RJ-11 connections between the wires that go into your house and the wires the phone company provides. Most of the time you cannot get to the phone company connections, and you are not supposed to touch them, although you could find and fix the problem there and save a lot of time. These outside boxes make nice homes for spiders and other bugs, and tend to collect a small amount of water and corrosion. The spider webs and dirt can be conductors and be a cause of line noise too.

Part of the telephone company's connections include a ground connector and a set of protection devices intended to prevent high voltages from getting into your phone system. These are lightning or surge protectors. Two kinds of these devices are in use — carbon and gas-tube. They appear on the outside as large (3/8 inch) hex-head bolts or as large, slotted screw heads. If any water has seeped into the box, you might find some corrosion has built-up across connections or in the protectors.

Reduced Signal Levels

If the signal between you and another party is always low in volume, the problem probably rests in the hands of the phone company, unless someone has installed some unknown line-reduction device in your lines. Specifications exist that govern the levels and quality of signal the phone company must deliver to you. Generally, the phone companies meet or exceed these specifications, giving you excellent signal level and quality.

If the protectors are the carbon-type, they may have already taken a lightning strike and become bad. The carbon-type have a very distinct button or bump of what appears to be thick pencil lead protruding to the inside contacts. The gas-tube protectors have nondistinct metal buttons or tabs that make contact inside the hole they screw into. The gas-tube protectors should never become damaged or noisy. You really cannot tell if either type is bad unless you remove it and then check the line, or know how to use a volt-ohmmeter to check it. If you have reached this point and have not found a problem, it is time to call the phone company.

If you feel you need or want additional protection for your modem, especially if you take it "on the road" to motels or places with unknown phone system types, take a look at the special protector illustrated in Appendix H. You might want to build one for yourself.

The phone system is required to deliver voice quality service between two callers. Voice quality is a certain signal level in the range of voice frequencies reaching the other end. This frequency range is from 300 to 3000 Hertz (cycles per second) — not exactly good for music, but voices are well within this range and make it through just fine.

You may request, and pay for, having your line conditioned specifically for data use. Different grades of lines can be requested, from low-speed to high-speed data and up to broadcast quality. The availability of these lines and the costs vary between locations. You should check with the phone company's business office for specific details, especially if they tell you that the quality of your voice grade line cannot be improved.

The laws that govern telephone operations make you responsible for the lines and devices inside your home, apartment, office, or other facility. The phone company is only responsible for repairing problems it finds outside your facility. You may request that the phone company inspect or repair your inside lines, but you usually have to pay a service charge.

Be aware that some telephone companies and laws consider the use of modems to be a business use of your telephone line, or that a higher charge applies to data over normal conversational use. If you get stuck with additional charges, be sure they are legal (check with your state regulatory agencies). If you have to pay extra, you might want to get a different service grade for your lines, including conditioning the line for data use so you get more reliable connections.

Long serial cables for local use

Our earlier discussion of line noise focused on the use of a modem and the telephone system for your serial connection, but the same concepts apply to a cable that you use to connect your computer to any serial device. Using twisted-pair cable (some are shielded and some are not) does increase the possible cable length between your computer and the other device. Shielded is generally better, meaning it supports greater speeds or greater length of cable, or both. If the connections are clean and tight and the cable is routed in such a way that it avoids noisy electronic equipment and devices, you may end up with a serial cable that is 2,000 feet long or more.

Erratic communications problems

There are many things that could cause erratic communications problems. They are listed here.

Symptoms

▶ Line noise or unwanted or poor signals getting into your modem.

Suspects

▶ Local (things you can fix yourself):

  • dirty connections at screws, plugs, jacks, and crimped or twisted fittings.

  • a dirty or defective line protection device at the outside telephone connection box.

  • bad or missing ground connection at the outside telephone box.

  • a nearby transmitter (TV, AM *or* FM broadcast, CB, ham, or other radio service).

  • a nearby appliance: motors, elevators, TVs, displays, neon signs, and so on.

  • noisy connections in nearby high voltage power lines.

  • bad connections in TV cable or antenna lines.

  • improper wiring (including two lines in one cable, nontwisted wires, and so on).

▶ Distant (things the phone company or the user on the other end needs to fix):

  • problems along the lines, in junction boxes or at the switch office.

  • line filters or equalization along the lines.

  • line-current reduction or build-out.

  • lightning or high static along the lines.

  • older/poor telephone facilities.

  • problems local to the other modem.

With all of the miles of wires, dozens of connections, and other possibilities affecting your lines and data flow, you still do not have to put up with all of it. Some simple steps enable you to prevent most causes of line noise.

Solutions

▶ The first step in getting rid of phone line problems is to identify what type of problem you are having. The type of noise you hear, or the quality of sounds, or if you have trouble hearing what other people say, helps define what you should or can do to begin solving the problem.

▶ Contact the appropriate utility company, an electrician, or technical person to help resolve.

 If you are not accustomed to working with wires, find someone who is, or call a trained repair person. The voltages present on a phone line when it is not in use can cause small shocks if you grab it tightly. If the phone then rings, there can be 130 volts, a lethal amount, present on the line.

The steps you need to take begin with working along all of the connections from your phone or modem, through all of the plugs, jacks and terminal blocks, to the telephone company connection points outside your house or office. If you find and fix problems in your own part of the system, you can save a significant amount of money for inside or outside service charges. Before calling the phone company, you should be able to repeat any problem found so they can see it for themselves and find the cause faster.

Erratic connection problems

The following Symptoms, Suspects, and Solutions section discusses crosstalk, a form of erratic connection problems.

Symptoms

▶ Crosstalk or interference. If you hear other conversations or tones on the line while you are using the telephone, you are hearing crosstalk. This is the effect of one line's information being induced into another.

Suspects

▶ Local phone wiring, phone electronics, remote phone wiring, or radio interference.

Solutions

The only cures for local crosstalk are to ensure that:

▶ You are using only twisted-pair wires between the telephone company's connections and your phone. This includes not using "station-wire" or "quad" cable for more than one telephone line if you have multiple lines.

▶ The wires are not crossed or touching between two different lines.

▶ The lines and connections are not wet or do not have corrosion between the terminals.

▶ You are not being subjected to radio interference.

Corrosion or water on the terminals can create an electrical path between lines, and crosstalk can be one of the symptoms. Any electrical path from a phone wire to ground causes a severe humming sound on the line. Be sure all connection points are clean and dry.

Appliances with motors — such as drills and refrigerators — may generate a static-type noise in your lines. Running your phone lines too near television sets, stereo systems or speakers, or electrical wiring can also induce unwanted signals.

If you hear garbled conversations, music or voices, you might be receiving radio interference. Before you blame the people next door with the big antenna on the house or your local radio station, some important things need to be considered:

▶ If you suspect radio interference from someone nearby, do not assume that the transmitter or antenna they are using is at fault. Many electronic and cordless phones, answering and fax machines, and modems are susceptible to overload or the reception of unintentional signals.

▶ A cordless phone is a radio device used by "nonradio people." It may be receiving a strong signal and placing it on your phone line. The transmitter nearby may be legal, but so strong as to have its signal penetrate your electronics. Most real, licensed, "radio people" are very considerate about these things and do their best not to interfere. They can also be your best source of simple fixes for your phone system to prevent most external interference.

▶ Radio interference is usually corrected with a simple filter, installed at the main phone connections, or sometimes at each phone connection in your house. It is possible that changing the length of the phone wires or tying some of the wire into a loop can cure the problem. A simplified filter and modem surge protector is illustrated in Appendix H. A skilled technician or radio operator might be able to build one of these for you, or add special components to it to correct your specific problem.

▶ If you cannot correct the crosstalk within your home, call the your local phone company and ask them to help correct the problems. They can correct the problem only if they can find it. If it generally happens when calling the same places, the problem is easier to trace.

When You Need a Faster Serial Connection

Many modem connections involve some cost, either in the form of telephone charges or the time or usage charges imposed by the system to which you connect. A serial printer without significant buffering can make you wait for quite a while during printing. These and other factors can make you want or need a faster serial connection.

Out-of-pocket expenses can justify the additional expense of newer and faster communications capabilities. However, you need to place some value on your own time. Waiting for something to finish costs whatever your time is worth, unless you can use that time to get other things done. If the sum of these values comes to more than the cost of a new modem, upgraded serial port capabilities, or both, do not hesitate to move up to higher speed and more efficient use of your time.

Symptoms

▶ Impatience, frustration, headaches from stressed deadline pushing, and envy for the faster modem and serial printer in the other person's office.

Suspects

▶ If you can almost read as fast as the data is being printed on your screen, you may be tempted to slow down the scroll so that you can read it. This increases connect time, which may be costly (if not in connection cost, certainly in terms of the cost of your own time). If the connection results in printing to your screen much too fast to read, you should capture the data to a file to be read later, which is the most efficient way to use communication connections.

▶ If you have large volumes to print or transfer from one device to another, it can take a long time. Maybe it is a good time for a break.

Solutions

▶ Upgrade to some newer and faster technology. Some ways exist of doing things in almost every area of communication between devices. Print spooling for a slow printer, a newer modem using higher speed capabilities, and local area networks to replace null modem connections between computers, are just a few examples.

High-speed connections and the 16550 UART

If you use very high rates or perform high-speed communications under a multitasking environment, you might need to replace the old 8250, 82450, MS62C50, or 16450 UART chips in your system with the NS16550AFN UARTs and others that include the FIFO buffering. The 16550 is pin-compatible with the 8250-type UART chips (including all of those just mentioned) but it provides FIFO buffering that enables the UART to operate at a faster speed. Lost characters, file transfers slowed due to multiple retries, and occasionally locked or failed communication connections are signs that you need to replace your current UART and use programs that take advantage of it.

Chip provides First-In-First-Out buffering

The NS16550AFN UART chip from National Semiconductor (other manufacturers' versions of this chip are usually referred to as *high speed serial port devices*) provides First-In-First-Out (FIFO) buffering that supports high-speed communications even under multi-tasking systems. However, if you think your serial port has a 16550 UART with FIFO buffering, even if the numbers of the chip show 16550, the FIFO buffering might not be present. Even National Semiconductor produced chips that have the 16550 number but do not support the FIFO buffering. A surface mount and other types of UART chips that do not use the 16550 number identification also exist.

The 16550 chips are available in single unit prices ranging from $10 to $20 so the expense is quite small. Installing the new chip is easy if your present UART chip is in a socket. Unsoldering a chip with 40 "legs" is not a simple task, but it can be done.

All current Windows platforms and current Unix related platforms support the use of the 16550 UART. Many of the newer serial port devices implement the same FIFO buffering as the 16550 UART. Most new internal modems also use the FIFO buffering like the 16550 so that they are able to provide the same high speed capabilities as an external modem connected to a high speed serial port.

High-Speed transfer problems

Here is some information to help you improve your data transfer rate.

Symptoms

▶ When operating your serial port at 9,600 bps or faster or when using your serial ports under a multi-tasking operating system, files lose characters or file transfers are slowed down due to multiple retries.

▶ Your communication connection occasionally locks up or the connection gets dropped or fails when using high speeds or working under a multi-tasking environment.

Suspects

▶ The UART used for the COM port cannot handle the higher speed.

Solutions

▶ Replace your current UART with an NS16550AFN UART chip and change to a communication program and multi-tasking environment that supports its use, if you use one.

The RS-232 Standard

RS-232 is the industry standard for serial connections between devices. RS-232 defines a set of signals used to send data from one hardware device to another, one bit at a time. The one-bit-at-a-time feature is what gives a serial port its name. Parallel ports handle data one byte (8-bits) at a time. In addition to the serial data bit lines (transmit and receive), other lines (signals) provide hardware flow control (the feature that assures that you do not lose data due to one side or the other not being ready to accept the data), and detecting the ringing phone (if being used for a modem). This standard defines how the COM port in our computers is setup and used.

Serial devices fall into two categories: Data Terminal Equipment (DTE) and Data Communications Equipment (DCE). DTE are devices, such as your PC, designed to connect to the other type, DCE. Serial modems are one type of DCE. DTE and DCE use the same signals, and the same definitions of those signals. However, they are a mirror image of each other. For instance, the transmit signal for the DTE is the receive signal for the DCE. Because the devices you may connect to your serial port refer to these signal definitions, see Table 22-3, which summarizes them..

Table 22-3 RS-232 Signal Definitions (DTE perspective)			
Signal Name	*9-pin #*	*25-pin #*	*Description (Telco Lead Designation)*
Protective Ground		1	Not used for the 9-pin connector. (AA/101)
Signal Ground	5	7	Ground reference for the other signals. (AB/102)
Transmit Data (TD or TXD)	3	2	Output pin for the data bits being sent to the device on the other end. (BA/103)
Receive Data (RD or RXD)	2	3	Input pin to receive the data bits being sent from the device on the other end. (BB/104)
Request to Send (RTS)	7	4	Output pin that tells the device on the other end that it is ready to send data bits. (CA/105)
Clear to Send (CTS)	8	5	Input pin that determines if the device on the other end is ready to receive data bits. (CB/106)
Data Set Ready (DSR)	6	6	Input pin that generally indicates that the connection between the devices is active and ready for transmitting data bits. (CC/107)

Continued

Table 22-3 (continued)			
Signal Name	**9-pin #**	**25-pin #**	**Description (Telco Lead Designation)**
Data Carrier Detect (DCD or CD or RLSD)	1	8	Input pin that indicates that a connection is established with the device on the other end. (CF/109)
Data Terminal Ready (DTR)	4	20	Output pin that informs the device on the other end that this device is available. (CD/108.2)
Ring Indicator (RI)	9	22	Input pin that determines when the telephone rings. (DE/125)

DCE devices use the same signals but, using the 9-pin definitions, pins three and two and pins seven and eight are switched. Specifically, the TD and RD signals and the CTS and RTS signals are switched. Another way to look at the difference is that the output signals of the DTE device are input signals for the DCE device, and vice versa.

Serial Cables

After the discussion of the RS-232 signals that must be passed between your computer and the serial device to which it is connected, you should see that a bad cable can cause all sorts of problems. The external device just may not work at all. It may seem to lose "data." Your computer may not be able to tell that the device is installed or available. Even if the problem seems like it is too complex to be caused by a "simple, little cable," check the cable. It is the easiest part of the communications link to fix. Most of the time the fix is just to replace the cable.

Connecting two serial devices (your PC's COM port and a modem or other device) is accomplished using a cable with the appropriate connectors on each end. By far, the most common connectors are the 25-pin and 9-pin D-Shell connectors (see Appendix G, for illustrations and diagrams). Devices that use other connectors, such as Microsoft's mouse, usually provide adapters to the 25-pin and 9-pin connectors or documentation showing how to connect to these most common connectors.

Most of the serial cable connections are made with straight through cables, meaning that pin 1 on one end is connected to pin 1 on the other end, pin 2 to pin 2, and so forth. This is not possible when one end is a 25-pin and the other is a 9-pin connector. It is also not possible when you are connecting two DTE devices such as connecting your computer's serial port to another computer's serial port. If you did use a straight through cable, TX would be hooked to TX, and RX to RX, and so forth. In this later case, a null modem is required. Figure 22-5 shows a null modem, which switches the appropriate input and output pins so that the signals go to the proper pins on the other end.

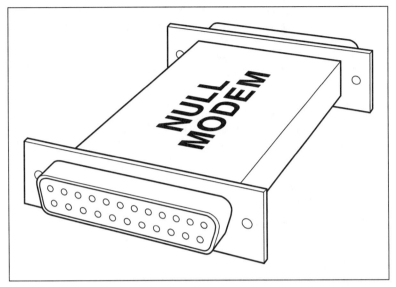

Figure 22-5: A null modem

Table 22-5 shows the connections for a 9-pin to 25-pin "straight through" connector (which is the same as 25-pin to 9-pin in the mirror) and the three possible combinations of 9-pin and 25-pin null modem connections:

Table 22-5 Serial Cables and Null Modems			
DB-9–DB-25 Straight Through	DB-9–DB-9 Null Modem	DB-25–DB-25 Null Modem	DB-9–DB-25 Null Modem
1 <–> 8	1,6 <–> 4	1 <–> 1	1,6 <–> 20
2 <–> 3	2 <–> 3	2 <–> 3	2 <–> 2
3 <–> 2	3 <–> 2	3 <–> 2	3 <–> 3
4 <–> 20	4 <–> 1,6	4 <–> 5	4 <–> 6,8
5 <–> 7	5 <–> 5	5 <–> 4	5 <–> 7
6 <–> 6	7 <–> 8	6,8 <–> 20	7 <–> 5
7 <–> 4	8 <–> 7	7 <–> 7	8 <–> 4
8 <–> 5	9 <–> 9	20 <–> 6,8	9 <–> 22
9 <–> 22		22 <–> 22	

Any serial device or cable that conforms to the RS-232 and PC compatible standards and uses the 9-pin or 25-pin D-Shell connectors is covered by the three previous tables. Other implementations of the RS-232 standard and different connectors exist. However, because the 9-pin and 25-pin connectors are by far the most common for PCs, most nonstandard implementations are accompanied by documentation pointing out the differences.

With a simple volt-ohmmeter (VOM), shown in Figure 22-6, a couple of straight pins to reach the contacts in the socket connector, and Table 22-5 shown previously, you can diagnose any standard serial cable or determine that the cable is nonstandard.

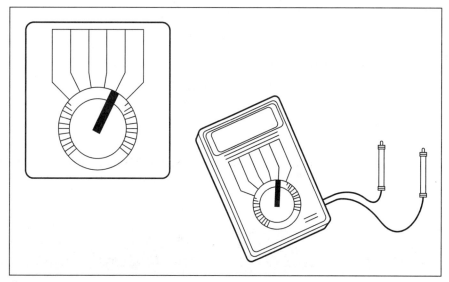

Figure 22-6: A VOM

With your VOM set to measure ohms, one lead connected to pin-1 on one end of the cable, and the other lead connected to pin-1 on the other end of the cable, you can determine whether a signal path exists between those two pins (resistance is near 0). A straight through cable has a signal path between each pin and the one with the same number on the other end. There should be no other signal path than those between pins of the same number.

Build your own cable tester

You may use two wires, a flashlight battery, and flashlight bulb to test a cable, as shown in Figure 22-7. One wire connects from the pin you want to test to one end of the battery. The other wire connects from the pin on the other end of the cable to the side of the flashlight bulb, and the tip of the flashlight bulb to the other end of the battery. This is a makeshift continuity checker and does the job just as well as the VOM. When the light is on, a signal path exists.

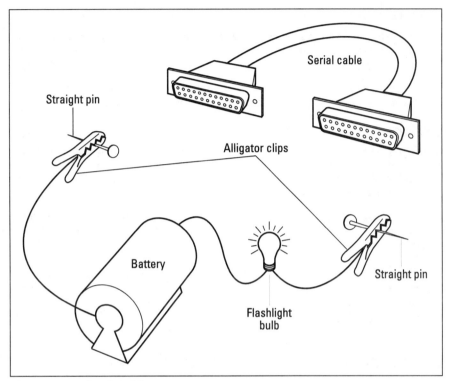

Figure 22-7: Simple cable tester

In Table 22-4, the connections that have two numbers on one side of the connection indicator (<–>) are pins that have been tied together. There should be a signal path from the one pin on the other end to both of these pins. A cable that does not provide all of the signal paths required is faulty and should be replaced or repaired. Again, see Appendix G, for cable diagrams.

Bad cables, poor connections

This section provides information to help you determine if your connection or cables are bad, and how to correct the problem.

Symptoms

▶ "It used to work and I have added no new hardware or software, and all the serial port and parameter settings are correct, but nothing happens."

▶ Same situation mentioned earlier, but the data transferred or received from the device or system on the other end is missing data or contains "garbage characters" mixed with what should be transmitted or received. (Again, this includes serial printers, modems, your mouse or track ball, and other serial devices.)

Suspects

▶ The cable attached to your computer or the other device is not properly connected. The screws might be loose or there might be corrosion on the pins or contacts in the connectors.

▶ A continuity check of the pins on each end of the cable, in accordance with Table 22-4, reveals that some pins are not properly connected.

Solutions

▶ Always check the connections before you assume that a cable is bad. Simply reseating the connectors and tightening the fasteners could save you a lot of time and trouble if nothing is wrong with the cables, connectors, or adapters between your computer and the serial device to which it is connected.

The quickest and easiest manner of fixing a serial cable is to replace it with a new one. This goes for null modem, "gender changers," and other serial cable adapters and connectors as well.

Cables may be repaired or fixed, temporarily or until you can get a replacement. However, it may involve some wiring and soldering activities that you may or may not be willing or able to perform. Table 22-4 contains the information you need to ensure that the cable connections are correct.

Null modems: When do you need them?

If you are connecting your computer's serial port directly to another device using a serial cable, it is possible that you may be connecting two Data Terminal Equipment (DTE)devices together. This is especially true if you are connecting to another computer. In this case, you need to use a null modem.

Null modem problems

The null modem, as specified in Table 22-3, switches the Transmit (TX) and Receive (RX) signals, the Ready to Send (RTS) and Clear to Send (CTS) signals, and the Data Set Ready (DSR) and Data Carrier Detect (DCD) signals.

Symptoms

▶ Data transmitted from one end of the serial cable is not received at the other end.

▶ Hardware flow control signals are ignored.

▶ Neither side knows the other is connected.

Suspects

▶ A straight-through cable results in no data being transmitted or received because the TX and RX signals are not properly connected.

▶ A cable missing the RTS/CTS switch cannot perform hardware flow control.

▶ A cable missing the DSR/DCD switch does not allow the devices on each end to know that the other is there and ready to receive or transmit data.

Solutions

▶ Install a proper null modem connector in the cable between the two devices (your computer and the other end of the cable).

Where We Were and Where We're Going

No more than about 17 years ago, a Bell 103 modem (the 1,200 bps standard that defines the telephone signals for this class of modems) was the greatest idea around. Just a few years later, the Bell 212 standard (2,400 bps modem signal definitions) identified the latest and greatest in general distribution. In fact, some of the modems in use today are of the 2,400 bps type.

The Microcom Network Protocol, Level 5, introduced a significant breakthrough in the process of error correction. A 2,400 bps modem equipped with MNP-5 could even run over noisy lines without the line noise affecting the data transmitted and received. This technology spurred the development of protocols for transmitting data in compressed form so that even higher speeds were becoming a reality.

There were a number of false starts for a 9,600 bps standard. Microcom introduced MNP levels six through nine, which defined modem signals with error correction and data compression that provided 9,600 bps (and 19,200 bps) capabilities. Hayes and other manufacturers introduced modems using the v.32 protocol that was similar to, but incompatible with, the new MNP protocols that provided 9,600 bps capabilities. The v.42 standard was introduced to try to reconcile the differences between the v.32 and MNP protocols. In the meantime, the international community developed the v.32bis and v.42bis standards that provided the final reconciliation for 9,600 bps protocols.

Modems using PEP, or Packetized Ensemble Protocol, may provide a throughput of up to 18,000 bps. The method of sending data between modems is designed for large data blocks. Using a transfer protocol such as 1K-XMODEM, YMODEM-G, or ZMODEM is preferred to reach maximum speed, rather than using standard XMODEM or KERMIT, which use small data blocks (128 bytes or smaller). The PEP/DAMQAM protocol is commonly used between UNIX systems and the UUCP transfer protocol. They use what is referred to as DAMQAM or, a method of modulating the modem tones to imbed more information into them.

Note   PEP does not perform well for text or online typing or common BBS or online system uses because it is optimized for large data blocks and continuous data streams. BBS is not normally associated with this type of modem.

As soon as the v.32 9,600 bps standards were approved, modem manufacturers started producing v.32bis modems with the ability to transmit and receive at 14,400 bps. These quickly became the greatest modems to use. The U.S. Robotics HST/Dual Standard modems were still faster sometimes but could not communicate at the higher speeds with any modems except other U.S. Robotics modems with the same capabilities.

One of the reasons that the 14,400 bps modems provided better throughput, apart from the faster speed, is that they used hardware flow control to enable the computer-to-modem connection to be implemented at a high bps rate (usually 38K or 57K bps) while the modem connected to the one at the other end at its highest-speed capability.

For a while, the community of modem users used a protocol called V.FAST. Prior to acceptance of the v.34 protocols, V.FAST modems offered transmit/receive bps rates of 19,200, 21,600, 24,000, and 28,800. These modems could not communicate with non-V.FAST modems at these higher speeds. Most of them do seem to do a good job at 14,400 bps (v.32bis/v.42bis) and lower speeds, so the older standards are still with us and working well.

The release of the v.34 standard by ITU-TSS (International Telecommunications Union–Telecommunications Standards Section that used to be called the CCITT — Consultative Committee for Telegraphy and Telephony) was released in 1995. The v.34 protocols provided modems that communicate with each other at 28,800 bps and higher.

To optimize the 14.4K and 28.8K bps modems, we use hardware flow control (RTS/CTS) and set the bps rate between our computer and modem at the highest possible speed — 19,200 or 38,400 for 14.4 modems and 57,600 or 115,200 bps for 28.8 modems, to enable internal data compression schemes to work to our advantage. If you connect to another 14.4K or 28.8K bps modem, the modems are set at the highest speed possible and even fluctuate between lower and higher speeds as line conditions change.

For a short while, we used 33.6K bps modems while waiting for the 56K modem wars to settle. The final version of the V.90 protocol occurred around September 1998. Most of the 56K modems being sold today (K-Flex and X2 are the most prominent among those competing to become the leader of the standard) are guaranteed by the manufacturer to have the ability to upgrade to the final standard. The Zoom modems — connected to the systems used to write the first version of this chapter — were upgraded more than once to the latest standard by connecting to the `www.zoomtel.com` site to get the upgrade programs.

This is probably the end of the line for asynchronous modems over standard voice grade phone lines. As a matter of fact, you are quite lucky if you are able to get connections that actually transmit anywhere close to 56K. If the distance between your phone and the telephone office that provides your service (called the Central Office or CO) is more than about 3 1/2 miles, no possible way exists for you to get a good enough connection to support 56K. We have just about run out of methods (error correction, compression, and so forth) that may be used to squeeze more into the bandwidth available using the standard voice connections. Even though it is possible, with special software, to combine multiple telephone lines for a faster combined connection, this is not the solution we all had hoped to see. Luckily we now have new kinds of modems including ISDN, Cable, and DSL Modems.

The demand for ever faster connections to the Internet is having quite an impact on the telecommunications industry. Phone companies are spending a good deal of resources on alternatives such as ISDN, ADSL, and other ways to use the copper wires already connecting us to their services. Cable and satellite companies are offering alternatives to using modems that, in some cases, may be quite a bit cheaper in the long run.

Today, cable modems and DSL (Digital Subscriber Line) connections are the more common ways to connect to the Internet at higher than modem speeds. Though cable modems provide the highest speeds, when enough users are on a cable segment to "use up" the bandwidth, the speed is slowed. Cable modems also provide security challenges because all persons on a particular cable segment are all using the same data path. DSL provides a lower speed but each user is connected directly to their Internet Service Provider so the speed is more constant. Though DSL presents *fewer* security concerns because no sharing of the connection occurs before it gets to the ISP, many security concerns still exist.

 Cross-Reference See Chapter 11 for information on dealing with a personal firewall.

Both of these faster options use a network adapter and connect your system directly to the Internet. If you are truly wishing for a faster connection to the Internet, get a cable modem or a DLS connection, *but* remember that optical fiber and gigabit speeds are on the way.

Going Wireless

Wireless modems (and lately, wireless networks) are a recent technology that is becoming popular in offices or facilities where it is not easy or economical to install dedicated wiring for networks or printer sharing. Many kinds of wireless modems exist, as the following section details. The types of settings, and the types of problems, associated with wired modems are also associated with these wireless counterparts. About the only difference is that no wire is present to wiggle to see if it is loose.

Cellular telephone modems

"on the go" you probably have a special cable attachment for your cellular telephone, and perhaps even a cellular-ready modem in your laptop computer. You need special equipment to use a modem with a cellular telephone system.

Considerable differences exist between modem use on a standard telephone line and on a cellular phone. A standard phone system (ideally) maintains a constant, uninterrupted connection during the call. A cellular telephone system breaks calls up intermittently as you move through and between different areas or "cells" of radio coverage with the phone.

This discontinuity is more or less acceptable for voice communications because our minds can piece together the bits of words to make sense, or it is easy for us to recognize when we have to ask someone to repeat a word or two if the connection gets noisy. Modems are not always smart enough to keep trying to keep data flowing and have a difficult time with interruptions.

Using cellular-specific equipment for portable computing adds a new layer of connection protection for data transmissions. For the telephone-side you need a way to get the modem signals into and out of the cellular phone/radio unit. This may be a simple adapter cable or a larger adapter module for your particular telephone. For the modem side, you may be able to use a conventional modem if the cellular signals are expected to be very stable, or a cellular specific modem that understands cellular phone signals and does not drop your data connection as you move about.

Radio modems

Using low-power, high-frequency radio waves is an effective way to transfer data without adding new wiring between systems. High-frequency radio and microwave transmitters and receivers designed for data communications are a form of wireless modems. They have fewer strict line-of-sight requirements than infrared modems.

Many of these units are intended for local use only and do not have the signal strength to carry the data very far. Use between buildings may be marginal, and any use where there may be other, stronger radio signals could present data loss problems.

Radio modems are also becoming common in service and delivery businesses, and in police and fire applications. Radio modems and vehicle-based data terminals have been in use for a number of years in the police and fire services. These allow patrol officers to get a driver's license and vehicle registration, or criminal record information directly from police computer networks. Fire services can get building use and content information and hazardous material data from their host computers. Many of these units share a frequency range used by government, business and hobby radio services, and the rules for radio services apply.

You may even see a form of wireless PC in use when you travel and return a rental car, and the lot attendant takes down your contract, mileage, and gas use information. The radio power level is too low to be harmful, but these units should not be placed where people might sit or walk past them, in order to avoid unnecessary RF exposure to the head or eyes.

Modems on the go

A company name Metracom, in Los Gatos, California, developed a set of dedicated wireless modems for data collection from remote utility sites. Relay modems are located on utility poles at frequent intervals throughout the area. These exchange information with other modems attached to a variety of utility devices.

Metracom also offers a radio-modem-based Internet service called Ricochet. When you sign up for their service they rent to you a small radio unit, about the size of a pocket cellular telephone, with a small flip-up antenna, a battery charger, a serial port cable, and software. The software is designed to operate with the modem, and provides a full range of Internet applications, from e-mail to surfing the Web. The modem attaches to your PCs serial port. This is an ideal solution for those "on the go" folks, or people who cannot always get access to a telephone line for long periods of time to use their standard modems. The connection speed of the service is about 38,000 bps—which is between 28.8 modem and single-channel ISDN connection speeds.

Infrared modems

Infrared modems use invisible light waves, much like the remote control for your TV or VCR, to convey data signals between two points. There must be a line-of-sight path between them. If anything obstructs the light path, or too much interfering light gets in the way of these units, the signal and data may be lost.

Wireless LAN

The latest wireless endeavors are focused on wireless LANs. It is not always convenient or possible to install network wiring in every situation. The latest wireless LANs offer connection speeds in the 1.6 Megabit speed range, making them equivalent to a T-1 line, which is still one of the ultimate speeds available to Internet users.

Most wireless LANs work within up to 100 feet. 300 feet is supported by some wireless LANs. However, users should be aware that wireless LAN systems from different vendors might not be interoperable. The three reasons for this are listed following:

✦ Different technologies do not interoperate. A system based on spread spectrum frequency hopping (FHSS) technology does not communicate with another based on spread spectrum direct sequence (DSSS) technology.

✦ Systems using different frequency bands do not interoperate even if they both employ the same technology.

✦ Systems from different vendors may not interoperate even if they both employ the same technology and the same frequency band, due to differences in implementation by each vendor.

Most wireless LANs provide for industry-standard interconnection with wired networks such as Ethernet or Token Ring. Wireless LAN nodes are supported by network operating systems in the same fashion as any other LAN node: through the use of the appropriate drivers. Once installed, the network treats wireless nodes like any other network component.

The unlicensed nature of radio-based wireless LANs means that other products that transmit energy in the same frequency spectrum can potentially provide some measure of interference to a wireless LAN system. Microwave ovens are a potential concern, but most wireless LAN manufacturers design their products to account for microwave interference. Another concern is the co-location of multiple wireless LANs. While wireless LANs from some manufacturers interfere with other wireless LANs, still others coexist without interference. This issue is best addressed directly with the appropriate vendors.

Users need very little new information to take advantage of wireless LANs. Because the wireless nature of a wireless LAN is transparent to a user's network operating system, applications work the same as they do on wired LANs. Wireless LAN products incorporate a variety of diagnostic tools to address issues associated with the wireless elements of the system; however, products are designed so that most users rarely need these tools.

Wireless LANs simplify many of the installation and configuration issues that plague network managers. Because only the access points of wireless LANs require cabling, network managers are freed from pulling cables for wireless LAN end users. Lack of cabling also turns moves, adds, and changes, into trivial operations on wireless LANs. Finally, the portable nature of wireless LANs lets network managers pre-configure and troubleshoot entire networks before installing them at remote locations.

Note   Once configured, wireless LANs can be moved from place to place with little or no modification.

Because wireless technology has roots in military applications, security has long been a design criterion for wireless devices. Security provisions are typically built into wireless LANs, making them more secure than most wired LANs. It is extremely difficult for unintended receivers (eavesdroppers) to listen in on wireless LAN traffic. Complex encryption techniques make it impossible for all but the most sophisticated to gain unauthorized access to network traffic. In general, individual nodes must be security-enabled before they are allowed to participate in network traffic.

The output power of wireless LAN systems is very low, much less than that of a hand-held cellular phone. Because radio waves fade rapidly over distance, very little exposure to RF energy is provided to those in the area of a wireless LAN system. Wireless LANs must meet stringent government and industry regulations for safety. No adverse health affects have ever been attributed to wireless LANs.

Wireless networks can be designed to be extremely simple or quite complex. Wireless networks can support large numbers of nodes and/or large physical areas by adding access points to boost or extend coverage.

No wonder anyone who has ever designed, wired, and maintained a LAN might be interested in gaining such advantages, especially for the kinds of constantly changing networks we use today.

Universal Serial Bus (USB) Problems

Computer manufacturers started adding the USB port to PC motherboards in 1996. Unfortunately, the industry standards were not completely settled until late 1997. This means you may have a USB port that accepts the plug for the device you want to install but your system may not be able to make it work correctly. On the other hand, some USB devices built before the standard, may not work with today's hardware.

An additional problem is that no one seems to be "enforcing" the USB standard. We have received reports of powered hubs that, none the less, draw power from the computer's USB port and have blown a motherboard fuse. This may not completely disable your computer but you are no longer able to use the USB port. There have also been reports of USB devices that have drawn too much power with similar effects. The real problem is we need a certification authority that tests, reports on, and provides authentication for USB systems and devices.

The USB operates at 12 Mbps and has the ability to support up to 127 devices simultaneously. Devices include keyboard, pointing devices, printers, video, digital cameras, and a host of products still in development. It is an exciting addition to the I/O for PCs. The newest versions of such devices, if they support connection to the USB port, should include the Plug-and-Play installation that takes care of the technical issues of finding their "place" among the other connected devices.

An exciting I/O channel using IEEE 1394, also known as FireWire, is available from companies such as Adaptec on a PCI add-in card that supports up to 63 devices connected simultaneously at up to 400 Mbps. It originated in the Apple world but is very quickly making inroads into consumer electronics and networking products. Because it is not built onto motherboards at this time, the kinds of problems we are covering here are not applicable. But stay tuned . . .

Symptoms

▶ Your PC has a USB port but the device you plug in does not work.

Suspects

▶ The USB port on your system is not enabled.

▶ The USB drivers installed in your system are not up to date.

▶ An add-on USB port is not being supported in your motherboard configuration.

▶ Your version of Windows 95 does not support the current standard.

▶ You have too many devices attached to your USB port drawing in internal power and using up the available bandwidth.

Solutions

▶ If you are using DOS and the manufacturer of the device you are installing did not provide a DOS driver, you have to obtain one from a manufacturer such as LCS/Telegraphics, a company that builds drivers for all sorts of devices.

For Windows 95 use the following as a guideline for checking your system:

▶ To verify that USB is enabled on your computer, go to the Control Panel//System Device Manager and select Universal Serial Bus. There should be a Host Controller and a USB Root Hub installed. If not, check the Other Devices panel and see if any USB components are listed. If so, highlight each component individually and click the Remove button. Yes, Remove. If these drivers are not working, they are most likely an older version. Unfortunately, no version number exists to check if yours is up to date.

▶ Once you have removed all USB components, click the Refresh button and See if your System installs them correctly into a Universal Serial Bus Section of your Device Manager. You may have to insert your Windows 95 installation diskettes or CD-ROM, hopefully the updated version.

▶ If USB is not mentioned in your Device Manager, it has not been properly installed. You should contact your computer manufacturer about properly installing the USB for your computer.

▶ One common cause of USB not functioning properly, is that the capability has not been properly enabled within your BIOS. If you are not familiar with your BIOS, you should contact the computer or motherboard manufacturer about enabling USB. Some BIOS' may only offer Keyboard or Mouse support for USB, which does not work with a bulk device (such as some of the latest video devices and digital cameras). If no mention of USB exists within your BIOS, it does NOT support USB and you are not able to utilize the USB plugs on your PC, unless you can get an updated or flash ROM upgrade for your BIOS.

▶ Many motherboards may have built-in USB support, but the physical ports are not installed. To enable USB you need to purchase the ports from a computer retailer. Simply adding the physical ports and enabling USB support within the BIOS may not be enough to get full functionality for USB devices. You may also need to adjust some jumpers on your motherboard to enable power to the ports. Consult your manual or contact your motherboard manufacturer for more details because their implementation may be unique.

▶ It is possible that you may have older devices that were created before the industry standard for USB was established in late 1997 (or even devices manufactured after the standard but that do not conform completely).

If you do, they might not run and the only option may be to get them replaced by the manufacturer or get a newer device.

▶ Finally, Windows 95B, also known as OSR2, is the first version of Windows 95 that correctly supports USB. Some patches exist which we have seen for Windows 95A, however these patches were created for unique devices on proprietary versions of Windows and may not work with newer devices.

▶ For more information about USB, go to the industry homepage at: www.usb.org though they are not advertising any possible problems yet. The specification is still too new.

▶ The USB standard provides up to 12 MHz bandwidth and 500 mA power which may be allocated in 100 mA unit load amounts in which a device may be allocated from one to five unit loads. The problem is that, once the bandwidth and power is used up by connected devices, no indication is given that no more bandwidth or power is available for an additional device. You connect another device and it just sits there, dormant. One solution is to connect your devices to a powered hub. That takes care of not having enough power (but you still need to be careful because not all powered hubs conform completely to the standard) but when you run out of bandwidth no place is left to turn. Well, not until the FireWire port becomes generally available with more than 33 times the bandwidth.

Summary

Serial communication is a part of every day life for many of us. We have special phones with data terminals, and standard modem and data interfaces for portable computers at major airports around the World. Many cities have Web sites to support distribution of public information and organize community activities. Most businesses have electronic mail and network capabilities that provide access to important information and programs at any time of the day or night and from remote locations. If you travel, you probably take a notebook computer with a built-in modem everywhere you go. We have provided a good look at serial communications, common problems with it, and helpful solutions for those problems. For more information on data communications, see Chapter 10 on networking and Chapter 11 on the Internet.

In this chapter we have covered:

✦ COM port assignment, selection, parameters, and problems

✦ Modem initialization, flow control, and problems

✦ Line noise and attenuation

✦ Ever faster connections

✦ The RS-232 standard, cables, connectors, adapters, and problems

✦ Alternative serial communications — going wireless, USB, and more

Despite evidence that we are well along the way up the road to the Information Age, every day we are surprised by even newer and more challenging opportunities. Serial Communications is just one path along that long road.

We're now ready to move on to Part VI in which we wrap up the troubleshooting concepts and methods we all should be using to manage our PCs. As a matter of fact, if you start with Chapter 23, when you are buying your first or your next PC, you are already on you way to preventing most of the problems or, at least, ensuring that you're able to handle any that sneak into your work environment.

✦   ✦   ✦

Maintaining Your PC

◆ ◆ ◆ ◆

In This Part

Chapter 23
Do it Yourself —
With Confidence!

◆ ◆ ◆ ◆

Part VI really should be the starting point for "Trouble-shooting Your PC." However, this is not the fun part. It is quite often the subject of what you hear from someone recovering from a computer or network disaster. "If only I had documented the model numbers and serial numbers of those components that we lost in the fire." "I wish I had kept better records of what was installed and how it was configured." "Can anyone find the name of the company we bought that from, and what is their phone number?" These are just a few of the exclamations (expletives deleted) that we hear all too often.

If you need or want to maintain your own PCs, if you want to get the most from your computer systems, networks, and remote communications, if you want to be prepared for getting the most from outside help — this is the place to start.

By using this section and the "Problem Index" (located after the Contents), you will be able to document exactly what equipment you have, get to the cause of problems quickly, and have the details you need to meet just about any problem with your PCs head on! (The "Problem Index" is a summary of all of the Symptoms, Suspects, and Solutions sections from every chapter.)

This section has just one chapter, so get on with it!

Do It Yourself – With Confidence!

As you may have realized by now, maintaining a PC can involve a lot of tools and processes. We have talked about the PC itself and its many options and their possible problems. We have revealed a lot of techniques and processes to get you from start to finish. Along the way we have also mentioned a few of the software tools to help you keep your PC in running order. It is time we shared more of what we know about these tools and how best to put them to work.

Later, we get into a more detailed discussion about these software tools and what they do well, and some of the things they do not do well. Because many of these tools are recommended as part of a regular PC maintenance routine, we delve into suggestions for a good self-maintenance program.

Rest assured, it is quite all right to step back and call someone else for help now and then. For those times when you just cannot fix the problems on your own, we also carry all of the information we have gone through to help you make a wise decision and get the most out of a technical support and repair service experience.

Finally, for the time when things are going smoothly and you just want that little extra boost, and to answer a lot of the questions we have been asked, we finish off with upgrade and performance enhancement suggestions.

Don't Neglect DOS

As we move closer and closer to a non command-line PC environment, as indicated by Windows Millennium, which doesn't include a "Command-prompt only" bootup option nor an "MS-DOS Prompt" selection on the Start Menu, we might be lulled into the feeling that we do not need DOS to setup or maintain our PCs. This has never been a more incorrect assumption than it was when Windows 95 was introduced. Even if DOS is dead, some form of command-line interface to get Windows started is still very much alive and well. Indeed, even Windows 2000 still provides a command prompt on demand, and offers a command-line driven installation recovery process.

The command-line interface, though scary to new users, can be your best friend when you need it most. It is crucial to installing and reinstalling the operating system. The command-line interface is also necessary when adding peripherals, such as a new disk drive that requires partitioning and formatting. If your Windows environment is infected with a computer virus, a command-line version is available for most virus protection software to get things cleaned up so Windows can run safely again. Windows' own SCANREG program comes in a command-line version for recovery of prior registry database files, should the current registry become corrupt. Disk drive diagnostics work best without Windows interfering in the process of sector testing and data recovery.

Thus, we need to mention a few of the basic DOS tools you need to work with, and toss in a few you may want to work with given that there may be no effective inside-Windows equivalent.

Hard drive setup

Everyone should know, that you need to partition and format a hard drive before it is available for use by the operating system. Three DOS programs are essential to this process — FDISK.EXE, FORMAT.COM and SYS.COM.

FDISK

The FDISK program is used to create or delete partitions and logical disk drive space on fixed disk drives; either IDE or SCSI. FDISK is the tool that determines whether a disk drive supports the FAT-12, FAT-16, or FAT-32 file systems. These tools calculate and set up the partitioning of the drive (whether or not a specific disk space is used for DOS or non-DOS operating systems) and the logical drive areas (DOS' drives C:, D:, and so on).

The file system type is determined when you answer yes or no to letting FDISK use large drive support when the FDISK program (from later versions of Windows 95 OSR2, 98, 98SE or Millennium) is run. If you select **No** the partition cluster sizes are calculated for FAT-16. If you select **Yes** the cluster sizes are calculated for FAT-32.

Partitioning is the process of assigning a specified amount of disk space to either DOS or non-DOS use. This process does not establish a file system or format that space. You can choose to allow the entire drive to be partitioned as one single DOS drive space, or break it into smaller partitions for DOS or non-DOS use.

FDISK can create three types of partitions — Primary DOS, Extended DOS, and non-DOS. Creating a Primary DOS partition also creates the space for the first DOS logical drive—typically C:, and makes that the Active or bootable partition. Within an Extended DOS partition, FDISK can also create subsequent logical drives, D:, E:, and so on. Extended DOS partitions are not normally bootable because boot information must reside in the first few sectors of the disk drive. Other operating systems may allow booting from other partitions. Non-DOS partitions are created as a place to install a non-DOS or non-Windows operating system such as FreeBSD or Linux.

 Tip Make sure that any partition you create, intended for installing an operating system that is used to boot your computer, conforms to the drive size limitation for that particular operating system.

Most users simply create one large Primary DOS partition as drive C: and make that the Active/bootable partition. No matter how you partition a drive, the partition must always be formatted to create a working file system for the operating system to be used on it. FDISK is for hard drives only and has no function on diskettes, tapes, Zip, LS-120 or CD-ROM media.

The FDISK program has one useful option, the /MBR "switch" that causes FDISK to rewrite the Master Boot Record on the active boot partition, in cases where the boot record may have become corrupt or over-written by the wrong version of DOS. Its use is:

```
FDISK /MBR
```

FORMAT

The format program uses the partition space created by the FDISK or other partitioning program to write out directory and file spaces on the partitioned area of the disk. This establishes the logical drive or, as in most cases, the DOS drive letter. FORMAT can also write the boot information and copy the basic operating system files to the drive area.

FORMAT is used on hard drives, diskettes, Zip, LS-120 and certain other removable media types (excluding tapes and CD-ROMs). Typical use is to format a diskette or a hard drive partition, such as:

```
FORMAT A:
```

or

```
FORMAT D:
```

To place the DOS boot and system files on a disk, use the /S (system) switch, as in:

```
FORMAT A: /S
```

or

```
FORMAT C: /S
```

SYS

The SYS program rewrites DOS boot information and basic DOS startup files to a formatted disk. The files it copies to your disk are the actual operating system used to start and run your computer.

Basic DOS features

When you are working with DOS quite a few useful programs exist that you need and may want to use as you set up and use your PC — among these are CD, MD (MKDIR), RD (RMDIR), DIR, COPY, ATTRIB, EDIT and XCOPY.

CD, MD, RD

CD or Change Directory, MD (MKDIR) or Make Directory, and RD (RMDIR) or Remove Directory are DOS' built-in navigation aids for getting around a logical disk drive. The Windows term, folder, is synonymous with a DOS directory.

CD enables you to move forward into and backward out of directory/folder areas on the disk. It can be used with a variety of command modifiers:

```
CD \
```

takes you back to the root directory of the current disk drive that you are working with

```
CD \WINDOWS\SYSTEM
```

takes you to the Windows system directory

```
CD \Progra~1
```

takes you to the directory that appears as "Program Files" under Windows. The "~1" is the DOS substitution for the remaining characters beyond the eight allowed in DOS.

```
CD ..
```

takes you up one directory level.

MD (MKDIR) and RD (RMDIR) enable you to create new, and delete empty, directories. They have similar options:

```
MD DOWNLOADS
```

for example creates a directory called downloads that is one level deeper than the current directory you are working in.

```
MD C:\DOWNLOADS
```

creates a directory called "downloads" below the root directory of drive C:.

Note Using RD instead of MD deletes the directory, if it does not contain any other files or sub-directories. If the directory indicated in the command-line still contains files, you get an error message, and must delete anything still in the directory before the directory itself can be removed.

DIR

The DIR program is built-in to the DOS command program, COMMAND.COM. It enables you to obtain a list and various details about files and directories. Use DIR /? to get a list of options and example uses for the DIR command.

COPY

The COPY program is built into the DOS command program, COMMAND.COM. It enables you to copy files from one filename to another and into different directories. Use COPY /? to get a list of options and example uses for this command.

ATTRIB

The ATTRIB program provides the simple feature of changing the Read-Only, System, Hidden, and Archive attributes that can be assigned to files and directories. Hidden files are those that cannot be viewed normally with the DIR command or the Windows Explorer program. System files are somewhat like Hidden files, often not seen with Explorer, and are considered critical to the operating system. Read-Only files are those that cannot be written to, deleted, or over-written by other data, as one way to protect them from accidental corruption. The Archive attribute is used by various file backup programs to indicate if the file has been changed or backed-up recently, otherwise it is a passive attribute that does not affect seeing, reading, writing or deleting the file.

The ATTRIB program is most often used to remove the Read-Only, System, or Hidden attributes of a file so that it can be "seen" by the DIR command *or* in Explorer, copied, deleted, or edited. The most common use we have for the ATTRIB program is to enable the Windows MSDOS.SYS boot control file to be edited, and to enable deletion of various Windows system files such as the registry databases. Examples are:

```
ATTRIB --R --A -S -H C:\MSDOS.SYS
```

to make the MSDOS.SYS boot configuration file editable, and

```
ATTRIB -R -A -S -H C:\Windows\USER.DAT
```

then

```
ATTRIB -R -A -S -H C:\Windows\SYSTEM.DAT
```

to make it possible to delete the registry files. Note that spaces exist between the -R and -A parameters, and so forth.

EDIT

The EDIT (filename EDIT.COM) program is as close to the Windows Notepad program as Microsoft offers for editing text files when in DOS. The menu bar, accessible with ALT+key combinations is about as simple as you can get for features. Not a very fancy editor, but it is great for editing C:\CONFIG.SYS, C:\AUTOEXEC.BAT, and C:\MSDOS.SYS and well as most ".INI." file types.

Note   Typically,".INI" files are plain ASCII text files, but not always. If you use EDIT, Notepad, or Wordpad to open ".INI" files and see only strange looking characters, chances are you ran across a special purpose file whose content is known only to the program that uses it. Do not edit the file; close it immediately.

XCOPY

The XCOPY (filename: XCOPY.EXE) program is a versatile program for copying groups of files and sub-directories from one place to another. The command-line options for this program are many, so run it with XCOPY /? to get onscreen help to see all of the options. Typical use is similar to:

```
XCOPY C:\WINDOWS\*.* D:\WINDOWS /s /e
```

which says, copy all of the files (*.*) and sub-directories (/s switch) of the C:\Windows (source) directory to the D:\Windows (destination) directory. This command is more useful than the COPY command because of the large number of parameters and the ability to literally copy a whole drive from one location to another.

Diagnostic and Utility Software

A book about PC troubleshooting is not complete without covering PC diagnostic and utility software. This section discusses why you need to use diagnostic and utility products, and how to select and use many of the best features they provide. Although this book cannot be a complete how-to guide for all of the software packages available, it discusses the programs that we found to be good for specific problems. Many operations, especially disk-partition, crash recovery, and exhaustive hardware tests, cannot be performed without the right software utility. Newer versions of operating systems include a few utilities but not enough to cover every problem you are likely to encounter.

If you cannot trace your particular PC problem to its source by one of the physical, audible, or visual clues outlined in Chapters 12 through 14, you probably need more capabilities than your system BIOS, DOS, DEBUG, CHKDSK, SCANDISK, UNDELETE, or UNFORMAT utilities can provide to find and resolve it.

Even the diagnostic programs included with the IBM PC/XT or PC/AT technical manuals, or with some other advanced systems, contain tests with more detail than simple memory checking or disk-directory snooping can provide. Digging a little deeper into your system requires you to get your hands on a public domain or shareware product, such as those listed here, or an appropriate commercial product.

Diagnostic software packages are the windows to the inside of your system. They provide details about memory, hardware, and, to some extent, the software contents of your system. They are the tools of service shops, consultants, and now everyday PC users.

Why utility software exists and when to use it

Until Peter Norton, Paul Mace, the folks at Central Point Software, and many public-domain and shareware programmers created utility software, there was no way short of raw technical expertise to recover information from a lost or damaged PC file. There was also no way an end user could test a system's functionality without trial-and-error, part swapping, or guesswork. With today's software tools, you can easily diagnose a system problem and perform much of the high-tech repair work yourself.

At one time or another, most users have lost, or almost lost, work because of a bad diskette *or* a power or system failure. All the methods and knowledge in the world is worthless unless you have the tools to repair a problem. As with backups, if you consider your work, time, and data valuable, little should stand in the way of making it safe or getting it back when you need it most. If nothing else, many utility programs are fun and interesting to use, and they can save you a lot of work while you enjoy them. As systems, peripherals, and operating software become more complex, it is also a good idea to use these programs to check out your system before faulting the software or device drivers for system failures.

Distinctions and occasional overlaps exist between diagnostic and utility software. These differences are sometimes subtle and depend on the nature of any corresponding services or repair functions involved and the depth to which each works in your system.

Utilities, such as Norton Disk Doctor (NDD.EXE), perform disk structure and file integrity diagnosis, making sure that the respective portions of your disk and file system are functioning within expected DOS or Windows definitions. The disk controller and file-sector checking has some diagnostic quality, but the value of this utility is in cross-checking file details and making corrections, where possible.

Most *utility software* works within BIOS, DOS, and various operating system or environment specifications and their limitations, providing little functional detail about the device on which the software is being used.

Diagnostic software normally does not provide corrective action, "repair" system components, or disk files that are found to be defective. Instead, diagnostic software provides the lowest level of system testing for functionality, proper timing, data storage reliability, and computational results.

Before using utility or diagnostic software

Unless you have a reason to test your system with all of the programs and memory areas configured for normal use, you should run all tests and diagnostic software on a "plain-Jane" PC system in DOS. This means you should not load memory managers (such as Microsoft's HIMEM.SYS or EMM386.SYS, Quarterdeck's QEMM, and so on), RAM disks (RAMDRIVE, VDISK), disk caches, device drivers, or terminate-and-stay-resident (TSR) programs when the system boots up.

Use only those device drivers required to make system components functional. ASPI drivers for SCSI devices, SCSI or IDE CD-ROM drivers and MSCDEX for CD-ROM drives, and sound card drivers are about all that should be required if you have these system components.

Device drivers and programs can alter the way hardware and memory are used, which may cause inaccurate results in the tests. After you test the bare-bones system, you can install your other device drivers and other system elements, one at a time, until you encounter a problem or your system is complete.

Take care of the items on the following checklist before you get too involved with a utility program, or you may find that it has "fixed" something (as with disk utilities) or reported a failure with a component that is not broken:

1. Use the sample CONFIG.SYS and AUTOEXEC.BAT files shown in the next section (which we saved with filenames CONFIG.TST and AUTOEXEC.TST).

2. Create and keep handy a set of bootable emergency DOS (or other operating system) and utility diskettes available in case something goes wrong, especially when testing your disk drives.

3. Create a current backup of your system (if the system in its present state allows you to do a backup).

4. Use the disk image-saving utility from the software package of your choice (again, if the system lets you do it). You should also have image files available from the last time the system was running. In either case, these files, and any "undo" files the utility software creates, can be the key to reconstructing the files on a bad disk.

5. Make sure you can leave the system unattended and undisturbed for the period of time it takes to run the tests. In-depth disk-sector testing can take over eight hours if you are just starting out, or if several bad areas exist on the disk.

You do not need to sit there watching the tests' progress for too long. The screen symbols can be mesmerizing. After five to ten minutes, you should have an idea of how long the tests take to complete, as most of the programs indicate percentage of completion or an anticipated completion time.

If you cannot leave the system powered up for the length of time it takes to do the full test, change the test pattern to a less in-depth process or wait until you can leave the system powered up that long.

6. If you are going to test serial or parallel ports, or the diskette drives, be sure you have the proper parts. Serial and parallel ports generally require a turn-around or loopback plug. Examples of these are shown in the cabling diagrams in the Reference section of this book. For the diskette drives, have formatted disks of the maximum capacity of the drives available. Using a 360K diskette to test a 1.2MB drive, or a 720K disk to test a 1.44MB drive may cause a failure.

Start with a simple system configuration

It is a good idea to create and use specific CONFIG.SYS and AUTOEXEC.BAT files for testing your system. You may find that similar examples are included with diagnostic software you buy, or in the documentation for the programs you download from an online library. You should make backup copies of your usual CONFIG.SYS and AUTOEXEC.BAT files. Next, before you run any tests, copy the test files (named here as CONFIG.TST and AUTOEXEC.TST) to CONFIG.SYS and AUTOEXEC.BAT, reboot the system, and start the testing software. In the following sample files, the d:\path\ means that you should put the drive letter and directory names for these files on your system in these places:

CONFIG.TST:
```
BREAK=ON
FILES=99
BUFFERS=6,2
SHELL=d:\path\COMMAND.COM d:\ /p /e:512
```

(Substitute your drive letter, typically A: or C: for the "d:" indicated previously.)

AUTOEXEC.TST:
```
ECHO OFF
CLS
PROMPT $p$g
PATH d:\path1;d:\path2,...C:\DIAGS
```

(Substitute your drive letter, typically A: or C: for the "d:" indicated previously. "C:\DIAGS" is an example of the directory containing your diagnostic software.)

With these files, no device drivers or memory-resident programs exist to get in the way, occupy extended or expanded memory, or obscure the locations of special BIOS chips that may be on your video or disk controller cards.

Note   You may need to use your CMOS RAM setup program (or select it at bootup) to disable any shadow RAM your system might place in the memory area between 640K and 1MB. Shadow RAM can obscure the hardware detail in the address range between 640K and 1MB (which may be the location of your problem in the first place).

When these files are in place and ready to use, reboot your system with the preceding configuration and begin your testing. To make this process a little easier, another batch file can do the copying and renaming of these files so you can switch back and forth between a normal working configuration and a test configuration. Here are two sample batch files to do this procedure:

TEST.BAT:
```
COPY C:\CONFIG.SYS C:\CONFIG.RUN /Y
COPY C:\CONFIG.TST C:\CONFIG.SYS /Y
COPY C:\AUTOEXEC.BAT C:\AUTOEXEC.RUN /Y
COPY C:\AUTOEXEC.TST C:\AUTOEXEC.BAT /Y
ECHO You may now reboot your system for Testing Mode
```

NORMAL.BAT:
```
ECHO OFF
CLS
COPY C:\CONFIG.RUN C:\CONFIG.SYS /Y
COPY C:\AUTOEXEC.RUN C:\AUTOEXEC.BAT /Y
ECHO You may now reboot your system for Normal Running Mode
```

Different flavors of diagnostic/utility software

Different classes of diagnostics exist, and each one gives a different depth and range of visibility of what is going on in your system. We group the programs into three general categories:

✦ viewers or informational programs

✦ diagnostics or testers

✦ preventive and repairing utilities

Some of each category may be combined in any one suite of programs you may purchase or obtain by downloading from the Internet, while those you might get from an online site or other source of noncommercial software generally contain only one type of software.

Disk-drive utility packages combine testing, prevention, and repair, in most cases. Some packages are test-only utilities, and some must be used with other advanced test equipment to perform repairs.

Note

Our discussion of repairing disk problems is limited to the recovery of lost data, formats, and protecting disks, rather than the operation of any physical or technical work inside drives.

Information viewers

Programs that merely let you see the contents of your system, from memory to disks to BIOS ROM, and those that assess the performance of your PC system, are viewers. Unless you ran the program while your system was working fine, you may not have a basis for comparison of the results of the analysis. However, if you have a specific problem in your system, the analysis should point to its cause.

This list shows some of the many programs that fall into this category:

✦ CHKDSK (without the /F option, an external DOS program).

✦ DIR (an internal command in DOS' COMMAND.COM).

✦ MEM.EXE (with MS-DOS 5.0 and higher).

✦ Microsoft's MSD or MSINFO (with DOS 5.0+ and Windows *and* available online from many sources), MSInfo32 (for Windows 9*x* and above, which is installed with most Microsoft Office programs).[MDW1]

✦ Norton Utilities' SysInfo (for your particular operating system).

✦ Advanced Personal System's SYSINFO.

✦ Quarterdeck's Manifest (provided with older versions of QEMM).

✦ Device Manager dialog boxes found in Windows 95 and 98.

✦ Windows NT Diagnostics installed in the Administrative Tools menu.

✦ Watergate Software's PC-Doctor.

✦ Microsoft's NTHQ utility, found in the \Support\Hqtool directory on your Windows NT 4.0 (both Workstation and Server) installation CD-ROM is one of the most comprehensive system viewer utilities available today. It is provided to check any PC with a 486 or higher CPU, at least 12MB memory, and a 3.5" diskette drive to determine whether NT may be installed., It provides tremendous information about your system and all of the devices that can be seen by NT including port addresses, IRQs, hardware configuration, CMOS settings, hardware conflicts, and more. The bootable diskette you create from this directory may be used on a computer regardless of the operating system installed. No technician's toolkit should be without a copy of this diskette.

Note

These programs report the status of your system and can identify its contents, including information such as the number and type of I/O ports, amount of memory, and so on. They do not show errors if the errors occur during operation, and they do not identify or correct problem areas.

The information these programs provide (See Figures 23-1 through 23-3, for example) can be quite valuable. They can survey a system, indicate whether a COM port or disk drive is present and, of particular interest with today's advanced memory use, report how much of which type of memory your system has installed and how it is being used. This is especially important if you suspect you have a memory problem or if you are working with Windows or some other operating environment with significant memory demands.

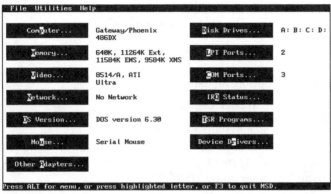

Figure 23-1: Typical system information from Microsoft's MSD

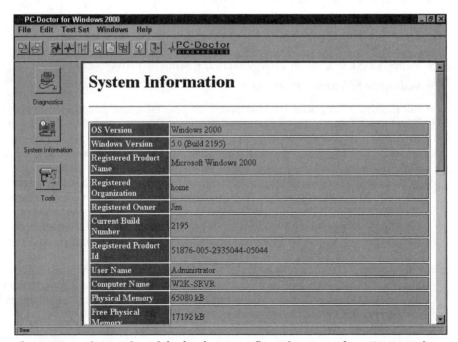

Figure 23-2: First portion of the hardware configuration report from Watergate's PC-Doctor Service Center 2000

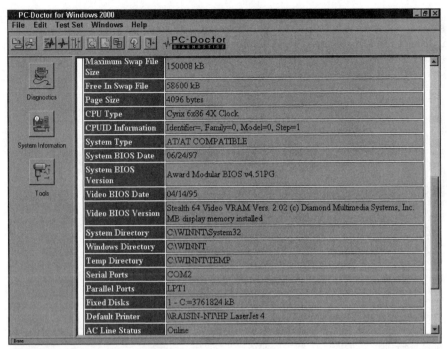

PC-Doctor for Windows 2000	
File Edit Test Set Windows Help	
Maximum Swap File Size	150008 kB
Free In Swap File	58600 kB
Page Size	4096 bytes
CPU Type	Cyrix 6x86 4X Clock
CPUID Information	Identifier=, Family=0, Model=0, Step=1
System Type	AT/AT COMPATIBLE
System BIOS Date	06/24/97
System BIOS Version	Award Modular BIOS v4.51PG
Video BIOS Date	04/14/95
Video BIOS Version	Stealth 64 Video VRAM Vers. 2.02 (c) Diamond Multimedia Systems, Inc. MB display memory installed
System Directory	C:\WINNT\System32
Windows Directory	C:\WINNT
Temp Directory	C:\WINNT\TEMP
Serial Ports	COM2
Parallel Ports	LPT1
Fixed Disks	1 - C=3761824 kB
Default Printer	\\RAISIN-NT\HP LaserJet 4
AC Line Status	Online

Figure 23-3: Second portion of the hardware configuration report from Watergate's PC-Doctor Service Center 2000

Note

The screens from PC-Doctor Service Center 2000 were taken from a system running Microsoft Windows 2000 Server. While Windows itself can provide this information from Device Manager and from the MSInfo32 program as well as diagnostics provided with Windows 2000, having this information validated by a third-party program is reassuring. You can always cross-check the settings by using the PC-Doctor utility for DOS and in your system BIOS.

Because memory allocation is very important to Windows, one of the best tools to help with installing or troubleshooting this environment is the Manifest program from Quarterdeck. You can get Manifest as a stand-alone utility, separate from QEMM. Manifest, the MEM program provided with MS-DOS Version 5.0 and higher, and the memory map programs listed previously, are among the most comprehensive indicators of memory status available (Figures 23-4 and 23-5). Although Manifest is no longer included in newer versions of Quarterdeck's QEMM, the older versions still work on your system while conducting tests, after booting with a plain, vanilla DOS system as described earlier.

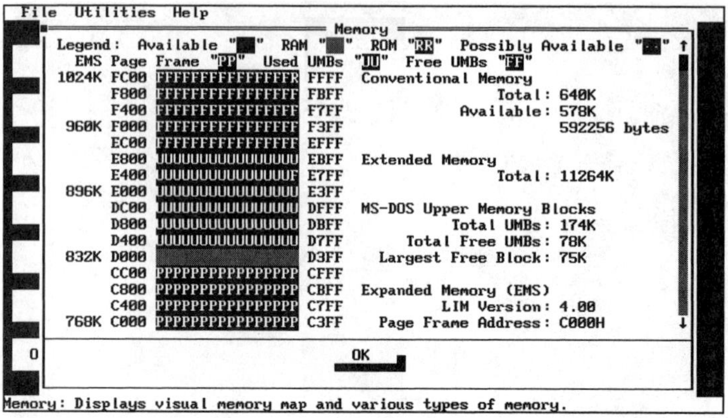

Figure 23-4: System memory map from Microsoft's MSD program

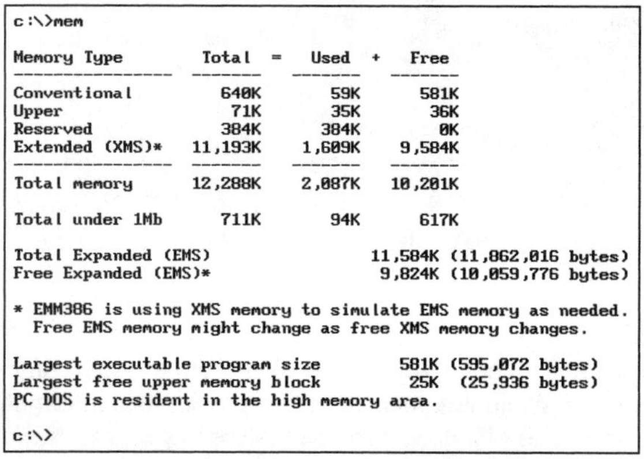

```
c:\>mem

Memory Type        Total  =   Used  +   Free
----------------  -------   -------   -------
Conventional         640K       59K      581K
Upper                 71K       35K       36K
Reserved             384K      384K        0K
Extended (XMS)*   11,193K    1,609K    9,584K
----------------  -------   -------   -------
Total memory      12,288K    2,087K   10,201K

Total under 1Mb      711K       94K      617K

Total Expanded (EMS)                11,584K (11,862,016 bytes)
Free Expanded (EMS)*                 9,824K (10,059,776 bytes)

* EMM386 is using XMS memory to simulate EMS memory as needed.
  Free EMS memory might change as free XMS memory changes.

Largest executable program size        581K (595,072 bytes)
Largest free upper memory block         25K  (25,936 bytes)
PC DOS is resident in the high memory area.

c:\>
```

Figure 23-5: DOS memory map from the DOS MEM program

Information about existing IRQ and DMA assignments is essential for ensuring proper performance and adding new devices to your system. Figure 23-6 shows an IRQ report from Microsoft's MSD. Figures 23-7 and 23-8 show the IRQ and DMA reports from PC-Doctor Service Center 2000. An important note here is that MSD assumes certain assignments and does not provide complete information about your current system, nor does it report on IRQs 8 through 15. In other words, MSD may not give correct or complete information. If you are looking for IRQs that are not used or that may be reassigned in order to resolve a conflict, you need that complete and accurate information. Use the best tools you can afford.

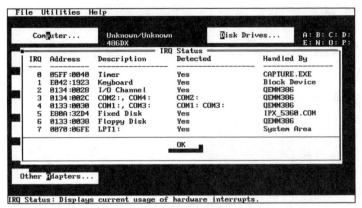

Figure 23-6: IRQ information from Microsoft's MSD program

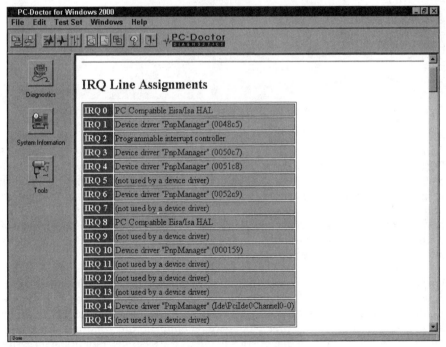

Figure 23-7: IRQ information from Watergate's PC-Doctor Service Center 2000

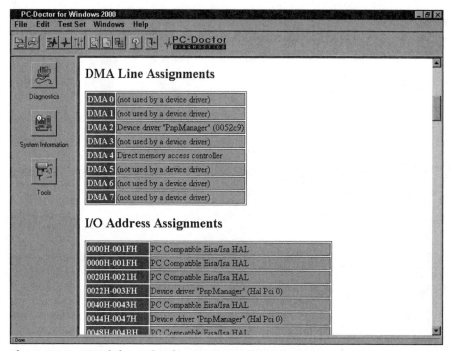

Figure 23-8: DMA information from Watergate's PC-Doctor Service Center 2000

Of note is that the PC-Doctor IRQ and DMA reports do not show the "IRQ Holder for PCI Steering" that Windows shows for many devices. When you have a device using an IRQ and the "IRQ holder" also assigned to that IRQ, this is not sharing IRQs. This is simply Windows' way of keeping track of who has what assignment. It is generally understood that, at the Windows device driver level, some form of translation occurs between the PCI and AGP bus and standard legacy IRQ allocations. The driver software holding a place for mapping internal and I/O bus, PCI and AGP resources, to the interrupt limitations of the x86 architecture chipsets, does this.

We have included a demo version of PC-Doctor Service Center 2000 to illustrate the power of such a program through its system information capabilities, and to give you a good deal of functionality to help get you past an immediate problem. The full version of PC-Doctor Service Center 2000 — we recommend the Windows version — also provides significant system diagnostics to check the system's functional integrity, locate bad modules, and verify subsequent repairs. The Windows version also provides detailed Windows task and running program module information, which can be quite handy for detecting performance bottlenecks and strange behaviors.

Benchmark programs

Benchmark programs fit into the viewer category, and provide basic and very detailed information about your system's performance. The benchmark tests have their pros and cons. The utility suites published by computer magazines and journals are setting some standards for compatibility checks of RAM, ROM, video, and adapters. Programs that report speed or computing performance are novelties. Sometimes they are useful, and on occasion they are misused to assess, compare, demonstrate, and sell systems.

You need to take the early versions of some speed tests with a grain of salt. They were easily fooled by BIOS or nonstandard PC timing applications, and sometimes this flaw indicated CPU speeds double, triple, or even ten times that of any known PC chip on the market. Rely only on industry standard figures for system performance, including MIPS, Dhrystones, and Whetstones for CPU and NPU performance, and the access and file transfer times for disk performance. The benchmarking in Symantec/Norton's System Information program (shown in Figure 23-9) is perhaps the best known and one of the most reliable tests, but it does not provide industry standard benchmark results. WinStone, WinBench, and similar tests from various magazine publishers seem to be the comparative guides many folks rely on these days.

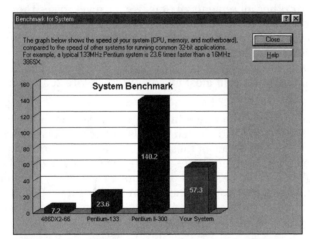

Figure 23-9: CPU Performance Benchmark from the Norton Utilities v 3.0

Many utilities evaluate and report the performance of video, memory, disk, and system boards available for use under Windows 3.x, Windows 95/98/NT, and Windows 2000. These are also limited by information available at the time the software was released. Be wary if you have an AMD, Cyrix, or IBM CPU that is not properly identified as such by the benchmark utility. This means that the utility is not up-to-date with current hardware. Do not rely on only one set of performance tests to evaluate a system unless you are familiar with and trust a particular set of system information reports and comprehensive tests.

If your Pentium III or Celeron chips show up as a Pentium II, you probably did not get short-changed. Windows 95 and 98 have limitations in CPU identification — they, of course, could not have been programmed with the ability to read, and associate specific CPU ID information, from the CPU chips with specific processors before said processors were available. Expect more of this kind of "misinformation" as new AMD and Intel chips come on the market.

Year 2000 tests and fixes

Although the year 2000 problem is behind us, experience tells us that the problem was bigger than just the fear of your computer's clock rolling back 100 years to January 1, 1900. The year 2000 issue brought attention to many other significant date problems, including the following:

✦ **Leap years.** Everyone we know seemed to get past this second-most significant date in the year 2000 which was a leap year even though most programs calculating leap years identify every century transition as NOT being a leap year.

✦ **Numbering system limitations.** Whether or not the numbering system in a clock chip, memory, logic, program, or data is large enough to count the seconds, minutes, days, or other increments of time. We have yet to see these limitations create problems, but look out for the years 2015 to 2038 because various programs and operating systems we know today can fail; let us hope we are past the Windows-whatever-version days by then. Even Unix with its 32-bit date handling will not accurately handle system dates beyond 2038. We need 64-bit date handling routines in most all computers before 2038 rolls around.

✦ **Significant default or "dummy" numbers in data.** We have commonly used 9/9/99, 00/00/00, or 99/99/99 to fill in unused records rather than leave them blank, and often test for the presence of these numbers as part of program operations. Again, no known problems here — but then many of us did prepare ahead of time. This may never surface as a problem. However, we should remember that the data files that contain these dummy dates have probably not been changed and future programmers may run into dates that may look real but mean nothing.

A type of utility program gained tremendous popularity in 1999 in the face of the year 2000 transition — programs that test PC system clock chips, BIOS, and operating systems for different types of date related functions. Among these tests are the following:

✦ **PC clock chip compliance.** Most pre-1997–98 clock chips do not have century capability and cannot roll over to 2000. You may expect this test to fail on many systems, but the BIOS, or a BIOS upgrade, may be able to patch-over the clock chip problem.

✦ **BIOS compliance.** BIOS comes into play in two ways. First, it can make up for the clock chip problem by evaluating the year (usually whether it is greater or less than "80") and place the right century data into memory. Second, whether or not the BIOS can handle the year 2000 properly; a BIOS that makes up for the clock problem should be able to perform into the next 100 years. If not, the operating system gets the wrong date.

✦ **Leap year checks.** The year 2000 is a leap year. If the clock chip and/or BIOS cannot handle this and subsequent leap years, the operating system is fed the wrong information and a lot of dates could be messed up. This may never be a problem unless you have old PCs kept around for doing noncritical work. Just remember not to use them for anything that may cause a date calculation problem.

Because many of the date milestones for the Year 2000 issue we faced last year still exist, you may still need a good Year 2000 diagnostic program. The data you've been collecting and storing for years may still have two-digit year dates and may still provide you with some challenges. Finding a year 2000 test program is very simple. Go to any Web search site or online file library and search with the words "year 2000" or just "2000" and take your pick. About 80 percent of the sites that are reported by the search engines are news or industry articles about the year 2000 problem. Another 10 percent are equipment manufacturer and software publisher sites reporting on their year 2000 compliance. The remainder is various year 2000 software and consulting companies that offer information and samples of software to download. Many of these sites also offer programs that can be run to make up for the clock chip and BIOS problems so that the operating system gets the right dates.

Testing the PC for the items listed previously is relatively easy. The real tough testing occurs not at the hardware, BIOS, or operating system level, but at the application and data level of our systems, and the other systems we depend on for work, utilities (power, gas, water, and communications), banking, and other critical functions. For these there can be no single or specific test other than making up data sets for your important dates in the year 2000 and putting the software through its paces, or auditing systems one piece at a time.

For as many Y2K test programs that existed there were almost as many Y2K-fix programs available—from those that would install in your system boot record, to supposedly intercept and correct simple date issues, to those that would somehow seem to intercept program instructions and correct date calculations on the fly. We have seen programs that would check the system date at bootup and make corrections (most of these are OK, if they are needed), to those that would claim to inspect actual program code and make in-line corrections to the code without harming it. Some of these programs were akin to the proverbial "snake oil", perhaps not intentionally but ineffective, and some of them actually made a legitimate correction for clock and BIOS deficiencies. Our recommendation, however, is if you have a system with significant clock chip or BIOS date issues, you should retire that system for something more up to date—it is cheaper and more reliable in the long run.

If you have any questions about your systems or software and their year 2000 compliance or other date issues, visit their Web site.

Diagnostics and testing

Diagnostic programs may check just one portion or all of a system and tell you what, if anything, is wrong. The most useful of these programs reports on all of your system components — memory, disk drives, I/O ports, internal functions, and the video adapter, modem, and keyboard.

One good thing a diagnostic program does best is to perform repetitive tests until an error is detected. A simple test of system RAM when you boot up (as provided by the POST) may not be a complete check of all possible memory patterns or addressing methods.

Only rarely does a CPU test fail on a system that you can still boot up and use to load the software. If you have an intermittent problem that suddenly occurs after the system warms up or after a specific program is used, repeating all of the system tests over the period of an hour or overnight might be the only way to identify clearly which part of the system is failing.

You can purchase, through mail order or off the shelf, the same diagnostic software that is used in manufacturing burn-in facilities (where the systems are sent for long-term testing after they are built) and by service technicians.

Armed with these tools, and access to parts support for your system, few problems exist that you cannot diagnose and fix yourself, providing that your system boots up.

The following programs fit into the diagnostic category:

✦ Watergate Software's PC-Doctor

✦ Eurosoft's PC-Check *aka* CheckIt

✦ Network Associates' PC Medic

✦ AMI's AMIDIAG and PC Care

✦ Norton Disk Doctor and NDIAG

✦ Steve Gibson's SpinRite

Few packages are as comprehensive as Watergate Software's PC-Doctor family of programs for testing all the nooks and crannies in your PC, whatever its model (refer back to Figure 23-8). These programs test in single or repetitive iterations, and you can configure them for the tests and the number of times they run. PC-Doctor is also the diagnostic suite of choice for most major PC manufacturers.

Although the Windows-based products, NAI's PC Medic, and AMI's PC Care are certainly clever, and in some cases very powerful and a lot friendlier to use than DOS-based programs, their operation, testing depth, and results are dependent upon the Windows configuration, device drivers, and the variables of Windows itself, meaning they may provide inaccurate information.

It is nice to know that your CPU, memory, disk and I/O systems work well under Windows. It is also nice to get a failure report based on what the programs see under Windows (which may lead to fixing configuration problems). However, if you really need to test something quickly and without interference from a lot of programs and graphics overhead, we recommend lower-level DOS-based diagnostics for the best testing you can perform without special test equipment. Certainly, by comparing DOS-level and Windows-level information, you can tell a lot about the system, but everything in a PC must be based on a proper hardware and BIOS setup first, and that is where you should start.

These diagnostic packages are commonly associated with technicians or manufacturers' quality control tests of systems needing repair or burn-in after manufacture or repair. They are certainly not everyday applications you need to run, but they are extremely valuable in identifying problems in broken systems, provided that the system boots up.

Beyond this category of programs are hardware products that may start the system without DOS (special diagnostic boot ROMs) or use a plug-in card to analyze the system through the data bus.

The hardest problems to pinpoint are the intermittent ones. By performing a comprehensive, full-system test without having to sit at the PC and interact with prompts or call up programs repetitively, you can exercise a PC for long periods of time. (After all, this is one of the things a computer is good for — repetitive, mundane tasks.)

If you repair systems, provide consulting services, or provide system quality checks or evaluation for purchasing, these are the packages to consider buying and using.

Memory tests

Memory testing of your system may be included in one of the system diagnostics, or it may be a separate selection or program. Which sections of memory are tested, need to be tested, and how well they are tested depends on your computer system, its configuration, the program you use to test memory, and the nature of any problems you encounter.

Many memory test programs are available within diagnostic packages such as CheckIt by TouchStone Software and PC-Doctor from Watergate Software.

Power-On Self Test

Your system BIOS does a quick memory test every time you boot your system. This is part of the power-on self test (POST) that is activated with a power-on or cold boot. If memory problems are detected at this step, you see an error message onscreen that reads something like this:

```
PARITY CHECK 1
10000 0200 202
```

or

```
PARITY CHECK 2
10000 0200 201 (202 or 203)
```

or

```
00640K OK
```

A parity check error indicates either that one of the actual parity bits, stored in a separate RAM chip from your data, is defective or that the memory contents did not match the test and set this flag instead of indicating the error location.

The numerical message indicates that the test found the first 640K of memory to be okay, but an error exists in higher memory. The next line shows the block of memory found defective (10000) and the row or chip location that was bad (0200), followed by the error message #202. In this case, the 64K bank of memory beginning at 1MB, and the column for bit 9, is bad.

To repair this problem, locate the memory section that contains the address range for the second megabyte of RAM, locate the chip for bit 9, and replace it. This location can be within a chip bank that covers a much larger range, or it may be an entire memory module. If your memory is not implemented in discrete chips, you have to replace the entire memory module containing the error.

Error 201 indicates a data-comparison or parity error, error 202 indicates that the error is in the address bits 00–15, and error 203 indicates a problem with address bits 16–23. (The appearance and detail of the error you receive from your system may be quite different, and so might the chip locations. This example simply shows the kind of information you can expect to see and have to interpret.)

Disk drive diagnostics

Norton Utilities is the most common, while NAI's Nuts & Bolts is a recent contender, but do not overlook Steve Gibson's SpinRite, which not only tests your drive but also repairs the problems caused by electro-magnetic and mechanical changes. This group of programs encompasses testing, prevention, and repair services for disk drives and file systems.

A good test of your disk subsystem should include the controller, the basic drive functions, the disk features (number of heads and cylinders), its configuration (partition and file structures), and its data integrity.

Adapters and controllers

Disk adapters and controllers must conform to a set of standards that enable your system BIOS, DOS, and any application programs to send a known set of commands and get back a known, expected set of responses. The commands tell the drive system what to do, and the returning information is the requested data, a response that data was written properly, or a report that an error occurred at the controller, in the drive, or in the data.

These standards are provided for in the controller's hardware or onboard BIOS. Most controllers use a small microprocessor specifically designed or programmed to control the disk hardware; and most also provide internal error correction of the data going to and from the disk drive, and some provide onboard disk data-caching to improve performance.

Your disk drive accepts commands from the controller and is expected to return or write good data or error messages if something goes wrong. The rest is up to the integrity of the disk surface, the read/write heads at the disk, and the data itself.

Probably your biggest concern is the integrity of data written to and read from the drive, where you rely on the electronic portions of the system to tell you if anything is wrong.

Disk test types

Many different ways exist for you to test these electronics to provide accurate data or an error message. The best way is to write and then read known data several times, perhaps changing the data slightly to ensure that writing works as well as reading. This is called destructive testing.

You can perform quick tests by reading only the data from the drive to check its integrity. This is nondestructive testing because your data is left as-is while the test program checks all the file areas on the drive.

The following programs provide read-only testing:

✦ DOS CHKDSK (without the /F option) or Windows' SCANDISK (which is actually a scaled down version of Norton's Disk Doctor).

✦ Norton Disk Doctor

✦ Steve Gibson's SpinRite

✦ AMIDIAG from American Megatrends

✦ Watergate's PC-Doctor

✦ Eurosoft's PC-Check / CheckIt

If you really have to know if your disk drive is working reliably, regardless of the format and file system to which it is formatted, use SpinRite.

The Norton Utilities package comes with disk-image logging programs that collect and save information to help the disk and data repair utilities reconstruct bad files or drive areas, or recover from accidental formatting.

Destructive Testing

Although destructive testing does not destroy your drive, it does wipe out your data. Any existing data is written over by test data. The drive may require a new low-level format (typically not for IDE drives), repartitioning, and a DOS format when the testing is complete. Destructive testing may be necessary if your system indicates continuous data errors, or you are trying to evaluate the drive for reliability. If data is present on the drive, and you can read data from the drive, use a backup program to save data before running these tests, unless you have dismissed the data. These tests can take a long time to exercise the drive mechanically and test all possible data patterns.

Disk surface testing utilities

If you really want to go beyond disk file integrity checking and scour a disk drive's sectors for bad data or determine the reliability of the data storing capability of your drive, the ultimate utility is Steve Gibson's SpinRite program. Vaguely comparable features to those of SpinRite are available by using both Norton Disk Doctor (NDD) and SpeedDisk programs from Norton Utilities and Microsoft's SCANDISK and DEFRAG programs (both are derived from, or are abbreviated versions of, the Norton programs). However, these do not perform a low-level format, change the interleave, or move data from bad sectors to good ones.

SpinRite (shown in Figures 23-10 and 23-11) scans your hard drive, identifying the optimum sector interleave for best performance, and tests for bad sectors. It dynamically reformats the drive, as needed, to correct the interleave setting or bad disk areas. Dynamic reformatting involves reading and saving the data from a disk sector to memory, performing a low-level format on the sector, and then replacing the data. It saves you from having to perform a backup of your data files, a complete reformat and repartitioning of the drive, and restoring the data files afterwards. Even if you stop the SpinRite process while it is running, your drive and data are available for immediate use. However, a complete backup of your data before you start is always a recommended procedure.

```
┌──────Determining 1st hard drive's operational characteristics──────┐
│ Partition C: with    210 megabyte capacity on the 1st physical drive. │
│         9 : heads              Yes : drive caches reads              │
│        32 : sectors            Yes : caches avoidable               │
│       832 : cylinders     3,609.12 : revolutions per minute         │
│   212.094 : total megabytes    8.97° : physical intersector angle   │
│   F000 hex : bios entry segment  1-to-1 : sector interleave         │
│   1st hard : bios drive          Yes : extreme sector translation   │
│    IDE/ATA : interaction method  Yes : zone bit recording           │
│        Yes : identify drive cmd  Yes : has engineering cylinder      │
│        Yes : retry suppression    No : drive caches writes          │
│         No : cache disable cmd    No : subtle sector translation     │
│        Yes : drive diagnostics    No : miscellaneous anomalies       │
│     32 bits : ecc data available  Yes : "dynastat" data recovery     │
└────────────────────────────────────────────────────────────────────┘
```

Figure 23-10: SpinRite Version 5.0 can probably tell you more about your disk drive than its manufacturer.

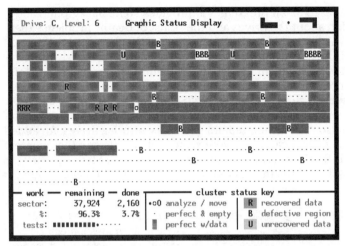

Figure 23-11: Status of a drive under test by SpinRite Version 5.0

The real key to SpinRite is that Gibson Research has invested a lot of time and effort into understanding disk drives and their operations, especially the features and tricks used in IDE drives from various manufacturers. We have to place this utility far ahead of Norton and other disk diagnostics for drive testing. It is nondestructive and inconsequential to long filenames or other file system issues (as long as DOS or Windows can see the drive) because it works with data sectors and the drive's electronics, preserving what is there, or helping the drive automatically move data to good, spare sectors.

The dynamic formatting capability offered by these utilities is a great time saver. When you are evaluating the drive for potential problems, this kind of reformatting can provide immediate correction, and prevent future problems.

Although you should back up data and files before performing this operation, dynamic or on-the-fly reformatting, with the existing data in-place, saves a lot of grief and thumb-twiddling. Performing these operations one step at a time takes hours of backing up, reformatting at a new interleave, repartitioning the drive, DOS formatting, and then restoring files from the backup.

Always exercise caution when using any software of this type with IDE, SCSI, and some ESDI drive interfaces and drives. Check the documentation that comes with the software and the product (system, drive, and adapter) before attempting any low-level testing, formatting, or partitioning operation.

Removable media drives

In response to a significant dilemma facing users who have experienced failing Iomega Zip drives, Steve Gibson has created a free program called TIP.EXE, which stands for Trouble In Paradise (a visit to the Gibson Research Web site—www.grc.com—explains all, and then some). TIP, shown in Figure 23-12, is a

Windows 95/98/NT-based 32-bit program. TIP provides some background and technical information about the drives and the "Click of Death" problem experienced with them, which leads to exhaustive testing of the drive and the currently inserted cartridge. All TIP testing is nondestructive, unless, of course, the drive has a preexisting massive hardware or electronic problem. The results are a detailed explanation of the condition of the cartridge being tested and, of course, the condition of your Zip drive. Steve's latest version of SpinRite, in addition to all the features we need to keep our disk media in good working order, has a much enhanced version of TIP that also detects and repairs problems with Jaz drives. An added feature helps you to maintain a catalog of your removable media and their contents. TIP.EXE is on the CD-ROM included with this book. Thanks to Steve's investigation into this problem, "Click of Death" issues have been pretty much wiped out.

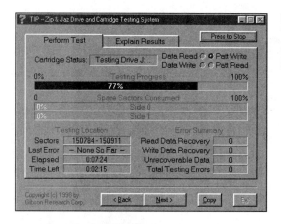

Figure 23-12: Steve Gibson's TIP.EXE examines Iomega Zip cartridges for defects and repairs bad sectors, if possible.

System utilities

In the past few years we have seen dozens of utility software packages spring up that offer a wide range of feature and function enhancements to your operating environment. These include the legendary disk and file utilities that test file and directory structures and fix them and the file and directory recovery, or undelete, utilities — the same category as the Norton Utilities. This category of utilities has grown up to handle myriad details under Windows that were once reserved for DOS-only operations — now they work equally well or better under Windows 95, 98, Me, NT, and 2000.

Many of the utilities mentioned here, and similar programs that run on your system in the background, automatically and normally consume some level of active, limited system resources — memory, CPU time, a certain amount of disk access time, and interception of normal memory, disk and peripheral I/O processes — to monitor and record system configuration, usage, and change details. Although these applications are designed and produced very carefully so as not to be destructive or overly intrusive, other applications may not tolerate the consumption of resources or the interception of functions.

These application conflicts or incompatibilities are becoming less common as standards and requirements are provided to developers. If in doubt about any program or system misbehaviors, you should disable these utilities and restart the system and the application or functions in question, as part of the process of elimination in determining related causes of problems.

Remember that the actual problem may not be within these utilities but within other programs that are intolerant or nonstandard in their design or function. Report any and all questionable errors to all software publishers involved — they are then able to cooperatively determine the best course of action to remedy any problems. Also, check the FAQs on the company's Web site for known issues regarding the problem at hand. Often, you are not alone in the problem you may be experiencing.

Application and excess file removal

Because Microsoft Windows and Windows applications are notorious in their misbehavior as far as maintaining good installation and setup file changes and tracking them, a new family of utilities monitors software installations and provides the ability to completely uninstall them and clean up excess files. These include Symantec's CleanSweep and McAfee's UnInstaller.

The object of these programs is to remove the normal bits and pieces of a software package's installation, from the installed files down to the entries they leave in DOS configuration files and Windows .INI files. The simplest implementations of these programs look for an application that you want to remove — say, Microsoft Word — and delete all associated files and subdirectories where it finds Word's files — or at least those put there by Word's installation.

The more sophisticated utilities actually scan your system to obtain a reference profile of its condition before an installation and then continuously monitor your system to determine and record exactly where an application installs itself and what files it modifies during the installation. This latter approach makes for a very exacting and complete removal of an installed application, so that the files and the modifications to .INI files are completely removed. Ideally, these utilities give you the option of storing rather than completely deleting a removed application in case you need it later, thus saving you the hassle of completely reinstalling the application. This latter capability is implemented in Quarterdeck's CleanSweep, Extra Strength.

Quarterdeck's CleanSweep, Extra Strength includes many other useful features. Among these are Zip-It, which makes a compressed archive of an application that you can recover later if you decide you want to use it, and options to enable you to move, backup, or transport an installed application from one disk drive or directory structure to another (or even another computer), moving or changing all references found in .INI files and desktop links as well. It also provides a Windows Registry Genie that enables you to view, edit, back up, and restore your Registry.

Another feature you may find useful in these utilities is the ability to detect files that are never used by any application at any time during the course of your normal

PC use, and then, at your request, present a list of these files and offer the ability to remove them to clean up your system and free up disk space. This is something that is highly recommended and should be done prior to using a disk file defragmentation utility.

Configuration monitors and updates

Recently there have been new utilities that offer to monitor and fix (or at least alert you to) system and software configuration problems. These begin to apply years of system experience, data collection, and the knowledge of expert developers and PC technicians to the everyday PC.

Windows diagnostics

There are several diagnostic programs on the market. McAfee's FirstAid 2000, offers an entire suite of utilities. and Symantec's Norton Utilities now has WinDoctor. First-Aid tries to present itself as just about everything you could want from hardware configuration checking, but it lacks robust system information, requiring you to tell it a few things about your hardware before it is able to diagnose your system. We have to question this because if a program needs you to tell it about your system, how is it going to know what is correct and what is not? The same applies to its software configuration tools.

Symantec's CleanSweep uses its tremendous, existing database of application installation details. In addition, it monitors the system activity for executable, DLL, and related file activities. Using your current Windows 95, 98, Me, NT, or 2000 configuration information, the install database information, and a lot of excellent logic and experience, it can pinpoint and tell you about mixed file versions, missing application and support files, misconfigured applications, and other details about applications and your computer's environment. It can also fix these misconfigurations or advise you of what to do to correct any problems found. This is a wonderful tool for those situations in which you find yourself with multiple versions of different DLL or driver files that create conflicts between applications.

Update and upgrade services

A number of utilities have started to include their own automatic update features, a process by which the utility uses a modem or the Internet to contact a host system, compares the version of software now installed to what is available, and offers to update your system. Anti-virus programs, which should be kept up-to-date regularly, are an excellent example of this trend.

These features have also found their way into a new family of utilities we call *updaters*. Updaters are used to take a snapshot of your system, recording the current operating system and the versions of all applications and drivers installed. This snapshot is then compared with an online database full of information about, and links to, file libraries that contain newer versions of these files. Some utilities or services provide the capability to download selected updates, install them, or, in the best of cases, track the new installation process and let you undo the changes if they do not work.

In 1996 CyberMedia introduced Oil Change, a retail package also available online as a subscription service. (CyberMedia has since been acquired by Network Associates/McAfee.) In 1997 a startup called TuneUp.com also developed and released a similar product called TuneUpdate. (TuneUp.com had since been acquired by Quarterdeck, and Quarterdeck by Symantec which killed this online support service.) Since these two services began operation, at least two different Web sites offer various forms of updates, `www.drivershq.com` and `www.manageable.com`. Symantec has also joined the fray with Norton LiveUpdate Pro at `www.nortonweb.com`.

In Windows 98 Microsoft has included the Windows Update utility to perform similar functions specific to the Windows 98 operating system, as a means to distribute updates and patches without a lot of complicated Web browsing. Microsoft is also embracing some form of online support with its "PCHealth" features in Windows Millennium, which may include featured services from many different vendors. Relatively new to the online support scene is the Attune service from Aveo, `www.aveo.com`. Attune is a unique service that can take the mystery out of obscure error messages, and provides advice when your are about to install a conflicting driver or application, as well as presenting many other types of helpful preemptive support messages — and best of all, the service is *free* to end-users.

These services are a tremendous idea, but they are in their infancy. In some cases accurate system information is missing, providing misleading driver or program update choices. Also missing from these utilities is a connection between any of the Windows configuration checkers or diagnostics and the update services to help you determine if you actually need or should download and apply a particular update. Users must be careful to read the information about any updates presented to see whether or not they apply to your system. Fortunately a good undo feature or an uninstaller utility is a good way out of the wrong update dilemma. We hope the firms offering these services plan to look at them more closely and determine ways to make them as comprehensive as they can be.

Disk system repair and file recovery tools

Beyond testing for and diagnosing disk problems, the greatest benefit of some utility packages is the recovery or correction of bad disk sectors, the transfer of good data out of bad areas, unerasing of files, and improving system performance by reinterleaving the drive or sorting and defragmenting files for faster access.

Disk-imaging routines

The imaging routines included with Norton Utilities and Nuts & Bolts are intended to be run on a regular (daily) basis so that you can maintain a current record of the files and organization of your drive. This imaging provides quick reference information for a recovery program, saving a lot of time in the recovery process and in post-recovery use of the system.

The steps to running these tests are straightforward. You should know the designation of the disk drive you want to test (A–Z). Also, if you are in doubt about allowing the test to write to the disk or automatically correct any errors found, configure the test for read-only, or "prompt before correcting," mode. The documentation for the program should help you here, but most of these programs also offer help if you invoke the program using a /? or /h parameter at the command line before actually running the tests.

Note Make a hard-copy print of the program's help screen for quick reference whenever you need it.

Disk and data recovery tools

Norton Disk Doctor, Nuts & Bolts, SpinRite (which can actually fix a failing drive), and SCANDISK provide tremendous help in recovering data and informing users of the status of their drives. What do you do when none of these solutions seem to work? What if your drive does not spin up? What if the drive spins up but does not sound quite right?

Two potential solutions to the problem exist — the first is to arrange to return the drive to the manufacturer's service facility for evaluation and possible repair, at some expense to you. Drive manufacturers do not warranty data loss and may otherwise offer to replace a defective drive, but no guarantee exists that the data will remain intact.

The second solution is to contact a data recovery service, such as OnTrack (www.ontrack.com). OnTrack first provides you with their DataAdvisor program. DataAdvisor is used to perform a quick analysis of your system and the condition of your disk drive. This information enhances OnTrack's ability to assess the situation and advise you of the alternatives for data recovery. Often they may be able to connect with your system online and execute testing, simple repairs, or further evaluation. If the online support does not work they should at least be able to give you an evaluation and an estimate of the cost of recovering the data from the drive. OnTrack has recovered data from drives that have been crushed, dropped, smashed, burned, mangled, crashed, or otherwise believed impossible to salvage.

This service is not inexpensive, but compared to the cost and time of recreating critical business and financial data from paper records, or asking your vendors and customers for help, the money is well spent. Of course, if you keep current backups of your data with a tape drive or other system, which costs a fraction of what recovery services charge, you are better off in the long run. Either way, you will probably still have to buy a new disk drive to replace the damaged one.

Configuration and Windows registry backups

Because many of us had all sorts of problems sorting through the multiple obscure possibilities presented in the ".INI" files of Windows 3.x, and were told to fear the Windows 95 registry database, many clever programmers devised simple utilities to backup, restore, and record changes to these files as we used Windows. One of the most effective and efficient programs is a little-known utility program called ConfigSafe from Imagine LAN, www.image-lan.com. ConfigSafe records an initial snapshot of your system configuration, and any changes that have been made to it from time to time.

A handful of other utilities are available for making backups of your Windows registry files so that you can return to a prior "point in time," essentially, when the system was known to be working well, should you or some program make a mistake and scramble the registry or try to run a driver or program that crashes your system. Recognizing this need, Microsoft first provided the SCANREG tool with Windows 98. SCANREG can make up to 5 backups of previous registry data for later recovery if needed. SCANREG can also check your registry for basic problems.

Software definitely worth mentioning

We have been fortunate enough to work with and review a number of software products that have been time and effort savers, in our travels, consulting, and routine work. We believe the items listed are just what you need when it comes to helpful software. Although these programs may not diagnose or fix problems with your PC, they may indeed help you solve some of those troubling tasks around the office.

For the Internet and the Web

Hot Off The Web (HOTW), a commercial product from Insight Development (www.hotofftheweb.com), has got to be the coolest program for sharing Web pages in a collaborative or "check this out" situation. HOTW enables you to capture any Web page of interest in its page-annotation tool. Within this tool you can highlight, circle, and make notes or callouts to any content appearing on the page, as if you had the page on a "whiteboard" and could scribble all over it. When you are done, save the page in the special HOTW format, which also includes a viewer utility, and then copy or attach the file to an e-mail message and send it to a friend for their viewing pleasure. Without HOTW you would be stuck making and marking up printouts, or simply sending off URL links and having to explain the items you want someone to look at. With HOTW, you don't have to worry about HTML, complicated screen captures, paint programs, and file format issues.

NetSwitcher is everything Microsoft should have included in Windows 95, 98, Me, NT, and 2000 for maintaining control and selection of different network and dial-up connections. If you travel, use a network in different places, change between portable and docking modes, or just want to play on a single network but have to change a few parameters, you know what a pain reconfiguring Windows networking can be. NetSwitcher is shareware, meaning you get some time to check it out before you are asked to register the program, and the $8 registration fee is *well* worth it. To get NetSwitcher, visit www.NetSwitcher.com/.

They still use text, right?

UltraEdit is *the* editor for all of those ASCII, HTML, source code, and similar files you encounter that do not require a full word processing system but do need more capabilities than just text editing. This $30 shareware program by IDM Computer Solutions is available from www.ultraedit.com. The program offers all the features of a technical editor, combined with the simplicity of NOTEPAD. You get column mode, word wrap, and known-format highlighting (meaning that when editing HTML files, the various tags and parameters are given different colors, making them more readable and easier to work with — and it works for C and other source code files as well). In addition, auto-selection and saving of files formatted for UNIX systems is possible. (This is a real time saver for those of us who refuse to learn "vi" but need to work with files on UNIX hosts.) You get both 16- and 32-bit Windows versions, and a DOS version as well.

Graphics galore and more

ThumbsPlus has got to be one of the most powerful graphics file viewing and modifying tools available. It is a $74.95 shareware program available from `www.thumbsplus.com`. ThumbsPlus enables you to view, modify the attributes (color depth, color shift, flips, inversions) of common graphics files, and convert them to other graphics file formats. This program is ideal for everyday graphics viewing as well as performing minor alterations, without having to invest in Photoshop or other expensive programs. ThumbsPlus was used extensively to help us capture and convert various graphics files for this book.

What is running back there?

Have you ever wondered what the heck is running in Windows? Has a technical support representative ever asked you to be sure nothing else is running on your system? DLL Master, a $25 shareware program from Shaftel Software (no Web site, but the program can be found on various sites through `www.download.com`), will probably provide the clues you are looking for. This program lists all of the drivers, DLLs, programs, and windows (open and hidden) that are active on your system. You might be amazed at all of the files and drivers it takes to make Windows and your applications tick. This program will show you these files and enable you to unload from memory those programs you do not want to have running or cannot seem to kill any other way. But be *careful* — unloading the wrong program can bring your system down like a house of cards in a hurricane.

Do-It-Yourself Advice

The best solution to a problem is to avoid it in the first place. The little time it takes to care for your system can save you a lot of time in the long run by preventing serious problems. Taking the time to make frequent backup copies of your software and data can save time when you run into problems, and in some cases, it can preserve your job or reputation. By following careful installation procedures (including documenting your configuration and updating the documentation you maintain on each of your systems) when adding new hardware or software to your system, you can prevent redundant procedures and new problems caused by faulty installation.

A megabyte or two of prevention

Use the following list of preventive measures to give yourself a little test. Are you comfortable with the measures you take to protect your system? If some of these practices sound foreign to you, consider how much time it would take to construct last week's work from scratch, and take a look at this list again:

✦ Always keep a set of system diskettes handy that you can use them to boot your computer.

These disks should contain the version of DOS (or other operating system) installed on your hard disk, all the device drivers that give access to the accessories added to your PC, the programs used in your CONFIG.SYS and AUTOEXEC.BAT files (or other operating system's device configuration files), and, of course, your CONFIG.SYS and AUTOEXEC.BAT files (or startup files used by your other operating system) and drivers for your CD-ROM.

✦ Back up your system often.

Your data and configuration are important elements, but the device drivers and programs used to start your computer have a special significance. If you cannot start your computer, you cannot work and you cannot modify your present configuration.

✦ Whenever you are installing new software and hardware, even new versions of software already running in your system, do not start it until you have a good backup of your system and the original software diskettes.

✦ If possible, store your backups at an alternate site.

It is best if that site can install your backup and give you access to your files at that alternate location. It is good to have friends and associates who can provide that sort of assistance. In some circumstances, it may be necessary.

✦ Develop a PC support "network" of people who know different things about hardware, applications, and so on in your office, company, or neighborhood.

Maintain contact with someone who knows enough about PCs, hardware, and software to help when things are not going right. User groups can be an excellent source for this kind of help. Refer to Appendix I, "Favorite Links," for WWW addresses of a few national and international user groups and other helpful companies and organizations. A more complete listing of user groups may be found by searching the Association of PC Users Group's Web site at www.apcug.org.

✦ Develop a personal library of the documentation for the hardware and software installed in your system.

Keep your system documentation handy and become familiar with it. It is a lot easier to get help if you can provide some basic information about your system. Remember, this includes both the documentation you received with the new software or hardware, along with the settings and configuration options you chose while installing it in your system.

✦ Keep your computer clean.

It is a good idea to cover your keyboard when it is not in use. Keep liquids away from all electronic components. Check air intake and outlet areas for dust and dirt buildup.

✦ Keep good records on the status of your system.

Sending in the registration cards for your hardware and software ensures that you can get help from the manufacturer, producer, or distributor, and makes it possible for you to receive updates, problem reports, and solutions that are sent to registered owners of products.

System diskettes

Chapters 12 through 22 cover the process of starting up and configuring your computer. Most systems today, even notebook and laptop computers, have hard disks. They make it convenient to turn on your computer and let the hard disk install device drivers to give access to the special hardware and to execute programs. However, when a problem occurs, especially if it involves your hard disk, it is critical that you have a set of diskettes you can use to boot your system.

As mentioned in the preceding checklist, these disks should contain the version of the operating system (DOS, Windows, OS/2, UNIX, or other O/S) on your hard disk, all the device drivers you have installed in your PC, the programs used in your operating system's configuration files (CONFIG.SYS, AUTOEXEC.BAT, Windows Registry and/or other files), and your CONFIG.SYS and/or AUTOEXEC.BAT, boot, and other files appropriate to the particular operating system. If you cannot fit everything on a bootable diskette, include at least the device drivers and programs that give access to your hard disk and other devices necessary for running your system.

Having several copies of these diskettes, rather than one, ensures that you can boot your computer, even if something goes wrong with one of the disks.

Tip   Every time you change your configuration, make a new backup. Keep at least one copy of your old configuration around, too, just in case something happens while you are developing your new one.

These diskettes are a backup of the crucial part of your system. Without them, you may have to call an expert to get your system going again.

The grandfather backup method

Use a "grandfather" approach to maintaining backups of your system diskettes. When you want to create a new set of system disks, the last set you made to start your system becomes the "grandfather," and it is not changed. Use the old "grandfather" set of disks, which become the "great-grandfather," to make a new set of disks that becomes the "father" of your system. This set of disks contains your most recent configuration and startup procedures. This way, you always have diskettes that can start your system, even if the new ones become corrupted or cannot do the job.

Tip

Before you store your backup system diskettes in a safe place, make sure they really will start your system by testing them. *Use* them to start your computer.

Backups

The term *backup* is almost always followed by *hard disk*. However, as indicated in the discussion of system diskettes earlier, backing up your hard disk is only part of this very important preventive measure. Make backup copies of the installation disks for the software installed in your system, separate from the hard disk backup as well. Copy your important data files to diskettes, tapes, CD-ROM, or other media, in addition to your normal hard disk backup. Store copies of your hard disk backup, system diskettes, software installation disks, and important data files in a place away from your computer.

Many companies "escrow" or keep backups of their work in progress and finished goods at other sites, use bank vaults, or contract with security services to archive and store the precious materials that record their businesses.

Many ways exist to back up your hard disk. The best method is the one you find convenient enough to use consistently. Dedicated tape drives and automated overnight backup utilities for individual workstations or networks are excellent time savers.

The simplest and most time-consuming method of backing up your system is to copy files to diskettes. If you run into problems because a file is too large to fit on a single diskette, try using one of the file compression utilities such as Winzip which can be found at www.winzip.com or others that use the ARJ, LHA, PAK, RAR, or ZIP formats to make the file smaller. These programs will even split a file that is too large to fit on a single diskette into multiple volumes, each on its own diskette and in a sequence that enables you to restore the large file from those multiple diskettes. Using a compression utility to compress seldom-used directories of files can free as much as 50 percent of your used disk space. This is similar to the methods used to provide DoubleSpace and other tricks to make your hard drive hold more data.

The DOS BACKUP and RESTORE programs have improved quite a bit over the past several years. Some of the commercial programs, such as Seagate's BackupExec and Norton's Backup Utilities, offer additional features, including the ability to rebuild a backup index from the backup diskettes and the ability to verify the files before restoring them.

Cross-Reference

See Chapters 18 and 19 for information on how to handle hard-disk problems.

Adding a tape drive to your system is a simple process, similar to adding a diskette drive or a hard disk. One or a few tapes can hold all of your data, and you do not have to stay at your system to constantly feed it more diskettes. You can start a backup before you settle back in your easy chair or head out to lunch, and come back refreshed and feeling a lot better about the work you have done.

A safe place

If the work your PC is helping you do is important, consider making arrangements with a friend or another office to be prepared to install and run your important jobs. This will require you to have a complete backup of the software and data files for the job. The alternate site will also have to provide the special hardware and software that your system uses to produce the finished product.

It may seem silly to hold a disaster drill and actually perform your work at the alternate site, but if the need actually arises and you are not prepared, you will be out of luck.

Careful installation procedures

The most important preventive measure is to be very careful about what you install in your system. The second is to make sure you have a complete backup of your system before you start. If you run into an installation problem, at least then you will not lose what you had before you started.

Manufacturers and producers of PC hardware and software are getting better about reporting known conflicts with their products; however, because these are not exactly selling points, they are not emphasized in any of the sales material. Anytime you add something new to your system and something goes wrong, the first suspect should be the new item. If in doubt, referring to your software and hardware vendors' Web sites, and the well-respected Bugnet (www.bugnet.com) Web site and subscription database is always a good idea.

Support networks

Many large companies have developed PC support groups. Sometimes these groups are implemented as company-wide user groups. Sometimes they form a new division and staff it with PC professionals whose job is to support the company's computer users. For smaller companies, involvement with a local PC user group can provide an avenue to getting help. If you work at home and you are really lucky, you might have a computer-savvy neighbor who can act as your guru and mentor.

Regardless of the form it takes, make sure that you have a place to turn when something goes wrong that you cannot fix yourself — even after reading this book.

Personal library

Get documentation for all computer software and hardware you purchase and install. These installation guides, manuals, and booklets are important. Keep them in a special place and make sure that new versions, as they become available, replace the old ones on your bookshelf.

The original and backup copies of the installation disks for your hardware and software are just as important as the documents. Keep these disks with the manuals if they have a special pocket or sleeve for storage. Otherwise, keep them in a covered disk box in a safe place.

When something goes wrong, check the documentation for the program you are using before you do anything else. Take notes on the steps that led to the problem before you forget what happened. The person you reach out to for help will need to know what happened to determine what may have gone wrong.

Keep it clean

Unless your system is used in an extremely dusty, damp, hot, or cold place, you should not have to clean it often. Soap and water are not good for your system. Use a damp cloth for dusting and wiping the outside of your system unit and external devices. Use a small vacuum and compressed air to get rid of the dust.

Office supply stores generally have cleaning kits for computers and other office equipment. The kit usually contains a cleaning solvent that is mostly alcohol, a lint-free cleaning cloth, tipped applicators for cleaning hard-to-reach places (such as around keys on your keyboard), an antistatic cleaning fluid for cleaning your computer screen, and cleaning solvent with special disks for cleaning your diskette drives.

Your diskette drives should be cleaned only when you suspect that they are not reading and writing disks correctly. Cleaning them too often increases the wear on the read/write heads. In a relatively clean office, your diskette drives should require cleaning no more than a few times a year.

Once or twice a year, use a vacuum cleaner to remove the dust from the vents around your system unit and the air screens on your monitor, modems, printers, and other devices.

Note   Avoid taking your system apart, even disconnecting cables, unless you need to move or test a component. Any time you disturb the connections in your system, you take a chance of introducing a problem that did not exist. The old saying "If it ain't broke, don't fix it" is good advice.

Keep good records

When you install new hardware and software in your system, send in the registration cards. Keep a copy for yourself with the serial and model numbers. Store these with your documentation or installation disks. When you need technical support, you will need to know exactly what is installed in your system and be able to provide the information that is on your registration cards.

Making a copy of the screens from installation programs is a simple way to document the specific installation settings for the hardware and software installed in your system. If you cannot use the PrtScn (Print Screen) key to get the screen printed, use a print-to-file utility or write the settings you have selected in the documentation for the hardware or software. This can save you time if you need to go through the installation process again.

 Note   The more information you have about your hardware and software, and the settings in your system, the fewer problems you will have troubleshooting and solving the problems that occur, or dealing with the people you call for help. See the "System Documentation and Technical Support Trouble Report Data Form" section at the end of this chapter.

Supporting yourself

Self-support can be a less expensive, immediate alternative to the high cost of service contracts that almost all vendors will try to sell you, or to the delays caused by visiting shops and ordering parts. Some of the following suggestions can assist you in providing your own technical support:

✦ Build a library of books such as this one. The collected experiences of those who have faced problems similar to yours can be valuable.

✦ Take classes at your local community college or university. You will have the opportunity to learn from experts and to meet other people in your area who have interests similar to yours.

✦ Join a user group. User groups offer help sessions, classes, and meeting discussions where you can broaden your knowledge and get tips from other users. A listing of user groups may be found by searching the Association of PC Users Group's World Wide Web site at www.apcug.org.

✦ Participate in discussions in news groups and use other Internet services. You will find online experts on nearly every facet of personal computing. You can often get an answer to even the toughest technical question in a matter of minutes. It is likely that the manufacturer or publisher of your troubled product has a bulletin board, online forum, or Web site. Check into these. Most of these have lists of frequently asked questions (FAQs) that feature common questions and answers about products, use, setup, and troubleshooting.

✦ Fill out the technical support form that appears later in this chapter and keep it handy as a reference.

Technical Support and Service

Unless you are a PC technician, all the books and tools in the world may still not provide the exact answer you need. In some cases technical support and service might be the ultimate solution.

Because even the most comprehensive testing does not reveal every possible problem that might arise with their products, most manufacturers and vendors provide some form of technical support, service, or both.

Computer manufacturers, software publishers, manufacturers of peripheral products such as modems and monitors, and sometimes even dealers who sell PC products, offer technical support for the products you have purchased. You must generally qualify for service or support at the time of purchase or within a specified period of time. This means you should complete and send in software and warranty registration cards as soon as possible, which will determine the level of service you may receive through the warranty period and beyond.

Software publishers often offer different levels of support based on the product you purchase and on whether you subscribe to and pay for enhanced support. System manufacturers and dealers all provide some form of warranty support, and may offer extended warranties, or carry-in or onsite service with various response times.

Software registration

Vendors who provide technical support usually do so only for their registered users. Most PC products include a product registration card in the package with the documentation or an Internet registration method—use it.

Send in the registration card or register over the Internet as soon as you install the product and prove that it works correctly. If the product is defective at installation, you should be able to return it to the place of purchase. If you have sent in the registration card, however, the dealer will probably send you to the manufacturer for repair or replacement.

Keep the purchase receipt in a safe place. The receipt will show the date of purchase, which many vendors require, to qualify you for upgrades. Some vendors only provide free technical support for a fixed time period after purchase; in this case, the dated purchase receipt provides proof of eligibility.

Registration is also a good way to protect yourself from losing support if someone has taken a copy of your product, uses it on another system, and tries to get help from the manufacturer. If your copy of the software spreads around a work environment, is subject to software piracy audits, or ends up on a pirate Internet site, registration and records are your only hope of proving that you are the proper license holder.

Service and support

Technical support and service is available in several ways. For software, support most often rests with the publisher and is usually handled by phone, fax, or through an online service, or the Internet. The last three methods can provide a broad range of information from other users, and possibly even supply files and updates available only to registered users. Registration, in fact, may be your key to unlocking a vast library of support files for the products you use.

For hardware, the selling vendor or the manufacturer may provide service and support at any of several levels, from phone calls to onsite service visits. Your employer may also provide in-house support for one or many products, or maintain the PC equipment the company provides.

Telephone technical support is available from almost all computer equipment manufacturers and software publishers. Support is usually free if you are calling long distance. Toll-free technical support is normally reserved for customers who have paid for extended support or some other type of premium service. A few vendors now offer 900-number technical support lines, but this can be very expensive, especially if you have to wait on hold for very long. Expect to provide some form of proof of registration at the time of the call.

Getting the most from any support experience

Support is becoming costly and time-consuming for everyone. It certainly can be improved in many ways. One of the reasons that more companies are charging for support, and why you have delays in getting support, is that the company has either poorly documented or poorly implemented the product, which you cannot help. Also, many users expect the technical support personnel to act as tutors to teach them how to use the application.

Note   Be sure that you fully understand the return policies of the store, dealer, mail-order house, or vendor from whom you purchase a product. Many "sidewalk" resellers out there have no connection with the originating company and thus no return method or agreement with them. Therefore, the manufacturer knows nothing about the reseller and cannot possibly be responsible for unknown sales. Many resellers will not fully or even partially credit software purchases after the shrink-wrap or tamper seals are opened.

Tip   Be sure you have done your best to select the right application by reading product reviews and understanding the application, and by knowing whether the application is suited to your needs. If in doubt, ask around and check the local users groups. You might find free support or classes to help you.

Remember, the technical support person is there to help as best they can. It is a job — no more, no less — just like yours. Having been behind the scenes for a number of successful and not so successful products, I've learned that support can be pretty grueling to provide as well as difficult to seek or get. Everyone involved should try to be positive—support is a positive concept in one way or another. If it becomes a negative experience, no one wins. The technician did not design, write, or build, the quality-assurance check, or review; nor did the technician release the product you purchased, or design the marketing campaign and packaging.

Indeed, some products out there are over-marketed in their claims or in relation to their compatibility or actual function. These are issues you can take up with the product's marketing department. Look for ways to improve things. If you have a serious problem with a product, simply state what you want—a refund, a fixed product, a workaround, whatever is reasonable to expect. You may only get what the company has to offer at the present time, so be prepared for a reasonable answer within those bounds. Threats of legal action without all the facts or without setting an expectation of what you want from the company or support effort make it difficult to serve any purpose. A simple statement of the outcome you desire from the support exchange may save everyone hours, days, or weeks of frustration and poor communication.

These are issues that we encourage the tech support staff to participate in where they work as well. They know best the problems to which they have to respond. This is valuable information for everyone from the company owners to the designers to the marketing and salespeople to have at hand.

Prior to the call

Regardless of which method of support you seek, the following tips will help you get the most from your contact with technical support personnel.

1. Information about your hardware and software environment will be important to the support technician you call to diagnose the problem. Prepare a listing of all the elements in your environment, preferably on paper. Keep the list updated as you change your hardware and software setup. This list should contain the following information:

   - A complete list of your hardware configuration, including computer manufacturer and model, serial and/or product numbers, processor type, amount and type of memory, display card type and manufacturer, monitor type, disk drive types and sizes, and the manufacturer and purpose of any boards installed in your system.

   - The operating system version you are using, if any.

   - A listing of your CONFIG.SYS file or other, startup configuration files.

   - A listing of your AUTOEXEC.BAT file or other startup programs and files.

   - A picture of your memory resources, such as that provided by MEM, MAP, or other utilities.

   - A listing of your subdirectory tree structure.

Cross-Reference

We have included a sample form at the end of this chapter, in Appendix H, and on this book's accompanying CD-ROM for recording this information. Keep a version of this document in hard-copy form. If your only copy is stored on a disk and your system will not boot, you cannot get to the data at the time when you and your support technician need it the most.

2. Make accurate notes describing the problem and the actions that you have taken while trying to solve it. Include as much detail as you can, and include screen prints of error messages if possible.

3. Check the hardware and software manuals to make sure that you have not missed a reference to the problem. Many manuals include a troubleshooting section. You may even find a solution there.

4. Check the company Web site support or FAQ sections to see if they have a fix listed there.

5. If you cannot resolve the problem on your own, take the following steps before calling technical support:

   • Gather the system information from Step 1 and the notes from Step 2.

   • Move a phone near the computer. This is very important. For your call to technical support to be truly effective, you must be at the keyboard of the computer having the problem. One of the first questions the technician will ask is, "Are you sitting at your computer now?"

Repair services

Your first efforts at getting hardware service or repair should be directed to the dealer from whom you bought the product. Many vendors will exchange a defective product that is within the warranty period if you have the proper documentation.

Some dealers have a service department for warranty and nonwarranty repairs, or a third-party arrangement. Many dealers offer their own services, or contract with another party in some areas. Some vendors serve as a drop-off or shipping point for you when a product must be returned to the manufacturer for repair or adjustment.

Tip

The vendor should be your first contact when you need technical support. Most large vendors, and many small ones, have a technical support department set up to answer your questions.

You dated receipt will serve as proof for most vendors offering service or support that the product was sold by their company; a dated receipt also serves as evidence of the warranty status. Be sure to ask dealers about their service and support policies when making your purchase.

When you solicit repair services, be sure you can get a copy of any diagnostic reports or verifications that the problem has been fixed. Diagnostics means a lot of different things to different shops, so do not expect that you will be able to get a printout from any one diagnostic program. Typically you may get a summary "Hard drive checked: _X_ Yes ___ No" type of listing.

For more information about typical PC repair experiences, check out `www.computeruser.com/magazine/national/1408/covr1408.html` for the scoop on how three shops dealt with (or did not deal with) some common PC problems. The bottom line here is this: Know as much as you can before you decide to call or take your system to the shop, and tell them exactly what you need and want done. If they try to sell you replacements or anything new, have them prove that you need it.

Service options

Some manufacturers offer service directly to the customer who purchased the product. Large firms dealing in many levels of computer products may have their own service plans, as do Hewlett-Packard, Compaq, and IBM. Others, such as Dell, offer service in the form of a contract or arrangement with a third-party maintenance company such as TRW, General Electric, or Honeywell. Service is available in several forms:

✦ Onsite service, where the service technician comes to your location. This is the most convenient and the most expensive type of service. If you plan to purchase an after-warranty service contract, expect to pay the most for onsite service.

✦ Carry-in service, where you will be expected to take your equipment to a factory-authorized repair center. This is less convenient, but it is also less expensive.

✦ Mail-in service, which is a variation of carry-in service. This is slower than carry-in service because of shipping times in both directions. It is also a bit riskier because your equipment is being handled by a third-party shipper. Mail-in service is usually a bit less expensive than carry-in service, however. Some companies, such as Dell and Gateway, may send you a new part or even a new computer based on your request for technical support. This kind of arrangement is very quick and convenient.

✦ Telephone service, in which a service technician attempts to coach you through your own repairs, based on your telephone descriptions of the problem. Some companies even send repair parts to you, but this form of service is usually marginal, at best, from smaller or less well-known companies.

Third-party arrangements sometimes look enticing, but they may not always be exactly what you expected. These firms service a variety of equipment, from cash registers to mainframe computers. If you are lucky, the service company will have a stock of parts for your particular brand of computer, but the farther you are from a major urban area, the less likely you are to find your part in stock. Confirm the level of parts and support available by calling the local service office before you spend money for this type of support.

In many cases, even local dealers with their own service shops do not stock the parts for all the systems they sell. They must send for them from their corporate stock or from a manufacturer, which may take at least a day.

For any of these service choices, you must assess your own needs, and be aware of what is available and how much it will cost. Onsite maintenance for a typical system costs from $150 to $300 per year, with some offset depending on where you live and the expected level of service.

Contract telephone support

As software publishers and manufacturers realize the cost of supporting their products and users realize that these costs are being passed along to them, it might help to seek support services from one of many new third-party telephone support companies.

These firms are often the same ones you are not supposed to know you are calling when you think you are calling the original software or hardware vendor. They charge by the call or on a fixed-fee basis for a period of time or number of calls. They can offer services for more than just one product, and often resolve problems for everything from booting up to printing, no matter the computer make, model, or included applications.

Tip   You can get more responsive, comprehensive support from third-party firms than from single-product support resources.

Remote or electronic support

Computer manufacturers, service and support vendors, in-house support departments, and friends are discovering the benefits and often fun of providing support electronically. Use online resources freely and often. You will find a wealth of information at your fingertips. The FAQ lists at most support sites handle a majority of the common problems you may encounter. This can take a little digging or Web surfing, but it is often well worth the effort.

Your computer system, utility, or diagnostic software package — and hopefully someday, common applications — may have communications software, of one type or another, bundled with it. Microsoft's Windows 95, 98, Me, NT, and 2000 include links to access the Internet and include Web access to their support sites. Windows 98 also brought Microsoft's new online update service that compares your system with a reference database at Microsoft, and offers updates for your operating system, saving you a lot of browsing and wondering.

More recently, system vendors who also bundle diagnostics are offering remote control support plans and software with system purchases. These efforts are aimed at providing direct, virtual onsite help. However, this is potentially time-consuming. By calling into an "electronic support center" the support technicians can operate your system and see the problems first hand. They can change the configuration or upload new files to get you going, or at least determine the problem more accurately and know which parts to send.

Even more exciting is the prospect of simply selecting the internal help in your software package and having remote support tools at your fingertips. These tools can be aware of your system configuration and the specific application, and they can forward detailed information to a support center electronically. Having this information at hand, rather than spending several minutes gathering it by voice over the phone, saves everyone time and money. Working out a solution and sending it back to you, formatted, within the context of the immediate situation, is much more effective.

This technique effectively automates the phone call or electronic mail to "see" the symptoms first hand. The support center can try your configuration and reply to your request for help without you waiting on hold, answering 20 questions, and having misunderstanding and frustration all around.

Expect present and future software packages to implement electronic support within the user environment or software package. Corporate help desks and other support providers find this to be a most effective way to support users. Just as you find emergency call boxes and service stations along the road to home, you will have them on your journey through your computer system.

Technical support form

The following pages contain the System Documentation and Technical Support Trouble Report Data Form referred to throughout this chapter. Many technical support and software beta test programs require very detailed technical information to identify or reproduce problems so they can be fixed. The following information is a compilation of that which is used by many hardware and software vendors. Without this information, it may not be possible to solve your problem. This information may also be provided from comprehensive diagnostic and system information software.

We intend for you to copy these pages and keep a report on file for every one of your systems. Attach or refer to this form every time you have a need to call for service or technical support.

We also recommend that you maintain a list of all software brands, names, versions, and serial numbers for quick reference. Do not forget to register your software and hardware to obtain special notices and upgrade information and to preserve your legal license to possess and use it and obtain technical support.

System Documentation and Technical Support Trouble Report Data Form

We have provided a comprehensive multipage form you may use to develop complete documentation of your computer system(s) and continue with additional pages for each problem you encounter throughout the system's life (see Appendix H for the form). Although we really cannot guarantee that developing and maintaining the form will ensure all of your computer problems are solved more quickly and completely, we still suggesting giving it a try to see how it works. The technical support representative of whatever company you call for support will be delighted that you know so much about your system before you place your call. It will make a *world* of difference in how your problem is handled.

Quick Performance and Upgrade Hints

We have explored a variety of hardware and software in the course of our work and writing this book, and we have come across many features, options, and add-ons that increase the performance of a system. This section contains some quick and economical recommendations.

Overall performance

Almost nothing beats upgrading from a 16 MHz 386 system board with 2MB of RAM and an 8 MHz I/O bus to a screaming 800 MHz Pentium III with 256MB of RAM and PCI and AGP I/O. However, more needs to be considered than the wholesale replacement of the entire system.

First, your present memory may be in 30-pin, 9-bit SIMM modules. A new system board will require 168-pin DIMMs (SDRAM), adding to the overall expense. A new system board costs anywhere from $100 to $500, without a CPU chip or RAM. If the CPU chip, RAM, and SRAM CPU cache components are not included, you may add another $500 or more to the cost.

Second, changing to PCI add-in cards for the disk and video interfaces adds another expense.

Once you add up all these items, you may be better off buying another system, and getting a faster, larger disk drive in the package.

CPU performance

A reasonable but aging alternative, if you just want speed, is to buy a Cyrix or AMD DX4 processor chip for your old 486 system. These CPUs come as direct plug-in replacements for your present 486 CPU, but they contain near-Pentium features and performance. A DX4 486 system performs, on average, as if it were a 90–100 MHz Pentium, for less than $100 and a few minutes of work. Note however, that your system board may support only 5-volt CPU chips, thus requiring you to buy a 3.3 volt regulator/adapter socket for the new CPU, and the only source for these may be computer stores or JDR Microdevices at www.jdr.com.

In many systems the Intel Slot-1 connection will support either Celeron, Pentium II, or Pentium III CPU chips. In many cases the economical Celeron is just fine, but the Pentium II and III offer larger internal caches for the CPU and various processing features that are desirable for multimedia and raw processing needs.

Note A new CPU will not solve your present memory limitations, but perhaps the speed will be enough to make the difference you need.

Memory

Adding RAM is one sure way to speed up all Windows systems because the operating system will require fewer swaps between RAM and your disk drive for virtual memory support.

In most cases Windows 3.x drastically improves when you increase memory from 4MB to 8MB, with 12–16MB being superior until you get to doing significant graphics, database, or spreadsheet work where 16–32MB of RAM begins to make another significant difference. Above 32 or 64MB of RAM, Windows 3.x doesn't seem to care.

For Windows 95/98/Me/NT and Windows 2000, you could try to survive on 16–32MB of RAM, but you will notice that your system is terribly sluggish and limited until you make the leap to 64MB or more. Going above 64MB may not gain you a lot of performance, unless you really need it for Windows 95/98 or Me. Certainly on NT and 2000 the more RAM the better — "NT" manages RAM access and avoids swapping more efficiently than 95/98/Me. Certainly if you are going to run more than one service — a Web site, e-mail, FTP, and so on, 64MB will just barely cut it, 128 is desirable and 256 is typical for serious server use.

Use the fastest RAM chips you can afford. EDO RAM provides an incremental increase in memory access speed from standard DRAM and Fast Page–mode RAM. SDRAM is much faster still. If your board supports it, go for it. You should not mix RAM types — use either all FPRAM, EDO, or SDRAM. Again, beware of the memory configuration — SIMMs or DIMMs.

Cross-Reference For the potentially "resource-confused" — well, the amount RAM has nothing to do with "system resources" errors and the Windows Resource Meter. Refer to Chapter 15 covering memory, and Chapters 6–9 for Windows resources issues

Disk performance

A faster disk drive alone can bring new life to your system. If your disk drive was made before 1996, chances are it is a 330–540MB drive with an access time of only 12 milliseconds. You may have compressed the drive with DoubleSpace or DriveSpace to fit all of your Windows applications on it, and loading Windows takes forever while the drive thrashes and chatters to collect all the information.

Two years ago, disk drive space cost roughly $1.00 per megabyte. Even further back than that many of us paid $400 for a 20MB 65 millisecond drive. Today, prices range from $0.05 to $0.30 per megabyte, with higher cost per megabyte for smaller drives, as a certain base cost for the drive technology exists. SCSI drives cost more, and you must account for the cost of the host adapter.

Drives with 10–20GB and larger capacities and with access times of 8 to 9 milliseconds are available for $150 to $250. Most have large (128K to 512K or larger) internal data caches to further increase transfer rates and reduce mechanical wear. Other speed factors include the rotation speed of the media. 5400 RPM is the norm today, with 7200 RPM units showing up here and there.

Tip   In 7200 RPM units there can be a problem with drives heating up, so check the case for high operating temperature and arrange suitable cooling as needed to keep the drive from burning itself up.

If you are depending on the operating system's permanent or temporary swap file on your disk to make up for a lack of RAM that Windows needs, a faster drive and disk caching software is certainly a beneficial way to go. For Windows 95, 98, ME, NT, and 2000 users, disk caching is built in and optimized for the operating system and available memory.

Video performance and clarity

You cannot beat PCI or AGP video accelerator cards for fast graphics. Even without AGP or PCI, the standard 16-bit video cards from Diamond, ATI, Matrox, and others are a vast improvement over the 8- and 16-bit cards that were standard around 1994. Most cards comply with the VESA VBE enhanced VGA specifications and contain incredibly fast video RAM and processing chips, so that whatever you choose to use on your PC for should be well supported.

A new video card will cost between $100 and $250, depending on your needs and preferences. You will need at least 512K of video RAM to use 800×600 modes, and a megabyte or two is preferred to use more than 256 colors or resolutions (higher than 800×600). Eight to sixteen megabytes of video RAM is now almost a standard on most cards. The speed and clarity of the newer cards is quite impressive, and it makes those hours of sitting at your computer much more pleasant.

Summary

Remember, you *can* solve most of the problems you will encounter on your PC. Even better, by following the tips in this book you should be able to prevent some of them. We would like to hear from you. If we have helped you solve a problem or if you run into a problem we did not cover here, see the author contact information in the front of this book and drop us a line.

The right tools—knowledge, familiarity with DOS and Windows, and a handful of utility programs can be quite beneficial in the hands of any PC user. If you can read the screen and press the keys, success is almost guaranteed (within limits, of course). Remember, software is no good if your system will not turn on or boot up. If there has been severe disk damage due to mechanical or electronic failure, no amount of software can perform the repairs. However, software may help diagnose or confirm the nature or location of the problem.

Periodically scanning your disks for errors using the disk imaging routines and the trash can or unerase protection facilities; implementing the appropriate user maintenance and preventive measures can save you many hours of problem solving and many files of otherwise lost work. While you are doing maintenance, run a full virus protection scan on your system, too.

If you do run into correctable problems, it is nice to know you can do something about them. You do not have to be a rocket scientist to take care of the more common and less technical problem situations you may encounter with your PC. The tools are right at your fingertips.

With all of the information we have presented to provide you with increased awareness, and by accumulating and becoming familiar with the proper tools, you are well on your way to being a successful PC user.

In this chapter we covered:

✦ Don't neglect DOS

✦ Diagnostic and utility software

✦ Do-it-yourself advice

✦ Technical support and repair services

✦ Performance and upgrade hints

Now, let's go on to the Appendixes where you will find one of the most comprehensive collections of useful details about what is in, around, and related to your PC.

✦   ✦   ✦

Memory Maps and BIOS Data Areas

One of the standard elements of PCs running DOS or using the PC hardware structure for other operating environments (UNIX, OS/2, and so on) is having the locations of the many bits of information about the hardware system in consistent, known places.

Some of this is predetermined by the use of Intel microprocessors, following the design conventions for starting the processor, loading an operating system, and running applications using standard devices. IBM established the rest in the Bits 7–1 Reserved design of the original IBM PC.

Although IBM established the initial standard, the least of which all PCs must follow to be "PC-compatible," other vendors, such as COMPAQ, American Megatrends, Phoenix Technologies, Chips and Technology, and Tandy, have taken advantage of the information IBM made available and the remaining "holes" that IBM left to be filled by enhancements.

Without getting into system architecture and programming details, the standards are meant to be followed. There are many ways around the standards, however, such as by replacing or redirecting device-handling program code, device locations, timing, and so on. Presented here are the standard PC device and parameter locations. Although we don't expect that everyone will need to use this information, it's nice to have it around just in case.

DOS Memory Map

Table A-1 is a gross memory map of PC systems. Following it are more detailed maps of specific areas.

Table A-1
DOS Memory Map

Address	Size	Contents/Use
0:0000–9:FFFFh	640K	System RAM (DOS)
0:0000–0:01DFh	480K	Interrupt vectors
0:01E0–0:02FFh	288K	User vectors
0:0300–0:03FFh	256K	BIOS stack/vectors (see Table A-2 for low memory details)
0:0400–0:04FFh	256K	BIOS data (see Table A-3 for BIOS data details)
0:0500–0:05FFh	256K	DOS and BASIC use
0:0600–9:FFFFh	638K	DOS and user RAM
A:0000–B:FFFFh	128K	Video buffer RAM
C:0000–E:FFFFh	192K	Adapter ROM/EMS page and/or Upper Memory Block (see Table A-4 for upper memory details)Au/ed: font OK?
F:0000–F:FFFFh	64K	ROM BIOS (Boot, POST) Also ROM BASIC (IBM) AMI also includes diagnostics and setup here
10:0000–up		Extended memory 14.9MB – 80286 30.9MB – 80386, 80486
10:0000–10:FFFFh	64K	Microsoft XMS/HMA using HIMEM.SYS, QEMM, or other drivers
10:0000–FD:FFFFh	14.9MB	Extended memory
FE:0000–FF:FFFFh	128K	AT ROM BIOS includes ROM BASIC (IBM only)

Remapping 384K Memory

Some non-IBM systems, such as those using some of the Chips and Technology or other specialized architectures, allow for remapping the 384K memory area above DOS RAM (640K) as shadow RAM and placing into it all basic input/output system (BIOS) and other information from the hardware in that region. This speeds certain operations (video, disk, BIOS calls) by having this information available in faster RAM memory rather than having to rely on the slow response of ROM chips. Sometimes the use of shadow RAM is optional, which allows other upper-memory-block memory-management applications to use this memory range, and sometimes it is forced, precluding its use, depending on the manufacturer. Without shadow RAM, any free memory blocks not used by other devices or applications may be mapped as upper-memory-block RAM for use here in loading device drivers and terminate-and-stay-residents (TSRs), providing more DOS RAM for applications and data.

Low DOS Memory Locations

The addresses shown in Table A-2 may be inspected for their content or, by careful programming, written to for direct device control.

Table A-2 DOS Low Memory Locations	
Address	**Description**
0000h	DMA Channel 0 Address Byte 0 (Low)
0001h	DMA Channel 0 Word Count Byte 0 (Low)
0002h	DMA Channel 1 Address Byte 0 (Low)
0003h	DMA Channel 1 Word Count Byte 0 (Low)
0004h	DMA Channel 2 Address Byte 0 (Low)
0005h	DMA Channel 2 Word Count Byte 0 (Low)
0006h	DMA Channel 3 Address Byte 0 (Low)
0007h	DMA Channel 3 Word Count Byte 0 (Low)
0008h	DMA Channel 0–3 Status/Command
0009h	DMA Write Request Register
000Ah	DMA Channel 0–3 Mask Register
000Bh	DMA Channel 0–3 Mode Register
000Ch	DMA Clear Byte Pointer
000Dh	DMA Read Temporary Register/Master Clear
000Eh	DMA Clear Mask Register
000Fh	DMA Write Mask Register
0019h	DMA Scratch Register
0020h	Programmable Interrupt Controller Init./Operation Command Word
0021h	PIC Init./Operation Command Word
0022–003Fh	8259 Program Interrupt Timer
0040h	Program Int. Timer R/W Center 0/Keyboard Channel 0
0041h	PIT Channel 1
0042h	PIT Channel 2
0043h	PIT Mode Port Control Word Register – Channel 0 and 2
0044h	PIT – Miscellaneous Register (EISA)

Continued

Table A-2 *(continued)*

Address	Description
0047h	PIT Control Word Register for Channel 0 (EISA)
0048h	For use by PIT
0060h	Keyboard Input Buffer (AT-ISA, EISA)
0060h	Keyboard Output Buffer (XT, AT-ISA, EISA)
0061h	Port B Control/Static Register (AT-ISA, EISA)
0061h	Program Peripheral Interface (XT)
0062h	Program Peripheral Interface (XT)
0063h	Program Peripheral Interface (XT only)
0064h	Keyboard Controller Rd Status (AT-ISA, EISA)
0064h	Keyboard Controller Input Buffer (AT-ISA, EISA)
0066–006Fh	Reserved for 8255 (XT) Reserved for 8042 (AT)
0070h	CMOS RAM Index Register (AT-ISA, EISA)
0071h	CMOS RAM Data Register (AT-ISA, EISA) 00h = Seconds in BCD 01h = Seconds Alarm in BCD 02h = Minutes in BCD 03h = Minutes Alarm in BCD 04h = Hour in BCD 05h = Hour Alarm in BCD 06h = Day of Week in BCD 07h = Day of Month in BCD 08h = Month in BCD 09h = Year in BCD (00–99) 0Ah = Status Register A 0Bh = Status Register B 0Ch = Status Register C 0Dh = Status Register D 0Eh = CMOS RAM Diagnostic Status 0Fh = Shutdown/Reboot Code 10h = Type of Diskette Drives (Bits 7–4 = Drive 0; Bits 3–0 = Drive 1) 0000 = None 0001 = 360K 0010 = 1.2MB 0011 = 720K 0100 = 1.44MB 0101–1111 = Reserved

Address	Description
0071h (continued)	11h = Reserved 12h = Fixed Drive Types (Bits 7–4 = Drive 0; Bits 3–0 = Drive 1) 13h = Reserved 14h = Equipment Byte 15h = Base Memory in K (Low) 16h = Base Memory in K (High) 17h = Extended Memory in K (Low) 18h = Extended Memory in K (High) 19h = Extended Drive Type (16+) – 1st Disk 1Ah = Extended Drive Type (16+) – 2nd Disk 1B–27h = Reserved 2Eh = High Byte, Checksum for 10–2Dh 2Fh = Low Byte, Checksum for 10–2Dh 30h = Extended Memory by POST (low byte) 31h = Extended Memory by POST (high byte) 32h = Century in BCD 33–3Fh = Reserved
0080h	Extra Page Register/Manufacturing Test Port
0081h	DMA Channel 2 Address Byte 2
0082h	DMA Channel 3 Address Byte 3
0083h	DMA Channel 1 Address Byte 2
0084h	Extra Page Register
0085h	Extra Page Register
0086h	Extra Page Register
0087h	DMA Channel 0 Address Byte 2
0088h	Extra Page Register
0089h	DMA Channel 6 Address Byte 2
008Ah	DMA Channel 7 Address Byte 2
008Bh	DMA Channel 5 Address Byte 2
008Ch	Extra Page Register
008Dh	Extra Page Register
008Eh	Extra Page Register
008Fh	DMA Refresh Page Register Cascade to Channel 5–7 (AT)
00A0h	NMI Mask Register (XT)
00A0h	Program Interrupt Controller 2 (AT-ISA, EISA)

Continued

Table A-2 *(continued)*

Address	Description
00A1h	PIC 2 Operation Command Word 1
00C0h	DMA Channel 4 Memory Address Bytes 1 and 0
00C2h	DMA Channel 4 Transfer Count Bytes 1 and 0 — AT Channel 0
00C4h	DMA Channel 5 Memory Address Bytes 1&0 — AT Channel 1
00C6h	DMA Channel 5 Memory Transfer Count Bytes 1 and 0 — AT Channel 1
00C8h	DMA Channel 6 Memory Address Bytes 1 and 0 — DMA Channel 2 — AT
00CAh	DMA Channel 6 Transfer Count Bytes 1 and 0 — AT Channel 2
00CCh	DMA Channel 7 Memory Address Bytes 1 and 0 — DMA Channel 3 — AT
00CEh	DMA Channel 7 Transfer Count Bytes 1 and0 — AT Channel 3
00D0h	DMA Channel 4–7 Status/Command Register (AT only)
00D2h	DMA Channel 4–7 Write Request Register (AT only)
00D4h	DMA Channel 4–7 Write Single Mask Register (AT only)
00D6h	DMA Channel 4–7 Mode Register (AT only)
00D8h	DMA Channel 4–7 Clear Byte Pointer (AT only)
00DAh	DMA Channel 4–7 Rd Temporary Register/Master Clear (AT only)
00DCh	DMA Channel 4–7 Clear Mask Register (AT only)
00DEh	DMA Channel 4–7 Write Mask Register (AT only)
00DF–00EFh	Reserved
00F0h	Math Coprocessor Clear Busy Latch
00F1h	Math Coprocessor Reset
00F2–FFh	Math Coprocessor
0100–016Fh	Reserved
0170h–0177h	AT-ISA and EISA Secondary Fixed Disk Addresses (see 01F0–01F7h for information)
01F0h	Fixed Disk 0 Data Register Port
01F1h	Fixed Disk 0 Error Register/WPC Register
01F2h	Fixed Disk 0 Sector Count
01F3h	Fixed Disk 0 Sector Number
01F4h	Fixed Disk 0 Cylinder Byte (Low)
01F5h	Fixed Disk 0 Cylinder Byte (High)

Address	Description
01F6h	Fixed Disk 0 Drive/Head Register
01F7h	Fixed Disk 0 Status/Command Register
0200–020Fh	Game Port Controller
0210–0217h	Expansion Unit (XT)
0278h	Parallel Port 3 Data
0279h	Parallel Port 3 Status
027Ah	Parallel Port 3 Control (see Note 1)
02B0–02DFh	Reserved
02E1h	GPIB (IEEE-488) Adapter 0
02E2h	Data Acquisition Adapter 0
02E3h	Data Acquisition Adapter 0
02E4–02F7h	Reserved
02F8h	Serial Port 2 Text/Rx Data/Division Latch (Low)
02F9h	Serial Port 2 Interrupt Enable/Division Latch (High)
02FAh	Serial Port 2 Interrupt ID Register
02FBh	Serial Port 2 Line Control Register
02FCh	Serial Port 2 Modem Control Register
02FDh	Serial Port 2 Line Status Register
02FEh	Serial Port 2 Modem Status Register
02FFh	Serial Port 2 Scratch Register
0300–031Fh	Prototype Card
0320h	Fixed Disk Adapter (8 or 16 bit)
0322h	Fixed Disk Adapter Control Register
0324h	Fixed Disk Adapter Attention Register
0325–0347h	Reserved
0348–0357h	DCA 3278
0360–036Fh	PC Network
0372–0377h	Secondary Diskette Controller (see 3F2–3F7 for information)
0378h	Parallel Port 2 Data
0379h	Parallel Port 2 Status
037Ah	Parallel Port 2 Control (see Note 1)

Continued

Table A-2 (continued)

Address	Description
0380–038Fh	SDLC and BSC Communications Adapter
0390–0393h	Cluster Adapter 0
03A0–03AFh	Primary BSC Communications
03B0–03B3h	Miscellaneous Video Registers
03B4h	MDA, EGA, VGA CRT Controller Index Register
03B5h	MDA, EGA, VGA CRT Controller Data Register (Index) 00h = Horizontal Total 01h = Horizontal Displayed 02h = Horizontal Sync. Position 03h = Horizontal Sync. Pulse Width 04h = Vertical Total 05h = Vertical Displayed 06h = Vertical Sync. Position 07h = Vertical Sync. Pulse Width 08h = Interlace Mode 09h = Maximum Scan Lines 0Ah = Cursor Start 0Bh = Cursor End 0Ch = Start Address (High) 0Dh = Start Address (Low) 0Eh = Cursor Location (High) 0Fh = Cursor Location (Low) 10h = Light Pen (High) 11h = Light Pen (Low)
03B8h	MDA Mode Control Register (buffer at B0000h)
03BAh	VGA Input Status Register EGA/VGA Feature Control Register
03BCh	Parallel Port 1 Data
03BDh	Parallel Port 1 Status
03BEh	Parallel Port 1 Control (see Note 1)
03BFh	Hercules Configuration Register
03C0h	EGA Index Register
03C2h	CGA, EGA, VGA Input Status Register and Misc. Output Register
03C4h	CGA, EGA, VGA Sequencer Index Register
03C5h	CGA, EGA, VGA Sequencer Data Register
03C6h	VGA Video DAC State Register DAC PEL Mask

Address	Description
03C7h	VGA Video DAC State Register
03C8h	VGA PEL Address, Read Mode
03C9h	VGA Video DAC Registers
03CAh	CGA, EGA, VGA Graphics Position Register 2
03CCh	CGA, EGA, VGA Graphics Position Register 1
03CDh	VGA Feature Control Register (color)
03CEh	VGA Control Index Register
03CFh	Other VGA Register (EGA also uses 03B4–5h, 03BAh, 03D4–5h, and 03DAh) (buffer at A0000h)
03D4h	Video CRT Controller Index Register
03D5h	Video CRTC Registers (Index) 00h = Horizontal Total 01h = Horizontal Displayed 02h = Horizontal Sync. Position 03h = Horizontal Sync. Pulse Width 04h = Vertical Total 05h = Vertical Displayed 06h = Vertical Sync. Position 07h = Vertical Sync. Pulse Width 08h = Interlace Mode 09h = Maximum Scan Lines 0Ah = Cursor Start 0Bh = Cursor End 0Ch = Start Address (High) 0Dh = Start Address (Low) 0Eh = Cursor Location (High) 0Fh = Cursor Location (Low) 10h = Light Pen (High) 11h = Light Pen (Low)
03D8h	Video Mode Control Register
03D9h	Video Palette Register (buffer at B8000h)
03DAh	CGA, EGA, VGA Register
03DBh	Video Register
03DCh	Video Register
03DDh	Video Register
03DEh	Video Register

Continued

Table A-2 *(continued)*

Address	Description
03DFh	Video Register
03F0h	Disk Controller Status Register A
03F1h	Disk Controller Status Register B
03F2h	Disk Controller Output Register
03F4h	Disk Controller Status Register
03F5h	Disk Controller Data Register
03F6h	Fixed Disk Control Port
03F7h	Disk Input/Data Transfer Rate Register
03F8h	Serial Port 1 Text/Rx Data Divisor Latch (Low Byte)
03F9h	Serial Port 1 Interrupt Enable Divisor Latch (High Byte)
03FAh	Serial Port 1 Interrupt ID Register
03FBh	Serial Port 1 Line Control Register
03FCh	Serial Port 1 Modem Control Register
03FDh	Serial Port 1 Line Status Register
03FEh	Serial Port 1 Modem Status Register
03FFh	Serial Port 1 Scratch Register (reserved) 0401–04D6h (Used in EISA Systems Only)
0401h	DMA Channel 0 Word Count Byte (High)
0403h	DMA Channel 1 Word Count Byte (High)
0405h	DMA Channel 2 Word Count Byte (High)
0407h	DMA Channel 3 Word Count Byte (High)
040Ah	DMA 0–3 Channel Mode Register/IRQ 13 Status
040Bh	DMA Channel 0–3 Extended Mode Register
0461h	Ext. NMI Status/Control Register
0462h	Software NMI Register
0464h	Bus Master Status Register (Slots 1–8)
0465h	Bus Master Status Register (Slots 9–16)
0481h	DMA Channel 2 Address Byte 3 (High)
0482h	DMA Channel 3 Address Byte 3 (High)
0483h	DMA Channel 1 Address Byte 3 (High)

Address	Description
0487h	DMA Channel 0 Address Byte 3 (High)
0489h	DMA Channel 6 Address Byte 3 (High)
048Ah	DMA Channel 7 Address Byte 3 (High)
048Bh	DMA Channel 5 Address Byte 3 (High)
04C6h	DMA Channel 5 Word Count Byte 2 (High)
04CAh	DMA Channel 6 Word Count Byte 2 (High)
04CEh	DMA Channel 7 Word Count Byte 2 (High)
04D0h	IRQ 0–7 Interrupt Edge/Level Registers
04D1h	IRQ 8–15 Interrupt Edge/Level Registers
04D4h	Ext. DMA 4–7 Chain. Mode/Status Register
04D6h	Ext. DMA 4–7 Mode Register
06E2–06E3h	Data Acquisition Adapter 1
0790–0793h	Cluster Adapter 1
0800–08FFh	I/O Port Register for External CMOS RAM
0AE2–0AE3h	Cluster Adapter 2
0B90–0B93h	Cluster Adapter 2
0C00h	Page Register for I/O or SRAM
0C80–0C83h	System Board ID Registers
1390–1393h	Cluster Adapter 3
2390–2393h	Cluster Adapter 4
3220h	Serial Port 3 Text/Rx Data Divisor Latch (Low Byte)
3221h	Serial Port 3 Interrupt Enable Divisor Latch (High Byte)
3222h	Serial Port 3 Interrupt ID Register
3223h	Serial Port 3 Line Control Register
3224h	Serial Port 3 Modem Control Register
3225h	Serial Port 3 Line Status Register
3226h	Serial Port 3 Modem Status Register
3227h	Serial Port 3 Scratch Register
3228h	Serial Port 4 Text/Rx Data Divisor Latch (Low Byte)
3229h	Serial Port 4 Interrupt Enable. Divisor Latch (High Byte)
322Ah	Serial Port 4 Interrupt ID Register

Continued

Table A-2 *(continued)*

Address	Description
322Bh	Serial Port 4 Line Control Register
322Ch	Serial Port 4 Modem Control Register
322Dh	Serial Port 4 Line Status Register
322Eh	Serial Port 4 Modem Status Register
322Fh	Serial Port 4 Scratch Register
3230–42E0h	Reserved
42E1h	GPIB (IEEE-488) Adapter 2
42E2–62E0h	Reserved
62E1h	GPIB (IEEE-488) Adapter 3
62E2–82E0h	Reserved
82E1h	GPIB (IEEE-488) Adapter 4
82E2–A2E0h	Reserved
A2E1h	GPIB (IEEE-488) Adapter 5
A2E2–AFFEh	Reserved
AFFFh	Video Plane 0–3 System Latch
B000–C2E0h	Reserved
C2E1h	GPIB (IEEE-488) Adapter 6
C2E2–E2E0h	Reserved
E2E1h	GPIB (IEEE-488) Adapter 7
E2E2–FFFFh	Reserved

Note Although the listed addresses of 3BCh for Port 1, 378h for Port 2, and 278h for Port 3 are common in many BIOS and programming references, most parallel port cards address Port 1 as 378h, Port 2 as 278h, and Port 3 (rarely used) as 3BCh. A function of BIOS, if only one port card exists, is to direct it as Port 1, despite the actual hardware address. This enables printing to a default device (PRN: or LPT:), if any port exists.

PC BIOS data area

As we mentioned, normal PC operations expect certain information about the system and interfaces to be located in specific places in memory. The BIOS data area, listed in Table A-3, is one such place.

This area of lower DOS RAM memory, at Offset 0, Location 400h, will contain information about serial and parallel ports (if they exist or were found at bootup) and other features of your system as listed in Table A-3.

This information may be viewed or changed with the DOS DEBUG program or other memory viewing/editing tools. To display this information, invoke DEBUG at a DOS prompt, type **d0:400**, and then press Enter. To view more addresses, type **d** and then press Enter until the address area of interest appears. Type **q** and press Enter to exit DEBUG.

Table A-3 BIOS Data Area		
Address	**Size**	**Contents**
0:400h	2	I/O address of 1st serial port
0:402h	2	I/O address of 2nd serial port
0:404h	2	I/O address of 3rd serial port
0:406h	2	I/O address of 4th serial port
0:408h	2	I/O address of 1st parallel port
0:40Ah	2	I/O address of 2nd parallel port
0:40Ch	2	I/O address of 3rd parallel port
0:40Eh	2	I/O address of 4th parallel port or segment address of extended data area
0:410h	2	Number of devices installed: Bits 15–14 Number of printers Bits 13–12 Reserved Bits 11–9 Number of serial ports Bit 8 Reserved Bits 7–6 Number of drives 00 = 1 Drive 01 = 2 Drives Bits 4–5 Bootup video mode 00 = PGA or EGA 01 = Color 40×25

Continued

		Table A-3 (continued)		

Address	Size	Contents
0:410h (continued)		10 = Color 80×25 11 = B&W 80×25 Bit 3 Reserved Bit 2 Pointing device Bit 1 Math coprocessor Bit 0 Disk for boot
0:412h	1	Bits 7–1 Reserved Bit 0–1 = Mfg. test mode 0 = Nontest mode
0:413h	2	Size of memory in kilobytes
0:417h	1	Keyboard flags: Bit 7 Insert on Bit 6 Caps Lock on Bit 5 Num Lock on Bit 4 Scroll Lock on Bit 3 Alt pressed Bit 2 Ctrl pressed Bit 1 Left Shift pressed Bit 0 Right Shift pressed
0:418h	1	Keyboard flags: Bit 7 Insert on Bit 6 Caps Lock on Bit 5 Num Lock on Bit 4 Scroll Lock on Bit 3 Ctrl+Num Lock on Bit 2 SysRq pressed Bit 1 Left Alt pressed Bit 0 Right Alt pressed
0:419h	1	Alt and Numeric keypad area
0:41Ah	2	Points to next character in keyboard buffer
0:41Ch	2	Points to 1st free spot in keyboard buffer
0:41Eh	32	Keyboard buffer area
0:43Eh	1	Disk drive recalibrate status: Bit 7 Disk hardware interrupt Bits 6–4 Not used Bits 3–2 Reserved Bit 1 Recalibrate drive 1 Bit 0 Recalibrate drive 0

Address	Size	Contents
0:43Fh	1	Disk motor status: Bit 7 Writing or formatting Bit 6 Reading or verifying 00 = Drive 0 01 = Drive 1 10 = Reserved 11 = Reserved Bits 3–2 Reserved Bit 1 If 1 = Drive 1 motor on Bit 0 If 1 = Drive 0 motor on
0:440h	1	Disk motor timeout count
0:441h	1	Disk status code: Bit 7–1 = Drive not ready Bit 6–1 = Seek error Bit 5 Disk controller failed Bits 4–0 Error codes 01h = Illegal function 02h = Address mark not found 03h = Write protect error 04h = Sector not found 06h = Change line active 08h = DMA overrun 09h = Data boundary error 0Ch = Media type not found 10h = Uncorrectable error 20h = General controller error 40h = Seek failed 80h = Timeout
0:442h	7	Disk controller status bytes
0:449h	1	Video mode
0:44Ah	2	Number of screen columns
0:44Ch	2	Page size in bytes
0:44Eh	2	Page address
0:450h	16	Cursor position on video page (2 bytes/page, 1st byte = column/2nd = row)
0:460h	2	Cursor size (start/end scan line)
0:462h	1	Current display page
0:463h	2	I/O port for current video mode (Mono = 3B4h/Color = 3D4h)
0:465h	1	Current mode select register

Continued

Table A-3 *(continued)*

Address	Size	Contents
0:466h	1	Current video palette
0:467h	2	Option ROM address offset (used by POST and XT)
0:469h	2	Option ROM address segment
0:46Bh	1	Last interrupt
0:46Ch	2	Timer count — least significant
0:46Eh	2	Timer count — most significant
0:470h	1	24-hour RTC rollover
0:471h	1	Control-Break flag
0:472h	2	RESET flag: 1234h = Bypass memory test 4321h = Preserve memory 64h = Special mode
0:474h	1	Last fixed-disk status: 00h = No error 01h = Invalid function request 02h = Address mark not found 04h = Sector not found 05h = Reset failed 07h = Parameter activity failed 08h = DMA overrun 09h = Data boundary error 0Ah = Bad sector flag detected 0Bh = Bad track detected 0Dh = Invalid no. sectors 0Eh = Control data address mark 0Fh = DMA arbitrate out of range 10h = Uncorrectable data error 11h = Corrected data error 20h = General controller failure 40h = Seek failed 80h = Timeout AAh = Drive not ready BBh = Undefined error CCh = Write fault on drive E0h = Status error FFh = Sense operation failed
0:475h	1	Number of fixed disk drives
0:476h	1	Fixed disk control byte
0:477h	1	Fixed disk port offset

Address	Size	Contents
0:478h	4	Parallel port timeout table
0:47Ch	4	Serial port timeout table
0:480h	2	Offset to start of keyboard buffer
0:482h	2	Offset to end of keyboard buffer
0:48Bh	1	Disk data transfer rate: Bits 7–6 = Last rate set by controller 00 = 500 kbs 01 = 300 kbs 10 = 250 kbs 11 = Reserved Bits 5–4 = Last drive step rate Bits 3–2 = Data transfer rate at start 00 = 500 kbs 01 = 300 kbs 10 = 250 kbs Bits 1–0 = Reserved
0:48Ch	1	Fixed disk status register (duplicate)
0:48Dh	1	Fixed disk error register (duplicate)
0:48Eh	1	Fixed disk interrupt flag
0:48Fh	1	Disk controller information: Bit 7 = Reserved Bit 6 = Drive 1 determined Bit 5 = Drive 1 is multi-rate Bit 4 = Drive 1 has change line Bit 3 = Reserved Bit 2 = Drive 0 determined Bit 1 = Drive 0 is multi-rate Bit 0 = Drive 0 has change line
0:490h	1	Drive 0 media type: Bits 7–6 = Transfer rate 00 = 500 kbs 01 = 300 kbs 10 = 250 kbs Bit 5 = Double step required Bit 4 = Known media in drive Bit 3 = Reserved Bits 2–0 = Media/drive 111 = OK – 720K in 720K drive or OK – 1.44 in 1.44MB drive 101 = OK – 1.2 in 1.2MB drive 100 = OK – 360K in 360K drive 011 = 360K in 1.2MB drive

Continued

Table A-3 *(continued)*

Address	Size	Contents
0:490h *(continued)*		010 = Try 1.2 in 1.2MB drive 001 = Try 360K in 1.2MB drive 000 = Try 360K in 360K drive
0:491h	1	Drive 1 media type: Bits 7–6 = Transfer rate 00 = 500 kbs 01 = 300 kbs 10 = 250 kbs Bit 5 = Double step required Bit 4 = Known media in drive Bit 3 = Reserved Bits 2–0 = Media/drive 111 = OK – 720K in 720K drive or OK – 1.44 in 1.44MB drive 101 = OK – 1.2 in 1.2MB drive 100 = OK – 360K in 360K drive 011 = 360K in 1.2 drive 010 = Try 1.2 in 1.2 drive 001 = Try 360K in 1.2 drive 000 = Try 360K in 360K drive
0:492h	2	Disk work area
0:494h	1	Current track for drive 0
0:495h	1	Current track for drive 1
0:496h	1	Keyboard status: Bit 7 = Read ID in progress Bit 6 = Last code was first ID Bit 5 = Forced Num Lock Bit 4 = Enhanced keyboard Bit 3 = Right Alt pressed Bit 2 = Right Ctrl pressed Bit 1 = Last code was E0h Bit 0 = Last code was E1h
0:497h	1	Status byte: Bit 7= Error flag for keyboard command Bit 6 = LED update Bit 5 = RESEND received from keyboard Bit 4 = ACK received from keyboard Bit 3 = Reserved Bit 2 = Caps Lock LED On Bit 1 = Num Lock LED On Bit 0 = Scroll Lock LED On

Address	Size	Contents
0:498h	2	User wait flag offset address
0:49Ah	2	User wait flag segment address
0:49Ch	2	Wait count (low word)
0:49Eh	2	Wait count (high word)
0:4A0h	1	Wait active flag: Bit 7 = Wait time elapsed Bits 6–1 = Reserved Bit 0 = INT 15h, AH = 86h
0:4B0h	6	Reserved

As shown in Tables A-4 and A-5, the memory above the standard 640K "program memory" in the first megabyte of a PC's memory is used to provide access to the video memory and to provide access to places to store and run adapter ROMs, as well as to provide access to the ROM BIOS, which provides the PC with its basic connections to the outside world.

Table A-4
PC High Memory Area Map

Address	Size	Contents
A:0000–B:FFFFh	128K	Video buffer RAM
A:0000–A:FFFFh	64K	Poss. extra DOS RAM (with MDA/CGA only)
A:0000–B:FFFFh	128K	EGA/VGA video buffer
B:0000–B:7FFFh	32K	MDA video buffer
B:8000–B:FFFFh	32K	CGA video buffer
C:0000–E:FFFFh	192K	Adapter ROM/EMS page; Upper Memory Block
C:0000–C:3FFFh	16k	EGA video BIOS
C:6000–C:63FFh	1K	PGA area
C:8000–C:BFFFh	16K	Hard disk BIOS (XT or non-IBM)
D:0000–D:FFFFh	64K	EMS page frame
D:0000–D:7FFFh	32K	Cluster adapter
E:0000–E:FFFFh	64K	ROM expanded/EMS page

The address range from E:0000–FFFF provides for many options, adapters, and application program use, depending on the chips used, installed devices, manufacturer, and other variables.

 Note   The Lotus/Intel/Microsoft Expanded Memory Specification (LIM-EMS) provides for up to 32MB of paged-RAM use through the EMS Page Frame.

Table A-5 BIOS and Extended Memory Area		
Address	*Size*	*Contents*
F:0000–F:FFFFh	64K	ROM BIOS (Boot, POST); also ROM BASIC (IBM), AMI (also includes diagnostics and CMOS SETUP here)
10:0000–up	Extended Memory: 14.9MB – 80286 30.9MB – 80386,80486	
10:0000–10:FFFFh	64K	Microsoft XMS/HMA using HIMEM.SYS, QEMM, or other drivers
10:0000–FD:FFFFh	14.9MB	Extended memoryl
FE:0000–FF:FFFFh	128K	AT ROM BIOS includes ROM BASIC (IBM only)

✦   ✦   ✦

Hardware Interrupt Requests and DMA Assignments

Hardware interrupt requests (IRQs) are issued by adapter or peripheral devices that need immediate or rapid processor/software attention to address incoming data or error conditions.

Although software running in the processor may be doing anything but paying attention to certain hardware activities, the processor is connected to a special integrated circuit that accepts these IRQ signals from the plug-in card sockets.

When these signals arrive, the processor must stop its present activity, look to see which IRQ was issued, and then determine which program is related to that IRQ.

An example of this is when you print or transfer a file to another system and the status of that activity is shown onscreen. The screen update activity is running under software control, but the hardware may have a problem that needs more immediate attention than the screen update indicates (loss of modem carrier, printer jam, and so on). This hardware method of getting the processor's attention handles that.

Events such as RAM parity, the routine tick of the PC timer, or keyboard input (perhaps to stop the software activity) take priority over other events. As shown in Table B-1, following the first three IRQ types (indicated by the * symbol), which are not user configurable, are the add-in devices in the order in which they might be expected to need attention.

Note that IRQs 8–15 (for AT or higher systems) actually have higher priority than IRQs 3–7 because by design they cause an IRQ 2-level interrupt. There are no IRQs 8–15 in PC or XT systems, so IRQ 2 is not to be used in these without some caution or special software, lest the software try to address nonexistent devices that would otherwise use IRQs 8–15.

Table B-1 Common IRQ Assignments	
IRQ #	**Device**
NMI	RAM memory parity error*
0	Timer (18 Hz/55 msec intervals)*
1	Keyboard*
2	Reserved-XT/Cascade Interrupt 8–15 — AT
3	COM2/COM4
4	COM1/COM3
5	Hard disk — XT/LPT2: AT
6	Floppy disk
7	LPT1: XT & AT
8	Real-time Clock
9	Directed to IRQ 2
10	Unassigned
11	Unassigned
12	Unassigned or PS/2 Mouse
13	Math coprocessor
14	Hard disk — AT
15	Unassigned

* IRQs 8–15 only on 80286, 80386, 80486, and Pentium (but this is ROM BIOS and not CPU-related)

OS/2 and Novell NetWare print servers work better using IRQs on LPT ports, but there are no known DOS applications or systems that require the printer hardware IRQ lines 5 or 7 for printing. These may be reused by other adapters and are particularly handy for adding serial ports 3 and/or 4, provided the software you need for these ports can be customized to accept nonstandard IRQ lines within the application and that you can rewire or set the switches or jumpers for the IRQ lines on the adapter card to IRQs 5 or 7. This avoids conflicts with IRQs 3 and 4, normally used by serial ports 1 and 2. Detecting and reporting IRQ activity with utility software requires that the software be capable of making an attached device active, which requires loop-back/test plugs on the port. Software that reports an IRQ assignment for a device without a test plug connected may be misleading you.

Direct Memory Access (DMA) channel assignments perform data transfers between devices and memory without using up processor resources. PC and XT systems have only four DMA channels, whereas the AT and higher systems have eight. Table B-2 lists common DMA assignments.

Table B-2 Common DMA Assignments	
DMA #	**Device**
0	Memory refresh
1	SDLC
2	Floppy disk
3	Unassigned
4	Unassigned
5	Unassigned
6	Unassigned
7	Unassigned

Note Devices such as sound cards, IDE, or SCSI host adapters that provide DMA services will require a unique DMA channel assignment and pairing of jumper settings for both DMA request lines and DMA acknowledge lines. There are no other common or standard assignments for DMA other than those shown previously. Information about this can only be found in the hardware's documentation.

✦   ✦   ✦

Keyboard Codes and ASCII Chart

A small microprocessor chip inside the keyboard controls the PC keyboard. Power and clock signals are provided from the system board, and data is returned in codes from the keyboard.

There are unique codes for each key pressed and special codes when certain keys are released. This is why there are some keys with no printable or transmittable code or characters, but the PC "knows" a key has been pressed. The keyboard also provides the status of the CapsLock, NumLock, and ScrollLock keys.

These codes are provided to the system board for interpretation and conversion into standard ASCII codes for the 128 characters of the ASCII character set.

IBM enhances the ASCII character set with some foreign language symbols and a set of line and block characters for graphics use, completing a 256-character code set.

The F1–F10 keys, as well as the Alt, SysReq, PrtSc, and Lock keys, have no ASCII equivalents. The PC and programs that know how to interpret the keyboard data use these internally.

Table C-1 provides the key name or character, the code sent to the PC system board (shown in both hex and decimal), and the key number — which is used by the PC to know which key is pressed. Note that some key operations produce two codes. This allows for Shift, Ctrl, and Alt extensions of key presses.

It is important to have all three codes available because different programs look for different representations of the keys. Also, the key number assignments differ between the PC and XT systems, the AT, and a variety of enhanced keyboards.

Table C-1
Keyboard Codes

Key Number	Key Label Lower Case	Key Label Upper Case	Scan Code Hex	Scan Code Decimal
1	`	~	2B	43
2	1	!	02	2
3	2	@	03	3
4	3	#	04	4
5	4	$	05	5
6	5	%	06	6
7	6	^	07	7
8	7	&	08	8
9	8	*	09	9
10	9	(	0A	10
11	0	)	0B	11
12	-	_	0C	12
13	=	+	0D	13
14	\			5D	93
15	Back Space	Back Space	0E	14
16	Tab	Back Tab	0F	15
17	q	Q	10	16
18	w	W	11	17
19	e	E	12	18
20	r	R	13	19
21	t	T	14	20
22	y	Y	15	21
23	u	U	16	22
24	I	I	17	23
25	o	O	18	24
26	p	P	19	25
27	[	{	1A	26
28	]	}	1B	27
29	Enter	Enter	1C	28

Key Number	Key Label Lower Case	Key Label Upper Case	Scan Code Hex	Scan Code Decimal
30	Caps Lock	Caps Lock	3A	58
31	a	A	1E	30
32	s	S	1F	31
33	d	D	20	32
34	f	F	21	33
35	g	G	22	34
36	h	H	23	35
37	j	J	24	36
38	k	K	25	37
39	l	L	26	38
40	;	:	27	39
41	'	"	28	40
44	Left Shift	Left Shift	2A	42
46	z	Z	2C	44
47	x	X	2D	45
48	c	C	2E	46
49	v	V	2F	47
50	b	B	30	48
51	n	N	31	49
52	m	M	32	50
53	,	<	33	51
54	.	>	34	52
55	/	?	35	53
57	Right Shift	Right Shift	36	54
58	Left Ctrl	Left Ctrl	1D	55
60	Left Alt	Left Alt	38	56
61	Space Bar	Space Bar	39	57
62	Right Alt	Right Alt	E0,38	
64	Right Ctrl	Right Ctrl	E0,1D	
75	Insert	Insert	E0,52	

Continued

Table C-1 *(continued)*

Key Number	Key Label Lower Case	Key Label Upper Case	Scan Code Hex	Scan Code Decimal
76	Delete	Delete	E0,53	
79	Left Arrow	Left Arrow	E0,4B	
80	Home	Home	E0,47	
81	End	End	E0,4F	
83	Up Arrow	Up Arrow	E0,48	
84	Down Arrow	Down Arrow	E0,50	
85	Page Up	Page Up	E0,49	
86	Page Down	Page Down	E0,51	
89	Right Arrow	Right Arrow	E0,4D	
90	Num Lock	Num Lock	45,C5	
91	Keypad 7	Home	47	71
92	Keypad 4	Left Arrow	4B	75
93	Keypad 1	End	4F	79
95	Keypad /	Keypad /	E0,35	
96	Keypad 8	Up Arrow	48	72
97	Keypad 5		4C	76
98	Keypad 2	Down Arrow	50	80
99	Keypad 0	Insert	52	82
100	Keypad *	Keypad *	E0,37	
101	Keypad 9	Page Up	49	73
102	Keypad 6	Right Arrow	4D	77
103	Keypad 3	Page Down	51	81
104	Keypad .	Keypad .	53	83
105	Keypad -	Keypad -	4A	74
106	Keypad +	Keypad +	4E	78
108	Keypad Enter	Keypad Enter	E0,1C	
110	Esc	Esc	01	1
112	F1	F1	3B	59
113	F2	F2	3C	60

Key Number	Key Label Lower Case	Key Label Upper Case	Scan Code Hex	Scan Code Decimal
114	F3	F3	3D	61
115	F4	F4	3E	62
116	F5	F5	3F	63
117	F6	F6	40	64
118	F7	F7	41	65
119	F8	F8	42	66
120	F9	F9	43	67
121	F10	F10	44	68
122	F11	F11	D9	217
123	F12	F12	DA	218
124	PrtSc/SysRq	PrtSc/SysRq	2A,37	
125	Scroll Lock	Scroll Lock	46	70
126	Pause Break	Pause Break	1D,E0,45, E0,C5,9D	

Complete ASCII Chart

The following 8-part table, in Figures C-1 through C-8, shows the most common (and one very uncommon) characters, codes, and symbols of the 256 possible values that an 8-bit character may represent. The first 128 (0 to 127) are the ASCII (American Standard Code for Information Interchange) codes and characters. The second 128 characters (128 to 255) are defined quite differently from one major platform to another. IBM first used them in the PC for foreign language characters and line drawing characters. With all of the fonts available today, one of these values could be a traffic sign or a weird looking symbol from the ZapfDingbats font's character set.

No ASCII chart would be considered complete without the PC version of the ASCII characters and the corresponding HEX values from 00 to FF. Few include the Octal numbers from 000 to 377. Sometimes you'll find an ASCII chart with the binary sequence from 00000000 to 11111111. Seldom do you find one with the EBCDIC characters, codes, and symbols (from IBM mainframes). The kicker in this chart are the EBCDIC card codes. Remember punch cards? Did you ever think about reading the information in those holes? Now, you too can be one of those "strange" people.

Binary	Octal	Decimal	Hex	(ASCII) PC Char	PC Char	(EBCDIC) IBM Char	(EBCDIC) Card Code
0000 0000	000	0	00	NUL	^@	NUL	12-0-1-8-9
0000 0001	001	1	01	SOH ☺	^A	SOH	12-1-9
0000 0010	002	2	02	STX ☻	^B	STX	12-2-9
0000 0011	003	3	03	ETX ♥	^C	ETX	12-3-9
0000 0100	004	4	04	EOT ♦	^D	SEL	12-4-9
0000 0101	005	5	05	ENQ ♣	^E	HT	12-5-9
0000 0110	006	6	06	ACK ♠	^F	RNL	12-6-9
0000 0111	007	7	07	BEL •	^G	DEL	12-7-9
0000 1000	010	8	08	BS ◘	^H	GE	12-8-9
0000 1001	011	9	09	HT ○	^I	SPS	12-1-8-9
0000 1010	012	10	0A	LF ◙	^J	RPT	12-2-8-9
0000 1011	013	11	0B	VT ♂	^K	VT	12-3-8-9
0000 1100	014	12	0C	FF ♀	^L	FF	12-4-8-9
0000 1101	015	13	0D	CR ♪	^M	CR	12-5-8-9
0000 1110	016	14	0E	SO ♫	^N	SO	12-6-8-9
0000 1111	017	15	0F	SI ☼	^O	SI	12-7-8-9
0001 0000	020	16	10	DLE ►	^P	DLE	12-11-1-8-9
0001 0001	021	17	11	DC1 ◄	^Q	DC1	11-1-9
0001 0010	022	18	12	DC2 ↕	^R	DC2	11-2-9
0001 0011	023	19	13	DC3 ‼	^S	DC3	11-3-9
0001 0100	024	20	14	DC4 ¶	^T	RES/ENP	11-4-9
0001 0101	025	21	15	NAK §	^U	NL	11-5-9
0001 0110	026	22	16	SYN ▬	^V	BS	11-6-9
0001 0111	027	23	17	ETB ↨	^W	POC	11-7-9
0001 1000	030	24	18	CAN ↑	^X	CAN	11-8-9
0001 1001	031	25	19	EM ↓	^Y	EM	11-1-8-9
0001 1010	032	26	1A	SUB →	^Z	UBS	11-2-8-9
0001 1011	033	27	1B	ESC ←	^[	CU1	11-3-8-9
0001 1100	034	28	1C	FS ∟	^\	IFS	11-4-8-9
0001 1101	035	29	1D	GS ↔	^]	IGS	11-5-8-9
0001 1110	036	30	1E	RS ▲	^^	IRS	11-6-8-9
0001 1111	037	31	1F	US ▼	^_	ITB/IUS	11-7-8-9

Figure C-1: ASCII chart, Part 1

Binary	Octal	Decimal	Hex	(ASCII) PC Char	(EBCDIC) IBM Char	(EBCDIC) Card Code
0010 0000	040	32	20	SP	DS	11-0-1-8-9
0010 0001	041	33	21	!	SOS	0-1-9
0010 0010	042	34	22	"	FS	0-2-9
0010 0011	043	35	23	#	WUS	0-3-9
0010 0100	044	36	24	$	BYP/INP	0-4-9
0010 0101	045	37	25	%	LF	0-5-9
0010 0110	046	38	26	&	ETB	0-6-9
0010 0111	047	39	27	'	ESC	0-7-9
0010 1000	050	40	28	(	SA	0-8-9
0010 1001	051	41	29	)	SFE	0-1-8-9
0010 1010	052	42	2A	*	SM/SW	0-2-8-9
0010 1011	053	43	2B	+	CSP	0-3-8-9
0010 1100	054	44	2C	,	MFA	0-4-8-9
0010 1101	055	45	2D	-	ENQ	0-5-8-9
0010 1110	056	46	2E	.	ACK	0-6-8-9
0010 1111	057	47	2F	/	BEL	0-7-8-9
0011 0000	060	48	30	0		12-11-0-1-8-9
0011 0001	061	49	31	1		1-9
0011 0010	062	50	32	2	SYN	2-9
0011 0011	063	51	33	3	IR	3-9
0011 0100	064	52	34	4	PP	4-9
0011 0101	065	53	35	5	TRN	5-9
0011 0110	066	54	36	6	NBS	6-9
0011 0111	067	55	37	7	EOT	7-9
0011 1000	070	56	38	8	SBS	8-9
0011 1001	071	57	39	9	IT	1-8-9
0011 1010	072	58	3A	:	RFF	2-8-9
0011 1011	073	59	3B	;	CU3	3-8-9
0011 1100	074	60	3C	<	DC4	4-8-9
0011 1101	075	61	3D	=	NAK	5-8-9
0011 1110	076	62	3E	>		6-8-9
0011 1111	077	63	3F	?	SUB	7-8-9

Figure C-2: ASCII chart, Part 2

Binary	Octal	Decimal	Hex	(ASCII) PC Char	(EBCDIC) IBM Char	(EBCDIC) Card Code
0100 0000	100	64	40	@	SP	(no punches)
0100 0001	101	65	41	A	RSP	12-0-1-9
0100 0010	102	66	42	B		12-0-2-9
0100 0011	103	67	43	C		12-0-3-9
0100 0100	104	68	44	D		12-0-4-9
0100 0101	105	69	45	E		12-0-5-9
0100 0110	106	70	46	F		12-0-6-9
0100 0111	107	71	47	G		12-0-7-9
0100 1000	110	72	48	H		12-0-8-9
0100 1001	111	73	49	I		12-1-8
0100 1010	112	74	4A	J	¢	12-2-8
0100 1011	113	75	4B	K	.	12-3-8
0100 1100	114	76	4C	L	<	12-4-8
0100 1101	115	77	4D	M	(	12-5-8
0100 1110	116	78	4E	N	+	12-6-8
0100 1111	117	79	4F	O	|	12-7-8
0101 0000	120	80	50	P	&	12
0101 0001	121	81	51	Q		12-11-1-9
0101 0010	122	82	52	R		12-11-2-9
0101 0011	123	83	53	S		12-11-3-9
0101 0100	124	84	54	T		12-11-4-9
0101 0101	125	85	55	U		12-11-5-9
0101 0110	126	86	56	V		12-11-6-9
0101 0111	127	87	57	W		12-11-7-9
0101 1000	130	88	58	X		12-11-8-9
0101 1001	131	89	59	Y		11-1-8
0101 1010	132	90	5A	Z	!	11-2-8
0101 1011	133	91	5B	[	$	11-3-8
0101 1100	134	92	5C	\	*	11-4-8
0101 1101	135	93	5D	]	)	11-5-8
0101 1110	136	94	5E	^	;	11-6-8
0101 1111	137	95	5F	_	¬	11-7-8

Figure C-3: ASCII chart, Part 3

Binary	Octal	Decimal	Hex	(ASCII) PC Char	(EBCDIC) IBM Char	(EBCDIC) Card Code
0110 0000	140	96	60	'	–	11
0110 0001	141	97	61	a	/	0-1
0110 0010	142	98	62	b		11-0-2-9
0110 0011	143	99	63	c		11-0-3-9
0110 0100	144	100	64	d		11-0-4-9
0110 0101	145	101	65	e		11-0-5-9
0110 0110	146	102	66	f		11-0-6-9
0110 0111	147	103	67	g		11-0-7-9
0110 1000	150	104	68	h		11-0-8-9
0110 1001	151	105	69	i		0-1-8
0110 1010	152	106	6A	j	¦	12-11
0110 1011	153	107	6B	k	,	0-3-8
0110 1100	154	108	6C	l	%	0-4-8
0110 1101	155	109	6D	m	_	0-5-8
0110 1110	156	110	6E	n	>	0-6-8
0110 1111	157	111	6F	o	?	0-7-8
0111 0000	160	112	70	p		12-11-0
0111 0001	161	113	71	q		12-11-0-1-9
0111 0010	162	114	72	r		12-11-0-2-9
0111 0011	163	115	73	s		12-11-0-3-9
0111 0100	164	116	74	t		12-11-0-4-9
0111 0101	165	117	75	u		12-11-0-5-9
0111 0110	166	118	76	v		12-11-0-6-9
0111 0111	167	119	77	w		12-11-0-7-9
0111 1000	170	120	78	x		12-11-0-8-9
0111 1001	171	121	79	y		1-8
0111 1010	172	122	7A	z	:	2-8
0111 1011	173	123	7B	{	#	3-8
0111 1100	174	124	7C	¦	@	4-8
0111 1101	175	125	7D	}	'	5-8
0111 1110	176	126	7E	~	=	6-8
0111 1111	177	127	7F	▲	"	7-8

Figure C-4: ASCII chart, Part 4

Binary	Octal	Decimal	Hex	(ASCII) PC Char	(EBCDIC) IBM Char	(EBCDIC) Card Code
1000 0000	200	128	80	Ç		12-0-1-8
1000 0001	201	129	81	ü	a	12-0-1
1000 0010	202	130	82	é	b	12-0-2
1000 0011	203	131	83	â	c	12-0-3
1000 0100	204	132	84	ä	d	12-0-4
1000 0101	205	133	85	à	e	12-0-5
1000 0110	206	134	86	å	f	12-0-6
1000 0111	207	135	87	ç	g	12-0-7
1000 1000	210	136	88	ê	h	12-0-8
1000 1001	211	137	89	ë	i	12-0-9
1000 1010	212	138	8A	è		12-0-2-8
1000 1011	213	139	8B	ï	{	12-0-3-8
1000 1100	214	140	8C	î	≤ ⁽ *	12-0-4-8
1000 1101	215	141	8D	ì	*	12-0-5-8
1000 1110	216	142	8E	Ä	+ *	12-0-6-8
1000 1111	217	143	8F	Å	+	12-0-7-8
1001 0000	220	144	90	É		12-11-1-8
1001 0001	221	145	91	æ	j	12-11-1
1001 0010	222	146	92	Æ	k	12-11-2
1001 0011	223	147	93	ô	l	12-11-3
1001 0100	224	148	94	ö	m	12-11-4
1001 0101	225	149	95	ò	n	12-11-5
1001 0110	226	150	96	û	o	12-11-6
1001 0111	227	151	97	ù	p	12-11-7
1001 1000	230	152	98	ÿ	q	12-11-8
1001 1001	231	153	99	Ö	r	12-11-9
1001 1010	232	154	9A	Ü		12-11-2-8
1001 1011	233	155	9B	¢	}	12-11-3-8
1001 1100	234	156	9C	£	¤	12-11-4-8
1001 1101	235	157	9D	¥	⁾ *	12-11-5-8
1001 1110	236	158	9E	₧	±	12-11-6-8
1001 1111	237	159	9F	ƒ	■	12-11-7-8

* Superscript

Figure C-5: ASCII Chart, Part 5

Binary	Octal	Decimal	Hex	(ASCII) PC Char	(EBCDIC) IBM Char	(EBCDIC) Card Code
1010 0000	240	160	A0	á	⁻ *	11-0-1-8
1010 0001	241	161	A1	í	~ °	11-0-1
1010 0010	242	162	A2	ó	s	11-0-2
1010 0011	243	163	A3	ú	t	11-0-3
1010 0100	244	164	A4	ñ	u	11-0-4
1010 0101	245	165	A5	Ñ	v	11-0-5
1010 0110	246	166	A6	ª	w	11-0-6
1010 0111	247	167	A7	º	x	11-0-7
1010 1000	250	168	A8	¿	y	11-0-8
1010 1001	251	169	A9	⌐	z	11-0-9
1010 1010	252	170	AA	¬		11-0-2-8
1010 1011	253	171	AB	½	L	11-0-3-8
1010 1100	254	172	AC	¼	Γ	11-0-4-8
1010 1101	255	173	AD	¡	[	11-0-5-8
1010 1110	256	174	AE	«	≥	11-0-6-8
1010 1111	257	175	AF	»	•	11-0-7-8
1011 0000	260	176	B0	░	ø *	12-11-0-1-8
1011 0001	261	177	B1	▒	1 *	12-11-0-1
1011 0010	262	178	B2	▓	2 *	12-11-0-2
1011 0011	263	179	B3	│	3 *	12-11-0-3
1011 0100	264	180	B4	┤	4 *	12-11-0-4
1011 0101	265	181	B5	╡	5 *	12-11-0-5
1011 0110	266	182	B6	╢	6 *	12-11-0-6
1011 0111	267	183	B7	╖	7 *	12-11-0-7
1011 1000	270	184	B8	╕	8 *	12-11-0-8
1011 1001	271	185	B9	╣	9 *	12-11-0-9
1011 1010	272	186	BA	║		12-11-0-2-8
1011 1011	273	187	BB	╗	⌐	12-11-0-3-8
1011 1100	274	188	BC	╝		12-11-0-4-8
1011 1101	275	189	BD	╜	]	12-11-0-5-8
1011 1110	276	190	BE	╛		12-11-0-6-8
1011 1111	277	191	BF	┐	⁻	12-11-0-7-8

✳ Superscript

Figure C-6: ASCII chart, Part 6

Binary	Octal	Decimal	Hex	(ASCII) PC Char	PC Char	(EBCDIC) IBM Char	(EBCDIC) Card Code
1100 0000	300	192	C0	L		{	12-0
1100 0001	301	193	C1	⊥		A	12-1
1100 0010	302	194	C2			B	12-2
1100 0011	303	195	C3	⊤		C	12-3
1100 0100	304	196	C4	—		D	12-4
1100 0101	305	197	C5	+		E	12-5
1100 0110	306	198	C6			F	12-6
1100 0111	307	199	C7			G	12-7
1100 1000	310	200	C8			H	12-8
1100 1001	311	201	C9			I	12-9
1100 1010	312	202	CA			SHY	12-0-2-8-9
1100 1011	313	203	CB				12-0-3-8-9
1100 1100	314	204	CC				12-0-4-8-9
1100 1101	315	205	CD	=			12-0-5-8-9
1100 1110	316	206	CE				12-0-6-8-9
1100 1111	317	207	CF				12-0-7-8-9
1101 0000	320	208	D0	⊥⊥		}	11-0
1101 0001	321	209	D1	⊤		J	11-1
1101 0010	322	210	D2			K	11-2
1101 0011	323	211	D3			L	11-3
1101 0100	324	212	D4			M	11-4
1101 0101	325	213	D5	F		N	11-5
1101 0110	326	214	D6			O	11-6
1101 0111	327	215	D7			P	11-7
1101 1000	330	216	D8			Q	11-8
1101 1001	331	217	D9			R	11-9
1101 1010	332	218	DA	⌐			12-11-2-8-9
1101 1011	333	219	DB	█			12-11-3-8-9
1101 1100	334	220	DC				12-11-4-8-9
1101 1101	335	221	DD	▌			12-11-5-8-9
1101 1110	336	222	DE	▐			12-11-6-8-9
1101 1111	337	223	DF				12-11-7-8-9

Figure C-7: ASCII chart, Part 7

Binary	Octal	Decimal	Hex	(ASCII) PC Char	PC Char	(EBCDIC) IBM Char	(EBCDIC) Card Code
1110 0000	340	224	E0	α		\	0-2-8
1110 0001	341	225	E1	β		NSP	11-0-1-9
1110 0010	342	226	E2	Γ		S	0-2
1110 0011	343	227	E3	π		T	0-3
1110 0100	344	228	E4	Σ		U	0-4
1110 0101	345	229	E5	σ		V	0-5
1110 0110	346	230	E6	μ		W	0-6
1110 0111	347	231	E7	τ		X	0-7
1110 1000	350	232	E8	Φ		Y	0-8
1110 1001	351	233	E9	Θ		Z	0-9
1110 1010	352	234	EA	Ω			11-0-2-8-9
1110 1011	353	235	EB	δ			11-0-3-8-9
1110 1100	354	236	EC	∞			11-0-4-8-9
1110 1101	355	237	ED	φ			11-0-5-8-9
1110 1110	356	238	EE	ε			11-0-6-8-9
1110 1111	357	239	EF	∩			11-0-7-8-9
1111 0000	360	240	F0	≡		0	0
1111 0001	361	241	F1	±		1	1
1111 0010	362	242	F2	≥		2	2
1111 0011	363	243	F3	≤		3	3
1111 0100	364	244	F4	⌠		4	4
1111 0101	365	245	F5	⌡		5	5
1111 0110	366	246	F6	÷		6	6
1111 0111	367	247	F7	≈		7	7
1111 1000	370	248	F8	°		8	8
1111 1001	371	249	F9	·		9	9
1111 1010	372	250	FA	·			12-11-0-2-8-9
1111 1011	373	251	FB	√			12-11-0-3-8-9
1111 1100	374	252	FC	η			12-11-0-4-8-9
1111 1101	375	253	FD	²			12-11-0-5-8-9
1111 1110	376	254	FE	■			12-11-0-6-8-9
1111 1111	377	255	FF			EO	12-11-0-7-8-9

Figure C-8: ASCII chart, Part 8

✦   ✦   ✦

Color Assignments and Video Modes Chart

The information given in this appendix can be useful for menu programs or other applications that enable you to customize screen colors by number.

Table D-1
IBM-PC Hexadecimal/Decimal Color Number Assignments

Background	Blk. 0		Blue 1		Green 2		Cyan 3		Red 4		Mag. 5		Yellow 6		White 7	
	Hex	Dec	Hex	Dec	Hex	Dec	Hex	Dec	Hex	Dec	Hex	Dec	Hex	Dec	Hex	Dec
Foreground																
BLACK=0	00	0	10	16	20	32	30	48	40	64	50	80	60	96	70	112
BLUE=1	01	1	11	17	21	33	31	49	41	65	51	81	61	97	71	113
GREEN=2	02	2	12	18	22	34	32	50	42	66	52	82	62	98	72	114
CYAN=3	03	3	13	19	23	35	33	51	43	67	53	83	63	99	73	115
RED=4	04	4	14	20	24	36	34	52	44	68	54	84	64	100	74	116
MAGENTA=5	05	5	15	21	25	37	35	53	45	69	55	85	65	101	75	117
YELLOW=6	06	6	16	22	26	38	36	54	46	70	56	86	66	102	76	118
WHITE=7	07	7	17	23	27	39	37	55	47	71	57	87	67	103	77	119
GREY=8	08	8	18	24	28	40	38	56	48	72	58	88	68	104	78	120
BRIGHT BLUE=9	09	9	19	25	29	41	39	57	49	73	59	89	69	105	79	121
BRIGHT GREEN=10	0A	10	1A	26	2A	42	3A	58	4A	74	5A	90	6A	106	7A	122
BRIGHT CYAN=11	0B	11	1B	27	2B	43	3B	59	4B	75	5B	91	6B	107	7B	123
BRIGHT RED=12	0C	12	1C	28	2C	44	3C	60	4C	76	5C	92	6C	108	7C	124
BRIGHT MAGENTA=13	0D	13	1D	29	2D	45	3D	61	4D	77	5D	93	6D	109	7D	125
BRIGHT YELLOW=14	0E	14	1E	30	2E	46	3E	62	4E	78	5E	94	6E	110	7E	126
BRIGHT WHITE=15	0F	15	1F	31	2F	47	3F	63	4F	79	5F	95	6F	111	7F	127
BLACK = 0	80	128	90	144	A0	160	B0	176	C0	192	D0	208	E0	224	F0	240

Background	Blk. 0		Blue 1		Green 2		Cyan 3		Red 4		Mag. 5		Yellow 6		White 7	
	Hex	Dec	Hex	Dec	Hex	Dec	Hex	Dec	Hex	Dec	Hex	Dec	Hex	Dec	Hex	Dec
Foreground																
BLUE = 1	81	129	91	145	A1	161	B1	177	C1	193	D1	209	E1	225	F1	241
GREEN = 2	82	130	92	146	A2	162	B2	178	C2	194	D2	210	E2	226	F2	242
CYAN = 3	83	131	93	147	A3	163	B3	179	C3	195	D3	211	E3	227	F3	243
RED = 4	84	132	94	148	A4	164	B4	180	C4	196	D4	212	E4	228	F4	244
MAGENTA = 5	85	133	95	149	A5	165	B5	181	C5	197	D5	213	E5	229	F5	245
YELLOW = 6	86	134	96	150	A6	166	B6	182	C6	198	D6	214	E6	230	F6	246
WHITE = 7	87	135	97	151	A7	167	B7	183	C7	199	D7	215	E7	231	F7	247
GREY = 8	88	136	98	152	A8	168	B8	184	C8	200	D8	216	E8	232	F8	248
BRIGHT BLUE = 9	89	137	99	153	A9	169	B9	185	C9	201	D9	217	E9	233	F9	249
BRIGHT GREEN = 10	8A	138	9A	154	AA	170	BA	186	CA	202	DA	218	EA	234	FA	250
BRIGHT CYAN = 11	8B	139	9B	155	AB	171	BB	187	CB	203	DB	219	EB	235	FB	251
BRIGHT RED = 12	8C	140	9C	156	AC	172	BC	188	CC	204	DC	220	EC	236	FC	252
BRIGHT MAGENTA = 13	8D	141	9D	157	AD	173	BD	189	CD	205	DD	221	ED	237	FD	253
BRIGHT YELLOW = 14	8E	142	9E	158	AE	174	BE	190	CE	206	DE	222	EE	238	FE	254
BRIGHT WHITE = 15	8F	143	9F	159	AF	175	BF	191	CF	207	DF	223	EF	239	FF	255

* Color numbers 0–127 (decimal) do not blink on solid background.
* Color numbers 128–255 (decimal) blink on solid background.
* Do not confuse these with the color hue settings that use numbers from 0 to 255 for each "color gun".

Table D-2
IBM-PC Video Modes

Mode	Type	Columns × Rows	Pixels	Number of Colors
0	Mono. text	40×25	320×200	2 – Black/White
1	Color text	40×25	320×200	Fore = 16/Back = 8 (EGA =16)
2	Mono. text	80×25	640×200	2 – Black/White
3	Color text	80×25	640×200	Fore = 16/Back = 8 (EGA =64)
4	Color graphics	40×25	320×200	4
5	Mono. graphics	40×25	320×200	2 – Black/White
6	Color graphics	80×25	640×200	2 – Black/White
7	Mono. text	80×25	720×350	2 – Black/White
8	Color graphics		160×200	16 (PCjr)
9	Color graphics	40×25	320×200	16 (PCjr)
10	Color graphics	80×25	640×200	4 (PCjr)
11	(Reserved – IBM)			
12	(Reserved – IBM)			
13	Color graphics	40×25	320×200	16 (EGA)
14	Color graphics	80×25	640×200	16 (EGA)
15	Mono. graphics	80×25	640×350	2 – Black/White (some 4color)
16	Color graphics	80×25	640×350	16 or 64 (EGA)
17	Color graphics	80×30	640×480	2 – Black/White (MCGA/VGA)
18	Color graphics	80×30	640×480	16 (VGA)
19	Color graphics	40×25	320×200	256 (MCGA/VGA)

✦   ✦   ✦

Hard Disk Drive Types (Standard, Extended, and Phoenix)

IBM defined the first 15 hard disk drive types within the BIOS for the IBM-AT and similar systems in January 1984. The table was expanded to include the following drive types:

- ✦ 22 types for the PC/AT in June 1985
- ✦ 23 types for the PC/AT in November 1985
- ✦ 24 types for the XT/286 in April 1986
- ✦ 26 types for the PS/2-30 in December 1986
- ✦ 32 types for the PS/2-80 in October 1987
- ✦ 33 types for the PS/2-50Z in April 1988

This information is stored in the CMOS RAM chip during system setup as part of the hard drive configuration and software handling. It is used in 80286, 80386, and 80486 and higher systems. However, this is a CMOS memory- and ROM BIOS-related item, not necessarily related to the installed CPU.

Most non-IBM systems have adopted these first 15 drive types and the subsequent additional drive types from 16 to 32. Compaq and others have defined their own drive types beyond this.

Some manufacturers or BIOS publishers have even made a provision for defining your own drive type with individual parameters in order to suit special situations or the use of drives not known at the time of BIOS distribution.

You should verify the drive type for your particular system with the BIOS or system board manufacturer or if this information is not otherwise available, consult the hard drive manufacturer.

The drive type is the number that should be keyed in during the setup process of your system. If this number does not match your drive, you will either not be able to access the drive or not be able to use all of the space available.

The number of cylinders, heads, and tracks refers to the physical and format characteristics of the drive. The write precompensation (WPC) value refers to a parameter used by the disk controller to allow for different data writing characteristics of the drive. Some format programs will also ask for a reduced-write-current (RWC) value. This should be obtained from the disk drive information, if necessary.

The drive capacity is typical of the space available after completing the DOS formatting process. The landing zone/head park track specifies the safe or nondata area on the disk where the heads automatically rest when the drive is not in use or where a head parking program will move the head on command. Table E-1 lists the IBM drive types.

Table E-1 IBM Drive Type Table						
Drive Type Number	Number of Tracks	Number of Heads	Number of Sectors Per Track	Write Precompensation Track	Drive Size (MB)	Landing Zone Track Number
1	306	4	17	128	10	305
2	615	4	17	300	20	615
3	615	6	17	300	32	615
4	940	8	17	512	64	940
5	940	6	17	512	48	940
6	615	4	17	65535	20	615
7	462	8	17	256	30	511
8	733	5	17	65535	30	733
9	900	15	17	65535	110	901
10	820	3	17	65535	20	820
11	855	5	17	65535	35	855

Drive Type Number	Number of Tracks	Number of Heads	Number of Sectors Per Track	Write Precompensation Track	Drive Size (MB)	Landing Zone Track Number
12	855	7	17	65535	50	855
13	306	8	17	128	20	319
14	733	7	17	65535	40	733
15	– DO	NOT	USE –			
16	612	4	17	0	20	663
17	977	5	17	300	40	977
18	977	7	17	65535	56	977
19	1024	5	17	512	60	1023
20	733	5	17	300	30	732
21	733	7	17	300	42	733
22	733	5	17	300	30	733
23	306	4	17	0	10	336
24	612	4	17	305	21	663
25	306	4	17	65535	10	340
26	612	4	17	65535	21	670
27	698	7	17	300	41	732
28	976	5	17	488	41	977
29	306	4	17	0	10	340
30	611	4	17	306	21	663
31	732	7	17	300	43	732
32	1023	5	17	65535	43	1023
33	614	4	25	65535	30	663

Types 34–47 are "reserved" for future allocation by IBM. They are otherwise unused, often allocated by other manufacturers (as shown in Table E-2), and not necessarily supported by IBM.

A type 0 indicates no hard disk drive or special BIOS supported drive specifications, usually on the controller.

A write precompensation value of 65535 or –1 equates to "none." A value of 0 indicates write precompensation applies to all tracks or cylinders. Any other cylinder number indicates the cylinder at which write precompensation begins. Table E-2 shows IBM-extended BIOS drive types.

Drive Type Number	Number of Tracks	Number of Heads	Number of Sectors Per Track	Write Precompen- sation Track	Drive Size (MB)	Landing Zone Track Number
			Table E-2 IBM-Extended BIOS Drive Types			
24	925	7	17	0	54	925
25	925	9	17	None	69	925
26	754	7	17	754	44	754
27	754	11	17	None	69	754
28	699	7	17	256	41	699
29	823	10	17	None	69	823
30	918	7	17	918	54	918
31	1024	11	17	None	98	1024
32	1024	15	17	None	133	1024
33	1024	5	17	1024	43	1024
34	612	2	17	128	10	612
35	1024	9	17	None	77	1024
36	1024	8	17	512	68	1024
37	615	8	17	128	41	615
38	987	3	17	987	25	987
39	987	7	17	987	58	987
40	820	6	17	820	41	820
41	977	5	17	977	41	977
42	981	5	17	981	41	981
43	830	7	17	512	49	830
44	830	10	17	None	69	830
45	917	15	17	None	115	918

Later versions of AMI BIOS allow a "define your own" drive type as Type 47, which is quite advantageous, considering the variety of drives available. Table E-3 lists Phoenix BIOS drive types.

Table E-3
Typical Phoenix BIOS Drive Types

Drive Type Number	Number of Tracks	Number of Heads	Number of Sectors Per Track	Write Precompen-sation Track	Drive Size (MB)	Landing Zone Track Number
24	– DO	NOT	USE –			
25	615	4	17	0	20	615
26	1024	4	17	–1	35	1024
27	1024	5	17	–1	44	1024
28	1024	8	17	–1	70	1024
29	512	8	17	256	35	512
30	615	2	17	615	10	615
31	989	5	17	0	42	989
32	1020	15	17	–1	130	1020
33	615	4	26	–1	32	615
34	820	6	26	–1	65	820
35	1024	9	17	1024	80	1024
36	1024	5	17	512	44	1024
37	1024	5	26	512	68	1024
38	823	10	17	256	70	824
39	615	4	17	128	21	664
40	615	8	17	128	42	664
41	917	15	17	–1	120	918
42	1023	15	17	–1	132	1024
43	823	10	17	512	71	823
44	820	6	17	–1	42	820
45	1024	5	17	–1	44	1023
46	925	9	17	–1	71	925

Continued

Table E-3 *(continued)*

Drive Type Number	Number of Tracks	Number of Heads	Number of Sectors Per Track	Write Precompen- sation Track	Drive Size (MB)	Landing Zone Track Number
47	699	7	17	256	42	700
48	User					
49	User					

✦   ✦   ✦

PC Error Codes, Beeps, and Diagnostic Messages

IBM PC–compatible systems provide a number of self-diagnostics to help you determine the nature of any major or minor flaws in your system's hardware. The following tables will help you in diagnosing the visual and audible error messages you could receive from many PC systems when a problem exists.

The first four audible indications listed in Tables F-1 through F-5 are standard for IBM systems and most compatibles. Following these are numerically coded audible indications used in some newer non-IBM systems, shown as a pattern of a number of beeps, with pauses between them.

Table F-1
Audible Indications

Indication	Possible Causes
None — dead system	No power, bad CPU, bad clock oscillator
Keyboard lights flickered	If the keyboard lights flicker and then go out, but the computer does not boot, check the CPU IC. If they always flicker, turn off the unit, wait 30 seconds, then turn the unit on again. There may have been a power-on sequence error or power glitch at turn-on.
One short speaker beep	System board POST passed.
One long and two short speaker beeps or two short speaker beeps	Display error — display type switch set incorrectly or bad display adapter.
One long speaker beep	See onscreen message; refer to Table F-2.

Table F-2
Fatal Error Beep Codes

Beep Sequence	Meaning
1-1-3	CMOS RAM failure
1-1-4	BIOS checksum failure
1-2-1	8253 timer failure
1-2-2	DMA setup failure
1-2-3	DMA page register failure
1-3-1	RAM refresh not verified
1-3-3	Low 64K RAM failure
1-3-4	Low 64K RAM odd/even failure
1-4-1	Low 64K RAM address failure
1-4-2	Low 64K RAM parity error
1-4-3	Fail-safe timer failure (EISA)
1-4-4	Software NMI port failure (EISA)
2-1-1	Low 64K RAM bit 0 error
2-1-2	Low 64K RAM bit 1 error
2-1-3	Low 64K RAM bit 2 error
2-1-4	Low 64K RAM bit 3 error

Beep Sequence	Meaning
2-2-1	Low 64K RAM bit 4 error
2-2-2	Low 64K RAM bit 5 error
2-2-3	Low 64K RAM bit 6 error
2-2-4	Low 64K RAM bit 7 error
2-3-1	Low 64K RAM bit 8 error
2-3-2	Low 64K RAM bit 9 error
2-3-3	Low 64K RAM bit 10 error
2-3-4	Low 64K RAM bit 11 error
2-4-1	Low 64K RAM bit 12 error
2-4-2	Low 64K RAM bit 13 error
2-4-3	Low 64K RAM bit 14 error
2-4-4	Low 64K RAM bit 15 error
3-1-1	DMA 2 register error
3-1-2	DMA 1 register error
3-1-3	8259 1 error
3-1-4	8259 2 error
3-2-4	8042 keyboard controller error
3-3-1	Slave DMA register test or failure
3-3-4	Video initialization error
3-4-1	Video retrace error
3-4-2	Video ROM scan in progress
3-4-3	Video ROM scan error

Table F-3
Nonfatal Error Beep Codes

Beep Sequence	Meaning
4-2-1	8253 timer tick test or failure
4-2-2	Shutdown/restart sequence test
4-2-3	Gate A20 failure

Continued

Table F-3 *(continued)*

Beep Sequence	Meaning
4-2-4	Unexpected virtual mode interrupt
4-3-1	RAM Test (>64K) in progress or failure
4-3-3	8253 timer channel 2 test or failure
4-3-4	Realtime clock test or failure
4-4-1	Serial port test or failure
4-4-2	Parallel port test or failure
4-4-3	Math coprocessor test or failure

Many vendors have adopted IBM's standard numerical error coding scheme for onscreen error messages. Table F-4 is a compilation of XT, AT, PS/2, and later model error messages. These messages may or may not be accompanied by audible indications (as described previously), or contain extra leading or trailing zeros. These messages are fairly specific as to the area, board, or component of the system that needs to be replaced.

Table F-4
IBM BIOS, POST, and Diagnostic Error Messages and Meanings

Error Code	Description
101	System board interrupt failure
102	System board timer failure
103	System board timer interrupt failure
104	Protected mode failure (AT)
105	Command not accepted at keyboard controller
106	Logic test failure, run diagnostics
107	NMI test failure (XT only, memory in PS/2)
108	Timer test failure, memory in PS/2
109	DMA test error, memory in PS/2
110	PS/2 system board error, parity check
111	PS/2 memory adapter error

Error Code	Description
112	PS/2 Micro Channel arbitration error, system board
113	PS/2 Micro Channel arbitration error, system board
114	Any adapter, ROM
115	System board, CPU
116	Run diagnostics, CPU
118	System board memory error
119	2.88MB diskette drive installed but not supported
120	System board processor, cache
121	Unexpected hardware interrupts occurred
122xx	Run diagnostics
130	POST—no operating system, check diskettes, configuration
131	Cassette interface test failed, PS/2 system board
132	DMA extended registers error, run diagnostics
133	DMA error, run diagnostics
134	DMA error, run diagnostics
151	System board realtime clock failure (or CMOS ERROR on 5170)
152	System board CMOS date and time error (5170)
161	Battery failure, replace and run setup
162	Configuration/CMOS error, run setup
163	Time/date incorrect, run setup (AT)
164	Memory size error, run setup (AT)
165	PS/2 system options not set
166	PS/2 Micro Channel adapter timeout error
199	Configuration not correct, check setup
201	Memory test failed, see chip location number
202	Memory address lines (00–15)
203	Memory address lines (16–23)
301	Keyboard did not respond to software reset correctly or a stuck key failure was detected; if a stuck key was detected, the scan code for the key is displayed (check keyboard connection)
302	User indicated error from the keyboard test, or key-switch locked

Continued

Table F-4 *(continued)*

Error Code	Description
303	Keyboard or system error
304	Keyboard clock line error
305	PS/2 keyboard fuse (system board) error
306	Check for unsupported keyboard
307	Keyboard, keyboard cable
365	Replace keyboard
366	Keyboard, replace interface cable
367	Replace enhancement card or cable
401	Monochrome memory test, horizontal sync frequency test, or video test failed or PS/2 system board parallel port failure
408	User indicated display mode failure
416	User indicated character set failure
424	User indicated 80×25 mode failure
432	Parallel port test failed (printer port on monochrome adapter card)
5xx	Display adapter, any type
501	Color memory test failed, horizontal sync frequency test, or video test failed
508	User indicated display mode failure
516	User indicated character set failure
524	User indicated 80×25 mode failure
532	User indicated 40×25 mode failure
540	User indicated 320×200 graphics mode failure
548	User indicated 640×200 graphics mode failure
556	Color adapter, light pen test failure
564	Color adapter, user indicated screen paging test failure
6xx	Diskette, diskette drive
601	Diskette POST diagnostics failed or diskette/drive error
602	Diskette diagnostic test failed or boot error, defective diskette
603	Diskette size failure
604	Wrong diskette drive type
605	Run advanced diagnostics

Error Code	Description
606	Diskette verify function failed
607	Write-protected diskette in drive
608	Bad command diskette status returned
610	Diskette initialization failed
611	Timeout, diskette status returned
612	Bad NEC diskette controller chip, diskette status returned
613	Bad DMA on system board or diskette controller (drive error)
614	Bad DMA on system board or diskette controller (boundary overrun)
615	Bad index timing, drive error
616	Drive speed error
621	Bad seek, diskette status returned, drive error
622	Bad CRC, diskette status returned, drive error
623	Record not found, diskette status returned, drive error
624	Bad address mark, diskette status returned, drive error
625	Bad NEC disk controller chip seek error
626	Diskette data compare error
627	Diskette line change error
628	Diskette removed
655	System board
662	Wrong diskette drive type
663	Wrong media type
668	Diskette drive (see 73xx series messages for 3.5-inch diskette drives)
7xx	Math coprocessor error
9xx	Printer or system board (parallel port) error
901	Parallel printer adapter test failed, add-on adapter card
914	Conflict between two parallel printer adapters.
11xx	System board
1101	ASYNC — asynchronous communications adapter test failed
1002	Alternate parallel printer adapter

Continued

Table F-4 (continued)

Error Code	Description
1047	16-bit AT SCSI fast adapter
10xx	Reserved for parallel printer adapter
1101	Asynchronous communications adapter test failed, serial or modem #1
1102	PS/2 system board asynchronous port or serial device error
1106	PS/2 system board asynchronous port or serial device error
1107	PS/2 system board asynchronous port or serial cable error
1108	PS/2 system board asynchronous port or serial device error
1109	PS/2 system board asynchronous port or serial device error
1110	ASYNC—Modem status register not clear
1111	ASYNC—Ring indicate failure
1112	ASYNC—Trailing edge ring indicate failure
1113	ASYNC—Receive and delta receive line signal detect failure
1114	ASYNC—Receive line signal detect failure
1115	ASYNC—Delta receive line signal detect failure
1116	ASYNC—Line control register (all bits cannot be set)
1117	ASYNC—Line control register (all bits cannot be reset)
1118	ASYNC—Transmit holding and/or shift register stuck on
1119	ASYNC—Data ready stuck on
1120	ASYNC—Interrupt enable register (all bits cannot be set)
1121	ASYNC—Interrupt enable register (all bits cannot be reset)
1122	ASYNC—Interrupt pending stuck on
1123	ASYNC—Interrupt ID register stuck on
1124	ASYNC—Modem control register (all bits cannot be set)
1125	ASYNC—Modem control register (all bits cannot be reset)
1126	ASYNC—Modem status register (all bits cannot be set)
1127	ASYNC—Modem status register (all bits cannot be reset)
1128	ASYNC—Interrupt ID failure
1129	ASYNC—Cannot force overrun error
1130	ASYNC—Bo modem status interrupt

Error Code	Description
1131	ASYNC — Invalid interrupt status pending
1132	ASYNC — No data ready
1133	ASYNC — No data available interrupt
1134	ASYNC — No transmit holding interrupt
1135	ASYNC — No interrupts
1136	ASYNC — No receive line status interrupt
1137	ASYNC — No receive data available
1138	ASYNC — Transmit holding register not empty
1139	ASYNC — No modem status interrupt
1140	ASYNC — Transmit holding register not empty
1141	ASYNC — No interrupts
1142	ASYNC — No IRQ4 interrupt
1143	ASYNC — No IRQ3 interrupt
1144	ASYNC — No data transferred
1145	ASYNC — Max baud rate failed
1146	ASYNC — Min baud rate failed
1148	ASYNC — Timeout error
1149	ASYNC — Invalid data returned
1150	ASYNC — Modem status register error
1151	ASYNC — No DSR to Delta DSR
1152	ASYNC — No data set ready
1153	ASYNC — No delta
1154	ASYNC — Modem status register not clear
1155	ASYNC — No CTS and delta CTS
1156	ASYNC — No clear to send
1157	ASYNC — No delta CTS (alternately, in the IBM PS/2 models)
1112	PS/2 system board asynchronous port error
1118	PS/2 system board asynchronous port error
1119	PS/2 system board asynchronous port error

Continued

Table F-4 *(continued)*

Error Code	Description
1201	Asynchronous communication adapter test failed, serial or modem #1
1202	PS/2 dual asynchronous port or serial device error
1206	PS/2 dual asynchronous port or serial device error
1207	PS/2 dual asynchronous port or serial cable error
1208	PS/2 dual asynchronous port or serial device error
1209	PS/2 dual asynchronous port or serial device error
1212	PS/2 dual asynchronous port or system board error
1218	PS/2 dual asynchronous port or system board error
1219	PS/2 dual asynchronous port or system board error
1227	PS/2 dual asynchronous port or system board error
1233	PS/2 dual asynchronous port or system board error
1234	PS/2 dual asynchronous port or system board error
12xx	Alternate serial port adapter
1201	ALT ASYNC—Asynchronous communications adapter test failed
1210	ALT ASYNC—Modem status register not clear
1211	ALT ASYNC—Ring indicate failure
1212	ALT ASYNC—Trailing edge ring indicate failure
1213	ALT ASYNC—Receive and delta receive line signal detect failure
1211	ALT ASYNC—Receive line signal detect failure
1215	ALT ASYNC—Delta receive line signal detect failure
1216	ALT ASYNC—Line control register (all bits cannot be set)
1217	ALT ASYNC—Line control register (all bits cannot be reset)
1218	ALT ASYNC—Transmit holding and/or shift register stuck on
1219	ALT ASYNC—Data ready stuck on
1220	ALT ASYNC—Interrupt enable register (all bits cannot be set)
1221	ALT ASYNC—Interrupt enable register (all bits cannot be reset)
1222	ALT ASYNC—Interrupt pending stuck on
1223	ALT ASYNC—Interrupt ID register stuck on
1224	ALT ASYNC—Modem control register (all bits cannot be set)

Error Code	Description
1225	ALT ASYNC — Modem control register (all bits cannot be reset)
1226	ALT ASYNC — Modem status register (all bits cannot be set)
1227	ALT ASYNC — Modem status register (all bits cannot be reset)
1228	ALT ASYNC — Interrupt ID failure
1229	ALT ASYNC — cannot force overrun error
1230	ALT ASYNC — No modem status interrupt
1231	ALT ASYNC — Invalid interrupt status pending
1232	ALT ASYNC — No data ready
1233	ALT ASYNC — No data available interrupt
1234	ALT ASYNC — No transmit holding interrupt
1235	ALT ASYNC — No interrupts
1236	ALT ASYNC — No receive line status interrupt
1237	ALT ASYNC — No receive data available
1238	ALT ASYNC — Transmit holding register not empty
1239	ALT ASYNC — No modem status interrupt
1240	ALT ASYNC — Transmit holding register not empty
1241	ALT ASYNC — No interrupts
1242	ALT ASYNC — No IRQ4 interrupt
1243	ALT ASYNC — No IRQ3 interrupt
1244	ALT ASYNC — No data transferred
1245	ALT ASYNC — Max baud rate failed
1246	ALT ASYNC — Min baud rate failed
1248	ALT ASYNC — Timeout error
1249	ALT ASYNC — Invalid data returned
1250	ALT ASYNC — Modem status register error
1251	ALT ASYNC — No DSR to delta DSR
1252	ALT ASYNC — No data set ready
1253	ALT ASYNC — No delta
1254	ALT ASYNC — Modem status register not clear

Continued

Table F-4 *(continued)*

Error Code	Description
1255	ALT ASYNC — No CTS and delta CTS
1256	ALT ASYNC — No clear to send
1257	ALT ASYNC — No delta CTS
1301	Game control adapter test failed
1302	Joystick test failed
13xx	Game controller
1401	Printer test failed, check cable/printer/card
14xx	Printer, check cable/printer/card
1510	8255 port B failure
1511	8255 port A failure
1512	8255 port C failure
1513	8253 timer 1 did not reach terminal count
1514	8253 timer 1 stuck on
1515	8253 timer 0 did not reach terminal count
1516	8253 timer 0 stuck on
1517	8253 timer 2 did not reach terminal count
1518	8253 timer 2 stuck on
1519	8273 port B error
1520	8273 port A error
1521	8273 command/read timeout
1522	Interrupt level 4 failure
1523	Ring indicate stuck on
1524	Receive clock stuck on
1525	Transmit clock stuck on
1526	Test indicate stuck on
1527	Ring indicate not on
1528	Receive clock not on
1529	Transmit clock not on
1530	Test indicate not on

Error Code	Description
1531	Data set ready not on
1532	Carrier detect not on
1533	Clear to send not on
1534	Data set ready stuck on
1536	Clear to send stuck on
1537	Level 3 interrupt failure
1538	Receive interrupt results error
1539	Wrap data miscompare
1540	DMA channel 1 error
1541	DMA channel 1 error
1542	Error in 8273 error checking or status
1547	Stray interrupt level 4
1548	Stray interrupt level 3
1549	Interrupt presentation sequence timeout
15xx	SLDC adapter
16xx	Display emulation error, 3270, 5520, 5250
1604	DSEA adapter error, or twin axial problem
1608	DSEA adapter error, or twin axial problem
1624	DSEA adapter error
1634	DSEA adapter error
1644	DSEA adapter error
1652	DSEA adapter error
1654	DSEA adapter error
1658	DSEA adapter error
1664	DSEA adapter error
1662	DSEA interrupt level switches set incorrectly or DSEA adapter error
1668	DSEA interrupt level switches set incorrectly or DSEA adapter error
1674	DSEA station address error or DSEA adapter error
1684	DSEA feature not installed or device address switches set incorrectly

Continued

Table F-4 *(continued)*

Error Code	Description
1688	DSEA feature not installed or device address switches set incorrectly
17xx	System board, hard disk drive, cable, power supply (see 104xx series messages for PS/2 ESDI hard disk errors)
1701	Fixed disk POST error, check disk drive address, cables
1702	Fixed disk adapter error
1703	Fixed disk drive error, check disk drive address, cables
1704	Fixed disk adapter or drive error
1705	No record round
1706	Write fault error
1707	Track "0" error
1708	Head select error
1709	Bad ECC
1710	Read buffer overrun
1711	Bad address mark
1712	Bad address mark
1713	Data compare error
1714	Drive not ready
1730	Replace adapter
1731	Replace adapter
1732	Replace adapter
1780	Hard disk 0 failed (XT only)
1781	Hard disk 1 failed (XT only)
1782	Hard disk controller error (XT only)
1790	Fixed disk 1 error (AT), check disk address, cables, setup
1791	Fixed disk 2 error (AT), check disk address, cables, setup
1801	I/O expansion unit POST error
1810	Enable/disable failure
1811	Extender card wrap test failed
1812	High order address lines failure
1813	Wait state failure

Error Code	Description
1814	Enable/disable could not be set on
1815	Wait state failure (enabled)
1816	Extender card wrap test failed (enabled)
1817	High order address failure (enabled)
1818	Disable not functioning
1819	Wait request switch not set correctly
1820	Receiver card wrap test failure
1821	Receiver high address lines failure
19xx	3270 PC attachment card errors
20xx	BSC adapter
2001	BSC—POST failed
2010	8255 port A failure
2011	8255 port B failure
2012	8255 port C failure
2013	8253 timer 1 did not reach terminal count
2014	8253 timer 1 stuck on
2016	8253 timer 2 did not reach terminal count or timer 2 stuck on
2017	8251 data set ready failed to come on
2018	8251 clear to send not sensed
2019	8251 data set ready stuck on
2020	8251 clear to send stuck on
2021	8251 hardware reset failed
2022	8251 software reset failed
2023	8251 software error reset failed
2024	8251 transmit ready did not come on
2025	8251 receive ready did not come on
2026	8251 could not force overrun error
2027	Interrupt failure—no timer interrupt
2028	Interrupt failure—transmit, replace card or system board

Continued

Table F-4 *(continued)*

Error Code	Description
2029	Interrupt failure — transmit, replace card
2030	Interrupt failure — receive, replace card or system board
2031	Interrupt failure — receive, replace card
2033	Ring indicate stuck on
2034	Receive clock stuck on
2035	Transmit clock stuck on
2036	Test indicate stuck on
2037	Ring indicate stuck on
2038	Receive clock not on
2039	Transmit clock not on
2040	Test indicate not on
2041	Data set ready not on
2042	Carrier detect not on
2043	Clear to send not on
2044	Data set ready stuck on
2045	Carrier detect stuck on
2046	Clear to send stuck on
2047	Unexpected transmit interrupt
2048	Unexpected receive interrupt
2049	Transmit data did not equal receive data (through turnaround)
2050	8251 detected overrun error
2051	Lost data set ready during data wrap
2052	Receive timeout during data wrap
209x	Diskette drive, cable, 16-bit SCSI fast adapter
21xx	SCSI device, if not below for XT, AT
2101	ALT BCC POST failed
2110	8255 port A failure
2111	8255 port B failure
2112	8255 port C failure

Error Code	Description
2113	8253 timer 1 did not reach terminal count
2114	8253 timer 1 stuck on
2116	8253 timer 2 did not reach terminal count or timer 2 stuck on
2117	8251 date set ready failed to come on
2117	8251 clear to send not sensed
2118	8251 data set ready stuck on
2119	8251 clear to send stuck on
2120	8251 hardware reset failed
2121	8251 software reset failed
2122	8251 software error reset failed
2123	8251 transmit ready did not come on
2124	8251 receive ready did not come on
2125	8251 could not force overrun error
2126	Interrupt failure — no timer interrupt
2128	Interrupt failure — transmit, replace card or system board
2129	Interrupt failure — transmit, replace card
2130	Interrupt failure — receive, replace card or system board
2131	Interrupt failure — receive, replace card
2133	Ring indicate stuck on
2134	Receive clock stuck on
2135	Transmit clock stuck on
2136	Test indicate stuck on
2137	Ring indicate stuck on
2138	Receive clock not on
2139	Transmit clock not on
2140	Test indicate not on
2142	Data set ready not on
2142	Carrier detect not on
2143	Clear to send not on

Continued

Table F-4 *(continued)*

Error Code	Description
2144	Data set ready stuck on
2145	Carrier detect stuck on
2146	Clear to send stuck on
2147	Unexpected transmit interrupt
2148	Unexpected receive interrupt
2149	Transmit data did not equal receive
2150	8251 detected overrun error
2151	Lost data set ready during data wrap
2152	Receive timeout during data wrap
2201	Cluster adapter — cluster adapter failure
2221	Cluster adapter — replace cluster adapter
23xx	Plasma monitor adapter errors
24xx	Enhanced graphics adapter errors
24xx	PS/2 system board VGA errors
2401	Display, system board
2402	Display, system board
2409	Display
2410	Display, system board
26xx	XT/3270 errors
27xx	AT/3270 errors
28xx	3278/3279 emulation adapter errors
29xx	Color graphics/printer errors
2901	Color printer — color graphics printer tests failed
3001	Primary PC network processor failure
3002	ROM checksum failure
3003	Unit ID PROM test failure
3004	RAM test failure
3005	Host interface controller test failure
3006	+/− 12 volt test failure

Error Code	Description
3007	Digital loop-back test failure
3008	Host detected host interface controller error
3009	Sync failure and no go bit
3010	Host interface controller test okay, no go bit
3011	Go bit and no command 41
3012	Card not present
3013	Digital failure, fall through
3015	Analog failure
3040	Network cable not attached?
3041	Hot carrier – not this card
3042	Hot carrier – this card
31xx	Alternate network adapter
3101	Sec. PC network processor test failure
3102	ROM checksum failure
3103	Unit ID PROM test failure
3104	RAM test failure
3105	Host interface controller test failure
3106	+/– 12 volt test failure
3107	Digital loop-back test failure
3108	Host detected host interface controller error
3109	Sync failure and no go bit
3110	Host interface controller test okay, no go bit
3111	Go bit and no Command 41
3112	Card not present
3113	Digital failure, fall through
3115	Analog failure
3140	Network cable not attached?
3141	Hot carrier – not this card
3142	Hot carrier – this card

Continued

Table F-4 *(continued)*

Error Code	Description
32xx	3270 PC Display Adapter errors
33xx	Compact printer errors
35xx	Enhanced Display Station Adapter errors
3504	EDSEA adapter connected to twin axial during offline tests
3508	EDSEA workstation address conflict, incorrect diagnostics or adapter
3588	EDSEA feature not installed or device address switches set
3588	EDSEA incorrect or adapter error
36xx	General-purpose interface bus errors
38xx	Data acquisition adapter errors
39xx	Professional graphics controller errors
401x	Recovered error, no error condition
44xx	3270/G/GX display errors
45xx	IEEE-488 adapter errors
50xx	Device/drive error
51xx	Device/drive error
52xx	Device/drive error (IDE)
56xx	Financial adapter error
60xx	SCSI device/adapter
61xx	SCSI device/adapter
62xx	Store loop adapter errors
64xx	Ethernet adapter
69xx	SYS 36/PC driver card error codes
71xx	Voice communications adapter errors
73xx	3.5-inch adapter errors
7306	Disk change line function failure, drive error
7307	Disk is write-protected, drive error
7308	Bad command, drive error
7310	Disk initialization failure, track 0 bad
7311	Timeout, drive error

Error Code	Description
7312	Bad controller chip
7313	Bad DMA, drive error
7314	Bad DMA, boundary overrun
7315	Bad index timing, drive error
7316	Drive speed error
7321	Bad seek, drive error
7322	Bad CRC, drive error
7323	Record not found, drive error
7324	Bad address mark, drive error
7325	Bad controller chip, seek error
74xx	PS/2, 8514/A display adapter (VGA) errors
75xx	Display adapter, any type
76xx	Page printer adapter
7601	Personal Pageprinter adapter failure
7602	Personal Pageprinter adapter failure
7603	Personal Pageprinter failure
7604	Personal Pageprinter cable problem
78xx	High-speed adapter
79xx	3117 scanner errors
7901	3117 scanner adapter failure
7902	3117 scanner lamp problem
7902	3117 scanner device card problem
7903	3117 scanner device card problem
80xx	PCMCIA adapter
82xx	4055 info window errors
84xx	Speech adapter
85xx	IBM expanded memory adapter (XMA) errors
86xx	Mouse, system board
8601	PS/2 pointing device error

Continued

Table F-4 *(continued)*

Error Code	Description
8602	PS/2 pointing device error
8603	PS/2 pointing device or system board error
89xx	Music feature card, MIDI card, bus adapter errors
91xx	3363 optical disk drive errors
9101	Optical disk POST error—drive #1 failed—reseat cables and adapter
9102	Optical disk POST Error—drive #1 failed—reinsert cartridge
9102	Reseat adapter
9103	Optical disk POST error—drive #1 failed—reseat cables and adapter
9104	Optical disk POST error—drive #2 failed—reseat cables and adapter
9105	Optical disk POST error—drive #2 failed—reinsert cartridge
9105	Reseat cables and adapter
9106	Optical disk POST error—drive #2 failed—reseat cables and adapter
9107	Optical disk POST error—adapter hung on BUSY—reseat cables and adapter
9110	Optical disk diagnostics error—data not recorded—check adapter, drive, cable
9111	Optical disk diagnostics error—data not readable—check adapter, drive, cable
9112	Optical disk diagnostics error—sector demarked—check adapter, drive, cable
9113	Optical disk diagnostics error—controller error—check adapter, drive, cable
9113	Check switch settings on adapter DS302 (8088 versus 80286)
9114	Optical disk diagnostics error—sector read/write error—check drive, adapter, or cable
9115	Optical disk diagnostics error—scramble buffer error—check drive, adapter
9115	Check cable
9116	Optical disk diagnostics error—data buffer error—check drive, adapter
9116	Check cable
9117	Optical disk diagnostics error—drive RAM/ROM error—check drive, adapter
9117	Check cable

Error Code	Description
9118	Optical disk diagnostics error — invalid command — check drive, adapter, cable
9119	Optical disk diagnostics error — track jump error — check drive, adapter, cable
9120	Optical disk diagnostics error — laser error — check drive, adapter, or cable
9121	Optical disk diagnostics error — focus error — check cartridge, drive, adapter, or cable
9122	Optical disk diagnostics error — motor sync error — cartridge upside down
9122	Check drive, adapter, cable
9123	Optical disk diagnostics error — write fault — check drive, adapter, or cable
9124	Optical disk diagnostics error — general drive error — check drive, adapter
9124	Check cable
9125	Optical disk diagnostics error — sense command failed — check drive, adapter
9125	Check cable
9126	Optical disk diagnostics error — invalid command — check drive, adapter, cable
9127	Optical disk diagnostics error — sense command failed — check drive, adapter
9127	Check cable
9128	Optical disk diagnostics error — disk not initialized — check drive, adapter
9128	Check cable
9129	Optical disk diagnostics error — disk ID did not match — check drive, adapter
9129	Check cable
9130	Optical disk diagnostics error — read-only disk installed — check disk
9130	Check drive, adapter
9130	Check cable
9131	Optical disk diagnostics error — no disk present — check disk
9131	Check drive, adapter, cable
9132	Optical disk diagnostics error — illegal disk detected — check disk
9132	Check adapter, drive

Continued

Table F-4 *(continued)*

Error Code	Description
9132	Check cable
9133	Optical disk diagnostics error—no disk change detected—check drive, adapter
9133	Check cable
9134	Optical disk diagnostics error—read-only disk detected—check drive, adapter
9134	Check cable
9135	Optical disk diagnostics error—illegal disk detected—check drive, adapter
9135	Check cable
9136	Optical disk diagnostics error—sense command failed—check adapter, drive
9136	Check cable
9138	Optical disk diagnostics error—no disk change detected—retry test again
9138	Check drive, adapter
9138	Check cable
9141	Optical disk diagnostics error—no disk change detected—retry tests
9141	Check drive, adapter
9141	Check cable
9144	Optical disk diagnostics error—write-protect window not opened—retry tests
9144	Check drive
9144	Check adapter
9144	Check cable
9145	Optical disk diagnostics error—no disk change detected—retry tests
9145	Check drive, adapter
9145	Check cable
9146	Optical disk diagnostics error—write-protect window not closed—retry tests
9146	Check drive
9146	Check adapter
9146	Check cable
9148	Optical disk diagnostics error—adapter card—check adapter, drive, or cable

Error Code	Description
9150	Optical disk diagnostics error — seek command railed — check drive, adapter
9150	Check cable
9151	Optical disk diagnostics error — not at track zero — check drive, adapter
9151	Check cable
9152	Optical disk diagnostics error — track address error — check drive, adapter
9152	Check cable
9153	Optical disk diagnostics error — not at track 17099 — check drive, adapter
9153	Check cable
9154	Optical disk diagnostics error — track address error — check drive, adapter
9154	Check cable
9155	Optical disk diagnostics error — track address 17K not found — check drive
9155	Check adapter
9155	Check cable
9156	Optical disk diagnostics error — seek time too long — check drive, adapter
9156	Check cable
9157	Optical disk diagnostics error — sense command failed — check drive, adapter
9157	Check cable
9158	Optical disk diagnostics error — no data read error found — check drive, adapter
9158	Check cable
9159	Optical disk diagnostics error — no null sector found — check drive, adapter
9159	Check cable
9160	Optical disk diagnostics error — sense command failed — check drive, adapter
9160	Check cable
9161	Optical disk diagnostics error — write command failed — check drive, adapter
9161	Check cable
9162	Optical disk diagnostics error — data compare error — check drive, adapter
9162	Check cable

Continued

Table F-4 *(continued)*

Error Code	Description
9163	Optical disk diagnostics error — read verify error — check drive, adapter
9163	Check cable
9164	Optical disk diagnostics error — demark verify failed — check drive, adapter
9164	Check cable
9165	Optical disk diagnostics error — demark bit not set — check drive, adapter
9165	Check cable
9166	Optical disk diagnostics error — seek 1/3 timing error — check drive, adapter
9166	Check cable
9167	Optical disk diagnostics error — seek 2/3 timing error — check drive, adapter
9167	Check cable
9168	Optical disk diagnostics error — seek 3/3 timing error — check drive, adapter
9168	Check cable
9170	Optical disk diagnostics error — seek error set — check drive, adapter, cable
9171	Optical disk diagnostics error — controller RAM/ROM error — check drive, adapter
9171	Check cable
9172	Optical disk diagnostics error — demark function error — check drive, adapter
9172	Check cable
9173	Optical disk diagnostics error — detected error set — check drive, adapter
9173	Check cable
9174	Optical disk diagnostics error — modulator/demodulator error — check drive
9174	Check adapter
9174	Check cable
9175	Optical disk diagnostics error — invalid command — check adapter, drive, cable
9176	Optical disk diagnostics error — Illegal disk error — check adapter, drive, cable
9177	Optical disk diagnostics error — Both drives set to same address or wrong address

Error Code	Description
9178	Optical disk diagnostics error—ID mismatch—check drive, adapter, or cable
9179	Optical disk diagnostics error—Sector not found—check drive, adapter, cable
9181	Optical disk diagnostics error—Sense command failed—check drive, adapter
9181	Check cable
9182	Optical disk diagnostics error—read command error—check drive, adapter, cable
9185	Optical disk diagnostics error—diagnostic track error—check drive, adapter
9185	Check cable
9186	Optical disk diagnostics error—diagnostic demark error—check drive, adapter
9186	Check cable
9187	Optical disk diagnostics error—no demark bit set—check drive, adapter, cable
9198	Optical disk diagnostics error—invalid command—Re-IPL CPU with on/off switch
100xx	Multiprotocol adapter errors
10001	DIAGS error—cannot detect presence of multiprotocol adapter
10002	DIAGS error—card selected feedback error
10003	DIAGS error—Port 102H failed register test
10004	DIAGS error—Port 103H failed register test
10006	DIAGS error—serial option cannot be put to sleep
10007	DIAGS error—cable error
10008	DIAGS error—ASYNC IRQ3 error
10009	DIAGS error—ASYNC IRQ4 error
10010	DIAGS error—16550 fails register test
10011	DIAGS error—internal wrap test of 16550 modem control lines failed
10012	DIAGS error—external wrap test of 16550 modem control lines failed
10013	DIAGS error—16550 transmit error
10014	DIAGS error—16550 receive error

Continued

Table F-4 *(continued)*

Error Code	Description
10015	DIAGS error — 16550 receive data not equal transmit data
10016	DIAGS error — 16550 interrupt function error
10017	DIAGS error — 16550 failed baud rate test
10018	DIAGS error — 16550 interrupt driven receive wrap failed
10019	DIAGS error — 16550 FIFO error
10026	DIAGS error — 8255 Port A error
10027	DIAGS error — 8255 Port B error
10028	DIAGS error — 8255 Port C error
10029	DIAGS error — 8254 timer 0 error
10030	DIAGS error — 8254 timer 1 error
10031	DIAGS error — 8254 timer 2 error
10032	DIAGS error — bisync DSR response to DTR error
10033	DIAGS error — bisync CTS response to RTS error
10034	DIAGS error — 8251 hardware reset test failed
10035	DIAGS error — 8251 function error
10035	DIAGS error — 8251 internal software rest failure
10035	DIAGS error — 8251 error reset command failed
10035	DIAGS error — 8251 cannot detect overrun error
10036	DIAGS error — 8251 status error
10036	DIAGS error — 8251 Tx ready error
10036	DIAGS error — 8251 Rx ready error
10037	DIAGS error — bisync timer interrupt error
10038	DIAGS error — bisync transmit interrupt error
10039	DIAGS error — bisync receive interrupt error
10040	DIAGS error — stray IRQ3 error
10041	DIAGS error — stray IRQ4 error
10042	DIAGS error — bisync external wrap error
10044	DIAGS error — bisync data wrap error
10045	DIAGS error — bisync line status/condition error

Error Code	Description
10046	DIAGS error — bisync timeout error during data wrap test
10050	DIAGS error — 8273 command acceptance or results ready timeout error
10051	DIAGS error — 8273 port A error
10052	DIAGS error — 8273 port B error
10053	DIAGS error — SDLC modem status change logic error
10054	DIAGS error — SDLC timer interrupt (IRQ4) error
10055	DIAGS error — SDLC modem status change interrupt (IRQ4) error
10056	DIAGS error — SDLC external wrap error
10057	DIAGS error — SDLC interrupt results error
10058	DIAGS error — SDLC data wrap error
10059	DIAGS error — SDLC transmit interrupt error
10060	DIAGS error — SDLC receive interrupt error
10061	DIAGS error — DMA channel 1 error (transmit)
10062	DIAGS error — DMA channel 1 error (receive)
10063	DIAGS error — 8273 status detect error
10064	DIAGS error — 8273 error detect failure (for the PS/2)
10002	PS/2 multiprotocol adapter error
10006	PS/2 multiprotocol adapter or serial device error
10007	PS/2 multiprotocol adapter error
10008	PS/2 multiprotocol adapter or serial device error
10009	PS/2 multiprotocol adapter or serial device error
10012	PS/2 multiprotocol adapter or serial device error
10018	PS/2 multiprotocol adapter or system board error
10019	PS/2 multiprotocol adapter or system board error
10042	PS/2 multiprotocol adapter or system board error
10056	PS/2 multiprotocol adapter or system board error
104xx	PS/2 ESDI fixed disk errors
10480	PS/2 ESDI fixed disk 0 errors
10481	PS/2 ESDI fixed disk 1 errors

Continued

Table F-4 *(continued)*

Error Code	Description
10482	PS/2 ESDI fixed disk controller errors
10483	PS/2 ESDI fixed disk controller errors
10490	PS/2 ESDI fixed disk 0 errors
10491	PS/2 ESDI fixed disk 1 errors
106xx	Ethernet adapter
106x1	Set configuration — Ethernet adapter
10635	Power off the computer — wait six seconds, restore power
149xx	Plasma display adapter errors
14901	Replace plasma display adapter, system board, or plasma display
14902	Replace plasma display adapter, system board, or plasma display
14922	Replace plasma display adapter, system board, or plasma display
14932	Replace external display, or plasma display adapter
152xx	Realtime clock error — run diagnostics (or if you have an XGA capable system)
152xx	XGA errors
156xx	Security error — cover removed without key
160xx	System board — run diagnostics
16000	Set configuration
161xx	Battery, processor board, system board
162xx	Power, battery
1630	Set date and time
16400	Set configuration
164xx	3.5-inch internal tape drive errors

Table F-5
Hardware Errors

Error Code	Description
16451	Not enough memory to operate the tape drive
16452	Cartridge presence error
16453	Servo electronics/mechanism failed

Error Code	Description
16454	Cartridge was not formatted, or read chain failed
16455	EOT test failed
16456	BOT test failed
16457	Track following error — servo electronics/mechanism failed
16458	Internal software error
16459	Diskette controller failure
16460	Internal software error
16461	Unrecoverable read error — drive failure
16462	Internal software error
16463	User changed the cartridge
16464	DMA controller failure
16465	General drive failure
16466	No internal tape drives were found
16467	Write-protect switch failed
16468	Unrecoverable write error — drive failure
16469	Defective cartridge
165xx	6157 tape attachment adapter errors
16520	6157 tape drive error
16540	Adapter of drive error FRU unknown
16600	Set configuration
16700	Set configuration
16xxxx	Display emulation error — 3270, 5520, 5250
166xx	Token ring adapter or run diagnostics
167xx	Token ring adapter
168xx	Realtime clock error — run diagnostics
169xx	Processor board, system board
170xx	Check/set configuration — serial port
171xx	Battery, processor board, system board
172xx	System board

Continued

Table F-5 *(continued)*

Error Code	Description
173xx	Set configuration
174xx	Set configuration, check devices, system board
175xx	Security failure, system board
176xx	Security failure, system board, use reference diskette
177xx	System board
178xx	System board
179xx	System error log full, note errors in log, clear log, run diagnostics
181xx	Run auto configuration, network adapter, hard disk, system board
182xx	Password corrupt – place JP2 to position 0 and restore password
183xx	Wrong password
184xx	Power-on password corrupt, see 182xx
185xx	Run select startup sequence utility
186xx	Security error, system board
187xx	Set system identification
188xx	Run automatic configuration
189xx	Wrong password entered three times – clear error log and restart
191xx	Run advanced diagnostics
194xx	System board memory, memory riser card, memory module
199xx	User configuration is invalid
1999xxxx	Default hard disk, SCSI adapter
1999	IML errors (model 90 and 95)
20xxy, 217xy	If *y* is from *G* to *V* suspect Model 90/95 processor board, otherwise suspect memory
210xx	Processor board, system board memory, memory riser card
211xx	Processor board, system board memory, memory riser card
21xxx	Processor board, system board memory, memory riser card
22xxx	Processor board, system board memory, memory riser card
231xx	Expanded memory option
24xxx	Processor board, system board, memory
252xx	Processor board

Error Code	Description
253xx	Processor cache
254xx	Processor cache
255xx	System board memory
290xx	Correct unsupported mix of ECC and parity memory modules
29xxx	Checksum value mismatch — run automatic configuration
298xx	System board memory
2xx00	(Not listed above) 486DX33 upgrade (Model 70/80)
100203	System board
17xxxx	Hard disk/hard file, see 17xx series
1803xx	System board
186xxx	Set configuration
18xxxx	System board expansion unit
240xxx	Display, see 24xx series
2410xx	System board
37xxxx	System board, (SCSI) hard disk drive or cable
46xxxx	Multiport/2 interface
56xxxx	Financial system controller adapter
62xxxx	1st store loop adapter
63xxxx	2nd store loop adapter
64xxxx	Network adapter
71xxxx	Voice adapter
101xxxx	Modem, fax/modem
10117xx	System speaker, PSTN cable, external DAA
104xxxx	Hard disk (ESDI)
106xxxx	Ethernet or network adapter
107xxxx	5.25-inch external diskette drive
109xxxx	ActionMedia adapter
110100	Serial adapter, system board — run advanced diagnostics
110xxx	Serial adapter, device, cable, system board

Continued

Table F-5 *(continued)*

Error Code	Description
111xxx	16550 UAR/T errors, system board
112xxxx	SCSI adapter
120xxx	Serial adapter, device, cable, system board
121xxxx	300/1200/2400 modem
129xxxx	Processor board error
129020	Cached processor option
137xxxx	System board
141xxxx	Realtime interface coprocessor
143xxxx	Japanese display adapter
147xxxx	System board display adapter
148xxxx	Display adapter
149xxxx	Display, display adapter
152xxxx	XGA display adapter
161xxxx	Fax adapter
164xxxx	Internal tape drive
165xxxx	Streaming tape
166xxxx	Token ring adapter
18001xx	Wizard adapter
18031xx	Wizard adapter cable
184xxxx	Unsupported memory configuration (386)
185xxxx	DBCS Japanese display adapter
194xxxx	Memory module, system board
2000xxx	Image adapter
201xxxx	Printer/scanner option
206xxxx	SCSI-2 adapter or device
208xxxx	Any SCSI device

✦　　✦　　✦

Cabling Diagrams: Serial, Video, Keyboard, Parallel, Network and More

This appendix is probably the most technical offering in this book. It contains diagrams for five common data cables and three common connectors used to interconnect PCs, modems, printers, and other peripherals through serial and parallel ports. A sixth cable, a parallel null modem, is useful as an extra cable between two systems using LapLink or similar direct-connection PC file transfer programs, which can transfer data between PCs through parallel printer ports at two to five times the rate of serial ports.

Connections are also listed for the four common video standards used on PCs — Monochrome, Color Graphics Adapter (CGA), Enhanced Graphics Adapter (EGA), and Video Graphics Array (VGA) — and for PC keyboard cables. We've also included a special circuit that can save your modem and possibly your PC system from excessive voltage that may appear on your telephone line during storms or other electrical disturbances.

Special Serial Connections

Many of the cables shown in the figures can be bought off the shelf at computer or electronics stores. All too often, we have found that there are three or four variations of null modems that are not correct. The null modem shown here is correct. If you have to build a cable, many snap-in wires and connectors are available that take only a few minutes to assemble with simple tools and no soldering. Refer to Chapter 20 for the specific details of each signal pin.

Our first diagram, Figure G-1, is for a proper 25-pin-to-25 pin serial null modem cable. A null modem cable is used to interconnect two PC systems for the purpose of transferring files or for remote operation of another PC. With some printers or other devices, a null modem is required to swap signals to their proper pins to enable devices to work properly with your PC.

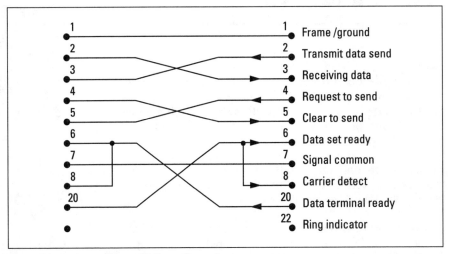

Figure G-1: A 25-pin-to-25-pin null modem

This is a full-function null modem, providing all the proper hardware handshaking and device status signals. Many null modems offered for sale or built by hand incorrectly connect the carrier detect signal to the standard hardware-handshake signal lines, or they loop the handshaking signals back to the originating device. These mis-wirings can cause loss of data or failure of information transfer. Properly built, one device should provide active signals to the other, whether the signal is a "ready" line or a "send" line. Looping signals from a device back to itself provides no information to another device—both will try to operate independently, and data loss can result.

The rules of proper interconnection are applied to the 25-pin-to-9-pin and the 9-pin-to-9-pin null modem cabling diagrams (Figures G-2, G-3, and G-4).

The numbered pin connections shown are valid whether the connectors are male plugs or female sockets. The pin orientations for each type of connector are shown at the end of this appendix.

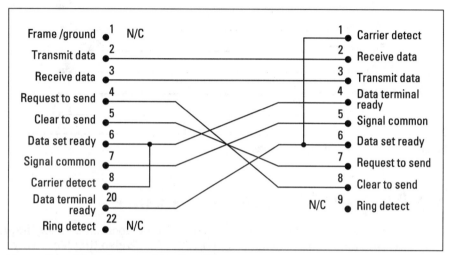

Figure G-2: A 25-pin-to-9-pin null modem

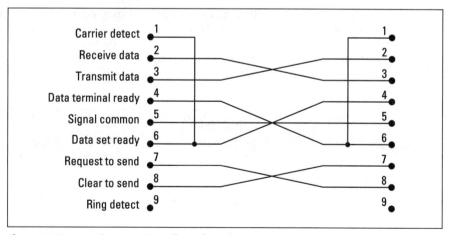

Figure G-3: A 9-pin-to-9-pin null modem

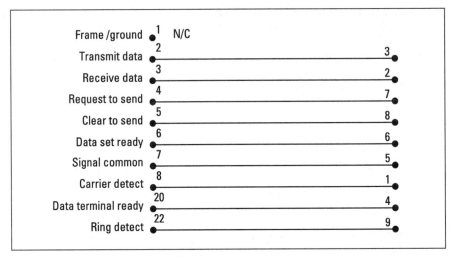

Figure G-4: A 25-pin-to-9-pin adapter

Video Adapter to Monitor Cabling

Tables G-1 through G-4 show the pin connections for monochrome, Color Graphics Adapter (CGA), Enhanced Graphics Adapter (EGA), and Video Graphics Array (VGA) display adapter to monitor cabling. Notice that the monochrome, CGA, and EGA cables use the same type and polarity of connector to attach to the display adapter. Because these cables use the same connections and there is no way to tell the difference between monochrome, CGA, or EGA display adapters from the connections, the connections on a PC can be confusing. Do not guess at the type of display adapter inside a PC. You will have to inspect the display-adapter card for markings or part numbers and seek technical support if it is not obvious which display adapter a system has.

	Table G-1
Monochrome Display Monitor and Adapter Connections	

Pin Number	Signal
1	Ground
2	Ground
3	n/c

Pin Number	Signal
4	n/c
5	n/c
6	Intensity bit
7	Video bit
8	Horizontal sync +
9	Vertical sync +

Table G-2
Color Graphics Display Monitor and Adapter Connections

Pin Number	Signal
1	Ground
2	Ground
3	Red signal
4	Green signal
5	Blue signal
6	Intensity signal
7	n/c
8	Horizontal sync
9	Vertical sync

Table G-3
Enhanced Graphics Adapter and Monitor Connections

Pin Number	Signal
1	Ground
2	Secondary red
3	Red signal
4	Primary green
5	Primary blue

Continued

Table G-3 *(continued)*

Pin Number	Signal
6	Secondary green
7	Secondary blue
8	Horizontal sync
9	Vertical sync

Table G-4
Video Graphics Array Monitor and Adapter Connections

Pin Number	Signal
1	Red video
2	Green video
3	Blue video
4	Monitor ID bit 2
5	Ground
6	Red return
7	Green return
8	Blue return
9	Key — no pin
10	Sync return
11	Monitor ID bit 0
12	Monitor ID bit 1
13	Horizontal sync
14	Vertical sync
15	Not used

Keyboard Connections

Most PCs use a standard 5-pin circular DIN connector for the keyboard-to-motherboard connections. Many newer systems, as well as the IBM PS/2 and later series, use a mini-DIN plug. The PS/2-style pointing devices use the same connections as the PS/2-style keyboard connectors (as shown in Table G-5).

Table G-5 Standard and PS/2 Keyboard Connectors		
Signal	**Standard PC Pin Number**	**PS/2-Style Signal Pin Number**
Clock	1	5
Data	2	1
Ground	4	3
+5 VDC	5	4
Not used	3	2 and 6

Parallel Port Cable Diagrams

The IBM PC parallel port has seen many uses from driving signals into a basic dot-matrix printer to being used as an interface for external disk drives, tape drives, and scanners. The basic cabling diagram connecting a DB-25 male plug to a Centronics 36-pin male plug is shown in Table G-6.

Table G-6 Standard PC Printer Cable Connections			
DB25 Male pins	**<= in => out**	**Centronics connector pins**	**Signal Name**
1	=>	1	-Strobe
2	=>	2	Data 0
3	=>	3	Data 1
4	=>	4	Data 2
5	=>	5	Data 3

Continued

Table G-6 *(continued)*			
DB25 **Male pins**	**<= in** **=> out**	**Centronics** **connector pins**	**Signal** **Name**
6	=>	6	Data 4
7	=>	7	Data 5
8	=>	8	Data 6
9	=>	9	Data 7
10	<=	10	-Ack
11	<=	11	+Busy
12	<=	12	+PaperEnd
13	<=	13	+SelectIn
14	=>	14	-AutoFd
15	<=	32	-Error
16	=>	31	-Init
17	=>	36	-Select
18–25	==	19–30	Ground
		33,17,16	n/a

Note For high-quality data transmission, each signal line should be one wire in a twisted pair of wires, the other of which is one of the ground lines connecting DB25 pins 18–25 to Centronics pins 19–30.

Table G-7 shows the interconnections between two DB-25 male connectors to make a direct-connect cable for PC-to-PC data transfer using Windows Direct Connection, Symantec's pcAnywhere, or Traveling Software's LapLink.

Table G-7 A Direct PC-to-PC Connection IEEE-1284 ECP Cable Diagram		
DB25 Male Pin #	**Connection**	**DB25 Male Pin #**
1	wire	10
2	1000 ohm resistor	2
3	1000 ohm resistor	3

DB25 Male Pin #	Connection	DB25 Male Pin #
4	1000 ohm resistor	4
5	1000 ohm resistor	5
6	1000 ohm resistor	6
7	1000 ohm resistor	7
8	1000 ohm resistor	8
9	1000 ohm resistor	9
10	wire	1
11	wire	14
12	wire	16
13	wire	17
14	wire	11
16	wire	12
17	wire	13
18–25	wire	18–25

Note   The 1000 ohm resistors in series with each of the data lines on pins 2–9 are optional in some configurations. They condition and protect signal lines on the driver chips on each end of the connection inside the PC. All other connections are a straight-through wire. Each signal line should be a twisted pair with the ground lines on pins 18–25, doubling up with the grounds from the nondata lines on pins 10–17.

Common PC Connector Diagrams

Figure G-5 shows the orientation and pin numbering of both the male plug and female/socket of bare connectors. Because most of the wiring you might do with these connectors is done from the wire or backside of the connectors, we emphasize that side here.

PC systems usually have female/socket connectors for the video and parallel printer cables andmale/plug connectors for the serial ports. Only a few odd systems make any change to this convention, and the change is typically the use of a female connector for the serial port. You may also find that the wiring is completely reversed for these serial ports, requiring a null modem cable or signal swap to enable interconnected devices to work properly.

Figure G-6 contains diagrams of the 9- and 25-pin serial loopback connectors that may be used for most diagnostic programs and the 25-pin parallel port loopback plug for DiagSoft's QAPlus diagnostic products.

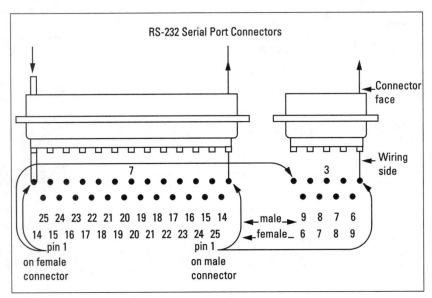

Figure G-5: 9-, 25-, and 36-pin connector layouts

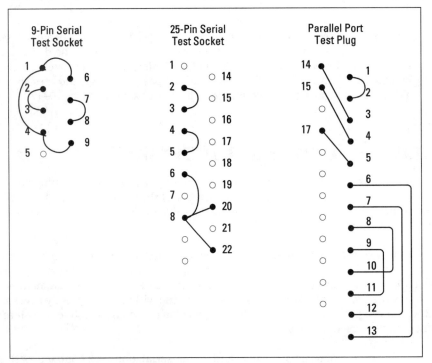

Figure G-6: Typical diagnostic loopback plugs

Save Your Modem

Figure G-7 shows a simple but effective protection circuit you can use with your modem, fax, or answering machine. This circuit is not FCC- or AT&T/Bell Systems-approved. Many modems, answering, and fax machines, as well as electronic and standard telephones, provide some form of internal protection against excessive voltage appearing across the phone lines. Unfortunately, the ratings for these protection devices are not always adequate for the line conditions you might encounter. The standard protection is for short-duration voltages in excess of 400 volts. Sustained voltages greater than 150 to 200 volts may damage many circuits.

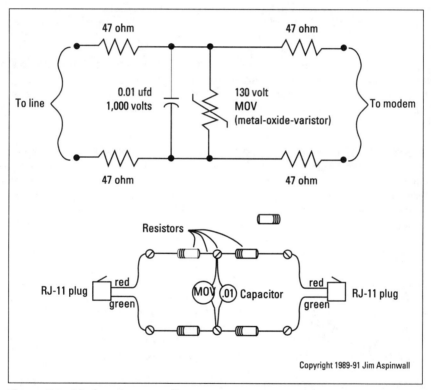

Copyright 1989-91 Jim Aspinwall

Figure G-7: Modem protector diagram

Theoretically, the voltage on your phone lines should never exceed 130 volts AC. This is the potential of the voltage that activates a ringer, a beeper, or a modem's ring detect circuit. The normal idle line voltage (phone on hook, no ringing) for a telephone line is 48 volts DC. This drops to between 6 and 24 volts when the line is in use. The devices you plug into a phone line should be able to operate at these levels. Lightning can impress well over 1,000 volts on the phone line, which can easily destroy delicate electronic equipment or your PC if this high voltage gets inside.

Some phone systems, connected between outside lines and a telephone set, can present different voltages at different times and may not be suitable for your modem. If you can prevent high voltages from reaching your equipment, it will suffer little or no damage. We recommend you use this circuit or a similar one if you anticipate connecting your modem to unfamiliar phone systems. If the phone system is not designed for modems, the circuit won't make your modem work with the line, but it can prevent it from being damaged.

The circuit shown in Figure G-7 was designed for a private, in-house phone system not directly attached to phone company circuits. It is an alternative to the expensive and less functional off-the-shelf units that costs ten times as much. It can also dramatically reduce line noise that can cause data errors. If your system or add-ons are susceptible to high voltage damage, and most are, you may want to try this circuit. This device is easy to build inside a common modular phone jack unit using parts available at most neighborhood electronics stores.

This device is not certified by the FCC or by telephone companies for use on standard direct lines. Its use on direct lines may violate your local telephone company or state tariffs. It does not damage lines or equipment, nor does it degrade the performance of your lines or equipment. In most cases, it improves the clarity and it certainly adds to the protection of equipment.

The four resistors help to slightly reduce the normal line current and absorb most of the excess energy of voltages over 130 volts. The metal-oxide-varistor (MOV) is the primary protection device. It sets the limit for the voltages that can pass between the line and the equipment. The 0.01 microfarad capacitor works with the resistors to reduce signals above the voice audio range (3 kHz). This has the effect of reducing clicks, pops, and static on the line.

If the resistors are replaced with 10 microhenry, 100 milliampere inductors, this circuit will provide much the same voltage protection and severely reduce any radio interference. Further reduction of radio interference may require the addition of a 0.001 microfarad capacitor from each end of the MOV to a solid nearby ground point. Using the capacitors and inductors is a long-standing method of removing radio interference (which is allowed and common in severe cases) as a repair or correction to phone lines. In effect, either circuit method should be allowed to be used as a repair if line noise is in excess of any standard limits.

Reducing the capacitor value from 0.01 microfarad to 0.0001 microfarad (100 picofarad) and changing the connectors to RJ-45 (6-pin) or RJ-48 (8-pin) will enable you to use this device on Integrated Services Digital Network (ISDN) interface units on either ISDN connection type S (requires separate NT-1 device) or U (NT-1 device included in unit).

10BaseT Network Connections

Most network connections today make use of economical twisted-pair cabling and connectors similar to those used for phone lines. However, the placement or attachment of the wires into the connectors is different to accommodate Ethernet use. You cannot reliably use a straight-through 8-pin or RJ-45 telephone cable for high-speed network cabling. The following diagrams, Figures G-8 and G-9, illustrate the pins and wire colors used for network cabling.

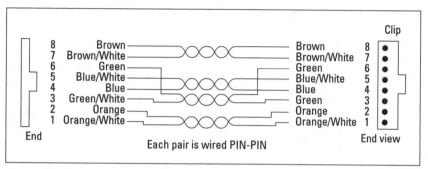

Figure G-8: Standard 10BaseT interconnections for connecting systems and devices to a hub

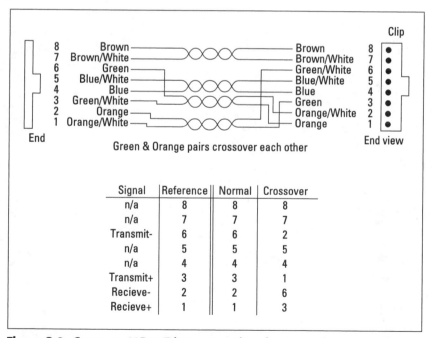

Figure G-9: Crossover 10BaseT interconnections for connecting two systems without a hub

Technical Support Trouble Report Data Form

This is the easy-to-use sample Technical Support form, which was discussed in Chapter 23. Make a copy and use it for every system you have. Much of this information may be obtained from system information software, but some of it will have to be obtained by visual inspection of the devices themselves. Keep this information handy for technical support staff and repair technicians, and for others who may need to assist you with any problems with your PC.

Technical Support Trouble Report Data Form

User Information (who you are and how to get in touch with you):

Name:_____ Phone:_____

Company:_____ E-mail:_____

System Information:

Dealer:_____   Date purchased:_____

Computer Mfr:_____   Model:_____

System Board Information:

Motherboard Mfr: _____

Motherboard Bus Types: ____ 8-Bit ISA   ____ 16-Bit ISA   ____ PCI

                            ____ EISA   ____ Local Bus   ____MicroChannel

Processor Make:

____ AMD   ____ Cyrix   ____ Intel   ____ NEC

CPU Speed: _____ MHz

____ 80386DX   ____ 80386SX   ____ 80386SLC   ____ 80486SX

____ 80486SX2   ____ 80486DX   ____ 80486DX2   ____ 80486DX4

____ Pentium   ____ Pentium-MMX   ____ Pentium II   ____ Celeron

Other processor: _____

Math coprocessor manufacturer and type: _____

BIOS mfr: _____   BIOS date/version: _____

Memory Information:

Base memory: ____ KBytes   Extended: ____ KBytes

Expanded-LIMS/EEMS: ____ KBytes   Ver: ____ 3.2   ____ 4.0

Memory manager and version: _____

Disk Drive Information:

Diskette drives (x):

	A:	B:
360K	_____	_____
1.2M	_____	_____
720K	_____	_____
1.44M	_____	_____
2.88M	_____	_____
LS-120	_____	_____
Zip	_____	_____

Hard Drives:

1st HD Mfr: _____ Model: _____ Size: ____ MB

Type: _____ MFM _____ RLL _____ ESDI _____ IDE _____ SCSI

2nd HD Mfr: _____ Model: _____ Size: ____ MB

Type: _____ MFM _____ RLL _____ ESDI _____ IDE _____ SCSI

3rd HD Mfr: _____ Model: _____ Size: ____ MB

Type: _____ MFM _____ RLL _____ ESDI _____ IDE _____ SCSI

4th HD Mfr: _____ Model: _____ Size: ____ MB

Type: _____ MFM _____ RLL _____ESDI _____ IDE _____ SCSI

1st HD adapter Mfr: _____ Model: _____ Internal? _____

2nd HD adapter Mfr: _____ Model: _____ Internal? _____

Partition sizes: C: _____ MB   D: _____ MB   E: _____ MB   F: _____ MB

Partitioning software: _____ FDISK _____ Other (name and version): _____

For SCSI devices, also identify the SCSI ID# of each device.

Disk Compression Software:

_____ Stacker™   _____ DoubleSpace™   _____ SuperStor™

_____ DoubleDisk™   _____ DriveSpace™

Video System:

Video Card mfr: _____ Model: _____

Type: ___ MDA ___ Hercules ___ CGA ___ EGA

___ PGA ___ VGA ___ XGA ___ SVGA ___AGP

Video on which Bus?   ___ISA   ___ PCI   ___ Local Bus

___ MicroChannel   ___ On-board

VESA VBE version: _____

Video Monitor mfr:_____ Model: _____

Operating System and User Interface:

___ PC-DOS	___ MS-DOS	___ Novell/DR-DOS	___ OS/2
___ Win 3.x	___ Win 95	___ Win 98	___ Win NT
___ DESQview	___ DESQview/X	___ LINUX	___ Solaris86

Other:_____

I/O Information:

Parallel Ports:

	LPT1	LPT2	LPT3
Address:	_____	_____	_____
IRQ:	_____	_____	_____

Parallel Port Devices (indicate port used for the device type):

Dot Matrix	_____	_____	_____
Laser	_____	_____	_____
Ink Jet	_____	_____	_____
Plotter	_____	_____	_____
Zip Drive	_____	_____	_____
SCSI Adapter	_____	_____	_____
Other:	_____	_____	_____

(Indicate devices like ZIP drives or scanners that are connected between your printer and PC system)

Serial Ports:

	COM1	COM2	COM3	COM4
Address:	_____	_____	_____	_____
IRQ:	_____	_____	_____	_____
Serial Devices (indicate port used for the device type):				
Modem (ext)	_____	_____	_____	_____
Modem (int)	_____	_____	_____	_____

Pointer   _____   _____   _____   _____

_____ Mouse _____ Trackball _____ Tablet/Pad

Printer   _____   _____   _____   _____

Plotter   _____   _____   _____   _____

Scanner   _____   _____   _____   _____

Network   _____   _____   _____   _____

Other   _____   _____   _____   _____

Network Interface Card(s):

Type: ____ NE1000 ____ NE2000 ____ NE3200 ____ 3Com

Other:_____

Cabling: ___ Coax/10Base2   ___ Twisted Pair/10BaseT   ___ AUI Adapter (15 pin)

Address: ___ IRQ   ___ DMA   ___ Boot ROM ?

Driver(s) required:_____

Other special-purpose cards/devices:

Attach the following if available:

— Printouts/copies of AUTOEXEC.BAT and CONFIG.SYS files

— Printout/copies of output from DOS SET > ENVIRON.TXT redirection

— Printouts/copies of WIN.INI, SYSTEM.INI, BOOTLOG.TXT

— Printouts/copies of NET.CFG and SHELL.CFG files (for network cards)

— Printouts/copies of BATch files you CALL in AUTOEXEC.BAT or that otherwise define or setup your system configuration

— System memory map (CHKDSK, MEM, Manifest or other)

— Printout of directory tree structure

— Attach PrintScreen or other printout of problem or other diagnostic log report

— Be sure to describe the problem(s) in detail, such as if you are in Windows or working from DOS; note any system changes since things worked fine; note if there are times when things work OK

Complete description of problem:

_____
_____
_____
_____

Can you reproduce the problem? __Y __N

How and when does/did the problem happen?

_____

_____

_____

_____

Record software brand, name, version and serial numbers:

_____

_____

_____

_____

_____

_____

Favorite Links

We've collected a few dozen favorite and useful Web site links that can help you get much more enjoyment and service out of your PC experience. Feel free to visit them often to check for the latest news, files, and PC tips, and let them know where you heard about them! Happy Surfing! Or, as we proclaimed at a recent dinner meeting we (the Internet Society Los Angeles Chapter) in honor of our guest speaker, Vint Cerf one of the primary developers of the Internet Protocol, "Cerf the Net!"

PC vendors

The following hardware and software companies are valuable resources for information.

Hardware companies

+ `www.3com.com`—3Com's comprehensive products site.

+ `www.adaptec.com`—Entrance to Adaptec's World Wide Web sites.

+ `www.ascend.com`—Ascend Communication's Web site.

+ `www.atitech.com`—ATI's graphics headquarters on the Web.

+ `www.compaq.com`—Compaq's presence on the Web.

+ `www.diamondmm.com`—Diamond Multi Media's Web site.

+ `www.gateway.com`—Gateway's Web presence. They are everywhere!

+ `www.ibm.com`—Need we say more?

+ `www.imation.com`—Imation has more products than you might imagine.

+ `www.iomega.com`—Iomega has been around a long time!

+ `www.matrox.com`—If you can see it, Matrox must be somewhere around.

♦ www.maxtor.com—Information storage is found here.

♦ www.quantum.com—A world of drives and storage technologies.

♦ www.seagate.com—Disk and tape drives and software are found here.

♦ www.usr.com—U. S. Robotics (modems and communications, no robots!—darn!)

♦ www.wdc.com—Western Digital's site for finding the drives you need.

Software companies

♦ www.adobe.com—They're everywhere but this is Adobe's home. Do you have Acrobat?

♦ www.ami.com—American Megatrends, Inc., provides more than BIOS chips!

♦ www.award.com—Phoenix and Award are the same company—see it here.

♦ www.netswitcher.com —All about networking your portable all around!

♦ www.checkit.com—Touchstone's latest diagnostic software suites are here.

♦ www.eudora.com—Qualcomm's Eudora Web site. Get the latest e-mail information.

♦ www.firmware.com—Your source for BIOS upgrades, motherboards, cables, and much more.

♦ www.ghostsoft.com—Ghost software brings the fun back into real computing! Check it out!

♦ www.grc.com—The best place to *try* to keep up with Steve Gibson. (SpinRite, TIP, and tons more!)

♦ www.intuit.com—Accounting made simple and complete. Quicken, QuickBooks, and more.

www.microsoft.com—Try home.microsoft.com, too. Customize your own information center.

♦ www.nai.com—Network Associates (McAfee) Virus protection and more for networks and PCs.

♦ www.ontrack.com—Data recovery help central! World headquarters for keeping your data.

♦ www.ora.com—Tim O'Reilly and Associates. The world's source for computing documentation.

♦ www.phoenix.com—Software developer for the world's PCs and information appliances.

♦ www.quarterdeck.com—CleanSweep, CrashDefender, VirusSweep, and more! (Now on Symantec's site)

✦ www.quicken.com—Another facet of Intuit's Web sites, focusing on Quicken.

✦ www.slonet.org/~doren—Home of the Rosenthal Utilities

Rosenthal Utilities can be found on this book's CD-ROM.

✦ www.symantec.com—Home of Norton Utilities, PC Anywhere, Visual Café, and much more!

✦ www.ultraedit.com—Home of IDM Computer Solutions's UltraEdit. Use it to believe it.

✦ www.unicore.com—BIOS and PC upgrades, Y2K software, and much more products and support!

✦ www.ws.com—Watergate Software, home of PC Doctor, used by IBM and more.

PC-Doctor is included on this book's CD-ROM.

General PC hints, tips, and references

The following sites offer a vast array of tips, advice, reference material, and much more.

✦ www.apcug.org—Association of PC User Groups. Get involved and connected!

✦ www.ISOC.org—Internet Society, International Organization that provides organization to the activities that provide the Internet World-wide!

✦ www.ISOC-LA.org—Internet Society Los Angeles Chapter. Mike Todd is currently the President of this Chapter that is setting the example for Chapters around the World.

✦ www.CPCUG.org—Capital PC User Group, Washington, DC. Mike Todd was the founder and first President of this, still one of the largest PC User Groups around the World.

✦ www.w3.org—World Wide Web Consortium. Leading the Web to its full potential.

✦ www.hwg.org—HTML Writers Guild. World's largest organization of HTML writers and those who are making the Web a better place to live.

✦ www.w3.org/WAI/—Web Accessibility Initiative. Access by everyone regardless of disability or other challenges.

✦ www.annoyances.org—If you are annoyed by Windows (95, 98, and more), go here!

♦ www.annoyances.org/win95 —Annoying features of Windows 95 and ways around most of them.

♦ www.annoyances.org/win98 —Installing, upgrading, customizing, tips, and much more!

♦ www.bugnet.com —The world's leading supplier of PC bug fixes. Many subscribers.

♦ www.currents.net —*Computer Currents* magazine online! News, downloads, help, and much more!

♦ www.download.com —clnet's online download libraries, with many suggestions and help.

♦ www.drivershq.com —Trouble finding a hardware or software driver for your PC? Go here!

♦ www.hardwaregroup.org —Hardware reviews, information, and links.

♦ www.idgbooks.com —Looking for the best computer books? You can find us here, too!

♦ www.manageable.com —Catch*UP provides online updates for your PC, drivers and all!

♦ www.motherboards.org —Upgrading? Links to more sites than the law allows!

♦ pcmech.pair.com —PC Mechanic (PCMech.com) for product reviews.

♦ sysdoc.pair.com —Tom's Hardware Guide (www.tomshardware.com) has tons of reviews!

♦ www.pcwebopedia.com —Computer acronyms and terms giving you problems? Learn them here!

♦ www.ping.be/bios —All about BIOS chips, settings, upgrades, flashes, and more.

♦ www.raisin.com/irq —Jim Aspinwall's page dedicated to the second edition of IRQ DMA and I/O.

♦ www.raisin.com/typc —Jim Aspinwall's page dedicated to the latest published edition of *Troubleshooting Your PC*!

♦ www.sysopt.com —System Optimization, the place to go when you need more help.

♦ www.shareware.com —Need the latest shareware program for anything from anywhere? Go here!

♦ www.whatis.com —At this site, learn all about the Internet, look up high-tech terminology, find and buy products —it's a veritable cornucopia.

♦ www.windrivers.com —Windows Drivers, more than any other site! Utilities, help, lost more.

Year 2000/Date related challenges sites

The following sites continue to be invaluable resources for resolving any residual year 2000 related problems

PC hardware and BIOS vendors

✦ `www.ami.com`—American Megatrends, Inc.

✦ `www.award.com`—Award Software

✦ `www.compaq.com/year2000`—COMPAQ

✦ `www.ibm.com/year2000`—IBM

✦ `www.mrbios.com`—Microid Research, Inc.

✦ `www.phoenix.com`—Phoenix Technologies, Inc.

✦ `www.resource800.com/`—Resource 800 (PC Clock and other batteries)

✦ `www.unicore.com`—Unicore Software, Inc.

Y2K information and PC test software

✦ `www.bozemanlegg.com/y2kanalyzer.html`—Bozeman Legg Consulting and Y2K solutions.

✦ `www.centennial.co.uk`—Centennial Ltd, year 2000 compliance software solutions.

✦ `www.clicknet.com`—Download free demo of software to test systems, software, and data.

✦ `www.computerexperts.co.uk/`—Download free demo of hardware/software test utility.

✦ `www.epri.com/`—Electric energy association with lots of information about Y2K and embedded systems.

✦ `www.eurosoft-uk.com`—Site for Eurosoft's PC-Check with Y2K features.

✦ `www.implement.co.uk/index.htm`—Implement Ltd. Fpro2000 demo download.

✦ `www.infoworld.com/cgi-bin/displayTC.pl?y2k.overview.htm`—InfoWorld's latest on Y2K.

✦ `www.netscapeworld.com/netscapeworld/nw-12-1996/nw-12-year2000.html`—Netscape's help for Webmasters!

✦ `www.rightime.com`—Get Test2000.EXE to test your system. Retail program fixes problems.

✦ `www.safetynet.com/yes2k/`—Download Yes2K to test and fix your personal PC. Retail version for the office.

Y2K fixes for PCs and LANs

Please read the information and get at least one of the listed utility programs to test your system (and in some cases to test your applications and data) to ensure your system is not a part of the year 2000 problem. Some of these are free for personal use and may even be used on small networks. If you need to test a lot of systems in your business, please start here and get an idea of the capabilities you will need in a commercial product. You may consider using the commercial version of one of these systems in your office at work. Your best bet is to access each site on the Internet and make your selection based on your system needs, work environment, and personal taste. There is no one best utility.

✦ www.bldrdoc.gov/timefreq/service—FTP index with files containing programs to set your clock.

✦ www.nrc.gov/NRC/NEWS/year2000.html—Nuclear Regulatory Commissions assessment of Y2K.

✦ www.schoolhs.demon.co.uk/—SchoolHouse Computers Ltd. Test2000 software.

✦ www.slonet.org/~doren—Home of the Rosenthal Utilities (included on our CD-ROM). Check it out!

✦ www.tecfacs.com/year2000/year2000.htm—Small European Company collecting info and offering help.

✦ www.year2000.com—Interesting articles and activities focused on Y2K.

✦   ✦   ✦

About the CD-ROM

This appendix provides a brief description of each of the utilities provided on the CD-ROM in the back of this book. We also include brief instructions for its use, and refer you to Chapter 23 for advice on how to best make use of utility software in general. We appreciate the generosity of the software providers who have allowed us to share these products with you, and hope that you will show your appreciation to them by purchasing their products.

Note We have chosen products that suit occasional use and still provide adequate functionality within the context of this book. This includes unregistered Shareware, evaluation versions of commercial software, as well as a suitable assortment of 'freeware' – all common practice with such book distributions of software.

We are unable to pre-register or license the Shareware because each package requires specific individual or corporate licensing, and we do not know who you are, yet. We also cannot anticipate if you are a personal, single-system user needing a one-copy license, or a multi-system commercial user requiring a multi-copy site license.

We believe it is best to allow you to make a choice of many available products that suit your needs, and to arrange any purchases and registrations accordingly.

Using These Programs

Most of the files on the CD-ROM are provided in ready-to-use form. You may execute many of them directly from the CD-ROM, but they are intended to be copied to or installed on your system or onto special diskettes for proper operation. These features will be noted with each program's description.

Note   Some of the products on this CD-ROM are demos or trial versions. They are intended to give you the opportunity to test the program out before you buy it. In order to purchase any of the individual programs, contact the vendors directly.

File Descriptions

The following products are included on this book's CD-ROM. Some of them are described in detail later in the appendix:

Software Name	Vendor
Acrobat Reader	Adobe Systems, Inc.
Diskeeper 5.0	Executive Software International, Inc.
Electronic version of book	IDG Books Worldwide. Inc.
Internet Explorer	Microsoft Corporation
Netscape Communicator	Netscape Communications
Norton Utilities 2000	Symantec
OptOut Spyware removal tool	Gibson Research Corporation
PC-Doctor for Windows	PC-Doctor, Inc.
PC-Doctor for Windows NT	PC-Doctor, Inc.
PC-Time v 2.0	Paul Scott
Rosenthal Utilities	Rosenthal Engineering
Sub-Pixel Font Rendering Demo	Gibson Research Corporation
Trouble In Paradise	Gibson Research Corporation
WinGate	Deerfield Communications Company
WinProxy 3.0	Ositis Software
WinZip	NicoMak

Please read the following descriptions before installing or using these utilities and programs. That way you will know what the program will do for you, what system requirements may affect your use, whether it is a real and free program or a demo of a more capable system, get some startup documentation.

PC-Doctor

Directory: PC-Doc
Filename: setup.exe
Program name: PC-Doctor for Windows and PC-Doctor for Windows NT
Vendor URL: www.pc-doctor.com

Intended installation and use: Hard drive; Windows 95, 98, 98SE, NT and 2000 systems.

Description: PC-Doctor is now the leading PC diagnostic product for all environments, DOS, Windows, PC factory, help desk, repair center and personal use. Once again we are able to provide you with this demo version of PC-Doctor, for Windows, that will show you what is available in the full version, and provide you with a tremendous amount of system information you will need for support work.

Rosenthal Utilities

Directory: Rosenthal
Filenames: Several .exe files are available under this utility demo.
Program name: Rosenthal Utilities
Vendor URL: www.slonet.org/~doren

Intended Installation and Use: hard drive or diskette; DOS, with appropriate ASPI, CD-ROM, network and/or sound card drivers loaded as may be needed for specific devices.

Description: Doren Rosenthal offers his Shareware utilities for your enjoyment. If you like them please register them! A brief description of each of them appears below:

CLEANER.EXE: The Disk Drive Cleaner, used in conjunction with a special media cleaning diskette helps to safely and effectively remove debris from the delicate read/write heads of diskette drives. This helps prevent data loss, unreliable performance and errors often traced to microscopic foreign particles, dirt, dust, oxides, and smoke that accumulates on drive heads. Preventive maintenance takes less than four minutes. It support standard diskette drives as well as commercial automatic mass disk duplicators.

R-FORMAT: R-Format replaces the standard diskette format so it no longer hangs the system during start up when the diskette is left in the A: drive. An embedded graphic and text message of your choice is displayed and the system then boots normally. The disk otherwise functions normally. The example graphic file R-FORMAT.PCX may be replaced with your own. This program may be run in DOS or Windows.

R-Y2KFIX: With the Rosenthal Year 2000 Fix and CMOS/Clock Battery Monitor Year 2000 compliance is enforced each time system power is restored. Tests and adjustments are performed independent of ROM BIOS, Real-Time clock (hardware) or system clock (virtual) versionsProgression including leap years is verified and a millennium counter displayed. R-Y2kFix is provided as a FREE bonus to non-commercial private users just for trying "The Rosenthal Utilities™". Please enjoy it with Doren's compliments as thanks for all the encouragement and support users have shown over the years. This program is *NOT* a TSR (terminate-and-stay-resident) utility, but it is intended to be included in your AUTOEXEC.BAT file to be effective, even for use with Windows 3.x, 95 or 98.

RCR.EXE: The Rosenthal Conflict Resolver provides hardware and software diagnostics combine to identify, resolve and prevent all PC system DMA and IRQ conflicts for DOS, Windows, Windows 95, Windows NT and OS/2. From the earliest PCs to today's most sophisticated Plug and Play components, all are supported even when systems mix old and new technologies. This program is a TSR (terminate-and-stay-resident) utility that should be included in your AUTOEXEC.BAT file, even for use with Windows 3.x, 95 or 98. RCR may be run inside of Windows to view IRQ and DMA activity detected by the resident portion of the program. It causes no known conflicts or problems with Windows.

RSW.EXE: This System Workout repeatedly exercises thousands of low level tests. System Workout confirms the reliable performance of new or upgraded systems and/or when changes are made like installing new hardware or software. Especially difficult problems like intermittent, marginal performance errors and conflicts are revealed. This program may be run only from DOS, with any required DOS-level drivers installed (mouse, sound card, CD-ROM, etc.)

SYSMON.EXE: The Rosenthal System Monitor provides professional diagnostics that are automatic enough for beginners. SYSMON evaluates your hardware and configuration each day during start up and maintains a diary log of changes to identify and quickly resolve future hardware/software conflicts. This program is a TSR (terminate-and-stay-resident) utility that should be included in your AUTOEXEC.BAT file, even for use with Windows 3.x, 95 or 98. SYSMON creates a log file of system changes at each boot-up. It causes no known conflicts or problems with Windows.

UN_DUP.EXE: Duplicate files waste valuable disk space, so "Rosenthal Un_Dup" finds any files that are redundant and may be removed. The path statement is optimized and directed to the remaining identical files. Files must be identical in name, size and contents to be considered duplicates. This is a DOS program.

UNINSTAL.EXE: Rosenthal UnInstall tracks installations to remove unwanted additions and restore things that have been changed. It will automatically removes unwanted files, directories and restores modified Windows and DOS programs, files, directories, the Windows Registry (USER.DAT and SYSTEM.DAT) and system files (AUTOEXEC.BAT, CONFIG.SYS, WIN.INI, SYSTEM.INI. This program is a TSR (terminate-and-stay-resident) utility that should be included in your AUTOEXEC. BAT file, even for use with Windows 3.x, 95 or 98. It causes no known conflicts or problems with Windows.

VIRSIM.COM and VIRSIMA.COM: The Virus Simulator from Rosenthal Engineering is an absolute necessity, for anyone seriously interested in defending against viruses. Government agencies, business, security consultants, law enforcement, institutions and system administrators, employ Virus Simulator when conducting internal security audits and training. This program may be run in DOS or Windows with your virus protection program active to test its capabilities.

The latest versions of these utilities are always available at Doren's web-site.

Symantec Norton Utilities Demo

Directory: NORTON
Filename: SETUP.EXE
Program name: Norton Utilities
Vendor URL: www.symantec.com

Intended Installation and Use: hard drive; Windows 95/98, with appropriate ASPI, CD-ROM, network and/or sound card drivers loaded as may be needed to access or check specific devices.

Description: This is a fully functional set of the Norton Utilities version 4.0 for Windows 95 and Windows 98. It will time out in 30-days. This demo allows you to review and exercise the features of the Norton Utilities, including the Norton Disk Doctor disk and file system tests and corrections, Norton SpeedDisk file optimization, and Norton WinDoctor to test application and Registry configuration, among others.

Gibson's OptOut

Directory: OptOut
Filename: optout.exe
Program name: OptOut
Vendor URL: www.grc.com

Intended Installation and Use: hard drive, Windows 95, 98, Me, NT, 2000

Description: The Internet community was recently rocked by rumors and reports that a popular system for creating advertiser-supported software was, in fact, functioning as an Internet "Trojan horse". The rumors stated that the unwitting user's computer was being "inventoried", the system registry was being scanned, and all manner of personal, private, and confidential information was being sent out across the Internet for collection by Aureate Media Corporation (pronounced: or'-ee-ate).

Although a complete technical analysis is ongoing, a preliminary examination of Aureate's web site and their privacy policy statements should immediately dispel most concerns about the company's intrinsic evilness."

That said, it is certainly the case that users should be made more aware than they have been of the potential privacy and security implications associated with the use of Aureate-hosted advertisement supported software.

This introduces Steve Gibson's program that analyzes your system for the existence of the Areate and other such software in your system that can compromise your personal information.

Gibson's Trouble In Paradise

Directory: Trouble
Filename: tip.exe
Program name: Trouble In Paradise
Vendor URL: www.grc.com

Intended Installation and Use: hard drive, Windows 95, 98, Me, NT, 2000

Description: TIP is the result of Steve Gibson's in-depth research into the causes and effects of various failures in Iomega's Zip and Jaz disk cartridges and drives. These problems have become widely known as the "click of death" – a name associated with the sound that Zip and Jaz drives make when they are trying to locate data on the disk media. TIP evaluates the inserted data cartridge, performing tests similar to Steve's popular and powerful SpinRite program. This free program tests your ZIP and JAZ drives and cartridges.

Diskeeper 5 (Trial Version)

Directory: Diskkeep
Filename: us_dk9xtr_i.exe
Program name: Diskeeper
Vendor URL: www.executive.com

Intended installation and use: Hard drive; Windows 95, 98, 98SE, NT and 2000 systems.

Description: A cut-down version of Diskeeper has been under the covers of many versions of Windows for the last several years, used to defrag your hard drive's files to help it run a lot faster. Many people have not known that you can purchase a much more robust version of Diskeeper for your personal computer or for large networks to keep all of your computer's hard drives working at top speed. The full commercial versions can even consolidate and optimize your directories, swap files, and the dreaded, corrupted Master File Table under Windows NT. If you want your hard drives running at top speed, you need Diskeeper!

WinGate

Directory: WinGate
Filename: wingate4.0.19.exe
Program name: WinGate
Vendor URL: www.wingate.com

Intended installation and use: Hard drive; Windows 95, 98, 98SE, NT and 2000 systems with Internet connection.

Description: WinGate is one of if not the first generally available programs that allowed multiple PCs to share a single Internet connection – via dial-up, ISDN, xDSL, cable modem or other access methods. WinGate serves as a proxy server that hides local area network workstations behind the single IP address of an Internet connection. The proxy server also caches web pages so that frequently visited pages can be recalled locally instead of from a new download over the Internet. WinGate can provide Network Address Translation and DHCP so that workstations can get private non-routed IP address assignments without being limited to the single IP address assigned by an ISP. Separate versions are provided for use on Windows 95, 98, and 98SE systems as well as for Windows NT and 2000.

WinProxy 3.0

Directory: Winproxy
Filename: Winproxy30.exe
Program name: WinProxy
Vendor URL: www.winproxy.com

Intended installation and use: Hard drive; Windows 95, 98, 98SE, NT and 2000 systems with Internet connection.

Description: WinProxy provides everything you need to simultaneously connect all your computers to the Internet through just one simple connection with your existing service provider. Plus, it includes innovative features like transparent proxy, a built-in firewall, centralized anti-virus protection, parental site restrictions and enhanced user privileges to put you in complete control of Internet access.

Netscape Communicator 4.72

Directory: Netscape
Filename: cc32d474.exe
Program name: Netscape Communicator
Vendor URL: www.netscape.com

Intended installation and use: Hard drive; Windows 95,98,Me,NT,2000; Web Browsing

Description: Integrated Web browser, e-mail, and groupware. The Communicator includes Netscape Navigator, Messenger, Composer, Collabra, Netcaster, Conference, AOL Instant Messenger, Netscape Calendar, AutoAdmin, and IBM Host On-Demand. Please see the documentation on the CD-ROM for installation and usage documentation.

Internet Explorer 5

Directory: MSIE
Filename: ie5setup.exe
Program name: Microsoft Internet Explorer
Vendor URL: www.microsoft.com

Intended installation and use: Hard drive; Windows 95,98,Me,NT,2000; Web Browsing

Description: This fully-functional release of Microsoft's award-winning Web browsing technology makes using the Web simpler than ever, more automated, and more flexible to let you use the Web the way you want. In short, Internet Explorer 5 brings IntelliSense to the Web to save you time on the things you do most often. Features like Web Accessories let you customize your browser to suit your needs. As part of this release, other Microsoft Internet tools are included such as Outlook Express 5 e-mail client, Windows Media Player 6, Chat 2.5, NetMeeting 2.11 conferencing software, Frontpage 2.0 web authoring software and more.

Troubleshooting Your PC Bible, 5th Edition

Directory: Book

Intended installation and use: Save the files to your hard drive. If you don't already have it, install Adobe Acrobat Reader, also included on this book's CD-ROM. Acrobat Reader will enable you to read the PDF files of the book.

Description: Search and read the entire text of *Troubleshooting Your PC Bible, 5th Edition* using your Internet Browser. This includes the Problem Index, all Chapters, the Appendices, References, and Index. Please treat it as part of your copy of Troubleshooting Your PC. In other words, do not copy it or upload it for others to read and use. It is your own copy.

Summary

We hope that you find these files and programs useful. If they provide some help, some education, or get some work done for you, then they have served their purpose.

Please, if you install and continue to use a user-supported or Shareware program, send in your registration to the author so that this wonderful type of program development and distribution may continue. It is only by giving these authors both financial and social encouragement that we will continue to benefit from these kinds of programs. In the same light, the commercial software vendors also deserve your support through purchases of their excellent products. We have had the pleasure of helping to influence the development of many of these types of products and feel that they all provide considerable value to any PC maintenance effort.

Good computing to you all!

✦   ✦   ✦

Glossary

10Base2 One of several types of Ethernet physical interconnections between networked devices. This specifies a 50 ohm coaxial cable and terminator arrangement, linking all devices on a specific network segment. It is capable of a data transfer rate of up to 10 megabits per second.

10BaseT One of several types of Ethernet physical interconnections between networked devices. This specifies four wires, specifically two twisted pairs of wires, linking devices on a specific network segment to one other network device, such as a hub or router. It is capable of a data transfer rate of up to 10 megabits per second.

100BaseT One of several types of Ethernet physical interconnections between networked devices. This specifies four wires, specifically two twisted pairs of wires, linking devices on a specific network segment to one other network device, such as a hub or router. It is capable of a data transfer rate of up to 100 megabits per second.

8086 An Intel 8-bit external, 16-bit internal data bus microprocessor capable of addressing up to 1MB of memory and operating at speeds up to 10 MHz. Its companion numerical coprocessor or math chip is the 8087. The 8086 is found in the IBM PS/2 Models 25 and 30, and some clones.

8088 An Intel 8-bit internal, 8-bit external data bus microprocessor capable of addressing up to 1MB of memory and operating at speeds up to 10 MHz. This chip is used in the IBM PC, XT, and compatible clone systems. Its companion numerical coprocessor or math chip is the 8087.

80286 An Intel 16-bit internal and external data bus microprocessor capable of addressing up to 16MB of memory and operating at speeds up to 12 MHz. Some non-Intel equivalents may run at 16 MHz. This chip's first use in PC systems was in the IBM PC/AT. Its companion numerical coprocessor or math chip is the 80287.

80386DX An Intel 32-bit internal and external data bus microprocessor capable of addressing up to 4GB of memory and operating at speeds up to 33 MHz. Some non-Intel equivalents may run at 40 MHz. This chip's first use in PC/AT-compatible systems was by Compaq. Its companion numerical coprocessor or math chip is the 80287 in some systems, otherwise the 80387.

80386SX An Intel 32-bit internal and 16-bit external data bus microprocessor capable of addressing up to 32MB of memory and operating at speeds up to 25 MHz. Its companion numerical coprocessor or math chip is the 80387SX.

80486DX An Intel 32-bit internal and external data bus microprocessor capable of operating at speeds up to 50 MHz. This processor contains an internal math coprocessor (floating-point processor) and an 8K internal instruction cache.

80486DX2 An Intel 32-bit internal and external data bus microprocessor capable of operating at speeds up to 66 MHz internally due to a doubling of the external clock speed. This processor contains an internal math coprocessor (floating-point processor) and an 8K internal instruction cache.

80486DX4 An Intel 32-bit internal and external data bus microprocessor capable of operating at speeds up to 100 MHz internally due to internal multiplication (tripling) of the external clock speed. This processor contains an internal math coprocessor (floating-point processor) and an 8K internal instruction cache.

80486SX An Intel 32-bit internal and external data bus microprocessor capable of operating at speeds up to 25 MHz. It is equivalent to the 80486DX, but it does provide the internal floating-point processor or the 8K cache.

80486SX2 An Intel 32-bit internal and external data bus microprocessor capable of operating at speeds up to 50 MHz internally due to doubling of the external clock speed. It is equivalent to the 80486DX, but it does provide the internal floating-point processor or the 8K cache.

access time The amount of time necessary for data to become available from a disk drive or memory area after a request is issued.

ACK *or* **Acknowledge** A signal sent by a receiving device confirming that information sent has been received. The opposite of NAK.

ACPI *See* Advanced Configuration and Power Interface (ACPI).

Active Directory Microsoft's implementation of the Internet Engineering Task Force's (IETF) Lightweight Directory Access Protocol (LDAP) standard that provides a common point for containing and sharing user and system resource information and secure access details.

adapter A hardware device, usually a set of connectors and a cable, used between two pieces of equipment to convert one type of plug or socket to another, or to convert one type of signal to another. Examples are a 9-to-25-pin serial port adapter cable, a serial-port-to-serial-port null modem, and a PC-printer-interface-to-printer cable.

adapter card A plug-in card used to exchange signals between the computer and internal or external equipment. *See also* video adapter card. Different types of adapter cards include multifunction cards, parallel adapter card, serial adapter card, USB adapter card, network adapter card (also called a NIC — network interface card), and very special adapter cards such as those used to provide TV programs on your screen and many more.

add-in card *See* adapter card.

address A location in memory or on a hardware bus of either a specific piece of data or a physical hardware device.

Advanced Configuration and Power Interface (ACPI) A standard specification and method for the monitoring of system activity and control of system configurations with power applied to or removed from system components, or switched to other components, depending on power states. Accommodates different modes of Sleep, Suspend, and Full-On system readiness of many system components.

Advanced Graphics Port (AGP) A high-speed data bus architecture used primarily for video adapters as an improvement over the PCI bus to enhance video graphics display performance.

Advanced Micro Devices (AMD) A manufacturer of microprocessors, primarily Intel *x*86-compatible devices, for use in PC systems.

Advanced Power Management (APM) A standard specification and method for the monitoring of system activity and control of power applied to, or removed from, system components, accommodating different modes of Sleep, Suspend, and Full-On system readiness. Sleep mode maintains current system activity with reduced power consumption, such as having disk drives and displays powered off but the CPU and memory retaining the last activities. Suspend mode maintains minimal if any current system activity with no power consumption. APM will be superceded by Advanced Configuration and Power Interface (ACPI) (*see also*).

Alt+key codes A combination of keystrokes using the Alt key plus one or more letter or number keys to initiate a particular program function or operation. The Alt key acts like a Shift or Ctrl key to change the function or use of a particular key. Alt+key combinations and their uses differ between many programs. One particular and common use for the Alt key is to enable entry of the decimal value of ASCII characters, especially the upper 128 special characters available with DOS, to draw lines and boxes. These keystrokes require use of any Alt key and the numeric data entry pad (rather than the top-row number keys). One example is pressing and holding the Alt key while entering the number sequence 1, 9, and 7, and then releasing the Alt key to enter and display a set of single crossed lines (a plus sign) the size of a character.

AMD Athlon An Advanced Micro Devices microprocessor operating at speeds of 750–1,000 MHz, with an I/O bus capable of 200 MHz speed, incorporating a 256K on-die L2 cache and 128K L1 cache, delivering industry-leading integer, floating point, and 3D multimedia functions in Socket A or Slot A physical configurations.

AMD Duron An Advanced Micro Devices microprocessor operating at speeds of 600–700 MHz, with a front side bus speed capable of 200 MHz, incorporating 192K of combined L1 and L2 cache, delivering integer, floating point, and 3D multimedia functions in Socket A physical configurations.

American National Standards Institute (ANSI) A governing body managing specifications for the computer industry and other disciplines. In terms of computing, ANSI maintains a set of standards for the coding and displaying of computer information, including certain "escape sequences" for screen color and cursor positioning. A device-driver file, ANSI.SYS, can be loaded in your PC's CONFIG.SYS file so your screen can respond properly to color and character changes provided from programs or terminal sessions between computers.

American Standard Code for Information Interchange (ASCII) ASCII defines the numerical or data representation of characters and numbers, and foreign language characters in computer data storage, text files, and display. There are 128 predefined characters, numbered 0–127, representing the alphabet, numbers, and data-terminal control functions that nearly any computer system will interpret properly. ASCII characters are represented or transferred in decimal or hexadecimal numeric representations, from 0–255 (decimal) or 00–FFh (hex). The upper 128 characters (128–255) vary between computer systems and languages and are known as the symbol set. IBM defined these as Extended ASCII characters, which include a variety of lines and boxes for pseudo-graphical screen displays. ASCII also defines the format of text files. ASCII text files generated on PCs differ slightly from the original ASCII standard and may appear with extra lines on other computer systems.

APM *See* Advanced Power Management (APM).

application A computer program or set of programs designed to perform a specific type or set of tasks to make a computer help you do your work or provide entertainment. Typical applications are games and word processing, database, or spreadsheet programs.

ANSI *See* American National Standards Institute (ANSI).

archive attribute *See* attributes.

ASCII *See* American Standard Code for Information Interchange (ASCII).

Asynchronous Transfer Mode (ATM) A high-speed, typically fiber optic, data communications circuit capable of between 25 and 622 megabit-per-second data transfer rates.

AT A model series of the IBM PC family known as Advanced Technology. This series includes those systems that use the 80286 microprocessor chip. The AT classification has been applied to 80386- and 80486-based systems that offer basic compatibility with and enhancements over the original specification.

AT-Attachments (ATA) An industry-wide specification for the interfacing of devices, typically hard disk drives, to the PC/AT standard data bus.

AT-compatible A description of a personal computer system that provides the minimum functions and features of the original IBM PC/AT system and is capable of running the same software and using the same hardware devices.

ATM *See* Asynchronous Transfer Mode (ATM).

attributes Every DOS file entry, including subdirectories, is accompanied by an attribute byte of information that specifies whether the file is read-only, hidden, system, or archived. *Read-only* indicates that no program operation should erase or write over a file with this attribute. *Hidden* indicates that the file should not be displayed or used in normal DOS DIR, COPY, or similar operations. The *system* attribute indicates that a file belongs to the operating system, which typically applies only to the hidden DOS files IO.SYS or IBMBIO.COM and MSDOS.SYS or IBMDOS.COM files. The *archive* attribute indicates that a file has been changed since the last backup, or that it should be backed up during the next backup session. Backup operations clear this attribute.

AUTOEXEC.BAT file An ASCII text file that may contain one or more lines of DOS commands that you want executed every time you boot up your PC. Also known as just the "autoexec" file, this file can be customized using a text editor program so you can specify a DOS prompt, set a drive and directory path to be searched when you call up programs, or load terminate-and-stay resident (TSR) programs that you want to have available all of the time.

back up The process of copying one, several, or all of the files on one disk to another disk, a set of diskettes, or tape cartridges for archival storage or routine protection against a system failure or loss of files. A backup should be done regularly and often.

barber pole A test pattern of data bytes written onto a disk drive's sectors such that if viewed as discrete 1s and 0s would appear as a spiral resembling a barber's red and white pole.

base address The initial or starting address of a device or memory location.

base memory *See* DOS memory.

basic input/output system (BIOS) The first set of program code to run when a PC system is booted up. The BIOS defines specific addresses and devices and provides software interface services for programs to use the equipment in a PC system. The PC system BIOS resides in a ROM chip on the system board. BIOS code also exists on add-in cards to provide additional adapter and interface services between hardware and software.

batch file An ASCII text file that may contain one or more lines of DOS commands that you want to execute by calling for one file, the name of the batch file, rather than keying them in individually. Also known as "bat" files, these files can be customized using a text editor program so you can specify a DOS prompt, set a drive and directory path to be searched when you call up programs, or load and execute specific programs. Batch files are used extensively as shortcuts for routine or repetitive tasks or those that you just don't want to have to remember each step for. These files always have the extension .BAT, as required by DOS.

battery backup The facility of providing power to a system or memory chip from a battery pack when AC power is not available. The battery may be a rechargeable or temporary type.

baud rate The rate, in bits per second, at which data is transferred between two systems or devices. The term *baud* actually applies to original 5-bit teletype code, developed by the term's namesake, J. M. E. Baudot, but it has been applied broadly to current 7- and 8-bit transfers between PCs, PCs and printers, and between modems. Modern transfer performance should be referred to as *bits per second* (of which there are 10 bits in each data character sent) or as *bytes per second* reflecting the actual amount of data that is transferred, without the data character overhead.

BBS *See* Bulletin Board Service *or* Bulletin Board System (BBS).

BIOS *See* basic input/output system (BIOS).

bit A bit is the smallest unit of information or memory possible in a digital or computer system. A bit has only two values: 1 (or on) and 0 (or off). A bit is the unit of measure in a binary (1/0) system. It might be thought of as a binary information term. A *bit* is one of eight pieces of information in a *byte*, one of 16 pieces in a *word* (16-bit words), or one of four pieces in a *nibble* (half a byte).

Bernoulli drive A disk drive system using the characteristics of specific data head design and air flow to draw the data head a predetermined distance to the data platter, as opposed to conventional drives that use air flow to push the heads away from the disk. These drives use removable cartridges containing the disk medium.

blue screen of death The all-too-familiar Windows error message text screen—white text characters on a blue background—indicating a critical failure of the operating system. A cold system restart (power down) is recommended after one of these errors occurs. Typically related to a corruption of memory or an illegal CPU instruction generated by a defective, improper, or conflicting program or device driver.

boot up The process of loading and running the hardware initialization program to enable access to hardware resources by applications.

BOOT.INI A plain-text format boot up configuration file used by the Microsoft Windows NT and 2000 operating systems.

bps *See* baud rate.

break *See* Control+Break.

BUFFERS A small area of memory used to temporarily store information being transferred between computer hardware and a disk drive. This is a settable parameter in the CONFIG.SYS file. Common values range from 3 to 30, as in BUFFERS=x.

built-in command A command or service that loads with and is available as part of the DOS command processor program, COMMAND.COM. DIR, COPY, DEL, TYPE, and CLS are examples of some internal DOS commands. *See also* internal command *and* your DOS manual.

Bulletin Board Service *or* **Bulletin Board System (BBS)** A public or private, local, or remote computer system accessed by modem for message and/or file sharing between users. A BBS may be operated by anyone with the time, equipment, and software to do so. User groups, clubs, companies, and government agencies operate BBSs to share information. You may be charged for the use of some systems. Listings of BBSs may be found accompanying some communications programs, in PC journals, or in the Yellow Pages. *See also* online services.

burn in The process of running diagnostic or repetitive test software on some or all components of and in a PC system for an extended period of time under controlled conditions. This process helps verify functionality and sort out weak or defective units before they are delivered or used under normal working conditions.

bus An internal wiring configuration between the CPU and various interface circuits carrying address, data, and timing information required by one or more internal, built-in, add-in, or external adapters and devices.

byte The common unit of measure of memory, information, file size, or storage capacity. A byte consists of 8 bits of information. There are typically two *bytes* to a *word* (typically 16 bits) of information; 1,024 bytes is referred to as a kilobyte or K, and contains 8,192 bits of information.

cache A reserved storage area used to hold information enroute to other devices, memory, or the CPU. Information that is called for during a disk-read operation can be read into a cache with additional information "stock-piled" ahead of time so that it is available for use, which is faster than having to wait for a disk's mechanical and electronic delays. Caching is becoming common between disks and the computer data bus or CPU and between the memory and CPU to speed up a system's operation. Some CPU chips and controller cards include caching as part of their design.

Cache on a Stick (COAST) A packing and connector system for add-in L2/external CPU cache memory.

cathode ray tube (CRT) The glass-faced vacuum tube housed inside your computer monitor that shows you the character and graphic display from your computer system.

Celeron An Intel microprocessor chip available in either Socket A or Slot 1 configurations providing 160K total L1 and L2 cache operating at speeds from 300–600 MHz with a bus speed of 66 MHz.

central processing unit (CPU) The main integrated circuit chip, processor circuit, or board in a computer system. For IBM PC-compatible systems the CPU may be an Intel or comparable 8088, 8086, 80286, 80386 (SX or DX), 80486 (SX or DX), Pentium, NEC V20 or V30, or other manufacturer's chip.

Certificates A method used to provide additional security in your connections over intranets and the Internet. Certificates are issued by a Certificate Authority that "knows" you and is trusted by others to be able to assure that you are the person holding that Certificate. They are usually associated with a Digital Signature (*see also*) that identifies you as the person involved in whatever transaction is being certified.

CGA *See* Color Graphics Adapter (CGA).

checksum An error-checking method used in file reading and writing operations to compare data sent with checksum information sent to verify correct reception of the information.

cluster The second smallest unit of measure of disk storage space under PC-DOS or MS-DOS. A cluster typically consists of four or more sectors of information storage space and contains 2,048 or more bytes of storage capacity. *See* sector.

CMOS Complimentary metal-oxide semiconductor. The type of memory usually used to store the configuration on an AT- or Pentium-class PC because it requires very little power to retain memory contents.

CMOS clock A special clock chip that runs continuously, either from the PC system power supply or a small battery, providing date and time information.

CMOS RAM A special memory chip used to store system configuration information. Rarely found in PC or XT models and usually found in 286 or higher models.

CMOS setup The process of selecting and storing configuration (device, memory, date, and time) information about your system for use during boot up. This process may be done through your PC's BIOS program or an external (disk-based) utility program.

COAST *See* Cache on a Stick (COAST).

code page A table stored in your computer's memory that defines the character set used by your keyboard and displayed on your screen. It is used to enable use of local or customary symbols and characters for various languages and countries.

code page switching A method of enabling you to change the character set used on your PC.

Color Graphics Adapter (CGA) The first IBM PC color display system, providing low-resolution (320×200) color graphics and basic text functions.

command A word used to represent a program or program function that you want your computer to perform. Commands are issued by you, through the keyboard or mouse, to tell the computer what to do.

command line The screen area immediately to the right of a prompt, where you key in commands to the computer or program. This is most commonly the "DOS command line," as indicated by the DOS prompt (C>, C:\>, or similar).

command-line editing The process of changing displayed commands before entering or starting the commanded activity.

communications program An application program that is used to simulate a computer data terminal when communicating with a computer at another location by modem or data communication line. Such programs often provide color display features, modem command setups, telephone number dialing directories, and script or batch-file-like automatic keystroke and file transfer functions.

CONFIG.SYS An ASCII text file that may contain one or more lines of special DOS commands that you want executed every time you boot up your PC. Also known as the "config" file, this file can be customized using a text editor program so you can specify one or more items specific to how your system should operate when it boots up. You may specify device drivers (with `DEVICE=`) such as memory management programs, disk caching, RAM disks, the number of files and buffers you want DOS to use, the location, name, and any special parameters for your command processor (usually COMMAND.COM), among other parameters. Refer to your DOS manual or device driver software manual for specific information.

Control+Alt+Delete *or* **Ctrl+Alt+Del** This is the special key sequence used to initiate a reboot of a PC system. If no alteration of the special reboot byte code in lower memory has taken place since the system was turned on, a warm boot or faster reset of the computer will occur. If the reboot code has been changed, the system may restart with a complete POST, including RAM memory count (*see also* power-on self test (POST)). Some systems contain special test code that may be activated in place of POST by setting the reboot byte and adding a test jumper on the system board. This latter feature is not well documented and may not be available on all systems.

Control+Break A combination entry of the Control (Ctrl) and Break (also Pause) keys that can interrupt and stop a program's operation and return the computer to the operating system. This is also a more robust or stronger version of the Ctrl+C key sequence used to abort a program. Checking for Control+Break is enhanced by setting BREAK ON in CONFIG.SYS or in DOS. Many programs intercept and do not allow Control+Break to pass to DOS because doing so might cause data loss or corrupt a number of open files in use by a program.

Control+C A keystroke combination of the Control (Ctrl) and C keys that can interrupt and stop the operation of many programs.

Control code A combination of keystrokes used by many programs, or during online sessions to cause special functions or operations to occur. Commonly used control codes are Ctrl+S to stop a DOS display from scrolling so it can be viewed more easily, and Ctrl+Q to cause the display to continue. These commands are entered by pressing the Ctrl key first, and then the accompanying single-letter code, much like using the Shift or Alt keys to change the action of a letter or number key.

controller *See* adapter.

conventional memory Also known as DOS memory, this is the range of your PCs memory from 0–640K where device drivers, DOS parameters, the DOS command processor (COMMAND.COM), your applications programs, and data are stored when you use your computer. *See* extended memory, expanded memory, video memory, high memory area (HMA), *and* upper memory.

cookie A tiny file placed on your computer that, if you allow it, is both placed by and used by Web sites to keep track of your current status at that Web site. It is one way to provide a sort of persistence to your connection to the site because the Internet Protocol is a connectionless type of network protocol. Cookies are usually harmless but some people choose not to accept cookies. They are probably a little more secure by making this choice but they also lose access to the full capabilities offered by the Web site that relies on cookies.

CPU *See* central processing unit (CPU).

crash The unexpected and unwanted interruption of normal computer operations. When a program crashes, all open data files may be corrupted or lost, and it is possible that hardware may get "stuck" in a loop with the computer appearing dead or "confused." Recovery from a program crash usually requires a reboot or turning off the power for a few seconds, and then restarting the system. A disk crash is normally associated with the improper mechanical contact of the read/write heads with the disk platter, although many people consider any disk error or data loss as a crash.

CRC *See* Cyclic Redundancy Check (CRC).

CRT *See* cathode ray tube (CRT).

current directory This is the subdirectory you or a program has last selected to operate from that is searched first before the DOS PATH is searched when calling a program. *See also* current disk drive *and* logged drive.

current disk drive The drive that you have selected for DOS and programs to use before searching the specified drives and directories in the DOS PATH (if specified). This may also be the drive indicated by your DOS prompt (typically C>, or C:\>, or similar) or that you have selected by specifying a drive letter followed by a colon in DOS and pressing the Enter key, as in A: Enter. This is also known as the *logged drive* (*see also*).

cursor A line or block character on your system display screen, usually blinking, that indicates where characters that you type will be positioned or where the current prompting for input is active. When at the DOS command line, the cursor is normally at the end of the DOS prompt string.

Cyclic Redundancy Check (CRC) An error-checking method used in file reading and writing operations to compare every two data bytes sent with transmitted CRC information sent to verify correct reception of the information.

D-connector An electronic connector style that appears as an exaggerated letter D when viewed from the face end; 9-, 15-, and 25-pin varieties are used for the monitor and I/O port connections on PCs.

default A predetermined or normal value or parameter used by a program or the computer as the selected value, if you do not or cannot change it by a command or by responding to a prompt for input.

defragment The process of reorganizing disk files so that they occupy contiguous sectors and clusters on a disk. This is done to reduce the access time (movement of the data read/write heads) needed to read a single data file.

Desktop Management Interface (DMI) One of many standards maintained by the Desktop Management Task Force that defines the collection and presentation of common computer system asset information.

Desktop Management Task Force (DMTF) A group of hardware and software companies studying, defining, and publishing standards for the advancement of local and remote computer system inventory and support features.

DESQview A multitasking user interface that facilitates the simultaneous operation of many programs. DESQview uses expanded memory to create virtual-DOS sessions and memory areas, and controls the amount of processor time given to each DOS session and the application using it.

DESQview/X A multitasking graphical user interface based on the MIT X-Window system client/server standard. It facilitates the simultaneous operation of many programs, on the local system and across other X-based systems on a network.

DESQview/X uses expanded memory to create virtual-DOS sessions and memory areas, and it controls the amount of processor time given to each DOS session and the application using it.

destructive testing Testing of memory or disk drives that overwrites the original or existing data without regard for restoring it upon completion of the test process.

device An actual piece of hardware interfaced to the computer to provide input or accept output. Typical devices are printers, modems, mice, keyboards, displays, and disk drives. Some special or virtual devices, handled in software, also act like hardware. The most common of these is called NUL, which is essentially nowhere. You can send screen or other output to the NUL device so that it does not appear. The NUL device is commonly used if the actual device to send something to does not exist, but a program requires that output be sent someplace. NUL is a valid "place" to send output to, although the output really doesn't go anywhere.

device driver A special piece of software required by some hardware or software configurations to interface your computer to a hardware device. Common device drivers are ANSI.SYS, used for display screen control; RAMDRIVE.SYS, which creates and maintains a portion of memory that acts like a disk drive; and HIMEM.SYS, a special device driver used to manage a specific area of extended memory called the high memory area (HMA). Device drivers are usually intended to be used in the CONFIG.SYS file, preceded by a `DEVICE=` statement.

diagnostics Software programs to test the functions of system components.

Digital Audio Tape (DAT) A high-capacity tape storage medium available in several formats (from 4 to 8mm in tape width) and capacities (to several gigabytes). Used for data backup systems and archival storage.

Digital Signature A security method using sophisticated encryption and decryption protocols, usually associated with Digital Certificates, that are becoming recognized by governments and courts as being just as valid as a physical signature. This one aspect of technology is beginning to change the way we do business and keep records, and may have much more impact than we are able to envision today.

digital subscriber line *See* DSL.

digital video disc (DVD) A type of CD-ROM with a capacity of 4.7GB or greater. The DVD specification supports disks with capacities of from 4.7GB to 17GB and access rates of 600 Kbps to 1.3 Mbps. DVD drives are backward-compatible with CD-ROMs.

DIMM *See* dual inline memory module (DIMM).

DIN connector A circular multiwire electronic connector based on international (German) standards. Available in normal and miniature sizes with three to seven connection pins. The PC uses five-pin normal and six-pin-mini DIN connectors for keyboards, and six-pin mini-DIN connectors for pointing devices.

DIP *See* dual inline package (DIP).

DIP switch A small board-mounted switch assembly resembling a DIP integrated circuit (IC) package in size and form. Used for the selection of system addresses and options.

direct memory access (DMA) A method of transferring information between a computer's memory and another device, such as a disk drive, without requiring CPU intervention.

directory File space on disks used to store information about files organized and referred to through a directory name. Each disk has at least one directory, called the root directory, which is a specific area reserved for other file and directory entries. A hard disk root directory may contain up to 512 other files or directory references, limited by the amount of disk space reserved for root directory entries. The files and directories referred to by the root directory may be of any size up to the limit of available disk space. Directories may be thought of as folders or boxes, as they may appear with some graphical user interfaces, although they are not visually represented that way by DOS. *See* root directory *and* subdirectory. All directories, except for the root directory, must have a name. The name for a directory follows the eight-character restriction that applies to filenames for DOS-only systems. Windows 95 and higher systems enjoy both longer file and directory names. *See also* filename.

directory services *See* Lightweight Directory Access Protocol (LDAP).

disk A rotating magnetic medium used for storing computer files. *See also* diskette *and* hard disk.

disk-bound servo track The data used by a disk drive to position and verify the location of the data read/write heads. This data may be mixed with the user's data, or on separate data tracks on the disk medium.

disk cache A portion of memory set aside to store information that has been read from a disk drive. The disk cache memory area is reserved and controlled by a disk caching program that you load in CONFIG.SYS or AUTOEXEC.BAT. The caching program intercepts a program or DOS request for information from a disk drive, reads the requested data, plus extra data areas, so it is available in memory, which is faster than a disk drive. This is commonly referred to as read-ahead caching. The cache may also be used for holding information to be written to disk, accepting the information more quickly than the disk can accept it and then writing the information to disk a short time later.

diskette Also called a *floppy disk*, this is a disk medium contained in a cover jacket that can be removed from a disk drive. The term *floppy* is deemed synonymous or descriptive of the flexible medium that is the magnetically coated disk of thin plastic material.

disk drive adapter A built-in or add-in card interface or controller that provides necessary connections between the computer system I/O circuits and a disk drive.

disk label A surface or sticker on the outside jacket of a diskette that is used for visually recording information about the contents of the disk. This label may contain as much information as you can write or type in the space provided.

A specific area on a disk used to record data as the disk's name or volume label. This area is written with the DOS LABEL command, or prompted for input during certain disk format processes. A volume label may be up to 11 characters long. The volume label appears onscreen during disk directory operations.

References to the disk label may not be clear about which "label" is to be used. You may use the two preceding definitions to help determine which label is being referred to by the limitations for each, and the reference you are given.

disk operating system (DOS) Software written for a specific computer system, disk, file, and application type to provide control over disk storage services and other input and output functions required by application programs and system maintenance. All computers using disk drives have some form of disk operating system containing applicable programs and services. For IBM PC-compatible computers, the term DOS is commonly accepted to mean the computer software services specific to PC systems.

DLL *See* dynamic-link library (DLL).

DMA *See* direct memory access (DMA).

DOS *See* disk operating system (DOS).

DOS diskette A diskette formatted for use with DOS-based PCs and file systems.

DOS memory Temporary memory used for storage of DOS boot and operating system information, programs, and data during the operation of a computer system. DOS memory occupies up to the first 640K of random access memory (RAM) space provided in your system's hardware. This memory empties out or loses its contents when your computer is shut off. *Lower memory* is the term used to describe a space in the first 640K of memory in which DOS stores status information about your system. *Upper memory* is in the space above DOS's 640K but below the 1MB limit imposed by the early CPU chips regarding their capability to directly access only the first megabyte. The high memory area (HMA) is the first 64K block of memory above the 1MB limit but is accessible by the early CPU chips.

DOS system diskette A diskette formatted for use with DOS-based PCs and file systems that also contains the two DOS-system hidden files and COMMAND.COM to enable booting up your system from a diskette drive.

double buffer A parameter used in and function provided by Windows 95, 98, 98SE, and Me operating systems, configured in the MSDOS.SYS file to provide additional memory buffering of SCSI and DMA I/O transfers. Often required and preset to be used by Windows when SCSI devices are detected to avoid data loss and transfer delays.

download The process of receiving or transferring information from another computer, usually connected via modem, onto your computer system. Downloading is a common method of obtaining public-domain and shareware programs from BBS and online services, obtaining software assistance and upgrades from many companies, or retrieving files or electronic mail from others.

DRAM *See* dynamic random access memory (DRAM).

drive The mechanical and electronic assembly that holds disk storage media and provides the reading and writing functions for data storage and retrieval.

DSL (also **xDSL, IDSL, ADSL, HDSL)** Digital subscriber line. A technique of providing high-speed digital communications over conventional telephone wires, using signaling above and different from voice-range frequencies. Implemented in various combinations of upward and downward bandwidth, telephone line, and equipment types. Typically lower cost and higher performance than ISDN depending on the implementation. It is possible to carry DSL signaling over some ISDN and frame relay circuits for 144–192 kilobit-per-second transfer rates, or on specially conditioned wire pairs to achieve T-1 (1.54 megabits per second) and higher data rates.

dual inline memory module (DIMM) A high-density memory packaging system consisting of 168 pins, similar to the edge connector used on larger printed circuit cards. DIMM is used in addition to or in place of SIMM memory design.

dual inline package (DIP) A form of integrated circuit housing and connection with two rows of pins on either side of a component body.

DVD Digital video (or versatile) disc is more highly compressed and, hence, able to store more data that a CD-ROM. It is the same size as a CD-ROM. DVDs are most commonly associated with movies but they can be used to store large amounts of data and may become a common backup system for PCs. *See also* digital video disc.

dynamic-link library (DLL) A file containing executable program functions that are invoked from another program. DLLs may be shared among many applications and are used only when a program requires the functions contained within, reducing program memory and disk space requirements by eliminating duplication of program elements and file size.

dynamic random access memory (DRAM) Relatively slow (50 to 200 nanoseconds access time) economical memory integrated circuits. These require a periodic refresh cycle to maintain their contents. Typically used for the main memory in the PC system, but occasionally also used for video memory. *See also* random access memory (RAM) *and* static random access memory (SRAM).

edge connector An electronic connector that is part of the circuit card, made of circuit foil extended to the edge of the board. A circuit card's edge connector mates with the fingers inside a complimentary female socket.

EGA *See* Enhanced Graphics Adapter (EGA).

EIA *See* Electronics Industries Association (EIA).

EISA *See* Extended Industry Standard Architecture (EISA).

Electronics Industries Association (EIA) An organization that provides and manages standards for many types of electronics designs and implementations. The RS-232C standard for serial data terminal and computer interconnection is the most commonly known EIA standard in the PC market.

EMM *See* Expanded Memory Manager (EMM).

EMS *See* Expanded Memory Specification (EMS).

Enhanced Graphics Adapter (EGA) A color graphics system designed by IBM, providing medium-resolution text and graphics, compatible also with monochrome text and CGA displays.

Enhanced Small Device Interface (ESDI) A standards definition for the interconnection of older high-speed disk drives. This standard is an alternative to earlier MFM, coincident applications of SCSI, and recent IDE drive interfaces.

Enter The command or line termination key, also known as Return on a computer keyboard. There are usually two Enter keys on your keyboard. Under some applications programs these two keys may have different functions; the numeric keypad Enter key may be used as an "enter data" key, while the alphanumeric keyboard Enter key may be used as a "carriage return."

environment An area of memory set up and used by the DOS software to store and retrieve a small amount of information that can be shared or referred to by many programs. Among other information that the DOS environment area could hold are the PATH, current drive, PROMPT, COMSPEC, and any SET variables.

escape sequence A set of commands or parameters sent between devices to control operations, printed text orientation or fonts, screen colors and displays, or to begin file transfer operations between systems. Many printers accept escape sequences to change typeface or between portrait and landscape modes. Screen displays and the DOS prompt may be controlled by ANSI escape sequences through the device driver ANSI.SYS. These sequences are started with the transmission or issuance of the ASCII ESC character (appearing similar to <-) or the ASCII control code Ctrl+Left Bracket (^[, decimal 27, 1B hex), and follow with lettered or numbered command definitions. A common sequence is ESC-2-j, possibly appearing as ^[2J on your screen, which is the Clear Screen ANSI escape sequence.

ESDI *See* Enhanced Small Device Interface (ESDI).

execute The action that a computer takes when it is instructed to run a program. A running program is said to "execute" or "be executing" when it is being used.

executable file A program file that may be invoked from the operating system. DLLs and overlay files also contain executable program information, but their functions must be invoked from within another program.

expanded memory This is an additional area of memory created and managed by a device driver program using the Lotus/Intel/Microsoft Expanded Memory Specifcation, known also as LIM-EMS. EMS comes in three common forms that conform to the LIM-EMS 3.2 standard for software-only access to this memory, LIM-EMS 4.0 in software, and LIM EMS 4.0 in hardware. With the proper hardware, this memory may exist and be used on all PC systems, from PCs to 486 systems. Expanded memory may be made up of extended memory (memory above 1MB) on 386 and 486 systems, or it may be simulated in extended memory on 286 systems. LIM-EMS 3.2, 4.0 (software) and 4.0 (hardware) are commonly used for additional data storage for spreadsheets and databases. Only LIM-EMS conforming to the 4.0 standard for hardware may be used for multitasking. Expanded memory resides at an upper memory address, occupying one 64K block between 640K and 1MB. The actual amount of memory available depends on your hardware and the amount of memory you can assign to be expanded memory. The 64K block taken up by expanded memory is only a window or port giving access to the actual amount of EMS available. There may be as little as 64K or as much as 32MB of expanded memory.

Expanded Memory Manager (EMM) The term often given to software or that refers to expanded memory chips and cards. *See also* expanded memory.

Expanded Memory Specification (EMS) The IBM PC-industry standards for software and memory hardware that make up expanded memory.

Extended Industry Standard Architecture (EISA) The definition of a PC internal bus structure that maintains compatibility with IBM's original PC, XT, and AT bus designs (known as the ISA, or Industry Standard Architecture) but offering considerably more features and speed between the computer system and adapter cards, including a definition for 32-bit PC systems that do not follow IBM's MCA (Micro Channel Architecture).

extended memory This is memory in the address range above 1MB, available only on 80286 or higher systems. It is commonly used for RAM disks, disk caching, and some applications programs. Using a special driver called HIMEM.SYS or similar services provided with memory management software, the first 64K of extended memory may be assigned as a high memory area, which some programs and DOS can be loaded into.

extended memory specification (XMS) A standard that defines access and control over upper, high, and extended memory on 286 and higher computer systems. XMS support is provided by loading the HIMEM.SYS device driver or other memory management software that provides XMS features.

external command A program or service provided as part of DOS that exists as separate programs on disk rather than built into the COMMAND.COM program that loads when you boot up your system. These programs have .COM or .EXE extensions. Some of these are FORMAT.COM, DISKCOPY.COM, DEBUG.EXE, LABEL.COM, MORE.COM, and PRINT.COM.

FAT *See* File Allocation Table (FAT).

FDDI *See* Fiber Distributed Data Interface (FDDI).

FDISK A special part of the hard disk formatting process required to assign and establish usable areas of the disk as either bootable, active, data-only for DOS, or as non-DOS for other operating system use. The FDISK process is to be performed between the low-level format and the DOS format of a hard disk prior to its use.

Fiber Distributed Data Interface (FDDI) A fiber optic digital data communications medium capable of transfer rates of 100 megabits per second. Used primarily as a local area network (LAN) backbone circuit between buildings or major workgroups.

file An area of disk space containing a program or data as a single unit, referred to by the DOS file directory. Its beginning location is recorded in the file directory, with reference to all space occupied by the file recorded in the DOS File Allocation Table (FAT). Files are pieces of data or software that you work with on your computer. They may be copied, moved, erased, or modified, all of which is tracked by DOS for the directory and FAT.

File Allocation Table (FAT) This is DOS's index to the disk clusters that files and directories occupy. It provides a table or pointer to the next disk cluster a file occupies. There are two copies of the FAT on a disk, for reliability. When files are erased, copied, moved, reorganized, or defragmented, the FAT is updated to reflect the new position of files or the availability of empty disk space. Files may occupy many different cluster locations on disk, and the FAT is the only reference to where all of the file pieces are.

file attributes *See* attributes.

filename The string of characters assigned to a disk file to identify it. A filename must be up to eight leading characters as the proper name for DOS-only systems, in which a filename may be followed by a three-character extension, separated from the proper name by a period (.). Windows 95, Windows 98, and Windows NT systems may have "long filenames" of up to 256 characters, including multiple period or "dot" separators. Allowable filename and extension characters are A–Z, 0–9, !, @, #, $, ^, &, _, -, {, }, (,),', `, or ~. Also, many characters of the IBM extended character set may be used. Reserved characters that cannot be used are %, *, +, =, ;, :, [,], <, >, ?, /, \, |, ", and spaces. Filenames must be unique for each file in a directory, but the same name may exist in separate directories. Filenames are assigned to all programs and data files.

filename extension A string of one to three characters used after a filename and a separating period (.), with the same character limitations as the filename, for DOS systems. The extension is often used to identify certain types of files to certain applications. DOS uses BAT, EXE, and COM as files it can load and execute, though this does not preclude the use of these extensions for non-executable files. The extensions SYS, DRV, and DVR are commonly used for device driver programs that are loaded and used in the CONFIG.SYS file prior to loading DOS (as COMMAND. COM). Refer to your software documentation for any limitations or preferences it has for filename extensions.

filespec Also known as the file specification or file specifier, this is a combination of a drive designation, directory path, and filename used to identify a specific file in its exact location on your system's disk drive. References to filespec may appear in examples or as prompts: `D:\path\filename.ext`, where `D:` indicates that you are supposed to place you disk drive information here, `\path\` indicates that you should specify the proper directory and subdirectory information here, and `filename.ext` indicates that you should specify the file's exact name and extension. In use, this might actually be `C:\DOS\COM\FORMAT.COM`.

firewall Either a hardware or software device used to control access to a network. It is most often associated with the Internet or intranets and controls access by either allowing or disallowing packets to pass through based on their port, address, and/or protocol.

FireWire Apple Computer's trade term for its implementation of the IEEE-1394 high-speed I/O communications protocol and physical connections. Typically used to interconnect video recording equipment and computers.

first-in, first-out (FIFO) *or* **FIFO buffering** A small-capacity data storage element, memory, or register that holds data flowing between a source and a destination. The data flow moves in the order in which it is received and cannot be accessed directly or randomly as with normal memory storage. A FIFO is commonly used in serial communication (COM) ports to retain data while applications software and storage devices catch up to and can store the incoming stream of data.

fixed disk *See* hard disk.

flag A hardware bit or register, or a single data element in memory that is used to contain the status of an operation, much like the flag on a mailbox signals that you have an item to be picked up.

floppy disk A slang term for diskette. *See* diskette.

format The process of preparing a disk (removable or fixed/hard) with a specific directory and file structure for use by DOS and applications programs. Formatting may consist of making the disk usable for data storage only, providing reserved space to make the disk bootable later on, or making the disk bootable, including the copying of the DOS hidden files and COMMAND.COM. FORMAT is the final process of preparing a hard disk, preceded by a low-level format and FDISK. All disk media require a format. RAM or virtual disks do not require formatting. Formatting, unless performed with certain types of software, erases all data from a disk.

frame relay A data communications circuit between two fixed points, a user and a frame relay routing service, capable of transfer rates between 64 kilobits per second up to T-1 rates. May be carried over part of a "Fractional T-1" circuit.

gigabyte (GB) A unit of measure referring to 1,024MB or 1,073,741,824 bytes of information, storage space, or memory. Devices with this capacity are usually large disk drives and tape backup units with 1.2GB to well over 12GB of storage area.

handshaking The process of two computer systems or modems exchanging information to determine and acknowledge first that a connection is possible and exists, and second, the best mode of operation for fastest or most reliable transmission.

hard disk A sealed disk drive unit with platters mounted inside on a fixed spindle assembly. The actual platter is a hard aluminum or glass surface coated with magnetic storage media. This definition also suits removable hard disks in which the hard platters are encased in a sealed casing and mate with a spindle similar to the attachment of a diskette to the drive motor. The platters are sealed to keep foreign particles from interfering with and potentially damaging the platters or the read/write heads that normally maintain a small gap between them during operation.

hardware interrupt A signal from a hardware device connected to a PC system that causes the CPU and computer program to act on an event that requires software manipulation, such as controlling mouse movements, accepting keyboard input, or transferring a data file through a serial I/O port.

head crash The undesired, uncontrolled mechanical contact of a disk drive's read/write heads with the disk surface. A minor crash may be recoverable with minimal data loss. A severe crash can render a disk or the head assembly completely useless. Minor to severe head crashes may be caused by mechanical shock, excessive vibration, or mishandling of a drive while it is operating. Not all disk errors or loss of data are the result of a physical crash and disk surface damage. Actual head crashes with disk damage are very rare compared with loss of data due to the weakening of magnetic properties of an area of the disk, and program, or operational errors.

Hercules An older medium-resolution monochrome graphics and text display system designed by Hercules Technology offering compatibility with IBM monochrome text. Hercules-specific graphics display was supported by many programs as a low-cost alternative and improvement to CGA displays before EGA was defined.

hexadecimal A base-16 numbering system made up of four digits or bits of information, where the least significant place equals 1 and the most significant place equals 8. A hexadecimal, or hex, number is represented as the numbers 0–9 and letters A–F, for the numerical range 0–15 as 0–F. A byte of hex information can represent from 0 to 255 different items, as 00 to FF.

HGC *See* Hercules.

hidden file *See* attributes.

high memory area (HMA) A 64K region of memory above the 1MB address range created by HIMEM.SYS or a similar memory utility. The HMA can be used by one program for program storage, leaving more space available in DOS or the lower memory area from 0 to 640K.

host adapter A built-in or add-in card interface between a device, such as a SCSI hard disk or CD-ROM drive, and the I/O bus of a computer system. A host adapter typically does not provide control functions, instead acting only as an address and signal conversion and routing circuit.

IA-64 Intel's term for 64-bit computing architecture products, to be supported by related Microsoft and Unix-family operating systems.

IBM PC-compatible A description of a personal computer system that provides the minimum functions and features of the original IBM PC system and is capable of running the same software and using the same hardware devices.

IDC *See* insulation displacement connector (IDC).

IDE *See* Integrated Device Electronics (IDE).

IEEE The Institute of Electrical and Electronics Engineers. An international standards organization responsible for fostering standard implementations of electronic methods and technology for compatibility between like systems.

iLink Sony Corporation's trade term for its implementation of the IEEE-1394 (*aka* FireWire) high-speed I/O communications protocol and physical connections. Typically used to interconnect video recording equipment and computers.

Industry Standard Architecture (ISA) The term given to the IBM PC, XT, and AT respective 8- and 16-bit PC bus systems. Non–32-bit, non–IBM Micro Channel Architecture systems are generally ISA systems.

input/output (I/O) The capability or process of software or hardware to accept or transfer data between computer programs or devices.

insulation displacement connector (IDC) The type of connector found on flat ribbon cables, used to connect I/O cards and disk drives.

Integrated Device Electronics (IDE) A standards definition for the interconnection of high-speed disk drives in which the controller and drive circuits are together on the disk drive and interconnect to the PC I/O system through a special adapter card. This standard is an alternative to earlier MFM, ESDI, and SCSI drive interfaces, and it is also part of the ATA standard.

Integrated Services Digital Network (ISDN) A technique of providing high-speed digital communications over conventional telephone wires, using signaling above and different from voice-range frequencies. ISDN uses three different signal channels over the same pair of wires, one D-channel for digital signaling such as dialing and several enhanced but seldom-used telephone calling features, and two B-channels, each capable of handling voice or data communications up to 64 kilobits per second. ISDN lines may be configured as Point-to-Point (both B-channels would connect to the same destination) or Multi-Point (allowing each B-channel to connect to different locations), and Data+Data (B-channels can be used for data-only) or Data+Voice (where either B-channel may be used for data or voice transmission). Interconnection to an ISDN line requires a special termination/power unit, known as an NT-1 (network termination 1), which may or may not be built into the ISDN modem or router equipment at the subscriber end. An ISDN modem may be used and controlled quite similarly to a standard analog modem, and may or may not also provide voice-line capabilities for analog devices. An ISDN router must be configured for specific network addresses and traffic control, and may or may not provide voice/analog line capabilities.

interleave The property, order, or layout of data sectors around disk cylinders to coincide with the speed of drive and controller electronics so that data can be accessed as quickly as possible. An improper interleave can make a sector arrive too soon or too late at the data heads, and thus be unavailable when the drive and controller are ready for it, slowing disk system performance. An optimal interleave will have the rotation of the disk, and placement of a data sector and electronics coincident so there is little or no delay in data availability. Interleave is set or determined at the time of a low-level format, which sets the order of the data sectors. consists of shuffling data sectors to a pattern optimal for best performance.

interlaced operation A method of displaying elements on a display screen in alternating rows of pixels (picture elements) or scans across a display screen, as opposed to non-interlaced operation, which scans each row in succession. Interlacing often produces a flickering or blinking of the illuminated screen.

internal command A command that loads with and is available as part of the DOS command processor program, COMMAND.COM. DIR, COPY, DEL, TYPE, and CLS are examples of some internal DOS commands. The same as *built-in command*. Also see your DOS manual.

International Standards Organization (ISO) A multifaceted, multinational group that establishes cross-border/cross-technology definitions for many industrial and consumer products. Related to the PC industry, it helps define electronic interconnection standards and tolerances.

Internet Engineering Task Force (IETF) The international body of experts chiefly responsible for drafting, accepting, and publishing data communications standards that affect the Internet.

interrupt *See* hardware interrupt, interrupt request (IRQ), *and* software interrupt.

interrupt request (IRQ) A set of hardware signals available on PC add-in card connections that can request prompt attention by the CPU when data must be transferred to/from add-in devices and the CPU or memory.

I/O *See* input/output (I/O).

IPX A device driver–type TSR program that connects a network interface card to the operating system. *See also* NETX.

IRQ *See* interrupt request (IRQ).

ISA *See* Industry Standard Architecture (ISA).

ISDN *See* Integrated Services Digital Network (ISDN).

ISO *See* International Standards Organization (ISO).

Joint Photographic Experts Group (JPEG) A working group of the International Standards Organization. The term also refers to a compression technique for digital images. A common file format for the transfer of images between computers and on Web sites.

Kermit A serial data transfer protocol developed by Columbia University. Kermit is available in some form on almost every type of computer system and in most all communications or terminal programs. A special version of Kermit called Sliding-Windows Kermit is commonly used on systems that connect to users by data networks such as SprintNet or Tymnet. Kermit is named after the Kermit the Frog puppet character and has no other special meaning.

keyboard A device attached to the computer system that provides for manual input of alpha, numeric, and function-key information to control the computer or place data into a file.

kilobyte (K) A unit of measure referring to 1,024 bytes or 8,192 bits of information, storage space, or memory.

label *or* **volume label** A 1- to 11-character name recorded on a disk to identify it during disk and file operations. The volume label is written to disk with the DOS LABEL or FORMAT programs or with disk utility programs. This may be confused with the paper tag affixed to the outside of a diskette. *See* disk label.

LAN *See* local area network (LAN).

language The specifically defined words and functions that form a programming language or method to control a computer system. At the lowest accessible level, programmers can control a CPU's operations with assembly language. Applications programs are created initially in different high-level languages such as BASIC, C, or Pascal, which are converted to assembly language for execution. DOS and applications may control the computer's operations with a batch (BAT) processing language or an application-specific macro language.

LCD *See* liquid crystal display (LCD).

Lightweight Directory Access Protocol (LDAP) The Internet Engineering Task Force's (IETF) Lightweight Directory Access Protocol (LDAP) standard provides a common point for containing and sharing user and system resource information and secure access details.

LIMS *See* extended memory.

Linux A Unix-like operating system created by Linus Torvolds with open-source code and ready-to-install public and commercial distributions. Linux is becoming a popular alternative to Windows NT/2000, FreeBSD, and Sun Solaris operating systems for private and commercial desktop and server uses.

liquid crystal display (LCD) A type of data display that uses microscopic crystals, which are sensitive to electrical energy to control whether they pass or reflect light. Patterns of crystals may be designed to form characters and figures, as are the small dots of luminescent phosphor in a CRT (display monitor or television picture tube).

loading high An expression for the function of placing a device driver or executable program in a high (XMS, above 1MB) or upper memory area (between 640K and 1MB.) This operation is performed by a DEVICEHIGH or LOADHIGH (DOS) statement in the CONFIG.SYS or AUTOEXEC.BAT file. High memory areas are created by special memory manager programs such as EMM386 (provided with versions of DOS) and Quarterdeck's QEMM386.

local area network (LAN) An interconnection of systems and appropriate software that enables the sharing of programs, data files, and other resources among several users.

Local Bus A processor to I/O device interface alternative to the PC's standard I/O bus connections, providing extremely fast transfer of data and control signals between a device and the CPU. It is commonly used for video cards and disk drive interfaces to enhance system performance. Local Bus is a trademark of the Video Electronics Standards Association (VESA).

logged drive The disk drive you are currently displaying or using, commonly identified by the DOS prompt (C> or A:\>). If your prompt does not display the current drive, you may issue a DIR or DIR/p command to see the drive information displayed.

logical device A hardware device that is referred to in DOS or applications by a name or abbreviation that represents a hardware address assignment, rather than by its actual physical address. The physical address for a logical device may differ. Logical device assignments are based on rules established by IBM and the ROM BIOS at boot up.

logical drive A portion of a disk drive assigned as a smaller partition of larger physical disk drive. Also a virtual or non-disk drive created and managed through special software. RAM drives (created with RAMDRIVE.SYS or VDISK.SYS) or compressed disk/file areas (such as those created by Stacker, DoubleDisk, or SuperStor) are also logical drives. A 40MB disk drive partitioned as drives C: and D: is said to have two logical drives. That same disk with one drive area referred to as C: has only one logical drive, coincident with the entire physical drive area. DOS may use up to 26 logical drives. Logical drives may also appear as drives on a network server or mapped by the DOS ASSIGN or SUBST programs.

logical pages Sections of memory that are accessed by an indirect name or reference rather than by direct location addressing, under control of a memory manager or multitasking control program.

loopback plug A connector specifically wired to return an outgoing signal to an input signal line for the purpose of detecting if the output signal is active or not, as sensed at the input line.

Lotus/Intel/Microsoft Standard (LIMS) *See* expanded memory.

lower memory *See* DOS memory.

LS-120 A high-capacity (120MB) diskette storage medium compatible with conventional 720K and 1.44MB diskette media.

math coprocessor An integrated circuit designed to accompany a computer's main CPU and speed up floating-point and complex math functions that would normally take a long time if done with software and the main CPU. Enables the main CPU to perform other work during these math operations.

MCA *See* Micro Channel Architecture (MCA).

MCGA *See* Multi-Color Graphics Array (MCGA).

MDA *See* Monochrome Display Adapter (MDA).

megabyte (MB) A unit of measure referring to 1,024K or 1,048,576 bytes of information, storage space, or memory. One megabyte contains 8,388,608 bits of information. One megabyte is also the memory address limit of a PC- or XT-class computer using an 8088, 8086, V20, or V30 CPU chip. 1MB is 0.001GB.

megahertz (MHz) A measure of frequency in millions of cycles per second. The speed of a computer system's main CPU clock is rated in megahertz.

memory Computer information storage area made up of chips (integrated circuits) or other components, which may include disk drives. Personal computers use many types of memory, from dynamic RAM chips for temporary DOS, extended, expanded, and video memory, to static RAM chips for CPU instruction caching to memory cartridges and disk drives for program and data storage.

memory disk *See* RAM disk.

Micro Channel An I/O card interconnection design created by IBM for use in IBM PS/2 series systems.

Micro Channel Architecture (MCA) IBM's system board and adapter card standards for the PS/2 (Personal System/2) series of computers. This is a non-ISA bus system requiring the use of different adapter cards and special configuration information than are used on early PC, XT, and AT compatible systems.

microprocessor A computer central processing unit contained within one integrated circuit chip package.

MIDI *See* Musical Instrument Digital Interface (MIDI).

Millennium *See* Windows Me (Windows Millennium).

modem An interface between a computer bus or serial I/O port and wiring, typically a dial-up telephone line, used to transfer information and operate computers distant from each other. The term *modem* stands for modulator/demodulator. It converts computer data into audible tone sounds that can be transferred by telephone lines to other modems that convert the tone sounds back into data for the receiving computer. Early modems transferred data at speeds of 110 to 300 bits per second (11 to 30 characters-per-second). Recent technology enables modems to transfer data at speeds of 56,700 bits per second (5,670 characters or bytes) and higher, often compressing the information to achieve these speeds and adding error correction to protect against data loss due to line noise. Modems typically require some form of UAR/T (Universal Asynchronous Receiver/Transmitter) as the interface to the computer bus.

Monochrome Display Adapter (MDA) The first IBM PC video system, providing text only on a one-color (green or amber) display. If you have one of these adapters, you own an antique!

Mosaic A user-interface program for access to WWW-based Internet services.

motherboard The main component or system board of your computer system. It contains the necessary connectors, components, and interface circuits required for communications between the CPU, memory, and I/O devices.

Moving Picture Experts Group (MPEG) A working group of the International Standards Organization. The term also refers to the family of digital video compression standards and file formats developed by the group. MPEG generally produces better-quality video than competing formats, such as Video for Windows, Indeo, and QuickTime. MPEG files can be decoded by special hardware or by software.

MPEG audio layer 3 (MP3) A digital file format typically containing audio information such as music, for playback on computer and personal digital audio devices.

MSDOS.SYS A plain-text format boot up configuration file used by the Microsoft Windows 95, 98, 98SE, and Me operating systems.

Multi-Color Graphics Array (MCGA) An implementation of CGA built into IBM PS/2 Model 25 and 30 systems using an IBM analog monitor and providing some enhancements for higher-resolution display and grayscale shading for monochrome monitors.

multimeter An electrical instrument combining measurement capabilities for voltage (voltmeter), current (ammeter), and ohms (ohmmeter). Available in analog (needle-indicating dial) and digital (numeric readout) versions, the latter giving a more accurate indication of the measured quantity, the former often more responsive to fluctuations in quantity.

multisync A display monitor that is capable of displaying information at a variety of resolutions, determined by the rate at which the internal electron beam scans across the front of the CRT. Non-multisync monitors are limited to fixed resolutions and display rates. This term is synonymous with multifrequency, multiscanning, and variable-frequency in the context of display monitors and video adapter cards.

multitasking The process of software control over memory and CPU tasks enabling the swapping of programs and data between active memory and CPU use to a paused or non-executing mode in a reserved memory area, while another program is placed in active memory and execution mode. The switching of tasks may be assigned different time values for how much of the processor time each program gets or requires. The program you see onscreen is said to be operating in the foreground and typically gets the most CPU time, while any programs you may not see are said to be operating in the background, usually getting less CPU time. DESQview and Windows are two examples of multitasking software in common use on PCs.

Musical Instrument Digital Interface (MIDI) An industry standard for hardware and software connections, control, and data transfer between like-equipped musical instruments and computer systems.

network The connection of multiple systems together or to a central distribution point for the purpose of information or resource sharing.

network interface card (NIC) An add-in card or external adapter unit used to connect a workstation (PC system) to a common network or distribution system.

NETX A TSR program that connects a network interface card driver program to an active network operating system, for access to LAN services.

nibble A nibble is one-half of a byte, or four bits, of information.

NiCad battery An energy cell or battery composed of nickel and cadmium chemical compositions, forming a rechargeable, reusable source of power for portable devices.

NIC *See* network interface card (NIC).

noninterlaced operation A method of displaying elements on a display screen at a fast rate throughout the entire area of the screen, as opposed to interlaced operation, which scans alternate rows of display elements or pixels, the latter often producing a flickering or blinking of the illuminated screen.

Norton *or* **Norton Utilities** A popular suite of utility programs used for PC disk and file testing and recovery operations, named after their author, Peter Norton. The first set of advanced utilities available for IBM PC-compatible systems.

NTF—No trouble found The status bestowed upon a piece of computer hardware returned to the manufacturer as defective, when no defect was found.

null modem A passive, wire-only data connection between two similar ports of computer systems, connecting the output of one computer to the input of another, and vice versa. Data flow control or handshaking signals may also be connected between systems. A null modem is used between two nearby systems, much as you might interconnect two computers at different locations by telephone modem.

offsets When addressing data elements or hardware devices, often the locations where data is stored or moved through is in a fixed grouping, beginning at a known or base address, or segment of the memory range. The offset is that distance, location, or number of bits or bytes that the desired information is from the base or segment location. Accessing areas of memory is done with an offset address based on the first location in a segment of memory. For example, an address of 0:0040h represents the first segment, and an offset of 40 bytes. An address of A:0040h would be the 40th (in hex) byte location (offset) in the tenth (Ah) segment.

ohmmeter An electrical test instrument for measuring the resistance of an electrical connection. Often used to determine whether wires or connections are in good condition (by exhibiting a low resistance to electrical flow). The unit of measurement for resistance to electrical flow is the ohm, and it is designated in diagrams and documentation by the Greek symbol omega.

OOBE Out-of-box experience. The initial phase of a computer user unpacking and setting up a new system. The "OOBE" is a subject of intense study and quality improvement among many computer system and peripheral device makers as well as software publishers and online service providers. A "good OOBE" partially accounts for the popularity of the America Online (AOL) service provider.

online A term referring to actively using a computer or data from another system through a modem or network connection.

online services These are typically commercial operations much like a BBS that charge for the time and services used while connected. Most online services use large computers designed to handle multiple users and types of operations. These services provide electronic mail, computer and software support conferences, online game playing, and file libraries for uploading and downloading public-domain and shareware programs. Often, familiar communities or groups of users form in the conferences, making an online service a favorite or familiar places for people to gather. Access to these systems is typically by modem, to either a local data network access number or through a WATS or direct-toll line. Delphi, GEnie, America Online, Prodigy, and CompuServe are among the many online services available in the United States and much of the world elsewhere.

operating system *See* disk operating system (DOS).

optical carrier data circuit type 1 (OC-1) A 51.85 megabits per second fiber optic data communications circuit.

optical carrier data circuit type 3 (OC-3) A 155 megabits per second fiber optic data communications circuit.

optical carrier data circuit type 12 (OC-12) A 622 megabits per second fiber optic data communications circuit.

optical carrier data circuit type 24 (OC-24) A 1.244 gigabits per second fiber optic data communications circuit.

optical carrier data circuit type 48 (OC-48) A 2.44 gigabits per second fiber optic data communications circuit.

optical carrier data circuit type 192 (OC-192) A 4 terabits per second fiber optic data communications circuit.

OS/2 A 32-bit operating system, multitasking control, and graphical user interface developed by Microsoft, currently sold and supported by IBM. OS/2 facilitates the simultaneous operation of many DOS, Windows, and OS/2-specific application programs.

overlays A portion of a complete executable program, existing separately from the main control program, that is loaded into memory only when it is required by the main program, thus reducing overall program memory requirements for most operations. Occasionally, overlays may be built into the main program file, but they are also not loaded into memory until needed.

page frame The location in DOS/PC system memory (between 640K and 1MB) where the pages or groups of expanded memory are accessed.

parallel I/O A method of transferring data between devices or portions of a computer where eight or more bits of information are sent in one cycle or operation. Parallel transfers require eight or more wires to move the information. At speeds from 12,000 to 92,000 bytes per second or faster, this method is faster than the serial transfer of data where one bit of information follows another. Commonly used for the printer port on PCs.

parallel port A computer's parallel I/O (LPT) connection, built into the system board or provided by an add-in card.

parameter Information provided when calling or within a program, specifying how or when it is to run with which files, disks, paths, or similar attributes.

parity A method of calculating the pattern of data transferred as a verification that the data has been transferred or stored correctly. Parity is used in all PC memory structures, as the 9th, 17th, or 33rd bit in 8-, 16-, or 32-bit memory storage operations. If an error occurs in memory, it usually shows up as a parity error, halting the computer so that processing does not proceed with bad data. Parity is also used in some serial data connections to ensure that each character of data is received correctly.

partition A section of a hard disk drive typically defined as a logical drive, which may occupy some or all of the hard-disk capacity. A partition is created by the DOS FDISK or other disk utility software.

path A DOS parameter stored as part of the DOS environment space, indicating the order and locations DOS is to use when you request a program to run. A path is also used to specify the disk and directory information for a program or data file. *See also* filespec.

PC The first model designation for IBM's family of personal computers. This model provided 64 to 256K of RAM on the system board, a cassette tape adapter as an alternative to diskette storage, and five add-in card slots. The term generally refers to all IBM PC-compatible models and has gained popular use as a generic term referring to all forms, makes, and models of personal computers.

PC-66 *and* **PC-100** These are designations for the bus speed of motherboards available for your PC. The need for higher bus speeds became very important as CPU and memory speeds increased past the capabilities of the original IBM PC specifications.

PC-compatible *See* IBM PC-compatible *and* AT-compatible.

PCI *See* Peripheral Component Interconnect (PCI).

PCMCIA *See* Personal Computer Memory Card International Association (PCMCIA).

Pentium A 64-bit Intel microprocessor capable of operating at 60–200+ MHz, containing a 16K instruction cache, floating-point processor, and several internal features for extremely fast program operations.

Pentium II A 64-bit Intel microprocessor capable of operating at 200–350+ MHz, containing a 16K instruction cache, floating-point processor, and several internal features for extremely fast program operations. Packaged in what is known as Intel's "Slot 1" module, containing the CPU and local chipset components.

Pentium III A 64-bit Intel microprocessor capable of operating at 400–1,000 MHz, containing a 64K L1 instruction cache and 256K L2 cache, floating-point processor, and several internal features for extremely fast program operations. Packaged in what is known as Intel's "Slot 1" module, containing the CPU and local chipset components.

peripheral A hardware device, internal or external, to a computer that is not necessarily required for basic computer functions. Printers, modems, document scanners, and pointing devices are peripherals to a computer.

Peripheral Component Interconnect (PCI) An Intel-developed standard interface between the CPU and I/O devices providing enhanced system performance. PCI is typically used for video and disk drive interconnections to the CPU.

Personal Computer Memory Card International Association (PCMCIA) An I/O interconnect definition used for memory cards, disk drives, modems, network and other connections to portable computers.

Personal System/2 (PS/2) A new series of IBM personal computer systems using new designs, bus, and adapter technologies. Early models did not support the many existing PC-compatible cards and display peripherals, although IBM has provided later models that maintain their earlier ISA expansion capabilities.

PGA *or* **PGC** *See* Professional Graphics Adapter (PGA) *or* Professional Graphics Controller (PGC) professional color graphics system.

PGP Pretty Good Privacy is one of the most secure and sophisticated security capabilities available for your PC today. It was pretty much certified by the United States government as being so capable at encryption that it disallowed it to be exported for fear of losing the capability to decrypt information encrypted by a foreign entity. It comes highly recommended.

physical drive The actual disk drive hardware unit, as a specific drive designation (A:, B:, or C:, and so on), or containing multiple logical drives, as with a single hard drive partitioned to have logical drives C:, D:, and so on. Most systems or controllers provide for two to four physical diskette drives and up to two physical hard disk drives, which may have several logical drive partitions.

pixel Abbreviation for picture element. A single dot or display item controlled by your video adapter and display monitor. Depending on the resolution of your monitor, your display may have the capability to display 320×200, 640×480, 800×600, or more picture elements across and down your monitor's face. The more elements that can be displayed, the sharper the image appears.

Plug and Play (PnP) A standard for PC BIOS peripheral and I/O device identification and operating system configuration established to reduce the manual configuration technicalities for adding or changing PC peripheral devices. Plug-and-Play routines in the system BIOS work with and around older, legacy, or otherwise fixed or manually configured I/O devices and reports device configuration information to the operating system. (The operating system does not itself control or affect PnP or I/O device configurations.)

PnP *See* Plug and Play (PnP).

pointing device A hardware input device (a mouse, trackball, cursor tablet, or keystrokes) used to locate or position graphic or character elements, or select position-activated choices (buttons, scroll bar controls, menu selections, and so on) displayed by a computer program.

port address The physical address within the computer's memory range that a hardware device is set to decode and allow access to its services through.

POST *See* power-on self test (POST).

power-on self test (POST) A series of hardware tests run on your PC when power is turned on to the system. POST surveys installed memory and equipment, storing and using this information for boot up and subsequent use by DOS and applications programs. POST provides either speaker beep messages, video display messages, or both if it encounters errors in the system during testing and boot up.

Professional Graphics Adapter (PGA) *or* **Professional Graphics Controller (PGC) professional color graphics system** This was an interim IBM high-resolution color graphics system in limited distribution between EGA and VGA.

program, programming A set of instructions provided to a computer specifying the operations the computer is to perform. Programs are created or written in any of several languages that appear at different levels of complexity to the programmer, or in terms of the computer itself. Computer processors have internal programming known as micro-code that dictates what the computer will do when certain instructions are received. The computer must be addressed at the lowest level of language, known as machine code, or one that is instruction-specific to the processor chip being used. Programming is very rarely done at machine-code levels except in development work.

The lowest programming level that is commonly used is assembly language, a slightly more advanced, easier-to-read level of machine code, also known as a second-generation language. Most programs are written in what are called third-generation languages such as BASIC, Pascal, C, or Fortran, more readable as a text file. Batch files, macros, scripts, and database programs are a form of third-generation programming, language-specific to the application or operating with whichever system they are used. All programs are either interpreted by an intermediate application or compiled with a special program to convert the desired tasks into machine code.

prompt A visual indication that a program or the computer is ready for input or commands. The native DOS prompt for input is shown as the A disk drive letter and "right arrow" or "caret" character (C>). The DOS prompt may be changed with the DOS PROMPT internal command to indicate the current drive and directory, include a user name, the date or time, or more creatively, flags or colored patterns.

PS/2 *See* Personal System/2 (PS/2).

public domain Items, usually software applications in this context, provided and distributed to the public without expectation or requirement of payment for goods or services, although copyrights and trademarks may be applied. Public-domain software may be considered shareware, but shareware is not always in the public domain for any and all to use as freely as they wish.

RAS Remote Access Service is a Windows feature that enables you to connect to other networks over a dial-up connection. In a way, it is an unsecure Virtual Private Network (VPN) or a simple representation of a wide area network (WAN). More commonly referred to as Dial-Up Networking.

RAM *See* random access memory (RAM).

RAMBUS An Intel and industry standard for more closely interconnecting memory to the central processor separate from using the typical I/O device bus.

RAM disk *or* **RAM drive** A portion of memory assigned by a device driver or program to function like a disk drive on a temporary basis. Any data stored in a RAM drive exists there as long as your computer is not rebooted or turned off.

random access memory (RAM) A storage area that information can be sent to and taken from by addressing specific locations in any order at any time. The memory in your PC and even the disk drives are a form of random access memory, although the memory is most commonly referred to as the RAM. RAM memory chips come in two forms, the more common dynamic RAM (DRAM), which must be refreshed often to retain the information stored in it, and static RAM (SRAM), which can retain information without refreshing, saving power and time. RAM memory chips are referred to by their storage capacity and maximum speed of operation in the part numbers assigned to them. Chips with 16K and 64K capacity were common in early PCs, but 256K and 1MB chips are now more common.

read-only An attribute assigned to a disk file to prevent DOS or other programs from erasing or writing over a file's disk space. *See* attributes.

read-only memory (ROM) This is a type of memory chip that is preprogrammed with instructions or information specific to the computer type or device it is used in. All PCs have a ROM-based BIOS that holds the initial boot up instructions that are used when your computer is first turned on or when a warm-boot is issued. Some video and disk adapters contain a form of ROM-based program that replaces or assists the PC BIOS or DOS in using a particular adapter.

refresh An internal function of the system board and CPU memory is to refresh timing circuits to recharge the contents of dynamic RAM so that contents are retained during operation. The standard PC RAM refresh interval is 15 microseconds. *See also* dynamic random access memory (DRAM), random access memory (RAM), static random access memory (SRAM), *and* wait states.

Remote Dial-Up Networking (RAN) Also called RAN, this is the capability of using a modem to connect your PC to a network (most often the Internet but also may be used to connect to your network at your office or your home system).

Return *See* Enter.

RMA Return Merchandise (*or* Material) Authorization. A tracking number and process for the return of unacceptable goods to the manufacturer. Something we try to avoid in this book!

ROM *See* read-only memory (ROM).

ROM BIOS The ROM-chip-based start-up or controlling program for a computer system or peripheral device. *See also* basic input/output system (BIOS) *and* read-only memory (ROM).

root directory The first directory area on any disk media. The DOS command processor and any CONFIG.SYS or AUTOEXEC.BAT file must typically reside in the root directory of a bootable disk. The root directory has space for a fixed number of entries, which may be files or subdirectories. A hard disk root directory may contain up to 512 files or subdirectory entries, the size of which is limited only by the capacity of the disk drive. Subdirectories may have nearly unlimited numbers of entries.

SCSI *See* Small Computer System Interface (SCSI).

SDRAM Synchronous dynamic random access memory is the most common type of memory used in PCs today. It is available in many forms (DIMM and other types of packaging) and speeds as low as a couple of nanoseconds for a complete memory cycle.

sector When used to describe a portion of a hard disk or diskette storage location, *sector* refers to the number of bytes that may be stored in the smallest part of a track. Because the tracks are concentric circles around the disk media, the sectors are sometimes referred to as "pie slices." All of the sectors within that slice have the same sector number. The data is "found" by knowing the sector number and the track number. These two numbers specify a unique location in which the number of bytes may be stored based on the format of the disk.

segments A method of grouping memory locations, usually in 64K increments or blocks, to make addressing easier to display and understand. Segment 0 is the first 64K of RAM in a PC. Accessing areas of memory within that segment is done with an offset address based on the first location in the segment. An address of 0:0040h would be the 40th (in hex) byte location in the first 64K of memory. An address of A:0040h would be the 40th (in hex) byte location in the tenth (Ah) 64K of memory.

serial I/O A method of transferring data between two devices one bit at a time, usually within a predetermined frame of bits that makes up a character, plus transfer control information (start and stop or beginning and end). Modems and many printers use serial data transfer. One-way serial transfer can be done on as few as two wires, with two-way transfers requiring as few as three wires. Transfer speeds of 110,000 to 115,000 bits per second (11,000 to 11,500 characters) are possible through a PC serial port.

serial port A computer's serial I/O (COM) connection, built into the system board or provided by an add-in card.

shadow RAM A special memory configuration that remaps some or all of the information stored in BIOS and adapter ROM chips to faster dedicated RAM chips. This feature is controllable on many PC systems that have it, enabling you to use memory management software to provide this and other features.

shareware Computer applications written by noncommercial programmers, offered to users with a try-before-you-buy understanding, usually with a requirement for a registration fee or payment for the service or value provided by the application. This is very much like a cooperative or user-supported development and use environment, as opposed to buying a finished and packaged product off the shelf with little or no opportunity to test and evaluate if the application suits your needs. Shareware is not public-domain software. Payment is expected or required to maintain proper, legal use of the application.

SIMM *See* single inline memory module (SIMM).

single inline memory module (SIMM) A dense memory packaging technique with small memory chips mounted on a small circuit board that clips into a special socket.

single inline package (SIP) Typically a dense memory module with memory chips mounted on a small circuit board with small pins in a single row that plugs into a special socket.

SIP *See* single inline package (SIP).

Small Computer System Interface (SCSI) An interface specification for interconnecting peripheral devices to a computer bus. SCSI allows for attaching multiple high-speed devices such as disk and tape drives through a single 50-pin cable.

software interrupt A (non-hardware) signal or command from a currently executing program that causes the CPU and computer program to act on an event that requires special attention, such as the completion of a routine operation or the execution of a new function.

Many software interrupt services are predefined and available through the system BIOS and DOS, while others may be made available by device driver software or running programs. Most disk accesses, keyboard operations, and timing services are provided to applications through software interrupt services.

SRAM *See* static random access memory (SRAM).

ST506/412 The original device interface specification for small hard drives, designed by Seagate and first commonly used in the IBM PC/XT.

start bit The first data bit in a serial data stream, indicating the beginning of a data element.

static random access memory (SRAM) Fast access (less than 50 nanoseconds), somewhat expensive, memory-integrated circuits that do not require a refresh cycle to maintain their contents. Typically used in video and cache applications. *See also* dynamic random access memory (DRAM) *and* random access memory (RAM).

stop bit The last data bit, or bits, in a serial data stream, indicating the end of a data element.

streaming media Relates to streaming audio and streaming video — the process of transferring, buffering and presenting digital content data from a server to a client system in a real-time or store-and-forward context. Examples: RealAudio live radio broadcast retransmissions and program archiving to a player program on a PC system. Useful for enjoying radio broadcasts and presentations over the Internet.

subdirectory A directory contained within the root directory or in other subdirectories, used to organize programs and files by application or data type, system user, or other criteria. A subdirectory is analogous to a file folder in a filing cabinet or an index tab in a book.

surface scan The process of reading and verifying the data stored on a disk to determine its accuracy and reliability, usually as part of a utility or diagnostic program's operation to test or recover data.

sysop The system operator of a BBS, online service forum, or network system.

system attribute *or* **system file** *See* attributes.

T-1 An analog (high-frequency carrier) communications circuit consisting of 24, 64 kilobit-per-second circuits, which may be split, or combined to create incremental transfer capacities, such as in the frame relay or Fractional-T-1 services. A T-1 is capable of 1.54 megabit-per-second data transfers (roughly three times as fast as 56K modems) originally used between telephone central offices to carry multiple phone call traffic. Used today to carry telephone and data traffic. While having a T-1 circuit is highly coveted by many Internet users, cable TV system data circuits and newer data circuit types far exceed T-1 capabilities.

T-3 An analog (high-frequency carrier) communications circuit consisting of 43, 64 kilobit-per-second circuits, which may be merged to form a single circuit capable of 43 megabit-per-second data rates.

TCP/IP The Transfer Control Program/Internet Protocol is the networking standard for the Internet and is rapidly becoming the preferred network protocol in almost any network. You have to listen to Vint Cerf's explanation about how it works (like postcards) in order to understand both its simplicity and power. Vint is one of TCP/IP's inventors and is now working on the Interplanetary Network Protocol. We'll probably have to add IPN to the next version of the Glossary — it's being used on Mars missions now!

terminate-and-stay-resident program (TSR) Also known as a memory-resident program. A program that remains in memory to provide services automatically or on request, through a special key sequence (also known as hot keys). Device drivers (MOUSE, ANSI, SETVER) and disk caches, RAM disks, and print spoolers are forms of automatic TSR programs. SideKick, Lightning, and assorted screen-capture programs are examples of hot-key–controlled TSR programs.

TorX fastener *and* **tool** A four-point special fastener and tool that differs from a normal slotted/flat edge, cross-head, or hexagonal fastener.

TSR *See* terminate-and-stay-resident program (TSR).

twisted-pair cable A pair of wires bundled together by twisting or wrapping them around each other in a regular pattern. Twisting the wires reduces the influx of other signals into the wires, preventing interference, as opposed to coaxial (concentric orientation), or parallel wire cabling.

UAR/T *See* Universal Asynchronous Receiver/Transmitter (UAR/T).

UltraDMA A high-speed data transfer method implemented in IDE disk drives and interface circuits providing 33 megabits per second, 66 megabits per second, and higher data transfers between computer systems and disk drives with minimal processor use.

UltraWide SCSI A high-speed data transfer method implemented in SCSI devices and interface circuits providing over 130 megabits per second data transfers between devices.

Universal Asynchronous Receiver/Transmitter (UAR/T) This is a special integrated circuit or function used to convert parallel computer bus information into serial transfer information and vice versa. A UAR/T also provides proper system-to-system online status, modem ring and data carrier detect signals, as well as start/stop transfer features. The most recent version of this chip, called the 16550A, is crucial to high-speed (greater than 2,400 bits per second) data transfers under multitasking environments.

Universal Serial Bus (USB) A high-speed (to 12 megabits per second in USB 1.1, to 480 megabits per seconds with USB 2.0 specification devices) I/O connection method and communications protocol used to allow for additional peripheral devices not suitable for parallel port, Ethernet, SCSI, or requiring IEEE-1394 interconnections. Available I/O devices include cameras, pointing and game devices, musical synthesizers, digital music players, printers, and document and image scanners.

Unix A high-performance multitasking operating system designed by AT&T/Bell Laboratories in the late 1960s. Today Unix has several offshoots and derivatives, including Linux, Sun OS/Solaris, FreeBSD, and others. Unix is the operating system of choice for many "enterprise" business applications, and most of the servers and Internet services we enjoy today.

upload The process of sending or transferring information from one computer to another, usually connected by modem or over a network. Uploading is done to BBS and online services when you have a program or other file to contribute to the system or to accompany electronic mail you send to others.

upper memory *and* **upper memory blocks** Memory space between 640K and 1MB that may be controlled and made available by a special device or UMB (EMM386.SYS, QEMM386, 386Max, and so on) for the purpose of storing and running TSR programs and leaving more DOS RAM (from 0 to 640K) available for other programs and data. Some of this area is occupied by BIOS, video, and disk adapters.

utilities Software programs that perform or assist with routine functions such as file backups, disk defragmentation, disk file testing, file and directory sorting, and so on. *See also* diagnostics.

V20 An NEC clone of the Intel 8088 8-bit internal and external data bus microprocessor, capable of addressing up to 1MB of memory and operating at speeds up to 10 MHz. NEC has optimized several of the internal micro-code commands so this CPU chip can perform some operations faster than the Intel chip it can replace. Its companion numerical coprocessor or math chip is the 8087. This chip can generally be used in any PC or XT system that uses an 8088 chip.

V30 An Intel 16-bit internal, 8-bit external data bus microprocessor capable of addressing up to 1MB of memory and operating at speeds up to 10 MHz. NEC has optimized several of the internal micro-code commands so this CPU chip can perform some operations faster than the Intel chip it can replace. Its companion numerical coprocessor or math chip is the 8087. This chip can only be used in IBM PS/2 Models 25 and 30 and in some clones.

variable Information provided when calling or within a program, specifying how or when it is to run with which files, disks, paths, or similar attributes. A variable may be allowed for in a batch file, using %1 through %9 designations to substitute or include values keyed-in at the command line when the batch file is called.

VGA *See* Video Graphics Array (VGA).

video adapter card The interface card between the computer's I/O system and the video display device.

Video Graphics Array (VGA) A high-resolution text and graphics system supporting color and previous IBM video standards using an analog-interfaced video monitor.

video memory Memory contained on the video adapter dedicated to storing information to be processed by the adapter for placement on the display screen. The amount and exact location of video memory depends on the type and features of your video adapter. This memory and the video adapter functions are located in upper memory between 640K and 832K.

virtual device driver (VXD) A special device driver type for the Windows 95, 98, 98SE, and Me operating systems.

virtual disk *See* RAM disk.

virtual memory Disk space allocated and managed by an operating system that is used to augment the available RAM memory, and is designed to contain inactive program code and data when switching between multiple computer tasks.

Virtual Private Network (VPN) A Virtual Private Network is a way of creating a network of computers that are only connected over the Internet but are viewed as a private network because of security and protocols that protect them as if they were connected only by direct wiring.

VMM32.VXD A special device driver file type for the Windows 95, 98, 98SE, and Me operating systems that combines several commonly used device drivers into one file during the system setup and update process that provides for efficient loading at boot time.

voltmeter An electrical instrument for measuring the potential energy in a circuit, indicated in terms of the volt, named for Voltaire, an early physics researcher.

volume label *See* disk label *and* label.

VPN *See* Virtual Private Network (VPN).

wait states A predetermined amount of time between the addressing of a portion of a memory location and when data may be reliably read from, or written to, that location. This function is controlled by the BIOS, and it is either permanently set or changed in CMOS setup. Setting this parameter too low may cause excessive delays or unreliable operation. Setting this parameter too high may slow down your system. *See also* dynamic random access memory (DRAM), random access memory (RAM), refresh, *and* static random access memory (SRAM).

WAN A wide area network involves computers and other networks that are connected, usually over long distances, using phone lines, leased lines, and wireless connections (such as microwave, satellite, even Internet connections) such that remote computers may act as if they are part of the local area network (LAN).

Windows A Microsoft multitasking and graphical user interface that enables multiple programs to operate on the same PC system and share the same resources.

Windows 2000 Microsoft's latest major upgrade to the Windows NT series of operating systems, including workstation, server, advanced server, and enterprise-level variations to suit a variety of critical applications.

Windows Me (Windows Millennium) Microsoft's latest major upgrade to the Windows 9x series of operating systems, featuring boot up without real-mode (8- and 16-bit DOS programs) operation prior to loading the 32-bit operating system kernel. Like Windows 98 and 98 SE, supporting the Universal Serial Bus, as well as IEEE-1394 *aka* FireWire (Apple Computer) *aka* iLink (Sony Corp.) I/O technologies.

Windows NT A Microsoft 32-bit multitasking operating system and graphical user interface.

Wireless Access Protocol (WAP) An industry-standard communications protocol for transferring data between wireless devices and network systems. Typically used to facilitate text messaging and non-graphical Web browsing in cellular telephones and wireless personal devices.

wireless networking Any number of possible implementations of Point-to-Point and Multi-Point Network communications over a radio frequency spectrum — typically using 900 MHz, 2.4 GHz or other band allocations.

workstation A user's computer system attached to a network. Workstations do not necessarily contain diskette or hard disk drives, instead using built-in programs to boot up and attach to a network server, from which all programs and data files are obtained.

World Wide Web (WWW) A term used to describe multiple inter-networked computer systems providing text and graphical content through the Hypertext Transfer Protocol (HTTP), usually over Internet Protocol (IP) networks.

write-protected The status of a diskette with a write-protection tab or slot. All 5¼-inch diskettes use a write-protect notch and stick-on tab to define write protected status. If the notch is covered, the disk is write-protected. All 3½-inch diskettes use a sliding window cover over a small hole in the near left corner of the casing (shutter door facing away from you). If the hole is uncovered, the disk is write protected.

WWW *See* World Wide Web (WWW).

WXMODEM A variation of the XMODEM file transfer protocol offering windowing or noncontiguous transfer of files during a single online/connected session, intended for use on data networks such as SprintNet and Tymnet. Originally developed by Peter Boswell on PCs and Tandem computers at the former PeopleLink online service.

XMODEM This is the first serial file transfer protocol and software program developed by Ward Christensen in 1977. XMODEM transfers data in 128-byte blocks, provides error-checking and correction, and is in the public domain. XMODEM has been copied, modified, and enhanced in several ways since it became available.

XMS *See* extended memory specification (XMS).

XT The second model of IBM PC series provided with "extended technology" enabling the addition of hard disks and eight add-in card slots. The original XT models had between 64K and 256K of RAM on board, a single diskette drive, and a 10MB hard disk.

YMODEM A serial file transfer protocol typically used between modems to copy data from one computer to another. YMODEM and YMODEM-G are variations of the original XMODEM transfer protocol, offering transfers of data in 1K blocks.

ZMODEM An enhancement to the XMODEM transfer protocol by Chuck Foresberg, providing filename and size transfer with the data, variable transmitted data block lengths, robust error checking, and automatic recovery and continuation of transfers if a connection is broken in midtransfer. ZMODEM is the first protocol to take advantage of the internal buffering of the 16550 UAR/T chip, providing the fastest transfer protocol available for many system environments.

✦   ✦   ✦

Index

Continued

Continued

Continued

Notes

Notes

Notes

IDG Books Worldwide, Inc.
End-User License Agreement

READ THIS. You should carefully read these terms and conditions before opening the software packet(s) included with this book ("Book"). This is a license agreement ("Agreement") between you and IDG Books Worldwide, Inc. ("IDGB"). By opening the accompanying software packet(s), you acknowledge that you have read and accept the following terms and conditions. If you do not agree and do not want to be bound by such terms and conditions, promptly return the Book and the unopened software packet(s) to the place you obtained them for a full refund.

1. **License Grant.** IDGB grants to you (either an individual or entity) a nonexclusive license to use one copy of the enclosed software program(s) (collectively, the "Software") solely for your own personal or business purposes on a single computer (whether a standard computer or a workstation component of a multiuser network). The Software is in use on a computer when it is loaded into temporary memory (RAM) or installed into permanent memory (hard disk, CD-ROM, or other storage device). IDGB reserves all rights not expressly granted herein.

2. **Ownership.** IDGB is the owner of all right, title, and interest, including copyright, in and to the compilation of the Software recorded on the disk(s) or CD-ROM ("Software Media"). Copyright to the individual programs recorded on the Software Media is owned by the author or other authorized copyright owner of each program. Ownership of the Software and all proprietary rights relating thereto remain with IDGB and its licensers.

3. **Restrictions On Use and Transfer.**

   (a) You may only (i) make one copy of the Software for backup or archival purposes, or (ii) transfer the Software to a single hard disk, provided that you keep the original for backup or archival purposes. You may not (i) rent or lease the Software, (ii) copy or reproduce the Software through a LAN or other network system or through any computer subscriber system or bulletin-board system, or (iii) modify, adapt, or create derivative works based on the Software.

   (b) You may not reverse engineer, decompile, or disassemble the Software. You may transfer the Software and user documentation on a permanent basis, provided that the transferee agrees to accept the terms and conditions of this Agreement and you retain no copies. If the Software is an update or has been updated, any transfer must include the most recent update and all prior versions.

4. Restrictions on Use of Individual Programs. You must follow the individual requirements and restrictions detailed for each individual program in Appendix J of this Book. These limitations are also contained in the individual license agreements recorded on the Software Media. These limitations may include a requirement that after using the program for a specified period of time, the user must pay a registration fee or discontinue use. By opening the Software packet(s), you will be agreeing to abide by the licenses and restrictions for these individual programs that are detailed in Appendix J and on the Software Media. None of the material on this Software Media or listed in this Book may ever be redistributed, in original or modified form, for commercial purposes.

5. Limited Warranty.

(a) IDGB warrants that the Software and Software Media are free from defects in materials and workmanship under normal use for a period of sixty (60) days from the date of purchase of this Book. If IDGB receives notification within the warranty period of defects in materials or workmanship, IDGB will replace the defective Software Media.

(b) **IDGB AND THE AUTHORS OF THE BOOK DISCLAIM ALL OTHER WARRANTIES, EXPRESS OR IMPLIED, INCLUDING WITHOUT LIMITATION IMPLIED WARRANTIES OF MERCHANTABILITY AND FITNESS FOR A PARTICULAR PURPOSE, WITH RESPECT TO THE SOFTWARE, THE PROGRAMS, THE SOURCE CODE CONTAINED THEREIN, AND/OR THE TECHNIQUES DESCRIBED IN THIS BOOK. IDGB DOES NOT WARRANT THAT THE FUNCTIONS CONTAINED IN THE SOFTWARE WILL MEET YOUR REQUIREMENTS OR THAT THE OPERATION OF THE SOFTWARE WILL BE ERROR FREE.**

(c) This limited warranty gives you specific legal rights, and you may have other rights that vary from jurisdiction to jurisdiction.

6. Remedies.

(a) IDGB's entire liability and your exclusive remedy for defects in materials and workmanship shall be limited to replacement of the Software Media, which may be returned to IDGB with a copy of your receipt at the following address: Software Media Fulfillment Department, Attn.: *Troubleshooting Your PC Bible, 5th Edition*, IDG Books Worldwide, Inc., 10475 Crosspoint Blvd., Indianapolis, IN 46256, or call 1-800-762-2974. Please allow three to four weeks for delivery. This Limited Warranty is void if failure of the Software Media has resulted from accident, abuse, or misapplication. Any replacement Software Media will be warranted for the remainder of the original warranty period or thirty (30) days, whichever is longer.

(b) In no event shall IDGB or the authors be liable for any damages whatsoever (including without limitation damages for loss of business profits, business interruption, loss of business information, or any other pecuniary loss) arising from the use of or inability to use the Book or the Software, even if IDGB has been advised of the possibility of such damages.

(c) Because some jurisdictions do not allow the exclusion or limitation of liability for consequential or incidental damages, the above limitation or exclusion may not apply to you.

7. U.S. Government Restricted Rights. Use, duplication, or disclosure of the Software by the U.S. Government is subject to restrictions stated in paragraph (c)(1)(ii) of the Rights in Technical Data and Computer Software clause of DFARS 252.227-7013, and in subparagraphs (a) through (d) of the Commercial Computer — Restricted Rights clause at FAR 52.227-19, and in similar clauses in the NASA FAR supplement, when applicable.

8. General. This Agreement constitutes the entire understanding of the parties and revokes and supersedes all prior agreements, oral or written, between them and may not be modified or amended except in a writing signed by both parties hereto that specifically refers to this Agreement. This Agreement shall take precedence over any other documents that may be in conflict herewith. If any one or more provisions contained in this Agreement are held by any court or tribunal to be invalid, illegal, or otherwise unenforceable, each and every other provision shall remain in full force and effect.

Do you have the right tools
to accurately diagnose your PC problems?

PC-Doctor
SERVICE CENTER 2000

The ultimate diagnostic testing and system information tool

Includes 3 products on one CD-ROM

PC-Doctor DOS
PC-Doctor for Windows 95/98
PC-Doctor for Windows NT and Windows 2000
Plus 5 Loopback Adapters -gameport, audio, serial, parallel and USB

POWERFUL FACTORY DIAGNOSTICS
Includes benchmarking, low-level hardware testing and maximum system load test that completes 10 days worth of testing in 24 hours!

PROFESSIONAL DIAGNOSTICS FOR PC PROFESSIONALS
Designed for VARs, PC manufacturers, assemblers, service centers and field support technicians.

ELIMINATE WRONGFUL RMAs AND INCREASE CUSTOMER SATISFACTION
Accurate testing of the latest hardware reduces wrongful RMAs and No Trouble Found (NTF) returns.

ALWAYS HAVE THE MOST CURRENT DIAGNOSTICS
e.Subscription program provides regular updates allowing you to test the newest technology with confidence.

THE SAME DIAGNOSTICS USED BY THE LEADERS IN THE INDUSTRY
IBM, Dell, Sony, Fujitsu Siemens, Acer, micronpc.com, SGI, Ingram Micro, NEC, Intel, Toshiba, Hewlett-Packard, Lucent Technologies and CompUSA.

Place your order now at www.pcdoctorstore.com!

Suggested retail price is $499

PC-Doctor, Inc. 2200 Powell Street, Suite 733, Emeryville, CA 94608 USA 510/596-2080 Fax: 510/596-2092
Copyright 2000 PC-Doctor, Inc. PC-Doctor is a registered trademark of PC-Doctor, Inc. All other trademarks are property of their respective owners.

my2cents.idgbooks.com

CD-ROM Installation Instructions

The CD-ROM that accompanies this book contains trial versions of commercial software discussed in the book, as well as fully-functional Internet Explorer and Netscape browsers. For a detailed list of the contents of the CD-ROM, refer to Appendix J.

To install any of these programs, place the disc in your CD-ROM drive and run the .exe file. Follow the prompts to complete installation.

For the PDF files of the book, copy the files to your hard rive, and open them using the complimentary copy of Adobe Acrobat Reader, also on the CD-ROM.